LIBERTY
EQUALITY
POWER

A HISTORY OF THE AMERICAN PEOPLE
VOLUME II: SINCE 1863

FOURTH EDITION

JOHN M MURRIN Princeton University

PAUL E. JOHNSON University of South Carolina

JAMES M. McPHERSON Princeton University

GARY GERSTLE University of Maryland

EMILY S. ROSENBERG Macalester College

NORMAN L. ROSENBERG Macalester College

THOMSON

WADSWORTH™

Australia • Canada • Mexico • Singapore • Spain
United Kingdom • United States

THOMSON

WADSWORTH

Publisher: Clark Baxter
Senior Development Editor: Margaret McAndrew Beasley
Senior Assistant Editor: Julie Yardley
Editorial Assistant: Anne Gittinger
Senior Technology Project Manager: Melinda Newfarmer
Executive Marketing Manager: Caroline Croley
Marketing Assistant: Mary Ho
Advertising Project Manager: Brian Chaffee
Project Manager, Editorial Production: Kimberly Adams
Print/Media Buyer: Barbara Britton
Permissions Editor: Joohee Lee

Production Service: Lachina Publishing Services
Text Designer: Norman Baugher
Photo Researcher: Lili Weiner
Musical Consultant: Harvey Cohen
Copy Editor: Ginjer Clarke
Production Specialist: Sona Lachina
Cover Designer: John Walker and Lisa Devenish
Cover Image: Smithsonian American Art Museum, Washington, DC/Art Resource, NY
Printer: Quebecor World/Versailles
Compositor: Lachina Publishing Services

Library of Congress Control Number: 2003116388
Student Edition: ISBN 0-534-62732-3

Wadsworth/Thomson Learning
10 Davis Drive
Belmont, CA 94002-3098
USA

Asia
Thomson Learning
5 Shenton Way #01-01
UIC Building
Singapore 068808

Australia/New Zealand
Thomson Learning
102 Dodds Street
Southbank, Victoria 3006
Australia

Canada
Nelson
1120 Birchmount Road
Toronto, Ontario M1K 5G4
Canada

Europe/Middle East/Africa
Thomson Learning
High Holborn House
50/51 Bedford Row
London WC1R 4LR
United Kingdom

Latin America
Thomson Learning
Seneca, 53
Colonia Polanco
11560 Mexico D.F.
Mexico

Spain/Portugal
Paraninfo
Calle Magallanes, 25
28015 Madrid, Spain

About the Authors

THE AUTHOR TEAM

From left: Norman Rosenberg, Emily Rosenberg, Paul Johnson, Gary Gerstle, John Murrin, and Jim McPherson.

One of the pleasures of this textbook project, now 15 years old, is the opportunity it has given us to work with each other. Before starting work on a new edition, we all gather for a lengthy period of time to evaluate past editions, discuss reviews that we have solicited from our textbook readers, and brainstorm about ways to improve our book and to make our history more lively, accurate, and up to date. These meetings are always interesting and energizing. After we scatter, the discussions continue through extensive e-mail and phone conversations in which we test and refine the initiatives that we have developed. The volume and richness of this communication over the years have deepened the collective nature of our endeavor and strengthened the quality of the history that we write. We are all proud to be part of the *Liberty, Equality, Power* author team.

JOHN M. MURRIN *Princeton University, Emeritus*
John M. Murrin is a specialist in American colonial and revolutionary history and the early republic. He has edited one multivolume series and five books, including two co-edited collections, *Colonial America: Essays in Politics and Social Development,* Fifth Edition (2001), and *Saints and Revolutionaries: Essays in Early American History* (1984). His own essays on early American history range from ethnic tensions, the early history of trial by jury, the rise of the legal profession, and the political culture of the colonies and the new nation, to the rise of professional baseball and college football in the 19th century. Professor Murrin

served as president of the Society for Historians of the Early American Republic in 1998–99.

PAUL E. JOHNSON *University of South Carolina*
A specialist in early national social and cultural history, Paul E. Johnson is also the author of *Sam Patch, the Famous Jumper* (2003); *A Shopkeeper's Millennium: Society and Revivals in Rochester, New York, 1815–1837,* 25th Anniversary Edition (2004); co-author (with Sean Wilentz) of *The Kingdom of Matthias: Sex and Salvation in 19th-Century America* (1994); and editor of *African-American Christianity: Essays in History* (1994). He has been awarded

the Merle Curti Prize of the Organization of American Historians (1980), the Richard P. McCormack Prize of the New Jersey Historical Association (1989), a John Simon Guggenheim Memorial Fellowship (1995), and the Gilder Lehrman Fellowship (2001).

JAMES M. McPHERSON   *Princeton University*
James M. McPherson is a distinguished Civil War historian and was president of the American Historical Association in 2003. He won the 1989 Pulitzer Prize for his book *Battle Cry of Freedom: The Civil War Era*. His other publications include *Marching Toward Freedom: Blacks in the Civil War*, Second Edition (1991); *Ordeal by Fire: The Civil War and Reconstruction*, Third Edition (2001); *Abraham Lincoln and the Second American Revolution* (1991); *For Cause and Comrades: Why Men Fought in the Civil War* (1997), which won the Lincoln Prize in 1998; and *Crossroads of Freedom: Antietam* (2002).

GARY GERSTLE   *University of Maryland*
Gary Gerstle—a specialist in labor, immigration, and political history—has published four books: *Working-Class Americanism: The Politics of Labor in a Textile City, 1914–1960* (1989); *The Rise and Fall of the New Deal Order, 1930–1980* (1989); *American Crucible: Race and Nation in the Twentieth Century* (2001), which won the Saloutos Prize in 2001 for the best work in immigration and ethnic history; and *E Pluribus Unum: Immigrants, Civic Culture, and Political Incorporation* (2001). His articles have appeared in the *American Historical Review, Journal of American History, American Quarterly,* and other journals.

His honors include a National Endowment for the Humanities Fellowship for University Teachers and a John Simon Guggenheim Memorial Fellowship.

EMILY S. ROSENBERG   *Macalester College*
Emily S. Rosenberg specializes in U.S. foreign relations in the 20th century and is the author of *Spreading the American Dream: American Economic and Cultural Expansion, 1890–1945* (1982); *Financial Missionaries to the World: The Politics and Culture of Dollar Diplomacy* (1999), which won the Ferrell Book Award; and *Pearl Harbor in American Memory* (2004). Her other publications include (with Norman L. Rosenberg) *In Our Times: America Since 1945,* Seventh Edition (2003), and numerous articles dealing with foreign relations in the context of international finance, American culture, and gender ideology. She has served on the board of the Organization of American Historians, on the board of editors of the *Journal of American History,* and as president of the Society for Historians of American Foreign Relations.

NORMAN L. ROSENBERG   *Macalester College*
Norman L. Rosenberg specializes in legal history with a particular interest in legal culture and First Amendment issues. His books include *Protecting the "Best Men": An Interpretive History of the Law of Libel* (1990) and (with Emily S. Rosenberg) *In Our Times: America Since 1945,* Seventh Edition (2003). He has published articles in the *Rutgers Law Review, UCLA Law Review, Constitutional Commentary, Law & History Review,* and many other journals and law-related anthologies.

Contents in Detail

Features

Maps

Americans Abroad

History through Film

Link to the Past

Musical Link to the Past

To the Student: Why Study History?

WHY TAKE A COURSE in American history? This is a question that many college and university students ask. In many respects, students today are like the generations of Americans who have gone before them: optimistic and forward looking, far more eager to imagine where we as a nation might be going than to reflect on where we have been. If anything, this tendency has become more pronounced in recent years, as the Internet revolution has accelerated the pace and excitement of change and made even the recent past seem at best quaint, at worst uninteresting and irrelevant.

But it is precisely in these moments of great change that a sense of the past can be indispensable in terms of guiding our actions in the present and future. We can find, in other periods of American history, moments, like our own, of dizzying technological change and economic growth, rapid alterations in the concentration of wealth and power, and basic changes in patterns of work, residence, and play. How did Americans at those times create, embrace, and resist these changes? In earlier periods of American history, the United States was home, as it is today, to a remarkably diverse array of ethnic and racial groups. How did earlier generations of Americans respond to the cultural conflicts and misunderstandings that often arise from conditions of diversity? How did immigrants perceive their new land? How and when did they integrate themselves into American society? To study how ordinary Americans of the past struggled with these issues is to gain perspective on the opportunities and problems that we face today.

History also provides an important guide to affairs of state. What should the role of America be in world affairs? Should we participate in international bodies such as the United Nations or insist on our ability to act autonomously and without the consent of other nations? What is the proper role of government in economic and social life? Should the government regulate the economy? To what extent should the government enforce morality regarding religion, sexual practices, drinking and drugs, movies, TV, and other forms of mass culture? And what are our responsibilities as citizens to each other and to the nation? Americans of past generations have debated these issues with verve and conviction. Learning about these debates and how they were resolved will enrich our understanding of the policy possibilities for today and tomorrow.

History, finally, is about stories—stories that we all tell about ourselves; our families; our communities; our ethnicity, race, region, and religion; and our nation. They are stories of triumph and tragedy, of engagement and flight, and of high ideals and high comedy. When telling these stories, "American history" is often the furthest thing from our minds. But, often, an implicit sense of history informs what we say about grandparents who immigrated many years ago; the suburb in which we live; the church, synagogue, or mosque that we attend; or the ethnic or racial group to which we belong. But how well do we really understand these individuals, institutions, and groups? Do we tell the right stories about them, ones that capture the complexities of their past? Or have we wittingly or unwittingly simplified, altered, or flattened them? A study of American history first helps us to ask these questions and then to answer them. In the process, we can engage in a fascinating journey of intellectual and personal discovery and situate ourselves more firmly than we had ever thought possible in relation to those who came before us. We can gain firmer self-knowledge and a greater appreciation for the richness of our nation and, indeed, of all humanity.

Preface

WE ARE PLEASED to present the fourth edition of *Liberty, Equality, Power*. Like the first three editions, this one captures the drama and excitement of America's past, from the pre-Columbian era through our own time. It integrates social and cultural history into a political story that is organized around the themes of liberty, equality, and power, and synthesizes the finest older historical scholarship with the best of the new to create a narrative that is balanced, lively, and accessible to a broad range of students.

The *Liberty, Equality, Power* Approach

In this book, we tell many small stories, and one large one: how America transformed itself, in a relatively brief era of world history, from a land inhabited by hunter-gatherer and agricultural Native American societies into the most powerful industrial nation on earth. This story has been told many times before, and those who have told it in the past have usually emphasized the political experiment in liberty and equality that took root here in the 18th century. We, too, stress the extraordinary and transformative impact that the ideals of liberty and equality exerted on American politics, society, and economics during the American Revolution and after.

We show how the creation of a free economic environment—one in which entrepreneurial spirit, technological innovation, and industrial production have flourished—underpinned American industrial might. We have emphasized, too, the successful struggles for freedom that, over the course of the last 225 years, have brought—first to all white men, then to men of color, and finally to women—rights and opportunities that they had not previously known.

But we have also identified a third factor in this pantheon of American ideals—that of power. We examine power in many forms: the accumulation of vast economic fortunes that dominated the economy and politics; the dispossession of American Indians from land that they regarded as theirs; the enslavement of millions of Africans and their African American descendants for a period of almost 250 years; the relegation of women and of racial, ethnic, and religious minorities to subordinate places in American society; and the extension of American control over foreign peoples, such as Latin Americans and Filipinos, who would have preferred to have been free and self-governing. We do not mean to suggest that American power has always been turned to these negative purposes. Subordinate groups have themselves marshaled power to combat oppression, as in the abolitionist and civil-rights crusades, the campaign for woman suffrage, and the labor movement. The state has used its power to moderate poverty and to manage the economy in the interests of general prosperity. And it has used its military power to defeat Nazi Germany, World War II Japan, the Cold War Soviet Union, and other enemies of freedom.

The invocation of power as a variable in American history forces us to widen the lens through which we look at the past and to complicate the stories we tell. Ours has been a history of freedom and domination; of progress toward realizing a broadly democratic polity and of delays and reverses, of abundance and poverty; of wars for freedom and justice and for control of foreign markets. In complicating our master narrative in this way, we think we have rendered American history more exciting and intriguing. Progress has not been automatic, but the product of ongoing struggles.

In this book, we have also tried to capture the diversity of the American past, both in terms of outcomes and in terms of the variety of groups who have participated in America's making. American Indians, in this book, are not presented simply as the victims of European aggression but as a people remarkably diverse in their own ranks, with a variety of systems of social organization and cultural expression. We give equal treatment to the industrial titans of American history—the likes of Andrew Carnegie and John D. Rockefeller—and to those, such as small farmers and poor workers, who resisted the corporate reorganization of economic life. We celebrate the great moments of 1863, when African Americans were freed from slavery, and of 1868, when they were made full citizens of the United States. But we also note how a majority of African Americans had to wait another 100 years, until the civil-rights movement of the 1960s, to gain full access to American freedoms. We tell similarly complex stories about women, Latinos, and other groups of ethnic Americans.

Political issues, of course, are only part of America's story. Americans have always loved their leisure and have created the world's most vibrant popular culture. They have embraced technological innovations, especially those promising to make their lives easier and more fun. We have, therefore, devoted considerable space to a discussion of American popular culture, from the founding of the first newspapers in the 18th century and the rise of movies, jazz, and the comics in the early 20th century, to the cable television and Internet revolutions in recent years. We have pondered, too, how American industry has periodically altered home and personal life by making new products—such as clothing, cars, refrigerators, and computers—available to consumers.

In such ways, we hope to give our readers a rich portrait of how Americans lived at various points in our history.

New to the Fourth Edition

The third edition won praise for its successful integration of political, cultural, and social history; its thematic unity; its narrative clarity and eloquence; its extraordinary coverage of pre-Columbian America; its extended treatment of the Civil War; its history of economic growth and change; and its excellent map and illustration programs. It also received high marks for its History through Film series, which discusses 31 different films (one per chapter) that treat important aspects of the American past. This very popular feature encourages students to think critically about what they see on screen and allows instructors to stimulate students' historical interest through a medium that they enjoy. The third edition earned plaudits, finally, for the inclusion of chapter outlines and focus questions at the beginning of each chapter and for the decision to move the Chronology boxes to each chapter's fore. We have preserved and enhanced all these strengths of the third edition in the fourth, and are pleased to announce that our History through Film series includes discussions of two new films, *The Gangs of New York* and *High Noon*. In preparing for this revision, we solicited feedback from professors and scholars throughout the country, many of whom have used the third edition of *Liberty, Equality, Power* in their classrooms. Their comments proved most helpful, and many of their suggestions have been incorporated into the fourth edition. For example, in response to reviewer comments, we have added captions to our outstanding map program, so that each map now comes with a brief commentary on how to interpret the geographical and topographical data it contains. Many of the maps are now animated on the Companion Web Site. We have also updated and condensed Suggested Readings and moved them to each chapter's end. Extensive bibliographic essays for each chapter are still available on the Web site. We have revised our Link to the Past feature so that the text of each

focuses more on specific primary sources, offering quotes, commentary, and questions while still linking these sources to online documents, images, or video or sound recordings. We think these improvements in the Links will add to their appeal.

In addition to making these pedagogical changes, we scrutinized each page of the textbook, making sure our prose was clear, the historical issues well presented, and the scholarship up to date. This review, guided by the scholarly feedback we received, caused us to make numerous revisions and additions throughout the textbook. We have also worked hard to bring our story to the present. Because of the changes in the final chapters, we now offer students historical perspective on such important recent events as George W. Bush's election in 2000, the destruction of the World Trade Center towers on September 11, 2001, and the war on terrorism and against Iraq.

Although a list of all the notable substantive changes appears below, we want to highlight one concentrated area of revision—the period from the 1880s through the 1930s, encompassing chapters 18–25. Although reviewers praised the high quality of the political history contained in these pages, some asked us to add more cultural and social history to the narrative mix. We have taken this request seriously, and have introduced more than 5,000 words of social and cultural commentary, much of it focusing on the following topics: the growth of the American middle class in both white and African American communities during the Gilded Age; middle-class patterns of urban living and consumption; the significance of the Philadelphia Centennial Exposition of 1876, the Chicago World's Fair of 1893, and museum exhibitions to late 19th century culture; turn-of-the-century changes in literary culture; the changing circumstances of women; Chinese and Japanese immigration to the United States in the late 19th and early 20th centuries; the decline of feminism in the 1920s; and the effects of the Great Depression on literary, cinematic, and musical culture during the 1930s. So as not to make the chapters in this time period overly long, we have made careful cuts in those chapters' political coverage; the net addition of text is much less than 5,000 words. The result, we believe, is a balanced and integrated political, social, and cultural history of the United States between the Civil War and the Second World War.

New Feature: Americans Abroad

We have also gone beyond our reviewers' suggestions and, in our group meetings to prepare for the fourth edition, committed ourselves to two new features for the textbook. The first, Americans Abroad, appearing in each chapter, focuses on an American who spent a significant portion of his or her life abroad. Some of those profiled carried U.S. political and cultural influence to other countries, while others became conduits through which foreign ideas and influences entered the United States. With our 31 features on both kinds of individuals, we wish to stress the interconnections between American history and world history, and examine the people who forged them. We have chosen a broad range of interesting and important figures—from Pocahontas to Thomas Jefferson, from the explorer Henry Morton Stanley to the anthropologist Margaret Mead, from the American industrialist Francis Cabot Lowell to the African American entertainer Josephine Baker, and from Civil War general Daniel Sickles to Secretary of State Madeleine Albright. We think students will both enjoy learning about these fascinating Americans, their travels, and their influence, and begin to develop, through such knowledge, a sense for the international context in which U.S. history has always unfolded. In the past, Americans (historians among them) have often ignored that context. But, as the events of September 11, 2001, tragically demonstrated, we ignore that context at our peril.

New Feature: Musical Link to the Past

Across their 200 plus years as a people, Americans have produced an extraordinarily rich and varied musical heritage. With the second new feature, Musical Link to the Past, we have embarked on a special effort to make aspects of this musical heritage integral to the history we present to our readers. In 15 features, we examine songs—the lyrics, the music, the performers, the historical context—from the middle of the 18th century to the present. These pieces range from revolutionary era odes to American liberty to 20th century country music laments about women's domestic burdens. Represented in this textbook are pieces by artists as diverse as Stephen Foster and Joni Mitchell, John Philip Sousa and Bob Dylan, Duke Ellington and Grandmaster Flash. All have made important contributions to the history of American music and enriched our musical heritage.

We hope that instructors and students alike will respond enthusiastically to our Musical Links to the Past. To make this feature come alive in classrooms, we have assembled a CD containing the musical selections that we discuss. All instructors who adopt our textbook will, upon request, receive a free copy of this CD, and will, as a result,

be able to play the music in their classrooms. For a small fee, students will be able to acquire their own CD copy.

In preparing this feature, we turned to Dr. Harvey Cohen, a cultural historian and music expert who teaches U.S. history at the University of Maryland. Possessing an extraordinary knowledge of the history of American music, and being an accomplished musician in his own right, Harvey was the ideal scholar to guide our choice of songs. He also drafted the texts of the 15 features, and, in the process, labored hard and imaginatively to turn his musical knowledge into history that, we think, will appeal to students. His work has been indispensable to us, and we are deeply grateful to him.

Specific Revisions to Content and Coverage

Chapter 18 New material on 1) the Native American perspective on destruction of the buffalo and the resulting effects on traditional Indian lifestyle; 2) how reality of life in the West differed from the myths and romanticized versions of "cowboys and Indians" popularized in fiction and traveling shows such as Buffalo Bill's Wild West show; and 3) how southern whites began to rebuild their way of life in the decades following the end of Reconstruction.

Chapter 19 Major new sections on American middle-class society and culture, the Columbian Exposition of 1893, and the New Woman.

Chapter 20 Major new section on Chinese and Japanese immigrants to the United States.

Chapter 24 Major new section on the decline of feminism in the 1920s; new material on Josh Gibson and the National Negro League.

Chapter 25 Major new section on the culture of the 1930s, covering the work of such artists as Studs Lonigan, Nathaniel West, and the Marx Brothers; new material on Woody Guthrie.

Chapter 27 Material on Eisenhower and on gender and women moved to chapter 28; more emphasis on race and gender in Cold War policies and the relationship of the economy to the Cold War.

Chapter 28 Section on women reorganized and strengthened.

Chapter 30 Reorganized through the removal of material on presidential administrations, which has now been placed in chapter 31.

Chapter 31 Brings American history to 2004, and includes full accounts of the first three years of the Bush administration; September 11, 2001, and its aftermath; and the war on terrorism and in Afghanistan and Iraq.

Supplements

For the Instructor

Instructor's Manual/Test Bank, Vols. I & II   The Instructor's Manual portion contains Chapter Outlines, Chronologies, Thematic Topics for Enrichment (critical thinking questions that could be used for classroom discussion or exams), Suggested Essay Topics, Comprehensive Lecture Outlines, and a Teaching Resources section that provides video ideas for lecture enrichment. The Test Bank section includes for each chapter: 50 multiple choice questions, 40 true/false questions, and approximately 10 fill-in-the-blank questions. All three of these question types are classified by type of question, whether they are analytical or factual, and the level of difficulty. Also included in the Test Bank are approximately 10 identification questions per chapter as well as five to seven short essays and two to four long essay questions with answers provided. The IM/TB is also available electronically on the Instructor's Resource CD and the pin-coded text Web site.

Instructor's Resource CD with ExamView (Windows/ Macintosh)   Includes the Instructor's Manual, Resource Integration Grid, ExamView® testing, and PowerPoint® slides with lecture outlines and images that can be used as offered, or customized by importing personal lecture slides or other material. ExamView allows you to create, deliver, and customize tests and study guides (both print and online) in minutes with this easy-to-use assessment and tutorial system. It offers both a Quick Test Wizard and an Online Test Wizard that guide you step by step through the process of creating tests, while its "what you see is what you get" capability allows you to see the test you are creating on the screen exactly as it will print or display online. You can build tests of up to 250 questions using up to 12 question types. Using ExamView's complete word processing capabilities, you can enter an unlimited number of new questions or edit existing questions.

New! Musical Links to the Past CD   Available free to adopters and for a small fee to students, this CD contains audio recordings of nearly all of the musical selections from the text's new Musical Link to the Past feature.

WebTutor Toolbox on WebCT or Blackboard   This online ancillary helps students succeed by taking the course beyond classroom boundaries to a virtual environment rich with study and mastery tools, communication tools, and course content. Professors can use WebTutor to provide virtual office hours, post their syllabi, set up threaded discussions, and track student progress with the quizzing material. For students, WebTutor offers real-time access to a full array of study tools, including flashcards (with audio), practice quizzes and tests, online tutorials, exercises, discussion questions, Web links, and a full glossary. Professors can customize the content in any way they choose, from uploading images and other resources, to adding Web links, to creating their own practice materials.

Transparency Acetates with Commentary for U.S. History   Contains more than 150 four-color map images from all of Wadsworth's U.S. History Texts. Packages are three-hole punched and shrink-wrapped. Correlation Guides for specific texts are included.

Wadsworth History Resource Center & *Liberty, Equality, Power* **Companion Web Site**

http://history.wadsworth.com/murrin_LEP4e

Provocative, exciting, and interactive, this site has something for everyone: instructors, students, and U.S. history buffs. Includes a wealth of documents and visuals with related activities, interactive maps (Timeline Maps and Discovery Maps), tutorial quiz questions, hyperlinks, and Internet and InfoTrac® College Edition exercises for each chapter. Also features activities utilizing American Journey Online for each chapter of the text. Each chapter includes Chapter Outlines, Learning Objectives, Glossaries (including flashcards with audio), Tutorial Quizzes (20 multiple choice, 5 to 10 fill-in-the-blank or true/false, and 5 essay/ short answers per chapter), Final Exam (incorporates all the quizzes by chapter into one "final" exam), Internet Exercises (centered around the *Liberty, Equality, Power* theme), InfoTrac Exercises, and Web Links.

Online Instructor's Resources include detailed plans and instructions for three Group Projects for classroom use: 1) Re-creating the '60s: Teaching History through Teach-ins; 2) Commemorating the Boston Massacre: Teaching History through Public Memory; and 3) Reconstruction and the Meaning of Freedom: Teaching History through Public Debate. In each of the projects, students examine the choices facing people in a particular era from the various perspectives of the different groups involved in the historical event.

Core Concept Lecture Launcher Videos   The Core Concept video package was created exclusively for *Liberty,*

Equality, Power by Films for the Humanities. Each video contains eight segments that include introductions by the respective author, concept clues, brief video segments, and concluding questions that take the student from image to text. Video segments are arranged chronologically and relate to topics of importance in the text. The video package is available free to instructors with adoption of the text.

Supplements are available to qualified adopters. Please consult your local sales representative for details.

For the Student

History Interactive: A Study Tool for *Liberty, Equality, Power* This valuable resource for students includes chapter summaries, chapter outlines, identification terms and definitions, fill-in the-blank and multiple choice quizzes, and extensive bonus materials including source readings, maps, and images. Also included are interactive versions of the text's maps plus Link to the Past and Americans Abroad features; two HistoryNOW modules; and a complete catalog of HistoryNOW interactive modules available for students and correlated chapter by chapter to *Liberty, Equality, Power*

U.S. History Atlas An invaluable collection of more than 50 clear and colorful historical maps covering all major periods in American history.

Wadsworth History Resource Center & *Liberty, Equality, Power* Companion Web Site

http://history.wadsworth.com/murrin_LEP4e

See description above.

American Journey Online Database

http://ajaccess.wadsworth.com

This text comes with free access to American Journey Online—16 primary source collections that capture the landmark events and major themes of the American experience through words and images from those who lived it. Each key topic in American history and culture addressed by the series encompasses hundreds of carefully selected rare documents, pictures, and archival audio and video, while essays, headnotes, and captions by scholars set the sources in context. Full text searchability and extensive hyperlinking provide fast and easy access and cross referencing. A new module on the Second World War is now available. For more information on how to search the database, please download the free User Guide, which highlights key features of American Journey Online in-

cluding search tips for each module, exercises, activities, and more.

U.S. History Documents Package The Documents Package, edited by Mark W. Beasley of Hardin-Simmons University, has been expanded to include more than 250 primary source documents interspersed with political cartoons and advertisements. Chapter openers and notes for each selection introduce the documents, provide essential background, and tie in the themes of liberty, equality, and power. Chapter discussion questions ask students to think critically about the ways the documents relate to each other and the text. The two-volume package is available to bundle with the textbook.

WebTutor Toolbox on WebCT or Blackboard See description above.

Acknowledgments

We recognize the contributions of reviewers who read portions of the manuscript in various stages:

William Allison, Weber State University
Angie Anderson, Southeastern Louisiana University
Kenneth G. Anthony, University of North Carolina, Greensboro
Paul R. Beezley, Texas Tech University
David Bernstein, California State University at Long Beach
Michael R. Bradley, Motlow College
Betty Brandon, University of South Alabama
Daniel Patrick Brown, Moorpark College
Ronald G. Brown, College of Southern Maryland
Phil Crow, North Harris College
Lorenzo M. Crowell, Mississippi State University
Amy E. N. Darty, University of Central Florida
Thomas M. Deaton, Dalton State College
Norman C. Delaney, Del Mar College
Ted Delaney, Washington and Lee University
Andrew J. DeRoche, Front Range Community College
Bruce Dierenfield, Canisius College
Brian R. Dirck, Anderson University
Maura Doherty, Illinois State University
R. Blake Dunnavent, Lubbock Christian University
Eileen Eagan, University of Southern Maine
Derek Elliott, Tennessee State University
B. Jane England, North Central Texas College
Van Forsyth, Clark College
Michael P. Gabriel, Kutztown University of Pennsylvania
Gary Gallagher, Pennsylvania State University
Gerald Ghelfi, Santa Ana College

Michael Goldberg, University of Washington, Bothell

David E. Hamilton, University of Kentucky

Michael J. Haridopolos, Brevard Community College

Mark Harvey, North Dakota State University

Mark Huddle, University of Georgia

Samuel C. Hyde, Jr., Southeastern Louisiana University

Thomas N. Ingersoll, Ohio State University

Frank Karpiel, Ramapo College of New Jersey

Michael Kazin, American University

Michael King, Moraine Valley Community College

Michael Krenn, Appalachian State

Frank Lambert, Purdue University

Pat Ledbetter, North Central Texas College

Jan Leone, Middle Tennessee State University

Craig Livingston, Montgomery College

Robert F. Marcom, San Antonio College

Suzanne Marshall, Jacksonville State University

Jimmie McGee, South Plains College

Nora E. McMillan, San Antonio College

Jerry Mills, Midland College

Charlene Mires, Villanova University

Rick Moniz, Chabot College

Michael R. Nichols, Tarrant County College, Northwest

Linda Noel, University of Maryland

Richard B. Partain, Bakersfield College

William Pencak, Penn State University, University Park
  Campus

Teresa Thomas Perrin, Austin Community College

David Poteet, New River Community College

Jonathan Rees, University of Southern Colorado

Anne Richardson, Texas Christian University

Lelia M. Roeckell, Molloy College

Roy Scott, Mississippi State University

Reynolds J. Scott-Childress, University of Maryland

Katherine A. S. Sibley, St. Joseph's University

Herb Sloan, Barnard College

John Smolenski, University of California, Davis

Jennifer Stollman, University of Mississippi

Siegfried H. Sutterlin, Indian Hills Community College

John Wood Sweet, The Catholic University of America

Xiansheng Tian, Metro State College of Denver

Vincent Vinikas, University of Arkansas, Little Rock

Vernon Volpe, University of Nebraska

Harry L. Watson, The University of North Carolina
  at Chapel Hill

William Benton Whisenhunt, College of DuPage

Laura Matysek Wood, Tarrant County College,
  Northwest

We wish to thank the members of the Wadsworth staff who embraced our textbook wholeheartedly when they inherited it from Harcourt and who have expertly guided the production of this fourth edition. Marcus Boggs, vice president and editor-in-chief, made it clear to us from the moment of acquisition that Wadsworth's support for this textbook would be strong. Clark Baxter, publisher, has brought great vision, enthusiasm, and savvy to this project and kept watch on the many different individuals in various locations who had responsibilities to this edition. Caroline Croley, executive marketing manager, has proven to be shrewd and imaginative in her efforts to make the match between our book and teachers of U.S. history a good one. Jennifer Ellis and Melinda Newfarmer, technology project managers, have helped us to glimpse vistas of multimedia use that we did not know existed. Kim Adams, production project manager, has expertly guided this book through the necessary stages from manuscript to finished book, while Ronn Jost, a project editor at Lachina Publishing Services, Inc., has expeditiously handled the complicated and seemingly endless tasks of copyediting, composition, proofreading, and indexing. Finally, a big thanks to all the Wadsworth salesmen and women who, from the moment we first presented our book to them in September 2001, have worked hard and creatively to generate interest in our book among university, college, and high school teachers across America. May this be one of many editions that we produce under the Wadsworth imprint.

We have been fortunate to be able, in this edition, to keep working with two freelancers who have made important contributions to several previous editions. Our photo editor, Lili Weiner, continues to dig up scores of new and interesting photographs and illustrations for us to examine. And our longtime developmental editor, Margaret McAndrew Beasley, has provided indispensable continuity and calm in a complicated time of transition. Margaret's editing skills, organizational expertise, good sense, and belief in this book and its authors keep us going.

In addition, each of us would like to offer particular thanks to those historians, friends, and family members who helped to bring this project to a successful conclusion.

JOHN M. MURRIN Mary R. Murrin has read each chapter, offered numerous suggestions, and provided the kind of moral and personal support without which this project would never have been completed. James Axtell and Gregory Evans Dowd saved me from many mistakes about Indians. John E. Selby and the late Eugene R. Sheridan were particularly helpful on what are now chapters 5 and 6. At an early phase, William J. Jackson and Lorraine E. Williams offered some very useful suggestions. Fred Anderson and Virginia DeJohns Anderson offered many acute suggestions for improvement. I am deeply grateful for their advice. Several colleagues and graduate students also have contributed in various ways, especially Stephen Aron, Ignacio Gallup-Diaz, Evan P. Haefeli, Geoffrey Plank, Nathaniel J. Sheidley, Jeremy Stern, and Beth Lewis Pardse.

PAUL E. JOHNSON My greatest debt is to the community of scholars who write about the United States between the Revolution and the Civil War. Closer to home, I owe thanks to the other writers of this book—particularly to John Murrin. The Department of History at the University of South Carolina provided time to work, while my wife, Kasey Grier, and a stray dog we named Lucy provided the right kinds of interruptions.

JAMES M. McPHERSON My family provided an environment of affection and stability that contributed immeasurably to the writing of my chapters, while undergraduate students at Princeton University who have taken my courses over the years provided feedback, questions, and insights that helped me to understand what students know and don't know, and what they need to know.

GARY GERSTLE When first drafting my parts of this textbook, I benefited enormously from the input of Roy Rosenzweig and Tom Knock, who gave each of my chapters an exceptionally thorough, thoughtful, and insightful critique. Kathleen Trainor was a gifted research assistant: She researched subjects I knew too little about, contributed to the design of charts and maps, checked facts, and solved countless thorny problems. To all these tasks she brought imagination, efficiency, and good cheer. Jerald Podair helped me to compile chapter bibliographies, offered me excellent ideas for maps and tables, and, on numerous occasions (and at all hours of the day and night), allowed me to draw on his encyclopedic knowledge of American history.

Reynolds Scott-Childress wrote the initial drafts for the new sections on cultural and social history in chapters 18 and 19 (and for the latter's Americans Abroad feature), while Linda Noel helped to research and write the Americans Abroad features for chapters 20–25. Kelly Ryan helped me to assemble the Link to the Past features, while Robert Chase worked to streamline and update the bibliographies. Marcy Wilson helped me out in a pinch with some

quick and careful proofreading. All of the last five individuals acknowledged are either recent Ph.D.s at the University or Maryland or soon will finish their degrees there. Four of them have taught for me in my U.S. history survey at Maryland and have used *Liberty, Equality, Power* in their sections. They know the book well (too well, some of them would say!), and the feedback they have given me over the years has helped to guide revisions. I thank them for their many contributions to this book. Finally, I thank my fellow authors for their intelligence, wit, and deep commitment to this project. By the time this book comes out, we will have been a team for 15 years. It has been an interesting, challenging, and satisfying journey.

EMILY AND NORMAN ROSENBERG We would like to thank our children—Sarah, Molly, Ruth, and Joe, who provided expert assistance on our charts. Students at Macalester College also deserve thanks, especially Sonya Michlin, Lorenzo Nencioli, Katie Kelley, Justin Brandt, Jessica Ford, and Mariah Howe. Paul Solon, a colleague at Macalester, provided his expertise in commenting on the maps. Anthony Todd, our research assistant at Macalester, made many important contributions to the fourth edition. We also want to acknowledge all of the people who offered their responses to the previous editions, including the historians who adopted the book and the students, especially those at San Diego State University, who read and evaluated it. Gary Gerstle, our collaborator, the late Richard Steele, a colleague at San Diego State, and Bruce Dierenfield provided wonderfully critical readings, and this edition is much better for their assistance.

Finally, no project of this scope is completely error free. We welcome all corrections and suggestions for improvement. Please send comments to:

Clark Baxter, Publisher
Wadsworth-Thomson
27R West Street #8
Beverly Farms, MA 01915

John M. Murrin, Paul E. Johnson, James M. McPherson, Gary Gerstle, Emily S. Rosenberg, Norman L. Rosenberg

Chapter 17

Reconstruction, 1863–1877

Winslow Homer, *Sunday Morning in Virginia*, 1877. Cincinnati Art Museum John J. Emery Fund. Acc. #1924.247.

SUNDAY MORNING IN VIRGINIA

This painting by Winslow Homer (1877) of four young black people and the grandmother of two of them is full of symbolism that illustrates important themes in both slavery and Reconstruction. The two lighter-skinned children, probably siblings, are reading the Bible while the dark-skinned children on either side—also probably brother and sister—follow along as they too learn to read. The grandmother listens with a wistful look into the distance, perhaps wishing that she was young enough to acquire the powerful tool of literacy denied to slaves. The religiosity of freedpeople, their humble homes, the partly white ancestry of some, and their thirst for education all are portrayed in this splendid painting.

CHAPTER OUTLINE

From the beginning of the Civil War, the North fought to "reconstruct" the Union. Lincoln first attempted to restore the Union as it had existed before 1861, but once the abolition of slavery became a Northern war aim, the Union could never be reconstructed on its old foundations. Instead, it must experience a "new birth of freedom," as Lincoln had said at the dedication of the military cemetery at Gettysburg.

But precisely what did "a new birth of freedom" mean? At the very least, it meant the end of slavery. The slave states would be reconstructed on a free-labor basis. But what would liberty look like for the 4 million freed slaves? Would they become citizens equal to their former masters in the eyes of the law? Would they have the right to vote? Should Confederate leaders and soldiers be punished for treason? On what terms should the Confederate states return to the Union? What would be the powers of the states and of the national government in a reconstructed Union?

CHAPTER FOCUS

♦ What were the positions of Presidents Abraham Lincoln and Andrew Johnson and of moderate and radical Republicans in Congress on the issues of restoring the South to the Union and protecting the rights of freed slaves?

♦ Why was Andrew Johnson impeached? Why was he acquitted?

♦ What were the achievements of Reconstruction? What were its failures?

♦ Why did a majority of the Northern people and their political leaders turn against continued federal involvement in Southern Reconstruction in the 1870s?

Wartime Reconstruction

Lincoln pondered the problems of Reconstruction long and hard. At first he feared that whites in the South would never extend equal rights to the freed slaves. After all, even most Northern states denied full civil equality to the few black people within their borders. In 1862 and 1863, Lincoln encouraged freedpeople to emigrate to all-black countries such as Haiti, where they would have a chance to get ahead without having to face the racism of whites. Black leaders, abolitionists, and many Republicans objected to that policy. Black people were Americans, they asserted. Why should they not have the rights of American citizens instead of being urged to leave the country?

Lincoln eventually acknowledged the logic and justice of that view, but in beginning the process of reconstruction, he first reached out to Southern *whites* whose allegiance to the Confederacy was lukewarm. On December 8, 1863, Lincoln issued his Proclamation of Amnesty and Reconstruction, which offered presidential pardon to Southern whites (with the exception of Confederate government officials and high-ranking military officers) who took an oath of allegiance to the United States and accepted the abolition of slavery. In any state where the number of white males aged 21 or older who took this oath equaled 10 percent of the number of voters in 1860, that nucleus could reestablish a state government to which Lincoln promised presidential recognition.

Because the war was still raging, this policy could be carried out only where Union troops controlled substantial portions of a Confederate state: Louisiana, Arkansas, and Tennessee in early 1864. Nevertheless, Lincoln hoped that once the process had begun in those areas, it might snowball as Union military victories convinced more and more Confederates that their cause was hopeless. In the end, those military victories were long delayed, and in most parts of the South, reconstruction did not begin until 1865.

Another problem that slowed the process was growing opposition within Lincoln's own party. Many Republicans believed that white men who had fought *against* the Union should not be rewarded with restoration of their political rights while black men who had fought *for* the Union were denied those rights. The Proclamation of Reconstruction had stated that

> any provision which may be adopted by [a reconstructed] State government in relation to the freed people of such State, which shall recognize and declare their permanent freedom, provide for their education, and which may yet be consistent, as a temporary arrangement, with their present condition as a laboring, landless, and homeless class, will not be objected to by the national Executive.

CHRONOLOGY

1863	Lincoln issues Proclamation of Amnesty and Reconstruction
1864	Congress passes Wade-Davis bill; Lincoln kills it by pocket veto
1865	Congress establishes Freedmen's Bureau • Andrew Johnson becomes president, announces his reconstruction plan • Southern states enact Black Codes • Congress refuses to seat Southern congressmen elected under Johnson's plan
1866	Congress passes civil rights bill and expands Freedmen's Bureau over Johnson's vetoes • Race riots in Memphis and New Orleans • Congress approves 14th Amendment • Republicans increase congressional majority in fall elections
1867	Congress passes Reconstruction acts over Johnson's vetoes • Congress passes Tenure of Office Act over Johnson's veto
1868	Most Southern senators and representatives readmitted to Congress under congressional plan of Reconstruction • Andrew Johnson impeached but not convicted • Ulysses S. Grant elected president • 14th Amendment is ratified
1870	15th Amendment is ratified
1871	Congress passes Ku Klux Klan Act
1872	Liberal Republicans defect from party • Grant wins reelection
1873	Economic depression begins with the Panic
1874	Democrats win control of House of Representatives
1875	Democrats implement Mississippi Plan • Congress passes civil rights act
1876	Centennial celebration in Philadelphia • Disputed presidential election causes constitutional crisis
1877	Compromise of 1877 installs Rutherford B. Hayes as president • Hayes withdraws troops from South
1883	Supreme Court declares civil rights act of 1875 unconstitutional

This seemed to mean that white landowners and former slaveholders could adopt labor regulations and other measures to control former slaves, so long as they recognized their freedom and made minimal provision for their education.

Radical Republicans and Reconstruction

These changes were radical advances over slavery, but for many Republicans they were not radical enough. Led by Thaddeus Stevens in the House and Charles Sumner in the Senate, the radical Republicans wanted to go much

LINCOLN'S FUNERAL PROCESSION IN CHICAGO, MAY 1, 1865
After a public funeral in Washington, D.C., on April 19, Lincoln's remains were transported by special train to New York City and then west to their final resting place in Springfield, Illinois, where Lincoln was buried on May 4, 1865. The funeral train stopped in major cities, where grieving citizens paid their last respects. An estimated 7 million people lined the tracks along the train's 1,000-mile journey, which reversed the route Lincoln had taken from Springfield to Washington, D.C., in February 1861.

further. If the freedpeople were landless, they said, provide them with land by confiscating the plantations of leading Confederates as punishment for treason. Radical Republicans also distrusted oaths of allegiance sworn by ex-Confederates. Rather than simply restoring the old ruling class to power, asked Charles Sumner, why not give freed slaves the vote, to provide a genuinely loyal nucleus of supporters in the South?

These radical positions did not command a majority of Congress in 1864. Yet the experience of Louisiana, the first state to reorganize under Lincoln's more moderate policy, convinced even nonradical Republicans to block Lincoln's program. With the protection of Union soldiers in the occupied portion of Louisiana (New Orleans and several parishes in the southern half of the state), enough white men took the oath of allegiance to satisfy Lincoln's

conditions. They adopted a new state constitution and formed a government that abolished slavery and provided a school system for blacks. But despite Lincoln's private appeal to the new government to grant literate blacks and black Union soldiers the right to vote, the reconstructed Louisiana legislature chose not to do so. It also authorized planters to enforce restrictive labor policies on black plantation workers. Louisiana's actions alienated a majority of congressional Republicans, who refused to admit representatives and senators from the "reconstructed" state.

At the same time, though, Congress failed to enact a reconstruction policy of its own. This was not for lack of trying. In fact, both houses passed the Wade-Davis reconstruction bill (named for Senator Benjamin Wade of Ohio and Representative Henry Winter Davis of Maryland) in July 1864. That bill did not enfranchise blacks, but it did impose such stringent loyalty requirements on Southern whites that few of them could take the required oath. Lincoln therefore vetoed it.

Lincoln's action infuriated many Republicans. Wade and Davis published a blistering "manifesto" denouncing the president. This bitter squabble threatened for a time to destroy Lincoln's chances of being reelected. Union military success in fall 1864, however, combined with sober second thoughts about the consequences of a Democratic electoral victory, reunited the Republicans behind Lincoln. The collapse of Confederate military resistance the following spring set the stage for compromise between the president and Congress on a policy for the postwar South. Two days after Appomattox, Lincoln promised that he would soon announce such a policy, which probably would have included voting rights for some blacks and stronger measures to protect their civil rights. But three days later, Lincoln was assassinated.

🌐 Andrew Johnson and Reconstruction

In 1864, Republicans had adopted the name Union Party to attract the votes of War Democrats and border-state Unionists who could not bring themselves to vote Republican. For the same reason, they also nominated Andrew Johnson of Tennessee as Lincoln's running mate.

Of "poor white" heritage, Johnson had clawed his way up in the rough-and-tumble politics of east Tennessee. This region of small farms and few slaves held little love for the planters who controlled the state. Andrew Johnson denounced the planters as "stuck-up aristocrats" who had no empathy with the Southern yeomen for whom Johnson became a self-appointed spokesman. Johnson, although a Democrat, was the only senator from a seceding state who refused to support the Confederacy. For this stance, the Republicans rewarded him with the vice presidential nomination, hoping to attract the votes of pro-war Democrats and upper-South Unionists.

Booth's bullet therefore elevated to the presidency a man who still thought of himself as primarily a Democrat and a Southerner. The trouble this might cause in a party that was mostly Republican and Northern was not immediately apparent, however. In fact, Johnson's enmity toward the "stuck-up aristocrats" whom he blamed for leading the South into secession prompted him to utter dire threats against "traitors." "Treason is a crime and must be made odious," he said soon after becoming president. "Traitors must be impoverished. . . . They must not only be punished, but their social power must be destroyed."

Radical Republicans liked the sound of this pronouncement. It seemed to promise the type of reconstruction they favored—one that would deny political power to ex-Confederates and would enfranchise blacks. They envisioned a coalition between these new black voters and the small minority of Southern whites who had never supported the Confederacy. These men could be expected to vote Republican. Republican governments in Southern states would guarantee freedom and would pass laws to provide civil rights and economic opportunity for freed slaves. Not incidentally, they would also strengthen the Republican Party nationally.

Johnson's Policy

Radical Republicans, with a combination of pragmatic, partisan, and idealistic motives, prepared to implement a progressive reconstruction policy, but Johnson unexpectedly refused to cooperate. Instead of calling Congress into special session, he moved ahead on his own. On May 29, 1865, Johnson issued two proclamations. The first provided a blanket amnesty for all but the highest-ranking Confederate officials and military officers, and those ex-Confederates with taxable property worth $20,000 or more—the "stuck-up aristocrats." The second named a provisional governor for North Carolina and directed him to call an election of delegates to frame a new state constitution. Only white men who had received amnesty and taken an oath of allegiance could vote. Similar proclamations soon followed for other former Confederate states. Johnson's policy was clear: He would exclude both blacks and upper-class whites from the reconstruction process. The backbone of the new South would be yeomen whites who, like himself, had remained steadfastly loyal to the Union, along with those who now proclaimed themselves loyal.

Although at first many Republicans supported Johnson's policy, the radicals were dismayed. They feared that restricting the vote to whites would lead to oppression of the newly freed slaves and restoration of the old power structure in the South. They began to sense that Johnson (who had owned slaves) was as dedicated to white supremacy as any Confederate. "White men alone must govern the South," he told a Democratic senator. After a tense confrontation with a group of black men led by Frederick Douglass, who had visited the White House to urge black suffrage, Johnson told his private secretary: "Those damned sons of bitches thought they had me in a trap! I know that damned Douglass; he's just like any nigger, and he would sooner cut a white man's throat than not."

Moderate Republicans believed that black men should participate to some degree in the reconstruction process,

From the Collections of the Library of Congress.

From the Collections of the Library of Congress.

ANDREW JOHNSON AND FREDERICK DOUGLASS

By 1866, the president and the leading black spokesman for equal rights represented opposite poles in the debate about Reconstruction. Johnson wanted to bring the South back into the Union on the basis of white suffrage; Douglass wanted black men to be granted the right to vote. Johnson's resistance to this policy as Republicans tried to enact it was a factor in his impeachment two years later.

but in 1865, they were not yet prepared to break with the president. They regarded his policy as an "experiment" that would be modified as time went on. "Loyal negroes must not be put down, while disloyal white men are put up," wrote a moderate Republican. "But I am quite willing to see what will come of Mr. Johnson's experiment." If the new Southern state constitutions failed to enfranchise at least literate blacks and those who had fought in the Union army, said another moderate, "the President then will be at liberty to pursue a sterner policy."

Southern Defiance

As it happened, none of the state conventions enfranchised a single black. Some of them even balked at ratifying the 13th Amendment (which abolished slavery). The rhetoric of some white Southerners began to take on a renewed anti-Yankee tone of defiance that sounded like 1861 all over again. Reports from Unionists and army officers in the South told of neo-Confederate violence against blacks and their white sympathizers. Johnson seemed to encourage such activities by his own rhetoric,

which sounded increasingly like that of a Southern Democrat, and by allowing the organization of white militia units in the South. "What can be hatched from such an egg," asked a Republican newspaper, "but another rebellion?"

Then there was the matter of presidential pardons. After talking fiercely about punishing traitors, and after excluding several classes of them from his amnesty proclamation, Johnson began to issue special pardons to many ex-Confederates, restoring to them all property and political rights. Moreover, under the new state constitutions, Southern voters were electing hundreds of ex-Confederates to state offices. Even more alarming to Northerners, who thought they had won the war, was the election to Congress of no fewer than nine ex-Confederate congressmen, seven ex-Confederate state officials, four generals, four colonels, and even the former Confederate vice president, Alexander H. Stephens. To apprehensive Republicans, it appeared that the rebels, unable to capture Washington in war, were about to do so in peace.

Somehow the aristocrats and traitors Johnson had denounced in April had taken over the reconstruction process.

Instead of weapons, they had resorted to flattering the presidential ego. Thousands of prominent ex-Confederates or their tearful female relatives applied for pardons confessing the error of their ways and appealing for presidential mercy. Reveling in his power over these once-haughty aristocrats who had disdained him as a humble tailor, Johnson waxed eloquent on his "love, respect, and confidence" toward Southern whites, for whom he now felt "forbearing and forgiving." More effective, perhaps, was the praise and support Johnson received from leading Northern Democrats. Although the Republicans had placed him on their presidential ticket in 1864, Johnson was after all a Democrat. That party's leaders enticed Johnson with visions of reelection as a Democrat in 1868 if he could manage to reconstruct the South in a manner that would preserve a Democratic majority there.

The Black Codes

That was just what the Republicans feared. Their concern that state governments devoted to white supremacy would reduce the freedpeople to a condition close to slavery was confirmed in fall 1865, when some of those governments enacted "Black Codes."

One of the first tasks of the legislatures of the reconstructed states was to define the rights of 4 million former slaves. The option of treating them exactly like white citizens was scarcely considered. Instead, the states excluded black people from juries and the ballot box, did not permit them to testify against whites in court, banned interracial marriage, and punished blacks more severely than whites for certain crimes. Some states defined any unemployed black person as a vagrant and hired him out to a planter, forbade blacks to lease land, and provided for the apprenticing to whites of black youths who did not have adequate parental support.

These Black Codes aroused anger among Northern Republicans, who saw them as a brazen attempt to reinstate a quasi-slavery. "We tell the white men of Mississippi," declared the *Chicago Tribune,* "that the men of the North will convert the State of Mississippi into a frog pond before they will allow such laws to disgrace one foot of the soil in which the bones of our soldiers sleep and over which the flag of freedom waves." And, in fact, the Union army's occupation forces did suspend the implementation of Black Codes that discriminated on racial grounds.

Land and Labor in the Postwar South

The Black Codes, although discriminatory, were designed to address a genuine problem. The end of the war had left black-white relations in the South in a state of limbo. The South's economy was in a shambles. Burned-out plantations, fields growing up in weeds, and railroads without tracks, bridges, or rolling stock marked the trail of war. Nearly half of the livestock in the former Confederacy and most other tangible assets except the land itself had been destroyed. Many people, white as well as black, lived from meal to meal. Law and order broke down in many areas. The war had ended early enough in the spring to allow the planting of at least some food crops, but who would plant and cultivate them? One-quarter of the South's white farmers had been killed in the war; the slaves were slaves no more. "We have nothing left to begin anew with," lamented a South Carolina planter. "I never did a day's work in my life, and I don't know how to begin."

Despite all of this trouble, life went on. Soldiers' widows and their children plowed and planted. Slaveless planters and their wives calloused their hands for the first time. Confederate veterans drifted home and went to work. Former slave owners asked their former slaves to work the land for wages or shares of the crop, and many did so. Others refused, because for them to leave the old place was an essential part of freedom. In slavery times, the only way to become free was to run away, and the impulse to leave the scene of bondage persisted. "You ain't, none o' you, gwinter feel rale free," said a black preacher to his congregation, "till you shakes de dus' ob de Ole Plantashun offen yore feet" (dialect in original source).

Thus the roads were alive with freedpeople who were on the move in summer 1865. Many of them signed on to work at farms just a few miles from their old homes. Others moved into town. Some looked for relatives who had been sold away during slavery or from whom they had been separated during the war. Some wandered aimlessly. Crime increased as people, both blacks and whites, stole food to survive—and as whites organized vigilante groups to discipline blacks and force them to work.

The Freedmen's Bureau

Into this vacuum stepped the U.S. Army and the Freedmen's Bureau. Tens of thousands of troops remained in the South as an occupation force until civil government could be restored. The Freedmen's Bureau (its official title was Bureau of Refugees, Freedmen, and Abandoned Lands), created by Congress in March 1865, became the principal agency for overseeing relations between former slaves and owners. Staffed by army officers, the bureau established posts throughout the South to supervise free-labor wage contracts between landowners and freedpeople. The Freedmen's Bureau also issued food rations to 150,000 people daily during 1865, one-third of them to whites.

Southern whites viewed the Freedmen's Bureau with hostility. Without it, however, the postwar chaos and devastation in the South would have been much greater—as some whites privately admitted. Bureau agents used their influence with black people to encourage them to sign free-labor contracts and return to work.

In negotiating labor contracts, the bureau tried to establish minimum wages. Lack of money in the South, however, caused many contracts to call for share wages—that is, paying workers with shares of the crop. At first, landowners worked their laborers in large groups (called gangs) under direct supervision, but many black workers resented this arrangement as reminiscent of slavery. Thus, a new system evolved, called sharecropping, whereby a black family worked a specific piece of land in return for a share of the crop produced on it.

THE FREEDMEN'S BUREAU

Created in 1865, the Freedmen's Bureau stood between freed slaves and their former masters in the postwar South, charged with the task of protecting freedpeople from injustice and repression. Staffed by officers of the Union army, the bureau symbolized the military power of the government in its efforts to keep peace in the South.

Land for the Landless

Freedpeople, of course, would have preferred to farm their own land. "What's de use of being free if you don't own land enough to be buried in?" asked one black sharecropper. "Might juss as well stay slave all yo' days" (dialect in original). Some black farmers did manage to save up enough money to buy small plots of land. Demobilized black soldiers purchased land with their bounty payments, sometimes pooling their money to buy an entire plantation on which several black families settled. Northern philanthropists helped some freedmen buy land. Most ex-slaves found the purchase of land impossible. Few of them had money, and even if they did, whites often refused to sell their land because it would mean losing a source of cheap labor and encouraging notions of black independence.

Several Northern radicals proposed legislation to confiscate ex-Confederate land and redistribute it to freedpeople, but those proposals went nowhere. The most promising effort to put thousands of slaves on land of their own also failed. In January 1865, after his march through Georgia, General William T. Sherman had issued a military order setting aside thousands of acres of abandoned plantation land in the Georgia and South Carolina low

SHARECROPPERS WORKING IN THE FIELDS

After the war, former planters tried to employ their former slaves in gang labor to grow cotton and tobacco, with the only difference from slavery being the grudging payment of wages. Freedpeople resisted this system as being too reminiscent of slavery. They compelled landowners to rent them plots of land on which these black families struggled to raise corn and cotton or tobacco, paying a share of the crop as rent—hence "sharecropping." This posed photograph was intended to depict the family labor of sharecroppers; in reality, most black farmers had a mule to pull their plow.

country for settlement by freed slaves. The army even turned over some of its surplus mules to black farmers. The expectation of "40 acres and a mule" excited freedpeople in 1865, but President Johnson's Amnesty Proclamation and his wholesale issuance of pardons restored most of this property to pardoned ex-Confederates. The same thing happened to white-owned land elsewhere in the South. Placed under the temporary care of the Freedmen's Bureau for subsequent possible distribution to freedpeople, by 1866 nearly all of this land had been restored to its former owners by order of President Johnson.

Education

Abolitionists were more successful in helping freedpeople obtain an education. During the war, freedmen's aid societies and missionary societies founded by abolitionists had sent teachers to Union-occupied areas of the South to set up schools for freed slaves. After the war, this effort was expanded with the aid of the Freedmen's Bureau. Two thousand Northern teachers, three-quarters of them women, fanned out into every part of the South. There they trained black teachers to staff first the mission schools and later the public schools established by Reconstruction state

governments. After 1870, the missionary societies concentrated more heavily on making higher education available to African Americans. Many of the traditionally black colleges in the South today were founded and supported by their efforts. This education crusade, which the black leader W. E. B. Du Bois described as "the most wonderful peace-battle of the nineteenth century," reduced the Southern black illiteracy rate to 70 percent by 1880 and to 48 percent by 1900.

☙ The Advent of Congressional Reconstruction

Political reconstruction shaped the civil and political rights of freedpeople. By the time Congress met in December 1865, the Republican majority was determined to control the process by which former Confederate states would regain full representation. Congress refused to admit the representatives and senators elected by the former Confederate states under Johnson's reconstruction policy and set up a special committee to formulate new

A BLACK SCHOOL DURING RECONSTRUCTION

In the antebellum South, teaching slaves to read and write was forbidden. Thus about 90 percent of the freedpeople were illiterate in 1865. One of their top priorities was education. At first, most of the teachers in the freedmen's schools established by Northern missionary societies were Northern white women. But as black teachers were trained, they took over the elementary schools, such as this one photographed in the 1870s.

terms. The committee held hearings at which Southern Unionists, freedpeople, and U.S. Army officers testified to abuse and terrorism in the South. Their testimony convinced Republicans of the need for stronger federal intervention to define and protect the civil rights of freedpeople. Many radicals wanted to go further and grant the ballot to black men, who would join with white Unionists and Northern settlers in the South to form a Southern Republican Party.

Most Republicans realized that Northern voters would not support such a radical policy, however. Racism was still strong in the North, where most states denied the right to vote to the few blacks living within their borders. Moderate Republicans feared that Democrats would exploit Northern racism in the congressional elections of 1866 if Congress made black suffrage a cornerstone of Reconstruction. Instead, the special committee decided to draft a constitutional amendment that would encour-

age Southern states to enfranchise blacks but would not require them to do so.

Schism between President and Congress

Meanwhile, Congress passed two laws to protect the economic and civil rights of freedpeople. The first extended the life of the Freedmen's Bureau and expanded its powers. The second defined freedpeople as citizens with equal legal rights and gave federal courts appellate jurisdiction to enforce those rights. To the dismay of moderates who were trying to heal the widening breach between the president and Congress, Johnson vetoed both measures. He followed this action with an intemperate speech to Democratic supporters in which he denounced Republican leaders as traitors who did not want to restore the Union

© Stock Montage, Inc.

"PARDON, Columbia—'Shall I Trust These Men'?"

© Stock Montage, Inc.

"FRANCHISE—'And Not This Man'?"

CARTOONS FOR FREEDOM

One of the best political cartoonists in American history, Thomas Nast drew scores of cartoons for *Harper's Weekly* in the 1860s and 1870s advocating the use of federal power to guarantee the liberty and enforce the equal rights of freed slaves. This illustration (1865) is an eloquent graphic expression of a powerful argument for giving freedmen the right to vote: black men who fought *for* the Union were more deserving of this privilege than white men who fought *against* it. Several of the kneeling figures are recognizable Confederate leaders: Alexander Stephens and Robert E. Lee in the foreground, Jefferson Davis to Lee's left, and John C. Breckinridge, Joseph E. Johnston, and Robert Toombs behind and to Davis's left.

except on terms that would degrade white Southerners. Democratic newspapers applauded the president for vetoing bills that would "compound our race with niggers, gypsies, and baboons."

The 14th Amendment

Johnson had thrown down the gauntlet to congressional Republicans, and they did not hesitate to take it up. With better than a two-thirds majority in both houses, they passed the Freedmen's Bureau and Civil Rights bills over the president's vetoes. Then on April 30, 1866, the special committee submitted to Congress its proposed 14th Amendment to the Constitution. After lengthy debate, the amendment received the required two-thirds majority in Congress on June 13 and went to the states for ratification. Section 1 defined all native-born or naturalized persons, including blacks, as American citizens and prohibited the states from abridging the "privileges and immunities" of citizens, from depriving "any person of life, liberty, or property without due process of law," and from denying to any person "the equal protection of the laws." Section 2 gave states the option of either enfranchising black males or losing a proportionate number of congressional seats and electoral votes. Section 3 disqualified a significant number of ex-Confederates from holding federal or state office. Section 4 guaranteed the national debt and repudiated the Confederate debt. Section 5 empowered Congress to enforce the 14th Amendment by "appropriate legislation." The 14th Amendment had far-reaching consequences. Section 1 has become the most important provision in the Constitution for defining and enforcing civil rights.

The 1866 Elections

Republicans entered the 1866 congressional elections campaign with the 14th Amendment as their platform. They made clear that any ex-Confederate state that ratified the amendment would be declared "reconstructed" and that its representatives and senators would be seated in Congress. Tennessee ratified the amendment, but Johnson counseled other Southern legislatures to reject the amendment, which they did. Johnson then prepared for an all-out campaign to gain a friendly Northern majority in the congressional elections.

Johnson began his campaign by creating a National Union Party made up of a few conservative Republicans who disagreed with their party, some border-state Unionists who supported the president, and Democrats. The inclusion of Democrats doomed the effort from the start. Many Northern Democrats still carried the taint of having opposed the war effort, and many Northern voters did not trust them. The National Union Party was further damaged by race riots in Memphis and New Orleans, where white mobs including former Confederate soldiers killed 80 blacks, among them several former Union soldiers. The riots bolstered Republican arguments that national power was necessary to protect "the fruits of victory" in the South. Perhaps the biggest liability of the National Union Party was Johnson himself. In a whistle-stop tour through the North, he traded insults with hecklers and embarrassed his supporters by comparing himself to Christ and his Republican adversaries to Judas.

Republicans swept the election: They gained a three-to-one majority in the next Congress. Having rejected the Reconstruction terms embodied in the 14th Amendment, Southern Democrats now faced far more stringent terms. "They would not cooperate in rebuilding what they destroyed," wrote an exasperated moderate Republican, so "we must remove the rubbish and rebuild from the bottom. Whether they are willing or not, we must compel obedience to the Union and demand protection for its humblest citizen."

The Reconstruction Acts of 1867

In March 1867, the new Congress enacted over Johnson's vetoes two laws prescribing new procedures for the full restoration of the former Confederate states (except Tennessee, which had already been readmitted) to the Union. These laws represented a complex compromise between radicals and moderates that had been hammered out in a confusing sequence of committee drafts, caucus decisions, all-night debates on the floor, and frayed tempers. The Reconstruction acts of 1867 divided the 10 Southern states into five military districts, directed army officers to register voters for the election of delegates to new constitutional conventions, and enfranchised males aged 21 and older (including blacks) to vote in those elections. The acts also disenfranchised (for these elections only) those ex-Confederates who were disqualified from holding office under the not-yet-ratified 14th Amendment—fewer than 10 percent of all white voters. When a state had adopted a new constitution that granted equal civil and political rights regardless of race and had ratified the 14th Amendment, it would be declared reconstructed and its newly elected congressmen would be seated.

These measures embodied a true revolution. Just a few years earlier, Southern whites had been masters of 4 million slaves and part of an independent Confederate nation. Now they were shorn of political power, with their former slaves not only freed but also politically empowered. To be sure, radical Republicans who warned that the

THE BURNING OF A FREEDMEN'S SCHOOL

Because freedpeople's education symbolized black progress, whites who resented and resisted this progress sometimes attacked and burned freedmen's schools, as in this dramatic illustration of a white mob burning a school during antiblack riots in Memphis in May 1866.

NEW YORK, SATURDAY, MAY 26, 1866.

Frank Leslie's Illustrated Newspaper.

revolution was incomplete as long as the old master class retained economic and social power turned out to be right in the end. In 1867, however, the emancipation and enfranchisement of black Americans seemed, as a sympathetic French journalist described it, "one of the most radical revolutions known in history."

Like most revolutions, the reconstruction process did not go smoothly. Many Southern Democrats breathed defiance and refused to cooperate. The presence of the army minimized antiblack violence, but thousands of white Southerners who were eligible to vote refused to do so, hoping that their nonparticipation would delay the process long enough for Northern voters to come to their senses and elect Democrats to Congress.

Blacks and their white allies organized Union leagues to inform and mobilize the new black voters into the Republican Party. Democrats branded Southern white Republicans as "scalawags" and Northern settlers as "carpetbaggers." By September 1867, the 10 states had 735,000 black voters and only 635,000 white voters registered. At least one-third of the registered white voters were Republicans.

President Johnson did everything he could to block Reconstruction. He replaced several Republican generals in command of Southern military districts with Democrats. He had his attorney general issue a ruling that interpreted the Reconstruction acts narrowly, thereby forcing a special session of Congress to pass a supplementary act

in July 1867. He encouraged Southern whites to obstruct the registration of voters and the election of convention delegates.

Johnson's purpose was to slow the process until 1868 in the hope that Northern voters would repudiate Reconstruction in the presidential election of that year, when Johnson planned to run as the Democratic candidate. Off-year state elections in fall 1867 encouraged that hope. Republicans suffered setbacks in several Northern states, especially where they endorsed referendum measures to enfranchise black men. "I almost pity the radicals," chortled one of President Johnson's aides after the 1867 elections. "After giving ten states to the negroes, to keep the Democrats from getting them, they will have lost the rest."

⬤ The Impeachment of Andrew Johnson

Johnson struck even more boldly against Reconstruction after the 1867 elections, despite warnings that he was risking impeachment. "What does Johnson mean to do?" an exasperated Republican asked another. "I am afraid his doings will make us all favor impeachment." In February 1868, Johnson took a fateful step. He removed from office Secretary of War Edwin M. Stanton, who had administered the War Department in support of the congressional Reconstruction policy. This appeared to violate the Tenure of Office Act, passed the year before over Johnson's veto, which required Senate consent for such removals. By a vote of 126 to 47 along party lines, the House impeached Johnson on February 24. The official reason for impeachment was that he had violated the Tenure of Office Act (which Johnson considered unconstitutional). The real reason was Johnson's stubborn defiance of Congress on Reconstruction.

Under the U.S. Constitution, impeachment by the House does not remove an official from office. It is more like a grand jury indictment that must be tried by a petit jury—in this case, the Senate, which sat as a court to try Johnson on the impeachment charges brought by the House. If convicted by a two-thirds majority of the Senate, he would be removed from office.

The impeachment trial proved long and complicated, which worked in Johnson's favor by allowing passions to cool. The Constitution specifies the grounds on which a president can be impeached and removed: "Treason, Bribery, or other high Crimes and Misdemeanors." The issue was whether Johnson was guilty of any of these acts. His able defense counsel exposed technical ambiguities in the Tenure of Office Act that raised doubts about whether

Johnson had actually violated it. Several moderate Republicans feared that the precedent of impeachment might upset the delicate balance of powers between the executive branch, Congress, and the judiciary that was an essential element of the Constitution. Behind the scenes, Johnson strengthened his case by promising to appoint the respected General John M. Schofield as secretary of war and to stop obstructing the Reconstruction acts. In the end, seven Republican senators voted for acquittal on May 16, and the final tally fell one vote short of the necessary two-thirds majority.

The Completion of Formal Reconstruction

The impeachment trial's end cleared the poisonous air in Washington, and Johnson quietly served out his term. Constitutional conventions met in the South during winter and spring 1867–68. Hostile whites described them as "Bones and Banjoes Conventions" and the Republican delegates as "ragamuffins and jailbirds." In sober fact, however, the delegates were earnest advocates of a new order, and the constitutions they wrote were among the

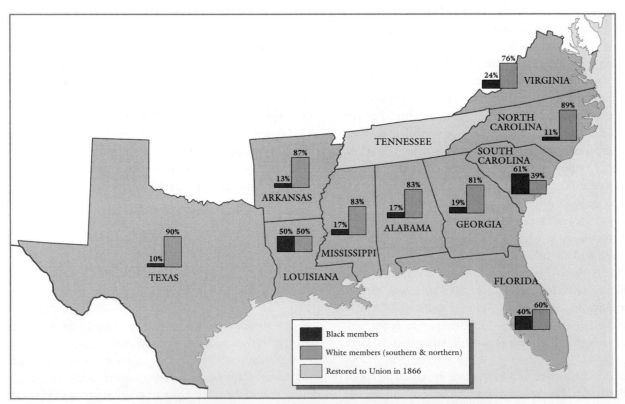

MAP 17.1 BLACK AND WHITE PARTICIPATION IN CONSTITUTIONAL CONVENTIONS, 1867–1868
Although black participation in these state constitutional conventions matched the African American percentage of the population only in South Carolina and Louisiana, the very presence of any black delegates in states where slavery had prevailed three years earlier was revolutionary.

most progressive in the nation. Three-quarters of the delegates to the 10 conventions were Republicans. About 25 percent of those Republicans were Northern whites who had relocated to the South after the war; 45 percent were native Southern whites who braved the social ostracism of the white majority to cast their lot with the despised Republicans; and 30 percent were blacks. Only in the South Carolina convention were blacks in the majority.

The new state constitutions enacted universal male suffrage, putting them ahead of most Northern states on that score. Some of the constitutions disenfranchised certain classes of ex-Confederates for several years, but by 1872, all such disqualifications had been removed. The constitutions mandated statewide public schools for both races for the first time in the South. Most states permitted segregated schools, but schools of any kind for blacks represented a great step forward. Most of the constitutions increased the state's responsibility for social welfare beyond anything previously known in the South.

Violence in some parts of the South marred the voting on ratification of these state constitutions. The Ku Klux Klan, a night-riding white terrorist organization, made its first appearance during the elections. Nevertheless, voters in seven states ratified their constitutions and elected new legislatures that ratified the 14th Amendment in spring 1868. That amendment became part of the U.S. Constitution the following summer, and the newly elected representatives and senators from those seven states, nearly all Republicans, took their seats in the House and Senate.

The 15th Amendment

The remaining three Southern states completed the reconstruction process in 1869 and 1870. Congress required them to ratify the 15th as well as the 14th Amendment. The 15th Amendment prohibited states from denying the right to vote on grounds of race, color, or previous condition of servitude. Its purpose was not only to prevent the reconstructed states from any future revocation of black suffrage, but also to extend equal suffrage to the border states and to the North. With final ratification of the 15th Amendment in 1870, the Constitution became truly color blind for the first time in U.S. history.

But the 15th Amendment still left half of the population disenfranchised. Many supporters of woman suffrage were embittered by its failure to ban discrimination on the grounds of gender as well as race. The radical wing of the suffragists, led by Elizabeth Cady Stanton and Susan B. Anthony, therefore opposed the 15th Amendment, causing a split in the woman suffrage movement.

This movement had shared the ideological egalitarianism of abolitionism since the Seneca Falls Convention of 1848. In 1866, male and female abolitionists formed the American Equal Rights Association (AERA) to work for both black and woman suffrage. Although some Republicans sympathized with the suffragists, they knew that no strong constituency among male voters favored granting the vote to women. A woman suffrage amendment to the state constitution of Kansas in 1867 suffered a lopsided defeat in a referendum. Most members of the AERA recognized that although Reconstruction politics made black enfranchisement possible, woman suffrage would have to wait until public opinion could be educated up to the standard of gender equality.

Stanton and Anthony refused to accept this reasoning. Why should illiterate Southern blacks have the right to vote, they asked, when educated Northern women remained shut out from the polls? It was "infinitely more important to secure the rights of 10 million women than to bring a million more men to the polls," declared Stanton. The 15th Amendment would establish "the most odious form of aristocracy the world has ever seen: an aristocracy of sex." When a majority of delegates at the 1869 convention of the AERA voted to endorse the 15th Amendment, several women led by Stanton and Anthony walked out and founded the National Woman Suffrage Association. The remainder reorganized themselves as the American Woman Suffrage Association. For the next two decades, these rival organizations, working for the same cause, remained at odds with each other.

The Election of 1868

Just as the presidential election of 1864 was a referendum on Lincoln's war policies, so the election of 1868 was a referendum on the Reconstruction policy of the Republicans. The Republican nominee was General Ulysses S. Grant. Although he had no political experience, Grant commanded greater authority and prestige than anyone else in the country. As general-in-chief of the army, he had opposed Johnson's Reconstruction policy in 1866 and had broken openly with the president in January 1868. That spring, Grant agreed to run for the presidency in order to preserve in peace the victory for Union and liberty he had won in war.

The Democrats turned away from Andrew Johnson, who carried too many political liabilities. They nominated Horatio Seymour, the wartime governor of New York, bestowing on him the dubious privilege of running against Grant. Hoping to put together a majority consisting of the South plus New York and two or three other Northern states, the Democrats adopted a militant platform denouncing the Reconstruction acts as "a flagrant usurpation of power . . . unconstitutional, revolutionary, and void."

A M E R I C A N S
A B R O A D

Dan Sickles Tries to Provoke
War with Spain

A lawyer and Democratic politician associated with the Tammany Hall machine in New York City, Sickles (1819–1914) went to London in 1853 to become secretary of the legation, where he helped draft the notorious Ostend Manifesto, which called for American acquisition of Cuba from Spain (see p. 429). At a Fourth of July dinner in 1854, Sickles refused to stand when a toast was offered to Queen Victoria, an act that generated outrage in Britain.

Sickles returned to New York in 1854 and was elected to Congress in 1856. A conspicuous womanizer and philanderer, Sickles found the shoe on the other foot when he discovered that his beautiful young wife Teresa was having an affair in Washington with Philip Barton Key (son of the composer of "The Star-Spangled Banner"). In 1859, Sickles shot Key dead in Lafayette Square near the White House. After a celebrated murder trial, Sickles was acquitted, partly on grounds of temporary insanity—the first time that plea had been used in American jurisprudence.

Shunned by polite society, Sickles sought to retrieve his reputation by raising an entire infantry brigade (five regiments) in New York City when the Civil War broke out. Partly through political influence, he rose to the rank of major general in 1863. At Gettysburg, he moved his corps forward without orders from the main Union position on Cemetery Ridge on July 2, and lost his leg in the subsequent Confederate attack that wrecked his corps.

After the war, Sickles became a Republican, campaigned for Grant in 1868, and received appointment as minister to Spain as a reward. Teresa had died in 1867, and he married a Spanish woman in 1871, converted to Roman Catholicism, and had two children with her. During Sickles's tenure in Madrid, Spain experienced political upheaval. Queen Isabella had been deposed because of the scandals caused by her constant succession of lovers. Regents, military rulers, republican leaders, and dictators came and went from 1869 to 1874. Behind the scenes, Sickles was active in various intrigues associated with these changes of regime.

In 1873, the *Virginius,* a vessel flying the American flag and running guns to rebels in Cuba fighting against Spanish rule of that island, was seized by the Spanish navy, and 53 Americans and Cuban rebels were executed. Sickles used this incident to try to provoke a war between the United States and Spain to liberate Cuba, but Secretary of State Hamilton Fish bypassed his loose-cannon minister and negotiated a peaceful settlement with Spain, provoking Sickles to resign in 1874.

Sickles thereupon moved to Paris and renewed a torrid affair with deposed Queen Isabella, earning a satirical reputation as "the Yankee King of Spain." In 1879, he returned to the United States, where he lived out the rest of his long life—without his wife and children, who remained in Europe. In 1898, the United States went to war with Spain to liberate Cuba a quarter-century after Sickles had tried to provoke such a war.

DANIEL SICKLES

© Corbis.

THE GRANT ADMINISTRATION   ■ 549

The platform also demanded "the abolition of the Freedmen's Bureau, and all political instrumentalities designed to secure negro supremacy."

The vice presidential candidate, Frank Blair of Missouri, became the point man for the Democrats. In a public letter, he proclaimed, "There is but one way to restore the Government and the Constitution, and that is for the President-elect to declare these [Reconstruction] acts null and void, compel the army to undo its usurpations at the South, disperse the carpet-bag State Governments, [and] allow the white people to reorganize their own governments."

The only way to achieve this bold counterrevolutionary goal was to suppress Republican voters in the South. This the Ku Klux Klan tried its best to do. Federal troops failed to prevent much of the violence because martial law had been lifted in the states where civilian governments had been restored. In Louisiana, Georgia, Arkansas, and Tennessee, the Klan or Klan-like groups committed dozens of murders and intimidated thousands of black voters. The violence helped the Democratic cause in the South, but probably hurt it in the North where many voters perceived the Klan as an organization of neo-Confederate paramilitary guerrillas. In fact, many Klansmen were former soldiers, and such famous Confederate generals as Nathan Bedford Forrest and John B. Gordon held high positions in the Klan.

Seymour did well in the South, carrying five former slave states and coming close in others despite the solid Republican vote of the newly enfranchised blacks. Grant, however, swept the electoral vote 214 to 80. Seymour actually won a slight majority of the white voters nationally; without black enfranchisement, Grant would have had a minority of the popular vote.

The Grant Administration

A great military commander, Grant is usually branded a failure as president. That indictment is only partly correct. Grant's inexperience and poor judgment betrayed him into several unwise appointments of officials who were later convicted of corruption, and his back-to-back administrations (1869–77) were plagued by scandals. His secretary of war was impeached for selling appointments to army posts and Indian reservations, and his attorney general and secretary of the interior resigned under suspicion of malfeasance in 1875.

Although he was an honest man, Grant was too trusting of subordinates. He appointed many former members of his military family, as well as several of his wife's relatives, to offices for which they were scarcely qualified. In an

era notorious for corruption at all levels of government, many of the scandals were not Grant's fault. The Tammany Hall "Ring" of "Boss" William Marcy Tweed in New York City may have stolen more money from taxpayers than all of the federal agencies combined. It was said that the only thing the Standard Oil Company could not do with the Ohio legislature was refine it. In Washington, one of the most widely publicized scandals, the Credit Mobilier affair, concerned Congress rather than the Grant administration. Several congressmen had accepted stock in the Credit Mobilier, a construction company for the Union Pacific Railroad, which received loans and land grants from the government. In return, the company expected lax congressional supervision, thereby permitting financial manipulations by the company.

What accounted for this explosion of corruption in the postwar decade, which one historian has called "The Era of Good Stealings"? During the war, expansion of government contracts and the bureaucracy had created new opportunities for the unscrupulous. Following the intense sacrifices of the war years came a relaxation of tensions and standards. Rapid postwar economic growth, led by an extraordinary rush of railroad construction, further encouraged greed and get-rich-quick schemes of the kind satirized by Mark Twain and Charles Dudley Warner in their 1873 novel *The Gilded Age*, which gave its name to the era.

Civil Service Reform

Some of the apparent increase in corruption during the Gilded Age was more a matter of perception. During a civil service reform movement to purify the government bureaucracy and make it more efficient, reformers focused a harsh light into the dark corners of corruption that was hitherto unilluminated because of the nation's preoccupation with war and reconstruction. Thus reformers' publicity may have exaggerated the actual extent of corruption. In reality, during the Grant administration, several government agencies made real progress in eliminating abuses that had flourished in earlier administrations.

The chief target of civil service reform was the "spoils system." With the slogan "To the victor belongs the spoils," the victorious party in an election rewarded party workers with appointments as postmasters, customs collectors, and the like. The hope of getting appointed to a government post was the glue that kept the faithful together when a party was out of power. An assessment of 2 or 3 percent on the beneficiaries' government salaries kept party coffers filled when the party was in power. The spoils system politicized the bureaucracy and staffed it with unqualified personnel who spent more time working for their party than for the government. It also plagued every incoming president (and other elected officials) with the "swarm of office seekers" that loom so large in contemporary accounts (including those of the humorist Orpheus C. Kerr, whose nom de plume was pronounced "Office Seeker").

Civil service reformers wanted to separate the bureaucracy from politics by requiring competitive examinations for the appointment of civil servants. This movement gathered steam during the 1870s and finally achieved success in 1883 with the passage of the Pendleton Act, which established the modern structure of the civil service. When Grant took office, he seemed to share the sentiments of civil service reformers; several of his cabinet officers inaugurated examinations for certain appointments and promotions in their departments. Grant also named a civil service commission headed by George William Curtis, a leading reformer and editor of *Harper's Weekly.* But many congressmen, senators, and other politicians resisted civil service reform. Patronage greased the political machines that kept them in office and all too often enriched them and their political chums. They managed to subvert reform, sometimes using Grant as an unwitting ally and thus turning many reformers against the president.

Foreign Policy Issues

A foreign policy controversy added to Grant's woes. The irregular procedures by which his private secretary had negotiated a treaty to annex Santo Domingo (now the Dominican Republic) alienated leading Republican senators, who defeated ratification of the treaty. Politically inexperienced, Grant acted like a general who needed only to give orders rather than as a president who must cultivate supporters. The fallout from the Santo Domingo affair widened the fissure in the Republican Party between "spoilsmen" and "reformers."

The Grant administration had some solid foreign policy achievements to its credit, however. Hamilton Fish, the able secretary of state, negotiated the Treaty of Washington in 1871 to settle the vexing Alabama Claims. These were damage claims against Britain for the destruction of American shipping by the C.S.S. *Alabama* and other Confederate commerce raiders built in British shipyards. The treaty established an international tribunal to arbitrate the U.S. claims, thus creating a precedent for the peaceful settlement of disputes. It resulted in the award of $15.5 million in damages to U.S. shipowners and a British expression of regret.

The events leading to the Treaty of Washington also resolved another long-festering issue between Britain and the United States: the status of Canada. The seven separate British North American colonies were especially vulnerable to U.S. desires for annexation. In fact, many bitter Northerners demanded British cession of Canadian colonies to the United States as fair payment for the wartime depredations of the *Alabama* and other commerce raiders. Such demands tended to strengthen the loyalty of many Canadians to Britain as a counterweight to the aggressive Americans. In 1867, Parliament passed the British North America Act, which united most of the Canadian colonies into a new and largely self-governing Dominion of Canada.

Canadian nationalism was further strengthened by the actions of the Irish American Fenian Brotherhood. A secret society organized during the Civil War, the Fenians believed that an invasion of Canada would strike a blow for the independence of Ireland. Three times from 1866 to 1871, small "armies" of Fenians, composed mainly of Irish American veterans of the Union Army, crossed the border into Canada, only to be driven back after comic-opera skirmishes. The Fenian raids intensified Canadian anti-Americanism and complicated the negotiations leading to the Washington Treaty, but after its signing, Canadian-American tensions cooled. The treaty also helped resolve disputes over American commercial fishing in Canadian waters. U.S. troops prevented further Fenian raids, and American demands for annexation of Canada faded away. These events gave birth to the modern nation of Canada.

Reconstruction in the South

During Grant's two administrations, the Southern Question was the most intractable issue. A phrase in Grant's acceptance of the presidential nomination in 1868 had struck a responsive chord in the North: "Let us have peace." With the ratification of the 15th Amendment, many people breathed a sigh of relief at this apparent resolution of "the last great point that remained to be settled of the issues of the war." It was time to deal with other matters that had been long neglected. Ever since the annexation of Texas a quarter-century earlier, the nation had known scarcely a moment's respite from sectional strife. "Let us have done with Reconstruction," pleaded the New York *Tribune* in 1870. "LET US HAVE PEACE." But there was no peace. Reconstruction was not over; it had hardly begun. State governments elected by black and white voters were in place in the South, but Democratic violence against Reconstruction and the instability of the Republican coalition that sustained it portended trouble.

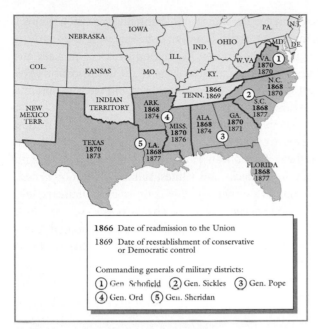

MAP 17.2   RECONSTRUCTION IN THE SOUTH
The dates for each state listed on this map show how short-lived "Radical Reconstruction" was in most Southern states.

Blacks in Office

Because the Republican Party had no antebellum roots in the South, most Southern whites perceived it as a symbol of conquest and humiliation. In the North, the Republican Party represented the most prosperous, educated, and influential elements of the population, but in the South, most of its adherents were poor, illiterate, and landless.

About 80 percent of Southern Republican voters were black. Although most black leaders were educated and many had been free before the war, most black voters were illiterate ex-slaves. Neither the leaders nor their constituents, however, were as ignorant or as venal as stereotypes have portrayed them. Of 14 black representatives and two black senators elected in the South between 1868 and 1876, all but three had attended secondary school and four had attended college. Several of the blacks elected to state offices were among the best-educated men of their day. Jonathan Gibbs, secretary of state in Florida from 1868 to 1872 and state superintendent of education from 1872 to 1874, was a graduate of Dartmouth College and Princeton Theological Seminary. Francis L. Cardozo, secretary of state in South Carolina for four years and treasurer for another four, was educated at the University of Glasgow and at theological schools in Edinburgh and London.

It is true that some lower-level black officeholders, as well as their constituents, could not read or write, but the fault for that situation lay not with them but with the slave regime that had denied them an education. Illiteracy did not preclude an understanding of political issues for them any more than it did for Irish American voters in the North, many of whom were also illiterate. Southern blacks thirsted for education. Participation in the Union League and the experience of voting were themselves forms of education. Black churches and fraternal organizations proliferated during Reconstruction and tutored African Americans in their rights and responsibilities.

Linked to the myth of black incompetence was the legend of the "Africanization" of Southern governments during Reconstruction. The theme of "Negro rule"—by which the "barbarous African" exercised "unbridled power" in the 10 Southern states—was a staple of Democratic propaganda. It was enshrined in folk memory and in generations of textbooks. In fact, blacks held only 15 to 20 percent of public offices, even at the height of Reconstruction in the early 1870s. No states had black governors (although the black lieutenant governor of Louisiana acted as governor for a month), and only one black man became a state supreme court justice. Nowhere except in South Carolina did blacks hold office in numbers anywhere near their proportion of the population; in that state, they constituted 52 percent of all state and federal elected officials from 1868 to 1876.

"Carpetbaggers"

Next to "Negro rule," carpetbagger corruption and scalawag rascality have been the prevailing myths of Reconstruction. Carpetbaggers did hold a disproportionate number of high political offices in Southern state governments during Reconstruction. More than half of the Republican governors and nearly half of the congressmen and senators were Northerners. A few did resemble the proverbial adventurer who came south with nothing but a carpetbag in which to stow the loot plundered from a helpless people. Most of the Northerners were Union army officers who stayed on after the war as Freedmen's Bureau agents, teachers in black schools, business investors, pioneers of a new political order—or simply because they liked the climate.

Like others who migrated to the West as a frontier of opportunity, those who settled in the postwar South hoped to rebuild its society in the image of the free-labor North. Many were college graduates at a time when fewer than 2 percent of Americans had attended college. Most brought not empty carpetbags but considerable capital, which they invested in what they hoped would become a new South. They also invested human capital—themselves—in a drive to modernize the region's social structure and democratize its politics. But they underestimated the hostility of Southern whites, most of whom regarded them as agents of an alien culture and leaders of an enemy army—as indeed they had been—in a war that for many Southerners was not yet over.

"Scalawags"

Most of the native-born whites who joined the Southern Republican Party came from the upcountry Unionist areas of western North Carolina and Virginia, eastern Tennessee, and elsewhere. Others were former Whigs who saw an opportunity to rebuild the South's economy in partnership with equally Whiggish Northern Republicans. Republicans, said a North Carolina scalawag, were the "party of progress, of education, of development. . . . Yankees and Yankee notions are just what we want in this country. We want their capital to build factories and work shops, and railroads."

But Yankees and Yankee notions were just what most Southern whites did not want. Democrats saw that the Southern Republican Party they abhorred was a fragile coalition of blacks and whites, Yankees and Southerners, hill-country yeomen and low-country entrepreneurs, illiterates and college graduates. The party was weakest along the seams where these disparate elements joined, especially the racial seam. Democrats attacked that weakness

HISTORY THROUGH FILM

The Birth of a Nation (1915)

Directed by D. W. Griffith. Starring Lillian Gish (Elsie Stoneman), Henry B. Walthall (Ben Cameron), Ralph Lewis (Austin Stoneman), George Siegmann (Silas Lynch).

Few, if any, films have had such a pernicious impact on historical understanding and race relations as *Birth of a Nation*. This movie popularized a version of Reconstruction that portrayed predatory carpetbaggers and stupid, brutish blacks plundering a prostrate South and lusting after white women. It perpetuated vicious stereotypes of rapacious black males. It glorified the Ku Klux Klan of the Reconstruction era, inspiring the founding of the "second Klan" in 1915, which became a powerful force in the 1920s (see chapter 24).

The first half of the film offers a conventional Victorian romance of the Civil War. The two sons and daughter of Austin Stoneman (a malevolent radical Republican who is a thinly disguised Thaddeus Stevens) become friends with the three sons and two daughters of the Cameron family of "Piedmont," South Carolina, through the friendship of Ben Cameron and Phil Stoneman at college. The Civil War tragically separates the families. The Stoneman and Cameron boys enlist in the Union and Confederate armies and—predictably—face each other on the battlefield. Two Camerons and one Stoneman are killed in the war, and Ben Cameron is badly wounded and captured, to be nursed back to health by—you guessed it—Elsie Stoneman.

After the war, the younger Camerons and Stonemans renew their friendship. During the Stonemans' visit to South Carolina, Ben Cameron and Elsie Stoneman, and Phil Stoneman and Flora Cameron, fall in love. If the story had stopped there, *Birth of a Nation* would have been just another Hollywood romance. But Austin Stoneman brings south with him Silas Lynch, an ambitious, leering mulatto demagogue who stirs up the animal passions of the ignorant black majority to demand "Equal Rights, Equal Politics, Equal Marriage." A "renegade Negro," Gus, stalks the youngest Cameron daughter, who saves herself from rape by jumping from a cliff to her death. Silas Lynch tries to force Elsie to marry him. "I will build a Black Empire," he tells the beautiful, virginal Elsie (Lillian Gish was the Hollywood beauty queen of silent films), "and you as my queen shall rule by my side."

Finally provoked beyond endurance, white South Carolinians led by Ben Cameron organize the Ku Klux Klan to save "the Aryan race." Riding to the rescue of embattled whites in stirring scenes that anticipated the heroic

with every weapon at their command, from social ostracism of white Republicans to economic intimidation of black employees and sharecroppers. The most potent Democratic weapon was violence.

The Ku Klux Klan

The generic name for the secret groups that terrorized the Southern countryside was the Ku Klux Klan, but some went by other names (the Knights of the White Camelia in Louisiana, for example). Part of the Klan's purpose was social control of the black population. Sharecroppers who tried to extract better terms from landowners, or black people who were considered too "uppity," were likely to receive a midnight whipping—or worse—from white-sheeted Klansmen. Scores of black schools, perceived as a particular threat to white supremacy, went up in flames.

The Klan's main purpose was political: to destroy the Republican Party by terrorizing its voters and, if necessary, by murdering its leaders. No one knows how many politically motivated killings took place—certainly hundreds, probably thousands. Nearly all of the victims were Republicans; most of them were black. In one notorious incident, the Colfax Massacre in Louisiana (April 18, 1873), a clash between black militia and armed whites left three whites and nearly 100 blacks dead. Half of the blacks were killed in cold blood after they had surrendered.

actions of the cavalry against Indians in later Hollywood Westerns, the Klan executes Gus, saves Elsie, disperses black soldiers and mobs, and carries the next election for white rule by intimidating black voters. The film ends with a double marriage that unites the Camerons and Stonemans in a symbolic rebirth of a nation that joins whites of the North and South in a new union rightfully based on the supremacy of "the Aryan race."

The son of a Confederate lieutenant colonel, David Wark (D. W.) Griffith was the foremost director of the silent movie era. He pioneered many precedent-setting cinematic techniques and profoundly influenced filmmaking throughout the world. *Birth of a Nation* was the first real full-length feature film, technically and artistically superior to anything before it. Apart from its place in the history of cinema, though, why should anyone today watch a movie that perpetuates such wrongheaded history and noxious racist stereotypes? Precisely *because* it reflects and amplifies an interpretation of Reconstruction that prevailed from the 1890s to the 1950s, and thereby shaped not only historical understanding but also contemporary behavior (as in its inspiration

Henry B. Walthall (Ben Cameron) kissing the hand of Elsie Stoneman (Lillian Gish) in *Birth of a Nation*.

for the Klan of the 1920s). Although *Birth of a Nation* aroused controversy in parts of the North and was picketed by the NAACP, some 200 million people saw the film in the United States and abroad from 1915 to 1946. The story, and director Griffith, demonstrated in dramatic fashion how the South, having lost the Civil War, won the battle for how the war and especially Reconstruction would be remembered for more than half a century.

© Bettmann/Corbis.

TWO MEMBERS OF THE KU KLUX KLAN

Founded in Pulaski, Tennessee, in 1866 as a social organization similar to a college fraternity, the Klan evolved into a terrorist group whose purpose was intimidation of Southern Republicans. The Klan, in which former Confederate soldiers played a prominent part, was responsible for the beating and murder of hundreds of blacks and whites alike from 1868 to 1871.

In some places, notably Tennessee and Arkansas, Republican militias formed to suppress and disarm the Klan, but in most areas the militias were outgunned and outmaneuvered by ex-Confederate veteran Klansmen. Some Republican governors were reluctant to use black militia against white guerrillas for fear of sparking a racial bloodbath—as happened at Colfax.

The answer seemed to be federal troops. In 1870 and 1871, Congress enacted three laws intended to enforce the 14th and 15th Amendments. Interference with voting rights became a federal offense, and any attempt to deprive another person of civil or political rights became a felony. The third law, passed on April 20, 1871, and popularly called the Ku Klux Klan Act, gave the president power to suspend the writ of habeas corpus and send in federal troops to suppress armed resistance to federal law.

Armed with these laws, the Grant administration moved against the Klan. Because Grant was sensitive to charges of "military despotism," he used his powers with restraint. He suspended the writ of habeas corpus in only nine South Carolina counties. Nevertheless, there and elsewhere federal marshals backed by troops arrested thousands of suspected Klansmen. Federal grand juries indicted more than 3,000 members, and several hundred defendants pleaded guilty in return for suspended sentences. To clear clogged court dockets so that the worst offenders could be tried quickly, the Justice Department dropped charges against nearly 2,000 others. About 600 Klansmen were convicted; most of them received fines or light jail sentences, but 65 went to a federal penitentiary for terms of up to five years.

The Election of 1872

These measures broke the back of the Klan in time for the 1872 presidential election. A group of dissident Republicans had emerged to challenge Grant's reelection. They believed that conciliation of Southern whites rather than continued military intervention was the only way to achieve peace in the South. Calling themselves Liberal Republicans, these dissidents nominated Horace Greeley, the famous editor of the New York *Tribune*. Under the slogan "Anything to beat Grant," the Democratic Party also endorsed Greeley's nomination, although he had long been their antagonist. On a platform denouncing "bayonet rule" in the South, Greeley urged his fellow Northerners to put the issues of the Civil War behind them and to "clasp hands across the bloody chasm which has too long divided" North and South.

This phrase would come back to haunt Greeley. Most voters in the North were still not prepared to trust Democrats or Southern whites. Powerful anti-Greeley cartoons by political cartoonist Thomas Nast showed Greeley shaking the hand of a Klansman dripping with the blood of a murdered black Republican. Nast's most famous cartoon portrayed Greeley as a pirate captain bringing his craft alongside the ship of state, while Confederate leaders, armed to the teeth, hid below waiting to board it.

Grant swamped Greeley on election day. Republicans carried every Northern state and 10 of the 16 Southern and border states. Blacks in the South enjoyed more freedom in voting than they would again for a century. This apparent triumph of Republicanism and Reconstruction would soon unravel.

The Panic of 1873

The U.S. economy had grown at an unprecedented pace since recovering from a mild postwar recession. In eight years, 35,000 miles of new railroad track were laid down, equal to all the track laid in the preceding 35 years. The first transcontinental railroad had been completed on May 10, 1869, when a golden spike was driven at Promontory Summit, Utah Territory, linking the Union Pacific and the Central Pacific. But the building of a second transcontinental line, the Northern Pacific, precipitated a Wall Street panic in 1873 and plunged the economy into a five-year depression.

Jay Cooke's banking firm, fresh from its triumphant marketing of Union war bonds, took over the Northern Pacific in 1869. Cooke pyramided every conceivable kind of equity and loan financing to raise the money to begin laying rails west from Duluth, Minnesota. Other investment firms did the same as a fever of speculative financing gripped the country. In September 1873, the pyramid of paper collapsed. Cooke's firm was the first to go bankrupt. Like dominoes, thousands of banks and businesses also collapsed. Unemployment rose to 14 percent, and hard times set in.

The Retreat from Reconstruction

It is an axiom of American politics that the voters will punish the party in power in times of economic depression. That axiom held true in the 1870s. Democrats made large gains in the congressional elections of 1874, winning a majority in the House for the first time in 18 years.

Public opinion also began to turn against Republican policies in the South. The campaign by Liberal Republicans and Democrats against "bayonet rule" and "carpetbag corruption" that left most Northern voters unmoved in 1872 found a growing audience in subsequent years. Intraparty battles among Republicans in Southern states enabled Democrats to regain control of several state governments. Well-publicized corruption scandals also discredited Republican leaders. Although corruption was probably no worse in Southern states than in many parts of the North, Southern postwar poverty made waste and extravagance seem worse. White Democrats scored propaganda points by claiming that corruption proved the incompetence of "Negro-carpetbag" regimes.

Northerners grew increasingly weary of what seemed to be the endless turmoil of Southern politics. Most of them had never had a strong commitment to racial equality, and they were growing more and more willing to let white supremacy regain sway in the South. "The truth is," confessed a Northern Republican, "our people are tired out with this worn out cry of 'Southern outrages'!!! Hard times & heavy taxes make them wish the 'nigger,' 'everlasting nigger,' were in hell or Africa."

By 1875, only four Southern states remained under Republican control: South Carolina, Florida, Mississippi, and Louisiana. In those states, white Democrats had revived paramilitary organizations under various names: White Leagues (Louisiana), Rifle Clubs (Mississippi), and Red Shirts (South Carolina). Unlike the Klan, these groups operated openly. In Louisiana, they fought pitched battles with Republican militias in which scores were killed. When the Grant administration sent large numbers of federal troops to Louisiana, people in both North and South cried out against military rule. The protests grew even louder when soldiers marched onto the floor of the Louisiana legislature in January 1875 and expelled several Democratic legislators after a contested election. Was this America? asked Republican Senator Carl Schurz in a widely publicized speech: "If this can be done in Louisiana, how long will it be before it can be done in Massachusetts and Ohio? How long before a soldier may stalk into the national House of Representatives, and, pointing to the Speaker's mace, say 'Take away that bauble!'"

The Mississippi Election of 1875

The backlash against the Grant administration affected the Mississippi state election of 1875. Democrats there devised a strategy called the Mississippi Plan. The first step was to "persuade" the 10 to 15 percent of white voters still calling themselves Republicans to switch to the Democrats. Only a handful of carpetbaggers could resist the economic pressures, social ostracism, and threats that made it "too damned hot for [us] to stay out," wrote one white Republican who changed parties. "No white man can live in the South in the future and act with any other than the Democratic Party unless he is willing and prepared to live a life of social isolation and remain in political oblivion."

The second step in the Mississippi Plan was to intimidate black voters because even with all whites voting Democratic, the party could still be defeated by the 55 percent black majority. Economic coercion against black sharecroppers and workers kept some of them away from the polls, but violence was the most effective method. Democratic "rifle clubs" showed up at Republican rallies, provoked riots, and shot down dozens of blacks in the ensuing melees. Governor Adelbert Ames—a native of Maine, a Union general who had won a congressional

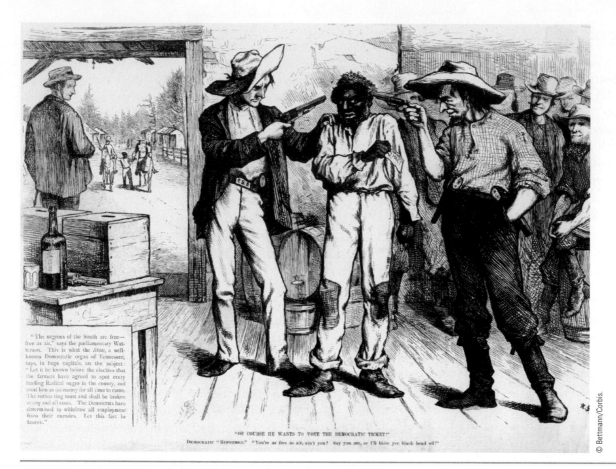

"The negroes of the South are free—free as air," says the parliamentary Watterson. This is what the *State*, a well-known Democratic organ of Tennessee, says, in huge capitals, on the subject: "Let it be known before the election that the farmers have agreed to spot every leading Radical negro in the county, and treat him as an enemy for all time to come. The rotten ring must and shall be broken at any and all costs. The Democrats have determined to withdraw all employment from their enemies. Let this fact be known."

"OF COURSE HE WANTS TO VOTE THE DEMOCRATIC TICKET."

DEMOCRATIC "REFORMER." "You're as free as air, ain't you? Say you are, or I'll blow yer black head off!"

© Bettmann/Corbis.

HOW THE MISSISSIPPI PLAN WORKED

This cartoon shows how black counties could report large Democratic majorities in the Mississippi state election of 1875. The black voter holds a Democratic ticket while one of the men, described in the caption as a "Democratic reformer," holds a revolver to his head and says: "You're as free as air, ain't you? Say you are, or I'll blow your black head off!"

medal of honor in the war, and one of the ablest of Southern Republicans—called for federal troops to control the violence. Grant intended to comply, but Ohio Republicans warned him that if he sent troops to Mississippi, the Democrats would exploit the issue of "bayonet rule" to carry Ohio in that year's state elections. Grant yielded—in effect giving up Mississippi for Ohio. The U.S. attorney general replied to Ames's request for troops:

> The whole public are tired out with these annual autumnal outbreaks in the South, and the great majority are now ready to condemn any interference on the part of the government. . . . Preserve the peace by the forces in your own state, and let the country see that the citizens of Mississippi, who are . . . largely Republican, have the courage to fight for their rights.

Governor Ames did try to organize a loyal state militia, but that proved difficult—and in any case, he was reluctant to use a black militia for fear of provoking a race war. "No matter if they are going to carry the State," said

Ames with weary resignation, "let them carry it, and let us be at peace and have no more killing." The Mississippi Plan worked like a charm. In five of the state's counties with large black majorities, the Republicans polled 12, 7, 4, 2, and 0 votes, respectively. What had been a Republican majority of 30,000 in 1874 became a Democratic majority of 30,000 in 1875.

The Supreme Court and Reconstruction

Even if Grant had been willing to continue intervening in Southern state elections, Congress and the courts would have constricted such efforts. The new Democratic majority in the House threatened to cut any appropriations for the Justice Department and the army intended for use in the South. In 1876, the Supreme Court handed down two decisions that declared parts of the 1870 and 1871 laws for enforcement of the 14th and 15th Amendments unconstitutional. In *U.S.* v. *Cruikshank* and *U.S.* v. *Reese*, the Court ruled on cases from Louisiana and Kentucky. Both cases grew out of provisions in these laws authorizing federal officials to prosecute *individuals* (not states) for violations of the civil and voting rights of blacks. But, the Court pointed out, the 14th and 15th Amendments apply to actions by *states*: "No State shall . . . deprive any person of life, liberty, or property . . . nor deny to any person . . . equal protection of the laws": the right to vote "shall not be denied . . . by any State." Therefore, the portions of these laws that empowered the federal government to prosecute individuals were declared unconstitutional.

The Court did not say what could be done when states were controlled by white-supremacy Democrats who had no intention of enforcing equal rights. (In the mid-20th century, the Supreme Court would reverse itself and interpret the 14th and 15th Amendments much more broadly.)

Meanwhile, in another ruling, *Civil Rights Cases* (1883), the Court declared unconstitutional a civil rights law passed by Congress in 1875. That law, enacted on the eve of the Democratic takeover of the House elected in 1874, was a crowning achievement of Reconstruction. It banned racial discrimination in all forms of public transportation and public accommodations. If enforced, it would have effected a sweeping transformation of race relations—in the North as well as in the South. Even some of the congressmen who voted for the bill doubted its constitutionality, however, and the Justice Department had made little effort to enforce it. Several cases made their way to the Supreme Court, which in 1883 ruled the law unconstitutional—again on grounds that the 14th Amendment applied only to states, not to individuals. Several states—all in the North—passed their own civil rights laws in the 1870s and 1880s, but less than 10 percent of the black population resided in those states. The mass of African Americans lived a segregated existence.

The Election of 1876

In 1876, the remaining Southern Republican state governments fell victim to the passion for reform. The mounting revelations of corruption at all levels of government ensured that reform would be the leading issue in the presidential election. In this centennial year of the birth

---

LINK TO THE PAST

Frederick Douglass on the Supreme Court and Civil Rights

The Civil Rights Act of 1875 anticipated many of the provisions of the Civil Rights Act of 1964, which is the law of the land and has been upheld by the U.S. Supreme Court. But the law of 1875 was ahead of its time, or at least ahead of the Supreme Court of its time, which declared it unconstitutional on the grounds that the Fourteenth Amendment prohibited discrimination by states but not by individuals. The black civil rights leader Frederick Douglass denounced the Court's decision in language that anticipated the Supreme Court's reasoning in the last third of the 20th century.

---

*T*his decision of the Supreme Court admits that the Fourteenth Amendment is a prohibition of the States. It admits that a State shall not abridge the privileges or immunities of citizens of the United States, but commits the seeming absurdity of allowing the people of a State to do what it prohibits the State itself from doing. . . . It is said that this decision will make no difference in the treatment of colored people; that the Civil Rights Bill was a dead letter, and could not be enforced. There is some truth in all this, but it is not the whole truth.

That bill, like all advance legislation, was a banner on the outer wall of American liberty, a noble moral standard, uplifted for the education of the American people. . . .

This law, though dead, did speak. It expressed the sentiment of justice and fair play. . . . If it is a bill for social equality, so is the Declaration of Independence, which declares that all men have equal rights; so is the Sermon on the Mount, so is the Golden Rule . . . so is the Constitution of the United States.

FREDERICK DOUGLASS

From a speech in Washington, D.C., October 22, 1883

---

1. What is Douglass's response to the argument that the Civil Rights Act was a dead letter even before the Supreme Court declared it so?

For additional sources related to this feature, visit the *Liberty, Equality, Power* Web site at:

http://history.wadsworth.com/murrin_LEP4e

of the United States, marked by a great exposition in Philadelphia, Americans wanted to put their best foot forward. Both major parties gave their presidential nominations to governors who had earned reform reputations in their states: Democrat Samuel J. Tilden of New York and Republican Rutherford B. Hayes of Ohio.

Democrats entered the campaign as favorites for the first time in two decades. It seemed likely that they would be able to put together an electoral majority from a "solid South" plus New York and two or three other Northern states. To ensure a solid South, they looked to the lessons of the Mississippi Plan. In 1876, a new word came into use to describe Democratic techniques of intimidation: *bulldozing*. To bulldoze black voters meant to trample them down or keep them away from the polls. In South Carolina and Louisiana, the Red Shirts and the White Leagues mobilized for an all-out bulldozing effort.

The most notorious incident, the Hamburg Massacre, occurred in the village of Hamburg, South Carolina, where a battle between a black militia unit and 200 Red Shirts resulted in the capture of several militiamen, five of whom were shot "while attempting to escape." This time Grant did send in federal troops. He pronounced the Hamburg Massacre "cruel, blood-thirsty, wanton, unprovoked . . . a repetition of the course that has been pursued in other Southern States."

The federal government also put several thousand deputy marshals and election supervisors on duty in the South. Although they kept an uneasy peace at the polls, they could do little to prevent assaults, threats, and economic coercion in backcountry districts, which reduced the potential Republican tally in the former Confederate states by at least 250,000 votes.

Disputed Results

When the results were in, Tilden had carried four Northern states, including New York with its 35 electoral votes. Tilden also carried all of the former slave states except—apparently—Louisiana, South Carolina, and Florida, which produced disputed returns. Because Tilden needed only one of them to win the presidency, while Hayes needed all three, and because Tilden seemed to have carried Louisiana and Florida, it appeared initially that he had won the presidency. But frauds and irregularities reported from several bulldozed districts in the three states clouded the issue. For example, a Louisiana parish that had recorded 1,688 Republican votes in 1874 reported only 1 in 1876. Many other similar discrepancies appeared. The official returns ultimately sent to Washington gave all three states—and therefore the presidency—to Hayes, but the Democrats refused to recognize the results, and they controlled the House.

The country now faced a serious constitutional crisis. Armed Democrats threatened to march on Washington. Many people feared another civil war. The Constitution offered no clear guidance on how to deal with the matter. A count of the state electoral votes required the concurrence of both houses of Congress, but with a Democratic House and a Republican Senate, such concurrence was not forthcoming. To break the deadlock, Congress created a special electoral commission consisting of five representatives, five senators, and five Supreme Court justices split evenly between the two parties, with one member, a Supreme Court justice, supposedly an independent—but in fact a Republican.

Tilden had won a national majority of 252,000 popular votes, and the raw returns gave him a majority in the three disputed states. But an estimated 250,000 Southern Republicans had been bulldozed away from the polls. In a genuinely fair and free election, the Republicans might have carried Mississippi and North Carolina as well as

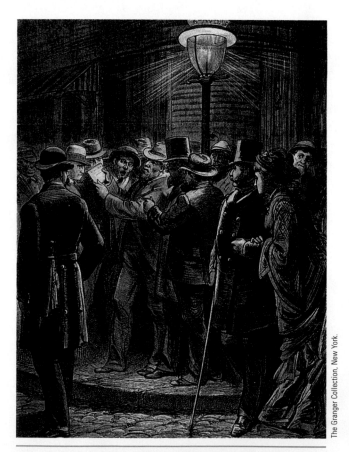

The Granger Collection, New York.

READING THE ELECTION BULLETIN BY GASLIGHT
In this drawing, eager voters scan the early returns, which seemed to give Samuel J. Tilden the presidency in 1876.

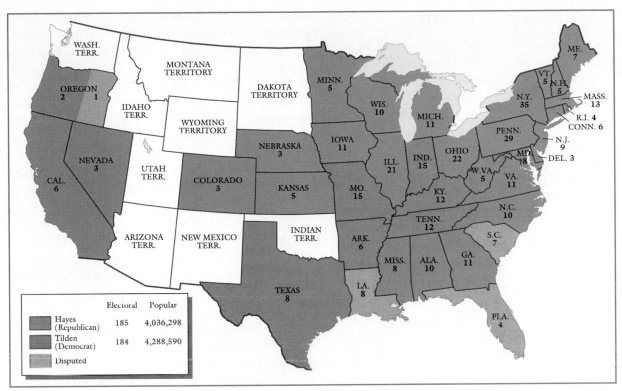

MAP 17.3 HAYES-TILDEN DISPUTED ELECTION OF 1876
A comparison of this map with those on pp. 546 and 551 shows the persistence of geographical voting patterns once
Southern Democrats had overthrown most Republican state governments and effectively disenfranchised many black voters.

the three disputed states. While the commission agonized, Democrats and Republicans in Louisiana and South Carolina each inaugurated their own separate governors and legislatures (Republicans in Florida gave up the fight at the state level). Only federal troops in the capitals at New Orleans and Columbia protected the Republican governments in those states.

The Compromise of 1877

In February 1877, three months after voters had gone to the polls, the electoral commission issued its ruling. By a partisan vote of 8 to 7—with the "independent" justice voting with the Republicans—the commission awarded all of the disputed states to Hayes. The Democrats cried foul and began a filibuster in the House to delay the final electoral count beyond the inauguration date of March 4, so as to throw the election to the House of Representatives, an eventuality that threatened to bring total anarchy. But, behind the scenes, a compromise began to take shape. Both Northern Republicans and Southern Democrats of Whig heritage had similar interests in liquidating the sectional rancor and in getting on with the business of

economic recovery and development. Among these neo-Whigs were Hayes and his advisers. To wean Southern Whiggish Democrats away from a House filibuster, Hayes promised his support as president for federal appropriations to rebuild war-destroyed levees on the lower Mississippi and federal aid for a southern transcontinental railroad. Hayes's lieutenants also hinted at the appointment of a Southerner as postmaster general, who would have a considerable amount of patronage at his disposal—the appointment of thousands of local postmasters.

Most important, Southerners wanted to know what Hayes would do about Louisiana and South Carolina. Would he withdraw the troops and allow the Democrats who already governed those states in fact to do so in law as well? Hayes signaled his intention to end "bayonet rule," which he had for some time considered a bankrupt policy. He believed that the goodwill and influence of Southern moderates would offer better protection for black rights than federal troops could provide. In return for his commitment to withdraw the troops, Hayes asked for—and received—promises of fair treatment of freedpeople and respect for their constitutional rights.

The End of Reconstruction

Such promises were easier to make than to keep, as future years would reveal. In any case, the Democratic filibuster collapsed, and Hayes was inaugurated on March 4. He soon fulfilled his part of the Compromise of 1877: ex-Confederate Democrat David Key of Tennessee became postmaster general; in 1878, the South received more federal money for internal improvements than ever before; and federal troops left the capitals of Louisiana and South Carolina. The last two Republican state governments collapsed. The old abolitionist and radical Republican warhorses denounced Hayes's actions as a sellout of Southern blacks. His was a policy "of weakness, of subserviency, of surrender," in the words of the venerable crusader William Lloyd Garrison, a policy that sustained "might against right . . . the rich and powerful against the poor and unprotected."

Voices of protest could scarcely be heard above the sighs of relief that the crisis was over. Most Americans—including even most Republicans—wanted no more military intervention in state affairs. "I have no sort of faith in a local government which can only be propped up by foreign bayonets," wrote the editor of the New York *Tribune* in April 1877. "If negro suffrage means that as a permanency then negro suffrage is a failure."

Conclusion

Before the Civil War, most Americans had viewed a powerful government as a threat to individual liberties. That is why the first 10 amendments to the Constitution (the Bill of Rights) imposed strict limits on the powers of the federal government. During the Civil War and especially during Reconstruction, however, the national government had to exert an unprecedented amount of power to free the slaves and guarantee their equal rights as free citizens.

That is why the 13th, 14th, and 15th Amendments to the Constitution contained clauses stating that "Congress shall have power" to enforce these provisions for liberty and equal rights.

During the post–Civil War decade, Congress passed civil rights laws and enforcement legislation to accomplish this purpose. Federal marshals and troops patrolled the polls to protect black voters, arrested thousands of Klansmen and other violators of black civil rights, and even occupied state capitals to prevent Democratic paramilitary groups from overthrowing legitimately elected Republican state governments.

By 1875, many Northerners had grown tired of or alarmed by this continued use of military power to intervene in the internal affairs of states. The Supreme Court stripped the federal government of much of its authority to enforce certain provisions of the 14th and 15th Amendments. Traditional fears of military power as a threat to individual liberties came to the fore again.

The withdrawal of federal troops from the South in 1877 constituted both a symbolic and a substantive end of the 12-year postwar era known as Reconstruction. Reconstruction had achieved the two great objectives inherited from the Civil War: (1) to reincorporate the former Confederate states into the Union, and (2) to accomplish a transition from slavery to freedom in the South. That transition was marred by the economic inequity of sharecropping and the social injustice of white supremacy. A third goal of Reconstruction, enforcement of the equal civil and political rights promised in the 14th and 15th Amendments, was betrayed by the Compromise of 1877. In subsequent decades, the freed slaves and their descendants suffered repression into segregated, second-class citizenship. Not until another war hero-turned-president sent troops into Little Rock (chapter 28), 80 years after they had been withdrawn from New Orleans and Columbia, did the federal government launch a second Reconstruction to fulfill the promises of the first.

SUGGESTED READINGS

The most comprehensive and incisive history of Reconstruction is **Eric Foner, *Reconstruction: America's Unfinished Revolution 1863–1872*** (1988). For a skillful abridgement of this book, see **Foner, *A Short History of Reconstruction*** (1990). Also valuable is **Kenneth M. Stampp, *The Era of Reconstruction, 1865–1877*** (1965). Important for their insights on Lincoln and the reconstruction question are **Peyton McCrary, *Abraham Lincoln and Reconstruction: The Louisiana Experiment*** (1978) and **LaWanda Cox, *Lincoln and Black Freedom: A Study in Presidential Leadership*** (1981). A superb study of the South Carolina Sea Islands as a laboratory of Reconstruction is **Willie Lee Rose, *Rehearsal for Reconstruction: The Port Royal Experiment*** (1964).

Three important studies of Andrew Johnson and his conflict with Congress over Reconstruction are **Eric L. McKitrick, *Andrew Johnson and Reconstruction*** (1960); **Hans L. Trefousse, *The Radical Republicans: Lincoln's Vanguard for Racial Justice*** (1969); and **Michael Les Benedict, *The Impeachment and Trial of Andrew Johnson*** (1973). Two books by **Michael Perman** connect events in the South and in Washington during Reconstruction: ***Reunion without Compromise: The South and Reconstruction, 1865–1868*** (1973) and ***The Road to Redemption: Southern Politics 1868–1879*** (1984). For counter-Reconstruction violence in the South, see **George C. Rable, *But There Was No Peace: The Role of Violence in the Politics of Reconstruction*** (1984). The evolution of sharecropping and other aspects of the transition from slavery to freedom are treated in **Roger L. Ransom and Richard Sutch, *One Kind of Freedom: The Economic Consequences of Emancipation*** (1977).

Of the many books on African Americans in Reconstruction, the following are perhaps the most valuable: **Thomas Holt, *Black over White: Negro Political Leadership in South Carolina during Reconstruction*** (1977) and **Laura F. Edwards, *Gendered Strife and Confusion: The Political Culture of Reconstruction***

(1997). An excellent collection of essays on the Freedmen's Bureau is **Paul A. Cimbala and Randall Miller, eds., *The Freedmen's Bureau and Reconstruction*** (1999). Both black and white churches are the subject of **Daniel Stowell, *Rebuilding Zion: The Religious Reconstruction of the South, 1863–1877*** (1998).

 AMERICAN JOURNEY ONLINE
AND
INFOTRAC COLLEGE EDITION

Visit the source collections at www.ajaccess.wadsworth.com and infotrac.thomsonlearning.com and use the Search function with the following key terms to explore documents, images, audio and video clips, articles, and commentary related to the material in this chapter.

Andrew Johnson	Transcontinental Railroad
Reconstruction	Ulysses S. Grant
Freedmen's Bureau	14th Amendment
Ku Klux Klan	15th Amendment

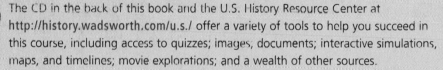

GRADE AIDS

Visit the Liberty Equality Power Companion Web site for resources specific to this textbook: http://history.wadsworth.com/murrin_LEP4e

The CD in the back of this book and the U.S. History Resource Center at http://history.wadsworth.com/u.s./ offer a variety of tools to help you succeed in this course, including access to quizzes; images; documents; interactive simulations; maps, and timelines; movie explorations; and a wealth of other sources.

Chapter 18

Frontiers of Change, Politics of Stalemate, 1865–1898

A DASH FOR TIMBER
Many of our images of the post–Civil War West derive from illustrations by the greatest artist of the Old West, Frederic Remington. In this dramatic painting, Remington combines realism and stereotype in a depiction of the kind of Cowboys-and-Indians conflict that became a staple of Hollywood portrayals of the West.

CHAPTER OUTLINE

Despite the nation's preoccupation with the politics of Reconstruction, one of the most remarkable developments in the post–Civil War generation was the accelerating westward expansion of the European-American frontier. From 1865 to 1890, the white population west of the 95th meridian (roughly a line from Galveston, Texas, through Kansas City to Bemidji, Minnesota) increased 400 percent to 8,628,000, a growth rate five times faster than the nation's growth as a whole. As much new agricultural and grazing land came under cultivation and exploitation by white Americans during these 25 years as during the previous 250 years. Through the Homestead Act, land grants to railroads, the Morrill Act (which turned land over to states to finance "agricultural and mechanical colleges"), and other liberal land laws enacted during and after the Civil War, some 400 million acres passed into private ownership. The number of American farms more than doubled, from 2.5 million to nearly 6 million. Their output of cattle, hogs, and hay more than doubled, while the production of corn, wheat, and oats nearly tripled—considerably outstripping the rate of population increase.

This growth enabled American farmers to increase agricultural exports tenfold during those 25 years thanks also partly to imports—of people. Many of the 4 million immigrants who came from Germany, the Czech region of the Austro-Hungarian empire, and the Scandinavian countries during this period settled in the Midwest or Far West and became farmers. To younger sons in Norwegian or German farm families who could expect to inherit no land at home, the opportunity to obtain 160 acres in Minnesota or Nebraska seemed miraculous. The power of a generous government to make equality of opportunity available to them, and to other white Americans of both native and foreign birth, underpinned the extraordinary expansion of population and agricultural production after the Civil War.

That growth and opportunity, however, came at great cost. The Indians were despoiled of their remaining open land and herded onto reservations. Buffalo were hunted almost to extinction. Millions of acres of forest and native grasslands were cut down or plowed up, setting the stage for destructive erosion, floods, and dust bowls in future generations. The overproduction of American agriculture drove prices down and contributed to a worldwide agricultural depression by the late 1880s.

CHAPTER FOCUS

♦ What was the balance between the economic gains and the social and environmental costs of westward expansion after the Civil War?

♦ How did the Indian peoples of the trans-Mississippi West respond to white settlement and U.S. government policies?

♦ What were the central themes of economic development and race relations in the post-Reconstruction South?

♦ What kind of national political structure emerged from the turmoil of war and reconstruction?

Agencies of Westward Expansion

One of the main engines of this postwar growth was the railroad. Five transcontinental railroads went into service between 1869 and 1893. At the end of the Civil War, only 3,272 miles of rail ran west of the Mississippi. By 1890, the total was 72,473 miles. Railroad access and mobility spurred settlement and economic development on the high plains and in the mountain valleys.

No longer did this region appear on maps as The Great American Desert. There was plenty of desert, to be sure, and the average normal rainfall on the plains west of the 98th meridian (a line running roughly from the center of the Dakotas through the center of Texas) was scarcely enough to support farming except in certain river valleys. Unfortunately, precipitation during the 1870s and early 1880s was heavier than normal, giving rise to the erroneous (as it turned out) notion that "rainfall follows the plow"—that settlement and cultivation somehow changed the weather.

This was the age of the "sodbuster," who adapted to the almost treeless prairies and plains by fencing with barbed wire (invented in 1874) and building his first house out of the sod that he broke with his steel plow, cutting deep furrows to bring up subsoil moisture. It was also the

C H R O N O L O G Y

1862	Sioux uprising in Minnesota; 38 Sioux executed
1864	Colorado militia massacres Cheyenne in village at Sand Creek, Colorado
1866	Cowboys conduct first cattle drive north from Texas
1869	President Grant announces his "peace policy" toward Indians
1876	Sioux and Cheyenne defeat Custer at Little Big Horn
1880	James A. Garfield elected president
1881	Garfield assassinated; Chester A. Arthur becomes president
1883	Pendleton Act begins reform of civil service
1884	Grover Cleveland elected president
1887	Dawes Severalty Act dissolves Indian tribal units and implements individual ownership of tribal lands
1888	Benjamin Harrison elected president
1889	Government opens Indian Territory (Oklahoma) to white settlement
1890	Wounded Knee massacre • New Mississippi constitution pioneers black disenfranchisement in South • Republicans try but fail to enact federal elections bill to protect black voting rights • Congress enacts McKinley Tariff
1892	Grover Cleveland again elected president
1895	Booker T. Washington makes his Atlanta Compromise address
1896	*Plessy* v. *Ferguson* legalizes "separate but equal" state racial segregation laws
1898	*Williams* v. *Mississippi* condones use of literacy tests and similar measures to restrict voting rights

THE SOD-HOUSE FRONTIER

On the prairies and plains of the regions west of the Mississippi, trees were scarce and the cost of lumber was prohibitive until railroads crisscrossed the land. So the settlers built their first houses from the tough prairie sod, which baked in the sun to almost the hardness of bricks.

Nebraska State Historical Society.

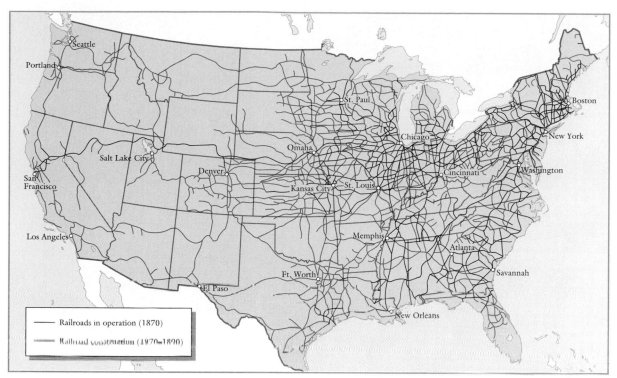

MAP 18.1 RAILROAD EXPANSION, 1870–1890
This map provides a vivid illustration of the spanning of the western half of the United States by steel rails in two short decades.

era of "bonanza farms"—huge wheat farms cultivated with heavy machinery and hired labor—in the Red River Valley of Dakota Territory and the Central Valley of California.

Perhaps even more important to the growth of the West, and surely more prolific of song and story, were the mining and ranching frontiers. This was the West of prospectors and boom towns that became ghost towns, of cowboys and cattle drives, of gold rushes and mother lodes, of stagecoach robbers and rustlers. It is a West so celebrated on stage, screen, radio, and television that it is hard to separate myth from reality—a reality in which thousands of black and Mexican American cowboys rode the Goodnight-Loving Trail; eastern capital and railroads came increasingly to control the mines and the grasslands; and gold or silver miners and cowboys came to resemble more closely the coal miners and farm laborers of the East than the romanticized independent spirits of legend.

The Mining Frontier

Gold discoveries had propelled the first waves of western settlement, but by the 1870s, silver eclipsed gold in volume and some years even in value. Other minerals also increased in value. Rich copper mines opened in Montana in concert with demand for thousands of tons of copper wire brought on by Alexander Graham Bell's invention

of the telephone (1876), Thomas A. Edison's invention of the incandescent lightbulb (1879), and construction of a successful electrical generator (1881).

Violence was never far from the surface in the mining frontier. In the early days, claim-jumping, robberies, and vigilante justice made life precarious. As placer mining of streams gave out, men ravaged the environment by hydraulic mining, by piling up tons of tailings from deep bores, and (especially in the copper industry) by creating strip-mining moonscapes. Mining became a highly capitalized and mechanized industry in which the biggest and richest mines were owned by corporations with headquarters in the East. Capital–labor relations were savage. Violent strikes at Coeur d'Alene, Idaho, in 1892; at Cripple Creek, Colorado, in 1894 and again in 1903; and at other places caused western governors to call out the militia 10 times from 1892 to 1904. From these conflicts emerged the Western Federation of Miners, founded in 1893, which became one of the most militant American labor unions.

The Ranching Frontier

Of course, the dominant symbol of the Old West is not the prospector or the hard-rock miner: It is the cowboy. The postwar boom in the range cattle industry had its beginnings in southern Texas. The Spaniards had introduced

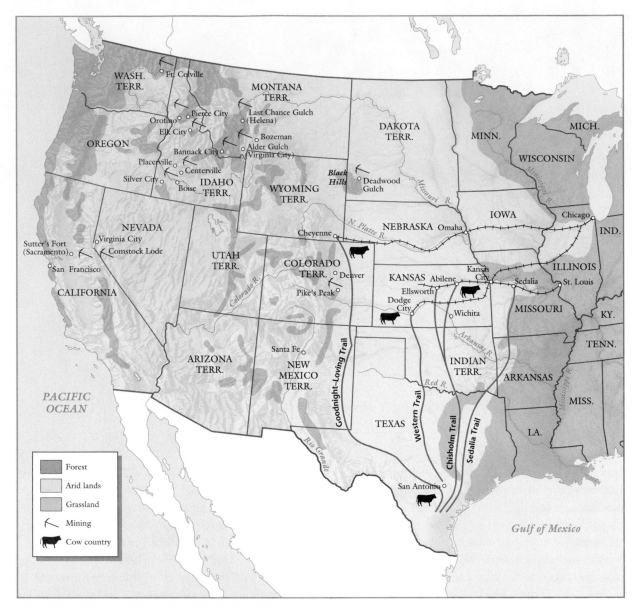

MAP 18.2 MINING AND CATTLE FRONTIERS, 1870s

Most of the mines shown on this map produced gold and silver. The next generation would begin to exploit the copper to be found in Montana and Arizona, and later generations would extract oil from Texas and Oklahoma and coal and oil from Wyoming.

longhorn cattle there in the 18th century. This hardy breed multiplied rapidly; by the 1850s, millions of them roamed freely on the Texas plains. The market for them was limited in this sparsely settled region; the nearest railhead was usually too far distant to make shipping them north and east economically feasible.

The Civil War changed all that. Beef supplies in the older states dropped drastically, and prices rose to the unheard-of sum of $40 per head. The postwar explosion of population and railroads westward brought markets and railheads ever closer to western cattle that were free to anyone who rounded them up and branded them.

Astute Texans quickly saw that the longhorns represented a fortune on the hoof—if they could be driven northward the 800 miles to the railhead at Sedalia, Missouri. In spring 1866, cowboys hit the trail with 260,000 cattle in the first of the great drives. Their experiences almost put an end to the range cattle industry before it was born. Disease, stampedes, bad weather, Indians, and irate farmers in Missouri (who were afraid that the Texas fever carried by some of the longhorns would infect their own stock) killed or ran off most of the cattle.

Only a few thousand head made it to Sedalia, but the prices they fetched convinced ranchers that the system would work, if only they could find a better route. By 1867, the rails of the Kansas Pacific had reached Abilene, Kansas, 150 miles closer to Texas, making it possible to drive the herds through a sparsely occupied portion of Indian Territory. About 35,000 longhorns reached Abilene that summer, where they were loaded onto cattle cars for the trip to Kansas City or Chicago. This success resulted in the interlocking institutions of the cattle drive and the Chicago stockyards. The development of refrigerated rail cars in the 1870s enabled Chicago to ship dressed beef all over the country. Abilene mushroomed overnight from a sleepy village whose one bartender spent his spare time catching prairie dogs into a boomtown where 25 saloons stayed open all night, and the railroad made almost as much money shipping liquor into town as it did shipping cattle out.

More than a million longhorns bellowed their way north on the Chisholm Trail to Abilene over the next four years while the railhead crept westward to other Kansas towns, chiefly Dodge City, which became the most wide-open and famous of the cow towns. As buffalo and Indians disappeared from the grasslands north of Texas, ranches moved northward to take their place. Cattle drives grew shorter as railroads inched forward. Ranchers grazed their cattle for free on millions of acres of open, unfenced government land. But clashes with "grangers" (the ranchers' contemptuous term for farmers), on the one hand, and with a growing army of sheep ranchers on the other—not to mention rustlers—led to several "range wars." Most notable was the Johnson County War in Wyoming in 1892. Grangers and small ranchers there (who had sometimes gotten their start by rustling) defeated the hired guns of the Stock Growers' Association, which represented larger ranchers.

By that time, however, the classic form of open-range grazing was already in decline. The boom years of the early 1880s had overstocked the range and driven down prices. Then came record cold and blizzards on the southern range in winter 1884–85, followed by even worse weather on the northern plains two years later. Hundreds of thousands of cattle froze or starved to death. These catastrophes spurred reforms that brought an end to open-range grazing. The ranchers who survived turned to growing hay and supplemental feed for the winter. They reduced the size of their herds, started buying or leasing land and fencing in their cattle, and invested in scientific breeding that crossed longhorns with higher-quality stock to produce a better grade of beef.

Although cowboys no longer rode the open range after the 1880s, the classic cowboy image became a staple of American popular culture. Cheap novels of the period created the myth of a proud and rugged white individual who overcame the West's hostile environment as easily

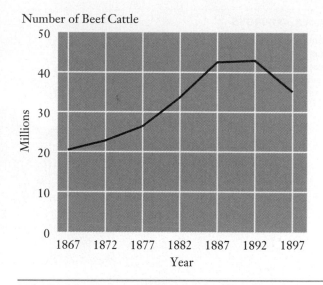

Number of Beef Cattle

BEEF CATTLE IN THE UNITED STATES, 1867–1897

as he overcame hostile Indians. Buffalo Bill's Wild West show presented thousands of Eastern urban Americans with a spectacle of cowboys conquering the West. Theatrical Indians in these spectacles attacked Buffalo Bill and his band of trick riders and sharp shooters. Buffalo Bill then led his forces in the dramatic slaughter of the Indian marauders. The entertainment presented a strong message to Easterners: White conquest of the West was necessary to protect the nation from aggressive Indians. Cheap novels and Western shows paid little attention to the realities of cowboy life: Thousands of cowboys were in fact black or Mexican. They were laborers paid wages for a difficult and grueling job. Few of them carried pistols tied to their legs.

Frederick Jackson Turner also turned the conquest of the West into a myth. It was nothing like Buffalo Bill's, for whom the bullet was "the pioneer of civilization." For Turner, the European confrontation with a vast, largely uninhabited wilderness created a new kind of democratic, egalitarian culture. Indians played almost no role in Turner's frontier myth. Both the cowboy myth and the frontier myth ignored perhaps the greatest reality of all: Neither individualistic cowboys nor community-oriented pioneers subdued the West. The U.S. army conquered the Indians who lived there while the federal government claimed and administered most of the land beyond the Mississippi.

❧ The Last Indian Frontier

The westward expansion of the ranching and farming frontiers after 1865 doomed the free range of the Plains Indians and the buffalo. In the 1830s, eastern tribes had been moved to preserves west of the Mississippi to end

BLACK COWBOYS

Some studies of cowboys estimate that one-quarter of them were black. That estimate is probably too high for all cowboys, but it might be correct for Texas, where this photograph was taken.

Erwin E. Smith Collection of the Library of Congress on deposit at the Amon Carter Museum, Fort Worth.

strife by separating whites and Indians. In scarcely a decade, white settlers had penetrated these lands via the overland trails to the Pacific Coast. In the 1850s, when the Kansas and Nebraska territories opened to white settlement, the government forced a dozen tribes living there to cede 15 million acres, leaving them on reservations totaling less than 1.5 million acres. Thus began what historian Philip Weeks has called the "policy of concentration": No longer were Indians to be pushed west onto the arid plains that early white explorers had christened The Great American Desert. Rather, as white settlers moved onto and through the plains and mountains, they began to covet these large spaces, which earlier treaties had assigned to the Indians for "as long as waters shall run and the grass shall grow."

Even before the Civil War, the nomadic Plains Indians, whose culture and economy were based on the buffalo, faced pressure not only from the advancing tide of white settlement but also from the forced migration of eastern tribes into their domain. In the aftermath of the Civil War, the process of concentrating Indian tribes on reservations accelerated. Chiefs of the five "civilized tribes"—Cherokees, Creeks, Choctaws, Chickasaws, and Seminoles—had signed treaties of alliance with the Confederacy. At that time, they were living in Indian Territory (most of present-day Oklahoma), where their economy was linked to the South. Many of them, especially members of the mixed-blood upper class, were slaveholders. Bitter toward the United States, the leaders of the "civilized tribes," on the principle that "the enemy of my enemy is my friend," cast their lot with the Confederacy. The Cherokee leader Stand Watie rose to brigadier general in the Confederate army and was the last Confederate commander to surrender, on June 23, 1865.

Siding with the Confederacy proved to be a costly mistake for the "civilized tribes." The U.S. government "reconstructed" Indian Territory more quickly and with less contention than it reconstructed the former Confederate states. Treaties with the five tribes in 1866 required them to grant tribal citizenship to their freed slaves and reduced tribal lands by half. The government then settled Indians who had been dispossessed from other areas on the land it had taken from the "civilized tribes."

Conflict with the Sioux

There was no shortage of dispossessed Indians. The Civil War had set in motion a generation of Indian warfare that was more violent and widespread than anything since the 17th century. During the war, the Union army was forced to pull many units out of frontier posts to fight the Confederacy. Moreover, the drain on the Union treasury to finance the war compounded the usual corruption of Indian agents and delayed annuity payments to tribes that had sold their land to the government. These events had dire consequences on the northern plains.

Herded onto reservations along the Minnesota River by the Treaty of Traverse des Sioux in 1851, the Santee Sioux grew restive when late annuity payments in summer 1862 threatened starvation. Angry braves began to speak openly of reclaiming ancestral hunting grounds. Then on August 17, a robbery in which five white settlers were murdered seemed to open the floodgates. The braves persuaded Chief Little Crow to take them on the warpath, and over the next few weeks, at least 500 white Minnesotans were massacred.

Hastily mobilized militia and army units finally suppressed the uprising. A military court convicted 319

Jennie Jerome Churchill's Contribution to the Anglo-American Alliance

Jennie Jerome (1854–1921) was born in Brooklyn of a mother who was one-quarter Iroquois and a father who made and lost two or three fortunes as a financial broker. Her mother gained a taste for European culture when her husband was American consul at Trieste, Italy, in 1852–53, a year before Jennie was born. Her father had a taste for fast racehorses and fast women. When his liaison with one of the latter became notorious in 1867, Clara Jerome took her three daughters to Europe. At a dance aboard a British warship in 1873, 19-year-old Jennie met Lord Randolph Churchill, younger son of the Duke of Marlborough. Three days later, he proposed to her and they were married in April 1874. Seven and one-half months later, Jennie gave birth to Winston Churchill—a premature birth caused by Jennie's fall while hunting, according to the family.

Winston and his younger brother John were raised by nurses and governesses, as was the custom among the British aristocracy. The relationship between Winston and his mother was not intimate, therefore; nevertheless, he later wrote that "she shone for me like the Evening Star. I loved her dearly—but at a distance."

Randolph Churchill's political career entered a steep decline in the 1880s, followed by his health, and Jennie was left a widow at the age of 41 in 1895.

Devoting herself to the promotion of closer Anglo-American ties, Jennie also gained a reputation for eccentricity when she married a man the same age as her son Winston, and after a subsequent divorce, married another man three years younger than Winston.

Jennie Churchill's greatest contribution to liberty and civilization came two decades after her death, when the man to whom she had given birth led the nation that stood alone against the Nazis and then forged the Anglo-American alliance that won a war fought on behalf of the Four Freedoms.

JENNIE JEROME CHURCHILL

By courtesy of the National Portrait Gallery, London.

Indians of murder and atrocities and sentenced 303 of them to death. Appalled by this ferocious retaliation, Lincoln personally reviewed the trial transcripts and reduced the number of executions to 38—the largest act of executive clemency in American history. Even so, the hanging of 38 Sioux on December 26, 1862, was the largest mass execution the country has ever witnessed. The government evicted the remaining Sioux from Minnesota to Dakota Territory.

In the meantime, the army's pursuit of fleeing Santee Sioux provoked other Sioux tribes farther west. By 1864 and for a decade afterward, fighting flared between the army and the Sioux across the northern plains. It reached a climax in 1874 and 1875 after gold-seekers poured into

the Black Hills of western Dakota, a sacred place to the Sioux. At the battle of Little Bighorn in Montana Territory on June 25, 1876, Sioux warriors led by Sitting Bull and Crazy Horse, along with their Cheyenne allies, wiped out George A. Custer and the 225 men with him in the Seventh Cavalry. In retaliation, General Philip Sheridan carried out a winter campaign in which the Sioux and Cheyenne were crushed.

Largest and most warlike of the Plains tribes, the Sioux were confined to a reservation in Dakota Territory where poverty, disease, apathy, and alcoholism reduced this once-proud people to desperation. In 1890, a current of hope arrived at the Sioux reservation in the form of a Ghost Dance, which had first appeared among the Paiutes

THE GHOST DANCE

This photograph shows a Sioux with a sacred whistle performing the Ghost Dance in 1890. The dance invoked the Great Spirit to restore the buffalo and drive away the whites, thereby revitalizing traditional Sioux culture. Instead, it provoked the U.S. Army into the confrontation that led to the massacre at Wounded Knee, South Dakota.

Smithsonian Institution, Bureau of American Ethnology.

HISTORY THROUGH FILM

Fort Apache (1948)

Directed by John Ford. Starring Henry Fonda (Lt. Col. Owen Thursday), John Wayne (Capt. Kirby York), Shirley Temple (Philadelphia Thursday).

With a cast containing some of the most famous actors in Hollywood history, directed by one of the most successful of Hollywood directors, *Fort Apache* lives up to expectations. In a career that spanned a half century from 1917 to 1966, John Ford did more than any other director to fix the images and legends of the Old West in the minds of Americans. He directed both John Wayne and Henry Fonda in some of their best films. In *Fort Apache,* he brought them together with a grown-up Shirley Temple in the starkly beautiful Arizona desert. The black-and-white footage resembles old glass-plate photographs from the 1870s.

The film opens with Lieutenant Colonel Owen Thursday traveling by stagecoach with his daughter Philadelphia to Arizona Territory to take command of the frontier outpost of Fort Apache. A Civil War veteran like most of the other soldiers in the film, Thursday had reached the rank of major general of volunteers in that war but reverted to his regular army rank of lieutenant colonel in the downsized postwar army. Resenting his assignment to this remote backwater, the spit-and-polish Thursday is determined to shape up the garrison, which had been under the relaxed temporary command of Captain Kirby York, a veteran Indian fighter, and the Irish-born sergeants who really run the post. Philadelphia Thursday falls in love with Lieutenant Michael O'Rourke, a recent West Point graduate and son of the sergeant major at the fort.

This setting offers Ford and scriptwriter Frank Nugent opportunity to explore class, ethnic, and gender relations as well as social customs in the frontier army of the 1870s. They succeed brilliantly. Thursday opposes his daughter's engagement to the Irish American son of a noncommissioned officer even though the son is a West Pointer and his father won the Medal of Honor in the Civil War. Although many tinges of Hollywood romance creep in, these relationships are sensitively portrayed. So are the efforts by wives of officers and noncoms to create a semblance of stable community and family life at the fort.

Not until halfway through the film does the inevitable conflict with the Indians begin to build. The movie avoids a stereotypical depiction of murderous Indians on the warpath and heroic cavalry coming to the rescue (a stereotype Ford had helped create in earlier films). A corrupt white Indian agent has been cheating the Mescalero Apaches led by Cochise, who leave the reservation after some of

of Nevada and spread quickly to other Indian nations. Similar to earlier revitalization movements among Indian peoples, the Ghost Dance expressed the belief that the Indians' god would destroy the whites and return their land. Alarmed by the frenzy of the dance, federal authorities sent soldiers to the Sioux reservation. A confrontation at Wounded Knee in the Dakota badlands led to a shootout that left 25 soldiers and at least 150 Sioux dead. Wounded Knee symbolized the death of 19th-century Plains Indian culture.

Suppression of Other Plains Indians

Just as the Sioux uprising in Minnesota had triggered war on the northern plains in 1862, a massacre of Cheyennes in Colorado in 1864 sparked a decade of conflict on the southern plains. The discovery of gold near Pike's Peak set off a rush to Colorado in 1858–59. The government responded by calling several Cheyenne and Arapaho chiefs to a council—and with a combination of threats, promises, and firewater, the agents persuaded the chiefs to sign a treaty giving up all claims to land in this region (guaranteed by an earlier treaty of 1851) in exchange for a reservation at Sand Creek in southeast Colorado.

In 1864, hunger and resentment on the reservation prompted many of the braves to return to their old hunting grounds and to raid white settlements. Skirmishes soon erupted into open warfare. In the fall, Cheyenne Chief Black Kettle, believing that he had concluded peace with the Colorado settlers, returned to the reservation. There, at dawn on November 29, militia commanded by Colonel John Chivington surrounded and attacked Black

Cochise's hotheaded braves kill two soldiers. Sensing a chance for glory and promotion if he can bring in Cochise, Thursday orders Captain York, whom Cochise trusts, to coax him back from Mexico. York does so, whereupon Thursday defies York's advice, provokes Cochise with impossible conditions, and leads an ill-advised attack against the more numerous Apaches that brings the death of Thursday and all of the men with him. In an ironic final twist, the national media make Thursday a heroic martyr, and York plays along with this image.

Two soldiers try to help a dying Henry Fonda (Lt. Col. Owen Thursday) in the climactic battle scene of *Fort Apache*.
© John Springer Collection/Corbis.

Fort Apache and Cochise were real, but the story in this film is entirely fictional. It is, in fact, a parable of a different conflict in which an entire detachment of U.S. Cavalry was wiped out: the battle of Little Big Horn in Montana Territory on June 26, 1876. The glory-hunting Owen Thursday represents George Armstrong Custer, and Cochise is a counterpart of Sitting Bull. Although not obvious, these parallels are clear. In some ways, Captain York also seems to be modeled on George Crook, a veteran Indian fighter who came to sympathize with the Native Americans and gained their confidence. In this reading of the film, *Fort Apache* transcends its particular time and place and becomes a broader story of the tragedy of Indian–white conflicts after the Civil War. This movie also represents a long step forward in John Ford's understanding and portrayal of the encounter between whites and Indians as truly tragic rather than as the triumph of Manifest Destiny, as it so often appeared to be in his earlier films.

DESTRUCTION OF THE BUFFALO

Historians estimate that as many as 30 million bison (popularly called buffalo) once roamed the grasslands of North America. By the mid-19th century, however, the expansion of European American settlement, the demand for buffalo robes in the European and eastern U.S. markets, and competition from Indian horses for grazing lands had reduced the herds by many millions. Such pressures intensified after the Civil War—as railroads penetrated the West and new technology enabled tanners to process buffalo hides for leather. Professional hunters flocked to the range and systematically killed the bison. By the 1880s, the buffalo were almost extinct, leaving behind millions of bones, which were gathered in piles, as in this photograph of buffalo skulls, and shipped to plants that ground them into fertilizer.

Kettle's unsuspecting camp, killing 200 Indians, half of them women and children.

The notorious Sand Creek massacre set a pattern for several similar attacks on Indian villages in subsequent years. Ever since the earliest battles between colonists and Indians in the 17th century, whites had followed the strategy of burning Indian crops and villages as a means of destroying or driving off the Indians. Sherman and Sheridan had adopted a similar strategy against the Confederates and followed it again as military commanders responsible for subduing the Plains Indians. Their purpose was to corral all of the Indians onto the reservations that were being created throughout the West. In addition to trying to defeat the Indians in battle—which proved to be difficult against the mounted Plains Indians—the army encouraged the extermination of the buffalo herds. Professional

hunters slaughtered the large, clumsy animals by the millions for their hides, thus depriving Plains Indians of both physical and spiritual sustenance. Indians continued to hunt the buffalo. They understood that the huge animals were disappearing, but they believed that the buffalo were retreating underground to avoid the mistreatment by the whites. The Indians believed the buffalo would reappear only after whites learned to respect them as the Indians did. But when the buffalo became nearly extinct in 1883, the Plains Indians understood that the old ways were gone forever. "Nothing happened after that," recalled one Crow warrior, "We just lived. There were no more war parties, no capturing horses from the Piegan and the Sioux, no buffalo to hunt. There is nothing more to tell."

The Indians were left with no alternative but to come into the reservations, and by the 1880s, nearly all of them

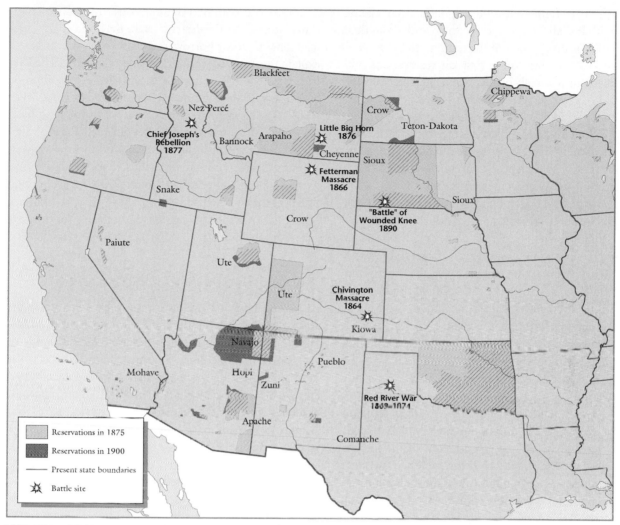

MAP 18.3 INDIAN RESERVATIONS, 1875 AND 1900

Before the Civil War, Indians had hunted and trapped over most of this vast region. The shrinking areas on which they were confined by the reservation policy vividly illustrates that for the first Americans, the story was not "the expansion of America" but "the contraction of America."

had done so. Chief Joseph of the Nez Percé pronounced the epitaph for their way of life when federal troops blocked the escape of his band from Montana to Canada in 1877:

> I am tired of fighting. Our chiefs are killed. The old men are all dead. It is cold and we have no blankets . . . no food. . . . The little children are freezing to death. . . . Hear me, my chiefs; I am tired; my heart is sick and sad. From where the sun now stands, I will fight no more forever.

The "Peace Policy"

Many Eastern reformers condemned America's violent repression of the Indians. One of the most prominent reformers was Helen Hunt Jackson, whose 1881 book, *A Century of Dishonor,* summed up their indictment of anti-Indian violence, exploitation, and broken treaties. Jackson may have romanticized Indian culture, especially

in her best-selling novel, *Ramona* (1884), but she also helped humanize the Indians. Nevertheless, most reformers believed that Indians must be compelled to give up their nomadic culture and settle down as the first step toward being assimilated into the American polity as citizens. Just as reformers wanted to reconstruct the South by assimilating emancipated slaves into a free-labor society, so they wished to reconstruct Indian culture into the white man's ways by means of schools and Christian missions.

President Grant, in his inaugural address in 1869, announced this new Peace Policy toward Indians. He urged "their civilization and ultimate citizenship." "Civilization" meant acceptance of white culture, including the English language, Christianity, and individual ownership of property. It also meant allegiance to the United States rather than to a tribe. In 1869, Grant established a Board of Indian Commissioners and staffed it with humanitarian reformers. In 1871, the century-long policy of negotiating treaties with Indian "nations" came to an end. From then on, Indians became "wards of the nation," to be civilized and prepared for citizenship, first on reservations and eventually on individually owned parcels of land that were carved out of the reservations.

With their military power broken and the buffalo gone, most Indians had acquiesced in the "reconstruction" that offered them citizenship by the 1880s. Also in the 1880s, the reformers found themselves in a strange alliance with land-hungry westerners, who greedily eyed the 155 million acres of land tied up in reservations. If part of that land could be allotted directly to individual ownership by Indian families, the remainder would become available for purchase by whites. The Dawes Severalty Act did just that in 1887. This landmark legislation called for the dissolution of Indian tribes as legal entities, offered Indians the opportunity to become citizens, and allotted each head of family 160 acres of farmland or 320 acres of grazing land.

For whites who were eager to seize reservation land, the Dawes Act brought a bonanza. At noon on April 22, 1889, the government threw open specified parts of the Indian Territory to "Boomers," who descended on the region like locusts and by nightfall had staked claim to nearly 2 million acres. In addition to the reservation lands legally opened for white settlement, many of the Indians who received individual land titles through the Dawes Act lost these lands to unscrupulous whites through fraud and misrepresentation. Eventually, whites gained title to 108 million acres of former reservation land.

For Indians, writes historian Philip Weeks, the Dawes Act "proved an unqualified failure." Private ownership of land was an alien concept to most tribes. And in many Indian cultures, farming was considered woman's work. To Americanize Indian males by compelling them to forsake hunting for farming was to strip them of their manhood. Some Indians were able to adapt to the new order, but many slipped further into depression, destitution, and alcoholism. Others worked to create a new culture out of the dust of the old.

Life went on for the Indians. They asserted their independence by subverting the power of governmental authorities whenever they could. Navajos forged ration coupons to obtain extra food from federal administrators. They refused to be herded into close living quarters as the administrators demanded. Instead, they followed traditional practices and built their homes far apart. Lakota Indians tricked census takers to obtain more provisions from reservation authorities. They would file past federal census counters giving their real names, then return to the line to be counted again. They would offer derisive fictitious names, such as the Lakota equivalent of "Dirty Prick."

Indians also found ways to reconstitute Native American cultures after the destruction of the buffalo. They created new rituals or borrowed rituals from other tribes to explain the changed world they had to negotiate. The Utes turned to the hallucinogenic drug peyote to commune with the spirit world and declare their difference from whites. The Navajo refused to accept white doctors' physical explanations for disease. They adapted the Apaches' ritual cures, the Chiricaha Windway and the Suckingway, to cure illnesses caused by winds, floods, snakes, and witches' darts. Some Indians found ways to use foreign practices to their own advantage. They turned to markets, selling their weaving and pottery, as a means for preserving traditional folkways.

Mexican Americans

Mexican Americans in the West were also forced to adjust to a new order. As with the Indians, some made this transition successfully, but many did not. At the hands of Anglo-American settlers, Mexican Americans lost their land, political influence, and much of their cultural identity. Even as early as 1849 in the northern California goldfields, resentment of "foreigners" provoked violence against Mexican American miners—and the Foreign Miners Tax of 1850 effectively forced Mexican Americans out of the goldfields (even though they were not "foreigners"). As the 19th century progressed, hordes of Anglo-American "squatters" invaded the expansive holdings of the Mexican American elite, who were forced to seek relief in the courts. Although their claims were generally upheld, these legal proceedings often stretched on for years. After exorbitant legal fees and other expenses were taken into account, a legal triumph was often a Pyrrhic victory. In the end, most Mexican American landholders in northern California had to sell the very lands they had fought to keep in order to pay their mounting debts. Similarly, ranchers in southern California had to sell their lands to pay outstanding debts after devastating droughts in the 1860s virtually destroyed the ranching industry. Forced off the land, California's Mexican Americans increasingly found themselves concentrated in segregated urban *barrios.*

The migration of Anglos into eastern Texas had played a role in fomenting the war for Texas independence and in bringing about the war with Mexico (see chapter 13). By the latter half of the 19th century, eastern Texas was overwhelmingly Anglo; most Mexican Americans were concentrated in the Rio Grande Valley of southern Texas. As in California, Anglos in Texas used force and intimidation, coupled with exploitative legal maneuvering, to disenfranchise the Mexican Americans. The vaunted Texas Rangers often acted as an Anglo vigilante force that exacted retribution for the real or imagined crimes of Mexican

THE NEW SOUTH ■ 575

Americans. Eventually, Mexican Americans in Texas were reduced to a state of peonage, dependent on their Anglo protectors for political and economic security.

Similar patterns prevailed in New Mexico, but the effects were mitigated somewhat because New Mexicans continued to outnumber Anglo-American settlers. Earlier in the 19th century, international trade along the Santa Fe Trail had strengthened the political and economic status of the New Mexican elites. Now these same elites consolidated their position by acting as power brokers between poorer New Mexicans and wealthy Anglos.

Despite all of these difficulties, Spanish-speaking peoples in the Southwest and California managed to preserve much of their distinctive culture. Moreover, Anglo-American immigrants adopted many Mexican American agricultural methods and mining techniques. Perhaps the most enduring legacy of the Spanish-speaking peoples is to be found in the areas of mining law, community property law, and—most important in the arid West—water law.

The New South

Southern whites began to rebuild their own culture in the decades following Reconstruction. Some refused to let go of the legacy of the defeated plantation South. They celebrated the Lost Cause by organizing fraternal and sororal organizations such as the United Daughters of the Confederacy (UDC). The UDC, like the Daughters of the American Revolution on which it was modeled, was open only to whites who could prove their relation to the "first families" of the South. Its members decorated the graves of Confederate soldiers, funded public statues of Confederate heroes, and sought to preserve a romanticized history of the slavery era. Several white Southern authors became famous writing stories about this fabled South. Thomas Nelson Page's story "Marse Chan" created a national craze for Southern literature in the 1880s. Published in a Northern magazine, the story was written in what Page claimed to be authentic black dialect. An aging freedman told of the glorious days "befo' de wah" when slaves "didn' hed nothin' 't all to do." Such stories made the romanticized Southern plantation, cleansed of the horrors of slavery, an appealing part of the national imagination.

Not all white Southerners revered the Lost Cause. Many looked to the future rather than the past. They attempted to modernize the South's economy and to diversify Southern agriculture. They encouraged Northern investment and the building of new railroads to tie the South into national and international markets. Rather than a Lost Cause, these Southerners looked to a New South.

The Republican Party did not disappear from the South after 1877. Nor was the black vote immediately and totally suppressed. Republican presidential candidates won about 40 percent of the votes in former slave states through the 1880s, and some blacks continued to win elections to state legislatures until the 1890s. Down to 1901, every U.S. Congress but one had at least one black representative from the South. Independent parties occasionally formed coalitions with Republicans to win local or state elections, especially in Virginia.

Even so, "bulldozing" of black voters (chapter 17) continued to keep the southern states solid for the Democrats. In 1880, the Democratic Party hoped to build on this foundation to win the presidency for the first time in a generation. Taking their cue from the Republicans, the Democrats nominated a Civil War hero, General Winfield Scott Hancock. His opponent was another Civil War general, James A. Garfield, who had served in Congress since the war. In an election with the closest popular vote in American history (Garfield had a plurality of only 10,000 votes out of 9 million cast), Hancock carried every southern state, while Garfield won all but three northern states—and the election.

According to legend, Hancock's defeat convinced forward-looking white Southerners that the way to salvation was not through politics. They rolled up their sleeves and went to work to build a New South of commerce, cotton mills, and steel. The legend embodies some truth. A new spirit of enterprise quickened Southern life in the 1880s. Some Southerners even went so far as to acknowledge that the Yankees had shown them the way, and they welcomed Northern investment. Henry Grady, editor of the Atlanta *Constitution,* was the leading spokesman for the New South ideology. In an 1886 speech to Northern businessmen, Grady boasted of the New South's achievements: "We have sown towns and cities in the place of theories, and put business above politics. . . . We have established thrift in city and country. We have fallen in love with work."

Southern Industry

Considerable reality underlay this rhetoric. The South's textile industry expanded rapidly during the 1880s. Along the piedmont from Virginia to Alabama, new cotton mills and company towns for their workers sprang up. The labor force was almost entirely white, drawn from farm families on the worn-out red clay soil of the piedmont. About 40 percent of the workers were women, and 25 percent were children aged 16 and younger. These "lintheads," as wealthier whites called them, labored long hours for wages about half the level prevailing in New England's mills. This cheap labor gave Southern mill owners a competitive advantage. In 1880, the South had only 5 percent of the country's textile-producing capacity; by 1900, it had 23 percent and was well on its way to surpassing New England a generation later. At first, Southerners supplied most of the capital for this expansion. After 1893, an increasing amount came from the North, as New England mill owners came to recognize the benefits of relocating in the low-wage, nonunion South.

Tobacco was another Southern industry that developed from a regional crop. Most of the initial capital for this effort also came from the South, and unlike the textile industry, many of the workers in the tobacco factories were black. James B. Duke of North Carolina transformed the tobacco industry when he installed cigarette-making machines at Durham in 1885. In 1890, he created the American Tobacco Company, which controlled 90 percent of the market, with himself at its head. After Duke moved to New York in the 1880s, Northern capital played an important role in this regional industry as well.

Railroads and iron were two New South industries that depended even more on outside capital. During the 1880s, railroad construction in the South outpaced the national average. In 1886, Southern railroads shifted their 5-foot gauge to the national standard of 4 feet 8½ inches. This change integrated Southern lines into the national network and symbolized Northern domination of the region's railroads. During those same years, Northern capital helped fuel the growth of an iron and steel industry in the South. In 1880, the former slave states produced only 9 percent of the nation's pig iron; by 1890, after a decade of extraordinary expansion for the industry nationwide, that proportion had doubled. Most of the growth was concentrated in northern Alabama, where the proximity of coal, limestone, and ore made the new city of Birmingham the "Pittsburgh of the South."

The heavy Northern investment in these industries meant that the South had less control over economic decisions that affected its welfare. Some historians have referred to the South's "colonial" relationship to the North in the late 19th century. The low wages prevailing in the South made for inequitable distribution of the economic benefits of industrial growth. Average Southern per capita income remained only two-fifths of the average in the rest of the country well into the 20th century.

Southern Agriculture

The main reason for the South's relative poverty, however, was its weak agriculture. A crucial reason for this problem was low-level investment in farming. Although manufacturing capital increased by 300 percent per capita in the ex-Confederate states from 1880 to 1900, the amount invested in agriculture increased by only 29 percent per capita.

One-crop specialization, overproduction, declining prices, and an exploitative credit system all contributed to the problem. The basic institution of the Southern rural economy was the crop lien system, which came into being because of the shortage of money and credit in the war-ravaged South. Few banks had survived the war, and land values had plummeted, which left farmers unable to secure a bank loan with their land as collateral. Instead, merchants in the crossroads country stores that sprang up across the South provided farmers with supplies and groceries in return for a lien on their next crop.

This system might have worked well if the merchants had charged reasonable interest rates and if cotton and tobacco prices had remained high enough for the farmer to pay off his debts after harvest with a little left over. But the country storekeeper charged a credit price 50 or 60 percent above the cash price, partly because he had no competition and partly because of the high risk of loss on his loans. And crop prices, especially for cotton, were dropping steadily. Cotton prices declined from an average of 12 cents per pound in the 1870s to 6 cents in the 1890s. As prices fell, many farmers went deeper and deeper into debt to the merchants. Sharecroppers and tenants incurred a double indebtedness: to the landowner whose land they sharecropped or rented, and to the merchant who furnished them supplies on credit. Because many landowners became merchants, and vice versa, that indebtedness was often to the same man. Many sharecroppers, particularly blacks, fell into virtual peonage.

One reason cotton prices fell was overproduction. Britain had encouraged the expansion of cotton growing in Egypt and India during the Civil War to make up for the loss of American cotton. After the war, Southern growers had to face international competition. By 1878, the Southern crop had reached the output of the best antebellum year, and during the next 20 years, output doubled. This overproduction drove prices ever lower. To obtain credit, farmers had to plant every acre with the most marketable cash crop—cotton. This practice exhausted the soil and required ever-increasing amounts of expensive fertilizer, which fed the cycle of overproduction and declining prices.

It also reduced the amount of land that could be used to grow food crops. Farmers who might otherwise have produced their own cornmeal and raised their own hogs for bacon became dependent on merchants for these supplies. Before the Civil War, the cotton states had been nearly self-sufficient in food; by the 1890s, they had to import nearly half their food at a price 50 percent higher than it would have cost to grow their own. Many Southerners recognized that only diversification could break this dependency, but the crop lien system locked them into it. "We ought to plant less [cotton and tobacco] and more of grain and grasses," said a North Carolina farmer in 1887, "but how are we to do it; the man who furnishes us rations at 50 percent interest won't let us; he wants money crop planted. . . . It is cotton! cotton! cotton! Buy everything and make cotton pay for it."

Race Relations in the New South

The downward spiral of the rural Southern economy caused frustration and bitterness in which blacks became the scapegoats of white rage. Lynching rose to an all-time high in the 1890s, averaging 188 per year. The viciousness of racist propaganda reached an all-time low. Serious anti-black riots broke out at Wilmington, North Carolina, in 1898 and in Atlanta in 1906. Several states adopted new constitutions that disenfranchised most black voters by means of literacy or property qualifications (or both), poll taxes, and other clauses implicitly aimed at black voters. The new constitutions contained "understanding clauses" or "grandfather clauses" that enabled registrars to register white voters who were unable to meet the new requirements. In *Williams v. Mississippi* (1898), the U.S. Supreme Court upheld these disenfranchisement clauses on the grounds that they did not discriminate "on their face" against blacks. Most blacks lost the right to vote, and the Republican Party almost disappeared from most southern states. State Democratic parties then established primary elections in which only whites could vote. For the next 60 years, the primary was the only meaningful election in the South.

During these same years, most southern states passed "Jim Crow" laws, which mandated racial segregation in public facilities of all kinds. In the landmark case of *Plessy* v. *Ferguson* (1896), the Supreme Court sanctioned such laws so long as the separate facilities for blacks were equal to those for whites—which, in practice, they never were.

One of the worst features of race relations in the New South was the convict leasing system. Before 1865, most crimes by slaves were punished on the plantations. The Southern prison system was therefore inadequate to accommodate the increase in convicted criminals after emancipation. Most states began leasing convicts to private contractors—coal-mining firms, railroad construction companies, planters, and so on. The state not only saved the cost of housing and feeding the prisoners but also received an income for leasing them; the lessees obtained cheap labor whom they could work like slaves. The cruelty and exploitation suffered by the convicts became a national scandal. Ninety percent of the convicts were black, the result in part of discriminatory law enforcement practices. The convicts were ill fed, ill clothed, victimized by sadistic guards, and worked almost to death—sometimes literally to death. Annual mortality rates among convicts in several states ranged up to 25 percent.

Northern reformers condemned what they called "this newest and most revolting form of slavery." Thoughtful Southerners agreed; an official investigation in Georgia pronounced convict leasing "barbaric," "worse than slavery," and "a disgrace to civilized people." Reform groups, many of them led by white women, sprang up in the South to work for the abolition of convict leasing. They achieved some success after 1900, although leasing was replaced in some states or counties by the chain gang—a dubious improvement.

At this "nadir" of the black experience in freedom, as one historian has called the 1890s, a new black leader emerged as successor of the abolitionists and Reconstruction politicians who were fading from the scene. Frederick Douglass died in 1895; but in that same year, Booker T. Washington, a 39-year-old educator who had founded Tuskegee Institute in Alabama, gave a speech at the Atlanta Exposition that made him famous. In effect, Washington accepted segregation as a temporary accommodation between the races in return for white support of black efforts for education, social uplift, and economic progress. "In all things that are purely social we can be as separate as the fingers," said Washington, "yet one as the hand in all things essential to mutual progress."

© The Granger Collection.

BOOKER T. WASHINGTON IN HIS OFFICE AT TUSKEGEE

The most powerful black leader of his time, Washington built an excellent secondary school and industrial training institute at Tuskegee, Alabama, and gained great influence with philanthropists and political leaders. But many northern blacks accused him of acquiescing in segregation and second-class citizenship for blacks in return for the crumbs of philanthropy.

Washington's goal was not permanent second-class citizenship for blacks, but improvement through self-help and uplift until they earned white acceptance as equals. Yet to his black critics, Washington's strategy and rhetoric seemed to play into the hands of white supremacists. The Atlanta Exposition speech of 1895 launched a debate over means and ends in the black struggle for equality that, in one form or another, has continued for more than a century.

The Politics of Stalemate

During the 20 years between the Panic of 1873 and the Panic of 1893, serious economic and social issues beset the American polity. As described in the next chapter, the strains of rapid industrialization, an inadequate monetary system, agricultural distress, and labor protest built up to potentially explosive force. The two mainstream political parties, however, seemed indifferent to these problems. Paralysis gripped the national government as the Civil War continued to cast its shadow, preventing political leaders from grappling with new issues facing the country because they remained mired in the passionate partisanship of the past.

Knife-Edge Electoral Balance

The five presidential elections from 1876 through 1892, taken together, were the most closely contested elections in American history. No more than 1 percent separated the popular vote of the two major candidates in any of these contests except 1892, when the margin was 3 percent. The Democratic candidate won twice (Grover Cleveland in 1884 and 1892), and in two other elections carried a tiny plurality of popular votes (Tilden in 1876 and Cleveland in 1888) but lost narrowly in the Electoral College. During the 20 years covered by these five administrations, the Democrats controlled the House of Representatives in seven Congresses to the Republicans' three, while the Republicans controlled the Senate in eight Congresses to the Democrats' two. During only 6 of those 20 years did the same party control the presidency and both houses, and then by razor-thin margins.

The few pieces of major legislation during these years—the Pendleton Civil Service Act of 1883, the Interstate Commerce Act of 1887, and the Sherman Antitrust Act of 1890—could be enacted only by bipartisan majorities, and only after they had been watered down by numerous compromises. Politicians often debated the tariff, but the tariff laws they passed had little real impact on the economy. Tariffs were still the principal source of federal tax revenue, but because the federal budget amounted to less than 3 percent of the gross national product (compared with 20 percent today), federal fiscal policies played only a marginal role in the economy.

Divided government and the even balance between the two major parties accounted for the political stalemate. Neither party had the power to enact a bold legisla-

Waving the Bloody Shirt

The Civil War cast a long shadow over the politics of the generation that had fought it. For decades after the war, political speakers in both North and South called on voters to "vote as you shot." In the North, this was called "waving the bloody shirt." Colonel Robert Ingersoll, who had commanded an Illinois cavalry regiment during the war, was a master of this genre; a speech he gave to Union veterans in 1876, urging them to vote Republican in the presidential election, is a classic example.

Every state that seceded from the United States was a Democratic State. . . . Every man that tried to destroy this nation was a Democrat. Every man that loved slavery better than liberty was a Democrat.

The man that assassinated Abraham Lincoln was a Democrat. . . . Every man that raised blood-hounds to pursue human beings was a Democrat. . . . Soldiers, every scar you have got on your heroic bodies was given to you by a Democrat.

1. Why did Ingersoll invoke the issues of the Civil War during an election that took place more than a decade after that war had ended?

For additional sources related to this feature, visit the *Liberty, Equality, Power* Web site at:

http://history.wadsworth.com/murrin_LEP4e

tive program; both parties avoided taking firm stands on controversial issues. Both parties practiced the politics of the past rather than the politics of the present. Individuals voted Republican or Democratic in the 1880s because they or their fathers had done so during the passionate years of the 1860s. Every Republican president from 1869 to 1901 had fought in the Union army; the one Democratic president, Grover Cleveland, had not. At election time, Republican candidates "waved the bloody shirt" to keep alive the memory of the Civil War. They castigated Democrats as former rebels or Copperheads who could not be trusted with the nation's destiny. Democrats, in turn, especially in the South, denounced racial equality and branded Republicans as the party of "Negro rule"—a charge that took on added intensity in 1890 when Republicans tried (and failed by one vote in the Senate) to enact a federal elections law to protect the voting rights of African Americans. From 1876 almost into the 20th century, scarcely anyone but a Confederate veteran could be elected governor or senator in the South.

Availability rather than ability or a strong stand on issues became the prime requisite for presidential and vice presidential nominees. Geographical availability was particularly important. The solid Democratic South and the rather less solid Republican North gave each party a firm bloc of electoral votes in every election. But in three large northern states—New York, Ohio, and Indiana—the two parties were so closely balanced that the shift of a few thousand votes would determine the margin of victory for one or the other party in the state's electoral votes. These three states alone represented 74 electoral votes, fully one third of the total necessary for victory. The party that carried New York (36 electoral votes) and either of the other two won the presidency.

It is not surprising that of 20 nominees for president and vice president by the two parties in five elections, 16 were from these three states. Only once did each party nominate a presidential candidate from outside these three states: Democrat Winfield Scott Hancock of Pennsylvania in 1880 and Republican James G. Blaine of Maine in 1884—both lost.

Civil Service Reform

The most salient issue of national politics in the early 1880s was civil service reform. Old-guard factions in both parties opposed it. Republicans split into three factions known in the colorful parlance of the time as Mugwumps (the reformers), Stalwarts (who opposed reform), and Half-Breeds (who supported halfway reforms). Mugwumps and Half-Breeds combined to nominate James A. Garfield for president in 1880. Stalwarts received a consolation

prize with the nomination of Chester A. Arthur for vice president. Four months after Garfield took office, a man named Charles Guiteau approached the president at the railroad station in Washington and shot him. Garfield lingered for two months before dying on September 19, 1881.

Described by psychiatrists as a paranoid schizophrenic, Guiteau was viewed by the public as a symbol of the spoils system at its worst. He had been a government clerk and a supporter of the Stalwart faction of the Republican Party but had lost his job under the new administration. As he shot Garfield, he shouted, "I am a Stalwart and Arthur is president now!" This tragedy gave a final impetus to civil service reform. If the spoils system could cause the assassination of a president, it was time to get rid of it.

Although a Stalwart, President Arthur supported reform. In 1883, Congress passed the Pendleton Act, which established a category of civil service jobs that were to be filled by competitive examinations. At first, only one-tenth of government positions fell within that category, but a succession of presidential orders gradually expanded the list to about half by 1897. State and local governments began to emulate federal civil service reform in the 1880s and 1890s.

Like the other vice presidents who had succeeded presidents who died in office (John Tyler, Millard Fillmore, and Andrew Johnson), Arthur failed to achieve nomination for president in his own right. The Republicans turned in 1884 instead to their most charismatic figure, James G. Blaine of Maine. His 18 years in the House and Senate had included six years (1869–75) as Speaker of the House. He had made enemies over the years, however, especially among Mugwumps, who believed that his cozy relationship with railroad lobbyists while Speaker and rumors of other shady dealings disqualified him for the presidency.

The Mugwumps, heirs of the old Conscience Whig element of the Republican Party, had a tendency toward elitism and self-righteousness in their self-appointed role as spokesmen for political probity. They were small in number but large in influence. Many were editors, authors, lawyers, college professors, or clergymen. Concentrated in the Northeast, particularly in New York, they admired the Democratic governor of that state, Grover Cleveland, who had gained a reputation as an advocate of reform and "good government." When Blaine won the Republican nomination, the Mugwumps defected to Cleveland.

In such a closely balanced state as New York, that shift could make a decisive difference, but Blaine hoped to neutralize it by shaving a few percentage points from the normal Democratic majority of the Irish vote. He made the most of his Irish ancestry on the maternal side. But that effort was rendered futile late in the campaign when a Protestant clergyman characterized the Democrats as the party of "Rum, Romanism, and Rebellion." Although Blaine was present when the Reverend Samuel Burchard made this remark, he failed to repudiate it. When the incident hit the newspapers, Blaine's hope for Irish support went glimmering. Cleveland carried New York State by 1,149 votes (a margin of one-tenth of 1 percent) and thus became the first Democrat to be elected president in 28 years.

The Tariff Issue

Ignoring a rising tide of farmer and labor discontent, Cleveland decided to make or break his presidency on the tariff issue. He devoted his annual State of the Union message in December 1887 entirely to the tariff, maintaining that lower duties would help all Americans by reducing the cost of consumer goods and by expanding American exports through reciprocal agreements with other nations. Republicans responded that low tariffs would flood the country with products from low-wage industries abroad, forcing American factories to close and throwing American workers out on the streets. The following year, the Republican nominee for president, Benjamin Harrison, pledged to retain the protective tariff. To reduce the budget surplus that had built up during the 1880s, the Republicans also promised more generous pensions for Union veterans.

The voters' response was ambiguous. Cleveland's popular-vote plurality actually increased from 29,000 in 1884 to 90,000 in 1888 (out of more than 10 million votes cast). Even so, a shift of six-tenths of 1 percent put New York in the Republican column and Harrison in the White House. Republicans also gained control of both houses of Congress. They promptly made good on their campaign pledges by passing legislation that almost doubled Union pensions and by enacting the McKinley Tariff of 1890. Named for Congressman William McKinley of Ohio, this law raised duties on a large range of products to an average of almost 50 percent, the highest since the infamous Tariff of Abominations in 1828.

The voters reacted convincingly—and negatively. They handed the Republicans a decisive defeat in midterm congressional elections, converting a House Republican majority of 6 to a Democratic majority of 147, and a Senate Republican majority of eight to a Democratic majority of six. Nominated for a third time in 1892, Cleveland built on this momentum to win the presidency by the largest margin in 20 years, but this outcome was deceptive. On March 4, 1893, when Cleveland took the oath of office for the second time, he stood atop a social and economic volcano that would soon erupt. When the ashes settled and the lava cooled, the political landscape would be forever altered.

Conclusion

In 1890, the superintendent of the U.S. Census made a sober announcement of dramatic import: "Up to and including 1880 the country had a frontier of settlement, but at present the unsettled area has been so broken into by isolated bodies of settlement that there can hardly be said to be a frontier line . . . any longer."

This statement prompted a young historian at the University of Wisconsin, Frederick Jackson Turner, to deliver a paper in 1893 that became the single most influential essay ever published by an American historian. For nearly 300 years, said Turner, the existence of a frontier of European-American settlement advancing relentlessly westward had shaped American character. To the frontier Americans owed their upward mobility, their high standard of living, and the rough equality of opportunity that made liberty and democracy possible. "American social development has been continually beginning over again on the frontier," declared Turner. He continued:

> This perennial rebirth, this fluidity of American life, this expansion westward with its new opportunities . . . furnish the forces dominating American character. . . . Frontier individualism has from the beginning promoted democracy [and] that restless, nervous energy, that dominant individualism . . . and withal that buoyancy and exuberance which comes with freedom—these are traits of the frontier, or traits called out elsewhere because of the existence of the frontier.

For many decades, Turner's insight dominated Americans' perceptions of themselves and their history. Today, however, the Turner thesis is largely discredited as failing to explain the experiences of the great majority of people throughout most of American history who lived and worked in older cities and towns or on farms or plantations hundreds of miles from any frontier, and whose culture and institutions were molded more by their place of origin than by a frontier. The whole concept of a frontier as a line of white settlement beyond which lay empty land has been discredited because other peoples had lived on that land for millennia.

The Turner thesis also ignored the environmental consequences of the westward movement. The virtual destruction of the bison, the hunting almost to extinction of other forms of wildlife, the ravaging of virgin forests by indiscriminate logging, and the plowing of semi-arid grasslands on the plains drastically changed the ecological balance in the West. They stored up trouble for the future in the form of soil erosion, dust bowls, and diminished biodiversity. Thoughtful Americans began to express concern about these problems in the 1890s, foreshadowing the launching of a conservation movement in the following decade.

The significance of the Turner thesis, however, is not whether he got everything right; in the 1890s, he expressed a widely shared belief among white Americans. They believed that liberty and equality were at least partly the product of the frontier, of the chance to go west and start a new life. And now that opportunity seemed to be coming to an end at the same time that the Panic of 1893 was launching another depression, the worst that the American economy had yet experienced. This depression caused the social and economic tinder that had been accumulating during the two preceding decades to burst into flame.

SUGGESTED READINGS

Wallace Stegner, *Beyond the Hundredth Meridian* (1954) is a readable and evocative description of the West from the plains to the Pacific. The various western frontiers are described in the following books, whose subjects are indicated by their titles: **William Greever,** *The Bonanza West: The Story of the Western Mining Rushes* (1963); **Edward E. Dale,** *The Range Cattle Industry,* rev. ed. (1969); **William Savage,** *The Cowboy Hero: His Image in American History and Culture* (1979); **Gilbert C. Fite,** *The Farmer's Frontier, 1865–1900* (1966); **Sandra Myres,** *Western Women and the Frontier Experience, 1880–1915* (1982); and **Robert M. Utley,** *The Indian Frontier of the American West 1846–1890* (1984). On the 19th- and 20th-century myths of the frontier, see **Richard White and Patricia Nelson Limerick,** *The Frontier in American Culture* (1994). The Indians' response to the reservation system after the 1860s is discussed in **Frederick Hoxie, Peter C. Mancall, and James H. Merrill,** eds., *American Nations: Encounters in Indian Country, 1850 to the Present* (2001).

The classic study of the New South is **C. Vann Woodward,** *Origins of the New South, 1877–1913* (1951). It can be supplemented by **Edward L. Ayers,** *The Promise of the New South: Life After Reconstruction* (1992). The lost cause ideology is examined in **Gaines M. Foster,** *Ghosts of the Confederacy: Defeat, the Lost Cause, and the Emergence of the New South* (1987). Disenfranchisement of black voters is analyzed in **J. Morgan Kousser,** *The Shaping of Southern Politics: Suffrage Restriction and the Establishment of the One-Party South*

1880–1910 (1974). The rising tide of white racism is chronicled by **Joel Williamson,** *The Crucible of Race: Black-White Relations in the American South Since Emancipation* (1984), which was also published in an abridged edition with the title *A Rage for Order: Black-White Relations in the American South Since Emancipation* (1986). See also **Leon F. Litwack,** *Trouble in Mind: Black Southerners in the Age of Jim Crow* (1998). A readable narrative of political history in the Gilded Age is **H. Wayne Morgan,** *From Hayes to McKinley* (1969).

 AMERICAN JOURNEY ONLINE AND INFOTRAC COLLEGE EDITION

Visit the source collections at www.ajaccess.wadsworth.com and infotrac.thomsonlearning.com and use the Search function with the following key terms to explore documents, images, audio and video clips, articles, and commentary related to the material in this chapter.

Ghost Dance
Dawes Severalty Act
Sand Creek Massacre
Jim Crow laws
Plessy v. *Ferguson*
Wounded Knee
Black cowboys
Sitting Bull
Crazy Horse
George A. Custer
Battle of Little Big Horn

GRADE AIDS

Visit the Liberty Equality Power Companion Web site for resources specific to this textbook: http://history.wadsworth.com/murrin_LEP4e

The CD in the back of this book and the U.S. History Resource Center at http://history.wadsworth.com/u.s./ offer a variety of tools to help you succeed in this course, including access to quizzes; images; documents; interactive simulations, maps, and timelines; movie explorations; and a wealth of other sources.

Chapter 19

Economic Change and the Crisis of the 1890s

The Kansas State Historical Society, Topeka, Kansas.

THE KANSAS LEGISLATURE, 1893
Agricultural depression in wheat and cotton states produced the third-party Populist movement in the 1890s. Populists won the Kansas governorship and state Senate by narrow margins in 1892, but contested returns for the lower House kept Kansas in turmoil for six weeks in early 1893. At one point, gun-toting Populists seized control of the capitol in Topeka, as shown in this dramatic photograph, and a shoot-out on the floor of the legislature seemed possible. A state court finally settled the dispute peacefully by certifying a Republican majority in the House.

CHAPTER OUTLINE

Alexis de Tocqueville visited the United States in 1831 and published his famous analysis, *Democracy in America*, in 1835. At that time, more than two-thirds of all Americans lived on farms, and only 10 percent lived in towns or cities with populations larger than 2,500. The overwhelming majority of white males owned property and worked for themselves rather than for wages. What impressed Tocqueville most was the relative absence of both great wealth and great poverty; the modest prosperity of the broad middle class created the impression—if not the literal reality—of equality, which Tocqueville made the central theme of *Democracy in America*.

During the next generation, the North began to industrialize, cities grew much faster than rural areas, and the inequality of wealth and income grew larger. The country's preoccupation with sectional issues before the Civil War and the gnawing problems of Reconstruction after the war diverted attention from the economic and social problems associated with industrialism and class inequality. With the depression that followed the Panic of 1873, however, these problems burst spectacularly into public view. For a time, economic growth promised to deflect class conflict. By the 1890s, however, no American could deny that Tocqueville's republic of equality had long since disappeared.

CHAPTER FOCUS

♦ What were the main engines of American economic growth in the last third of the 19th century?

♦ How did post–Civil War economic changes affect working people? How did they respond?

♦ What provoked the farmer protest movements in the last third of the 19th century?

♦ What issues were at stake in the contest between "free silver" and the "gold bugs"?

⚓ Economic Growth

During the 15 years between recovery from one depression in 1878 and the onset of another in 1893, the American economy grew at one of the fastest rates in its history. The gross national product (GNP) almost doubled, and per capita GNP increased by 35 percent. All sectors of the economy were expanding. The most spectacular growth was in manufacturing, which increased by 180 percent, whereas agriculture grew by 26 percent. Manufacturing passed agriculture in value added for the first time in the early 1880s, and by 1900 the value added of manufacturing was almost twice that of agriculture.

Railroads

The railroad was the single most important agent of economic growth during these years. Track mileage increased by 113 percent, from 103,649 to 221,864 miles; the number of locomotives and revenue cars (freight and passenger) increased by a similar amount. Railroads converted from iron to steel rails and wheels, boosting steel production from 732,000 tons in 1878 to 10,188,000 tons by 1900. Railroads were the largest consumers of coal, the largest carriers of goods and people, and the largest single employer of labor.

The power wielded by the railroad companies inevitably aroused hostility. Companies often charged less for long hauls than for short hauls in areas with little or no competition. The rapid proliferation of tracks produced overcapacity in some areas, which led to rate-cutting wars that benefited some shippers at the expense of others—usually large shippers at the expense of small ones. To avoid

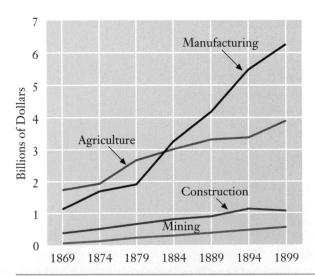

VALUE ADDED BY ECONOMIC SECTOR, 1869–1899 (IN 1879 PRICES)

C H R O N O L O G Y

1869 Knights of Labor founded

1873 "Crime of 1873" demonetizes silver

1877 Railroad strikes cost 100 lives and millions of dollars in damage

1878 Bland-Allison Act to remonetize silver passed over Hayes's veto

1879 Henry George publishes *Progress and Poverty*

1883 Railroads establish four standard time zones

1886 Knights of Labor membership crests at 700,000 • Haymarket riot causes antilabor backlash • American Federation of Labor founded

1887 Edward Bellamy publishes *Looking Backward* • Interstate Commerce Act creates the first federal regulatory agency

1890 Congress passes Sherman Antitrust Act • Congress passes Sherman Silver Purchase Act

1892 Homestead strike fails • Populists organize the People's Party

1893 Financial panic begins economic depression • Congress repeals Sherman Silver Purchase Act

1894 "Coxey's army" of the unemployed marches on Washington • Pullman strike paralyzes the railroads and provokes federal intervention

1896 William McKinley defeats William Jennings Bryan for the presidency

"ruinous competition" (as the railroads viewed it), companies formed "pools" by which they divided traffic and fixed their rates. Some of these practices made sound economic sense; others appeared discriminatory and exploitative. Railroads gave credence to farmers' charges of monopoly exploitation by keeping rates higher in areas with no competition (most farmers lived in areas served by only one line) than in regions with competition. Grain elevators, many of which were owned by railroad companies, came under attack for cheating farmers by rigging the classification of their grain.

Farmers responded by organizing cooperatives to sell crops and buy supplies. The umbrella organization for many of these cooperatives was the Patrons of Husbandry, known as the Grange, founded in 1867. But because farmers could not build their own railroads, they organized "antimonopoly" parties and elected state legislators who enacted "Granger laws" in several states. These laws established railroad commissions that fixed maximum freight rates and warehouse charges. Railroads challenged the laws in court. Eight challenges made their way to the U.S. Supreme Court, which in *Munn* v. *Illinois* (1877) ruled that states could regulate businesses clothed with a "public interest"—railroads and other common carriers, millers, innkeepers, and the like. It was a landmark decision.

The welter of different and sometimes conflicting state laws, plus rulings by the U.S. Supreme Court in the 1880s that states could not regulate interstate railroad traffic, brought a drive for federal regulation. After years of discussion, Congress passed the Interstate Commerce Act in 1887. This law, like most such laws, reflected compromise between the varying viewpoints of shippers, railroads, and other pressure groups. It outlawed pools, discriminatory rates, long-haul versus short-haul differentials, and rebates to favored shippers. It required that freight and passenger rates must be "reasonable and just." What that meant was not entirely clear, but the law created the Interstate Commerce Commission (ICC) to define the requirement on a case-by-case basis. Because the ICC had minimal enforcement powers, however, federal courts frequently refused to issue the orders the ICC requested. Staffed by men who were knowledgeable about railroading, the ICC often sympathized with the viewpoint of the industry it was supposed to regulate. Nevertheless, its powers of publicity had some effect on railroad practices, and freight rates continued to decline during this period as railroad operating efficiency improved.

The outstanding example of the railroads' impact on everyday life was the creation of standard time zones. Before 1883, many localities and cities kept their own time, derived from the sun's meridian in each locality. When it was noon in Chicago, it was 11:27 A.M. in Omaha, 11:56 A.M. in St. Louis, 12:09 P.M. in Louisville, and 12:17 P.M. in Toledo. This situation played havoc with railroad timetables. In 1883, a consortium of railroads established four standard time zones—much the same as they exist in the 48 contiguous states today. They put new timetables into effect for these zones on November 18, 1883. Some grumbling followed about the arrogance of railroad presidents changing "God's time." The U.S. attorney general ruled that government agencies need not change their clocks until authorized to do so by Congress; the next day, he missed a train by eight minutes because he had not reset his watch to the new Eastern Standard Time. For the most part, however, the public accepted the change, and Congress finally sanctioned standard time zones in 1918.

Technology

Technological advances during this era had an enormous impact: the railroads gained automatic signals, air brakes, and knuckle couplers; steel mills added the Bessemer and then the open-hearth process. The 1870s produced the telephone, electric light, and typewriter; the elevator and structural steel made possible the first "skyscrapers" in the 1880s; and in the 1890s, the phonograph and motion pictures provided new forms of entertainment. This era also introduced the electric dynamo (generator), the basis for such household items as refrigerators and washing machines and a new source of industrial power that gradually replaced water power and the steam engine; and the internal combustion engine, which made possible the first automobiles (1890s) and the first airplane flight by the Wright brothers in 1903.

● The American Middle Class

The American middle class became conscious of itself as a group situated between laborers and wealthy elites in the decades following the Civil War. New forms of corporate organization, growing per capita income, an increasingly complex social order, and ever faster national communications provided those Americans of moderate means with a set of common interests that distinguished them from other Americans. As they became more aware of these class interests, middle-class Americans attempted to re-create the nation in their own image. In the process, they changed American culture in profound ways.

The Philadelphia Centennial Exposition

The Philadelphia Centennial Exposition of 1876 became a defining moment for this middle class. Americans celebrated their 100th anniversary with an enormous economic fair. Its organizers wanted it to rival famous European fairs, which began with the 1851 Crystal Palace Exhibition in London. Organizers erected 249 temporary buildings, housing more than 30,000 exhibits, on 300 acres of land. Countries from all over the world displayed their economic and cultural products. Anxious to prove their economic might, these foreign countries spent extravagantly. British firms alone spent more than $4 million (in current U.S. dollars) on commercial displays, and Japan sent more than 7,000 packages of material to stock its exhibit. But the country most on display was the United States. Alexander Graham Bell and Christopher Sholes exhibited their new inventions: the telephone and the typewriter. Engineers unveiled the world's largest power generator, the Corliss Steam Engine, capable of driving more than 75 miles of belts and shafts running row after row of industrial machinery. Visitors were awed by recent industrial, agricultural, and cultural innovations, including elevators, monorails, streetcars, linoleum floor coverings, canned food, and dry yeast. Many Americans also had their first taste of bananas and hot popcorn at the fair.

Almost 10 million people visited the fair, and far more read about it in newspaper and magazine articles. The fair demonstrated that the antebellum Market Revolution had become a full-fledged Industrial Revolution. The fruits of economic growth and innovation on display in Philadelphia demonstrated how vigorous American industry and technology had become.

Gilded Age Cities

Cities grew at a rapid pace in the late 1880s and 1890s. In 1860, about one in five Americans lived in cities. By 1900, this number had doubled to two in five. Chicago alone shot up from 30,000 residents in 1850 to 500,000 in 1880 and 1,700,000 by 1900. Cities rapidly expanded in physical terms, as well. Before 1850, urban Americans lived in "walking cities," which they could traverse on foot. This was no longer doable after the war. Streetcars, made possible by advances in railroad engineering and in electrical power generation, took citizens across vast urban distances. The expanding cities changed their look, too. Many of the people flocking to the expanding cities were for-eign immigrants or native-born rural laborers displaced from agricultural work by innovations in farm machinery. They moved into cramped, stuffy, poorly lit tenement buildings. Newly wealthy capitalists, meanwhile, built ostentatious homes and threw extravagant parties that came to symbolize the Gilded Age. The middle class, however, had no access to this aristocratic world. They boarded the streetcars and moved to new suburban communities located on the edges of large cities beyond urban noise and congestion.

Streetcars allowed middle-class Americans to conjure up images of living a rural ideal. Suburbanites inhabited private, single-family homes surrounded by trees, lawns, and gardens. They owned a spot of land they could call their own. Of course, these middle-class Americans did not want to live in the isolated rural world of their parents' generation. They advocated for communities built around two new social institutions: the high school and the public library. Growing suburbs required the development of large systems for sanitation, power, and communication. The control of these systems—whether by private companies or public utilities—would be a major point of socioeconomic conflict after the turn of the 20th century as Progressives fought to bring order to the hodge-podge development of the Gilded Age city.

The American Museum

Other middle-class institutions changed the cultural face of U.S. cities. The American museum evolved from a warehouse of curiosities to an ornate space for the display of fine art and scientific artifacts, spurred by the proliferation of wealthy donors and the growth of universities. Newly rich art patrons donated huge collections to establish museums such as the Metropolitan and Natural History museums in New York, the Field Museum and the Art Institute in Chicago, and the Fine Arts Museum in Boston.

The Museum of the City of New York.

NEW YORK CITY IN 1885

This photograph shows the crowded, chaotic nature of lower Manhattan in the 1880s. The scene is Broadway at Cortlandt Street looking south from Maiden Lane. Note the proliferation of utility poles and wires: the telephone and electric lighting had become part of American urban life in the past half-dozen years, radically changing the face of city streets.

William Randolph Hearst: Collecting the Art of Europe

Many Gilded Age Americans feared that they lived in a nation without culture. Wealthy Americans discovered a way to solve the problem without having to wait for the development of indigenous schools of art. Increasing numbers of rich Americans bought European art and brought it back to the United States. American museums greatly benefited. Museumgoers could now experience firsthand the masterpieces of Rembrandt, Vermeer, El Greco, Gainsborough, and Titian.

Collecting European art was William Randolph Hearst's passion. The future newspaper tycoon, movie producer, and politician first traveled to Europe at age 10. His mother, Phoebe, flush with the fortune his father George Hearst had made in mining, took him on a grand tour of European museums, churches, and historic sights that lasted 18 months. Young Hearst simultaneously developed a deep love of art and the desire to spend money. Phoebe Hearst wrote home to George that their son "wants all sorts of things. [He] gets so fascinated, his reason and judgment forsake him." In London, he pleaded with his mother to buy him four of the magnificent white horses that pulled the king's carriage. In Germany, he bought himself boy things, such as coins, stamps, and comic books. He also bought things few boys wanted or could afford: beer steins and porcelain statues. In Venice, he collected hand-blown art glass. He also developed, his sympathetic mother sighed, "a mania for antiquities, poor old boy."

Hearst traveled to Europe on his own in 1889 at age 26. Now the publisher of a San Francisco newspaper, he was surprised to find that he still suffered from the "art fever." "I never miss a gallery now," he wrote his mother, "I mosey about the pictures and statuary and admire them and wish they were mine. My artistic longings are not altogether distinct from avarice. . . ." In later years, he indulged his collecting passion by taking friends on exhausting journeys to explore the wonders of Old World art.

Hearst and his fellow wealthy art patrons became American cultural icons. The expatriate American novelist Henry James made a career of writing about them. James, who lived in London for most of his adult life, wrote novels such as *The American* and *The Portrait of a Lady*, which chronicled the inner struggles of naive, newly wealthy Americans as they confronted sophisticated yet corrupt European aristocrats. His books brim with American collectors of European art, such as Breckinridge Bender of *The Outcry*, who hunted Europe in pursuit of some "ideally expensive thing" armed "with huge cheque-books instead of with spears and battle axes." Bender was something of a caricature. Although some art patrons were as shallow, others were genuinely committed to making the great works of Europe available to all Americans in the nation's new museums of art.

The homes of many wealthy Americans came to resemble museums. Isabella Stewart Gardner and Henry Clay Frick built grand homes in Boston and New York as personal museums to display their vast collections of European art. Hearst, himself, built an immense mansion complex at San Simeon, California, to house his Old World art treasures. He had it designed to resemble a Mediterranean villa of the Spanish Renaissance.

The homes of Gardner, Frick, and Hearst are all now museums open to the public.

This photograph of the reflecting pool at William Randolph Hearst's estate, San Simeon, portrays the fabulous lifestyle he created for himself in the foothills of central California's coastal range. San Simeon today is a popular tourist attraction.

© Bob Krist/Corbis.

Although these museums were public institutions heavily funded by state and local governments, wealthy trustees often saw them as upper-class institutions. When other classes protested, museums could become class battlegrounds. In the late 1880s, labor unions in New York City began demanding that trustees open the Metropolitan and Natural History museums on Sundays, the only day of the week workers had free. More than 100 labor organizations, representing some 50,000 workers, petitioned the museums to open on Sundays. In 1891, social reformers gathered 80,000 signatures from the poor for the same cause. The press, the state legislature, and even some wealthy New Yorkers joined in the movement. By 1892, both museums capitulated. But museum administrators, under pressure from wealthy trustees, were determined that middle-class decorum should be maintained. They discouraged such practices as blowing the nose with one's fingers, bringing dogs, whistling, yelling, and even urinating in the galleries. They experimented with dress codes, barring overalls for a time, and they required visitors to check coats and canes at the door. Mark Twain, ever the curmudgeon, sarcastically complained, "Leave my cane! Then how do you expect me to poke holes through the oil paintings?"

The Department Store and Mail-Order Catalogs

Middle-class Americans changed the ways they obtained household goods. As cities grew, so did the stores that supplied city dwellers. Before the Civil War, shops usually sold only a single line of goods. The shoemaker sold shoes, and the dressmaker sold dresses. Shoppers went from shop to shop to purchase items from proprietors they often knew personally. Personal acquaintance allowed shopkeepers to extend credit to customers, believing they could trust their neighbors to settle accounts sooner or later. Then when John Wanamaker's in Philadelphia opened its doors in 1876, the department store was born. Wanamaker took a series of single-line shops and put them in one huge space. This concentrated arrangement of shops had two major advantages over the old shops. Department stores sold goods more cheaply because they made their profit through high-volume sales, and they brought a multitude of items under one roof.

The changes wrought by the department stores created a new experience of shopping. The profuse display of goods overwhelmed many customers. Author Theodore Dreiser captured this feeling in describing young Carrie Meeker's first visit to a department store in his novel *Sister Carrie*. She felt "the drag of desire for all which was new and pleasing in apparel for women, but she noticed too,

with a touch at the heart, the fine ladies who elbowed and ignored her, brushing past in utter disregard of her presence, themselves eagerly enlisted in the materials which the store contained." To make the department store experience more enticing, store owners modeled their interiors on the displays of museums and world's fairs. They ornately decorated store interiors with marble, richly colored textiles, and mirrored glass. They cut huge display windows into street-level walls to exhibit fancy jewelry, clothing, and housewares. The idea was to turn shopping into entertainment.

For those who lived in rural areas and could not travel to the big city, mail-order companies emerged. Montgomery Ward and Sears, Roebuck used the nation's rapidly expanding rail system to speed goods across the country. They published thick catalogues, offering everything from women's underclothing to entire houses. The chain store was another retail strategy that spread throughout the country. The Great Atlantic and Pacific Tea Company (A&P) and Woolworth's developed extensive systems of food and dry goods stores built in small towns and large cities alike.

The department stores, mail-order houses, and chain stores would not have been possible without the standardization of the goods they sold. Standardization had long been central to the American system of manufactures. Already in the 1850s, the American system had allowed for the mass production of many items built with interchangeable parts. Numerous entrepreneurs after the Civil War adapted these basic techniques to the production of additional consumer goods. Fashionable items of clothing and housewares, once obtainable only by the wealthy, could now be made relatively cheaply and quickly. After 1885, the clothing industry grew two to three times faster than any other industry. By 1915, it was the nation's third largest industry, ranking just behind steel and oil. Such rapid production required consumer goods manufacturers to devise new ways of selling their mass-produced wares.

Advertising and Magazines

Advertising soon became a major American industry. Ad agencies created personal images consumers could identify with particular products, such as Cream of Wheat's Rastus, Aunt Jemima, or the Quaker on Quaker Oats boxes. Seeking to distance themselves from the outlandishly false claims of the quacks who sold "patent" medicines and other fakery, advertising agencies justified their labors as the publicity of honest information and as a sign of the nation's moral progress. By the 1890s, advertising had revolutionized the sale of consumer goods. "Advertising is to the field of distribution," claimed a copywriter for

Wanamaker's department store, "what the railroad is to transportation." Advertisements were distributed by way of printed catalogs, booklets, posters, cigarette cards, and numerous other devices. The most widespread advertising medium was probably the American magazine. By the middle 1890s, the nation's most prestigious popular magazines filled almost half their pages with advertisements for a panoply of name-brand consumer goods, from Pond's Soap to Remington Typewriters.

The American magazine signaled the nation's cultural arrival to itself and to the world. Magazines such as the *Century, Harper's New Monthly,* and *Scribner's* were created by editors who had themselves risen from modest circumstances into middle-class lives. These magazines were lavishly illustrated. Their art directors invented new methods of image reproduction that allowed them to print sumptuously detailed illustrations. The magazines pushed American culture in two different directions. On the one hand, they featured highlights of Western civilization with articles on venerated authors from Dante to Wordsworth and reproductions of art masterpieces from ancient Greece to Rembrandt. On the other hand, they pioneered new artistic and literary movements, such as impressionism and realism. The magazines became the site of intense conflicts over the function of literature. *Harper's,* for instance, became the platform from which William Dean Howells called for a realist literature that was based on close observation of the facts of life. His novels explored issues that had rarely been touched by American authors, including divorce, the moral bankruptcy of capitalism, and miscegenation. Henry James survived as an author only because magazine editors deeply admired his penetrating psychological studies. They persisted in publishing his novels, even though the public seemed largely indifferent to his work. Although they published an author like James from time to time, magazine editors never lost sight of their commercial status. They published romantic works that were popular, but which presented whitewashed pictures of the American past, particularly the era of slavery. White Southern author Thomas Nelson Page's fame, based on his "negro" dialect stories, was due chiefly to his association with the *Century* and *Harper's.* But no matter their particular stand in the debate between realism and romanticism, all magazine editors believed that their mission was to hold up a cultural mirror in which the American people could see themselves. They pioneered the development of the short story and made it as much a symbol of the American nation as the flag or Niagara Falls.

The magazines revolutionized newspaper journalism. Before the Civil War, newspapers refused to make much use of illustration. Technological limitations to the old methods of reproduction made it impossible for illustrators to produce pictures as fast as writers could report events. But the innovations invented by the magazines did away with these technological limitations. Photographic processes invented in the 1890s made it possible to transmit and reproduce newspaper pictures as quickly as telegraph lines carried journalists' words. Newspapers could now reproduce illustrations on a daily basis. Another limitation on the newspaper had been the prohibition of Sunday publication, enforced by religious-minded consumers and community leaders. Taking a cue from the magazines, newspaper publishers began to issue Sunday editions after the Civil War that added special sections devoted to culture and leisure. Book reviews, fashion layouts, extended sports sections—these new features made Sunday editions extremely popular. Towering over all of these features borrowed from the magazines was an innovative art form, the newspaper comic strip. A blend of magazine cartoons and streetwise attitude, the first Sunday strip with continuing characters was James Swinnerton's *California Bears,* carried by the *San Francisco Examiner* beginning in 1892. But the most famous early strip was *The Yellow Kid,* created by Richard Outcault for Joseph Pulitzer's *New York World.* The slang-speaking, slum-dwelling, yellow-shirted "Kid" quickly became a national craze. His image proliferated beyond the newspapers, appearing on lapel pins, cigarette packs, and all sorts of consumer items.

African American Middle-Class Culture

African Americans built a middle-class culture of their own. White racial separatism throughout the country forced many blacks to organize economic and social institutions that catered specifically to their race. One African American woman, Maggie Lena Walker of Richmond, Virginia, founded and managed a black-owned bank. She went on to head the Richmond Council of Negro Women, and spearheaded efforts to support a girl's training school, a tuberculosis sanitarium, a community center, and a nursing home. Black barbers, who traditionally had served white clientele, often were leading business figures in African American communities. Urban blacks in particular founded a plethora of businesses and amassed sizable estates. These middle-class blacks launched magazines, such as *The Colored American* and *The Voice of the Negro,* to rival the cultural magazines aimed at the nation at large. Novelist Frances E. W. Harper, in *Iola Leroy, Or Shadows Uplifted,* framed the problem of the color line in quintessentially middle-class terms: Either blacks would lift themselves up into the middle class or continue to be dominated by whites. Several black intellectuals and writers made headway in national periodicals. Paul Laurence Dunbar was a regular contributor to the *Century,* Charles Chesnutt published several stories in the prestigious *Atlantic Monthly,* and Booker T. Washington's *Up from Slavery* first appeared as a series of articles in the *Outlook.* W. E. B. Du Bois, a Harvard-educated and German-trained professor, published essays in the *Atlantic,* which he later collected in his forceful examination of African American life, *The Souls of Black Folk.*

The New Woman

The rise of the middle class changed women's lives. For most of the 19th century, the ideal of "separate spheres" had dominated relations between the sexes, especially among middle-class Americans. The male sphere was one of work, politics, and public events. The female sphere, by contrast, was one of domesticity, moral education, and child rearing. Men and women were not supposed to intrude into each other's spheres. It was "unnatural" for women to work outside the home, to enter the corrupting world of politics, or to engage in pleasurable sex. It was equally "unnatural" for men to devote themselves to child rearing, to "idle" themselves with domestic chores, or to live a life bereft of sexual passion. This doctrine of separate spheres frustrated increasingly educated women who wanted to work and play outside the home. It also meant that men and women spent substantial portions of their daily lives apart from each other. The ceremonial occasions, meals, and leisure activities that brought them together tended to be closely regulated. The lives of the young, in particular, were closely watched, guided, and supervised by parents, teachers, and ministers.

After the Civil War, women challenged the separate-sphere ideal in a variety of ways. Some women, ironically, transformed the ideal by trying to live it out in the rapidly changing world of consumerism. Books such as *The House Beautiful* instructed women on tasteful yet economical styles and methods for furnishing the middle-class home. To procure these furnishings, women had to leave their suburban houses to shop in downtown department stores. Old urban institutions evolved to meet women's new needs for public spaces for rest and amusement. Department stores and hotels added soda fountains to provide women with nonalcoholic drinks (including "tonics" such as the drug-laced Coca-Cola). Restaurants, once off-limits to women unaccompanied by men, began serving a female clientele.

The needs of corporate America for increasingly educated workers led to changes in American education that diminished the amount of time women devoted to child care. School enrollments went up in general. The educa-

tion of children also expanded both up and down the age scale. The kindergarten movement brought thousands of American children to school at an earlier age than had been deemed advisable in previous decades. At the other end of the scale, the number of high schools grew rapidly in the late 1800s. Middle-class daughters benefited from this explosion of education. The number of female high school graduates rose steeply between 1870 and 1900 from 9,000 to 57,000. Some of the nation's most prestigious women's colleges were founded in the 1870s and 1880s, including Wellesley, Smith, Bryn Mawr, Radcliffe, and Barnard. The number of female college graduates increased in these same decades from 1,378 to 5,237.

Women's rising employment rates transformed the separate-spheres ideal. Women made up 20 percent of the nation's workforce in 1876. The total number of female workers doubled by 1900. Once limited chiefly to factory labor and domestic service, women increased their numbers in professional and white-collar occupations. Childhood education became even more of a female profession than it had been before the Civil War. Women replaced men as telephone operators because they purportedly did not talk back to callers and accepted lower wages. Women surged into new clerical jobs multiplying in corporate offices. At one office, the Metropolitan Life Insurance Company, more than half of the employees were women in the middle 1890s. By 1900, one-third of all clerical positions in the country were held by women. Department stores not only served increasing numbers of female customers, but they also hired women to work the counters that were once reserved for male clerks.

Work gave women a new sense of social independence. Their jobs were distant from their homes and from parental supervision. They received all of their pay in the form of wages, which, although low, heightened their sense of economic freedom. Working women came into close proximity both with one another and with men at work and in public, unsupervised places. To prevent male and female interaction at work, business managers often segregated functions according to sex. All stenographers were women, while men staffed the mailroom. Where men and women worked together, women were limited to strictly defined tasks that usually required little or no expert knowledge. Nonetheless, new forms of employment for working-class women propelled them into the lower middle classes. They, along with established middle-class women, found increased means and time for public amusement.

Women expressed their newfound sense of freedom in a variety of ways. They flocked out of doors. They took up physical exercise—many on a new invention, the modern two-wheeled bicycle. Croquet became a major fad of the post–Civil War era. Other women pursued intellectual activities, forming book clubs to read the classics of Western literature as well as contemporary American works. Many women formed volunteer associations, from women's professional organizations to social reform efforts such as the Young Women's Christian Association and the settlement house movement.

The New Woman became a dominant figure of American popular culture in the 1890s. She replaced the earlier middle-class ideal of the voluptuous, plump, round-faced matron who wore richly adorned dresses. The New Woman, as drawn by artist Charles Dana Gibson in numerous magazine portraits, was tall, slender, and athletic. She rejected the ornate fashions of her mother's generation. Instead, she adopted a more practical style of clothing, wearing a simple skirt below a shirtwaist fashioned after men's clothing. The boundaries between the once separate spheres of men and women had begun to blur.

The World's Columbian Exhibition

The middle-class revolution culminated in 1893 at the Chicago World's Fair. Opened in the midst of an economic depression, the fair counted almost 30 million admissions at a time when the total U.S. population was 63 million. The Chicago fair, organized to celebrate the 400th anniversary of Columbus's discovery of America, dwarfed the Philadelphia exposition. Some 400 buildings spread across 700 acres housed 65,000 exhibits. The total cost of constructing and stocking the fair was more than $28 million ($550 million in current U.S. dollars). Size alone, however, was not what distinguished the fair.

The Chicago World's Fair was split into two distinct parts with strikingly different atmospheres. The first part, the White City, represented the middle-class ideal for the future of America. It was a majestic realm of neo-classical Beaux-Arts architecture, with broad, open courts, studded with statuary, and interspersed with lagoons, canals, fountains, and parks designed by the famous landscape architect Frederick Law Olmsted. The White City was a triumph of the City Beautiful movement, whose advocates called for urban planning and unity of style to combat the helter-skelter development of the modern city. The colossal white

buildings also had political motives. On the one hand, they stood as memorials to the expanding power of Chicago's corporate leaders over workers, blacks, and immigrants. On the other hand, by appropriating classical European styles, they announced the triumph of the United States as a world-class empire.

The majestic buildings housed miles of displays celebrating middle-class consumerism. Visitors were inundated with exhibits on housekeeping, home furnishings, and even model homes. One exhibit featured the furnished, two-story, wood-frame Workingman's Model Home that instructed young couples on how to achieve a middle-class lifestyle. Another model home displayed the electrified future house. It was stocked with electric stoves, washing machines, doorbells, fire alarms, and lighting fixtures. The Manufacturers and Liberal Arts Building, the largest building in the world in 1893, was one endless department store. Its 44-acre hall resembled an enormous railroad shed with exposed steel arches holding up a glass roof. Under the roof, hundreds of pavilions exhibited a myriad of manufactured consumer goods, all of which bore price tags to allow visitors to compare costs of similar items. Visitors could order for future purchase anything from firearms and Swiss clocks to garden furniture and baby carriages. The new communications technology on display included the phonograph and the kinetoscope (an early film projector). Visitors were awed by the power

From the Collections of the Library of Congress.

CHICAGO WORLD'S FAIR, 1893

A photograph of the canal and some of the exhibit buildings at the Chicago World's Fair in 1893. These structures have an air of permanence about them, but within a few years they were gone.

of electricity. Westinghouse's electric dynamos produced vastly greater amounts of power than the Corliss steam engines of the Philadelphia fair. A quarter of a million electric bulbs suffused the White City with white light after sunset.

The second part of the fair, the Midway Plaisance, was a mile-long collection of amusements, "ethnological" displays, cabarets, wild-animal acts, and exotic dancing. Anthropologists of the Smithsonian had originally planned the Midway as a living exhibition of the cultures of humankind. These displays were to be arranged hierarchically from lowest human civilizations at the west end progressing to the highest at the east end, where the midway abutted the White City. But the conception of the Midway changed several times. When the fair opened, Sol Bloom, an entrepreneur who specialized in popular culture, had transformed the Midway into what one observer called "a strange land, peopled with outlandish folk, echoing barbaric noises, and given over to strange customs, costumes, tongues, diets, dwellings and gods." The Midway, unlike the White City, gave visitors no sense of spatial arrangement or advance planning. The dominating feature, set at the center of the Midway, was the world's first Ferris Wheel. It stood 246 feet high and carried 36 cars, which could hold 60 passengers each. When fully loaded, the wheel spun more than 2,100 people around its axis.

The Chicago World's Fair was a phantasmagoria of the middle class's venerable dreams and repressed desires. While Frederick Jackson Turner gave his famous paper on the closing of the frontier at a conference of historians, Buffalo Bill ran his Wild West Show just beyond the Midway's western gates. Francis J. Bellamy, the editor of a popular magazine for youth, wrote and introduced the Pledge of Allegiance to the American flag at the fair. Numerous staples of the mass market debuted, including the stereotypical faces of Aunt Jemima and Cream of Wheat's Rastus and such goods as Juicy Fruit gum, Postum, and Shredded Wheat cereal. Historian Henry Adams, great-grandson of President John Adams and grandson of President John Quincy Adams, was overwhelmed by what he saw: "[S]ince Noah's ark, no such Babel of loose and ill-joined, such vague and ill-defined and unrelated thoughts and half-thoughts and experimental outcries as the Exposition, had ever ruffled the surface of the Lake [Michigan]."

No one knew what to do with the buildings when the fair closed in November 1893. Built to last only temporarily, none was suitable for any sort of permanent exhibition. A series of small fires and vandalism damaged much of the decorative work and some of the smaller buildings as tramps and transients moved into the remains of the White City. Finally, on the night of July 5, 1894, a massive fire destroyed the great buildings surrounding the central Court of Honor. The specific source of the fire was unclear, but it came in the midst of clashes between federal troops and railway workers striking against the Pullman Palace Car Company. In two hours, the buildings that once housed so many middle-class dreams went up in smoke.

Wealth and Inequality

All of the wonders of economic growth and technological change exhibited at the Chicago fair came at great human cost. One such cost was a widening gulf between rich and poor. Although the average per capita income of all Americans increased by 35 percent from 1878 to 1893, real wages advanced only 20 percent. That advance masked sharp inequalities of wages by skill, region, race, and gender. Many unskilled and semiskilled workers made barely enough to support themselves, much less a family; many families, especially recent immigrants (who formed a large part of the blue-collar workforce), needed two or three wage earners to survive.

The perception of class inequality was even greater than the reality. The estimated number of *millionaires* (a word that came into use during this era) was 300 in 1860; by 1892, the number was 4,000. Many of them practiced what the eccentric but brilliant economist Thorstein Veblen described in his book *The Theory of the Leisure Class* (1899) as "conspicuous consumption." They sent agents to Europe to buy paintings and tapestries from impoverished aristocrats. In their mansions on Fifth Avenue and their summer homes at Newport, they entertained lavishly, sometimes spending on a single party an amount that would have supported a tenement full of immigrant families for a year. These extravagant habits gave substance to the labeling of this era as the Gilded Age. Their well-publicized activities, while millions lived on the edge of poverty, sharpened the growing sense of class consciousness.

Some of the millionaires made their money by methods that critics considered predatory, providing another vivid epithet of the period: "robber barons." Some of the most conspicuous figures who bore this epithet, whether deserved or not, were William Vanderbilt (who once allegedly burst out in response to criticism: "The public be damned!"), Jay Gould, Jim Fisk, and Collis P. Huntington in railroading; John D. Rockefeller in oil; Andrew Carnegie and Henry Clay Frick in steel; James B. Duke in tobacco; and John Pierpont Morgan in banking.

Criticism of the robber barons sometimes focused more on the immense power commanded by their wealth than on the wealth itself. Fisk and Gould bribed legislators, manipulated the stock market, exploited workers,

HISTORY THROUGH FILM

The Molly Maguires (1970)

Directed by Martin Ritt. Starring Richard Harris (James McParlan), Sean Connery (Jack Kehoe), Samantha Eggar (Mary Raines).

The gritty realism of *The Molly Maguires* offers a compelling portrait of labor conditions in 19th-century coal mines. Filmed on location in the anthracite region of eastern Pennsylvania, the film takes the viewer deep into the earth where Irish American miners labored long hours for a pittance at the dangerous, back-breaking, health-destroying job of bringing out the coal that heated American homes and fueled American industry.

These mining communities constituted a microcosm of ethnic and class tensions in American society. Most of the mine owners were Scots-Irish Presbyterians; many foremen, skilled workers, and police were English or Welsh Protestants; most of the unskilled workers were Irish Catholics. This was a volatile mixture, as vividly depicted in the movie. The skilled miners had formed the Workingmen's Benevolent Association, which had won modest gains for its members by 1873. Many Irish belonged to the Ancient Order of Hibernians, which aided sick miners and supported the widows and orphans of those who died—and there were many such. The inner circle of this order called itself the Molly Maguires, after an antilandlord organization in Ireland that resisted the eviction of tenants. In Pennsylvania, the Mollies retaliated against exploitative owners, unpopular foremen, and the police with acts of sabotage, violence, intimidation, and murder.

The economic depression following the Panic of 1873 exacerbated tensions and violence. The owners hired the Pinkerton detective agency to infiltrate and gather criminal evidence against the Mollies. Detective James McParlan went to work in the mines, gained the confidence of his fellow Irish Americans, and was eventually admitted to the Molly Maguires. For more than two years, he lived a dangerous double existence (foreshortened in the movie) that would have meant instant death if the Mollies had discovered his mole role. In a series of widely publicized trials from 1875 to 1877 in which McParlan was the main witness, dozens of Molly Maguires were convicted and 20 were hanged.

Richard Harris and Sean Connery are superb as McParlan and Jack Kehoe, the Mollies' leader. The real Jamie McParlan courted the sister-in-law of one of the Mollies; the film expands this into a poignant romance between McParlan and a retired miner's beautiful daughter. The love interest fits with the film's effective presentation of McParlan's conflicted conscience and the moral ambiguity of his role as the agent of justice (as defined by the ruling class), which requires him to betray the men with whom he had lived, sung, plotted, swapped stories, and carried out raids. What were McParlan's real motives? The film does not successfully answer that question, but neither does history. Most viewers, however, will take from this movie a feeling of empathy with the Mollies, whose protest against terrible conditions drove them to desperate acts of violence.

© Bettmann/Corbis.

Sean Connery (Jack Kehoe, right) and Art Lund (a fellow Molly Maguire) prepare to dynamite a coal train in *The Molly Maguires*.

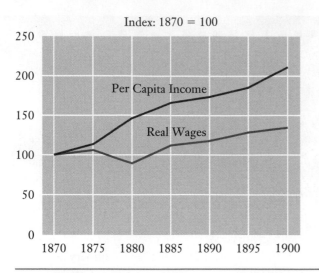

Index: 1870 = 100

REAL WAGES OF WORKERS AND PER CAPITA INCOME OF ALL AMERICANS, 1870–1900

and cheated stockholders in their various schemes to corner the gold market, milk the Erie Railroad for personal profit, and create a railroad empire in the Southwest. Rockefeller either bought out or ruined his competitors, obtained rebates and drawbacks on rail shipments of oil, and created a monopoly in his determined efforts to gain control of oil refining—efforts that culminated in the formation of the Standard Oil Trust in 1879. Carnegie and Frick pushed laborers to the limit in 72-hour workweeks, redefined skill levels and changed work rules, and sped up the pace in steel mills in a ceaseless quest for greater efficiency and lower labor costs. Morgan's banking firm built an empire of leveraged financing and interlocking corporate directorates, often using a New Jersey incorporation law passed in 1889 that permitted holding companies to gain control or dominant influence in several firms.

These activities could be—and were—defended on grounds of entrepreneurial innovation and efficiency, and the enterprises these men created did enable the United States to leap ahead of Britain as an industrial power. By 1913, American manufacturing output equaled that of the next three industrial nations combined—Germany, Britain, and France. The robber barons created wealth for all Americans—poorly distributed though it was—as well as for themselves, and not all of them practiced conspicuous consumption. Professing a gospel of stewardship, Carnegie, Rockefeller, and others gave away much of their wealth to educational and philanthropic institutions, establishing the basis for modern multibillion-dollar foundations.

The Antitrust Movement

Nevertheless, many Americans feared the power wielded by these tycoons. Their monopoly or near-monopoly share of the market in oil, steel, tobacco, sugar, transportation, and other products seemed to violate the ideal of fair competition. To curb that power, an "antitrust" movement emerged in the 1880s. The word *trust* derived from an investment strategy pioneered by Rockefeller, in which the stockholders of several refining companies turned over their shares to Standard Oil in return for so-called trust certificates. The term came to be applied to all large corporations that controlled a substantial share of any given market. In response to pressures to curb such trusts, several states passed antitrust laws in the 1880s.

Because the larger corporations operated across state lines, reformers turned to Congress, which responded in 1890 by passing the Sherman Antitrust Act (named for Senator John Sherman of Ohio, brother of the Civil War general). On the face of it, the Sherman Act seemed to mean business: "Every contract, combination in the form of trust or otherwise, or conspiracy, in restraint of trade or commerce among the several States is hereby declared to be illegal." But what constituted "restraint of trade"? For that matter, what constituted a trust? Did a holding company incorporated under New Jersey's 1889 law violate the Sherman Act? Of eight cases against corporations brought before federal courts from 1890 to 1893, the government lost seven. In 1895, the Supreme Court dealt the Sherman Act a crippling blow in *U.S. v. E. C. Knight Company*. In this case, which concerned a sugar-refining monopoly, the Court ruled that manufacturing was not commerce and therefore did not fall under jurisdiction of the law. For the time being, the Sherman Act was almost a dead letter.

Labor Strife

The drive for even greater speed and productivity on railroads and in factories gave the United States the unhappy distinction of having the world's highest rate of industrial accidents. Workmen's compensation was almost unknown; many families were impoverished by workplace accidents that killed or maimed their chief breadwinner. This was one source of a rising tide of labor discontent. Another was the erosion of worker autonomy in factories, where new machinery took over tasks once performed by skilled workers and where managers made decisions about the procedures and pace of operations once made by workers themselves. Many crafts that had once been a source of pride to those who practiced them became just a job that could be performed by anyone. Labor increasingly became a commodity bartered for wages rather than a craft whereby the worker sold the product of his labor rather than the labor itself. For the first time in American history, the census of 1870 reported that a majority of employed persons worked for wages paid by others rather than working for themselves.

Skilled artisans considered this an alarming trend. Their efforts to preserve or recapture independence from bosses and robber barons fueled much of the labor unrest in the 1870s and 1880s. In 1866, the leaders of several craft unions had formed the National Labor Union. Labor parties sprang up in several states; the Labor Reform candidate for governor of Massachusetts in 1870 won 13 percent of the vote. In response to growing labor political activism, several states established bureaus or departments of labor that had little substantive power but that did begin to gather and report data for the first time. These pressures filtered up to Washington, where Congress created the Bureau of Labor in 1884 and elevated it to cabinet rank in 1903. In 1894, Congress also made the first Monday in September an official holiday—Labor Day—to honor working people.

The National Labor Union withered away in the depression of the 1870s, but industrial violence escalated. In the anthracite coal fields of eastern Pennsylvania, the Molly Maguires (an amalgam of a labor union and a secret order of Irish Americans) carried out guerrilla warfare against mine owners. In the later 1870s, the Greenbackers (a group that urged currency expansion to end deflation) and labor reformers formed a coalition that elected several local and state officials plus 14 congressmen in 1878. In 1880, the Greenback-Labor candidate for president won 3 percent of the popular vote.

The Great Railroad Strike of 1877

Railroads became an early focal point of labor strife. Citing declining revenues during the depression that followed the Panic of 1873, several railroads cut wages by as much as 35 percent between 1874 and 1877 (during that same period, the price index fell only 8 percent). When the Baltimore and Ohio Railroad announced its third 10 percent wage cut on July 16, 1877, workers struck. The strike spread rapidly to other lines. Traffic from St. Louis to the East Coast came to a halt. Ten states called out their militias. Strikers and militia fired on each other, and workers set fire to rolling stock and roundhouses. By the time federal troops gained control in the first week of August, at least 100 strikers, militiamen, and bystanders had been killed, hundreds more had been injured, and uncounted millions of dollars of property had gone up in smoke.

© Bettmann/Corbis.

THE RAILROAD STRIKES OF 1877

This illustration shows striking workers on the Baltimore and Ohio Railroad forcing the engineer and fireman from a train at Martinsburg, West Virginia, on July 17, 1877.

It was the worst labor violence in U.S. history to that time; the specter of class conflict frightened many Americans and generated a desperate view of the future.

The Knights of Labor

The principal labor organization that emerged in the 1880s was the Knights of Labor. Founded in Philadelphia in 1869, the Knights began as a secret fraternal society. Under the leadership of Terence V. Powderly, a machinist by trade, the Knights abandoned secrecy in 1879 and emerged as a potent national federation of unions—or "assemblies," as they were officially known. The Knights of Labor departed in several respects from the norm of labor organization at that time. Most of its assemblies were organized by industry rather than by craft, giving many unskilled and semiskilled workers union representation for the first time. Some assemblies admitted women; some also admitted blacks. Despite this inclusiveness, however, tendencies toward exclusivity of craft, gender, and race divided and weakened many assemblies.

A paradox of purpose also plagued the Knights. Most members wanted to improve their lot within the existing system through higher wages, shorter hours, better working conditions—the bread-and-butter goals of working people. This meant collective bargaining with employers; it also meant strikes. The assemblies won some strikes and lost some. Powderly and the Knights' national leadership discouraged strikes, however, partly out of practicality:

A losing strike often destroyed an assembly, as employers replaced strikes with strikebreakers, or "scabs."

Another reason for Powderly's antistrike stance was philosophical. Strikes constituted a tacit recognition of the legitimacy of the wage system. In Powderly's view, wages siphoned off to capital a part of the wealth created by labor. The Knights, he said, intended "to secure to the workers the full enjoyment of the wealth they create." This was a goal grounded both in the past independence of skilled workers and in a radical vision of the future—a vision in which workers' cooperatives would own the means of production. "There is no reason," said Powderly, "why labor cannot, through cooperation, own and operate mines, factories, and railroads."

The Knights did sponsor several modest workers' cooperatives. Their success was limited, partly from lack of capital and of management experience and partly because even the most skilled craftsmen found it difficult to compete with machines in a mass-production economy. Ironically, the Knights gained their greatest triumphs through strikes. In 1884 and 1885, successful strikes against the Union Pacific and Missouri Pacific railroads won enormous prestige and a rush of new members, which by 1886 totaled 700,000. But defeat in a second strike against the Missouri Pacific in spring 1886 was a serious blow. Then came the Haymarket bombing in Chicago.

Haymarket

Chicago was a hotbed of labor radicalism. In 1878, the newly formed Socialist Labor Party won 14 percent of the vote in the city, electing five aldermen and four members of the Illinois legislature. With recovery from the depression after 1878, the Socialist Labor Party fell onto lean times. Four-fifths of its members were foreign-born, mostly Germans. Internal squabbles generated several offshoots of the party in the 1880s. One of these embraced anarchism and called for the violent destruction of the capitalist system so that a new socialist order could be built on its ashes. Anarchists infiltrated some trade unions in Chicago and leaped aboard the bandwagon of a national movement centered in that city for a general strike on May 1, 1886, to achieve the eight-hour workday. Chicago police were notoriously hostile to labor organizers and strikers, so the scene was set for a violent confrontation.

The May 1 showdown coincided with a strike at the McCormick farm machinery plant in Chicago. A fight outside the gates on May 3 brought a police attack on the strikers in which four people were killed. Anarchists then organized a protest meeting at Haymarket Square on May 4. Toward the end of the meeting, when the rain-soaked crowd was already dispersing, the police suddenly arrived in force. When someone threw a bomb into their midst, the police opened fire. When the wild melee was over, 50 people lay wounded and 10 dead, 6 of them policemen.

This affair set off a wave of hysteria against labor radicals. Police in Chicago rounded up hundreds of labor leaders. Eight anarchists (seven of them German-born) went on trial for conspiracy to commit murder, although no evidence turned up to prove that any of them had thrown the bomb. All eight were convicted; seven were sentenced to hang. One of the men committed suicide; the governor commuted the sentences of two others to life imprisonment; the remaining four were hanged on November 11, 1887. The case became a cause célèbre that bitterly divided the country. Many workers, civil libertarians, and middle-class citizens who were troubled by the events branded the verdicts judicial murder, but most Americans applauded the summary repression of un-American radicalism.

The Knights of Labor were caught in this antilabor backlash. Although the Knights had nothing to do with the Haymarket affair and Powderly had repeatedly denounced anarchism, his opposition to the wage system sounded suspiciously like socialism, perhaps even anarchism, to many Americans. Membership in the Knights plummeted from 700,000 in spring 1886 to fewer than 100,000 by 1890.

As the Knights of Labor waned, a new national labor organization waxed. Founded in 1886, the American Federation of Labor (AFL) was a loosely affiliated association of unions organized by trade or craft: cigar-makers, machinists, carpenters, and so on. Under the leadership of Samuel Gompers, an immigrant cigar-maker, the AFL accepted capitalism and the wage system, and worked for better conditions, higher wages, shorter hours, and occupational safety within the system—"pure and simple unionism," as Gompers called it. Most AFL members were skilled workers, and few were women or blacks—a strategy that enabled the AFL to survive and even to prosper in a difficult climate. Its membership grew from 140,000 in 1886 to nearly a million by 1900.

Labor militancy survived Haymarket, however. Two best-selling books helped keep alive the vision of a more equalitarian social order. Although their impact was less powerful than that of *Uncle Tom's Cabin* a generation earlier (see chapter 13), they nevertheless affected the millions who read them.

Henry George

The first, a book on economics titled *Progress and Poverty* (1879), seemed an unlikely candidate for best-seller status. Henry George, a self-educated author, had spent 15 years working as a sailor, printer, and prospector before becoming a newspaper editor in California. In his travels, George had been struck by the appalling contrast between wealth and poverty. He fixed on "land monopoly" as the cause: the control of land and resources by the few at the expense of the many. His solution was 100 percent taxation on the "unearned increment" in the value of land—that is, on the difference between the initial purchase price and the eventual market value (minus improvements), or what today we would call capital gains. Such gains were created by society, he insisted, not by the landowner, and the total amount should be confiscated by taxation for the benefit of society. This would eliminate the need for all other taxes, George maintained; it would free productive capital and labor and would narrow the gulf between rich and poor.

Progress and Poverty achieved astonishing success. By 1905, it had sold 2 million copies and had been translated into several languages. But few economists endorsed the single tax, and the idea made little headway. The real impact of George's book came from its portrayal of the injustice of poverty in the midst of plenty. George became a hero to labor. He joined the Knights of Labor, moved to New York City, and ran for mayor as the candidate of the United Labor Party in 1886. He narrowly lost, but his campaign dramatized the grievances of labor and alerted the major parties to the power of that constituency. George's influence cast a long shadow into the next century; numerous Progressive leaders were first sensitized to social issues by their reading of *Progress and Poverty.*

Edward Bellamy

The other book that found a wide audience was a novel, *Looking Backward,* by Edward Bellamy. Like Harriet Beecher Stowe, Bellamy was a New England writer imbued with the tenets of Christian reform. *Looking Backward* is a utopian romance that takes place in the year 2000 and contrasts the America of that year with the America of 1887. In 2000, all industry is controlled by the national government, everyone works for equal pay, no one is rich and no one is poor, there are no strikes, no class conflict. Bellamy was not a Marxian socialist—he criticized the Marxian emphasis on class conflict—and he preferred to call his collectivist order Nationalism, not socialism. His vision of a world without social strife appealed to middle-class Americans, who bought a half million copies of *Looking Backward* every year for several years in the early 1890s. More than 160 Nationalist clubs sprang up to support the idea of public ownership, if not of all industries, then at least of public utilities.

Some of Bellamy's followers called themselves Christian Socialists. They formed the left wing of a broader movement, the Social Gospel, that deeply affected mainstream Protestant denominations (and many Catholic leaders as well) in the rapidly growing cities of the Gilded Age. Shocked by poverty and overcrowding in the sprawling tenement districts of urban America, clergymen and laypeople associated with the Social Gospel embraced a theology that considered aiding the poor as important as saving souls. They supported the settlement houses being established in many cities during the 1890s (see chapter 21) and pressed for legislation to curb the exploitation of the poor and provide them with opportunities for betterment. These efforts gathered strength during the 1890s and contributed to the rise of the Progressive movement after 1900.

The Homestead Strike

The 1890s provided plenty of evidence to feed middle-class fears that America was falling apart. Strikes occurred with a frequency and a fierceness that made 1877 and 1886 look like mere preludes to the main event. The most dramatic confrontation took place in 1892 at the Homestead plant (near Pittsburgh) of the Carnegie Steel Company. Carnegie and his plant manager, Henry Clay Frick, were determined to break the power of the country's strongest union, the Amalgamated Association of Iron, Steel, and Tin Workers. Frick used a dispute over wages and work rules as an opportunity to close the plant (a "lockout"), preparatory to reopening it with nonunion workers. When the union called a strike and refused to leave the plant (a "sitdown"), Frick called in 300 Pinkerton guards to oust them. (The Pinkerton detective agency had evolved since the Civil War era into a private security force that specialized in antiunion activities.) A full-scale gun battle between strikers and Pinkertons erupted on July 6, leaving nine strikers and seven Pinkertons dead and scores wounded. Frick persuaded the governor to send in 8,000 militia to protect the strikebreakers, and the plant reopened. Public sympathy, much of it pro-union at first, shifted when an anarchist tried to murder Frick on July 23. The failed Homestead strike crippled the Amalgamated Association; another strike against U.S. Steel (successor of Carnegie Steel) in 1901 destroyed it.

The Depression of 1893–1897

By the 1890s, the use of state militias to protect strikebreakers had become common. Events after 1893 brought an escalation of conflict. The most serious economic crisis since the 1873–78 depression was triggered by the Panic of

North Wind Picture Archives.

PENNSYLVANIA MILITIA AT CARNEGIE'S HOMESTEAD STEEL MILL, 1892
After the shoot-out between striking workers and Pinkerton guards, the Pennsylvania militia reopened the mills and protected strikebreakers from striking workers. This photograph shows the militia using steel beams manufactured by the mill as a makeshift barricade.

1893, a collapse of the stock market that plunged the economy into a severe four-year depression. Its complex origins included an economic slowdown abroad, which caused British banks to call some of their American loans, thereby draining gold from the United States at a time of political controversy about the American monetary system and nervousness in financial circles. Other causes included declining farm prices and attendant rural unrest and the overly rapid expansion of railroad construction and manufacturing capacity after 1885. The bankruptcy of the Reading Railroad and the National Cordage Company in early 1893 set off a process that by the end of the year had caused 491 banks and 15,000 other businesses to fail. By mid-1894, the unemployment rate had risen to more than 15 percent.

An Ohio reformer named Jacob Coxey conceived the idea of sending Congress a "living petition" of unemployed workers to press for appropriations to put them to work on road building and other public works. "Coxey's army," as the press dubbed it, inspired other groups to hit the road and ride the rails to Washington during 1894. This descent of the unemployed on the capital provoked arrests by federal marshals and troops, and ended in anticlimax when Coxey and others were arrested for trespassing on the Capitol grounds. Coxey's idea for using public works to relieve unemployment turned out to be 40 years ahead of its time.

The Pullman Strike

Even more alarming to middle-class Americans than Coxey's army was the Pullman strike of 1894. George M. Pullman had made a fortune in the manufacture of sleeping cars and other rolling stock for railroads. Workers in his large factory complex lived in the company town of Pullman just south of Chicago, where they enjoyed paved streets, clean parks, and decent houses rented from the company. But Pullman controlled many aspects of their lives, including banning liquor from the town and punishing workers whose behavior did not suit his ideas of decorum. When the Panic of 1893 caused a sharp drop in orders for Pullman cars, the company laid off one-third of its workforce and cut wages for the rest by 30 percent, but did not reduce company house rents or company store prices. Pullman refused to negotiate with a workers' committee, which called a strike and appealed to the American Railway Union (ARU) for help.

COXEY'S ARMY ON THE MARCH

Reformer Jacob Coxey organized a group of unemployed workers, who traveled to Washington, D.C., as a "petition in boots" to lobby for a public works program to put them back to work in 1894. They failed on this occasion, but their efforts planted a seed that bore fruit during the Great Depression of the 1930s.

The Railway Union had been founded the year before by Eugene V. Debs. A native of Indiana, Debs had been elected secretary of the Brotherhood of Locomotive Firemen in 1875 at the age of 20. By 1893, he had become convinced that the conservative stance of the various craft unions in railroading (firemen, engineers, brakemen, and so forth) was divisive and contrary to the best interests of labor. He formed the ARU to include all railroad workers in one union. With 150,000 members, the union won a strike against the Great Northern Railroad in spring 1894. When George Pullman refused the ARU's offer to arbitrate the strike of Pullman workers, Debs launched a boycott by which ARU members would refuse to run any trains that included Pullman cars. When the railroads attempted to fire the ARU sympathizers, whole train crews went on strike and quickly paralyzed rail traffic.

Over the protests of Illinois Governor John P. Altgeld, who sympathized with the strikers, President Grover Cleveland sent in federal troops. That action inflamed violence instead of containing it. The U.S. attorney general (a former railroad lawyer) obtained a federal injunction against Debs under the Sherman Antitrust Act on grounds that the boycott and the strike were a conspiracy in restraint of trade. This creative use of the Sherman Act, whose purpose had been to curb corporations, was upheld by the Supreme Court in 1895 and became a powerful weapon against labor unions in the hands of conservative judges.

For a week in July 1894, the Chicago railroad yards resembled a war zone. Millions of dollars of equipment went up in smoke. Thirty-four people, mostly workers, were killed. Finally, 14,000 state militia and federal troops restored order and broke the strike. Debs went to jail (for violation of the federal injunction) for six months. He emerged from prison a socialist.

To many Americans, 1894 was the worst year of crisis since the Civil War. The Pullman strike was only the most dramatic event of a year in which 750,000 workers went on strike and another 3 million were unemployed. But it was a surge of discontent from down on the farm that wrenched American politics off its foundations in the 1890s.

Farmers' Movements

After the Civil War, farmers from the older states and immigrants from northern Europe poured into the territories and states of Dakota, Nebraska, Kansas, Texas, and—after 1889—Indian Territory. Some went on to the Pacific Coast states or stopped in the cattle-grazing and mining territories in between. This wave of settlement brought nine new states into the Union between 1867 and 1896 that almost equaled in total size all the states east of the Mississippi.

The vagaries of nature and weather were magnified in the West. Grasshopper plagues wiped out crops from Minnesota to Kansas several times in the 1870s. Dry, searing summer winds alternated with violent hailstorms to scorch or level whole fields of wheat and corn. Winter blizzards intensified the isolation of farm families and produced loneliness and depression, especially among women. Adding to these woes, the relatively wet years of the 1870s and early 1880s gave way to an abnormally dry cycle the following decade, causing many farmers who had moved beyond the zone of 20 inches of annual precipitation (roughly the 98th meridian) to give up and return east, sometimes with a sign painted on their wagon: "In God we trusted, in Kansas we busted."

RETURNING TO ILLINOIS, 1894

This photograph shows one of the thousands of farm families who had moved into Kansas, Nebraska, and other plains states in the wet years of the 1870s and 1880s, only to give up during the dry years of the 1890s. Their plight added fuel to the fire of rural unrest and protest during those years.

Kansas State Historical Society.

Despite these problems, America's soaring grain production increased three times as fast as the American population from 1870 to 1890. Only rising exports could sustain such expansion in farm production. But by the 1880s, the improved efficiency of large farms in eastern Europe brought intensifying competition and consequent price declines, especially for wheat, just as competition from Egypt and India had eroded prices for American cotton. Prices on the world market for these two staples of American agriculture—wheat and cotton—fell about 60 percent from 1870 to 1895, while the wholesale price index for all commodities (including other farm products) declined by 45 percent during the same period. Not surprisingly, distress was greatest and protest loudest in the wheat-producing West and the cotton-producing South.

Credit and Money

Victims of a world market largely beyond their control, farmers lashed out at targets nearer home: banks, commission merchants, railroads, and the monetary system. In truth, these institutions did victimize farmers, although not always intentionally. The long period of price deflation from 1865 to 1897, unique in American history, exacerbated the problem of credit. A price decline of 1 or 2 percent per year added that many points cumulatively to the nominal interest rate. If a farmer's main crop was wheat or cotton, whose prices declined even further, his real inter-

est rate was that much greater. Thus it was not surprising that farmers who denounced banks or country-store merchants for gouging them also attacked a monetary system that brought deflation.

The federal government's monetary policies worsened deflation problems. The 1862 emergency wartime issuance of treasury "greenback" notes (see chapter 15) had created a dual currency—gold and greenbacks—with the greenback dollar's value relative to gold rising and falling according to Union military fortunes. After the war, the Treasury moved to bring the greenback dollar to par with gold by reducing the amount of greenbacks in circulation. This limitation of the money supply produced deflationary pressures. To complicate matters further, national banknotes backed by the banks' holding of government bonds continued to circulate as money. Because national banks were concentrated in the Northeast, the South and West suffered from downward pressures on prices they received for their crops because of money scarcity. Western farmers were particularly vociferous in their protests against this situation, which introduced a new sectional conflict into politics—not North against South, but East against West.

Because parity between greenbacks and gold would not be reached until 1879, a controversy arose in the postwar years over whether Union war bonds should be paid off in greenbacks or in gold. Congress resolved this issue in 1869 by passing the Public Credit Act, which required

Index: 1913 = 100

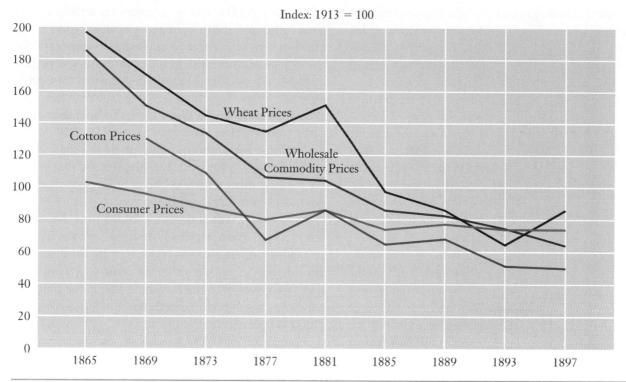

WHOLESALE AND CONSUMER PRICE INDEXES, 1865–1897

payment in gold. Because little silver had been coined into money for years, Congress enacted a law in 1873 that ended the coinage of silver dollars, thus putting the United States on the road to joining the international gold standard. In 1874, President Grant vetoed a bill sponsored by antideflation western congressmen to increase the number of greenbacks in circulation, setting the stage for enactment of the important Specie Resumption Act in 1875. When the provisions of this act went fully into effect on January 1, 1879, the U.S. dollar reached par with the gold dollar on the international market.

Grant's role in bringing about these steps toward "sound money" is more important than is generally recognized, but the benefits of his achievement were sharply debated then and remain controversial today. On the one hand, they strengthened the dollar, placed government credit on a firm footing, and helped create a financial structure for the remarkable economic growth that tripled the GNP during the last quarter of the 19th century. On the other hand, the restraints on money supply hurt the rural economy in the South and West; they hurt debtors who found that deflation enlarged their debts by increasing the value of greenbacks; and they probably worsened the two major depressions of the era (1873–78 and 1893–97) by constraining credit.

The Greenback and Silver Movements

Many farmers in 1876 and 1880 supported the Greenback Party, whose platform called for the issuance of more U.S. Treasury notes (greenbacks). Even more popular was the movement for "free silver." Until 1873, government mints had coined both silver and gold dollars at a ratio of 16 to 1—that is, 16 ounces of silver were equal in value to one ounce of gold. However, when new discoveries of gold in the West after 1848 placed more gold in circulation relative to silver, that ratio undervalued silver, so that little was being sold for coinage. This was the principal reason for the law of 1873 demonetizing silver, except for small coins. Antideflationists later branded this law as "the Crime of 1873"—a conspiracy to destroy silver, the people's money, in favor of gold, the bankers' money.

Ironically, just when the law of 1873 was enacted, the production of new silver mines began to increase dramatically, which soon brought the price of silver below the old ratio of 16 to 1. Silver miners joined with farmers to demand a return to silver dollars. In 1878, Congress responded by passing, over President Hayes's veto, the Bland-Allison Act requiring the Treasury to purchase and coin not less than $2 million nor more than $4 million of silver monthly. Once again, silver dollars flowed from the mint, but those amounts failed to absorb the increasing production of silver and did little, if anything, to slow deflation. The market price of silver dropped to a ratio of 20 to 1.

Pressure for "free silver"—that is, for government purchase of all silver offered for sale at a price of 16 to 1 and its coinage into silver dollars—continued through the 1880s. The admission of five new western states in 1889 and 1890 contributed to the passage of the Sherman Silver Purchase Act in 1890. That act increased the amount of silver coinage, but not at the 16-to-1 ratio. Even so, it went too far to suit "gold bugs," who wanted to keep the United States on the international gold standard.

President Cleveland blamed the Panic of 1893 on the Sherman Silver Purchase Act, which caused a run on the Treasury's gold reserves triggered by uncertainty over the future of the gold standard. Cleveland called a special session of Congress in 1893 and persuaded it to repeal the Sherman Silver Purchase Act, setting the stage for the most bitter political contest in a generation.

The Farmers' Alliance

Agrarian reformers supported the free silver movement, but many had additional grievances concerning problems of credit, railroad rates, and the exploitation of workers and farmers by the "money power." A new farmers' organization emerged in the 1880s, starting in Texas as the Southern Farmers' Alliance and expanding into other southern states and the North. By 1890, it had evolved into the National Farmers' Alliance and Industrial Union, which was affiliated with the Colored Farmers' Alliance and also with the Knights of Labor.

Reaching out to 2 million farm families, the Alliance set up marketing cooperatives to eliminate the middlemen who profited as "parasites" on the backs of farmers. The Alliance served the social needs of farm families as well as their economic needs. Alliance farm families came together in what one historian has termed a "movement culture" that helped overcome their isolation, especially in the sparsely settled regions of the West. The Alliance also gave farmers a sense of pride and solidarity to counter the image of "hick" and "hayseed" being purveyed by an increasingly urban American culture.

The Farmers' Alliance developed a comprehensive political agenda. At a national convention in Ocala, Florida, in December 1890, it set forth these objectives: (1) a graduated income tax; (2) direct election of U.S. senators (instead of election by state legislatures); (3) free and unlimited coinage of silver at a ratio of 16 to 1; (4) effective government control and, if necessary, ownership of railroad, telegraph, and telephone companies; and (5) the establishment of "subtreasuries" (federal warehouses) for the storage of crops, with government loans at 2 percent interest on those crops. The most important of these goals, especially for southern farmers, was the subtreasuries. Government storage would allow farmers to hold their crops until market prices were more favorable. Low-interest government loans on the value of these crops would enable farmers to pay their annual debts and thus escape the ruinous interest rates of the crop lien system in the South and bank mortgages in the West.

These were radical demands for the time. Nevertheless, most of them eventually became law: the income tax and the direct election of senators by constitutional amendments in 1913; government control of transportation and communications by various laws in the 20th century; and the subtreasuries in the form of the Commodity Credit Corporation in the 1930s.

Anticipating that the Republicans and the Democrats would resist these demands, many Alliancemen were eager to form a third party. In Kansas they had already done so, launching the People's Party (whose members were known as Populists) in summer 1890. Southerners, mostly Democrats, opposed the idea of a third party for fear that it might open the way for the return of the Republican Party to power—with the Reconstruction bogey of "Negro rule." That this antiblack position could coexist alongside the Alliance's affiliation with black farmers suggests the schizophrenic nature of southern politics at the time.

In 1890, farmers helped elect numerous state legislators and congressmen who pledged to support their cause, but the legislative results were thin. By 1892, many Alliance members were ready to take the third-party plunge. The two-party system seemed fossilized and unable to respond to the explosive problems of the 1890s.

The Rise and Fall of the People's Party

Enthusiasm for a third party was particularly strong in the plains and mountain states, five of which had been admitted since the last presidential election: North and South Dakota, Montana, Wyoming, and Idaho. The most prominent leader of the Farmers' Alliance was Leonidas L. Polk of North Carolina. A Confederate veteran, Polk commanded support in the West as well as in the South. He undoubtedly would have been nominated for president by the newly organized People's Party had not death cut short his career at the age of 55 in June 1892.

The first nominating convention of the People's Party met at Omaha a month later. The preamble of their platform expressed the grim mood of delegates. "We meet in the midst of a nation brought to the verge of moral, political, and material ruin," it declared. "The fruits of the toil of millions are boldly stolen to build up colossal fortunes for a few. . . . From the same prolific womb of governmental injustice we breed the two great classes—tramps and millionaires." The platform called for unlimited coinage of silver at 16 to 1; creation of the subtreasury program for crop storage and farm loans; government ownership of railroad, telegraph, and telephone companies; a graduated income tax; direct election of senators; and laws to protect labor unions against prosecution for strikes and boycotts. To ease the lingering tension between southern and western farmers, the party nominated Union veteran James B. Weaver of Iowa for president and Confederate veteran James G. Field of Virginia for vice president.

Despite winning 9 percent of the popular vote and 22 electoral votes, Populist leaders were shaken by the outcome. In the South, most of the black farmers who were allowed to vote stayed with the Republicans. Democratic bosses in several southern states dusted off the racial demagoguery and intimidation machinery of Reconstruction days to keep white farmers in line for the party of white supremacy. Only in Alabama and Texas, among southern states, did the Populists get more than 20 percent of the vote. They did even worse in the older agricultural states of the Midwest, where their share of the vote ranged from 11 percent in Minnesota down to 2 percent in Ohio. Only in distressed wheat states such as Kansas, Nebraska, and the Dakotas and in the silver states of the West did the Populists do well, carrying Kansas, Colorado, Idaho, and Nevada.

The party remained alive, however, and the anguish caused by the Panic of 1893 seemed to boost its prospects. In several western states, Populists or a Populist-Democratic coalition controlled state governments for a time, and a Populist-Republican coalition won the state elections of 1894 in North Carolina.

President Cleveland's success in getting the Sherman Silver Purchase Act repealed in 1893 drove a wedge into the Democratic Party. Southern and western Democrats turned against Cleveland. In what was surely the most abusive attack on a president ever delivered by a member of his own party, Senator Benjamin Tillman of South Carolina told his constituents in 1894: "When Judas betrayed Christ, his heart was not blacker than this scoundrel, Cleveland, in deceiving the Democracy. He is an old bag of beef and I am going to Washington with a pitchfork and prod him in his fat ribs."

The Silver Issue

Democratic dissidents stood poised to take over the party in 1896. They adopted free silver as the centerpiece of their program. This stand raised possibilities for a fusion with the Populists, who hoped the Democrats would adopt other features of their platform as well. Meanwhile, out of the West came a new and charismatic figure, a silver-tongued orator named William Jennings Bryan, whose shadow would loom large across the political landscape for the next generation. A one-term congressman from Nebraska, Bryan had taken up the cause of free silver. He came to the Democratic convention in 1896 as a young delegate—only 36 years old. Given the opportunity to make the closing speech in the debate on the silver plank in the party's platform, Bryan brought the house to its feet in a frenzy of cheering with his peroration: "You shall not press down upon the brow of labor this crown of thorns, you shall not crucify mankind upon a cross of gold."

The Granger Collection, New York.

AN ANTI-BRYAN CARTOON, 1896

This cartoon in *Judge* magazine, entitled "The Sacrilegious Candidate," charged William Jennings Bryan with blasphemy in his "Cross of Gold" speech at the Democratic national convention. Bryan grinds his Bible into the dust with his boot while waving a crown of thorns and holding a cross of gold. In the background, a bearded caricature of an anarchist dances amid the ruins of a church and other buildings.

This speech catapulted Bryan into the presidential nomination. He ran on a platform that not only endorsed free silver but also embraced the idea of an income tax, condemned trusts, and opposed the use of injunctions against labor. Bryan's nomination created turmoil in the People's Party. Although some Populists wanted to continue as a third party, most of them saw fusion with silver Democrats as the road to victory. At the Populist convention, the fusionists got their way and endorsed Bryan's nomination. In effect, the Democratic whale swallowed the Populist fish in 1896.

The Election of 1896

The Republicans nominated William McKinley, who would have preferred to campaign on his specialty, the tariff. Bryan made that impossible. Crisscrossing the country in an unprecedented whistle-stop campaign covering 18,000 miles, Bryan gave as many as 30 speeches a day, focusing almost exclusively on the free silver issue. Republicans responded by denouncing the Democrats as irresponsible inflationists. Free silver, they said, would mean a 57-cent dollar and would demolish the workingman's gains in real wages achieved over the preceding 30 years.

Under the skillful leadership of Ohio businessman Mark Hanna, chairman of the Republican National Committee, McKinley waged a "front-porch campaign" in which various delegations visited his home in Canton, Ohio, to hear carefully crafted speeches that were widely publicized in the mostly Republican press. Hanna sent out an army of speakers and printed pamphlets in more than a dozen languages to reach immigrant voters. His propaganda portrayed Bryan as a wild man from the prairie whose monetary schemes would further wreck an economy that had been plunged into depression during a

LINK TO THE PAST

William Jennings Bryan's Cross of Gold Speech

William Jennings Bryan's famous "Cross of Gold" speech at the Democratic convention in 1896 made him the youngest presidential candidate in American history—at age 36, only a year older than the minimum stipulated by the Constitution. In that age before radio and television, Bryan's speech became the standard by which to measure political oratory, which had to move readers of cold print as well as listeners in a hot convention hall.

If the gold standard advocates win, this country will be dominated by the financial harpies of Wall Street. I am trying to save the American people from that disaster—which will mean the enslavement of the farmers, merchants, manufacturers, and laboring classes to the most merciless and unscrupulous gang of speculators on earth—the money power. . . . We have petitioned, and our petitions have been scorned; we have entreated, and our entreaties have been disregarded; we have begged, and they have mocked when our calamity came. We beg no longer; we entreat no more; we petition no more. We defy them. . . . If they dare to come out in the open . . . we will fight them to the uttermost. Having behind us the producing masses of this nation and the world, supported by the commercial interests, the laboring interest, and the toilers everywhere, we will answer their demand for a gold standard by saying to them: You shall not press down upon the brow of labor this crown of thorns, you shall not crucify mankind upon a cross of gold.

1. What did Bryan mean by referring to the "enslavement" of farmers, merchants, manufacturers, and workers to the gold standard? Was he right?

For additional sources related to this feature, visit the *Liberty, Equality, Power* Web site at:

http://history.wadsworth.com/murrin_LEP4e

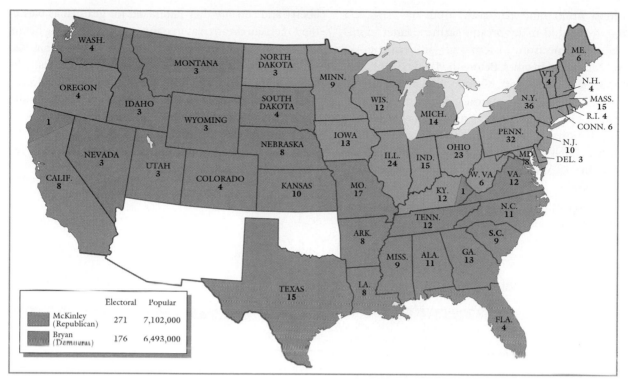

MAP 19.1 PRESIDENTIAL ELECTION OF 1896

Once again, note the continuity of voting patterns over the two generations from the 1850s to the 1890s by comparing this map with those on pages 444, 469, and 559.

Democratic administration. McKinley's election, by contrast, would maintain the gold standard, revive business confidence, and end the depression.

The 1896 election was the most impassioned and exciting in a generation. Many Americans believed that the fate of the nation hinged on the outcome. The number of voters jumped by 15 percent over the 1892 election. The sectional pattern of South and West versus Northeast and North Central was almost as pronounced as the North–South split of 1860. Republicans won a substantial share of the urban, immigrant, and labor vote by arousing fear about the Democratic 57-cent dollar and by inspiring hope with the slogan of McKinley as "the advance agent of prosperity." McKinley rode to a convincing victory by carrying every state in the northeast quadrant of the country. Bryan carried most of the rest. Republicans won decisive control of Congress as well as the presidency. They would maintain control for the next 14 years. The election of 1896 marked a crucial turning point in American political history away from the stalemate of the preceding two decades.

Whether by luck or by design, McKinley did prove to be the advance agent of prosperity. The economy pulled out of the depression during his first year in office and entered into a long period of growth—not because of anything the new administration did (except perhaps to encourage a revival of confidence) but because of the mysterious workings of the business cycle. With the discovery of rich new goldfields in the Yukon, in Alaska, and in South Africa, the silver issue lost potency, and a cascade of gold poured into the world economy. The long deflationary trend since 1865 reversed itself in 1897. Farmers entered a new—and unfamiliar—era of prosperity. Bryan ran against McKinley again in 1900 but lost even more emphatically. The nation seemed embarked on a placid sea of plenty. But below the surface, the currents of protest and reform that had boiled up in the 1890s still ran strong. They would soon surface again.

Conclusion

The 1890s were a major watershed in American history. On the past side of that divide lay a largely rural society and agricultural economy, and on the future side lay the cities and a commercial-industrial economy. Before the

1890s, most immigrants had come from northern and western Europe, and many became farmers. Later immigrants largely came from eastern and southern Europe, and nearly all settled in cities. Before the 1890s, the old sectional issues associated with slavery, the Civil War, and Reconstruction remained important forces in American politics; after 1900, racial issues would not play an important part in national politics for another 60 years. The election of 1896 ended 20 years of even balance between the two major parties and led to more than a generation of Republican dominance.

Most important, the social and political upheavals of the 1890s shocked many people into recognition that the liberty and equality they had taken for granted as part of the American dream was in danger of disappearing before the onslaught of wrenching economic changes that had widened and deepened the gulf between classes. The strikes and violence and third-party protests of the decade were a wake-up call. As the forces of urbanization and industrialism increased during the ensuing two decades, many middle-class Americans supported greater government power to carry out progressive reforms to cure the ills of an industrializing society.

SUGGESTED READINGS

For the impact of the railroad on the Gilded Age economy and culture, see **George R. Taylor and Irene D. Neu, *The American Railroad Network, 1861–1890*** (2003). For the rise of industry and "big business," the following are useful: **Glenn Porter, *The Rise of Big Business, 1860–1910,*** rev. ed. (1992), and **Harold G. Vatter, *The Drive to Industrial Maturity: The U.S. Economy, 1865–1914*** (1975). For the social and political response to these developments, see **Samuel P. Hay, *The Response to Industrialism, 1885–1914*** (1957).

The rise of the department store is examined in **William Leach, *Land of Desire: Merchants, Power, and the Rise of a New American Culture*** (1993). The effects of white-collar work on men and women are detailed in **Olivier Zunz, *Making America Corporate, 1870–1920*** (1990), and **Sue Porter Benson, *Counter Cultures: Saleswomen, Managers, and Customers in American Department Stores, 1890–1940*** (1986). The effects of the streetcar on suburbanization are covered in **Sam B. Warner, Jr., *Streetcar Suburbs: The Process of Growth in Boston, 1870–1900*** (1962). The cultural development of American museums is the subject of **Steven Conn, *Museums and American Intellectual Life, 1876–1926*** (1998). Four conflicting visions of the Chicago World's Fair can be found in **Alan Trachtenberg, *The Incorporation of America: Culture and Society in the Gilded Age*** (1982); **Robert W. Rydell, *All the World's a Fair: Visions of Empire at the American International Expositions,*** *1876–1916* (1984); **James Gilbert, *Perfect Cities: Chicago's Utopias of 1893*** (1991); and **Christopher Robert Reed, *"All the World Is Here": The Black Presence at the White City*** (2000). Several interesting essays on late 19th-century middle-class culture appear in **Burton J. Bledstein and Robert D. Johnston, eds., *The Middling Sorts: Explorations in the History of the American Middle Class*** (2001).

The labor movement is treated in **Melvin Dubofsky, *Industrialism and The American Worker, 1865–1920,*** rev. ed. (1985), and **Robert E. Weir, *Beyond Labor's Veil: The Culture of the Knights of Labor*** (1996). Two of the spectacular labor conflicts of the era are described in **Robert V. Bruce, *1877: Year of Violence*** (1959), and **Leon Wolff, *Lockout, The Story of the Homestead Strike of 1892*** (1965). The best modern survey of the Populist movement is **Lawrence Goodwyn, *Democratic Promise: The Populist Moment in America*** (1976), which was published in an abridged edition with the title *The Populist Moment* (1978). The politics of the 1890s culminating in the climactic election of 1896 are treated in **J. Rogers Hollingsworth, *The Whirligig of Politics: The Democracy of Cleveland and Bryan*** (1963), and **Paul W. Glad, *McKinley, Bryan, and the People*** (1964). For the beginnings of Progressive reform during this era, see the early chapters of **Michael McGerr, *A Fierce Discontent: Rise and Fall of the Progressive Movement in America, 1870–1920*** (2003).

AMERICAN JOURNEY ONLINE
AND
INFOTRAC COLLEGE EDITION

Visit the source collections at www.ajaccess.wadsworth.com and infotrac.thomsonlearning.com and use the Search function with the following key terms to explore documents, images, audio and video clips, articles, and commentary related to the material in this chapter.

John D. Rockefeller

Andrew Carnegie

Homestead strike

Knights of Labor

Haymarket riots

Edward Bellamy

Pullman strike

Farmers' Alliance

William McKinley

William Jennings Bryan

Sherman Antitrust Act

GRADE AIDS

Visit the Liberty Equality Power Companion Web site for resources specific to this textbook: http://history.wadsworth.com/murrin_LEP4e

 The CD in the back of this book and the U.S. History Resource Center at http://history.wadsworth.com/u.s./ offer a variety of tools to help you succeed in this course, including access to quizzes; images; documents; interactive simulations, maps, and timelines; movie explorations; and a wealth of other sources.

Chapter 20

An Industrial Society, 1890–1920

John Sloan, The City from Greenwich Village, 1922. National Gallery of Art. Gift of Helen Farr Sloan, 1970.1. 1

THE CITY FROM GREENWICH VILLAGE
This 1922 painting by John Sloan, one of America's foremost early-20th-century painters, captures both the expanse and night-time vitality of New York City. Cities such as New York were the most dynamic centers of business and culture during America's industrial age.

CHAPTER OUTLINE

With the collapse of populism in 1896 and the end of the depression in 1897, the American economy embarked on a remarkable stretch of growth. By 1910, America was unquestionably the world's greatest industrial power.

Corporations were changing the face of America. Their railroad and telegraph lines crisscrossed the country. Their factories employed millions. Their production and management techniques became the envy of the industrialized world. A new kind of building—the skyscraper—came to symbolize America's corporate power. These modern towers were made possible by the use of steel rather than stone framework and by the invention of electrically powered elevators.

Impelled upward by rising real estate values, they were intended to evoke the same sense of grandeur as Europe's medieval cathedrals. But these monuments celebrated man, not God; material wealth, not spiritual riches; science, not faith; corporations, not the commonweal. Reaching into the sky, dwarfing Europe's cathedrals, they were convincing embodiments of America's worldly might.

This chapter explores how the newly powerful corporations transformed America: how they revolutionized production and management; how the jobs they generated attracted millions of immigrants, southern blacks, and young single women to northern cities; and how they triggered an urban cultural revolution that made amusement parks, dance halls, vaudeville theater, and movies integral features of American life.

The power of the corporations dwarfed that of individual wage earners, but wage earners sought to limit the power of corporations through labor unions and strikes and by organizing institutions of collective self-help within their own ethnic or racial communities. Many found opportunities and liberties they had not known before. Immigrant entrepreneurs invented ways to make money through legal and illegal enterprise; young, single, working-class women pioneered a sexual revolution; and radicals dared to imagine building a new society where no one suffered from poverty, inequality, and powerlessness. The power of the new corporations, in other words, did not go unchallenged. Even so, a more egalitarian society would prove difficult to attain.

C H A P T E R F O C U S

♦ How did corporations and workers respond to the social and economic turmoil of the late 19th century?

♦ Why did American elites become obsessed with physical and racial fitness? How did this obsession affect attitudes toward immigrants and blacks?

♦ What hardships and successes did immigrants experience in America? How does the immigrant experience compare to that of African Americans?

♦ What explains the new sexuality and the rise of feminism?

Sources of Economic Growth

A series of technological innovations in the late 19th century fired up the nation's economic engine, but technological breakthroughs alone do not fully explain the nation's spectacular economic boom. New corporate structures and new management techniques—in combination with the new technology—created the conditions that powered economic growth.

Technology

Two of the most important new technologies were the harnessing of electric power and the invention of the gasoline-powered internal combustion engine. Scientists had long been fascinated by electricity, but only in the late 19th century did they find ways to make it practically useful. The work of Thomas Edison, George Westinghouse, and Nikola Tesla produced the incandescent bulb that brought electric lighting into homes and offices and the alternating current (AC) that made electric transmission possible over long distances. From 1890 to 1920, the proportion of American industry powered by electricity rose from virtually nil to almost one-third. Older industries switched from expensive and cumbersome steam power to more efficient and cleaner electrical power. New sectors of the metalworking and machine-tool industries arose in response to the demand for electric generators and related equipment. Between 1900 and 1920, virtually every major city built electric-powered transit systems to replace horse-drawn trolleys and carriages. By 1912, some 40,000 miles of electric railway and trolley track had been laid. In New York City, electricity made possible the construction of the first subways. Electric lighting—on city streets, in department store windows, in brilliantly lit amusement parks such as New York's Coney Island—gave cities a new allure.

C H R O N O L O G Y

1897	Depression ends; prosperity returns
1899	Theodore Roosevelt urges Americans to live the "strenuous life"
1900–14	Immigration averages more than 1 million per year
1901	U.S. Steel is formed from 200 separate companies • Andrew Carnegie devotes himself to philanthropic pursuits • 1 of every 400 railroad workers dies on the job
1904	20 percent of the North's industrial population lives below poverty line
1905	*Lochner* v. *New York:* Supreme Court declares unconstitutional a New York state law limiting the workday of bakery employees • Industrial Workers of the World (IWW) founded
1907	Henry Ford unveils his Model T
1907–11	73 of every 100 Italian immigrants return to Italy
1909	Immigrants and their children constitute more than 96 percent of labor force building and maintaining railroads
1910	Black skilled tradesmen in northern cities reduced to 10 percent of total skilled trades workforce • 20,000 nickelodeons dot northern cities
1911	Triangle Shirtwaist Company fire kills 146 workers • Frederick Winslow Taylor publishes *The Principles of Scientific Management*
1913	Henry Ford introduces the first moving assembly line; employee turnover reaches 370 percent a year • 66 men, women, and children killed in "Ludlow massacre" • John D. Rockefeller establishes Rockefeller Foundation
1914	Henry Ford introduces the $5-per-day wage • Theda Bara, movies' first sex symbol, debuts • *The Masses,* a radical journal, begins publication
1919	Japanese farmers in California sell $67 million in agricultural goods, 10 percent of state's total
1920	Nation's urban population outstrips rural population for first time
1921	1,250,000 Model Ts sold, a 16-fold increase over 1912

The public also fell in love with the movies, which depended on electricity to project images onto a screen. Electric power, in short, stimulated capital investment and accelerated economic growth.

The first gasoline engine was patented in the United States in 1878, and the first "horseless carriages" began appearing on European and American roads in the 1890s, but few thought of them as serious rivals to trains and horses. Rather, they were seen as playthings for the wealthy, who liked to race them along country roads.

In 1900, Henry Ford was just an eccentric 37-year-old mechanic who built race cars in Michigan. In 1909, Ford

SURF AVENUE AND LUNA PARK, CONEY ISLAND, 1913

With its 1 million lights, Surf Avenue in Brooklyn, New York, advertised itself as the most brilliantly lit thoroughfare in the world. The avenue included the entrance to Luna Park, one of Coney Island's most popular attractions.

LUNA PARK, SURF AVENUE, BY NIGHT, CONEY ISLAND, N. Y.

© Lake County Museum/Corbis.

unveiled his Model T: an unadorned, even homely car, but reliable enough to travel hundreds of miles without servicing and cheap enough to be affordable to most working Americans. Ford had dreamed of creating an automobile civilization with his Model T, and Americans began buying his car by the millions. The stimulus this insatiable demand gave to the economy can scarcely be exaggerated. Millions of cars required millions of pounds of steel alloys, glass, rubber, petroleum, and other material. Millions of jobs in coal and iron-ore mining, oil refining and rubber manufacturing, steelmaking and machine tooling, road construction and service stations came to depend on automobile manufacturing.

Corporate Growth

Successful inventions such as the automobile required more than the mechanical ingenuity and social vision of inventors such as Henry Ford. They relied on corporations with sophisticated organizational and technical know-how to mass-produce and mass-distribute the newly invented products. Corporations had played an important role in the nation's economic life since the 1840s, but in the late 19th and early 20th centuries, they underwent significant changes. The most obvious change was in their size. Employment in Chicago's International Harvester factory, where agricultural implements were built, nearly quadrupled from 4,000 in 1900 to 15,000 in 1916. Delaware's DuPont Corporation, a munitions and chemical manufacturer, employed 1,500 workers in 1902 and 31,000 workers in 1920. Founded with a few hundred employees

in 1903, the Ford Motor Company employed 33,000 at its Detroit Highland Park plant by 1916 and 42,000 by 1924. That same year, the 68,000 workers employed at Ford's River Rouge plant (just outside Detroit) made it the largest factory in the world.

This growth in scale was in part a response to the enormous domestic market. By 1900, railroads provided the country with an efficient transportation system that allowed corporations to ship goods virtually anywhere in the United States. A national network of telegraph lines allowed constant communication between buyers and sellers separated by thousands of miles. And the population, which was expanding rapidly, demonstrated an ever-growing appetite for goods and services.

Mass Production and Distribution

Manufacturers responded to this burgeoning domestic market by developing mass-production techniques that increased production speed and lowered unit costs. Mass production often meant replacing skilled workers with machines that were coordinated to permit high-speed, uninterrupted production at every stage of the manufacturing process. Mass-production techniques had become widespread in basic steel manufacturing and sugar refining by the 1890s, and they spread to the machine-tool industry and automobile manufacturing in the first two decades of the 20th century.

Such production techniques were profitable only if large quantities of output could be sold. Although the domestic market offered a vast potential for sales,

MAP 20.1 INDUSTRIAL AMERICA, 1900–1920

This map shows that the Northeast, Midwest, and California dominated factory production in the United States from 1900 to 1920. It also reveals the state-by-state distribution of various industries—clothing in New York, automobiles in Michigan, petroleum refining in Texas and Oklahoma, and lumber in Oregon, Washington, and Idaho.

 View an animated version of this map or related maps at http://history.wadsworth.com/murrin_LEP4e.

manufacturers often found distribution systems inadequate. This was the case with North Carolina smoking tobacco manufacturer James Buchanan Duke, who almost single-handedly transformed the cigarette into one of the best-selling commodities in American history. In 1885, at a time when relatively few Americans smoked, Duke invested in several Bonsack cigarette machines, each of which manufactured 120,000 cigarettes per day. To create a market for the millions of cigarettes he was producing,

Duke advertised his product aggressively throughout the country. He also established regional sales offices so that his sales representatives could keep in touch with local jobbers and retailers. As cigarette sales skyrocketed, more corporations sought to emulate Duke's techniques. Over the course of the next 20 years, those corporations that integrated mass production and mass distribution, as Duke did in the 1880s, came to define American "big business."

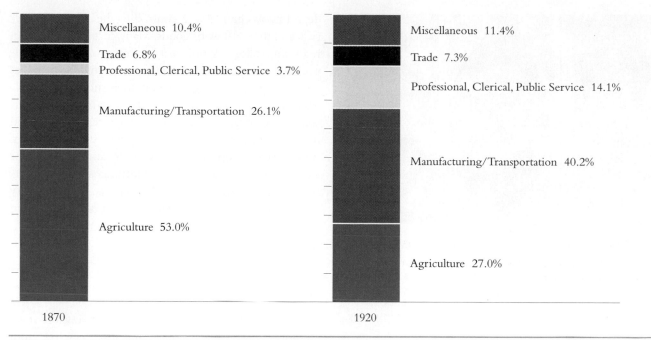

Miscellaneous 10.4%

Trade 6.8%

Professional, Clerical, Public Service 3.7%

Manufacturing/Transportation 26.1%

Agriculture 53.0%

1870

Miscellaneous 11.4%

Trade 7.3%

Professional, Clerical, Public Service 14.1%

Manufacturing/Transportation 40.2%

Agriculture 27.0%

1920

CHANGE IN DISTRIBUTION OF THE AMERICAN WORKFORCE, 1870–1920

Source: Data from Alba Edwards, *Comparative Occupational Statistics for the United States 1870–1940,* U.S. Bureau of the Census, *Sixteenth Census of the United States, 1940, Population* (Washington, D.C., 1943).

Corporate Consolidation

Corporate expansion also reflected a desire to avoid market instability. The rapid industrial growth of the late 19th century had unsettled industrialists. As promising economic opportunities arose, more industrialists sought to take advantage of them, but overexpansion and increasingly furious competition often turned rosy prospects into less-than-rosy results. Bankrupting busts quickly followed buoyant booms. Soon, corporations began looking for ways to insulate themselves from harrowing downturns in the business cycle.

The railroads led the way in tackling this problem. Rather than engaging in ruinous rate wars, railroads began cooperating. They shared information on costs and profits, established standardized rates, and allocated discrete portions of the freight business among themselves. These cooperative arrangements were variously called "pools," "cartels," or "trusts." The 1890 Sherman Antitrust Act declared such cartel-like practices illegal, but the law's enforcement proved to be short-lived (see chapter 19). Still, the railroads' efforts rarely succeeded for long because they depended heavily on voluntary compliance. During difficult economic times, the temptation to lower freight rates and exceed one's market share could become too strong to resist.

Corporations' efforts to restrain competition and inject order into the economic environment continued unabated, however. Mergers now emerged as the favored instrument of control. By the 1890s, investment bankers, such as J. P. Morgan, possessed both the capital and the financial skills to engineer the complicated stock transfers and ownership renegotiations that mergers required. James Duke again led the way in 1890 when he and four competitors merged to form the American Tobacco Company. Over the next eight years, the quantity of cigarettes produced by Duke-controlled companies quadrupled, from 1 billion to almost 4 billion per year. Moreover, American Tobacco used its powerful position in cigarette manufacture to achieve dominance in pipe tobacco, chewing tobacco, and snuff manufacture as well.

The merger movement intensified as the depression of the 1890s lifted. In the years from 1898 to 1904, many of the corporations that would dominate American business throughout most of the 20th century acquired their modern form: Armour and Swift in meatpacking, Standard Oil in petroleum, General Electric and Westinghouse in electrical manufacture, American Telephone and Telegraph in communications, International Harvester in the manufacture of agricultural implements, and DuPont in munitions and chemical processing. The largest merger occurred in steel in 1901, when Andrew Carnegie and J. P.

© Bettmann/Corbis.

AN EARLY CIGARETTE ADVERTISEMENT (1885–1900)

This particular advertisement—including three trading cards, each featuring an attractive female stage star—was aimed at theatergoers, who were encouraged to "light up" between acts. Ads such as this one were part of an intensive promotional campaign to generate interest in smoking among a consuming public that was unaccustomed to the practice.

Morgan together fashioned the U.S. Steel Corporation from 200 separate iron and steel companies. U.S. Steel, with its 112 blast furnaces and 170,000 steelworkers, controlled 60 percent of the country's steelmaking capacity. Moreover, its 78 iron-ore boats and 1,000 miles of railroad gave it substantial control over procuring raw materials and distributing finished steel products.

Revolution in Management

The growth in the number and size of corporations revolutionized corporate management. The ranks of managers mushroomed, as elaborate corporate hierarchies defined both the status and the duties of individual managers. Increasingly, senior managers took over from owners the responsibility for long-term planning. Day-to-day operations fell to middle managers who oversaw particular departments (e.g., purchasing, research, production, labor) in corporate headquarters or who supervised regional sales offices or directed particular factories. Middle managers also managed the people—accountants, clerks, foremen, engineers, salesmen—in these departments, offices, or factories. The rapid expansion within corporate managerial ranks created a new middle class, whose members were intensely loyal to their employers but at odds both with blue-collar workers and with the older middle class of shopkeepers, small businessmen, and independent craftsmen.

As management techniques grew in importance, companies tried to make them more scientific. Firms introduced cost-accounting methods into purchasing and other departments charged with controlling the inflow of materials and the outflow of goods. Many corporations began requiring college or university training in science, engineering, or accounting for entry into middle management. Corporations that had built their success on a profitable invention or discovery sought to maintain their competitive edge by creating research departments and hiring professional scientists—those with doctorates from American or European universities—to come up with new technological and scientific breakthroughs. Such departments were modeled on the industrial research laboratory set up by the inventor-entrepreneur Thomas Edison in Menlo Park, New Jersey, in 1876.

Scientific Management on the Factory Floor

The most controversial and, in some respects, the most ambitious effort to introduce scientific practices into management occurred in production. Managers understood that improvements in factory organization as well as technological innovation could enhance the speed and efficiency of mass production. So, in league with engineers, they sought optimal arrangements of machines and deployments of workers that would achieve the highest speed in production with the fewest human or mechanical interruptions. Some of these managers, such as Frederick Winslow Taylor, the chief engineer at Philadelphia's Midvale Steel Company in the 1880s, styled themselves as the architects of scientific management. They examined every human task and mechanical movement involved in each production process. In "time-and-motion studies," they recorded every distinct movement a worker made in performing his or her job, how long it took, and how often it was performed. They hoped thereby to identify and eliminate wasted human energy. Eliminating waste might mean reorganizing a floor of machinery so as to reduce "down time" between production steps; it might mean instructing workers to perform their tasks differently; or it might mean replacing uncooperative skilled workers with machines tended by unskilled, low-wage laborers. Regardless of the method chosen, the goal was the same: to make human labor emulate the smooth and apparently effortless operation of an automatic, perfectly calibrated piece of machinery.

Taylor publicized his vision, first through speeches to fellow engineers and managers, and then through his writings. By the time he published *The Principles of Scientific Management* (1911), his ideas had already captivated countless corporate managers and engineers, many of whom sought to introduce "Taylorism" into their own production systems.

Introducing scientific management practices rarely proceeded easily. Time-and-motion studies were costly, and Taylor's formulas for increasing efficiency and reducing waste often were less scientific than he claimed. Taylor also overestimated workers' willingness to play the mechanical role he assigned them; the skilled workers and general foremen, whom Taylor sought to eliminate, often resisted his schemes. In the end, managers and engineers who persisted in their efforts to apply scientific management usually modified Taylor's principles.

Henry Ford's engineers initially adopted Taylorism and with apparent success. By 1910, they had broken down automobile manufacturing into a series of simple, sequential tasks. Each worker performed only one task—adding a carburetor to an engine, inserting a windshield, mounting tires onto wheels. Then, in 1913, Ford's engineers introduced the first moving assembly line, a continuously moving conveyor belt that carried cars in production through each workstation. This innovation eliminated precious time previously wasted in transporting car parts (or partially built cars) by crane or truck from one work area to another. It also limited the time available to workers to perform their assigned tasks. Only the foreman, not the workers, could stop the line or change its speed.

By 1913, the continuous assembly line made Ford Motor Company's new Highland Park plant the most tightly integrated and continuously moving production system in American industry. The pace of production exceeded all expectations. Between 1910 and 1914, production time on Ford Model Ts dropped by 90 percent, from an average of more than 12 hours per car to 1.5 hours. A thousand Model Ts began rolling off the assembly line each day. This striking increase in the rate of production enabled Ford to slash the price of a Model T from $950 in 1909 to only $295 in 1923, a reduction of 70 percent. The number of Model Ts purchased by Americans increased 16-fold between 1912 and 1921, from 79,000 to 1,250,000. The assembly line quickly became the most admired—and most feared—symbol of American mass production.

Problems immediately beset the system, however. Repeating a single motion all day long induced mental stupor, and managerial efforts to speed up the line produced physical exhaustion—both of which increased the incidence of error and injury. Some workers tried to organize

© Bettmann/Corbis.

THE WORLD'S FIRST AUTOMOBILE ASSEMBLY LINE
Introduced by Henry Ford at his Highland Park plant in 1913, this innovation cut production time on Ford Model Ts by 90 percent, allowing Ford to reduce the price of his cars by more than half and to double the hourly wages of his workers.

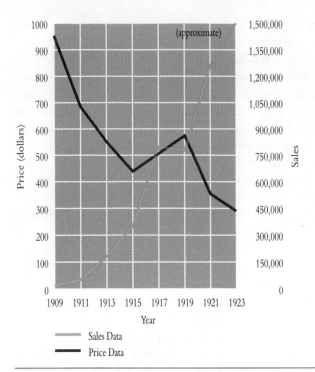

MODEL T PRICES AND SALES, 1909–1923

Source: From Alfred D. Chandler, Jr., ed., *Giant Enterprise: Ford, General Motors, and the Automobile Industry* (New York: Harcourt, Brace and World, 1964), pp. 32–33.

a union to gain a voice in production matters, but most Ford workers expressed their dissatisfaction simply by quitting. By 1913, employee turnover at Highland Park had reached the astounding rate of 370 percent per year. At that rate, Ford had to hire 51,800 workers every year just to keep his factory fully staffed at 14,000.

A problem of that magnitude demanded a dramatic solution. Ford provided it in 1914 by raising the wage he paid his assembly-line workers to $5 per day, double the average manufacturing wage then prevalent in American industry. The result: Workers, especially young and single men, flocked to Detroit. Highland Park's high productivity rate permitted Ford to absorb the wage increase without cutting substantially into profits.

Taylor had believed that improved efficiency would lead to dramatic wage gains. With his decision to raise wages, Ford was being true to Taylor's principles, but Ford went even further in his innovations. He set up a sociology department, forerunner of the personnel department, to collect job, family, and other information about his employees. He sent social workers into workers' homes to inquire into (and "improve") their personal lives. For the foreign-born, he instituted Americanization classes. He offered his employees housing subsidies, medical care, and other benefits. In short, Ford recognized that workers were more complex than Taylor had allowed and that high wages alone would not transform them into the perfectly functioning parts of the mass-production system Taylor had envisioned.

Although Ford's success impelled others to move in his direction, it would take time for modern management to come of age. Not until the 1920s did a substantial number of corporations establish personnel departments, institute welfare and recreational programs for employees, and hire psychologists to improve human relations in the workplace.

♔ "Robber Barons" No More

Innovations in corporate management were part of a broader effort among elite industrialists to shed their "robber baron" image. The swashbuckling entrepreneurs of the 19th century—men such as Cornelius Vanderbilt, Jay Gould, and Leland Stanford—had wielded their economic power brashly and ruthlessly, while lavishing money on European-style palaces, private yachts, personal art collections, and extravagant entertainments. But the depression of the 1890s—along with the populist political movement and labor protests such as the Homestead and Pullman strikes—shook the confidence of members of this elite. Industrialists were terrified when in 1892 anarchist Alexander Berkman marched into the office of Henry Clay Frick, Andrew Carnegie's right-hand man, and shot him at point-blank range (Frick survived). Although such physical assaults were rare, anger over ill-gotten and

LEADING INDUSTRIALIST PHILANTHROPIC FOUNDATIONS, 1905–1930

Foundation	Date of Origin	Original Endowment
Buhl Foundation	1927	$ 10,951,157
Carnegie Corporation of New York	1911	125,000,000
Carnegie Endowment for International Peace	1910	10,000,000
Carnegie Foundation for the Advancement of Teaching	1905	10,000,000
Carnegie Institution of Washington	1902	10,000,000
Duke Endowment	1924	40,000,000
John Simon Guggenheim Memorial Foundation	1925	3,000,000
W. K. Kellogg Foundation	1930	21,600,000
Rockefeller Foundation	1913	100,000,000
Rosenwald Fund	1917	20,000,000
Russell Sage Foundation	1907	10,000,000

Source: Joseph C. Kiger, *Operating Principles of the Larger Foundations* (New York: Russell Sage Foundation, 1957), p. 122.

The Luce Family and China: Missionary Work, Education, and the Origins of an American Media Empire

Steeped in the Social Gospel, Elizabeth Root and Henry Winters Luce resembled significant numbers of young Protestants in the late 19th century who rejected conventional lifestyles in favor of becoming missionaries for Christ and for American democratic values among the world's poor. Before marriage, Elizabeth Root worked with factory women, while Luce had turned down an invitation to join a law practice to pursue a divinity degree. Soon after marrying, the two became Presbyterian missionaries in Tengchow, China, where they hoped both to convert the Chinese to Christianity and to educate them in Western science, politics, and values. They and their thousands of missionary allies built both churches and colleges in China.

The Luces also raised a family in China. Their oldest child, Henry, born in 1898, would, upon returning to the United States as a young man, build one of the great American media empires, consisting of the mass circulation magazines *Life*, *Look*, *Time*, and *Fortune*. Henry's youth in China influenced his business and politics in America. First, because Henry was exposed early and often to a depth of poverty that most Americans never encountered, he acquired his parents' zeal for helping to improve life and culture in other parts of the world. He would become a leading internationalist, by which he meant that America ought to develop strong relationships with other countries and use its wealth, economic ingenuity, and democratic habits to raise up the world's less fortunate. In the late 1930s, at a time when many newspaper and magazine publishers worried about involving the United States in another world war, Luce argued for expanding American influence in the world.

Second, in China, especially through his private boarding school experience, Luce came to dislike the upper-class British students who taunted the poorer British as well as the American students. He was equally critical of the Germans in China who, he believed, treated Chinese workers in condescending ways. Such experiences helped to shape Luce's belief that America should supplant European countries as the world's leading nation and that it should use its power to spread its democratic message of free enterprise, individualism, and equality to the world. The crusade that Luce embraced in the 1940s to make the 20th century the "American Century" had begun to take shape in his imagination many years earlier in China.

Finally, Luce developed a lifelong love for China and its people and hoped to nurture a special relationship between the country of his birth and the country of his nationality. When, in the 1940s, the Chinese communists were threatening to cut ties between their country and the United States, Luce became an anticommunist, using the might of his publishing empire to attack communists both in China and the United States. In such ways did the experiences of living abroad influence the thinking and practices of this notable American.

THE LUCE CHILDREN IN CHINA

Henry Luce is flanked by his two sisters, Emmavail on the left and Elisabeth on the right.

ill-spent wealth was widespread. In the 1890s, popular rage forced Mrs. Bradley Martin and her husband to flee to England after she spent $370,000 (roughly $3.5 million in 2005 dollars) on an evening of entertainment for her friends in New York's high society.

Seeking a more favorable image, some industrialists began to restrain their displays of wealth and use their private fortunes to advance the public welfare. As early as 1889, Andrew Carnegie had advocated a "gospel of wealth." The wealthy, he believed, should consider all income in excess of their needs as a "trust fund" for their communities. In 1901, the year in which he formed U.S. Steel, Carnegie withdrew from industry and devoted himself to philanthropic pursuits, especially in art and education. By the time he died in 1919, he had given away or entrusted to several Carnegie foundations 90 percent of his fortune. Among the projects he funded were New York's Carnegie Hall, Pittsburgh's Carnegie Institute (now Carnegie-Mellon University), and 2,500 public libraries throughout the country.

Other industrialists, including John D. Rockefeller, soon followed Carnegie's lead. A devout Baptist with an ascetic bent, Rockefeller had never flaunted his wealth (unlike the Vanderbilts and others), but his ruthless business methods in assembling the Standard Oil Company and in crushing his competition made him one of the most reviled of the robber barons. In the wake of journalist Ida Tarbell's stinging 1904 exposé of Standard Oil's business practices, and of the federal government's subsequent prosecution of Standard Oil for monopolistic practices in 1906, Rockefeller transformed himself into a public-spirited philanthropist. Between 1913 and 1919, his Rockefeller Foundation dispersed an estimated $500 million. His most significant gifts included money to establish the University of Chicago and the Rockefeller Institute for Medical Research (later renamed Rockefeller University). His charitable efforts did not escape criticism, however; many Americans interpreted them as an attempt to establish control over American universities, scientific research, and public policy. Still, Rockefeller's largesse helped build for the Rockefeller family a reputation for public-spiritedness and good works, one that grew even stronger in the 1920s and 1930s. Many other business leaders, such as Julius Rosenwald of Sears Roebuck and Daniel and Simon Guggenheim of the American Smelting and Refining Company, also dedicated themselves to philanthropy during this time.

Obsession with Physical and Racial Fitness

The fractious events of the 1890s also induced many wealthy Americans to engage in what Theodore Roosevelt dubbed "the strenuous life." In an 1899 essay with that title, Roosevelt exhorted Americans to live vigorously, to test their physical strength and endurance in competitive athletics, and to experience nature through hiking, hunting, and mountain climbing. He articulated a way of life that influenced countless Americans from a variety of classes and cultures.

The 1890s were a time of heightened enthusiasm for competitive sports, physical fitness, and outdoor recreation. Millions of Americans began riding bicycles and eating healthier foods. A passion for athletic competition

Brown University Archives.

BROWN UNIVERSITY GOES TO THE ROSE BOWL

Seeking to demonstrate their physical prowess and racial fitness, the sons of the nation's elite took up the rough game of football. In the early years of the 20th century, Ivy League schools such as Brown fielded some of the country's best teams.

gripped American universities. The power and violence of football helped make it the sport of choice at the nation's elite campuses, and for 20 years Ivy League schools were the nation's football powerhouses. In athletic competition, as in nature, one could discover and recapture one's manhood, one's virility. The words "sissy" and "pussyfoot" entered common usage in the 1890s as insults hurled at men whose masculinity was found wanting.

Ironically, this quest for masculinity had a liberating effect on women, many of whom had internalized Victorian moral codes that frowned on strenuous outdoor activity for the "weaker" sex. In the vigorous new climate of the 1890s, young women began to engage in sports and other activities. They put away their corsets and long dresses and began wearing simple skirts, shirtwaists, and other clothing that gave them more comfort and freedom of movement. By the standards of the 1920s, these changes would seem mild, but in the 1890s, they were radical.

In the country at large, the new enthusiasm for athletics and the outdoor life reflected a widespread dissatisfaction with the growing regimentation of industrial society. Among wealthy Americans the quest for physical superiority reflected a deeper and more ambiguous anxiety: their *racial* fitness. Most of them were native-born Americans whose families had lived in the United States for several generations and whose ancestors had come from the British Isles, the Netherlands, or some other region of northwestern Europe. They liked to attribute their success and good fortune to their "racial superiority." They saw themselves as "natural" leaders, members of a noble Anglo-Saxon race endowed with uncommon intelligence, imagination, and discipline. But events of the 1890s had challenged the legitimacy of the elite's wealth and authority, and the ensuing depression mocked their ability to exert economic leadership. The immigrant masses laboring in factories, despite their poverty and alleged racial inferiority, seemed to possess a vitality that the "superior" Anglo-Saxons lacked. Immigrant families were overflowing with children. The city neighborhoods where these families lived exhibited social and cultural energy (especially apparent in popular entertainments—vaudeville, amusement parks, nickelodeons, and dance halls) that were missing in the sedate environs of the wealthy.

Some rich Americans, such as Henry Adams, Henry Cabot Lodge, and other members of Boston's declining political elite, reacted to the immigrants' vigor and industry by calling for a halt to further immigration, but not the ebullient Roosevelt; he argued instead for a return to fitness, superiority, and numerical predominance of the "English-speaking" races. He called on American men to live the strenuous life and on women to devote themselves to reproduction. The only way to avoid "race suicide," he declared, was for every American mother to have at least four children.

Such racialist thought was not limited to wealthy elites. Many other Americans, from a variety of classes and regions, also thought that all people demonstrated the characteristics of their race. Racial stereotypes served to describe not only blacks, Asians, and Hispanics, but also Italians ("violent"), Jews ("nervous"), and Slavs ("slow"). Such aspersions flowed as easily from the pens of compassionate reformers, such as Jacob Riis, who wanted to help the immigrants, as from the pens of bitter reactionaries, such as Madison Grant, who argued in *The Passing of the Great Race* (1916) that America should rid itself of "inferior" races.

Social Darwinism

Racialist thinking even received "scientific" sanction from distinguished biologists and anthropologists, who argued that racially inherited traits explained variations in the economic, social, and cultural lives of ethnic and racial groups. Many intellectuals believed that human society developed according to the "survival of the fittest" principle articulated by the English naturalist Charles Darwin to describe plant and animal evolution. Human history could be understood in terms of an ongoing struggle among races, with the strongest and the fittest invariably triumphing. The wealth and power of the Anglo-Saxon race was ample testimony, in this view, to its superior fitness.

This view, which would become known as Social Darwinism, was rooted in two developments of the late 19th century, one intellectual and one socioeconomic. Intellectually, it reflected a widely shared belief that human society operated according to principles that were every bit as scientific as those governing the natural world. The ability of 19th-century biologists, chemists, and physicists to penetrate the mysteries of the natural world generated confidence in science, in people's ability to know and control their physical environment. That confidence, in turn, prompted intellectuals to apply the scientific method to the human world. The social sciences—economics, political science, anthropology, sociology, psychology—took shape in the late 19th century, each trying to discover the scientific laws governing individual and group behavior. Awed by the accomplishments of natural scientists, social scientists were prone to exaggerate the degree to which social life mimicked natural life; hence the appeal of Social Darwinism, a philosophy that allegedly showed how closely the history of human beings resembled the history of animal evolution.

Social Darwinism was also rooted in the unprecedented interpenetration of the world's economies and peoples. Cheap and rapid ocean travel had bound together continents as never before. International trade, immigration, and imperial conquest made Americans more conscious of the variety of peoples inhabiting the earth. Although awareness of diversity sometimes encourages tolerance and cooperation, in the economically depressed years of the late 19th century, it encouraged intolerance and suspicion, fertile soil for the cultivation of Social Darwinism.

➤ Immigration

Perhaps the most dramatic evidence of the nation's growing involvement in the international economy was the high rate of immigration. The United States had always been a nation of immigrants, but never had so many come in so short a time. Between 1880 and 1920, some

23 million immigrants came to a country that numbered only 76 million in 1900. From 1900 to 1914, an average of 1 million immigrants arrived each year. In many cities of the Northeast and Midwest, immigrants and their children constituted a majority of the population. In 1920s Boston, New York City, Chicago, and Milwaukee, immigrants accounted for more than 70 percent of the total population; in Buffalo, Detroit, and Minneapolis, more than 60 percent; and in Philadelphia, Pittsburgh, and Seattle, more than 50 percent. Everywhere in the country, except in the South, the working class was overwhelmingly ethnic.

European immigration accounted for approximately three-fourths of the total. Some states received significant numbers of non-European immigrants—Chinese, Japanese, and Filipinos in California; Mexicans in California and the Southwest; and French Canadians in New England. Although their presence profoundly affected regional economies, politics, and culture, their numbers, relative to the number of European immigrants, were small. Immigrants from Latin America were free to enter the United States throughout this period, but few did until 1910, when the social disorder caused by the Mexican Revolution propelled a stream of refugees to southwestern parts of the United States. One-half million French Canadians had migrated to New England and the upper Midwest between 1867 and 1901. After that, the rate slowed as the pace of industrialization in their Quebec homeland quickened.

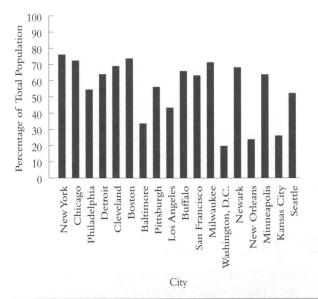

IMMIGRANTS AND THEIR CHILDREN AS A PERCENTAGE OF THE POPULATION OF SELECTED CITIES, 1920

Source: Data from U.S. Department of Commerce, Bureau of the Census, *Fourteenth Census of the United States, 1920, Population* (Washington, D.C.).

European Immigration

Most of the European immigrants who arrived between 1880 and 1914 came from Eastern and Southern Europe. Among them were 3 to 4 million Italians, 2 million Russian and Polish Jews, 2 million Hungarians, an estimated 4 million Slavs (including Poles, Bohemians, Slovaks, Russians, Ukrainians, Bulgarians, Serbians, Croatians, Slovenians, Montenegrins, and Macedonians), and 1 million from Lithuania, Greece, and Portugal. Hundreds of thousands came as well from Turkey, Armenia, Lebanon, Syria, and other Near Eastern lands abutting the European continent.

These post-1880 arrivals were called "new immigrants" to underscore the cultural gap separating them from the "old immigrants," who had come from northwestern Europe—Great Britain, Scandinavia, and Germany. Old immigrants were regarded as racially fit, culturally sophisticated, and politically mature. The new immigrants, by contrast, were often regarded as racially inferior, culturally impoverished, and incapable of assimilating American values and traditions. This negative view of the new immigrants reflected in part a fear of their alien languages, religions, and economic backgrounds. Few spoke English, and most adhered to Catholicism, Greek Orthodoxy, or Judaism rather than Protestantism. Most, with the exception of the Jews, were peasants, unaccustomed to urban industrial life. But they were not as different from the old immigrants as the label implied. For example, many of the earlier-arriving Catholic peasants from Ireland and Germany had had no more familiarity with American values and traditions than did the Italians and Slavs who arrived later.

In fact, the old and new European immigrants were more similar than different. Both came to America for the same reasons: either to flee religious or political persecution or to escape economic hardship. The United States attracted a small but steady stream of political refugees throughout the 19th century: labor militants from England; nationalists from Ireland; socialists and anarchists from Germany, Russia, Finland, and Italy. Many of these people possessed unusual talents as skilled workers, labor organizers, political agitators, and newspaper editors and thus exercised considerable influence in their ethnic communities. However, only the anti-Semitic policies of Russia in the late 19th and early 20th centuries triggered a mass emigration (in this case Jewish) of political refugees.

Most mass immigration was propelled instead by economic hardship. Europe's rural population was growing faster than the land could support. European factories absorbed some, but not all, of the rural surplus. Industrialization and urbanization were affecting the European

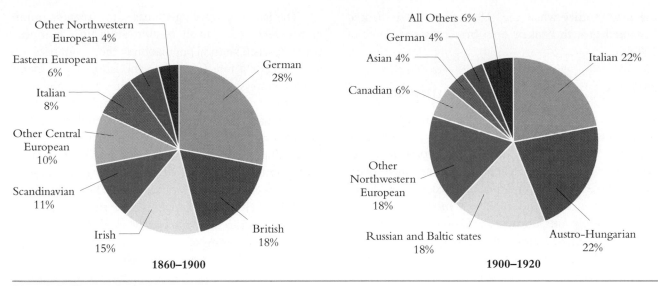

1860–1900

1900–1920

SOURCES OF IMMIGRATION

Source: Data from *Historical Statistics of the United States, Colonial Times to 1970* (White Plains, N.Y.: Kraus International, 1989), pp. 105–109.

countryside in ways that disrupted rural ways of life. As railroads penetrated the countryside, village artisans found themselves unable to compete with the cheap manufactured goods that arrived from city factories. These handicraftsmen were among the first to emigrate. Meanwhile, rising demand for food in the cities accelerated the growth of commercial agriculture in the hinterland. Some peasant families lost their land. Others turned to producing crops for the market, only to discover that they could not compete with larger, more efficient producers. In addition, by the last third of the 19th century, peasants faced competition from North American farmers. Prices for agricultural commodities plummeted everywhere. The economic squeeze that spread distress among American farmers in the 1880s and 1890s caused even more hardship among Europe's peasantry, and many of them decided to try their luck in the New World.

An individual's or family's decision to emigrate often depended on having a contact—a family member, relative, or fellow villager—already established in an American city. These people provided immigrants with a destination, inspiration (they were examples of success in America), advice about jobs, and financial aid. Sometimes whole villages in southern Italy or western Russia—or at least all of the young men—seemed to disappear, only to reappear in a certain section of Chicago, Pittsburgh, or New York. Villages without contacts in the United States were relatively unaffected by the emigration mania.

Most immigrants viewed their trip to the United States as a temporary sojourn. They came not in search of

permanent settlement but in search of high wages that would enable them to improve their economic standing in their homeland. For them, America was a land of economic opportunity, not a land to call home. This attitude explains why men vastly outnumbered women and children in the migration stream. From 1899 to 1910, three-fourths of the immigrants from Southern and Eastern Europe were adult men. Some had left wives and children behind; more were single. Most wanted merely to make enough money to buy a farm in their native land. True to their dream, many did return home. For every 100 Italian immigrants who arrived in the United States between 1907 and 1911, for example, 73 returned to Italy. Before the First World War, an estimated 60 to 80 percent of all Slavic immigrants eventually returned to the land of their birth.

The rate of return was negligible among certain groups, however. Jews had little desire to return to the religious persecution they had fled, and only 5 percent returned to Europe. The rate of return was also low among the Irish, who saw few opportunities in their long-suffering (although much-loved) Emerald Isle. In the early 20th century, however, such groups were exceptional. Most immigrants looked forward to returning to Europe. Not until the First World War shut down transatlantic travel did most immigrants begin to regard their presence in the United States as permanent.

Immigration tended to move in rhythm with the U.S. business cycle. It rose in boom years and fell off during depressions. It remained high during the first 14 years of the new century when the U.S. economy experienced sustained growth broken only briefly by the Panic of 1907–08.

Chinese and Japanese Immigration

The relatively small numbers of Chinese and Japanese immigrants who came to the United States in the late 19th and early 20th centuries reflected the efforts of native-born Americans and their allies to keep them out. As many as 300,000 Chinese immigrants arrived in the United States between 1851 and 1882, and more than 200,000 Japanese immigrants journeyed to Hawaii and the western continental United States between 1891 and 1907. They contributed in major ways to the development of two of the West's major industries: railroad building and commercial agriculture. These two immigrant groups might have formed two of America's largest, each numbering in the millions, but the U.S. government began to exclude Chinese immigrant laborers in 1882 (The Chinese Exclusion Act) and Japanese immigrant laborers in 1907 (see chapter 22). The government also interpreted a 1790 law to mean that Chinese, Japanese, and other East Asian immigrants were ineligible for citizenship. These exclusions remained in force until the 1940s and 1950s. They expressed the racial prejudice felt by most native-born white Americans toward nonwhite Asian immigrants, and they also revealed how determined America was to remain a nation of European immigrants and their descendants.

The factors propelling Chinese and Japanese immigrants were similar to those motivating their European counterparts. The rural population in those countries was increasing at a rate faster than the labor requirements of the countryside's agricultural sector. Chinese and Japanese rural peasants were being integrated into an international market for agriculture, contributing to the global oversupply of agricultural goods and depressing prices. Many Chinese and Japanese immigrants, like their European counterparts, conceived of their movement beyond their countries' borders as temporary. They intended to move abroad just long enough to make enough money to establish themselves economically in their homelands. Thus the early streams of Chinese and Japanese migration to the United States were overwhelmingly composed of men looking for work. Similar to the European immigrants, the Chinese and Japanese sojourners tended to follow precise migratory paths—from one region or village in China or Japan to one city or region in the United States.

Conditions in China were more desperate than those in Japan, where industrialization had begun to generate new wealth and absorb some of the rural population. Chinese immigrants, as a result, often suffered greater hardship than did their Japanese counterparts. In the 19th century, many were forced to sign contracts with suppliers of overseas laborers that subjected them to slave-like conditions: They were herded onto boats for the transpacific voyage, bound to particular employers for years on end,

IMMIGRANT JAPANESE CHILDREN ARRIVE AT ANGEL ISLAND, SAN FRANCISCO HARBOR, 1905

Beginning in 1907, as a result of the "gentlemen's agreement" between the United States and Japanese governments, it would no longer be possible for Japanese immigrants such as these children to come to the United States.

© Bettmann/Corbis.

thrust into dangerous working conditions, and paid paltry wages. The conditions of their labor in the western states where they tended to settle inflamed the sentiments of white working men, who saw the Asian migration as a threat to their own wages and livelihoods. These white workers might have made common cause with Asian immigrant workers, but the racial prejudice they harbored toward the "yellow hordes" was simply too great. White workers became leaders of the movements in the western states to keep these immigrants out.

Significant numbers of Chinese and Japanese immigrants continued to try to enter the United States during the period of Asian immigrant exclusion—after 1882 in the case of the Chinese and 1907 in the case of the Japanese. Some were desperate to reunite themselves with family members already living in the United States, while others were driven by deteriorating economic circumstances in their homeland. Many attempted to enter the United States with forged papers declaring them to be merchants (a permitted class of Chinese and Japanese immigrants) when they were not, or to have been resident in the United States before the exclusion laws had gone into effect (and thus entitled to return). San Francisco was their principal port of entry, and Angel Island, in San Francisco harbor, became the counterpart of Ellis Island in New York harbor: the place where inspectors for the U.S. Bureau of Immigration interrogated them and scrutinized their documents and, more often than not, sent them back to Asia.

Others East Asian immigrants attempted to enter the United States through Canada or Mexico, hoping to find an unpatrolled part of the land border and to cross into the United States undetected. They became, in effect, America's first illegal aliens. That a certain percentage of East Asian immigrants were illegals subject to deportation generated considerable fear among the Asian immigrant populations resident in the United States, deepening tendencies within these communities to secrecy and to separation from mainstream American culture and society. Despite these considerable hardships, Asian immigrants would prove to be resourceful and to find ways to build homes and livelihoods in America.

Immigrant Labor

In the first decade of the 20th century, immigrant men and their male children constituted 70 percent of the workforce in 15 of the 19 leading U.S. industries. They concentrated in industries where work was the most backbreaking. Immigrants built the nation's railroads and tunnels; mined its coal, iron ore, and other minerals; stoked its hot and sometimes deadly steel furnaces; and slaughtered and packed its meat in Chicago's putrid packinghouses.

In 1909, first- and second-generation immigrants—especially Greeks, Italians, Japanese, and Mexicans—constituted more than 96 percent of the labor force that built and maintained the nation's railroads. Of the 750,000 Slovaks who arrived in America before 1913, at least 600,000 headed for the coal mines and steel mills of western Pennsylvania. The steel mills of Pittsburgh, Buffalo, Cleveland, and Chicago also attracted disproportionately large numbers of Poles and other Slavs.

Immigrants also performed "lighter" but no less arduous work. Jews and Italians predominated in the garment manufacturing shops of New York City, Chicago, Philadelphia, Baltimore, and Boston. In 1900, French-Canadian immigrants and their children held one of every two jobs in New England's cotton textile industry. By 1920, the prosperity of California's rapidly growing agricultural industry depended primarily on Mexican and Filipino labor. In these industries, immigrant women and children, who worked for lower wages than men, formed a large part of the labor force. Few states restricted child labor. More than 25 percent of boys and 10 percent of girls aged 10 to 15 were "gainfully employed."

Immigrants were as essential as fossil fuels to the smooth operation of the American economic machine. Sometimes, however, the machine consumed workers as well as coal and oil. Those who worked in heavy industry, mining, or railroading were especially vulnerable to accident and injury. In 1901, for instance, 1 in every 400 railroad workers died on the job and 1 in every 26 suffered injury. Between the years 1906 and 1911, almost one-quarter of the recent immigrants employed at the U.S. Steel Corporation's South Works (Pittsburgh) were injured or killed on the job. Lax attention to safety rendered even light industry hazardous and sometimes fatal. In 1911, a fire broke out on an upper floor of the Triangle Shirtwaist Company, a New York City garment factory. The building had no fire escapes. The owners of the factory, moreover, had locked the entrances to each floor as a way of keeping their employees at work. A total of 146 workers, mostly young Jewish and Italian women, perished in the fire or from desperate nine-story leaps to the pavement below.

Chronic fatigue and inadequate nourishment increased the risk of accident and injury. Workweeks averaged 60 hours—10 hours every day except Sunday. Workers who were granted Saturday afternoons off—thus reducing their workweek to a mere 55 hours—considered themselves fortunate. Steelworkers were not so lucky. They labored from 72 to 89 hours per week and were required to work one 24-hour shift every two weeks.

Most workers had to labor long hours simply to eke out a meager living. In 1900, the annual earnings of American manufacturing workers averaged only $400 to $500 per year. Skilled jobs offered immigrants far more (as much as $1,500 to $2,000 per year), but most of them were held by Yankees and by the Germans, Irish, Welsh, and other Europeans who had come as part of the old immigration. Through their unions, workers of Northern European extraction also controlled access to new jobs that opened up and usually managed to fill them with a son, relative, or fellow countryman. Consequently, relatively few of the new immigrants rose into the prosperous ranks of skilled labor. In any case, employers were replacing many skilled workers with machines operated by cheaply paid operatives.

From the 1870s to 1910, real wages paid to factory workers and common laborers did rise, but not steadily. Wages fell sharply during depressions, and the hope for increases during periods of recovery often collapsed under the weight of renewed mass immigration, which brought hundreds of thousands of new job seekers into the labor market. One of every five industrial workers was unemployed, even during the boom years of the early 20th century.

Most working families required two or three wage earners to survive. If a mother could not go out to work because she had small children at home, she might rent rooms to some of the many single men who had recently immigrated. But economic security was difficult to attain. In his book, *Poverty*, published in 1904, social investigator Robert Hunter conservatively estimated that 20 percent of the industrial population of the North lived in poverty.

Living Conditions

Strained economic circumstances confined many working-class families to cramped and dilapidated living quarters. Many of them lived in two- or three-room apartments, with several sleeping in each room. To make ends meet, one immigrant New York City family of eight living in a two-room apartment took in six boarders. Some boarders considered themselves lucky to have their own bed. That luxury was denied the 14 Slovaks who shared eight beds in a small Pittsburgh apartment and the New York City printer who slept on a door he unhinged every night and balanced across two chairs. The lack of windows in city

Victor Joseph Gatto Triangle Fire, March 25, 1911. Oil on canvas. 19 x 28 inches. Museum of the City of New York, 54.75, Gift of Mrs. Henry L. Moses.

TRIANGLE SHIRTWAIST COMPANY FIRE

In 1911, a fire at the Triangle Shirtwaist Company in New York City claimed the lives of 146 workers, most of them young Jewish and Italian women. Many died because they could not escape the flames. The building had no fire escapes, and their employer had locked the entrances to each floor to keep workers on the job. The tragedy spurred the growth of unions and the movement for factory reform in New York.

tenements allowed little light or air into these apartments, and few had their own toilets or running water. Crowding was endemic. The population density of New York City's Lower East Side—where most of the city's Jewish immigrants settled—reached 700 per acre in 1900, a density greater than that of the poorest sections of Bombay, India. Overcrowding and poor sanitation resulted in high rates of infectious diseases, especially diphtheria, typhoid fever, and pneumonia.

By 1900, this crisis in urban living had begun to yield to the insistence of urban reformers that cities adopt housing codes and improve sanitation. Between 1880 and 1900, housing inspectors condemned the worst of the tenements and ordered landlords to make improvements. City governments built reservoirs, pipes, and sewers to carry clean water to the tenements and to carry away human waste. Newly paved roads lessened the dirt, mud, and stagnant pools of water and thus further curtailed the spread of disease. As a result, urban mortality rates fell in the 1880s and 1890s.

Nevertheless, improvements came far more slowly to the urban poor than they did to the middle and upper classes. Cities such as Pittsburgh built extensive systems of paved roads in wealthy districts but not in working-class areas. Water supplies and pressures were far better in prosperous than in poor neighborhoods. At the outbreak of the First World War, many working-class families still lacked running water in their homes.

Building Ethnic Communities

The immigrants may have been poor, but they were not helpless. Migration had required a good deal of resourcefulness, self-help, and mutual aid—assets that survived in the new surroundings of American cities.

A Network of Institutions

Each ethnic group quickly established a network of institutions that supplied a sense of community and multiplied sources of communal assistance. Some immigrants simply reproduced those institutions that had been important to them in the Old Country. The devout established churches and synagogues. Lithuanian, Jewish, and Italian radicals reestablished Old World socialist and anarchist organizations. Irish nationalists set up clandestine chapters of the Clan Na Gael to keep alive the struggle to free Ireland from the English. Germans felt at home in their traditional *Turnevereins* (athletic clubs) and musical societies.

Immigrants developed new institutions as well. In the larger cities, foreign language newspapers disseminated news, advice, and culture. Each ethnic group created fraternal societies to bring together immigrants who had known each other in the Old Country, or who shared the same craft, or who had come from the same town or region. Most of these societies provided members with a death benefit (ranging from a few hundred to a thousand dollars) that guaranteed the deceased a decent burial and the family a bit of cash. Some fraternal societies made small loans as well. Among those ethnic groups that prized home ownership, especially the Slavic groups, the fraternal societies also provided mortgage money. And all of them served as centers of sociability—places to have a drink, play cards, or simply relax with fellow countrymen. The joy, solace, and solidarity these groups generated helped countless immigrants adjust to American life.

The Emergence of an Ethnic Middle Class

Within each ethnic group, a sizable minority directed their talents and ambitions toward economic gain. Some of these entrepreneurs first addressed their communities' needs for basic goods and services. Immigrants preferred to buy from fellow countrymen with whom they shared a language, a history, and presumably a bond of trust. Enterprising individuals responded by opening dry-goods stores, food shops, butcher shops, and saloons in their ethnic neighborhoods. Those who could not afford to rent a store hawked their fruit, clothing, or dry goods from portable stands, wagons, or sacks carried on their backs. The work was endless and the competition tough. Men often enlisted the entire family—wife, older children, younger children—in their undertakings. Few family members were ever paid for their labor, no matter how long or hard they worked. Although many of these small businesses failed, enough survived to give some immigrants and their children a toehold in the middle class.

Other immigrants turned to small industry, particularly garment manufacture, truck farming, and construction. A clothing manufacturer needed only a few sewing machines to become competitive. Many Jewish immigrants, having been tailors in Russia and Poland, opened such facilities. If a rented space proved beyond their means, they set up shop in their own apartments. Competition among these small manufacturers was fierce, and work environments were condemned by critics as "sweatshops." Workers suffered from inadequate lighting, heat, and ventilation; 12-hour workdays and 70-hour workweeks during peak seasons, with every hour spent bent over a sewing machine; and poor pay and no employment security, especially for the women and children who made up a large part of this labor force. Even at this level of exploitation, many small manufacturers failed, but over time, many of them managed to firm up their position as manufacturers and to evolve into stable, responsible employers. Their success contributed to the emergence of a Jewish middle class.

The story was much the same in urban construction, where Italians who had established themselves as labor contractors, or *padroni*, went into business for themselves to take advantage of the rapid expansion of American cities. Although few became general contractors on major downtown projects, many of them did well building family residences or serving as subcontractors on larger buildings.

One who did make the leap from small to big business was Amadeo P. Giannini, the son of Italian immigrants, who used his savings from a San Francisco fruit and vegetable stand to launch a career in banking. Determined to make bank loans available and affordable to people of ordinary means, Giannini generated a huge business in small loans. Expanding on his ethnic base of small depositors, he eventually made his bank—the Bank of America—into the country's largest financial institution.

In southern California, Japanese immigrants chose agriculture as their route to the middle class. Working as agricultural laborers in the 1890s, they began to acquire their own land in the early years of the 20th century. Altogether, they owned only 1 percent of California's total farm acreage. Their specialization in fresh vegetables and fruits (particularly strawberries), combined with their family-labor-intensive agricultural methods, was yielding $67 million in annual revenues by 1919—one-tenth of the total California agriculture revenue that year. Japanese farmers sold their produce to Japanese fruit and vegetable wholesalers in Los Angeles, who had chosen a mercantile route to middle-class status. The success of Japanese farmers was all the more impressive given that the state of California had passed the Alien Land Law in 1913, prohibiting Japanese and other Asian aliens from owning property in the state. Japanese immigrant farmers thus depended on their native-born children or friendly whites to acquire land for them, arrangements that made them more vulnerable to losing the land—or control of it—than if they had been able to own it outright themselves.

Each ethnic group created its own history of economic success and social mobility. From the emerging middle classes came many leaders who would provide their ethnic groups with identity, legitimacy, and power and would lead the way toward Americanization and assimilation. Their children tended to do better in school than the children of working-class ethnics, and academic success served as a ticket to upward social mobility in a society that increasingly depended on university-trained engineers, managers, lawyers, doctors, and other professionals.

Political Machines and Organized Crime

The underside of this success story was the rise of government corruption and organized crime. Many ethnic entrepreneurs operated on the margins of economic failure and bankruptcy, and some accepted the help of those who promised financial assistance. Sometimes the help came from honest unions and upright government officials, but other times it did not. Unions were generally weak, and some government officials, lacking experience and economic security, were susceptible to bribery. Economic necessity became a breeding ground for government corruption and greed. A contractor who was eager to win a city contract—to build a trolley system, a sewer line, or a new city hall, for example—would find it necessary to pay off government officials who could throw the contract his way. By 1900, such payments, referred to as "graft," had become essential to the day-to-day operation of government in most large cities. The graft, in turn, made local officeholding a source of economic gain. Politicians began building political organizations called machines to guarantee their success in municipal elections. The machine "bosses" used a variety of legal and illegal means to bring victory on election day. They won the loyalty of urban voters—especially immigrants—by providing poor neighborhoods with paved roads and sewer systems. They helped newly arrived immigrants find jobs (often on city payrolls) and occasionally provided food, fuel, or clothing to families in dire need. Many of their clients were grateful for these services in an age when government provided little public assistance.

The bosses who ran the political machines—including "King Richard" Croker in New York, James Michael Curley in Boston, Tom Pendergast in Kansas City, Martin Behrman in New Orleans, and Abe Ruef in San Francisco—served their own needs first. They saw to it that construction contracts went to those who offered the most graft, not to those who were likely to do the best job. They protected gamblers, pimps, and other purveyors of urban vice who contributed large amounts to their machine coffers. They often required city employees to contribute to their campaign chests, to solicit political contributions, and to get out the vote on election day. And they engaged in widespread election fraud by rounding up truckloads of newly arrived immigrants and paying them to vote a certain way; having their supporters vote two or three times; and stuffing ballot boxes with the votes of phantom citizens who had died, moved away, or never been born.

© Bettmann/Corbis.

"KEEPING TAMMANY'S BOOTS SHINED"

This 1880s cartoon by Joseph Keppler declares that the real boss of New York City was not its elected mayor, Hugh Graham, here depicted as a lowly shoe-shiner, but the Tammany Hall political machine. The loose strap underneath the boot, used to control both City Hall and Tammany, belongs to Richard Croker, Tammany's leader from 1886 to 1901.

Big-city machines, then, were both positive and negative forces in urban life. Reformers despised them for disregarding election laws and encouraging vice, but many immigrants valued them for providing social welfare services and for creating opportunities for upward mobility.

The history of President John F. Kennedy's family offers one example of the economic and political opportunities opened up by machine politics. Both of Kennedy's grandfathers, John Francis ("Honey Fitz") Fitzgerald and Patrick Joseph Kennedy, were the children of penniless Irish immigrants who arrived in Boston in the 1840s. Fitzgerald excelled at academics and won a coveted place in Harvard's Medical School, but left Harvard that same year, choosing a career in politics instead. Between 1891 and 1905, Fitzgerald served as a Boston city councilor, Massachusetts state congressman and senator, U.S. congressman, and mayor of Boston. For much of this period, he derived considerable income and power from his position as the North End ward boss, where he supervised the trading of jobs for votes and favors for cash in his section of Boston's Democratic and Irish-dominated political machine.

Patrick Kennedy, an East Boston tavern owner and liquor merchant, became an equally important figure in Boston city politics. In addition to running the Democratic Party's affairs in Ward Two, he served on the Strategy Board, a secret council of Boston's machine politicians that met regularly to devise policies, settle disputes, and divide up the week's graft. Both Fitzgerald and Kennedy derived a substantial income from their political work and used it to lift their families into middle-class prosperity. Kennedy's son (and the future president's father), Joseph P. Kennedy, would go on to make a fortune as a Wall Street speculator and liquor distributor and to groom his sons for Harvard and the highest political offices in the land. But his rapid economic and social ascent had been made possible by his father's and father-in-law's earlier success in Boston machine politics.

Underworld figures, too, influenced urban life. In the early years of the 20th century, gangsterism was a scourge of Italian neighborhoods, where Sicilian immigrants had established outposts of the notorious Mafia, and in Irish, Jewish, Chinese, and other ethnic communities as well. Favorite targets of these gangsters were small-scale manufacturers and contractors, who were threatened with violence and economic ruin if they did not pay a gang for "protection." Gangsters enforced their demands with physical force, beating up or killing those who failed to abide by the "rules." In Chinese communities, secret societies originating in China, or *tongs*, and initially set up in America to strengthen communal life among the immigrants, occasionally crossed the line into crime. Some-

times this transition resulted from good intentions—for example, tong members might smuggle into the United States the wife and children of an immigrant Chinese man who had no legal way of reuniting his family—but other times, tongs enmeshed themselves in far more damaging criminal activities such as the opium trade, prostitution, and gambling.

Greedy for money, power, and fame, and willing to use any means necessary, many immigrant and ethnic criminals considered themselves authentic entrepreneurs cut from the American mold. By the 1920s, petty extortion had escalated in urban areas, and underworld crime had become big business. Al Capone, the ruthless Chicago mobster who made a fortune from gambling, prostitution, and bootleg liquor during Prohibition, once claimed: "Prohibition is a business. All I do is to supply a public demand. I do it in the best and least harmful way I can." New York City's Arnold Rothstein, whose financial sophistication won him a gambling empire and the power to fix the 1919 World Series, nurtured his reputation as "the J. P. Morgan of the underworld." Mobsters like Rothstein and Capone were charismatic figures, both in their ethnic communities and in the nation at large. Few immigrants, however, followed their criminal path to economic success.

African American Labor and Community

Unlike immigrants, African Americans remained a predominantly rural and southern people in the early 20th century. Most blacks were sharecroppers and tenant farmers. The markets for cotton and other southern crops had stabilized in the early 20th century, but black farmers remained vulnerable to exploitation. Landowners, most of whom were white, often forced sharecroppers to accept artificially low prices for their crops. At the same time, they charged high prices for seed, tools, and groceries at the local stores they controlled. Few rural areas generated enough business to support more than one store or to create a competitive climate that might force prices down. Those sharecroppers who traveled elsewhere to sell their crops or purchase their necessities risked retaliation—either physical assaults by white vigilantes or eviction from their land. Thus most remained beholden to their landowners, mired in poverty and debt.

Some African Americans sought a better life by migrating to industrial areas of the South and the North. In the South, they worked in iron and coal mines, in furniture and cigarette manufacture, as railroad track layers and longshoremen, and as laborers in the steel mills of

COTTON AND AFRICAN AMERICAN LABOR

Cotton remained one of the South's most important commodities into the 20th century, and much of it was cultivated and harvested by African Americans who worked as sharecroppers, tenant farmers, and agricultural laborers.

Birmingham, Alabama. By the early 20th century, their presence was growing in the urban North as well, where they worked on the fringes of industry as janitors, elevator operators, teamsters, longshoremen, and servants of various kinds. Altogether, about 200,000 blacks left the South for the North and West between 1890 and 1910.

In southern industries, blacks were subjected to hardships and indignities that even the newest immigrants were not expected to endure. Railroad contractors in the South, for example, treated their black track layers like prisoners. Armed guards marched them to work in the morning and back at night. Track layers were paid only once a month and forced to purchase food at the company commissary, where the high prices claimed most of what they earned. Their belongings were locked up to discourage them from running away. Although other southern employers of black workers did not engage in labor practices as harsh as those of the railroad contractors, they still confined blacks to the dirtiest and most grueling jobs. The "Jim Crow" laws passed by every southern state legislature in the 1890s legalized this rigid separation of the black and white races (see chapter 18).

The nation's worsening racial climate adversely affected southern blacks who came north, even though these migrants had moved to states that had no Jim Crow laws. Northern industrialists generally refused to hire black migrants for manufacturing jobs, preferring the labor of European immigrants. Only when those immigrants went on strike did employers turn to African Americans. Black workers first gained a foothold in the Chicago meatpacking industry in 1904, when 28,000 immigrant packinghouse workers walked off their jobs. Employers hoped that the use of black strike-breakers would inflame racial tensions between white and black workers and thus undermine labor unity and strength.

African Americans who had long resided in northern urban areas also experienced intensifying discrimination in the late 19th and early 20th centuries. In 1870, about one-third of the black men in many northern cities had been skilled tradesmen: blacksmiths, painters, shoemakers, and carpenters. Serving both black and white clients, these men enjoyed steady work and good pay, but by 1910 only 10 percent of black men made a living in this way. In many cities, the number of barber shops and food catering businesses owned by blacks also went into sharp decline, as did black representation in the ranks of restaurant and hotel waiters. These barbers, food caterers, and waiters had formed a black middle class whose livelihood depended on the patronage of white clients. By the early 20th century, this middle class was in decline, the victim of growing racism. Whites were no longer willing to engage the services of blacks, preferring to have their hair cut, beards shaved, and food prepared and served by European immigrants. The residential segregation of northern blacks also rose in these years, as whites excluded them from urban neighborhoods.

Although northern blacks at the turn of the 20th century had to cope with a marked deterioration in their working and living conditions, they did not lack for resourcefulness. Urban blacks laced their communities with the same array of institutions—churches, fraternal insurance societies, political organizations—that solidified ethnic neighborhoods. A new black middle class arose, consisting of ministers, professionals, and businesspeople who

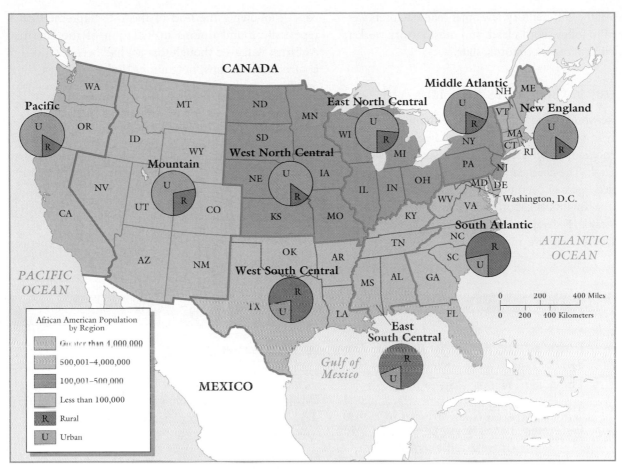

MAP 20.2   AFRICAN AMERICAN POPULATION, 1910

This map reveals that African Americans in 1910 were concentrated largely in rural areas of the South. Those who lived outside the South, although relatively few in number, were predominately urban.

serviced the needs of their racial group. Black-owned real estate agencies, funeral homes, doctors' offices, newspapers, groceries, restaurants, and bars opened for business on the commercial thoroughfares of African American neighborhoods. Many businessmen had been inspired by the words of black educator Booker T. Washington, and specifically by his argument that blacks should devote themselves to self-help and self-sufficiency. Madame C. J. Walker offers one example of a black woman who built a lucrative business from the hair and skin lotions she devised and sold to black customers throughout the country. In many cities, African American real estate agents achieved significant wealth and power. Nevertheless, entrepreneurial success remained a tougher task among African Americans than among immigrants. Black communities were often smaller and poorer than their white ethnic counterparts; economic opportunities were fewer, and black businessmen found it more difficult than their white ethnic counterparts to cultivate customers outside of their core community. Racial prejudice stood as an obstacle to

black business success. Meanwhile, blacks were so marginalized in politics that they had little opportunity to gain power or wealth through holding political office or controlling a political machine. Thus the African American middle class remained smaller and more precarious than did its counterpart in ethnic communities, less able to lead the way toward affluence and assimilation.

Workers and Unions

Middle-class success eluded most immigrants and blacks in the years before the First World War. Even among Jews, whose rate of social mobility was rapid, most immigrants were working class. For most workers, the path toward a better life lay in improving their working conditions, not in escape from the working class. Henry Ford's $5-per-day wage, double the average manufacturing wage, raised the hopes of many. Young immigrant men, in particular, flocked to Detroit to work for Ford. But in the early decades of the 20th century, few other manufacturers were prepared to follow Ford's lead, and most factory workers remained in a fragile economic state.

Samuel F. Gompers and the AFL

For those workers, the only hope for economic improvement lay in organizing unions powerful enough to wrest wage concessions from reluctant employers. This was not an easy task. The charged, often violent labor protests of the Gilded Age had been put down. Labor organizations, such as the Knights of Labor, that had unified workers had been defeated. Federal and state governments had shown themselves ready to use military force to break strikes. The

courts, following the lead of the U.S. Supreme Court, repeatedly found unions in violation of the Sherman Antitrust Act, even though that act had been intended to control corporations, not unions. Judges in most states usually granted employer requests for injunctions—court orders that barred striking workers from picketing their place of employment (and thus from obstructing employer efforts to hire replacement workers). Before 1916, no federal laws protected workers' right to organize or required employers to bargain with the unions to which their workers belonged.

This hostile legal environment retarded the growth of unions from the 1890s through the 1930s. It also made the major labor organization of those years, the American

---

MUSICAL LINK TO THE PAST

Before Jazz: An Early African American Orchestra

Composer: Wilbur C. Sweatman

Title: "Down Home Rag"

Performer: James Reese Europe's Society Orchestra (December 29, 1913)

The dense, smeared, and exciting sound of "Down Home Rag," with its frenetic tempo that approximates the speed of today's punk rock, represented one of the first attempts to define black musical identity before jazz became a commercial force. The band on this disc, the first black orchestra to secure a major recording contract, was led by James Reese Europe, the son of an Alabama slave.

Jim Crow segregation laws and practices extended into the world of professional music, limiting the opportunities and respect accorded to black musicians and composers. The strict color line in musicians' unions meant that blacks earned lesser wages and were often asked to wash dishes or work more hours than white musicians to keep their nonunion jobs. African Americans were also kept from performing and writing in the more high-brow world of classical music. To combat these problems, Europe became the leading force behind the Clef Club, a New York City trade union and booking agency created in 1910 for and by African American musicians. The Club's signature event was their May 2, 1912, staging of a "Concert of Negro Music" at Carnegie Hall, America's premiere venue for classical music, a place where no African American performers or compositions had previously been featured. Blacks and whites

sat in equal numbers in the capacity crowd, probably for the first time at an American concert. Following the show, more black composers and musicians received jobs, although the classical market was still heavily skewed toward whites.

Europe believed that African American orchestras needed to demonstrate their own character apart from white orchestral music. In "Down Home Rag," we hear a scaled-down 18-piece version of the 125-piece orchestra that showcased Europe's musical vision at Carnegie. The orchestra boasted a full-bodied, percussive, and singular sound, including 14 upright pianos and unorthodox instruments such as banjos, mandolins, and guitars combined with more traditional string instruments and percussion. Europe's mixing of violin-led melodies that sounded like 19th-century Virginia reels with an aggressive and layered rhythmic foundation provided an early preview of the mixing of black and white genres that characterized American music in the 20th century.

1. How would you describe the music that James Reese Europe created with his orchestra?
2. Why do you think Europe argued that African American orchestral music had to be different in character from that usually performed in America's classical concert halls?

For additional sources related to this feature, visit the *Liberty, Equality, Power* Web site at:

http://history.wadsworth.com/murrin_LEP4e

MEN AT WORK

This photo of male workers stoking a boiler conveys some of the grime and heat associated with much turn-of-the-20th-century blue-collar work as well as the strength and concentration required of workmen.

Underwood Photo Archives.

Federation of Labor (AFL), more timid and conservative than it had been before the depression of the 1890s. In the aftermath of that depression, the AFL focused on organizing craft, or skilled, workers such as carpenters, typographers, plumbers, painters, and machinists. Because of their skills, these workers commanded more respect from employers than did the unskilled laborers. Employers negotiated contracts, or trade agreements, with craft unions that stipulated the wages workers were to be paid, the hours they were to work, and the rules under which new workers would be accepted into the trade. These agreements were accorded the same legal protection that American law bestowed on other commercial contracts.

As the AFL emphasized these bread-and-butter issues, it withdrew from the political activism that had once occupied its attention. It no longer agitated for governmental regulation of the economy and the workplace. The AFL had concluded that labor's powerful opponents in the legislatures and the courts would find ways to undermine whatever governmental gains organized labor managed to achieve. That conclusion was reinforced by a 1905 ruling, *Lochner* v. *New York,* in which the U.S. Supreme Court declared unconstitutional a seemingly innocent New York state law limiting bakery employees to a 10-hour day.

The AFL's "business" unionism took its most forceful expression from its president, Samuel F. Gompers. A one-time Marxist and cigarmaker who had helped found the AFL in 1886, Gompers was reelected to the AFL presidency every year from 1896 until his death in 1924. The AFL showed considerable vitality under his leadership, especially in the early years when its membership quadrupled

from less than a half million in 1897 to more than 2 million in 1904. Aware of the AFL's growing significance and conservatism, the National Civic Federation, a newly formed council of corporate executives, agreed to meet periodically with the organization's leaders to discuss the nation's industrial and labor problems.

Nevertheless, the AFL had limited success. Its 2 million members represented only a small portion of the industrial workforce. Its concentration among craft workers, moreover, distanced it from most workers, who were not skilled. Unskilled and semiskilled workers could only be organized into an industrial union that offered membership to all workers in a particular industry. Gompers understood the importance of such unions and allowed several of them, including the United Mine Workers (UMW) and the International Ladies Garment Workers Union (ILGWU), to participate in the AFL. But AFL ranks remained dominated by skilled workers who looked down upon the unskilled. Ethnic background intensified these craftsmen's sense of superiority over the unskilled. Most skilled workers were from old immigrant stock—particularly English, Scottish, German, and Irish—and they shared the common prejudice against immigrants from Southern and Eastern Europe.

AFL members demonstrated even worse prejudice toward black workers. In the early 20th century, more than 10 AFL unions excluded African Americans from membership. The AFL's racist policies partially account for the shrinking numbers of black tradesmen between 1870 and 1910. White and black workers sometimes managed to set aside their suspicions of each other and cooperate. The

UMW allowed black workers to join and to rise to positions of leadership. In New Orleans, black and white dockworkers constructed a remarkable experiment in biracial unionism that flourished from the 1890s through the early 1920s. But these moments of cooperation were rare.

Although blacks made up too small a percentage of the working class to build alternative labor organizations that would counteract the influence of the AFL, the new immigrants from Eastern and Southern Europe were too numerous to be ignored. Their participation in the UMW enabled that union to grow from only 14,000 in 1897 to more than 300,000 in 1914. In 1909, a strike of 20,000 women workers against the owners of New York City's garment factories inspired tens of thousands of workers, male and female, to join the ILGWU.

"Big Bill" Haywood and the IWW

When the AFL failed to help them organize, immigrants turned to other unions. The most important was the Industrial Workers of the World (IWW), founded by western miners in 1905 and led by William "Big Bill" Haywood. The IWW rejected the AFL principle of craft organization, hoping instead to organize all workers into "one big union." It scorned the notion that only a conservative union could survive in American society, declaring its commitment to revolution instead.

The IWW refused to sign collective bargaining agreements with employers, arguing that such agreements only trapped workers in capitalist property relations. Capitalism had to be overthrown through struggles between workers and their employers at the point of production. Although hundreds of thousands of workers passed through its ranks or participated in its strikes, the IWW's membership rarely exceeded 20,000. Nevertheless, few labor organizations inspired as much fear. The IWW organized the poorest and most isolated workers—lumbermen, miners, and trackmen in the West, textile workers and longshoremen in the East. Emboldened by IWW leaders, these workers waged strikes against employers who were unaccustomed to having their authority challenged. Violence lurked beneath the surface of these strikes and occasionally erupted in bloody skirmishes between strikers and police, National Guardsmen, or the private security forces hired by employers. Some blamed the IWW for the violence, seeing it as a direct outgrowth of calls for a "class war." Others understood that the IWW was not solely responsible. Employers had shown themselves quite willing to resort to violence to enforce their will on employees. In 1913, for example, at Ludlow, Colorado, the Colorado Fuel and Iron Company, a subsidiary of Rockefeller's Standard Oil Company, brought in a private security force and the local

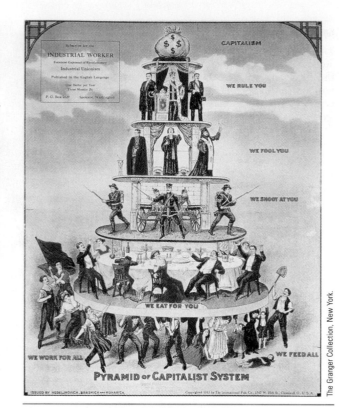

The Granger Collection, New York.

THE RADICAL CRITIQUE OF CAPITALISM

This "Pyramid of the Capitalist System" humorously illustrates how radicals analyzed capitalism—as an economic system that oppressed workers, rewarded the wealthy, and worshipped money. In this pyramid, the police, political leaders, and clerics are all depicted as the opponents of workers and the servants of capital.

militia (which it controlled) to break up a UMW strike. When the company evicted strikers and their families from their homes, the union set up 13 tent colonies to obstruct the entrances to the mines. The standoff came to a bloody conclusion in April 1914 when company police, firing into one colony of tents, killed 66 men, women, and children.

The "Ludlow massacre" outraged the nation. At hearings of the U.S. Commission on Industrial Relations, John D. Rockefeller, Jr., was humiliated by Commissioner Frank Walsh's disclosure that the industrialist had been complicit in the events leading up to the violence. The massacre revealed yet again what the IWW strikes had already demonstrated: that many American workers resented their low wages and poor working conditions; that neither the government nor employers offered workers a mechanism for airing and peacefully resolving their grievances; and that workers, as a result, felt compelled to protest through joining unions and waging strikes, even if it meant risking their lives. On the eve of the First World War, almost 40 years after the Great Railroad Strike of 1877 (chapter 19), industrial conflict still plagued the nation.

The Joys of the City

Industrial workers might be missing their fair share of the nation's prosperity, but they were crowding the dance halls, vaudeville theaters, amusement parks, and ballparks offered by the new world of commercial entertainment. Above all, they were embracing a new technological marvel, the movies.

Movies were well suited to poor city dwellers with little money, little free time, and little command of the English language. Initially, the movies cost only a nickel. The "nickelodeons" where they were shown were usually converted storefronts in working-class neighborhoods. Movies required little leisure time because at first they lasted only 15 minutes on average. Viewers with more time on their hands could stay for a cycle of two or three films (or for several cycles). And even non-English-speakers could understand what was happening on the "silent screen." By 1910, at least 20,000 nickelodeons dotted northern cities.

These early "moving pictures" were primitive by today's standards, but they were thrilling just the same. The figures appearing on the screen were "larger than life." Moviegoers could transport themselves to parts of the world they would otherwise never see, encounter people they would otherwise never meet, and watch boxing matches they could otherwise not afford to attend. The darkened theater provided a setting in which secret desires, especially sexual ones, could be explored. As one newspaper innocently commented in 1899: "For the first time in the history of the world it is possible to see what a kiss looks like."

No easy generalizations are possible about the content of these early films, more than half of which came from France, Germany, and Italy. American-made films tended toward slapstick comedies, adventure stories, and romances. Producers did not yet shy away, as they soon would, from the lustier or seedier sides of American life.

THEDA BARA AS CLEOPATRA (1917)

Bara was the first movie actress to gain fame for her roles as a "vamp"—a woman whose irresistible sexual charm led men to ruin. Because little effort was made to censor movies before the early 1920s, movie directors were able to explore sexual themes and to film their female stars in erotic, and partially nude, poses.

The Hollywood formula of happy endings had yet to be worked out. In fact, the industry, centered in New York City and Fort Lee, New Jersey, had yet to locate itself in cheery southern California. In 1914, the movies' first sex symbol, Theda Bara, debuted in a movie that showed her tempting an upstanding American ambassador into infidelity and ruin. She would be the first of the big screen's

NICKELODEONS IN MAJOR AMERICAN CITIES, 1910

Cities	Population	Nickelodeons (estimate)	Seating Capacity	Population per Seat
New York	4,338,322	450	150,000	29
Chicago	2,000,000	310	93,000	22
Philadelphia	1,491,082	160	57,000	26
St. Louis	824,000	142	50,410	16
Cleveland	600,000	75	22,500	27
Baltimore	600,000	83	24,900	24
San Francisco	400,000	68	32,400	12
Cincinnati	350,000	75	22,500	16
New Orleans	325,000	28	5,600	58

Source: Garth Jowett, *Film: The Democratic Art* (Boston: Little, Brown, 1976), p. 46.

many "vamps," so-called because the characters they portrayed, like vampires, thrived on the blood (and death) of men.

The New Sexuality and the Rise of Feminism

The appearance of the "vamp" was one sign of a growing popular dissatisfaction with the separate-sphere ideology that dominated American life in the 19th century (see chapter 19) and, in particular, of one notion central to it: that women were naturally chaste and passionless creatures. The leaders of this revolt against separate spheres included middle-class women who, after achieving first-rate educations at elite women's colleges, were told they could not participate in the nation's economic, governmental, or professional enterprises. Now they began to demand that they be allowed to enter what had been a man's world. The revolt drew as well on young, single, working-class women who were entering the workforce in large numbers and mixing at workplaces, in loosely supervised ways, with men their own age.

The associations between young men and women that sprang up at work carried over into their leisure. Young people of both sexes flocked to the dance halls that were opening in every major city. They rejected the stiff formality of earlier ballroom dances such as the cotillion or the waltz for the freedom and intimacy of newer forms, such as the fox trot, tango, and bunny-hug. They went to movies and to amusement parks together, and they engaged, far more than their parents had, in premarital sex. It is estimated that the proportion of women having sex before marriage rose from 10 percent to 25 percent in the generation that was coming of age between 1910 and 1920.

Feminism

This movement toward sexual freedom was one expression of women's dissatisfaction with the restrictions that had been imposed on them by earlier generations. By the

HISTORY THROUGH FILM

The Great White Hope (1970)

Directed by Martin Ritt. Starring James Earl Jones (Jack Jefferson) and Jane Alexander (Eleanor Backman).

This movie is a fictional retelling of the life of Jack Johnson, the first black world heavyweight boxing champion, and of the furor that his dominance over white boxers, his outspokenness, and his relationships with white women generated in early 20th-century America. The movie opens with white boxing promoters persuading a former white champion (James Bradley) to come out of retirement to battle the black champion, here called Jack Jefferson (rather than Johnson). In a subsequent scene, Jefferson destroys Bradley in the ring and reacts with defiant cheeriness to the boos and racial epithets that rain down upon him from the predominantly white crowd.

Jefferson refuses to accept any of the limitations that white society placed on black men at the time. He is neither submissive nor deferential toward whites, and he openly dates white women. One evening, federal agents burst in on Jefferson and his white lover, Eleanor Backman (Jane Alexander), and accuse Jefferson of violating the Mann Act, a 1910 law that made it illegal to transport women across state lines for sexual purposes (see page 635). At Jefferson's trial, prosecutors expected to convince a jury that Backman was coerced into sex, for no white woman, they intended to argue, would have freely chosen to consort with a black man in this way.

Jefferson manages to evade the authorities and flee to Europe, where Backman joins him. The early months abroad are invigorating for both, as Jefferson is celebrated for his fighting prowess and the couple's love for each other flourishes. Soon, however, the opponents dry up, money stops coming in, and a sense of despair grows between the two lovers. Their exile ends disastrously in Mexico, where Backman kills herself after an argument with Jefferson. Jefferson, his spirit finally broken, agrees to throw a fight against the newest Great White Hope, Jess Willard, in

second decade of the 20th century, eloquent spokeswomen had emerged to make the case for full female freedom and equality. The author Charlotte Perkins Gilman called for the release of women from domestic chores through the collectivization of housekeeping. Social activist Margaret Sanger insisted, in her lectures on birth control, that women should be free to enjoy sexual relations without having to worry about unwanted motherhood. The anarchist Emma Goldman denounced marriage as a kind of prostitution and embraced the ideal of "free love"—love unburdened by contractual commitment. Alice Paul, founder of the National Women's Party, brought a new militancy to the campaign for woman suffrage (see chapter 21).

These women were among the first to use the term *feminism* to describe their desire for complete equality with men. Some of them came together in Greenwich Village, a community of radical artists and writers in lower Manhattan, where they found a supportive environment in which to express and live by their feminist ideals. Crystal Eastman, a leader of the feminist Greenwich Village group called Heterodoxy, defined the feminist challenge as "how to arrange the world so that women can be human beings, with a chance to exercise their infinitely varied gifts in infinitely varied ways, instead of being destined by the accident of their sex to one field of activity."

The movement for sexual and gender equality aroused considerable anxiety in the more conservative sectors of American society. Parents worried about the promiscuity of their children. Conservatives were certain that the "new women" would transform American cities into dens of iniquity. Vice commissions sprang up in every major city to clamp down on prostitution, drunkenness, and pornography. The campaign for prohibition—a ban on the sale of alcoholic beverages—gathered steam. Movie theater owners were pressured into excluding "indecent" films from their screens. Many believed the lurid tales of international vice lords scouring foreign lands for innocent girls who could be delivered to American brothel owners. This "white slave trade" inspired passage of the 1910 Mann Act, which made the transportation of women across state lines for immoral purposes a federal crime.

return for an opportunity to end his fugitive status and return to the United States.

Made in 1970, the *Great White Hope* was inspired by the brash heavyweight champion of the 1960s, Muhammad Ali. The film is quite faithful to the story of the real Jack Johnson, who dated white women, was arrested for "violating" the Mann Act, fled the country rather than submit to jail, and ultimately lost a heavyweight bout to Jess Willard. The film endows Backman, a fictional character, with more "class" and refinement than the real women who associated with Johnson usually possessed. The film also fictionalizes Johnson's fight against Willard by suggesting that Johnson could have won the fight had he not been required to throw it. Despite these changes, the film successfully re-creates the climate of the early years of the 20th century and the white hostility imperiling a black man who dared to assert his pride and independence.

James Earl Jones as Jack Jefferson.

MARGARET SANGER ON TRIAL, 1916

Feminist Margaret Sanger, left, was put on trial for using the U.S. mail service to circulate her book *The Woman Rebel,* which advocated birth control. A federal law barred the use of the mails to spread birth control advice or techniques.

© Bettmann/Corbis.

Nor did it escape the attention of conservatives that Greenwich Village was home not only to the dangerous exponents of "free love" but also to equally dangerous advocates of class warfare. Prominent IWW organizer Elizabeth Gurley Flynn was a member of Heterodoxy; her lover, Carlo Tresca, was an IWW theoretician. "Big Bill" Haywood also frequented Greenwich Village, where he was lionized as a working-class hero. When Greenwich Village radicals began publishing an avant-garde artistic journal in 1914, they called it *The Masses;* its editor was Max Eastman, the brother of Crystal. This convergence of labor and feminist militancy intensified conservative feeling that the nation had strayed too far from its roots.

Cultural conservatism was strongest in those areas of the country that were least involved in the ongoing industrial and sexual revolutions—in farming communities and small towns; in the South, where industrialization and urbanization were proceeding at a slower rate than elsewhere; and among old social elites, who felt pushed aside by the new corporate men of power.

Conservatives and radicals alike shared a conviction that the country could not afford to ignore its social problems—the power of the corporations; the poverty and powerlessness of wage earners; the role of women and African Americans. Conservatives were as determined to restore 19th-century moral standards as radicals were determined to achieve working-class emancipation and women's equality. But in politics, neither would become the dominant force. That role would fall to the so-called progressives, a diverse group of reformers who confidently and optimistically believed they could bring order and justice to the new society.

Conclusion

Between 1890 and 1920, corporate power, innovation, and demands had stimulated the growth of cities, attracted millions of immigrants, enhanced commercial opportunities, and created the conditions for a vibrant urban culture. Many Americans thrived in this new environment, taking advantage of business opportunities or, as in the case of women, discovering liberties in dress, employment, dating, and sex that they had not known. Millions of Americans, however, remained impoverished, unable to rise in the social order or to earn enough in wages to support their families. African Americans who had migrated to the North in search of economic opportunity suffered more than any other single group, as they found themselves shut out of most industrial and commercial employment.

Henry Ford, whose generous $5-per-day wage drew tens of thousands to his Detroit factories, was an exceptional employer. Although other employers had learned to restrain their crass displays of wealth and had turned toward philanthropy in search of a better public image, they remained reluctant to follow Ford's lead in improving the conditions in which their employees labored.

Working-class Americans proved resourceful in creating self-help institutions to serve their own and each other's needs. In some cities, they gained a measure of power through the establishment of political machines. Labor unions arose and fought for a variety of reforms, but their success was limited. How to inject greater equality and opportunity into an industrial society in which the gap between rich and poor had reached alarming proportions remained a daunting challenge.

SUGGESTED READINGS

For a general overview of the period, see **Alan Dawley, *Struggles for Justice: Social Responsibility and the Liberal State*** (1991), and **Nell Irvin Painter, *Standing at Armageddon: The United States, 1877–1919*** (1987). On economic growth and corporate development, see **Harold G. Vatter, *The Drive to Industrial Maturity: The United States Economy, 1860–1914*** (1975), **Glenn Porter, *The Rise of Big Business, 1860–1910*** (1973), and **Robert Kanigel, *The One Best Way: Frederick Winslow Taylor and the Enigma of Efficiency*** (1997). For a discussion of Ford's labor policies and their impact on immigrant workers, see **Stephen Meyer III, *The Five Dollar Day: Labor Management and Social Control in the Ford Motor Company, 1908–1921*** (1981). On the influence of Darwinist thinking on American culture, see **Robert Bannister, *Social Darwinism: Science and Myth in Anglo-American Social Thought*** (1970). For an excellent overview concerning immigration, consult **Roger Daniels, *Coming to America: A History of Immigration and Ethnicity in American Life*** (2002). The best single-volume history of European immigrants is **John Bodnar, *The Transplanted: A History of Immigration*** (1985). For an innovative account of European immigrants' encounters with racial patterns in the United States, see **Matthew Frye Jacobson, *Whiteness of a Different Color: European Americans and the Alchemy of Race*** (1998). The experience of Chinese immigrants during the period of American exclusion is discussed in **Erika Lee, *At America's Gates: Chinese Immigration During the Exclusion Era, 1882–1943*** (2003), while **Steven P. Erie, *Rainbow's End: Irish Americans and the Dilemmas of Urban Machine Politics 1840–1945*** (1988), insightfully examines the benefits and costs of big city machines. **David Montgomery, *The Fall of the House of Labor, 1865–1925*** (1987), and **Herbert Gutman, *Work, Culture, and Society in Industrializing America*** (1976), are essential sources on both immigrant and nonimmigrant labor during this period. **John Hope Franklin and Alfred A. Moss Jr., *From Slavery to Freedom: A History of Negro Americans,*** 8th ed. (2000) offers a comprehensive account of African American life, while an important account of black female workers can be found in **Jacqueline Jones, *Labor of Love Labor of Sorrow: Black Women, Work and the Family from Slavery to the Present*** (1985). On the rise of mass culture, see **David Nasaw, *Going Out: The Rise and Fall of Public Amusements*** (1993), and **Warren I. Susman, *Culture as History: the Transformation of American Society in the Twentieth Century*** (1984). On the new woman and feminism, consult **Nancy F. Cott, *The Grounding of Modern Feminism*** (1987), and **Christine Stansell, *American Moderns: Bohemian New York and the Creation of a New Century*** (2000).

AMERICAN JOURNEY ONLINE AND INFOTRAC COLLEGE EDITION

Visit the source collections at www.ajaccess.wadsworth.com and infotrac.thomsonlearning.com and use the Search function with the following key terms to explore documents, images, audio and video clips, articles, and commentary related to the material in this chapter.

Sherman Antitrust Act	Andrew Carnegie
Alice Paul	Frederick W. Taylor
"Big Bill" Haywood	doctrine of separate spheres
J. P. Morgan	Triangle Shirtwaist Company

GRADE AIDS

Visit the Liberty Equality Power Companion Web Site for resources specific to this textbook: http://history.wadsworth.com/murrin_LEP4e

The CD in the back of this book and the U.S. History Resource Center at http://history.wadsworth.com/u.s./ offer a variety of tools to help you succeed in this course, including access to quizzes; images; documents; interactive simulations; maps, and timelines; movie explorations; and a wealth of other sources.

Chapter 21

Progressivism

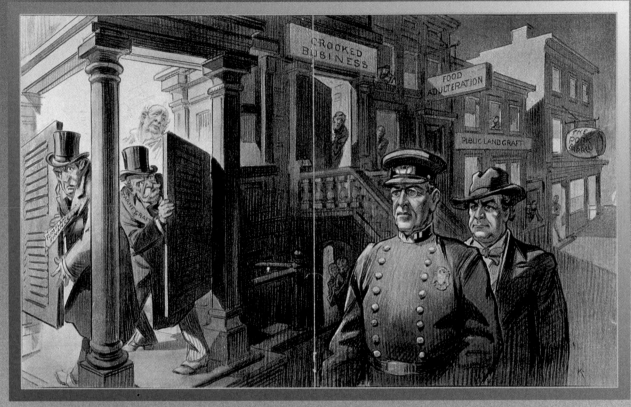

Culver Pictures.

"A NEW CAPTAIN IN THE DISTRICT"
This cartoon depicts newly elected President Woodrow Wilson as a police captain who is determined to clean up Washington politics and regulate "crooked business." It illustrates a key belief shared by Wilson, Theodore Roosevelt, and most other progressives: that an activist government was society's best hope for solving the nation's political and economic problems.

CHAPTER OUTLINE

Progressivism was a reform movement that took its name from individuals who left the Republican Party in 1912 to join Theodore Roosevelt's new party, the Progressive Party. The term *progressive*, however, refers to a much larger and more varied group of reformers than those who gathered around Roosevelt in 1912.

As early as 1900, these reformers had set out to cleanse and reinvigorate an America whose politics and society they considered in decline. Progressives wanted to rid politics of corruption, tame the power of the "trusts," and, in the process, inject more liberty into American life. They fought against prostitution, gambling, drinking, and other forms of vice. They first appeared in municipal politics, organizing movements to oust crooked mayors and to break up local gas or streetcar monopolies. They carried their fights to the states and finally to the nation. Two presidents, Theodore Roosevelt and Woodrow Wilson, placed themselves at the head of this movement.

Progressivism was popular among a variety of groups who brought to the movement distinct, and often conflicting, aims. On one issue, however, most progressives agreed: the need for an activist government to right political, economic, and social wrongs. Some progressives wanted government to become active only long enough to clean up the political process, root out vice, upgrade the electorate, and break up trusts. These problems were so difficult to solve that many other progressives endorsed the notion of a permanently active government—with the power to tax income, regulate industry, protect consumers from fraud, empower workers, safeguard the environment, and provide social welfare. Many progressives, in other words, came to see the federal government as the institution best equipped to solve social problems.

Such positive attitudes toward government power marked an important change in American politics. Americans had long been suspicious of centralized government, viewing it as the enemy of liberty. The Populists had broken with that view (see chapter 19), but they had been defeated. The progressives had to build a new case for strong government as the protector of liberty and equality.

CHAPTER FOCUS

♦ What was progressivism, and which groups spearheaded the movement?

♦ What, in your opinion, were the three most important Progressive Era reforms? Be prepared to defend your choices.

♦ What was disenfranchisement and can it be considered a progressive reform?

♦ What were the key similarities and differences in the progressive politics of Theodore Roosevelt and Woodrow Wilson?

Progressivism and the Protestant Spirit

Progressivism emerged first and most strongly among young, mainly Protestant, middle-class Americans who felt alienated from their society. Many had been raised in devout Protestant homes in which religious conviction had often been a spur to social action. They were expected to become ministers or missionaries or to serve their church in some other way. They had abandoned this path, but they never lost their zeal for righting moral wrongs and for uplifting the human spirit. They were distressed by the immorality and corruption in American politics and by the gap that separated rich from poor. They became, in the words of one historian, "ministers of reform."

CHRONOLOGY

1889	Hull House established
1890–1904	All ex-Confederate states pass laws designed to disenfranchise black voters • Virtually all states adopt the Australian (secret) ballot
1900	La Follette elected governor of Wisconsin • City commission plan introduced in Galveston, Texas
1901–14	More than 1,000 African Americans lynched
1901	Johnson elected reform mayor of Cleveland • McKinley assassinated; Roosevelt becomes president
1902	Direct primary introduced in Mississippi • Initiative and referendum introduced in Oregon • Roosevelt sides with workers in coal strike
1903	*McClure's Magazine* publishes Standard Oil exposé • Federal court dissolves Northern Security Company
1904	Roosevelt defeats Alton B. Parker for presidency
1905	National Forest Service established
1906	La Follette elected to U.S. Senate • Congress passes Hepburn Act • Upton Sinclair publishes *The Jungle* • Congress passes Pure Food and Drug Act and Meat Inspection Act
1907	Reformer Hughes elected New York governor • Financial panic shakes economy
1908	Taft defeats Bryan for presidency
1909	Congress passes Payne-Aldrich tariff bill
1910	Ballinger-Pinchot controversy • NAACP founded • Wilson elected governor of New Jersey
1911	National Urban League founded • City manager plan introduced in Sumter, South Carolina • Wisconsin Industrial Commission established
1912	Roosevelt forms Progressive Party • Wilson defeats Roosevelt, Taft, and Debs for presidency
1913	16th and 17th Amendments ratified • Congress passes Underwood-Simmons Tariff • Congress establishes Federal Reserve system
1914	Congress establishes Federal Trade Commission • Congress passes Clayton Antitrust Act
1916	Louis Brandeis appointed to Supreme Court • Kern-McGillicuddy Act, Keating-Owen Act, and Adamson Act passed • National Park Service formed • National Women's Party founded
1919	18th Amendment ratified
1920	19th Amendment ratified

Other Protestant reformers retained their faith. This was true of William Jennings Bryan, the former Populist leader who became an ardent progressive and evangelical. Throughout his political career, Bryan always insisted that Christian piety and American democracy were integrally related. Billy Sunday, a former major league baseball player who became the most theatrical evangelical preacher of his day, elevated opposition to saloons and the "liquor trust" into a righteous crusade. And Walter Rauschenbusch led a movement known as the Social Gospel, which emphasized the duty of Christians to work for the social good.

Protestants, of course, formed a large and diverse population, sizable sections of which showed little interest in reform. Thus it is important to identify smaller and more cohesive groups of reformers. Of the many that arose, three were of particular importance, especially in the early years: investigative journalists, who were called "muckrakers"; the founders and supporters of settlement houses; and socialists.

Muckrakers, Magazines, and the Turn toward "Realism"

The term *muckraker* was coined by Theodore Roosevelt, who had intended it as a criticism of newspaper and magazine reporters who, for no purpose other than monetary reward, wrote stories about scandalous situations. But the label became a badge of honor among journalists who were committed to exposing the repugnant aspects of American life. During the first decade of the 20th century, they presented the public with one startling revelation after another. Ida Tarbell revealed the shady practices by which John D. Rockefeller had transformed his Standard Oil Company into a monopoly. Lincoln Steffens unraveled the webs of bribery and corruption that were strangling local governments in the nation's cities. George Kibbe Turner documented the extent of prostitution and family disintegration in the ethnic ghettos of those cities. These muckrakers wanted to shock the public into recognizing the shameful state of political, economic, and social affairs and to prompt "the people" to take action.

The tradition of investigative journalism reached back at least to the 1870s, when newspaper and magazine writers exposed the corrupt practices of New York City's Boss Tweed and his Tammany Hall machine. The 20th-century rise of the muckrakers reflected two factors, one economic—expanded newspaper and magazine circulation—and the other intellectual—increased interest in "realism." Together they transformed investigative reporting into something of national importance.

Increased Newspaper and Magazine Circulation

From 1870 to 1909, daily newspapers rose in number from 574 to 2,600, and their circulation increased from less than 3 million to more than 24 million. During the first decade of the 20th century, the magazine revolution of

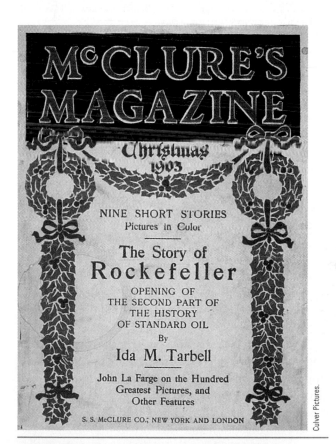

Culver Pictures.

PIONEERING INVESTIGATIVE JOURNALISM

This Christmas 1903 issue of *McClure's Magazine* featured the second part of Ida Tarbell's exposé of John D. Rockefeller's business practices. Tarbell's revelations were regarded as sensational, and they convinced many middle-class Americans of the need for economic and political reform.

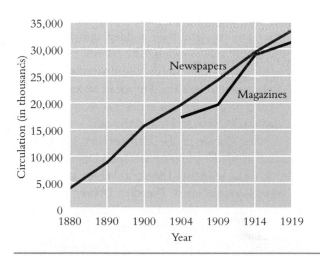

CIRCULATION OF DAILY NEWSPAPERS AND MAGAZINES, 1880–1919

Source: Data from *Historical Statistics of the United States, Colonial Times to 1970* (White Plains, N.Y.: Kraus International, 1989).

the 1880s and 1890s (see chapter 19) accelerated. Cheap, 10-cent periodicals such as *McClure's Magazine* and *Ladies Home Journal,* with circulations of 400,000 to 1 million, began to displace genteel and relatively expensive 35-cent publications such as *Harper's* and *The Atlantic Monthly.* The expanded readership brought journalists considerably more money and prestige and attracted many talented and ambitious men and women to the profession. Wider circulation also made magazine publishers more receptive to stories—particularly sensational ones about ill-gotten economic power, government corruption, and urban vice—that might appeal to their newly acquired millions of readers.

The Turn toward "Realism"

The American middle class's growing intellectual interest in "realism" also favored the muckrakers. "Realism" was a way of thinking that prized detachment, objectivity, and skepticism. Those who embraced it pointed out that constitutional theory, with its emphasis on citizenship, elections, and democratic procedures, had little to do with the way government in the United States actually worked. What could one learn about bosses, machines, and graft from studying the Constitution? There was also a sense that the nation's glorification of the "self-made man" and of "individualism" was preventing Americans from coping effectively with large-scale organizations—corporations, banks, labor unions—and their sudden centrality to the nation's economy and to society. The realists, finally, criticized the tendency, which was prevalent among American writers and artists, to emulate European styles, and they called on them to pioneer new styles that would be better able to "capture" American life and thought.

By the first decade of the 20th century, intellectuals and artists of all sorts—philosophers John Dewey and William James; social scientists Thorstein Veblen and Charles Beard; novelists Frank Norris, Theodore Dreiser, and Upton Sinclair; painters John Sloan, George Bellows, and other members of the "Ashcan School"; photographers Jacob Riis and Lewis Hine; architects Louis Sullivan and Frank Lloyd Wright; jurists Oliver Wendell Holmes and Louis Brandeis—were attempting to create truer, more realistic

George Bellows. "Cliff Dwellers" 1913. Oil on canvas. Los Angeles County Museum of Art, Los Angeles County Fund.

CLIFF DWELLERS

George Bellows was a member of the Ashcan School, a group of painters who sought to create a distinctly American and "realist" style. Here Bellows portrays the urban masses sympathetically and in a way that evokes their connection to a group of quintessential Americans, the cliff-dwelling Pueblo Indians.

ways of representing and analyzing American society. Many of them were inspired by the work of investigative journalists, and some had been newspapermen. Years of firsthand observation enabled them to describe American society as it "truly was." They brought shadowy figures vividly to life. They pictured for Americans the captain of industry who ruthlessly destroyed his competitors; the con artist who tricked young people new to city life; the innocent immigrant girl who fell prey to the white slave traders; the corrupt policeman under whose protection urban vice flourished.

A large middle class, uneasy about the state of American society, applauded the muckrakers for telling these stories and became interested in reform. Members of this class put pressure on city and state governments to send crooked government officials to jail and to stamp out the sources of corruption and vice. Between 1902 and 1916, more than 100 cities launched investigations of the prostitution trade. At the federal level, all three branches of government felt compelled to address the question of "the trusts"—the concentration of power in the hands of a few industrialists and financiers. Progressivism began to crystallize into a political movement centered on the abuses the muckrakers had exposed.

Settlement Houses and Women's Activism

Established by middle-class reformers, settlement houses were intended to help the largely immigrant urban poor cope with the harsh conditions of city life. Much of the inspiration for settlement houses came from young, college-educated, Protestant women from comfortable but not particularly wealthy backgrounds. Some had imbibed a commitment to social justice from parents and grandparents who had fought to abolish slavery. Highly educated, talented, and sensitive to social injustice, they rebelled against being relegated solely to the roles of wife and mother and sought to assert their independence in socially useful ways.

Hull House

Jane Addams and Ellen Gates Starr established the nation's first settlement house, in Chicago, in 1889. The two women had been inspired by a visit the year before to London's Toynbee Hall, where a small group of middle-class men had been living and working with that city's poor since 1884. Addams and Starr bought a decaying mansion that had once been the country home of a prominent Chicagoan, Charles J. Hull. By 1889, "Hull House" stood amidst factories, churches, saloons, and tenements inhabited by poor, largely foreign-born working-class families.

Addams quickly emerged as the guiding spirit of Hull House. She moved into the building and demanded that

Brown Brothers.

JANE ADDAMS

The founder of the settlement house movement, Addams was the most famous woman reformer of the progressive era. This photograph dates from the 1890s or 1900s, Hull House's formative period.

WOMEN ENROLLED IN INSTITUTIONS OF HIGHER EDUCATION, 1870–1930

Year	Women's Colleges (thousands of students)	Coed Institutions (thousands of students)	Total (thousands of students)	Percentage of All Students Enrolled
1870	6.5	4.6	11.1	21.0%
1880	15.7	23.9	39.6	33.4
1890	16.8	39.5	56.3	35.9
1900	24.4	61.0	85.4	36.8
1910	34.1	106.5	140.6	39.6
1920	52.9	230.0	282.9	47.3
1930	82.1	398.7	480.8	43.7

Source: From Mabel Newcomer, *A Century of Higher Education for American Women* (New York: Harper and Row, 1959), p. 46.

all who worked there do the same. She and Starr enlisted extraordinary women such as Florence Kelley, Alice Hamilton, and Julia Lathrop. They set up a nursery for the children of working mothers, a penny savings bank, and an employment bureau, soon followed by a baby clinic, a neighborhood playground, and social clubs. Determined to minister to cultural as well as economic needs, Hull House sponsored an orchestra, reading groups, and a lecture series. Members of Chicago's widening circle of reform-minded intellectuals, artists, and politicians contributed their energies to the enterprise. John Dewey taught philosophy and Frank Lloyd Wright lectured on architecture. Clarence Darrow, the workingman's lawyer, and Henry Demarest Lloyd, Chicago's radical muckraker, spent considerable time at Hull House. In 1893, Illinois Governor John P. Altgeld named Hull House worker Florence Kelley as the state's chief factory inspector. Her investigations led to Illinois's first factory law, which prohibited child labor, limited the employment of women to eight hours a day, and authorized the state to hire inspectors to enforce the law.

The Hull House activists seemed to have unlimited energy, imagination, and commitment. Julia Lathrop used her appointment to the State Board of Charities to agitate for improvements in the care of the poor, the handicapped, and the delinquent. With Edith Abbott and Sophonisba Breckinridge, she established the Department of Social Research at the University of Chicago (which would evolve into the nation's first school of social work). Alice Hamilton, who had overcome gender discrimination to become a doctor, pioneered in the field of public health.

The Hull House leaders did not command the instant fame accorded the muckrakers. Nevertheless, they were steadily drawn into the public arena. Thousands of women across the country were inspired to build their own settlement houses on the Hull House model (eventually more than 400 settlement houses would open nationwide). By 1910, Jane Addams had become one of the nation's most famous women. She and other settlement house workers played a critical role in fashioning the progressive agenda and in drafting pieces of progressive legislation.

The Cultural Conservatism of Progressive Reformers

In general, settlement house workers were more sympathetic toward the poor, the illiterate, and the downtrodden than the muckrakers were. Although she disapproved of machine politics, Jane Addams saw firsthand the benefits machine politicians delivered to their constituents. She respected the cultural inheritance of the immigrants and admired their resourcefulness. Although she wanted them to become Americans, she encouraged them to integrate their "immigrant gifts" into their new identities. Those attitudes were more liberal than those of other reformers, who considered many immigrants to be culturally, even racially, inferior.

But there were limits even to Addams's sympathy for the immigrants. In particular, she disapproved of the new working-class entertainments that gave adolescents extensive and unregulated opportunities for intimate association. She was also troubled by the emerging sexual revolution (see chapter 20). Addams tended to equate female sexuality with prostitution, and she joined many other women reformers in a campaign to suppress both. Addams and others had identified a serious problem in American cities, where significant numbers of immigrant and rural women new to urban life were lured into prostitution or chose it as a job preferable to 65 poorly paid hours per week in a sweatshop.

The reformers' zeal on this matter, however, exaggerated the dimensions of the problem and led to some questionable legislation, such as the Mann Act (1910), which made it illegal to transport a woman across state lines "for immoral purposes." If this law permitted the prosecution of true traffickers in women, it also allowed the government to interfere in the private sexual relations of consenting adults. This is what happened in the case of Jack Johnson, the African American heavyweight champion, who was arrested and convicted for "transporting" his white secretary, Lucy Cameron, across state lines (see History through Film, chapter 20). That Johnson's and Cameron's relationship was consensual and would culminate in marriage did not deter the authorities, who wanted to punish Johnson for his dominance of white boxers and his relationship with a white woman.

The cultural conservatism evident in the attitudes of Jane Addams and others on female sexuality also emerged in their attitudes toward alcohol. Drinking rivaled prostitution as a problem in poor, working-class areas. Many men wasted their hard-earned money on drinks at the local saloon, a drain on meager family resources that created tension between these men and their wives. Domestic fights and family violence sometimes ensued. Settlement house workers were well aware of the ill effects of alcoholism (250 saloons did business in Chicago's 19th Ward alone) and sought to combat it. They called on working people to refrain from drink and pushed legislation that would shut down the saloons. The progressives joined forces with the Women's Christian Temperance Union (245,000 members strong by 1911) and the Anti-Saloon League. By 1916, through their collective efforts, these groups had won prohibition of the sale and manufacture of alcoholic beverages in 16 states. In 1919, their

Florence Kelley: A European-Inspired Search of Social Justice

Between 1890 and 1910, Florence Kelley became one of America's most famous progressives, an indefatigable advocate of the rights of American workers in general and of women workers and child laborers in particular. Some of her crusading zeal came from her family. Her aunt had been a Quaker abolitionist, her father a pro-labor U.S. congressman. But the time that Kelley spent in France, England, and Switzerland in the 1880s was equally important to her political development.

In the late 19th century, touring Europe had become a rite of passage for many upwardly mobile Americans. Most of those who went simply wanted to acquire culture and refinement (see the Americans Abroad feature for chapter 19). But a significant minority found in these trips an opportunity to acquire the kind of high-quality university education and strategies for social and political transformation not easily accessible to them in the United States. Ambitious and talented women were well represented in this minority. Encouraged by their parents to be intellectually adventurous, these women discovered, upon graduation from their American colleges, that they were expected to put their intellectual and occupational goals aside and to settle into the customary female roles of wife and mother.

Florence Kelley was one of those who found in European travel an escape from this future. On a trip to France in 1882, Kelley learned that the University of Zurich, almost alone among the world's universities, was willing to grant women advanced degrees. Before enrolling, Kelley, with her father, toured areas of England devastated by industrialization. At Zurich, Kelley settled in to a thriving university community that drew its students from everywhere on the continent. No issue concerned students more than the inequalities caused by capitalism; no solution attracted more attention than socialism. Students debated the politics of socialism in their classes, in Zurich's cafés, and in long walks through the city's streets. Kelley found these intense political discussions exhilarating, and she became a socialist, immersing herself in the works of Karl Marx, Friedrichs Engels, and other socialist theoreticians. She even merged socialism and romance by marrying Lazare Wischnewetzky, a fellow student and socialist refugee from Russia.

Kelley returned to the United States with her husband convinced that nothing less than the replacement of capitalism with socialism would suffice. This would never be an easy campaign in the United States, in part because Kelley did not like the strategies of the American socialists (she was thrown out of the Socialist Labor Party in 1887) and in part because so many American workers were hostile to any kind of socialist ideals. Thus, Kelley had to adjust her radical European ideas to fit the more conservative American political environment in which she was operating. Nevertheless, her time in Europe provided her with a lifetime of inspiration and helped to make her one of America's leading advocates for working-class rights.

Florence Kelley (pregnant) with her husband, Lazare Wischnewetzky, in Europe, ca. 1885.

crowning achievement was the 18th Amendment to the U.S. Constitution, making prohibition the law of the land (see chapter 23).

In depicting alcohol and saloons as unmitigated evils, however, the prohibition movement ignored the role saloons played in ethnic, working-class communities. On Chicago's South Side, for example, saloons provided tens of thousands of workers with the only decent place to eat lunch. The meatpacking plants where they labored had no cafeterias, and few workers could stomach eating their lunch where animals were slaughtered, dressed, and packed. Some saloons catered to particular ethnic groups: They served traditional foods and drinks, provided meeting space for fraternal organizations, and offered camaraderie to men longing to speak in their native tongue. Saloon-keepers sometimes functioned as informal bankers, cashing checks and making small loans. Not surprisingly, many immigrants shunned the prohibition movement. They had no interest in being "uplifted" and "reformed" in this way. Here was a gulf separating the immigrant masses from the Protestant middle class that even compassionate reformers such as Jane Addams could not bridge.

A Nation of Clubwomen

Settlement house workers comprised only one part of a vast network of female reformers. Hundreds of thousands of women belonged to local women's clubs. Conceived as self-help organizations in which women would be encouraged to sharpen their minds, refine their domestic skills, and strengthen their moral faculties, these clubs began taking on tasks of social reform. Clubwomen typically focused their energies on improving schools, building libraries and playgrounds, expanding educational and vocational opportunities for girls, and securing fire and sanitation codes for tenement houses. In so doing, they made traditional female concerns—the nurturing and education of children, the care of the home—questions of public policy.

Clubwomen rose to prominence in black communities, too, and addressed similar sorts of issues; on matters of sexuality and alcohol, they often shared the conservative sentiments of their white counterparts. Some groups of black clubwomen ventured into community affairs more boldly than their white counterparts, however, especially in southern states, where black men were being stripped of the right to vote, to serve on juries, and to hold political office. Whites were prepared to punish any African American, male or female, who showed too much initiative or was thought to be challenging the principles of white supremacy. Even so, many black female activists persevered in the face of such threats, determined to provide leadership in their communities and voice their people's concerns.

☙ Socialism and Progressivism

Issues such as women's sexuality and men's alcoholism drew progressives in a conservative direction, but other issues drew them to socialism. In the early 20th century, socialism stood for the transfer of control over industry from a few industrialists to the laboring masses. Socialists believed that such a transfer, usually defined in terms of government ownership and operation of economic institutions, would make it impossible for wealthy elites to control society.

The Socialist Party of America, founded in 1901, became a political force during the first 16 years of the century, and socialist ideas influenced progressivism. In 1912, at the peak of its influence, the Socialist Party enrolled more than 115,000 members. Its presidential candidate, the charismatic Eugene Victor Debs of Terre Haute, Indiana, attracted almost a million votes—6 percent of the total votes cast that year. In that same year, 1,200 Socialists held elective office in 340 different municipalities. Of these, 79 were mayors of cities as geographically and demographically diverse as Schenectady, New York; Milwaukee, Wisconsin; Butte, Montana; and Berkeley, California. More than 300 newspapers and periodicals, with a combined circulation exceeding 2 million, spread the socialist gospel. The most important socialist publication was *Appeal to Reason,* published by Kansan Julius Wayland and sent out each week to 750,000 subscribers. In 1905, Wayland published, in serial form, a novel by an obscure muckraker named Upton Sinclair, which depicted the scandalous working conditions in Chicago's meatpacking industry. When it was later published in book form in 1906, *The Jungle* created such an outcry that the federal government was forced to regulate the meat industry.

The Many Faces of Socialism

Socialists came in many varieties. In Milwaukee, they consisted of predominantly German working-class immigrants and their descendants; in New York City, their numbers were strongest among Jewish immigrants from Eastern Europe. In the Southwest, tens of thousands of disgruntled native-born farmers who had been Populists in the 1890s now flocked to the socialist banner. In Oklahoma alone, these erstwhile Populists were numerous enough by 1912 to support 11 socialist weeklies. In that same year, Oklahoma voters gave a higher percentage of their votes, more than 16 percent, to the Socialist candidate Debs than did the voters of any other state. In the West, socialism was popular among miners, timber cutters, and others who labored in isolated areas where industrialists possessed extraordinary power over work and community matters. These radicals gravitated to the militant labor union, the Industrial Workers of the World (IWW) (see chapter 20), which found a home in the Socialist Party from 1905 to 1913.

Socialists differed from each other not only in their occupations and ethnic origins but also in their politics. The IWW was the most radical socialist group, with its

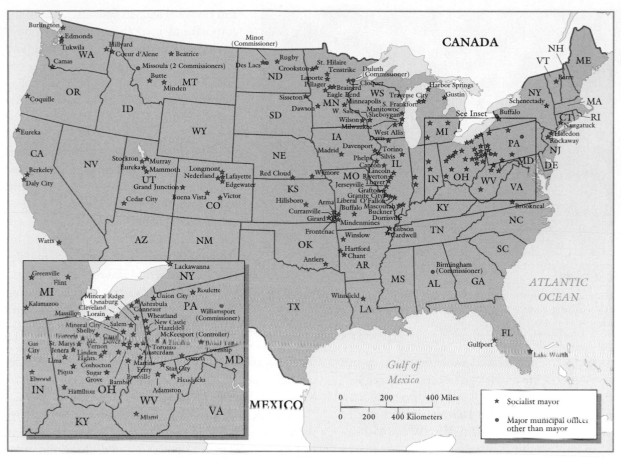

MAP 21.1   CITIES AND TOWNS ELECTING SOCIALIST MAYORS OR OTHER MAJOR MUNICIPAL OFFICERS, 1911–1920
This map reveals the strength of socialist electoral support in some unexpected areas: western Pennsylvania, Ohio, Illinois, Minnesota, a cluster of towns where Oklahoma, Missouri, and Kansas meet, Colorado, and Utah.

incessant calls for revolution. By contrast, mainstream socialism, as articulated by Debs, was more respectful of American political, cultural, and religious traditions. Mainstream socialists saw themselves as the saviors rather than the destroyers of the American republic—as the true heirs of Thomas Jefferson. Their confidence that the nation could be redeemed through conventional politics—through the election of Debs as president—is evidence of their affection for American democracy. And their faith in redemption reveals the degree to which Protestant religious beliefs underlay their quest for social justice and what they called a "cooperative commonwealth." Evolutionary socialists, led by Victor Berger of Milwaukee, abandoned talk of revolution altogether and chose instead an aggressive brand of reform politics. They were dubbed "gas and water socialists" because of their interest in improving city services.

These differences would, after 1912, fragment the socialist movement. For a decade or so, however, all of these divergent groups managed to coexist in a single political party thanks, largely, to the leadership of Debs.

When he was released from a Chicago jail in 1895 after serving time for his role in the strike against the Pullman Company (see chapter 19), Debs declared to a gathering of 100,000 admirers: "Manifestly the spirit of '76 still survives. The fires of liberty and noble aspirations are not yet extinguished. . . . The vindication and glorification of American principles of government, as proclaimed to the world in the Declaration of Independence, is the high purpose of this convocation."

Socialists and Progressives

Debs's speeches both attracted and disturbed progressives. On the one hand, he spoke compellingly about the dangers of unregulated capitalism and excessively concentrated wealth, both progressive concerns. His confidence that a strong state could bring the economic system under control mirrored the progressives' own faith in the positive uses of government. Progressives often worked hand-in-hand with socialists to win economic and political reforms, especially at the municipal and state levels, and

EUGENE V. DEBS

This photograph captures something of the energy and charisma of Debs as he addresses a working-class audience in New York during his 1912 presidential campaign.

many intellectuals and reformers easily moved back and forth between socialism and progressivism. Florence Kelley, Hull House reformer and Illinois factory inspector, was one such person; Clarence Darrow, a Chicago trial lawyer who successfully defended the IWW's William Haywood in 1907 against charges that he had murdered a former Idaho governor, was another. Walter Lippmann, who would become a close adviser to President Wilson during the First World War, began his political career in 1912 as an assistant to the Socialist mayor of Schenectady. Several of the era's most prominent intellectuals, including John Dewey, Richard Ely, and Thorstein Veblen, also traveled back and forth between the socialist and progressive camps. So did Helen Keller, the country's leading spokesperson for the disabled.

On the other hand, Debs's talk of revolution scared progressives, as did his efforts to organize a working-class political movement independent of middle-class involvement or control. Although progressives wanted to tame capitalism, they stopped short of wanting to eliminate it. They wanted to improve working and living conditions for the masses but not cede political control to them. The progressives hoped to offer a political program with enough socialist elements to counter the appeal of Debs's more radical movement. In this, they were successful.

Municipal Reform

Progressive-era reform battles first erupted over control of municipal transportation networks and utilities. Private corporations typically owned and operated street railways and electrical and gas systems. Many of the corporations used their monopoly power to charge exorbitant fares and rates, and they often won that power by bribing city officials who belonged to one of the political machines. Corporations achieved generous reductions in real estate taxes in the same way.

The attack on private utilities and their protectors in city government gained momentum in the mid-1890s. In Detroit, reform-minded Mayor Hazen S. Pingree led successful fights to control the city's gas, telephone, and trolley companies. In Chicago in 1896 and 1897, a group of middle-class reformers ousted a corrupt city council and elected a mayor, Carter Harrison, Jr., who promised to protect Chicago's streetcar riders from exploitation. In Cleveland, the crusading reformer Tom Johnson won election as mayor in 1901, curbed the power of the streetcar interests, and brought honest and efficient government to the city.

Occasionally, a reform politician of Johnson's caliber would rise to power through one of the regular political parties. But this path to power was a difficult one, especially in cities where the political parties were controlled by machines. Consequently, progressives worked for reforms that would strip the parties of their power. Two of their favorite reforms were the city commission and the city manager forms of government.

The City Commission Plan

First introduced in Galveston, Texas, in 1900, in the wake of a devastating tidal wave, the city commission shifted municipal power from the mayor and his aldermen to five city commissioners, each responsible for a different department of city government. In Galveston and elsewhere, the impetus for this reform came from civic-minded businessmen who were determined to rebuild government on the same principles of efficient and scientific management that had energized the private sector. The results were often impressive. The Galveston commissioners restored the city's credit after a brush with bankruptcy, improved the city's harbor, and built a massive seawall to protect the city from future floods. They accomplished all of this on budgets that had been cut by one-third. In Houston, Texas; Des Moines, Iowa; Dayton, Ohio; Oakland, California; and elsewhere, city commissioners similarly improved urban infrastructures, expanded city ser-

POLITICAL REFORM IN THE STATES ■ **649**

vices, and strengthened the financial health of the cities. Many commissions established publicly owned utilities. By 1913, more than 300 cities, most of them small to middling in size, had adopted the city commission plan.

The City Manager Plan

The city commission system did not always work to perfection, however. Sometimes the commissioners used their position to reward electoral supporters with jobs and contracts; other times, they pursued power and prestige for their respective departments. The city manager plan was meant to overcome such problems. Under this plan, the commissioners continued to set policy, but policy implementation now rested with a "chief executive." This official, who was not elected but appointed by the commissioners, would curtail rivalries among commissioners and ensure that no outside influences interfered with the impartial, businesslike management of the city. The job of city manager was explicitly modeled after that of a corporation executive. First introduced in Sumter, South Carolina, in 1911 and then in Dayton, Ohio, in 1913, by 1919 the city manager plan had spread to 130 cities.

The Costs of Reform

Although these reforms limited corruption and improved services, they were not universally popular. Poor and minority voters, in particular, found that their influence in local affairs was weakened by the shift to city commissioners and city managers. Previously, candidates for municipal office (other than the mayor) competed in ward elections rather than in citywide elections. Voters in working-class wards commonly elected workingmen to represent them, and voters in immigrant wards made sure that fellow ethnics represented their interests on city councils. Citywide elections diluted the strength of these constituencies. Candidates from poor districts often lacked the money needed to mount a citywide campaign, and they were further hampered by the nonpartisan nature of such elections. Denied the support of a political party or platform, they had to make themselves personally known to voters throughout the city. That was a much easier task for the city's "leading citizens"—manufacturers, merchants, and lawyers—than it was for workingmen. In Dayton, the percentage of citizens voting Socialist rose from 25 to 44 percent in the years following the introduction of the commission manager system, while the number of Socialists elected to office declined from five to zero. Progressive political reforms thus frequently had the effect of reducing the influence of radicals, minorities, and the poor in elections.

Political Reform in the States

As at the local level, political parties at the state level were often dominated by corrupt politicians who did the bidding of powerful private lobbies. In New Jersey in 1903, for example, industrial and financial interests, working through the Republican Party machine, controlled numerous appointments to state government, including the chief justice of the state supreme court, the attorney general, and the commissioner of banking and insurance. Such webs of influence ensured that New Jersey would provide large corporations such as the railroads with favorable political and economic legislation.

Restoring Sovereignty to "the People"

Progressives introduced reforms designed to undermine the power of party bosses, restore sovereignty to "the people," and encourage honest, talented individuals to enter politics. One such reform was the direct primary, a mechanism that enabled voters, rather than party bosses, to choose party candidates. Mississippi introduced this reform in 1902 and Wisconsin in 1903. By 1916, all but three states had adopted the direct primary. Closely related was a movement to strip state legislatures of their power to choose U.S. senators. State after state enacted legislation that permitted voters to choose Senate candidates in primary elections. In 1912, a reluctant U.S. Senate was obliged to approve the 17th Amendment to the Constitution, mandating the direct election of senators. The state legislatures ratified this amendment in 1913.

Populists had first proposed direct election of U.S. senators in the 1890s; they also proposed the initiative and the referendum, both of which were adopted first by Oregon in 1902 and then by 18 other states between 1902 and 1915. The initiative allowed reformers to put legislative proposals before voters in general elections without having to wait for state legislatures to act. The referendum gave voters the right in general elections to repeal an unpopular act that a state legislature had passed. Less widely adopted but important nevertheless was the recall, a device that allowed voters to remove from office any public servant who had betrayed his trust. As a further control over the behavior of elected officials, numerous states enacted laws that regulated corporate campaign contributions and restricted lobbying activities in state legislatures.

These laws neither eliminated corporate privilege nor destroyed the power of machine politicians. Nevertheless, they made politics more honest and strengthened the influence of ordinary voters.

Creating a Virtuous Electorate

Progressive reformers focused as well on creating a responsible electorate that understood the importance of the vote and that resisted efforts to manipulate elections. To create this ideal electorate, reformers had to see to it that all of those citizens who were deemed virtuous could cast their votes free of coercion and intimidation. At the same time, reformers sought to disenfranchise citizens who were considered irresponsible and corruptible. In pursuing these goals, progressives substantially altered the composition of the electorate and strengthened government regulation of voting. The results were contradictory. On the one hand, progressives enlarged the electorate by extending the right to vote to women; on the other hand, they either initiated or tolerated laws that barred large numbers of minority and poor voters from the polls.

The Australian Ballot

Government regulation of voting had begun in the 1890s when virtually every state adopted the Australian, or secret, ballot. This reform required voters to vote in private rather than in public. It also required the government, rather than political parties, to print the ballots and supervise the voting. Before this time, each political party had printed its own ballot with only its candidates listed. At election time, each party mobilized its loyal supporters. Party workers offered liquor, free meals, and other bribes to entice voters to the polls and to "persuade" them to cast the party ballot. Because the ballots were cast in public, few voters who had accepted gifts of liquor and food dared to cross watchful party officials. Critics argued that the system corrupted the electoral process. They also pointed out that it made "ticketsplitting"—dividing one's vote between candidates of two or more parties—virtually impossible.

The Australian ballot solved these problems. Although it predated progressivism, it embodied the progressives' determination to use government power to encourage citizens to cast their votes responsibly and wisely.

Personal Registration Laws

That same determination was apparent in the progressives' support for the personal registration laws that virtually every state passed between 1890 and 1920. These laws allowed prospective voters to register to vote only if they appeared at a designated government office with proper identification. Frequently, these laws also mandated a certain period of residence in the state before registration and a certain interval between registration and actual voting.

Personal registration laws were meant to disenfranchise citizens who showed no interest in voting until election day, when a party worker arrived with a few dollars and offered a free ride to the polls. However, they also excluded many hardworking, responsible, poor people who wanted to vote but had failed to register, either because their work schedules made it impossible or because they were intimidated by the complex regulations. The laws were particularly frustrating for immigrants with limited knowledge of American government and of the English language.

Disenfranchisement

Progressives also promoted election laws expressly designed to keep noncitizen immigrants from voting. In the 1880s, 18 states had passed laws allowing immigrants to vote without first becoming citizens. Progressives reversed this trend. At the same time, the newly formed Bureau of Immigration and Naturalization (1906) made it more difficult to become a citizen. Applicants for citizenship now had to appear before a judge who interrogated them, in the English language, on American history and civics. In addition, immigrants were required to provide two witnesses to vouch for their "moral character" and their "attachment to the principles of the Constitution." Finally, immigrants had to swear (and, if necessary, prove) that they were not anarchists or polygamists and that they had resided continuously in the United States for five years.

Most progressives defended the new rigor of the process. U.S. citizenship, they believed, carried responsibilities; it was not to be bestowed lightly. This position was understandable, given the electoral abuses progressives had exposed. Nevertheless, the reforms also had the effect of denying the vote to a large proportion of the population. In cities and towns where immigrants dominated the workforce, the numbers of registered voters fell steeply. Nowhere was exclusion more startling than in the South, where between 1890 and 1904 every ex-Confederate state passed laws designed to strip blacks of their right to vote. Because laws explicitly barring blacks from voting would have violated the Fifteenth Amendment, this exclusion had to be accomplished indirectly—through literacy tests, property qualifications, and poll taxes mandated by the legislatures of the ex-Confederate states. Any citizen who failed a reading test, or who could not sign his name, or

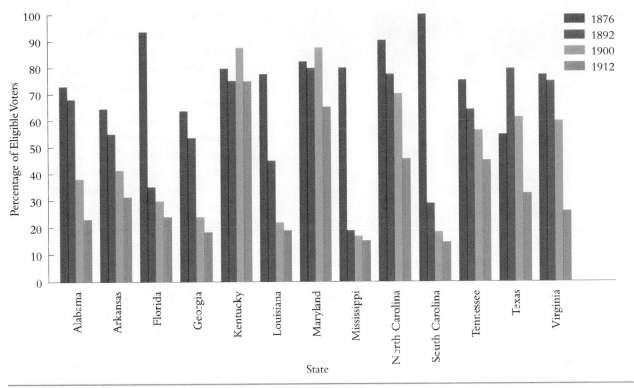

VOTER PARTICIPATION IN 13 SOUTHERN STATES, 1876, 1892, 1900, 1912

Source: Data from *Historical Statistics of the United States, Colonial Times to 1970* (White Plains, N.Y.: Kraus International, 1989).

who did not own a minimum amount of property, or who could not pay a poll tax, lost his right to vote. The citizens who failed these tests most frequently were blacks, who formed the poorest and least educated segment of the southern population, but a large portion of the region's poor whites also failed the tests. The effects of disenfranchisement were stark. In 1900 only 1,300 blacks voted in Mississippi elections, down from 130,000 in the 1870s. Virginia's voter turnout dropped from 60 percent of adult men (white and black) in 1900 to 28 percent in 1904.

Many progressives in the North, such as Governor Robert La Follette of Wisconsin, criticized southern disenfranchisement. Some, including Jane Addams and John Dewey, joined in 1910 with W. E. B. Du Bois and other black reformers to found the National Association for the Advancement of Colored People (NAACP), an interracial political organization that made black equality its primary goal. In the South, however, white progressives rarely challenged disenfranchisement, and most had little difficulty justifying it with progressive ideology. Because progressives everywhere considered the right to vote a precious gift granted only to those who could handle its responsibilities, they equally believed that it must be withheld from people deemed racially or culturally unfit. Progressives

in the North excluded many immigrants on just those grounds. Progressives in the South saw the disenfranchisement of African Americans in the same light.

Disillusionment with the Electorate

In the process of identifying those groups "unfit" to hold the franchise, some progressives soured on the electoral process altogether. The more they looked for rational and virtuous voters, the fewer they found. In *Drift and Mastery* (1914), Walter Lippmann developed a theory that ordinary people had been overwhelmed by industrial and social changes. Because these changes seemed beyond their comprehension or control, they "drifted," unable to "master" the circumstances of modern life or take charge of their own destiny. Lippmann did not suggest that such ordinary people should be barred from voting, but he did argue that more political responsibility should rest with appointed officials who possessed the training and knowledge necessary to make government effective and just. The growing disillusionment with the electorate, in combination with intensifying restrictions on the franchise, created an environment in which fewer and fewer Americans

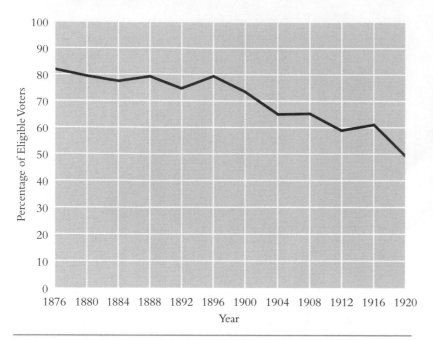

VOTER PARTICIPATION IN PRESIDENTIAL ELECTIONS, 1876–1920

Source: Data from *Historical Statistics of the United States, Colonial Times to 1970* (White Plains, N.Y.: Kraus International, 1989).

more nurturing nature would tame and civilize the men who had populated the frontier.

This notion reflected a subtle but important change in the thrust of the suffrage movement. Earlier generations had insisted that women were fundamentally equal to men, but the new suffragists argued that women were different from men. Women, they stressed, possessed a moral sense and a nurturing quality that men lacked. Consequently, they understood the civic obligations implied by the franchise and could be trusted to vote virtuously. Their votes would hasten to completion the progressive task of cleansing the political process of corruption. Their experience as mothers and household managers, moreover, would enable them to guide local and state governments in efforts to improve education, sanitation, family wholesomeness, and the condition of women and children in the workforce. In other words, the enfranchisement of women would enhance the quality of both public and private life without insisting they were the equals of men in all respects.

actually went to the polls. Voting participation rates fell from 79 percent in 1896 to only 49 percent in 1920.

Woman Suffrage

The major exception to this trend was the enfranchisement of women. This momentous reform was adopted by several states during the 1890s and the first two decades of the 20th century and became federal law with the ratification of the 19th Amendment to the Constitution in 1920.

Launched in 1848 at the famous Seneca Falls convention (see chapter 11), the women's rights movement floundered in the 1870s and 1880s. In 1890, suffragists came together in a new organization, the National American Woman Suffrage Association (NAWSA), led by Elizabeth Cady Stanton and Susan B. Anthony. Thousands of young, college-educated women campaigned door-to-door, held impromptu rallies, and pressured state legislators.

Wyoming, which attained statehood in 1890, became the first state to grant women the right to vote, followed in 1893 by Colorado and in 1896 by Idaho and Utah. The main reason for success in these sparsely populated western states was not egalitarianism but rather the conviction that women's supposedly gentler and

WOMAN SUFFRAGE

This confident, torch-bearing suffragist striding across the continent in this 1915 cartoon conveys the conviction of woman suffragists everywhere that their most cherished goal, gaining the vote for women, was within reach. The cartoon also reveals the interesting split among the states: western states had already granted women the vote whereas eastern states had not.

Suffragists were slow to ally themselves with blacks, Asians, and other disenfranchised groups. In fact, many suffragists, especially those in the South and West, opposed the franchise for Americans of color. They, like their male counterparts, believed that members of these groups lacked moral strength and thus did not deserve the right to vote. Unlike the suffrage pioneers of the 1840s and 1850s, many Progressive-era suffragists were little troubled by racial discrimination and injustice.

Washington, California, Kansas, Oregon, and Arizona followed the lead of the other western states by enfranchising women in the years from 1910 to 1912. After a series of setbacks in eastern and midwestern states, the movement regained momentum under the leadership of the strategically astute Carrie Chapman Catt, who became president of NAWSA in 1915 and successfully coordinated myriad grassroots campaigns. Equally important was Alice Paul, a radical who founded the Congressional Union in 1913 and later renamed it the National Woman's Party. Paul and her supporters focused their attention on the White House, picketing President Wilson's home 24 hours a day, unveiling large posters charging him with abandoning his democratic principles, and daring the police to arrest them. Several suffrage demonstrators were jailed, where

LINK TO THE PAST

Humor and the Woman Suffrage Movement

The length and difficulty of the struggle for woman suffrage have left many Americans with an image of suffragists as a rather serious and humorless group. But the poem reproduced below, from a book by suffragist Alice Duer Miller, *Are Women People? A Book of Rhymes for Suffrage Times* (New York: George H. Doran Company, 1915), suggests that we need to rethink this image. The poems in this book make the case for woman suffrage and attack anti-suffragists (known at the time simply as "antis") in a humorous, lighthearted way. The poem below ridicules a "consistent anti," meaning someone opposed to woman suffrage. The poem imagines this anti to be a mother anguished by the knowledge that her son, Willie, who has just turned 21 (then the voting age for men), must soon confront the "danger" of the polls, those "dark and dreadful places where many lose their souls." By making the fear of voting seem ludicrous, the poem attempts to discredit all those who dreaded the consequences of extending the franchise to women.

A Consistent Anti to Her Son

You're twenty-one to-day, Willie,
And a danger lurks at the door,
I've known about it always,
But I never spoke before;
When you were only a baby
It seemed so very remote,
But you're twenty-one to-day, Willie,
And old enough to vote.

You must not go to the polls, Willie,
Never go to the polls,

They're dark and dreadful places
Where many lose their souls;

They smirch, degrade and coarsen,
Terrible things they do
To quiet, elderly women—
What would they do to you!

If you've a boyish fancy
For any measure or man,
Tell me, and I'll tell Father,
He'll vote for it, if he can.
He casts my vote, and Louisa's,
And Sarah, and dear Aunt Clo;
Wouldn't you let him vote for you?
Father, who loves you so?

I've guarded you always, Willie,
Body and soul from harm;
I'll guard your faith and honor,
Your innocence and charm
From the polls and their evil spirits,
Politics, rum and pelf;
Do you think I'd send my only son
Where I would not go myself?

1. What does this poem reveal about the arguments of the antis (those who opposed woman suffrage)?
2. Is the poem successful in its effort to poke fun at (and thus to undermine) these arguments?

For additional sources related to this feature, visit the *Liberty, Equality, Power* Web site at:

http://history.wadsworth.com/murrin_LEP4e

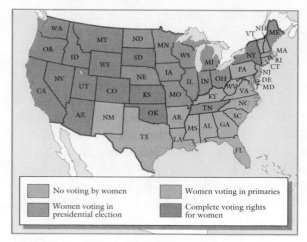

MAP 21.2 WOMAN SUFFRAGE BEFORE 1920
This map illustrates how woman suffrage prior to 1920 had advanced furthest in the West.

they continued their protests by going on hunger strikes (refusing to eat). Aided by a heightened enthusiasm for democracy generated by America's participation in the First World War (see chapter 23), which generated a more positive popular response to Paul's tactics than might otherwise have been the case, the suffragists achieved their goal of universal woman suffrage in 1920.

Predictions that suffrage for women would radically alter politics turned out to be false. The political system was neither cleansed of corruption, nor did the government rush headlong to address the private needs of women and their families. Although the numbers of voters increased after 1920, voter participation rates continued to decline. Still, the extension of the vote to women, 144 years after the founding of the nation, was a major political achievement.

Economic and Social Reform in the States

In some states, progressive reform extended well beyond political parties and the electorate. Progressives also wanted to limit corporate power, strengthen organized labor, and offer social welfare protection to the weak. State governments were pressured into passing such legislation by progressive alliances of middle-class and working-class reformers and by dynamic state governors.

Robert La Follette and Wisconsin Progressivism

Nowhere else did the progressives' campaign for social reform flourish as it did in Wisconsin. The movement arose first in the 1890s, in hundreds of Wisconsin cities and towns, as citizens began to mobilize against the state's corrupt Republican Party and the special privileges the party had granted to private utilities and railroads. These reform-minded citizens came from varied backgrounds. They were middle class and working class, urban and rural, male and female, intellectual and evangelical, Scandinavian Protestant and German Catholic. Wisconsin progressivism had already gained considerable momentum by 1897, when Robert La Follette assumed its leadership.

La Follette was born into a prosperous farming family in 1855. He entered politics as a Republican in the 1880s and embraced reform in the late 1890s. Elected governor in 1900, he secured for Wisconsin both a direct primary and a tax law that stripped the railroad corporations of tax exemptions they had long enjoyed. In 1905, he pushed through a civil service law mandating that every state employee meet a certain level of competence.

A tireless campaigner and a spellbinding speaker, "Fighting Bob" won election to the U.S. Senate in 1906. Meanwhile, Wisconsin's advancing labor and socialist movements forced progressive reformers to focus their legislative efforts on issues of corporate greed and social welfare. By 1910, reformers had passed state laws that reg-

© Bettmann/Corbis.

ROBERT LA FOLLETTE, WISCONSIN PROGRESSIVE
This cartoon, "Mr. La Follette's Strongest Card," used Robert La Follette's record as governor of Wisconsin (1900–06) to promote his 1912 campaign for the presidency. During La Follette's governorship, Wisconsin became the nation's leading "laboratory" for social and economic reform, although his accomplishments failed to win him the presidential nomination.

ulated railroad and utility rates, instituted the nation's first state income tax, and provided workers with compensation for injuries, limitations on work hours, restrictions on child labor, and minimum wages for women.

Many of these laws were written by social scientists at the University of Wisconsin, with whom reformers had close ties. In the first decade of the 20th century, John R. Commons, University of Wisconsin economist, drafted Wisconsin's civil service and public utilities laws. In 1911, Commons designed and won legislative approval for the Wisconsin Industrial Commission, which brought together employers, trade unionists, and professionals and gave them broad powers to investigate and regulate relations between industry and labor throughout the state. Never before had a state government so plainly committed itself to the cause of industrial justice. For the first time, the rights of labor would be treated with the same respect as the rights of industry. Equally important was the responsibility the commission delegated to nonelected professionals: social scientists, lawyers, engineers, and others. These professionals, Wisconsin reformers believed, would succeed where political parties had failed—namely, in providing the public with expert and honest government.

The "Wisconsin idea" found quick adoption in Ohio, Indiana, New York, and Colorado; and in 1913, the federal government established its own Industrial Relations Commission and hired Commons to direct its investigative staff. In other areas, too, reformers began urging state and federal governments to shift the policy making initiative away from political parties and toward administrative agencies staffed by professionals.

Progressive Reform in New York

New York seemed second only to Wisconsin in the vigor and breadth of its progressive movement. As in Wisconsin, New York progressives focused first on fighting political corruption. Revelations of close ties between leading Republican politicians and life insurance companies vaulted reform lawyer Charles Evans Hughes into the governor's mansion in 1907. Hughes immediately established several public service commissions to regulate railroads and utility companies. Also, as in Wisconsin, labor had its effect. New York City garment workers struck and forced state legislators to regulate working conditions. With the establishment of the Factory Investigating Committee, New York, like Wisconsin, became a pioneer in labor and social welfare policy.

New York state legislators also faced pressure from middle-class reformers—settlement house workers such as Lillian Wald of the Henry Street Settlement and lawyers such as Louis Brandeis—who had become convinced of the need for new laws to protect the disadvantaged. This combined pressure from working-class and middle-class constituencies impelled some state Democrats, including Assemblyman Alfred E. Smith and Senator Robert F. Wagner, to convert from machine to reform politics. Their appearance in the progressive ranks represented the arrival of a new reform sensibility. Wagner and Smith were both ethnic Catholics (Wagner was born in Germany, and Smith was the grandchild of Irish immigrants). They opposed prohibition, city commissions, voter registration laws, and other reforms whose intent seemed anti-immigrant or anti-Catholic. Meanwhile, they supported reforms meant to improve the working and living conditions of New York's urban poor. They agitated for a minimum wage, factory safety, workmen's compensation, the right of workers to join unions, and the regulation of excessively powerful corporations. Their participation in progressivism accelerated the movement's shift, first in New York and then elsewhere, away from preoccupation with political parties and electorates and toward questions of economic justice and social welfare.

🌎 A Renewed Campaign for Civil Rights

At the same time that politicians such as Smith and Wagner introduced an ethnic sensibility into progressivism, a new generation of African American activists began insisting that the issue of racial equality also be placed on the reform agenda.

The Failure of Accommodationism

Booker T. Washington's message that blacks should accept segregation and disenfranchisement as unavoidable and focus their energies instead on self-help and self-improvement—faced increasing criticism from black activists such as W. E. B. Du Bois, Ida B. Wells, Monroe Trotter, and others. Washington's accommodationist leadership (see chapter 18), in their eyes, brought southern blacks no reprieve from racism. More than 100 blacks had been lynched in 1900 alone; between 1901 and 1914, at least 1,000 others would be hanged.

Increasingly, unsubstantiated rumors of black assaults on whites became occasions for white mobs to rampage through black neighborhoods and indiscriminately destroy life and property. In 1908, a mob in Springfield, Illinois, attacked black businesses and individuals; a force of 5,000 state militia was required to restore order. The troops were too late, however, to stop the lynching of two innocent black men, one a successful barber and the other

© Bettmann/Corbis.

ANTIBLACK VIOLENCE

In 1913, a white mob destroyed a large part of the black section of Omaha, Nebraska. Race riots of this scale and devastation in early 20th-century America convinced many blacks that Booker T. Washington's message of accommodation was not working.

an 84-year-old man who had been married to a white woman for more than 30 years. There was a sad irony in the deaths of these African Americans. Murdered in Abraham Lincoln's hometown and within walking distance of his grave, they died just as black and white Americans everywhere were preparing to celebrate the centennial of the Great Emancipator's birth.

Booker T. Washington had long believed that blacks who educated themselves or who succeeded in business would be accepted as equals by whites. As Du Bois and other black militants observed, however, white rioters made no distinction between rich blacks and poor, or between solid citizens and petty criminals. All that had seemed to matter was the color of one's skin. Similarly, many black militants knew from personal experience that individual accomplishment was not enough to overcome racial prejudice. Du Bois was a brilliant scholar who became, in 1899, the first African American to receive a doctorate from Harvard University. Had he been white, Du Bois would have been asked to teach at Harvard or another elite academic institution, but no prestigious white university, in the South or North, ever made him an offer.

From the Niagara Movement to the NAACP

Seeing no future in accommodation, Du Bois and other young black activists came together at Niagara Falls in 1905 to fashion a new political agenda. They demanded that African Americans regain the right to vote in states that had taken it away; that segregation be abolished; and that the many discriminatory barriers to black advancement be removed. They declared their commitment to freedom of speech, the brotherhood of all men, and respect for the working man. Although their numbers were small, the members of the so-called Niagara movement were inspired by the example of the antebellum abolitionists. Meeting in Boston, Oberlin, and Harpers Ferry—all places of special significance to the abolitionist cause—they hoped to rekindle the militant, uncompromising spirit of that earlier crusade (see chapters 12 and 14).

The 1908 Springfield riot had shaken many whites. Some, especially those already working for social and economic reform, now joined in common cause with the Niagara movement. Together, black and white activists planned a conference for Lincoln's birthday in 1909 to revive, in the words of author William English Walling, "the spirit of the abolitionists" and to "treat the Negro on a plane of absolute political and social equality." Oswald Garrison Villard, the grandson of William Lloyd Garrison, called on "all believers in democracy to join in a National conference for the discussion of present evils, the voicing of protests, and the renewal of the struggle for civil and political liberty." The conference brought together distinguished progressives, white and black, including Mary White Ovington, Jane Addams, John Dewey, William Dean Howells, Ida B. Wells, and Du Bois. They drew up plans to establish an organization dedicated to fighting racial discrimination and prejudice. In May 1910, the National Association for the Advancement of Colored People (NAACP) was officially launched, with Moorfield Storey of Boston as president, Walling as chairman of the executive committee, and Du Bois as the director of publicity and research.

The formation of the NAACP marked the beginning of the modern civil-rights movement. The organization launched a magazine, the *Crisis*, edited by Du Bois, to publicize and protest the lynchings, riots, and other abuses directed against black citizens. Equally important was the Legal Redress Committee, which initiated lawsuits against city and state governments for violating the constitutional rights of African Americans. The committee scored its first major success in 1915, when the U.S. Supreme Court ruled that the so-called grandfather clauses of the Oklahoma and Maryland constitutions violated the 15th Amend-

W. E. B. DU BOIS

Du Bois was one of the founders of the National Association for the Advancement of Colored People (NAACP), and the editor of its magazine, the *Crisis*. This photograph shows him in the offices of the *Crisis*. Du Bois would become one of the most important African American intellectuals and activists of the 20th century.

ment. (These clauses allowed poor, uneducated whites—but not poor, uneducated blacks—to vote, even if they failed to pay their state's poll tax or to pass its literacy test, by exempting the descendants of men who had voted before 1867.) NAACP lawyers won again in 1917 when the Supreme Court declared unconstitutional a Louisville, Kentucky, law that required all blacks to reside in predetermined parts of the city.

By 1914, the NAACP had enrolled thousands of members in scores of branches throughout the United States. The organization's success generated other civil-rights groups. The National Urban League, founded in 1911, worked to improve the economic and social conditions of blacks in cities. It pressured employers to hire blacks, distributed lists of available jobs and housing in African American communities, and developed social programs to ease the adjustment of rural black migrants to city life.

Progress toward racial equality was slow. Attacking segregation and discrimination through lawsuits was, by its nature, a slow strategy that would take decades to complete. The growing membership of the NAACP, although impressive, was not large enough to qualify it as a mass movement. And its interracial character made the organi-

zation seem dangerously radical to millions of whites. White NAACP leaders responded to this hostility by limiting the number and power of African Americans who worked for the organization. This policy, in turn, outraged black militants who argued that no civil-rights organization should be in the business of appeasing white racists.

Despite its limitations, the NAACP made significant strides. The NAACP gave Du Bois the security and visibility he needed to carry on his fight against Booker T. Washington's accommodationist philosophy. Even before his death in 1915, Washington's influence in black and white communities had begun to recede. The NAACP, more than any other organization, helped resurrect the issue of racial equality at a time when many white Americans had accepted as normal the practices of racial segregation and discrimination.

🌐 National Reform

The more progressives focused on economic and social matters, the more they sought to increase their influence in national politics. Certain problems demanded national solutions. No patchwork of state regulations, for example, could curtail the power of the trusts, protect workers, or monitor the quality of consumer goods. Moreover, state and federal courts often were hostile toward progressive goals: They repeatedly struck down as unconstitutional reform laws regulating working hours or setting minimum wages, on the grounds that they impinged on the freedom of contract and trade. A national progressive movement could force passage of laws that were less vulnerable to judicial veto or elect a president who could overhaul the federal judiciary with progressive-minded judges.

National leadership would not emerge from Congress. The Democratic Party had been scarred by the Populist challenge of the 1890s. Divided between the radical Bryanites and the conservative followers of Grover Cleveland, and consequently unable to speak with one voice on questions of social and economic policy, after 1896 the Democrats seemed incapable of winning a national election or offering a national agenda. The Republican Party was more unified and popular, but it was controlled by a conservative Old Guard. Led by Senator Nelson Aldrich of Rhode Island and House Speaker Joseph G. Cannon of Illinois, the Republican Old Guard was pro-business and devoted to a 19th-century style of backroom patronage. When Robert La Follette arrived in the Senate from Wisconsin in 1907, the Old Guard ostracized him as a dangerous radical.

National progressive leadership came from the executive rather than the legislative branch, and from two presidents in particular, Republican Theodore Roosevelt and Democrat Woodrow Wilson. These two presidents sponsored reforms that profoundly affected the lives of Americans and altered the nature of the American presidency.

The Roosevelt Presidency

When the Republican bosses chose Theodore Roosevelt as William McKinley's running mate in 1900, their purpose was more to remove this headstrong, unpredictable character from New York state politics than to groom him for national leadership. As governor of New York, Roosevelt had been a moderate reformer, but even his modest efforts to rid the state's Republican Party of corruption and to institute civil service reform were too much for the state party machine, led by Thomas C. Platt. Consigning Roosevelt to the vice presidency seemed a safe solution. McKinley was a young, vigorous politician, fully in control of his party and his presidency.

Less than a year into his second term, in September 1901, McKinley was shot by an anarchist assassin. The president clung to life for nine days, and then died. Upon succeeding McKinley, Theodore Roosevelt, age 42, became the youngest chief executive in the nation's history.

Born to an aristocratic New York City family, Roosevelt nevertheless developed an uncommon affection for "the people." Asthmatic, sickly, and nearsighted as a boy, he remade himself into a vigorous adult. With an insatiable appetite for high-risk adventure—everything from "dude ranching" in the Dakota Territory, to big-game hunting in Africa, to wartime combat—he was also a voracious reader and an accomplished writer. Aggressive and swaggering in his public rhetoric, he was in private a skilled, patient negotiator. A believer in the superiority of the English-speaking peoples, he nevertheless appointed members of "inferior" races to important posts in his administration. Rarely has a president's personality so enthralled the American public. He is the only 20th-century president immortalized on Mount Rushmore.

Regulating the Trusts

Roosevelt quickly revealed his flair for the dramatic. In 1902, he ordered the Justice Department to prosecute the Northern Securities Company, a $400 million monopoly that controlled all railroad lines and traffic in the Northwest from Chicago to Washington state. Never before had an American president sought to use the Sherman Antitrust Act to break up a business monopoly. The news shocked J. P. Morgan, the banker who had brokered the Northern Securities deal. Morgan rushed to the White House, where he is said to have told Roosevelt, "If we have done anything wrong, send your man to my man and they can fix it up." Roosevelt would have none of this "fixing." In 1903, a federal court ordered Northern Securities dissolved, and the U.S. Supreme Court upheld the decision the next year. Roosevelt was hailed as the nation's "trust-buster."

Roosevelt, however, did not believe in breaking up all, or even most, large corporations. Industrial concentration, he believed, brought the United States wealth, productivity, and a rising standard of living. Rather than bust them up, Roosevelt argued, government should regulate the industrial giants and punish those that used their power improperly.

This new role would require the federal government to expand its powers. A newly fortified government—the centerpiece of a political program that Roosevelt would later call the New Nationalism—was to be led by a forceful president, who was willing to use all of the powers at his disposal to achieve prosperity and justice.

Toward a "Square Deal"

Roosevelt displayed his willingness to use government power to protect the economically weak in a 1902 coal miners' strike. Miners in the anthracite fields of eastern Pennsylvania wanted recognition for their union, the United Mine Workers (UMW). They also wanted a 10 to 20 percent increase in wages and an eight-hour day. When their employers, led by George F. Baer of the Reading Railroad, refused to negotiate, they went on strike. In October, the fifth month of the strike, Roosevelt summoned the mine owners and John Mitchell, the UMW president, to the White House. Baer expected Roosevelt to threaten the striking workers with arrest by federal troops if they failed to return to work. Instead, Roosevelt supported Mitchell's request for arbitration and warned the mine owners that if they refused to go along, 10,000 federal troops would seize their property. Stunned, the mine owners agreed to submit the dispute to arbitrators, who awarded the unionists a 10 percent wage increase and a nine-hour day.

The mere fact that the federal government had ordered employers to compromise with their workers carried great symbolic weight. Roosevelt enjoyed a surge of support from Americans convinced that he shared their dislike for ill-gotten wealth and privilege. He also raised the hopes of African Americans when, only a month into his presidency, he dined with Booker T. Washington at the White House and then shrugged off the protests of white southerners who accused him of undermining segregation.

In his 1904 election campaign, Roosevelt promised that, if reelected, he would offer every American a "square deal." The slogan resonated with voters and helped carry Roosevelt to a victory (57 percent of the popular vote) over the conservative Democrat Alton B. Parker. To the surprise of many observers, Roosevelt had aligned the Republican Party with the cause of reform.

Expanding Government Power: The Economy

Emboldened by his victory, the president intensified his efforts to extend government regulation of economic affairs. His most important proposal was to give the government power to set railroad shipping rates and thereby to eliminate the industry's discriminatory marketing practices. The government, in theory, already possessed this power through the Interstate Commerce Commission (ICC), a regulatory body established by Congress in 1887, but the courts had so weakened the ICC's oversight and regulatory functions as to render it virtually powerless. Roosevelt achieved his goal in 1906, when Congress passed the Hepburn Act, which significantly increased the ICC's powers of rate review and enforcement. Roosevelt supported the Pure Food and Drug Act, passed by Congress that same year, which protected the public from fraudulently marketed and dangerous foods and medications. He also campaigned for the Meat Inspection Act (1906), which committed the government to monitoring the quality and safety of meat being sold to American consumers.

Expanding Government Power: The Environment

Roosevelt also did more than any previous president to extend federal control over the nation's physical environment. Roosevelt was not a "preservationist" in the manner of John Muir, founder of the Sierra Club, who insisted that the beauty of the land and the well-being of its wildlife should be protected from all human interference. Instead, Roosevelt viewed the wilderness as a place to live strenuously, to test oneself against the rough outdoors, and to match wits against strong and clever game. Roosevelt further believed that in the West—that land of ancient forests, lofty mountain peaks, and magnificent canyons—Americans could learn something important about their nation's roots and destiny. To preserve this West, Roosevelt oversaw the creation of 5 new national parks, 16 national monuments, and 53 wildlife reserves. The work of his administration led directly to the formation of the National Park Service in 1916.

From the Collections of the Library of Congress.

ENVIRONMENTALIST JOHN MUIR MEETS WITH THEODORE ROOSEVELT, 1903

This photo was taken on Glacier Point, Yosemite Park, where the two men were camping and discussing how best to preserve the U.S. wilderness.

Roosevelt also emerged a strong supporter of the "conservationist" movement. Conservationists cared little for national parks or grand canyons. They wanted to manage the environment, so as to ensure that the nation's resources were put to the most efficient use for economic development. Roosevelt shared the conservationists' belief that the plundering of western timberlands, grazing areas, water resources, and minerals had reached crisis proportions. Only broad regulatory controls would restore the West's economic potential.

To that end, Roosevelt appointed a Public Lands Commission in 1903 to survey public lands, inventory them, and establish permit systems to regulate the kinds and numbers of users. Soon after, the Departments of Interior and Agriculture placed certain western lands rich in natural resources and waterpower off-limits to agricultural users. Government officials also limited waterpower development by requiring companies to acquire permits and pay fees for the right to generate electricity on their sites. When political favoritism and corruption within the Departments of the Interior and Agriculture threatened these efforts at regulation, Roosevelt authorized the hiring of university-trained experts to replace state and local politicians. Scientific expertise, rather than political connections, would now determine the distribution and use of western lands.

Gifford Pinchot, a specialist in forestry management and Roosevelt's close friend, led the drive for scientific management of natural resources. In 1905, he persuaded Roosevelt to relocate jurisdiction for the national forests from the Department of the Interior to the Department of Agriculture, which, Pinchot argued, was the most appropriate department to oversee the efficient "harvest" of the nation's forest crop. The newly created National Forest Service, under Pinchot's control, quickly instituted a system of competitive bidding for the right to harvest timber on national forest lands. Pinchot and his expanding staff of college-educated foresters also implemented a new policy that exacted user fees from livestock ranchers who had previously used national forest grazing lands for free. Armed with new legislation and authority, Pinchot and fellow conservationists in the Roosevelt administration declared vast stretches of federal land in the West off-limits to mining and dam construction.

The Republican Old Guard disliked these initiatives. When Roosevelt recommended prosecution of cattlemen and lumbermen who were illegally using federal land for private gain, congressional conservatives struck back with legislation (in 1907) that curtailed the president's power to create new government land reserves. Roosevelt responded by seizing another 17 million acres for national forest reserves before the new law went into effect. To his conservative opponents, excluding commercial activity from public land—a program they regarded as socialistic—was bad enough, but flouting the will of Congress with a 17-million-acre land grab violated constitutional principles governing the separation of powers. Yet, to millions of American voters, Roosevelt's willingness to defy western cattle barons, mining tycoons, and other "malefactors of great wealth" increased his popularity.

Progressivism: A Movement for the People?

Historians have long debated how much Roosevelt's economic and environmental reforms altered the balance of power between the "interests" and the people. Some have demonstrated that many corporations were eager for federal government regulation—that railroad corporations wanted relief from the rate wars that were driving them into bankruptcy, for example, and that the larger meatpackers believed that the costs of government food inspections would drive smaller meatpackers out of business. So, too, historians have shown that large agribusinesses, timber companies, and mining corporations in the West believed that government regulation would aid them and hurt smaller competitors. According to this view, government regulation benefited the corporations more than it benefited workers, consumers, and small businessmen.

This view has some validity. These early reforms often curtailed corporate power only to a limited extent. Corporations fought with some success to turn the final versions of the reform laws to their advantage. But in 1907, the progressive program was still evolving. Popular anger over corporate power and political corruption remained a driving force of progressivism. The presence in the Senate of La Follette, Albert Beveridge of Indiana, and other anticorporate Republicans gave that anger an influential national voice. Whether the corporations or the people would benefit most from progressive reforms had yet to be determined.

The Republicans: A Divided Party

The financial panic of 1907 further strained relations between Roosevelt reformers and Old Guard conservatives. When several New York banks failed in a speculative effort to corner the copper market, they triggered a run on banks, a short but severe dip in industrial production, and widespread layoffs. Everywhere, people worried that a major depression, like that of the 1890s, was in the offing.

Only the timely decision of J. P. Morgan and his fellow bankers to pour private cash into the collapsing banks saved the nation from an economic crisis. Prosperity quickly returned, but the panic jitters lingered. Conservatives blamed Roosevelt's "radical" economic policies for the fiasco. To Roosevelt and his fellow progressives, however, the panic merely pointed out how little impact their reforms had actually made on the reign of "speculation, corruption, and fraud."

Roosevelt, as a result, began calling for an overhaul of the banking system and regulation of the stock market. The Republican Old Guard, meanwhile, was more determined than ever to run the "radical" Roosevelt out of the White House. Sensing that he might fail to win his party's nomination, and mindful of a rash promise he had made in 1904 not to run again in 1908, Roosevelt decided not to seek reelection. It was a decision he would soon regret. Barely 50, he was too young and energetic to end his political career, and much of his reform program had yet to win Congressional approval.

The Taft Presidency

Roosevelt thought he had found in William Howard Taft, his secretary of war, an ideal successor. Taft had worked closely with Roosevelt on foreign and domestic policies. He had supported Roosevelt's progressive reforms and offered him shrewd advice on countless occasions. Roosevelt believed he possessed both the ideas and the skills to complete the reform Republican program.

To reach that conclusion, however, Roosevelt had to ignore some obvious differences between Taft and himself. Taft neither liked nor was particularly adept at politics. With the exception of a judgeship in an Ohio superior court, he had never held elective office. He was by nature a cautious and conservative man. As Roosevelt's hand-picked successor, Taft easily won the election of 1908, defeating Democrat William Jennings Bryan with 52 percent of the vote. His conservatism soon revealed itself in his choice of corporation lawyers, rather than free-thinking reformers, for cabinet positions.

Battling Congress

Taft's troubles began when he appeared to side against progressives in an acrimonious congressional battle over tariff legislation. Progressives had long desired tariff reduction, believing that competition from foreign manufacturers would benefit American consumers and check the economic power of American manufacturers. Taft had raised expectations for tariff reduction when he called Congress into special session to consider a reform bill that called for a modest reduction of tariffs and an inheritance tax. The bill passed the House but was gutted in the Senate. When congressional progressives pleaded with Taft to use his power to whip conservative senators into line, he pressured the Old Guard into including a 2 percent corporate income tax in their version of the bill, but he did not insist on tariff reductions. As a result, the Payne-Aldrich Tariff he signed into law on August 5, 1909, did nothing to encourage imports. Progressive Republicans, bitterly disappointed, held Taft responsible.

They were further angered when Taft withdrew his support of their efforts to strip Speaker Joe Cannon of his legislative powers. By 1910, Republican insurgents had entered into an alliance with reform-minded congressional Democrats. Then a bruising fight over Taft's conservation policies brought relations between Taft and the insurgent Republicans to the breaking point.

The Ballinger-Pinchot Controversy

Richard A. Ballinger, secretary of the interior, had aroused progressives' suspicions by reopening for private commercial use 1 million acres of land that the Roosevelt administration had previously brought under federal protection. Then Gifford Pinchot, still head of the National Forest Service, obtained information implicating Ballinger in the sale of Alaskan coal deposits to a private syndicate. Pinchot showed the information, including an allegation that Ballinger had personally profited from the sale, to Taft. Taft defended Ballinger, Pinchot went public with his charges, and a contentious congressional investigation ensued. Whatever hope Taft may have had of escaping political damage disappeared when Roosevelt, returning from an African hunting trip by way of Europe in spring 1910, staged a highly publicized rendezvous with Pinchot in England. In so doing, Roosevelt signaled his continuing support for his old friend Pinchot and his displeasure with Taft.

Roosevelt's Return

When Roosevelt arrived in the United States later that summer, he quickly returned to politics. In September, Roosevelt embarked on a speaking tour, the high point of which was his elaboration at Osawatomie, Kansas, of his New Nationalism, an ambitious reform program that called for the federal government to stabilize the economy, protect the weak, and restore social harmony.

The 1910 congressional elections confirmed the popularity of Roosevelt's positions. Insurgent Republicans trounced conservative Republicans in primary after primary, and the Democrats' embrace of reform brought them a majority in the House of Representatives for the first time since 1894. When Robert La Follette, who was challenging Taft for the Republican presidential nomination, seemed to suffer a nervous breakdown in February 1912, Roosevelt announced his own candidacy. In the 13 states sponsoring preferential primaries, Roosevelt won nearly 75 percent of the delegates, but the party's national leadership remained in the hands of the Old Guard, and they were determined to deny Roosevelt the Republican nomination. At the Republican convention in Chicago, Taft won renomination on the first ballot.

The Bull Moose Campaign

Roosevelt had expected this outcome. The night before the convention opened, he had told an assembly of 5,000 supporters that the party leaders would not succeed in derailing their movement. "We stand at Armageddon," he declared, and "we battle for the Lord." The next day, Roosevelt and his supporters withdrew from the convention and from the Republican Party. In August, the reformers reassembled as the new Progressive Party, nominated Roosevelt for president and California governor Hiram W. Johnson for vice president, and hammered out the reform platform they had long envisioned: sweeping regulation of the corporations, extensive protections for workers, a sharply graduated income tax, and woman suffrage. "I am as strong as a bull moose," Roosevelt roared as he readied for combat; his proud followers took to calling themselves "Bull Moosers."

Some of them, however, probably including Roosevelt, knew that their mission was futile. They had failed to enroll many of the Republican insurgents who had supported Roosevelt in the primaries but who now refused to abandon the GOP. Consequently, the Republican vote would be split between Roosevelt and Taft, making them both vulnerable to the Democrats' candidate, Woodrow Wilson.

The Rise of Woodrow Wilson

Few would have predicted in 1908 that the distinguished president of Princeton University, Woodrow Wilson, would be the 1912 Democratic nominee for president of the United States. Before 1910, Wilson had never run for elective office, nor had he ever held an appointed post in a local, state, or federal administration. The son of a Presbyterian minister from Virginia, Wilson had practiced law for a short time after graduating from Princeton (then still the College of New Jersey) in 1879 before settling on an academic career. Earning his doctorate in political science from Johns Hopkins in 1886, he taught history and political science at Bryn Mawr and Wesleyan (Connecticut) before returning to Princeton in 1890. He became president of Princeton in 1902, a post he held until he successfully ran for the governorship of New Jersey in 1910.

Brown Brothers.

THEODORE ROOSEVELT LAUNCHES HIS NEW NATIONALISM CAMPAIGN, 1910
This photograph of Roosevelt at Osawatomie, Kansas, captures some of the strength and exuberance of Roosevelt's public style. Roosevelt's appearance at Osawatomie marked his formal return to politics. For the occasion, he unveiled his New Nationalism, a far-reaching program of reform that called on the government to control the powerful corporations in the interests of the commonweal.

Identifying himself with the anti-Bryan wing of the Democratic Party, Wilson attracted the attention of wealthy conservatives, who saw him as a potential presidential candidate. They convinced the bosses of the New Jersey Democratic machine to nominate Wilson for governor in 1910. Wilson accepted the nomination and won the governorship handily. He then shocked his conservative backers by declaring his independence from the state's Democratic machine and moving New Jersey into the forefront of reform. Wilson's Presbyterian upbringing had instilled in him a strong sense that society should be governed by God's moral law. As a young man in the 1880s, he had come to believe that the social consequences of unregulated industrialization were repugnant to Christian ethical principles. Although these beliefs had receded from view somewhat during his tenure as Princeton University president, they had not disappeared. Their presence in his consciousness helps explain his emergence in 1911 and 1912 as one of the nation's leading progressives.

The Election of 1912

At the Democratic convention of 1912, Wilson was something of a dark horse, running a distant second to House Speaker Champ Clark of Missouri. When the New York delegation gave Clark a simple majority of delegates, virtually everyone assumed that he would soon command the two-thirds majority needed to win the nomination. But Wilson's managers held onto Wilson's delegates and began chipping away at Clark's lead. On the fourth day, on the 46th ballot, Wilson finally won the nomination. The exhausted Democrats closed ranks behind their candidate.

Given the split in Republican ranks, Democrats had their best chance in 20 years of regaining the White House. A Wilson victory, moreover, would give the country its first southern-born president in almost 50 years. Finally, whatever its outcome, the election promised to deliver a hefty vote for reform. Both Roosevelt and Wilson were running on reform platforms, and the Socialist Party candidate, Eugene V. Debs, was attracting larger crowds and generating greater enthusiasm than had been expected. Taft was so certain of defeat that he barely campaigned.

Debate among the candidates focused on the trusts. All three reform candidates—Roosevelt, Wilson, and Debs—agreed that corporations had acquired too much economic power. Debs argued that the only way to ensure popular control of that power was for the federal government to assume ownership of the trusts. Roosevelt called for the establishment of a powerful government that

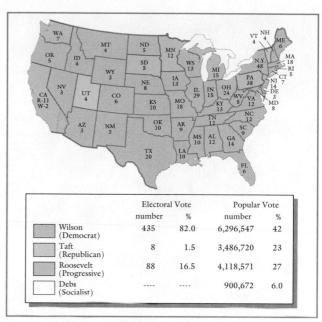

		Electoral Vote		Popular Vote	
		number	%	number	%
	Wilson (Democrat)	435	82.0	6,296,547	42
	Taft (Republican)	8	1.5	3,486,720	23
	Roosevelt (Progressive)	88	16.5	4,118,571	27
	Debs (Socialist)	----	----	900,672	6.0

MAP 21.3 PRESIDENTIAL ELECTION, 1912
Taft and Roosevelt split the Republican vote, allowing Wilson to win with a plurality of the popular vote (42 percent) and a big majority (82 percent) of the electoral vote.

would regulate and, if necessary, curb the power of the trusts. This was the essence of his New Nationalism, the program he had been advocating since 1910.

Rather than regulate the trusts, Wilson desired to break them up. He wanted to reverse the tendency toward economic concentration and thus restore opportunity to the people. This philosophy, which Wilson labeled the New Freedom, called for a temporary concentration of governmental power in order to dismantle the trusts. But once that was accomplished, Wilson promised, the government would relinquish its power.

Wilson won the November election with 42 percent of the popular vote to Roosevelt's 27 percent and Taft's 23 percent; Debs made a strong showing with 6 percent, the largest in his party's history. The three candidates who had pledged themselves to reform programs—Wilson, Roosevelt, and Debs—together won a remarkable 75 percent of the vote.

The Wilson Presidency

Wilson quickly assembled a cabinet of talented men who could be counted on for wise counsel, loyalty, and influence over vital Democratic constituencies. He cultivated a public image of himself as a president firmly in charge of his party and as a faithful tribune of the people.

Reproduced from the Collections of the Library of Congress.

WOODROW WILSON

Wilson entered politics after a long career in academia, where he had been a distinguished political scientist, historian, and university president. Here he sits for a full-length portrait soon after his election to the presidency.

Tariff Reform and a Progressive Income Tax

Like his predecessor, Wilson first turned his attention to tariff reform. The House passed a tariff-reduction bill within a month, and Wilson used his leadership skills to push the bill through a reluctant Senate. The resulting Underwood-Simmons Tariff of 1913 reduced tariff barriers from approximately 40 to 25 percent. To make up for revenue lost to tariff reductions, Congress then passed an income tax law. The 16th Amendment to the Constitution, ratified by the states in 1913, had already given the government the right to impose an income tax. The law passed by Congress made good on the progressive pledge to reduce the power and privileges of wealthy Americans

by requiring them to pay taxes on a greater *percentage* of their income than the poor.

The Federal Reserve Act

Wilson then asked Congress to overhaul the nation's financial system. Virtually everyone in both parties agreed on the need for greater federal regulation of banks and currency, but they differed sharply over how to proceed. The banking interests and their congressional supporters wanted the government to give the authority to regulate credit and currency flows either to a single bank or to several regional banks. Progressives opposed the vesting of so much financial power in private hands and insisted that any reformed financial system must be publicly controlled. Wilson worked out a compromise plan that included both private and public controls and marshaled the votes to push it through both the House and the Senate. By the end of 1913, Wilson had signed the Federal Reserve Act, the most important law passed in his first administration.

The Federal Reserve Act established 12 regional banks, each controlled by the private banks in its region. Every private bank in the country was required to deposit an average of 6 percent of its assets in its regional Federal Reserve bank. The reserve would be used to make loans to member banks and to issue paper currency (Federal Reserve notes) to facilitate financial transactions. The regional banks were also instructed to use their funds to shore up member banks in distress and to respond to sudden changes in credit demands by easing or tightening the flow of credit. A Federal Reserve Board appointed by the president and responsible to the public rather than to private bankers would set policy and oversee activities within the 12 reserve banks.

The Federal Reserve system strengthened the nation's financial structure and was in most respects an impressive political achievement for Wilson. In its final form, however, it revealed that Wilson was retreating from his New Freedom pledge. The Federal Reserve Board was a less powerful and less centralized federal authority than a national bank would have been, but it nevertheless represented a substantial increase in government control of banking. Moreover, the bill authorizing the system made no attempt to break up private financial institutions that had grown too powerful or to prohibit the interlocking directorates that large banks used to augment their power. Because it sought to work with large banks rather than to break them up, the Federal Reserve system seemed more consonant with the principles of Roosevelt's New Nationalism than with those of Wilson's New Freedom.

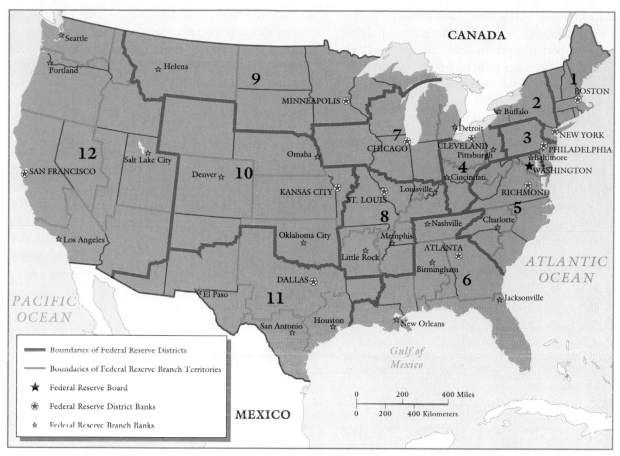

MAP 21.4 FEDERAL RESERVE DISTRICTS

This map demonstrates in visual terms how the Federal Reserve (FR) attempted to impose order on the nation's financial system: 12 districts, each with an FR district bank. Most of the districts were subdivided into branches, in which the FR also established a banking presence.

From the New Freedom to the New Nationalism

Wilson's failure to mount a vigorous antitrust campaign confirmed his drift toward the New Nationalism. For example, in 1914, Wilson supported the Federal Trade Commission Act, which created a government agency by that name to regulate business practices. The Federal Trade Commission (FTC) had wide powers to collect information on corporate pricing policies and on cooperation and competition among businesses. The FTC might have attacked trusts for "unfair trade practices," but the Senate stripped the FTC Act's companion legislation, the Clayton Antitrust Act, of virtually all provisions that would have allowed the government to prosecute the trusts. Wilson supported this weakening of the Clayton Act, having decided that the breakup of large-scale industry was no longer practical or preferable. The FTC, in Wilson's eyes, would help businesses, large and small, to regu-

late themselves in ways that contributed to national well-being. In accepting giant industry as an inescapable feature of modern life and in seeking to regulate industrial behavior by means of government agencies such as the FTC, Wilson had become, in effect, a New Nationalist.

At first, Wilson's drift to New Nationalist policies led him to support business interests. His nominations to the Federal Reserve Board, for example, were generally men who had worked for Wall Street firms and large industrial corporations. At the same time, he usually refused to use government powers to aid organized groups of workers and farmers. Court rulings had made worker and farmer organizations vulnerable to prosecution under the terms of the Sherman Antitrust Act of 1890. AFL president Samuel Gompers and other labor leaders tried but failed to convince Wilson to insert into the Clayton Antitrust Act a clause that would unambiguously grant labor and farmer organizations immunity from further antitrust prosecutions.

Nor did Wilson, at this time, view with any greater sympathy the campaign for African Americans' political equality. He supported efforts by white southerners in his cabinet, such as Postmaster General Albert Burleson and Treasury Secretary William McAdoo, to segregate their government departments, and he ignored pleas from the NAACP to involve the federal government in a campaign against lynching.

In late 1915, however, Wilson moved to the left, in part because he feared losing his reelection in 1916. The Bull Moosers of 1912 were retreating back to the Republican Party. Wilson remembered how much his 1912 victory, based on only 42 percent of the popular vote, had depended on the Republican split. To halt the progressives' rapprochement with the GOP, he made a bid for their support. In January 1916, he nominated Louis Brandeis to the Supreme Court. Not only was Brandeis one of the country's most respected progressives, but he was also the first Jew nominated to serve on the country's highest court. Congressional conservatives did everything they could to block the confirmation of a man they regarded as dangerously radical, but Wilson, as usual, was better organized, and by June his forces in the Senate had emerged victorious.

Wilson followed up this victory by pushing through Congress the first federal workmen's compensation law (the Kern-McGillicuddy Act, which covered federal employees), the first federal law outlawing child labor (the Keating-Owen Act), and the first federal law guaranteeing workers an eight-hour day (the Adamson Act, which covered the nation's 400,000 railway workers). The number of Americans affected by these acts was rather small. Never-

HISTORY THROUGH FILM

Wilson (1941)

Hollywood films about presidents are rare, and *Wilson* reveals some of the challenges confronting those who are willing to undertake such projects: achieving an impartial point of view on a president's political achievements, balancing the president's affairs of state and family affairs, and developing a perspective on the presidential figure that is neither fawning nor excessively hostile.

The makers of this movie considered Woodrow Wilson to be a great man and president: intelligent, principled, courageous, visionary, and devoted to his family. Wilson's greatness lies ultimately, the movie suggests, in his willingness to stand up for what's right—for the common man against wealthy elites; for democracy against the party bosses; for keeping America out of war when some Americans were too eager to fight; and for a new world order of peace, diplomacy, and fairness and against those who wanted to rule through war and conquest. Numerous his-

Directed by Henry King. Starring Alexander Knox (Wilson), Thomas Mitchell (Joseph Tumulty), Ruth Nelson (Ellen Wilson—first wife), Geraldine Fitzgerald (Edith Wilson—second wife), and Cedric Hardwicke (Henry Cabot Lodge).

torians were consulted to assemble this portrait, and no expense was spared in an effort to re-create historically accurate sets.

Nevertheless, the relentless celebration of Wilson's qualities endows the film with a ponderousness, evident in its excessive length, the too-frequent efforts to stir the emotions of audiences by playing bars from "My Country 'Tis of Thee," and a numbing visual emphasis on the majesty of the White House quarters. The movie, too, makes a great deal of Wilson's love for both of his wives and his three daughters, and of their devotion to him, and too many scenes have the family gathered around the piano, singing songs that express their domestic bliss. The movie would have benefited from exploring Wilson's rigidities and blind spots as well as his strengths and from more fully examining the controversy surrounding his second wife, Edith, especially her role in managing Wilson and the government after his 1919 stroke.

theless, Wilson had reoriented the Democratic Party to a New Nationalism that cared as much about the interests of the powerless as the interests of the powerful.

Trade unionists flocked to Wilson, as did most of the prominent progressives who had followed the Bull Moose in 1912. Meanwhile, Wilson had appealed to the supporters of William Jennings Bryan by supporting legislation that made federal credit available to farmers in need. He had put together a reform coalition capable of winning a majority at the polls. In the process, he had transformed the Democratic Party. From 1916 on, the Democrats, rather than the Republicans, became the chief guardians of the American reform tradition.

That Wilson did so is a sign of the strength of the reform and radical forces in American society. By 1916, the ranks of middle-class progressives had grown broad and deep. Working-class protest had also accelerated in scope and intensity. In Lawrence, Massachusetts, in 1912, and in Paterson, New Jersey, in 1913, for example, the IWW organized strikes of textile workers that drew national attention, as did the 1914 strike by Colorado mine workers that ended with the infamous Ludlow massacre (see chapter 20). These protests reflected the mobilization of those working-class constituencies—immigrants, women, the unskilled—long considered inconsequential both by mainstream labor leaders and party politicians. Assisted by radicals, these groups had begun to fashion a more inclusive and politically contentious labor movement. Wilson and other Democrats understood the potential strength of this new labor movement, and the president's pro-labor legislative agenda in 1916 can be understood, in part, as an effort to channel labor's new constituents into

Alexander Knox as Woodrow Wilson, addressing Congress.

Kobal Collection/20th Centur- Fox.

Nevertheless, the movie has significant virtues. It features several lavish sets, such as those for the 1912 Democratic Party convention and for Wilson's appearances before Congress in 1917 and 1918, that impressively re-create the look and feel of contemporary building interiors and political assemblies. Once America enters the war, moreover, the movie acquires the momentum and focus it earlier lacked. Wilson's eloquent speeches for world peace and his tense interchanges with key political antagonists, such as Senator Henry Cabot Lodge and Premier Georges Clem- enceau of France, are brilliantly done; moreover, they are intercut with authentic World War I newsreel footage in effective and illuminating ways. Finally, Wilson's last, and debilitating, campaign to sell the Treaty of Versailles to the American people after opposition had appeared to block its passage in the Senate gives the movie a dramatic climax. For the textbook's analysis of that campaign, see chapter 23, pages 721–723. The film thus retains considerable interest and power.

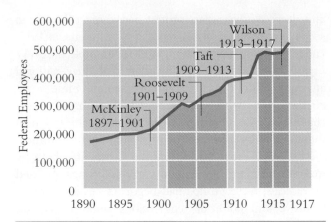

GROWTH IN FEDERAL EMPLOYMENT, 1891–1917

Source: Reprinted by permission from *The Federal Government Service,* ed. W. S. Sayre (Englewood Cliffs, N.J.: Prentice-Hall, 1965), p. 41, The American Assembly.

the Democratic Party. It was a successful strategy that contributed to Wilson's reelection in 1916.

Conclusion

By 1916, the progressives had accomplished a great deal. They demonstrated that traditional American concerns with democracy and liberty could be adapted to an industrial age. They exposed and curbed some of the worst abuses of the American political system. They enfranchised women and took steps to protect the environment. They broke the hold of laissez-faire economic policies on national politics and replaced it with the idea of a strong federal government committed to economic regulation and social justice. They transformed the presidency into a

post of legislative and popular leadership. They enlarged the executive branch by establishing new commissions and agencies charged with administering government policies.

The progressives, in short, had presided over the emergence of a new national government, one in which power increasingly flowed away from municipalities and states and toward Washington. This reorientation followed a compelling logic: A national government stood a better chance of solving the problems of growing economic inequality, mismanagement of natural resources, and consumer fraud than did local and state governments. The promise of effective remedies, however, brought new dangers. In particular, the new national government was creating a bureaucratic elite whose power rested on federal authority rather than private wealth or political machines. Progressives argued that the university-educated experts and scientific managers who staffed the new federal agencies would bring to the political process the very qualities that party politicians allegedly lacked: knowledge, dedication, and honesty. Few of these new public servants, however, were entirely disinterested. Some had close ties to the corporations and businesses that their agencies were expected to regulate. Others allowed their prejudices against women, immigrants, and minorities to shape social policy. Still others believed that "the people" could not be trusted to evaluate the government's work intelligently. For these reasons, the progressive approach to governance sometimes failed to enhance democracy and secure the people's sovereignty. America's imperial expansion and involvement in a world war would further demonstrate how a powerful state could serve illiberal ends.

SUGGESTED READINGS

No topic in 20th century American history has generated as large and rapidly changing a scholarship as has progressivism. Today, few scholars treat this political movement in the terms set forth by the progressives themselves: as a movement of "the people" against the "special interests." In *The Age of Reform: From Bryan to FDR* (1955), **Richard Hofstadter** argues that progressivism was the expression of a declining Protestant middle class at odds with the new industrial order. In *The Search for Order, 1877–1920* (1967), **Robert Wiebe** finds the movement's core in a rising middle class, closely allied to the corporations and bureaucratic imperatives that were defining this new order. **Gabriel Kolko,** *The Triumph of Conservatism: A Reinterpretation of American History* (1963), and **James**

Weinstein, *The Corporate Ideal in the Liberal State, 1900–1918* (1969), both argue that progressivism was the work of businessmen themselves, who were eager to ensure corporate stability and profitability in a dangerously unstable capitalist economy. Without denying the importance of this corporate search for order, **Nell Irvin Painter,** *Standing at Armageddon: The United States, 1877–1919* (1987), and **Alan Dawley,** *Struggles for Justice: Social Responsibility and the Liberal State* (1991), insist on the role of the working class, men and women, whites and blacks, in shaping the progressive agenda. **James T. Kloppenberg,** *Uncertain Victory: Social Democracy and Progressivism in European and American Thought, 1870–1920* (1986), and **Thomas J. Knock,** *To End All Wars: Woodrow Wilson and* *the Quest for a New World Order* (1992), emphasize the influence of socialism on progressive thought, while **Martin J. Sklar,** *The Corporate Reconstruction of American Capitalism, 1900–1916: The Market, the Law and Politics* (1988), stresses the role of progressivism in "containing" or taming socialism. **Nick Salvatore** superbly captures the charisma and enigma of Debs in his *Eugene V. Debs: Citizen and Socialist* (1982). **Paul Boyer,** *Urban Masses and Moral Order in America, 1820–1920* (1978), treats progressivism as a cultural movement to enforce middle-class norms on an unruly urban and immigrant population. **Theda Skocpol,** *Protecting Soldiers and Mothers: The Political Origins of Social Policy in the United States* (1992), and **Robyn Muncy,** *Creating a Female Dominion in American Reform, 1890–1935* (1991), reconstruct the central role of middle-class Protestant women in shaping progressive social policy, while **Robert M. Crunden,** *Ministers of Reform: The Progressives' Achievement in American Civilization, 1889–1920* (1982), stresses the religious roots of progressive reform. **Alexander Keyssar,** *The Right to Vote: The Contested History of Democracy in the United States* (2000), is an indispensable guide to political reform during this period. An impressive recent attempt to synthesize the literature on progressivism is **Michael McGerr,** *A Fierce Discontent: The Rise and Fall of the Progressive Movement in America, 1870–1920* (2003).

 AMERICAN JOURNEY ONLINE
AND
INFOTRAC COLLEGE EDITION

Visit the source collections at www.ajaccess.wadsworth.com and infotrac.thomsonlearning.com and use the Search function with the following key terms to explore documents, images, audio and video clips, articles, and commentary related to the material in this chapter.

Eugene V. Debs
Helen Keller
Ida Tarbell
Jane Addams
John Muir
Robert La Follette
W. E. B. Du Bois

National Association for the Advancement of Colored People (NAACP)
Woman Suffrage
Theodore Roosevelt
Woodrow Wilson
Federal Reserve Act

GRADE AIDS

Visit the Liberty Equality Power Companion Web Site for resources specific to this textbook: http://history.wadsworth.com/murrin_LEP4e

  The CD in the back of this book and the U.S. History Resource Center at http://history.wadsworth.com/u.s./ offer a variety of tools to help you succeed in this course, including access to quizzes; images; documents; interactive simulations, maps, and timelines; movie explorations; and a wealth of other sources.

Chapter 22

Becoming a World Power, 1898–1917

Culver Pictures.

UNCLE SAM GETS COCKY, 1901

From 1898 to 1917, the United States broadened its influence in world affairs and especially sought to establish its dominance in Latin America. This cartoon illustrates that dominance through the figure of a giant Uncle Sam rooster that dwarfs both the European chickens (gamely protesting, "you're not the only rooster in South America") and the diminutive Latin American republics.

For much of the 19th century, most Americans were preoccupied by continental expansion. They treasured their distance from European societies, monarchs, and wars. Elections rarely turned on international events, and presidents rarely made their reputations as statesmen in the world arena. The diplomatic corps, like most agencies of the federal government, was small and inexperienced. The government projected its limited military power westward and possessed virtually no capacity or desire for involvement overseas.

The nation's rapid industrial growth in the late 19th century forced a turn away from such continentalism. Technological advances, especially the laying of transoceanic cables and the introduction of steamship travel, diminished America's physical isolation. The babel of languages one could hear in American cities testified to how much the Old World had penetrated the New. Then, too, Americans watched anxiously as England, Germany, Russia, Japan, and other industrial powers intensified their competition for overseas markets and colonies, and some believed America too needed to enter this contest. The voices making this argument grew more insistent and persuasive as the long economic depression of the 1890s stripped the United States of its prosperity and pride.

A war with Spain in 1898 gave the United States an opportunity to upgrade its military and acquire colonies and influence in the Western Hemisphere and Asia. Under Presidents William McKinley and Theodore Roosevelt, the United States pursued these initiatives and established a small but strategically important empire. Not all Americans supported this imperial project, and many protested the subjugation of the peoples of Cuba, Puerto Rico, and the Philippines that imperial expansion seemed to entail. In the eyes of anti-imperialists, the United States seemed to be becoming the kind of nation that many Americans had long despised—one that valued power more than liberty. Roosevelt brushed aside these objections and set about creating an international system in which a handful of industrial nations pursued their global economic interests, dominated world trade, and kept the world at peace. Woodrow Wilson, however, was more troubled by America's imperial turn. His doubts became apparent in his efforts to devise a policy toward postrevolutionary Mexico that restrained American might and respected Mexican desires for liberty. It was a worthy ambition but one that proved exceedingly difficult to achieve.

CHAPTER FOCUS

♦ What were the causes of the Spanish-American War?

♦ Over what countries did the United States exert control between 1898 and 1917, and what were the mechanisms of control? How did American expansion compare with that of other industrial powers?

♦ What were the similarities and differences in the foreign policies of Theodore Roosevelt, William Howard Taft, and Woodrow Wilson?

♦ What happened on Kettle and San Juan Hills, and why was the prominent role of one group in those battles excised from historical memory?

The United States Looks Abroad

By the late 19th century, sizable numbers of Americans had become interested in extending their country's influence abroad. The most important groups were Protestant missionaries, businessmen, and imperialists.

Protestant Missionaries

Protestant missionaries were among the most active promoters of American interests abroad. Overseas missionary activity grew quickly between 1870 and 1900, most of it directed toward China. Between 1880 and 1900, the number of women's missionary societies doubled, from 20 to 40; by 1915, these societies enrolled 3 million women. Convinced of the superiority of the Anglo-Saxon race, Protestant missionaries considered it their Christian duty to teach the Gospel to the "ignorant" Asian masses and save their souls. Missionaries also believed that their efforts would free those masses from their racial destiny, enabling them to become "civilized." In this "civilizing" effort, missionaries resembled progressive reformers who sought to uplift America's immigrant masses at home. (For the story of one missionary family in China, see the Americans Abroad feature in chapter 20, p. 617.)

Businessmen

For different reasons, industrialists, traders, and investors also began to look overseas, sensing that they could make fortunes in foreign lands. Exports of American manufactured goods rose substantially after 1880. By 1914, American foreign investment already equaled a sizable 7 percent of the nation's gross national product. Companies

CHRONOLOGY

1893	Frederick Jackson Turner publishes an essay announcing the end of the frontier
1898	Spanish-American War (April 14–August 12) • Treaty of Paris signed (December 10), giving U.S. control of Philippines, Guam, and Puerto Rico • U.S. annexes Hawaii
1899–1902	American-Filipino War
1899–1900	U.S. pursues Open Door policy toward China
1900	U.S. annexes Puerto Rico • U.S. and other imperial powers put down Chinese Boxer Rebellion
1901	U.S. forces Cuba to adopt constitution favorable to U.S. interests
1903	Hay–Bunau-Varilla Treaty signed, giving U.S. control of Panama Canal Zone
1904	"Roosevelt corollary" to Monroe Doctrine proclaimed
1905	Roosevelt negotiates end to Russo-Japanese War
1906–17	U.S. intervenes in Cuba, Nicaragua, Haiti, Dominican Republic, and Mexico
1907	Roosevelt and Japanese government reach a "gentlemen's agreement" restricting Japanese immigration to U.S. and ending discrimination against Japanese schoolchildren in California
1907–09	Great White Fleet circles the world
1909–13	William Howard Taft conducts "dollar diplomacy"
1910	Mexican Revolution
1914	Panama Canal opens
1914–17	Wilson struggles to develop a policy toward Mexico
1917	U.S. purchases Virgin Islands from Denmark

such as Eastman Kodak (film and cameras), Singer Sewing Machine Company, Standard Oil, American Tobacco, and International Harvester had become multinational corporations with overseas branch offices.

Some industrialists became entranced by the prospect of clothing, feeding, housing, and transporting the 400 million people of China. James B. Duke, who headed American Tobacco, was selling 1 billion cigarettes per year in East Asian markets. Looking for ways to fill empty boxcars heading west from Minnesota to Tacoma, Washington, the railroad tycoon James J. Hill imagined stuffing them with wheat and steel destined for China and Japan. He actually published and distributed wheat cookbooks throughout East Asia to convince Asians to shift from a rice-based to a bread-based diet (so that there would be a market for U.S. flour exports). Although export trade with East Asia during this period never fulfilled the expectations of Hill and other industrialists, their talk about the "wealth of the Orient" impressed on politicians its importance to American economic health.

Events of the 1890s only intensified the appeal of foreign markets. First, the 1890 U.S. census announced that the frontier had disappeared and that America had completed the task of westward expansion. Then, in 1893, a young historian named Frederick Jackson Turner published an essay, "The Significance of the Frontier in American History," that articulated what many Americans feared: that the frontier had been essential to the growth of the economy and to the cultivation of democracy. Living in the wilderness, Turner argued, had transformed the Europeans who settled the New World into Americans. They shed their European clothing styles, social customs, and political beliefs, and acquired distinctively "American" characteristics—rugged individualism, egalitarianism, and a democratic faith. How, Turner wondered, could the nation continue to prosper now that the frontier had gone?

In recent years, historians of the American West have criticized Turner's "frontier thesis." They have argued that the very idea of the frontier as uninhabited wilderness overlooked the tens of thousands of Indians who occupied the region and that much else of what Americans believed about the West was based more on myth than on reality. They have also pointed out that it makes little sense to view the 1890s as a decade in which opportunities for economic gain disappeared in the West.

Even though these points are valid, they would have meant little to Americans living in Turner's time. For them, as for Turner, concern about the disappearing frontier expressed a fear that the increasingly urbanized and industrialized nation had lost its way. Turner's essay appeared just as the country was entering the deepest, longest, and most conflict-ridden depression in its history (see chapter 19). What could the republic do to regain its economic prosperity and political stability? Where would it find its new frontiers? One answer to these questions focused on the pursuit of overseas expansion. As Senator Albert J. Beveridge of Indiana declared in 1899: "We are raising more than we can consume. . . . We are making more than we can use. Therefore, we must find new markets for our produce, new occupation for our capital, new work for our labor."

Smithsonian Institution Photo No. 85-14366.

SINGER SEWING MACHINE ADVERTISEMENT
The Singer Sewing Machine Company was one of the first American multinational corporations. This advertisement, with its maps of the Western Hemisphere and its description of Singer as "the universal sewing machine," stresses Singer's global orientation.

Imperialists

Eager to assist in the drive for overseas expansion was a group of politicians, intellectuals, and military strategists who viewed such expansion as a key ingredient in the pursuit of world power. They wanted the United States to take its place alongside Britain, France, Germany, and Russia as a great imperial nation. They believed that the United States should build a strong navy, solidify a sphere of influence in the Caribbean, and extend markets into Asia. Their desire to control ports and territories beyond the continental borders of their own country made them imperialists. Many of them were also Social Darwinists (see chapter 20), who believed that America's destiny required that it prove itself the military equal of the strongest European nations and the master of the "lesser" peoples of the world.

One of the best-known imperialists of the period was Admiral Alfred Thayer Mahan. In an influential book, *The Influence of Sea Power upon History, 1660–1783* (1890), Mahan argued that all the world's great empires, beginning with Rome, had relied on their capacity to control the seas. Mahan called for the construction of a U.S. navy with enough ships and firepower to make its presence felt everywhere in the world. To be effective, that global fleet would require a canal across Central America through which U.S. warships could pass swiftly from the Atlantic to the Pacific Oceans. It would also require a string of far-flung service bases from the Caribbean to the southwestern Pacific. Mahan recommended that the U.S. government take possession of Hawaii and other strategically located Pacific islands with superior harbor facilities.

Henry Morton Stanley:
Journalist, Explorer, Colonizer

Henry Morton Stanley was a journalist and explorer who probably did more than any other single American to open up Africa to European colonization.

Born in Wales in 1841 and abandoned by his mother shortly thereafter, Stanley arrived in New Orleans as a penniless immigrant in 1858. He enlisted in the Confederate Army in 1861, was captured by the Union in 1862, and fought for the Union Army for a time before deserting. After the war, Stanley worked as a journalist.

His big break came in 1871 when his boss at the *New York Herald*, James Bennett, asked Stanley to find and resupply Dr. David Livingstone, the famous British missionary and explorer who in 1866 had set off to find the source of the Nile but was feared lost and dead. Stanley actually found his man, greeting him with the words that would immortalize both men: "Dr. Livingstone, I presume?"

Fascinated with Africa, Stanley returned in 1874. Authorized by his sponsors to explore the Lualaba River in Central Africa, the suspected source of the Nile, Stanley proved that the Lualaba was instead part of the Congo River. Stanley then proceeded to become the first white person to travel the length of the mighty Congo from its origins in Central Africa to the Atlantic Ocean and to chart not just the river's path but all the territory that surrounded it. It was an exploring feat of the highest magnitude, and it claimed the lives of more than half of Stanley's expedition. But Stanley, despite losing 60 pounds, survived and became celebrated in the West as Africa's greatest explorer.

When Stanley could interest neither the United States nor Great Britain in colonizing Central Africa, he went to work for King Leopold II of Belgium, driving his African workforce mercilessly to carve a city, Leopoldville, out of African wilderness and to connect that city and other parts of the interior by road and fleets of ships to the Atlantic. By the early 1880s, largely as a result of Stanley's work, Leopold laid claim to 900,000 square miles of Africa's interior, calling it the Congo "Free State." As the Congo began to yield up its riches to Leopold, the scramble for Africa on the part of the other European powers began in earnest. Stanley had done much to trigger this imperialist movement. In helping to set up the Belgian Congo, Stanley also brought to Africa the cruelest of the European colonizers, Leopold, who exploited his African subjects heartlessly and punished resistance with torture and death.

As the United States proved slow to join the race for African colonies, Stanley found himself drawn back to Britain. In 1892, he relinquished his American citizenship and formally returned to Britain, where he lived until he died in 1904. But, it had been his time in America and the opportunities he had gained as an American journalist that launched his career as an African explorer.

HENRY MORTON STANLEY

In this 1871 portrait, shot on the eve of his expedition to find Dr. Livingstone, Stanley poses as the "great white hunter" with a diminutive African at his side.

© Hulton-Deutsch Collection/Corbis.

Presidents William McKinley and Theodore Roosevelt would eventually make almost the whole of Mahan's vision a reality, but in the early 1890s, Mahan doubted that Americans would accept the responsibility and costs of empire. Although the imperialists counted in their ranks such prominent figures as Theodore Roosevelt and Sena-

tor Henry Cabot Lodge of Massachusetts, many Americans still insisted that the United States should not aspire to world power by acquiring overseas bases and colonizing foreign peoples.

Mahan underestimated, however, the government's alarm over the scramble of Europeans to extend their im-

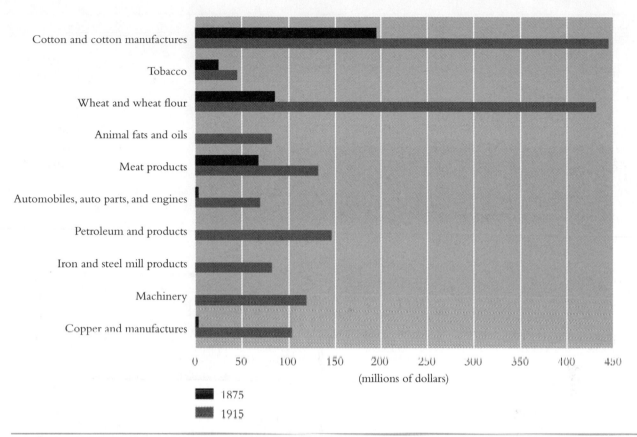

LEADING U.S. EXPORTS, 1875 AND 1915

Source: Data from *Historical Statistics of the United States, Colonial Times to 1970* (White Plains, N.Y.: Kraus International, 1989).

perial control. Every U.S. administration from the 1880s on committed itself to a "big navy" policy. By 1898, the U.S. Navy ranked fifth in the world and by 1900, it ranked third. Already in 1878, the United States had secured rights to Pago Pago, a superb deep-water harbor in Samoa (a collection of islands in the southwest Pacific inhabited by Polynesians), and in 1885, it had leased Pearl Harbor from the Hawaiians. Both harbors were expected to serve as fueling stations for the growing U.S. fleet.

These attempts to project U.S. power overseas had already deepened the government's involvement in the affairs of distant lands. In 1889, the United States established a protectorate over part of Samoa, a move meant to forestall German and British efforts to weaken American influence on the islands. In the early 1890s, President Grover Cleveland's administration was increasingly drawn into Hawaiian affairs, as tensions between American sugar plantation owners and native Hawaiians upset the islands' economic and political stability. In 1891, plantation owners succeeded in deposing the Hawaiian king and putting into power Queen Liliuokalani. But when Liliuokalani strove to establish her independence from American in-

terests, the planters, assisted by U.S. sailors, overthrew her regime, too. Cleveland declared Hawaii a protectorate in 1893, but he resisted the imperialists in Congress who wanted to annex the islands.

Still, imperialist sentiment in Congress and throughout the nation continued to gain strength, fueled by "jingoism." Jingoists were nationalists who thought that a swaggering foreign policy and a willingness to go to war would enhance their nation's glory. They were constantly on the alert for insults to their country's honor and swift to call for military retaliation. This predatory brand of nationalism emerged in each of the world's big powers in the late 19th century. In the United States, it manifested itself in terms of an eagerness for war. The anti-imperialist editor of the *Nation*, E. L. Godkin, exclaimed in 1894: "The number of men and officials of this country who are now mad to fight somebody is appalling." Recent feminist scholarship has emphasized the degree to which men of the 1890s saw war as an opportunity to revive frontier-like notions of masculinity—of men as warriors and conquerors—that were proving difficult to sustain in an increasingly industrialized and bureaucratized America.

THE U.S. NAVY, 1890–1914: EXPENDITURES AND BATTLESHIP SIZE

Fiscal year	Total Federal Expenditures	Naval Expenditures	Naval Expenditures as Percentage of Total Federal Expenditures	Size of Battleships (average tons displaced)
1890	$318,040,711	$ 22,006,206	6.9%	11,000
1900	520,860,847	55,953,078	10.7	12,000
1901	524,616,925	60,506,978	11.5	16,000
1905	657,278,914	117,550,308	20.7	16,000
1909	693,743,885	115,546,011	16.7	27,000 (1910)
1914	735,081,431	139,682,186	19.0	32,000

Sources: (for expenditures) E. B. Potter, *Sea Power: A Naval History* (Annapolis: Naval Institute Press, 1982), p. 187; (for size of ships) Harold Sprout, *Toward a New Order of Sea Power* (New York: Greenwood Press, 1976), p. 52.

Spain's behavior in Cuba in the 1890s gave those men the war they sought.

☀ The Spanish-American War

By the 1890s, the islands of Cuba and Puerto Rico were virtually all that remained of the vast Spanish empire in the Americas. Relations between the Cubans and their Spanish rulers had long been deteriorating. The Spanish had taken 10 years to subdue a revolt begun in 1868. In 1895, the Cubans staged another revolt, sparked by their continuing resentment of Spanish control and by a depressed economy caused in part by an 1894 U.S. tariff law that made Cuban sugar too expensive for the U.S. market. The fighting was brutal. Cuban forces destroyed large areas of the island to make it uninhabitable by the Spanish. The Spanish army, led by General Valeriano Weyler, responded in kind, forcing large numbers of Cubans into concentration camps. Denied adequate food, shelter, and sanitation, an estimated 200,000 Cubans—one-eighth of the island's population—died of starvation and disease.

Such tactics, especially those ascribed to "Butcher" Weyler (as he was known in much of the U.S. press), inflamed American opinion. Many Americans sympathized with the Cubans, who seemed to be fighting the kind of anticolonial war Americans themselves had waged more than 100 years earlier. Americans stayed well informed about the atrocities by reading the *New York Journal*, owned by William Randolph Hearst, and the *New York World*, owned by Joseph Pulitzer. Hearst and Pulitzer were transforming newspaper publishing in much the same way Sam McClure and others had revolutionized the magazine business (see chapter 21). To boost circulation, they sought out sensational and shocking stories and described them in lurid detail. They were accused of engaging in

UNCLE SAM

The Spanish-American War was popular among Americans. Here, a proud Uncle Sam salutes the U.S. Navy for its role in winning the "latest, greatest, and shortest war."

"yellow journalism"—embellishing stories with titillating details when the true reports did not seem dramatic enough.

The sensationalism of the yellow press and its frequently jingoistic accounts failed to bring about American intervention in Cuba, however. In the final days of his administration, President Cleveland resisted mounting pressure to intervene. William McKinley, who succeeded him in 1897, denounced the Spanish even more harshly, with the aim of forcing Spain into concessions that would satisfy the Cuban rebels and bring an end to the conflict. Initially, this strategy seemed to be working: Spain relieved "Butcher" Weyler of his command, stopped incarcerating Cubans in concentration camps, and granted Cuba limited autonomy. Still, Spaniards living on the island refused to be ruled by a Cuban government, and the Cuban rebels continued to demand full independence. Late in 1897, when riots broke out in Havana, McKinley ordered the battleship *Maine* into Havana harbor to protect U.S. citizens and their property. Two unexpected events then set off a war.

The first was the February 9, 1898, publication in Hearst's *New York Journal* of a letter stolen from Depuy de Lôme, the Spanish minister to Washington, in which he described McKinley as "a cheap politician" and a "bidder for the admiration of the crowd." The de Lôme letter also implied that the Spanish cared little about resolving the Cuban crisis through negotiation and reform. The news embarrassed Spanish officials and outraged U.S. public opinion. Then, only six days later, the *Maine* exploded in Havana harbor, killing 260 American sailors. Although subsequent investigations revealed that the most probable cause of the explosion was a malfunctioning boiler, Americans were certain that it had been the work of Spanish agents. "Remember the Maine!" screamed the headlines in the yellow press. On March 8, Congress responded to the clamor for war by authorizing $50 million to mobilize U.S. forces. In the meantime, McKinley notified Spain of his conditions for avoiding war: Spain would pay an indemnity for the *Maine*, abandon its concentration camps, end the fighting with the rebels, and commit itself to Cuban independence. On April 9, Spain accepted all the demands but the last. Nevertheless, on April 11, McKinley asked Congress for authority to go to war. Three days later, Congress approved a war resolution, which included a declaration (spelled out in the Teller Amendment) that the United States would not use the war as an opportunity to acquire territory in Cuba. On April 24, Spain responded with a formal declaration of war against the United States.

"A Splendid Little War"

Secretary of State John Hay called the fight with Spain "a splendid little war." Begun in April, it ended in August. More than 1 million men volunteered to fight, and fewer than 500 were killed or wounded in combat. The American victory over Spain was complete, not just in Cuba but in the neighboring island of Puerto Rico and in the Philippines, Spain's strategic possession in the Pacific.

Actually, the war was more complicated than it seemed. The main reason for the easy victory was U.S. naval superiority. In the war's first major battle, a naval engagement in Manila harbor in the Philippines on May 1, a U.S. fleet commanded by Commodore George Dewey destroyed an entire Spanish fleet and lost only one sailor (to heat stroke). On land, the story was different. On the eve of war, the U.S. Army consisted of only 26,000 troops. These soldiers were skilled at skirmishing with Indians but ill-prepared and ill-equipped for all-out war. A force of 80,000 Spanish regulars awaited them in Cuba, with another 50,000 in reserve in Spain. Congress immediately increased the army to 62,000 and called for an additional 125,000 volunteers. The response to this call was astounding, but outfitting, training, and transporting the new recruits overwhelmed the army's capacities. Its standard-issue, blue flannel uniforms proved too heavy for fighting in tropical Cuba. Rations were so poor that soldiers referred to one common item as "embalmed beef." Most of the volunteers had to make do with ancient Civil War rifles that still used black, rather than smokeless, powder. The initial invasion force of 16,000 men took more than five days to sail the short distance from Tampa, Florida, to Daiquiri, Cuba. Moreover, the army was unprepared for the effects of malaria and other tropical diseases.

That the Cuban revolutionaries were predominantly black also came as a shock to the

Chicago Historical Society.

"REMEMBER THE *MAINE!*"

The explosion of the battleship *Maine* in Havana harbor on February 15, 1898, killed 260 American sailors and helped drive the United States into war with Spain.

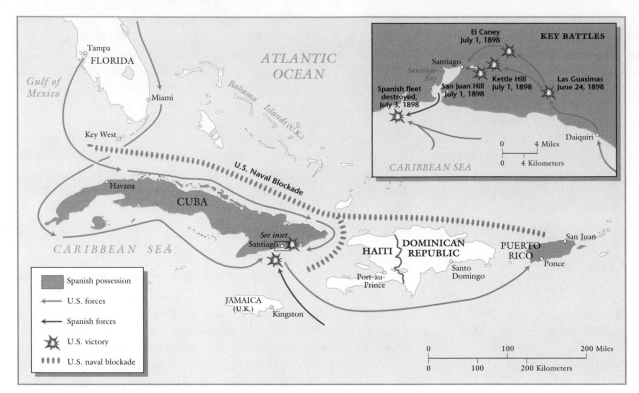

MAP 22.1 SPANISH-AMERICAN WAR IN CUBA, 1898

This map shows the following: the routes taken by U.S. ships transporting troops from Florida to Cuba; the concentration of troop landings and battles around Santiago, Cuba; and a U.S. naval blockade, stretching hundreds of miles from Puerto Rico to Cuba, that attempted to keep the Spanish troops in Cuba and Puerto Rico from being reinforced.

 View an animated version of this map or related maps at http://history.wadsworth.com/murrin_LEP4e.

U.S. forces. In their attempts to arouse support for the Cuban cause, U.S. newspapers had portrayed the Cuban rebels as fundamentally similar to white Americans. They were described as intelligent, civilized, and democratic, possessing an "Anglo-Saxon tenacity of purpose." And, they were "fully nine-tenths" white, according to one report. The Spanish oppressors, by contrast, were depicted as dark complexioned—"dark cruel eyes, dark swaggering men" wrote author Sherwood Anderson—and as possessing the characteristics of their "dark race": barbarism, cruelty, and indolence. The U.S. troops' first encounters with Cuban and Spanish forces dispelled these myths. Their Cuban allies appeared poorly outfitted, rough in their manners, and primarily black-skinned. The Spanish soldiers appeared well disciplined, tough in battle, and light complexioned.

The Cuban rebels were actually skilled guerrilla fighters, but racial prejudice prevented most U.S. soldiers and reporters from crediting their military expertise. Instead, they judged the Cubans harshly—as primitive, savage, and incapable of self-control or self-government. White U.S. troops preferred not to fight alongside the Cubans; increasingly, they refused to coordinate strategy with them.

At first, the U.S. Army's ineptitude and its racial misconceptions did little to diminish the soldiers' hunger

for a good fight. No one was more eager for battle than Theodore Roosevelt who, along with Colonel Leonard Wood, led a volunteer cavalry unit composed of Ivy League gentlemen, western cowboys, sheriffs, prospectors, Indians, and small numbers of Hispanics and ethnic European Americans. Roosevelt's Rough Riders, as the unit came to be known, landed with the invasion force and played an active role in the three battles fought in the hills surrounding Santiago. Their most famous action, the one on which Roosevelt would build his lifelong reputation as a military hero, was a furious charge up Kettle Hill into the teeth of Spanish defenses. Roosevelt's bravery was stunning, although his judgment was faulty. Nearly 100 men were killed or wounded in the charge. Reports of Roosevelt's bravery overshadowed the equally brave performance of other troops, notably the 9th and 10th Negro Cavalries, which played a pivotal role in clearing away Spanish fortifications on Kettle Hill and allowing Roosevelt's Rough Riders to make their charge. One Rough Rider commented: "If it had not been for the Negro cavalry, the Rough Riders would have been exterminated." Another added: "I am a Southerner by birth, and I never thought much of the colored man. But . . . I never saw such fighting as those Tenth Cavalry men did. They didn't seem to know what fear was, and their battle hymn was

From the Collections of the Library of Congress.

LEADERS OF THE CUBAN STRUGGLE FOR INDEPENDENCE

By 1898, Cubans had been fighting to free their country from Spain for 30 years. This lithograph, a souvenir of the Grand Cuban-American Fair held in New York in 1896, depicts five key leaders of the Cuban struggle: Máximo Gómez (upper left), Antonio Maceo (upper right), Calixto García (bottom right), and Salvador Cisneros (bottom left). At the center is José Martí, the "Father of the Revolution," killed in battle in 1895.

'There'll be a hot time in the old town tonight.'" The 24th and 25th Negro Infantry Regiments performed equally vital tasks in the U.S. Army's conquest of the adjacent San Juan Hill.

Theodore Roosevelt saw the Rough Rider regiment that he commanded in the Spanish-American War as a melting pot of different groups of white Americans. Combat, he further believed, would forge these many groups into one, as war had always done in the American past. African Americans were the group most conspicuously absent from this mix. Yet the fury of the fighting on Kettle Hill and San Juan Hill so scrambled the white and black regiments that by the time the troops reached the San Juan summit, they were racially intermixed. Combat had brought blacks into the great American melting pot, a phenomenon that Roosevelt celebrated at the time. The black troops, he declared, were "an excellent breed of Yankee," and no "Rough Rider will ever forget," he added, "the tie that binds us to the Ninth and Tenth Cavalry."

But Roosevelt did not truly believe that blacks were the equals of whites or that they could be absorbed into the American nation. So, a few months after returning home, he began downplaying the role of black troops and questioned their ability to fight. The heroic role of black soldiers disappeared not only from Roosevelt's own memory but also from accounts and illustrations of the great charge. The attack on black fighting abilities would become so widespread that by the start of the First World War, the U.S. military had excluded black troops from combat roles altogether. Thus, an episode that had demonstrated the possibility of interracial cooperation in America ended in the hardening of racial boundaries.

The taking of Kettle Hill, San Juan Hill, and other high ground surrounding Santiago gave the U.S. forces a substantial advantage over the Spanish defenders. Nevertheless, logistical and medical problems nearly did them in. The troops were short of food, ammunition, and medical facilities. Their ranks were devastated by malaria, typhoid, and dysentery; more than 5,000 soldiers died from disease. Even the normally ebullient Roosevelt was close to despair: "We are within measurable distance of a terrible military disaster," he wrote his friend Henry Cabot Lodge on July 3.

Fortunately, the Spanish had lost the will to fight. On the very day Roosevelt wrote to Lodge, Spain's Atlantic fleet tried to retreat from Santiago harbor and was promptly destroyed by a U.S. fleet. The Spanish army in Santiago surrendered on July 16; on July 18, the Spanish government asked for peace. While negotiations for an armistice proceeded, U.S. forces overran the neighboring island of Puerto Rico. On August 12, the U.S. and Spanish governments agreed to an armistice, but before the news could reach the Philippines, the United States had captured Manila and had taken prisoner 13,000 Spanish soldiers.

The armistice required Spain to relinquish its claim to Cuba, cede Puerto Rico and the Pacific island of Guam to the United States, and tolerate the American occupation of Manila until a peace conference could be convened in Paris on October 1, 1898. At that conference, American diplomats startled their Spanish counterparts by demanding that Spain also cede the Philippines to the United States. After two months of stalling, the Spanish government agreed to relinquish their coveted Pacific colony for $20 million, and the transaction was sealed by the Treaty of Paris on December 10, 1898.

© Bettmann/Corbis.

ROUGH RIDERS AND 10TH CAVALRY

Roosevelt poses with his Rough Riders (to the right) while members of the 10th Cavalry appear below. Both groups played pivotal roles in the battles of San Juan and Kettle Hills, but America would celebrate only the Rough Riders, not the black cavalrymen.

The Granger Collection.

The United States Becomes a World Power

America's initial war aim had been to oust the Spanish from Cuba—an aim that both imperialists and anti-imperialists supported, but for different reasons. Imperialists hoped to incorporate Cuba into a new American empire; anti-imperialists hoped to see the Cubans gain their independence. But only the imperialists condoned the U.S. acquisition of Puerto Rico, Guam, and particularly the Philippines, which they viewed as integral to the extension of American interests into Asia. Soon after the war began, President McKinley had cast his lot with the imperialists.

First, he annexed Hawaii, giving the United States permanent control of Pearl Harbor. Next, he set his sights on setting up a U.S. naval base at Manila. Never before had the United States sought such a large military presence outside the Western Hemisphere.

In a departure of equal importance, McKinley announced his intent to administer much of this newly acquired territory as U.S. colonies. Virtually all territory the United States had acquired in the 19th century had been part of the North American continent. These lands had been settled by Americans, who had eventually petitioned for statehood. By 1900, most of these territories had been admitted to the Union with the same rights as existing states; others, such as New Mexico, Arizona, and Oklahoma, soon would acquire statehood status. In the case of the new overseas territories, however, only Hawaii would be allowed to follow this traditional path toward statehood. There, the powerful American sugar plantation owners prevailed on Congress to pass an act in 1900 extending U.S. citizenship to all Hawaiian citizens and putting Hawaii on the road to statehood. No such influential group of Americans resided in the Philippines. The country was made an American colony and placed under a U.S. administration that took its orders from Washington rather than from the Filipino people. Such colonization was necessary, in the eyes of U.S. imperialists, to prevent other powers, such as Japan and Germany, from gaining a

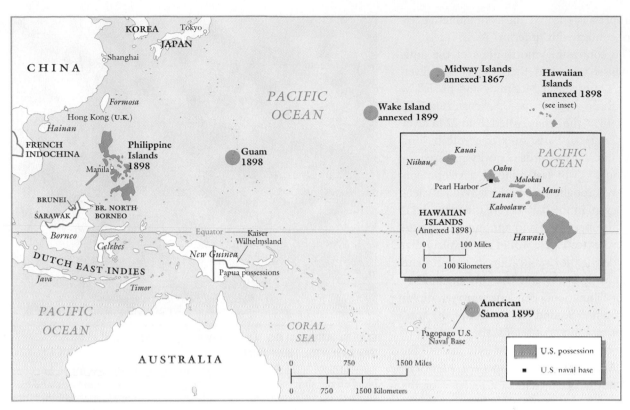

MAP 22.2 AMERICAN SOUTH PACIFIC EMPIRE, 1900
By 1900, the American South Pacific empire consisted of a series of strategically located islands with superior harbor facilities, stretching from the Hawaiian Islands and Samoa in the middle of the Pacific to the Philippines on the ocean's western edge.

foothold somewhere in the 400-island archipelago and launching attacks on the American naval base in Manila.

The McKinley administration might have taken a different course. The United States might have negotiated a deal with Emilio Aguinaldo, the leader of an anticolonial movement in the Philippines, that would have given the Philippines independence in exchange for a U.S. naval base at Manila. An American fleet stationed there would have been able to protect both American interests and the fledgling Philippine nation from predatory assaults by Japan, Germany, or Britain. Alternatively, the United States might have annexed the Philippines outright and offered Filipinos U.S. citizenship as the first step toward statehood. McKinley and his supporters, however, believed that the "inferior" Filipino people lacked the capacity for self-government. The United States would undertake a solemn mission to "civilize" the Filipinos and thereby prepare them for independence, but until that mission was complete, the Philippines would submit to rule by presidentially appointed American governors.

The Debate over the Treaty of Paris

The proposed acquisition of the Philippines aroused opposition both in the United States and in the Philippines.

The Anti-Imperialist League, strong in the Northeast, enlisted the support of several elder statesmen in McKinley's own party, as well as the former Democratic President Grover Cleveland, the industrialist Andrew Carnegie, and the labor leader Samuel Gompers. William Jennings Bryan, meanwhile, marshaled a vigorous anti-imperialist protest among Democrats in the South and West, while Mark Twain, William James, William Dean Howells, and other men of letters lent the cause their prestige. Some anti-imperialists believed that subjugating the Filipinos would violate the nation's most precious principle: the right of all people to independence and self-government. Moreover, they feared that the military and diplomatic establishment needed to administer the colony would threaten political liberties at home.

Other anti-imperialists were motivated more by self-interest than by democratic ideals. U.S. sugar producers, for example, feared competition from Filipino producers. Trade unionists worried that poor Filipinos would flood the U.S. labor market and depress wage rates. Some businessmen warned that the costs of maintaining an imperial outpost would exceed any economic benefits that the colony might produce. Many Democrats, meanwhile, simply wanted to gain partisan advantage by opposing the Republican administration's foreign policy. Still other anti-imperialists feared the contaminating effects of contact with "inferior" Asian races.

The contrasting motivations of the anti-imperialists weakened their opposition. Even so, they almost dealt McKinley and his fellow imperialists a defeat in the U.S. Senate. On February 6, 1899, the Senate voted 57 to 27 in favor of the Treaty of Paris, only one vote beyond the minimum two-thirds majority required for ratification. Two last-minute developments may have brought victory. First, William Jennings Bryan, in the days before the vote, abandoned his opposition and announced his support for the treaty. (He would later explain that he had decided for ratification in order to end the war with Spain and that he intended to work for Filipino independence through diplomatic means.) Second, on the eve of the vote, Filipinos rose in revolt against the U.S. army of occupation. With another war looming and the lives of American soldiers imperiled, a few senators who had been reluctant to vote for the treaty may have felt obligated to support the president.

© Corbis.

EMILIO AGUINALDO AND FILIPINO ANTICOLONIAL INSURGENTS, 1899–1901

Aguinaldo is in the first row, second from the right (he has his right hand on the shoulder of the man sitting in the center). Aguinaldo and his supporters initially welcomed the U.S. war against Spain in the Philippines but then fought U.S. efforts to turn the Philippines into an American colony.

The American-Filipino War

The acquisition of the Philippines immediately embroiled the United States in a long, brutal war to subdue the Filipino rebels. In four years of fighting, more than 120,000 American soldiers served in the Philippines and more than 4,200 of them died. The war cost $160 million, or eight times what the United States had paid Spain to acquire the archipelago. The war brought Americans face-to-face with an unpleasant truth: that American actions in the Philippines were virtually indistinguishable from Spain's actions in Cuba. Like Spain, the United States refused to acknowledge a people's aspiration for self-rule. Like "Butcher" Weyler, American generals permitted their soldiers to use savage tactics. Whole communities suspected of harboring guerrillas were driven into concentration camps, and their houses, farms, and livestock were destroyed. American soldiers executed so many Filipino rebels (whom they called "goo-goos") that the ratio of Filipino dead to wounded reached 15 to 1, a statistic that made the American Civil War, in which one soldier had died for every five wounded, seem relatively humane. One New York infantryman wrote home that his unit had killed 1,000 Filipinos—men, women, and children—in retaliation for the murder of a single American soldier: "I am in my glory when I can sight my gun on some dark skin and pull the trigger," he exclaimed. A total of 15,000 Filipino sol-

diers died in the fighting. Estimates of total Filipino deaths from gunfire, starvation, and disease range from 50,000 to 200,000.

The United States finally gained the upper hand in the war after General Arthur MacArthur (father of Douglas) was appointed commander of the islands in 1900. MacArthur did not lessen the war's ferocity, but he understood that it could not be won by guns alone. He offered amnesty to Filipino guerrillas who agreed to surrender, and he cultivated close relations with the islands' economic elites. McKinley supported this effort to build a Filipino constituency sympathetic to the U.S. presence. To that end, he sent William Howard Taft to the islands in 1900 to establish a civilian government. In 1901, Taft became the colony's first "governor-general" and declared that he intended to prepare the Filipinos for independence. He transferred many governmental functions to Filipino control and launched a program of public works (roads, bridges, schools) that would give the Philippines the infrastructure necessary for economic development and political independence. By 1902, this dual strategy of ruthless war against those who had taken up arms and concessions to those who were willing to live under benevolent American rule had crushed the revolt. Though sporadic fight-ing continued until 1913, Americans had secured control of the Philippines. The explicit commitment of the United States to Philippine independence (a promise that was deferred until 1946), together with an extensive program of internal improvements, eased the nation's conscience.

Controlling Cuba and Puerto Rico

Helping the Cubans achieve independence had been a major rationalization for the war against Spain. Even so, in 1900, when General Leonard Wood, now commander of American forces in Cuba, authorized a constitutional convention to write the laws for a Cuban republic, the McKinley administration made clear it would not easily relinquish control of the island. At McKinley's urging, the U.S. Congress attached to a 1901 army appropriations bill the Platt Amendment (Orville Platt was the Republican senator from Connecticut), delineating three conditions for Cuban independence. First, Cuba would not be permitted to make treaties with foreign powers. Second, the United States would have broad authority to intervene in Cuban political and economic affairs. Third, Cuba would sell or

MUSICAL LINK TO THE PAST

Music for Patriots

Composer: John Philip Sousa
Title: "Stars and Stripes Forever"
(c. 1895)

In the five years following the writing of "Stars and Stripes Forever," John Philip Sousa was probably the most famous musician in America. When he and his band arrived in town, a holiday atmosphere ensued: schools were closed, businesses released their workers for the day, and special flags were flown. He furthered international respect for American music and helped dispel the pervasive stereotype that the United States could not produce musical works and performers worthy of the highest cultural respect. Sousa frowned upon symphonies, the musical form on which most famous composers had built their reputation. For him, symphonies were pretentious, full of padding, and dawdled excessively before they reached their most crowd-pleasing sections. Instead, Sousa favored short, snappy, and often patriotic three-minute pieces such as "Stars and Stripes Forever."

Sousa viewed music as entertainment and insisted on giving audiences what they wanted, and plenty of it. He did not mandate what audiences should hear as most classical conductors did; instead, he allowed them to render democratically their choices with applause. He mixed high-brow and low-brow material, classical themes with march music, and frequently used humor in his arrangements, purposely avoiding what he regarded as the stuffiness of classical concerts. If audiences wished to hear "Stars and Stripes Forever" as an encore over and over (and they consistently did, until he died in 1932), then Sousa and his men would service them, with no withering of enthusiasm.

Besides his own works, Sousa championed the works of young and struggling American composers, but he demanded to know the stories behind their compositions. Musical inspiration, in Sousa's opinion, needed to be generated from "glorious events," and he avoided material from "atheistic composers" or those "crazily in love," because such works would not produce the appropriate nationalist feelings that he wished to cultivate in his audiences. "This was my mission. The point was to move all of America, while busied in its everyday pursuits, by the power of direct and simple music," he proclaimed in 1910. "I wanted to make a music for the people, a music to be grasped at once."

It was hardly an accident that Sousa's period of greatest popularity coincided with the wave of patriotic feeling that swept over America during the second half of the 1890s. The economy was recovering from the depression, and America was successfully flexing its muscles in a war with Spain. Many Americans wanted to wave the stars and stripes and found special inspiration in Sousa's music.

1. Does music, even instrumental music such as Sousa's, have the power to generate a patriotic mood?
2. Have recent years in America—from 1895 until 2005—produced music whose influence on Americans has been similar to that of Sousa's in the 1890s?

Listen to an audio recording of this music on the Musical Links to the Past CD.

lease land to the United States for naval stations. The delegates to Cuba's constitutional convention were so outraged by these conditions that they refused even to vote on them. But the dependence of Cuba's vital sugar industry on the U.S. market and the continuing presence of a U.S. army on Cuban soil rendered resistance futile. In 1901, by a vote of 15 to 11, the delegates reluctantly wrote the Platt conditions into their constitution. "There is, of course, little or no independence left Cuba under the Platt Amendment," Wood candidly admitted to his friend Theodore Roosevelt, who had recently succeeded the assassinated McKinley as president.

Cuba's status, in truth, differed little from that of the Philippines. Both were colonies of the United States. In the case of Cuba, economic dependence closely followed political subjugation. Between 1898 and 1914, American trade with Cuba increased more than tenfold (from $27 million to $300 million), while investments more than quadrupled (from $50 million to $220 million). The United States intervened in Cuban political affairs five times between 1906 and 1921 to protect its economic interests and those of the indigenous ruling class with whom it had become closely allied. The economic, political, and military control that the United States imposed on Cuba would fuel anti-American sentiment there for years to come.

Puerto Rico received somewhat different treatment. The United States did not think independence appropriate, even though under Spanish rule the island had enjoyed a large measure of political autonomy and a parliamentary form of government. Nor did the United States follow its Cuban strategy by granting Puerto Rico nominal independence under informal economic and political controls. Instead, it annexed the island outright with the Foraker Act (1900). This act, unlike every previous annexation authorized by Congress since 1788, contained no provision for making the inhabitants of Puerto Rico citizens of the United States. Instead, Puerto Rico was designated an "unincorporated" territory, which meant that Congress would dictate the island's government and specify the rights of its inhabitants. Puerto Ricans were allowed no role in designing their government, nor was their consent to its establishment sought. With the Foraker Act, Congress had, in effect, invented a new, imperial mechanism for ensuring sovereignty over lands deemed vital to U.S. economic and military security. The U.S. Supreme Court upheld the constitutionality of this mechanism in a series of historic decisions, known as the Insular Cases, in the years from 1901 to 1904.

In some respects, Puerto Rico fared better than "independent" Cuba. Puerto Ricans were granted U.S. citizenship in 1917 and won the right to elect their own governor in 1947. Still, Puerto Ricans enjoyed fewer political rights than Americans in the 48 states. Moreover, throughout the 20th century, they endured a poverty rate far exceeding that of the mainland. As late as 1948, for example, three-fourths of Puerto Rican households subsisted on $1,000 or less annually, a figure below the U.S. poverty line. In its skewed distribution of wealth and its lack of industrial development, Puerto Rico resembled the poorly developed nations of Central and South America more than it did the affluent country that took over its government in 1900.

The subjugation of Cuba and the annexation of Puerto Rico troubled Americans far less than the U.S. takeover in the Philippines. Since the first articulation of the Monroe Doctrine in 1823, the United States had, in effect, claimed the Western Hemisphere as its sphere of influence. Within that sphere, many Americans believed, the United States possessed the right to act unilaterally to protect its interests. Before 1900, most of its actions (with

RECRUITING AMERICAN YOUTH FOR MILITARY SERVICE OVERSEAS

This U.S. Army advertisement portrays military duty in tropical areas under U.S. control as educational, leisurely, and exotic. The real work of such forces, maintaining social order and defeating anticolonial insurrections, is entirely effaced from this portrait, as are the native peoples who inhabited these lands.

The Granger Collection, New York.

the exception of the Mexican War) had been designed to limit the influence of European powers—Britain, France, Russia and Spain—on the countries of the hemisphere. After 1900, however, the United States assumed a more aggressive role, seizing land, overturning governments it did not like, forcing its economic and political policies on weaker neighbors in order to turn the Caribbean Sea into what policy makers called an American Mediterranean.

China and the "Open Door"

Except for the Philippines and Guam, the United States made no effort to take control of Asian lands. Such a policy might well have triggered war with other world powers that were already well established in the area. Nor were Americans prepared to tolerate the financial and political costs Asian conquest would have entailed. The United States opted for a diplomatic rather than a military strategy to achieve its foreign policy objectives. For China, in 1899 and 1900, it proposed the policy of the "open door."

The United States was concerned that the actions of the other world powers in China would block its own efforts to open up China's markets to American goods. Britain, Germany, Japan, Russia, and France each coveted their own chunk of China, where they could monopolize trade, exploit cheap labor, and establish military bases. By the 1890s, each of these powers was building a sphere of influence, either by wringing economic and territorial concessions from the weak Chinese government or by seizing outright the land and trading privileges they desired.

To prevent China's breakup and to preserve American economic access to the whole of China, McKinley's secretary of state, John Hay, sent "open door" notes to the major world powers. The notes asked each power to open its Chinese sphere of influence to the merchants of other nations and to grant them reasonable harbor fees and railroad rates. Hay also asked each power to respect China's sovereignty by enforcing Chinese tariff duties in the territory it controlled.

None of the world powers embraced either of Hay's requests, although Britain and Japan gave provisional assent. France, Germany, Russia, and Italy responded evasively, indicating their support for the Open Door policy in theory but insisting that they could not implement it until all of the other powers had done so. Hay put the best face on their responses by declaring that all of the powers had agreed to observe his Open Door principles and that he regarded their assent as "final and definitive." Americans took Hay's bluff as evidence that the United States had triumphed diplomatically over its rivals. The rivals may have been impressed by Hay's diplomacy, but whether

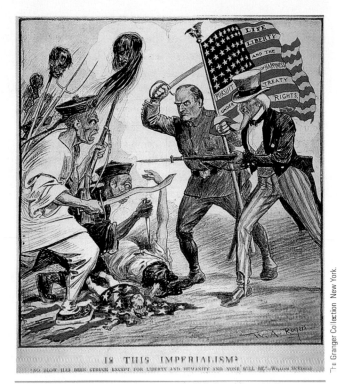

IS THIS IMPERIALISM?
NO BLOW HAS BEEN STRUCK EXCEPT FOR LIBERTY AND HUMANITY, AND NONE WILL BE.—WILLIAM McKINLEY

The Granger Collection, New York.

A DEFENSE OF AMERICA'S CHINA OPEN DOOR POLICY

This cartoon portrays a courageous William McKinley and standard bearer Uncle Sam engaging the vicious Chinese Boxers who had risen up to defeat the Western imperialists. "Is This Imperialism?" the cartoon asks, answering in McKinley's own words: "No blow has been struck except for liberty and humanity, and none will be."

they intended to uphold the United States' Open Door policy was not at all clear.

The first challenge to Hay's policy came from the Chinese. In May 1900, a Chinese organization, colloquially known as the "Boxers," sparked an uprising to rid China of all "foreign devils" and foreign influences. Hundreds of Europeans were killed, as were many Chinese men and women who had converted to Christianity. When the Boxers laid siege to the foreign legations in Beijing and cut off communication between that city and the outside world, the imperial powers raised an expeditionary force to rescue the diplomats and punish the Chinese rebels. The force, which included 5,000 U.S. soldiers, rushed over from the Philippines, broke the Beijing siege in August, and ended the Boxer Rebellion soon thereafter.

Hay feared that other major powers would use the rebellion as a reason to demand greater control over Chinese territory. He sent out a second round of Open Door notes, now asking each power to respect China's political independence and territorial integrity, in addition to guaranteeing unrestricted access to its markets. Impressed by America's show of military strength and worried that the

Chinese rebels might strike again, the imperialist rivals responded more favorably to this second round of notes. Britain, France, and Germany endorsed Hay's policy outright. With that support, Hay was able to check Russian and Japanese designs on Chinese territory. Significantly, when the powers decided that the Chinese government should pay them reparations for their property and personnel losses during the Boxer Rebellion, Hay convinced them to accept payment in cash rather than in territory. By keeping China intact and open to free trade, the United States had achieved a major foreign policy victory. Americans began to see themselves as China's savior as well.

● Theodore Roosevelt, Geopolitician

Roosevelt had been a driving force in the transformation of U.S. foreign policy during the McKinley administration. As assistant secretary of the navy, as a military hero, as a speaker and writer, and then as vice president, Roosevelt worked tirelessly to remake the country into one of the world's great powers. He believed that the Americans were a racially superior people destined for supremacy in

economic and political affairs. He did not assume, however, that international supremacy would automatically accrue to the United States. A nation, like an individual, had to strive for greatness and demand of its citizens physical and mental fitness. It had to build a military force that could convincingly project power overseas. And it had to be prepared to fight. All great nations, Roosevelt declared, ultimately depended on the skill and dedication of their warriors.

Roosevelt's appetite for a good fight caused many people to rue the ascension of this "cowboy" to the White House after McKinley's assassination in 1901. But behind his blustery exterior lay a shrewd analyst of international relations. As much as he craved power for himself and the nation, he understood that the United States could not rule every portion of the globe through military or economic means. Consequently, he sought a balance of power among the industrial nations through negotiation rather than war. Such a balance would enable each imperial power to safeguard its key interests and contribute to world peace and progress.

Absent from Roosevelt's geopolitical thinking was concern for the interests of less powerful nations. Roosevelt had little patience with the claims to sovereignty of small countries or the human rights of weak peoples.

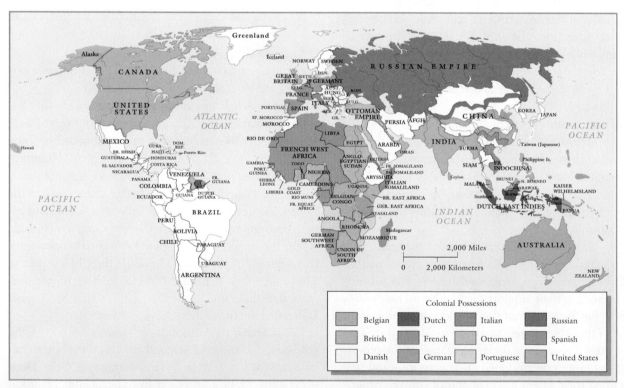

MAP 22.3   COLONIAL POSSESSIONS, 1900

In 1900, the British Empire was the largest in the world, followed by the French and Russian Empires. The U.S. Empire, if measured by the square miles of land held as colonial possessions, was small by comparison.

In his eyes, the peoples of Latin America, Asia (with the exception of Japan), and Africa were racially inferior and thus incapable of self-government or industrial progress. They were better suited to subservience and subsistence than to independence and affluence.

The Roosevelt Corollary

Ensuring U.S. dominance in the Western Hemisphere ranked high on Roosevelt's list of foreign policy objectives. In 1904, he issued a "corollary" to the Monroe Doctrine, which had asserted the right of the United States to keep European powers from meddling in hemispheric affairs. In his corollary, Roosevelt declared that the United States possessed a further right: the right to intervene in the domestic affairs of nations in the Western Hemisphere to quell disorder and forestall European intervention. The Roosevelt corollary formalized a policy that the United States had already deployed against Cuba and Puerto Rico in 1900 and 1901. Subsequent events in Venezuela and the Dominican Republic had further convinced Roosevelt of the need to expand the scope of U.S. intervention in hemispheric affairs.

Both Venezuela and the Dominican Republic were controlled by corrupt dictators. Both had defaulted on debts owed to European banks. Their delinquency prompted a German-led European naval blockade and bombardment of Venezuela in 1902 and a threatened invasion of the Dominican Republic by Italy and France in 1903. The United States forced the German navy to retreat from the Venezuelan coast in 1903. In the Dominican Republic, after a revolution had chased the dictator from power, the United States assumed control of the nation's customs collections in 1905 and refinanced the Dominican national debt through U.S. bankers.

The willingness of European bankers to loan money to Latin America's corrupt regimes had created the possibility that the countries ruled by these regimes would suffer bankruptcy, social turmoil, and foreign intervention. The United States, under Roosevelt, did not hesitate to intervene to make sure that loans were repaid and social stability was restored. But rarely in Roosevelt's tenure did the United States show a willingness to help the people who had suffered under these regimes establish democratic institutions or achieve social justice. When Cubans seeking true national independence rebelled against their puppet government in 1906, the United States sent in the Marines to silence them.

The Panama Canal

Roosevelt's varied interests in Latin America embraced the building of a canal across Central America. The president had long believed, along with Admiral Mahan, that the

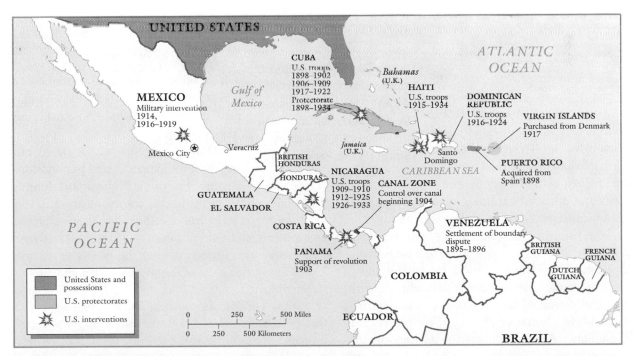

MAP 22.4   UNITED STATES PRESENCE IN LATIN AMERICA, 1895–1934
The United States possessed few colonies in Latin America but intervened (often repeatedly) in Mexico, Cuba, Nicaragua, Panama, Haiti, the Dominican Republic, and Venezuela to secure its economic and political interests.

nation needed a way of moving its ships swiftly from the Pacific Ocean to the Atlantic Ocean, and back again. Central America's narrow width, especially in its southern half, made it the logical place to build a canal. In fact, a French company had obtained land rights and had begun construction of a canal across the Colombian province of Panama in the 1880s. But even though a "mere" 40 miles of land separated the two oceans, the French were stymied by technological difficulties and by the financial costs of literally moving mountains. Moreover, French doctors found they were unable to check the spread of malaria and yellow fever among their workers. By the time Roosevelt entered the White House in 1901, the French Panama Company had gone bankrupt.

Roosevelt was not deterred by the French failure. He first presided over the signing of the Hay-Pauncefote Treaty with Great Britain in 1901, releasing the United States from an 1850 agreement that prohibited either country from building a Central American canal without the other's

participation. He then instructed his advisers to develop plans for a canal across Nicaragua. The Panamanian route chosen by the French was shorter than the proposed Nicaraguan route, and the canal begun by the French was 40 percent complete, but the French company wanted $109 million for it, more than the United States was willing to pay. In 1902, however, the company reduced the price to $40 million, a sum that Congress deemed appropriate. Secretary of State Hay quickly negotiated an agreement with Tomas Herran, the Colombian chargé d'affaires in Washington. The agreement, formalized in the Hay-Herran Treaty, accorded the United States a six-mile-wide strip across Panama on which to build the canal. Colombia was to receive a onetime $10 million payment and annual rent of $250,000.

The Colombian legislature, however, rejected the proposed payment as insufficient and sent a new ambassador to the United States with instructions to ask for a onetime payment of $20 million and a share of the $40 million

HISTORY THROUGH FILM

Tarzan, the Ape Man (1932)

Directed by W. S. Van Dyke. Starring Johnny Weismuller (Tarzan), Maureen O'Sullivan (Jane Parker), Neil Hamilton (Harry Holt), C. Aubrey Smith (James Parker), and Cheeta the Chimp.

This movie introduced Americans to Tarzan, one of the most popular screen figures of the 1930s, 1940s, and 1950s. Based on the best-selling novels of Edgar Rice Burroughs, this Tarzan movie, like the ones that followed, was meant to puncture the civilized complacency in which Americans and other Westernized, imperial peoples had enveloped themselves. The movie opens with an American woman, Jane Parker, arriving in Africa to join her father, James, and the crew he has assembled to search for the mythic elephant graveyard thought to contain untold riches in ivory tusks. Jane is depicted as bright, energetic, attractive, and defiant of female gender conventions. The rest of the white adventurers, however, are portrayed as greedy, haughty, contemptuous of the African environment, or just ignorant. The Africans who act as their servants and guides are presented as primitive and superstitious, more like animals than humans. This expedition in search of ivory is destined for disaster, and the movie provides thrills by showing expedition members succumbing to attacks by wild animals and "wild humans" who inhabit this "dark continent."

During one such attack by hippos and pygmies, Tarzan, played by handsome Olympic swimming champion Johnny Weismuller, comes to the rescue, scaring off the attackers by mobilizing a stampede of elephants with his piercing, high-pitched, and unforgettable jungle cry. He takes Jane, who has become separated from the group, to his tree house. Thus begins one of the more unusual and famous screen romances.

Tarzan's origins are not explained, although one knows that he somehow lost his white family and was raised by apes. He has none of the refining features of civilization—decent clothes, language, manners—but he possesses strength, honesty, and virtue. As Jane falls in love with Tarzan and decides to share a jungle life with him, we, the viewers, are asked to contemplate, with Jane, the benefits of

being paid to the French company. Actually, the Colombians (not unreasonably) were hoping to stall negotiations until 1904, when they would regain the rights to the canal zone and consequently to the $40 million sale price promised to the French company.

As negotiations failed to deliver the result he desired, Roosevelt encouraged the Panamanians to revolt against Colombian rule. The Panamanians had staged several rebellions in the previous 25 years, all of which had failed, but the 1903 rebellion succeeded, mainly because a U.S. naval force prevented the Colombian government from landing troops in its province of Panama. Meanwhile, the U.S.S. *Nashville* put U.S. troops ashore to help the new nation secure its independence. The United States formally recognized Panama as a sovereign state only two days after the rebellion against Colombia began.

Philippe Bunau-Varilla, a director of the French company from which the United States had bought the rights to the canal, declared himself Panama's diplomatic representative, even though he was a French citizen operating out of a Wall Street law firm and hadn't set foot in Panama in 15 years. Before the true Panamanian delegation (appointed by the new Panamanian government) even reached the United States for negotiations over the canal, Bunau-Varilla had gone to Washington, where he and Secretary of State Hay signed the Hay–Bunau-Varilla Treaty (1903). The treaty granted the United States a 10-mile-wide canal zone in Panama in return for the package Colombia had rejected—$10 million down and $250,000 annually. Thus the United States secured its canal, not by dealing with the newly installed Panamanian government, but with Bunau-Varilla's French company. When the Panamanian delegation arrived in Washington and read the treaty, one of them became so enraged that he knocked Bunau-Varilla cold. Under the circumstances, however, the Panamanian delegation's hands were tied. If it objected to the counterfeit treaty, the United States might withdraw its troops from Panama, leaving the new country at the

Johnny Weismuller and
Maureen O'Sullivan as
Tarzan and Jane.

© Bettmann/Corbis.

peeling off the layers of civilized life (which seem to drop away from Jane along with many of her clothes) and returning to a simpler, more wholesome, and more natural form of existence.

The movie critiques and lampoons the imperial pretensions and smugness of the West, but it never asks viewers to see the indigenous African peoples as anything other than savage. Tarzan may have been ignorant of civilized customs, but he was white and, as such, equipped with the "native" intelligence and character of his race. The Africans depicted in the movie show no such intelligence or character. They are presented as weak and superstitious or as brutally aggressive and indifferent to human life. Thus *Tarzan, the Ape Man* manages to critique the West without asking Western viewers to challenge the racism that justified the West's domination of non-Western peoples and territories.

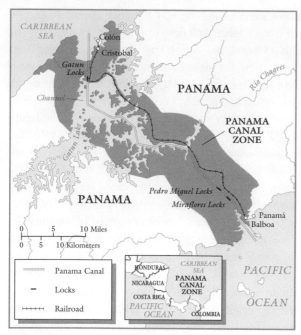

MAP 22.5 PANAMA CANAL ZONE, 1914

This map shows the route of the completed canal through Panama and the 10-mile-wide zone surrounding it that the United States controlled. The inset map locates the Canal Zone in the context of Central and South America.

mercy of Colombia. The instrument through which the United States secured the Canal Zone is known in Panamanian history as "the treaty which no Panamanian signed," and it bedeviled relations between the two countries for much of the 20th century.

Roosevelt's severing of Panama from Colombia prompted angry protests in Congress. The Hearst newspapers decried the Panama foray as "nefarious" and "a quite unexampled instance of foul play in American politics." Roosevelt was not perturbed. Elihu Root (secretary of state in Roosevelt's second administration), after hearing Roosevelt defend his action before a meeting of his cabinet, jokingly told the president, "You have shown that you were accused of seduction and you have conclusively proved that you were guilty of rape." Roosevelt later gloated, "I took the Canal Zone and let Congress debate!"

Roosevelt turned the building of the canal into a test of American ingenuity and willpower. Engineers overcame every obstacle; doctors developed drugs to combat malaria and yellow fever; armies of construction workers "made the dirt fly."

The canal remains a testament to the labor of some 30,000 workers, imported mainly from the West Indies, who, over a 10-year period, labored 10 hours a day, 6 days a week, for 10 cents an hour. Roosevelt visited the canal site in 1906, the first American president to travel overseas while in office. When the canal was triumphantly opened to shipping in 1914, the British ambassador James Bryce described it as "the greatest liberty Man has ever taken with Nature." The canal shortened the voyage from San Francisco to New York by more than 8,000 miles and significantly enhanced the international prestige of the United States. The strategic importance of the canal, in turn, made the United States even more determined to preserve political order in Central America and the Caribbean.

In 1921, the United States paid the Colombian government $25 million as compensation for its loss of Panama. Panama waited more than 70 years, however, to regain control of the 10-mile-wide strip of land that Bunau-Varilla, in connivance with the U.S. government, had bargained away in 1903. President Jimmy Carter signed a treaty in 1977 providing for the reintegration of the Canal Zone into Panama, and the canal was transferred to Panama in 2000.

Keeping the Peace in East Asia

In East Asia, Roosevelt strove to preserve the Open Door policy in China and the balance of power throughout the region. The chief threats came from Russia and Japan, both of whom wanted to seize large chunks of China.

BUILDING THE PANAMA CANAL

This photograph underscores the enormity of the construction task involved in digging out the canal and how much the work depended on workers using only pickaxes, shovels, and wheelbarrows. The headdresses of the workers suggest that they are immigrant laborers from the Indian subcontinent.

© Underwood & Underwood/Corbis.

At first, Russian expansion into Manchuria and Korea prompted Roosevelt to support Japan's 1904 attack on the Russian Pacific fleet anchored at Port Arthur, China. Once the ruinous effects of the war on Russia became clear, however, Roosevelt entered into secret negotiations to arrange a peace. He invited representatives of Japan and Russia to Portsmouth, New Hampshire, and prevailed on them to negotiate a compromise. The settlement favored Japan by perpetuating its control over most of the territories it had won during the brief Russo-Japanese War. Its chief prize was Korea, which became a protectorate of Japan, but Japan also acquired the southern part of Sakhalin Island, Port Arthur, and the South Manchurian Railroad. Russia avoided paying Japan a huge indemnity and it retained Siberia, thus preserving its role as an East Asian power. Finally, Roosevelt protected China's territorial integrity by inducing the armies of both Russia and Japan to leave Manchuria. Roosevelt's success in ending the Russo-Japanese War won him the Nobel Prize for Peace in 1906; he was the first American to earn that award.

Although Roosevelt succeeded in negotiating a peace between these two world powers, he subsequently ignored, and sometimes encouraged, challenges to the sovereignty of weaker Asian nations. In a secret agreement with Japan (the Taft-Katsura Agreement of 1905), for example, the United States agreed that Japan could dominate Korea in return for a Japanese promise not to attack the Philippines. And in the Root-Takahira Agreement of 1908, the United States tacitly reversed its earlier stand on the inviolability of Chinese borders by recognizing Japanese expansion into southern Manchuria.

In Roosevelt's eyes, the overriding need to maintain peace with Japan justified ignoring the claims of Korea and, increasingly, of China. Roosevelt admired Japan's industrial and military might and regarded Japanese expansion into East Asia as a natural expression of its imperial ambition. The task of American diplomacy, he believed, was first to allow the Japanese to build a secure sphere of influence in East Asia (much as the United States had done in Central America), and second to encourage them to join the United States in pursuing peace rather than war. This was a delicate diplomatic task that required both sensitivity and strength, especially when anti-Japanese agitation broke out in California in 1906.

White Californians had long feared the presence of East Asian immigrants (see chapter 20). They had pressured Congress into passing the Chinese Exclusion Act of 1882, which ended most Chinese immigration to the United States. They next turned their racism on Japanese immigrants, whose numbers in California had reached 24,000. In 1906, the San Francisco school board ordered the segregation of Asian schoolchildren so that they would not "contaminate" white children. In 1907, the California legislature debated a law to end Japanese immigration to the state. Anti-Asian riots erupted in San Francisco and Los Angeles, encouraged in part by hysterical stories in the press about the "Yellow Peril."

Outraged militarists in Japan began talking of a possible war with the United States. Roosevelt assured the

ANTI-ASIAN HYSTERIA IN SAN FRANCISCO

In 1906, in the midst of a wave of anti-Asian prejudice in California, the San Francisco school board ordered the segregation of all Asian schoolchildren. Here, a nine-year-old Japanese student submits an application for admission to a public primary school and is refused by the principal, Miss M. E. Dean.

North Wind Picture Archives.

Japanese government that he too was appalled by the Californians' behavior. In 1907, he reached a "gentlemen's agreement" with the Japanese, by which the Tokyo government promised to halt the immigration of Japanese adult male laborers to the United States in return for Roosevelt's pledge to end anti-Japanese discrimination. Roosevelt did his part by persuading the San Francisco school board to rescind its segregation ordinance.

At the same time, Roosevelt worried that the Tokyo government would interpret his sensitivity to Japanese honor as weakness. So he ordered the main part of the U.S. fleet, consisting of 16 battleships, to embark on a 45,000-mile world tour, including a splashy stop in Tokyo Bay. Many Americans deplored the cost of the tour and feared that the appearance of the U.S. Navy in a Japanese port would provoke military retaliation. Roosevelt brushed his critics aside, and, true to his prediction, the Japanese were impressed by the Great White Fleet's show of strength. Their response seemed to lend validity to the African proverb Roosevelt often invoked: "Speak softly and carry a big stick."

In fact, Roosevelt's handling of Japan was arguably the most impressive aspect of his foreign policy. Unlike many other Americans, he refused to let racist attitudes cloud his thinking. He knew when to make concessions and when to stand firm. His policies lessened the prospect of a war with Japan while preserving a strong U.S. presence in East Asia.

William Howard Taft, Dollar Diplomat

William Howard Taft brought impressive foreign policy credentials to the job of president. He had gained valuable experience in colonial administration as the first governor-general of the Philippines. As Roosevelt's secretary of war and chief negotiator for the Taft-Katsura agreement of 1905, he had learned a great deal about conducting diplomacy with imperialist rivals. Yet Taft lacked Roosevelt's grasp of balance-of-power politics and capacity for leadership in foreign affairs. Furthermore, Taft's secretary of state,

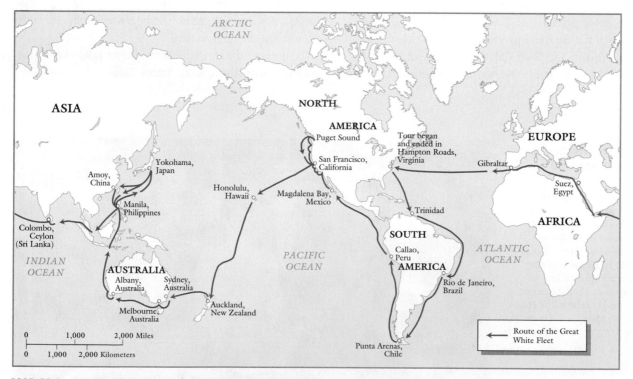

MAP 22.6 ROUTE OF THE GREAT WHITE FLEET, 1907–1909

A 16-battleship-strong U.S. fleet left Virginia in 1907 for a 45,000-mile world tour, whose most important stop was Japan. The map reveals the enormous distance ships had to travel to cross from the Atlantic to the Pacific in the days before the Panama Canal.

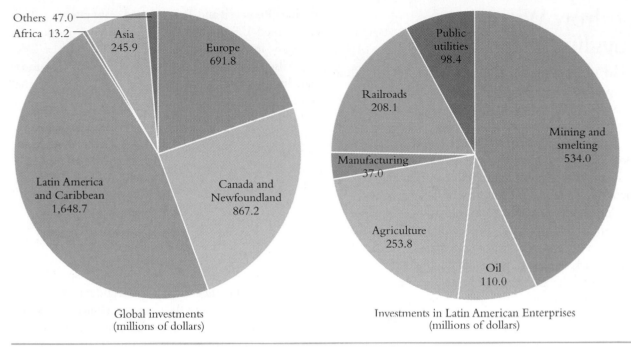

Global investments
(millions of dollars)

Investments in Latin American Enterprises
(millions of dollars)

U.S. GLOBAL INVESTMENTS AND INVESTMENTS IN LATIN AMERICA, 1914

Source: From Cleona Lewis, *America's Stake in International Investments* (Washington, D.C.: The Brookings Institute, 1938), pp. 576–606.

Philander C. Knox, a corporation lawyer from Pittsburgh, lacked diplomatic expertise. Knox's conduct of foreign policy seemed directed almost entirely toward expanding opportunities for corporate investment overseas, a disposition that prompted critics to deride his policies as "dollar diplomacy."

Taft and Knox believed that U.S. investments would effectively substitute "dollars for bullets," and thus offer a more peaceful and less coercive way of maintaining stability and order. Taking a swipe at Roosevelt's "big stick" policy, Taft announced that "modern diplomacy is commercial."

The inability of Taft and Knox to grasp the complexities of power politics, however, led to a diplomatic reversal in East Asia. Knox, prodded by banker associates, sought to expand American economic activities in China—even in Manchuria, where they encroached on the Japanese sphere of influence. In 1911, Knox proposed that a syndicate of European and American bankers buy the Japanese-controlled South Manchurian Railroad to open up North China to international trade. Japan reacted by signing a friendship treaty with Russia, its former enemy, which signaled their joint determination to exclude American, British, and French goods from Manchurian markets. Knox's plan to purchase the railroad collapsed, and the United States' Open Door policy suffered a serious blow.

Knox's further efforts to increase American trade with Central and South China triggered further hostile responses from the Japanese and the Russians and contributed to the collapse of the Chinese government and the onset of the Chinese Revolution in 1911.

Dollar diplomacy worked better in the Caribbean, where no major power contested U.S. policy. Knox encouraged American investment. Companies such as United Fruit of Boston, which established extensive banana plantations in Costa Rica and Honduras, grew powerful enough to influence both the economies and the governments of Central American countries. When political turmoil threatened their investments, the United States simply sent in its troops. Thus, when Nicaraguan dictator José Santos Zelaya reportedly began negotiating with a European country to build a second trans-Isthmian canal in 1910, a force of U.S. Marines toppled his regime. Marines landed again in 1912 when Zelaya's successor, Adolfo Diaz, angered Nicaraguans with his pro-American policies. This time the Marines were instructed to keep the Diaz regime in power. Except for a brief period in 1925, U.S. troops would remain in Nicaragua continuously from 1912 until 1933. Under Taft, the United States continued to do whatever American policy makers deemed necessary to bolster friendly governments and maintain order in Latin America.

Woodrow Wilson, Struggling Idealist

Woodrow Wilson's foreign policy in the Caribbean initially appeared no different from that of his Republican predecessors. In 1915, the United States sent troops to Haiti to put down a revolution; they remained as an army of occupation for 21 years. In 1916, when the people of the Dominican Republic (who shared the island of Hispaniola with the Haitians) refused to accept a treaty making them more or less a protectorate of the United States, Wilson forced them to accept the rule of a U.S. military government. When German influence in the Danish West Indies began to expand, Wilson purchased the islands from Denmark, renamed them the Virgin Islands, and added them to the U.S. Caribbean empire. By the time Wilson left office in 1921, he had intervened militarily in the Caribbean more often than any American president before him.

Wilson's relationship with Mexico in the wake of its revolution, however, reveals that he was troubled by a foreign policy that ignored a less powerful nation's right to determine its own future. He deemed the Mexicans capable of making democracy work and, in general, showed a concern for morality and justice in foreign affairs—matters to which Roosevelt and Taft had paid scant attention. Wilson wanted U.S. foreign policy to advance democratic ideals and institutions in Mexico.

Wilson's Mexican dealings were motivated by more than his fondness for democracy. He also feared that political unrest in Mexico could lead to violence, social disorder, and a revolutionary government hostile to U.S. economic interests. With a U.S.-style democratic government in Mexico, Wilson believed, property rights would be respected and U.S. investments would remain secure. Wilson's desire both to encourage democracy and to limit the extent of social change made it difficult to devise a consistent foreign policy toward Mexico.

The Mexican Revolution broke out in 1910 when dictator Porfirio Diaz, who had ruled for 34 years, was overthrown by democratic forces led by Francisco Madero. Madero's talk of democratic reform frightened many foreign investors, especially those in the United States and Great Britain, who owned more than half of all Mexican real estate, 90 percent of its oil reserves, and practically all of its railroads. Thus, when Madero himself was overthrown early in 1913 by Victoriano Huerta, a conservative general who promised to protect foreign investments, the dollar diplomatists in the Taft administration and in Great Britain breathed a sigh of relief. Henry Lane Wilson, the

Brown Brothers.

PANCHO VILLA

Francisco "Pancho" Villa was the charismatic commander of a rebel Mexican army during the years of the Mexican Revolution (1910–17). Failing to attract the support of President Wilson, Villa became a bitter enemy of the United States. After Villa's forces murdered more than 30 U.S. civilians, Wilson dispatched an army to Mexico to hunt him down. U.S. forces pursued him 300 miles into Mexico but never caught him.

U.S. ambassador to Mexico, had helped engineer Huerta's coup. Before close relations between the United States and Huerta could be worked out, however, Huerta's men murdered Madero.

Woodrow Wilson, who became president shortly after Madero's assassination in 1913, might have overlooked it (as did the European powers) and entered into close ties with Huerta on condition that he protect American property. Instead, Wilson refused to recognize Huerta's "government of butchers" and demanded that Mexico hold democratic elections. Wilson favored Venustiano Carranza and Francisco ("Pancho") Villa, two enemies of Huerta who commanded rebel armies and who claimed to be democrats. In April 1914, Wilson used the arrest of several U.S. sailors by Huerta's troops as a reason to send a fleet into Mexican waters. He ordered the U.S. Marines to occupy the Mexican port city of Veracruz and to prevent a German ship there from unloading munitions meant for Huerta's army. In the resulting battle between U.S. and Mexican forces, 19 Americans and 126 Mexicans were killed. The battle brought the two countries dangerously close to war. Eventually, however, American control over Veracruz weakened and embarrassed Huerta's regime to the point where Carranza was able to take power.

Carranza did not behave as Wilson had expected. Rejecting Wilson's efforts to shape a new Mexican government, he announced a bold land reform program. That program called for the distribution of some of Mexico's agricultural land to impoverished peasants and the transfer of developmental rights on oil lands from foreign corporations to the Mexican government. If the program went into effect, U.S. petroleum companies would lose control of their Mexican properties, a loss that Wilson deemed unacceptable. Wilson now threw his support to Pancho Villa, who seemed more willing than Carranza to protect U.S. oil interests. When Carranza's forces defeated Villa's forces in 1915, Wilson reluctantly withdrew his support of Villa and prepared to recognize the Carranza government.

Furious that Wilson had abandoned him, Villa and his soldiers pulled 18 U.S. citizens from a train in northern Mexico and murdered them, along with another 17 in an attack on Columbus, New Mexico. Determined to punish Villa, Wilson received permission from Carranza to send a U.S. expeditionary force under General John J. Pershing into Mexico to hunt down Villa's "bandits." Pershing's troops pursued Villa's forces 300 miles into Mexico but failed to catch them. The U.S. troops did, however, clash twice with Mexican troops under Carranza's command,

once again bringing the countries to the brink of war. The United States, about to enter the First World War, could not afford a fight with Mexico; in 1917, Wilson quietly ordered Pershing's troops home and grudgingly recognized the Carranza government.

Wilson's policies toward Mexico in the years from 1913 to 1917 seemed to have produced few concrete results, except to reinforce an already deep antagonism among Mexicans toward the United States. His repeated changes in strategy, moreover, seemed to indicate a lack of skill and decisiveness in foreign affairs. Actually, however, Wilson recognized something that Roosevelt and Taft had not: that more and more peoples of the world were determined to control their own destinies. The United States, under Wilson, was looking for a way to support these peoples' democratic aspirations while also safeguarding its own economic interests. The First World War would make this quest for a balance between democratic principles and national self-interest all the more urgent.

Conclusion

We can assess the dramatic turn in U.S. foreign policy after 1898 either in relation to the foreign policies of rival world powers or against America's own democratic ideals. By the first standard, U.S. foreign policy looks impressive. The United States achieved its major objectives in world affairs: It tightened its control over the Western Hemisphere and projected its military and economic power into Asia. It did so while sacrificing relatively few American lives and while constraining the jingoistic appetite for truly extensive military adventure and conquest. The United States added only 125,000 square miles to its empire in the years from 1870 to 1900, while Great Britain, France, and Germany enlarged their empires by 4.7, 3.5, and 1.0 million square miles, respectively. Relatively few foreigners were subjected to American colonial rule. By contrast, in 1900, the British Empire extended more than 12 million square miles and embraced one-fourth of the world's population. At times, American rule could be brutal, as it was to Filipino soldiers and civilians alike, but on the whole it was no more severe than British rule and significantly less severe than that of the French, German, Belgian, or Japanese imperialists. McKinley, Roosevelt, Taft, and Wilson all placed limits on American expansion and avoided, until 1917, extensive foreign entanglements and wars.

If measured against the standard of America's own democratic ideals, however, U.S. foreign policy after 1898 must be judged more harshly. It demeaned the peoples of the Philippines, Puerto Rico, Guam, Cuba, and Colombia as inferior and primitive and denied them the right to govern themselves. In choosing to behave like the imperialist powers of Europe, the United States abandoned its long-standing claim to being a different kind of nation—one that valued liberty more than power.

Many Americans of the time judged their nation by both standards and thus faced a dilemma that would ex-tend throughout the 20th century. On the one hand, they believed with Roosevelt that the size, economic strength, and honor of the United States required it to accept the role of world power and policeman. On the other hand, they continued to believe with Wilson that they had a mission to spread the values of 1776 to the farthest reaches of the earth. The Mexico example demonstrates how hard it was for the United States to reconcile these two very different approaches to world affairs.

SUGGESTED READINGS

General works on America's imperialist turn in the 1890s and early years of the 20th century include **John Dobson,** *America's Ascent: The United States Becomes a Great Power, 1880–1914* (1978), **Walter LaFeber,** *The Cambridge History of Foreign Relations: The Search for Opportunity, 1865–1913* (1993), and **Emily Rosenberg,** *Spreading the American Dream: American Economic and Cultural Expansion, 1890–1945* (1982). **David F. Trask,** *The War with Spain in 1898* (1981), is a comprehensive study of the Spanish-American War, but it should be supplemented with **Philip S. Foner,** *The Spanish-Cuban-American War and the Birth of American Imperialism,* 2 vols. (1972). **Gerald F. Linderman,** *The Mirror of War: American Society and the Spanish-American War* (1974), brilliantly recaptures the shock that overtook Americans who discovered that their Cuban allies were black and the Spanish enemies were white. The role of gender in the Spanish-American War is explored in **Kristin L. Hoganson,** *Fighting for American Manhood: How Gender Politics Provoked the Spanish-American and Philippine-American Wars* (1998). **Stuart Creighton Miller,** *"Benevolent Assimilation": The American Conquest of the Philippines, 1899–1903* (1982), analyzes the Filipino-American war, **Louis A. Perez,** *Cuba under the Platt Amendment, 1902–1934* (1986), examines the extension of U.S. control over Cuba,

while **Marilyn B. Young,** *The Rhetoric of Empire: American China Policy, 1895–1901* (1968), explores the unfolding Open Door policy. The acquisition of Guam and Samoa is examined in **Paul M. Kennedy,** *The Samoan Tangle* (1974), and the history of Puerto Rico following its annexation by the United States is explored in **Raymond Carr,** *Puerto Rico: A Colonial Experiment* (1984). The anti-imperialist movement is analyzed in **E. Berkeley Tompkins,** *Anti-Imperialism in the United States, 1890–1920: The Great Debate* (1970). **Howard K. Beale,** *Theodore Roosevelt and the Rise of America to World Power* (1956), is still a crucial work on Roosevelt's foreign policy, but it should be supplemented with **Richard H. Collin,** *Theodore Roosevelt's Caribbean: The Panama Canal, the Monroe Doctrine and the Latin American Context* (1990). Consult **Emily Rosenberg,** *Financial Missionaries to the World: The Politics and Culture of Dollar Diplomacy, 1900–1930* (1999), on the "dollar diplomacy" that emerged during the Taft Administration. On Wilson's foreign policy, consult **Thomas J. Knock,** *To End All Wars: Woodrow Wilson and the Quest for a New World Order* (1992), **Lloyd C. Gardner,** *Safe for Democracy: The Anglo-American Response to Revolution, 1913–1923* (1984), and **John S. D. Eisenhower,** *Intervention: The United States and the Mexican Revolution, 1913–1917* (1993).

AMERICAN JOURNEY ONLINE
AND
INFOTRAC COLLEGE EDITION

Visit the source collections at www.ajaccess.wadsworth.com and infotrac.thomsonlearning.com and use the Search function with the following key terms to explore documents, images, audio and video clips, articles, and commentary related to the material in this chapter.

William McKinley
Imperialism
Spanish-American War
Treaty of Paris
Theodore Roosevelt
Rough Riders

American-Filipino War
Roosevelt Corollary
Panama Canal
William Howard Taft
Woodrow Wilson

GRADE AIDS

Visit the Liberty Equality Power Companion Web Site for resources specific to this textbook: http://history.wadsworth.com/murrin_LEP4e

The CD in the back of this book and the U.S. History Resource Center at http://history.wadsworth.com/u.s./ offer a variety of tools to help you succeed in this course, including access to quizzes; images; documents; interactive simulations; maps, and timelines; movie explorations; and a wealth of other sources.

Chapter 23

War and Society, 1914–1920

THE SINKING OF THE LUSITANIA
On May 7, 1915, a German U-boat torpedoed and sank the British passenger liner *Lusitania*, killing 1,198 people, 128 of them Americans. The event turned U.S. opinion sharply against the Germans, especially because the civilians on board had been given no chance to escape or surrender.

CHAPTER OUTLINE

The First World War broke out in Europe in August 1914. The Triple Alliance of Germany, Austria-Hungary, and the Ottoman Empire squared off against the Triple Entente of Great Britain, France, and Russia. The United States entered the war on the side of the Entente (the Allies, or Allied Powers, as they came to be called) in 1917. Over the next year and a half, the United States converted its large, sprawling economy into a disciplined war production machine, raised a 5-million-man army, and provided both the war matériel and troops that helped propel the Allies to victory. The United States emerged from the war as the world's mightiest country. In these and other respects, the war was a great triumph.

But the war also convulsed American society more deeply than any event since the Civil War. This was the first "total" war, meaning that combatants devoted virtually all of their resources to the fight. Thus the U.S. government had no choice but to pursue a degree of industrial control and social regimentation that was unprecedented in American history. Needless to say, this degree of government control was a controversial measure in a society that had long distrusted state power. Moreover, significant numbers of Americans from a variety of constituencies opposed the war. To overcome this opposition, Wilson couched American war aims in disinterested and idealistic terms: The United States, he claimed, wanted a "peace without victory," a "war for democracy," and liberty for the world's oppressed peoples. Because these words drew deeply on American political traditions, Wilson believed that Americans would find them inspiring, put aside their suspicions, and support him.

Although many people in the United States and abroad responded enthusiastically to Wilson's ideals, Wilson needed England and France's support to deliver peace without victory, and this support never came. At home, disadvantaged groups stirred up trouble by declaring that American society had failed to live up to its democratic and egalitarian ideals. Wilson supported repressive policies to silence these rebels and to enforce unity and conformity on the American people. In the process, he tarnished the ideals for which America had been fighting. Only a year after the war ended, Wilson's hopes for peace without victory abroad had been destroyed, and America was being torn apart by violent labor disputes and race riots at home.

CHAPTER FOCUS

♦ Why did the United States become involved in the First World War?

♦ What problems did the U.S. government encounter as it sought to mobilize its people and economy for war, and how were they overcome?

♦ What were Woodrow Wilson's peace proposals and how did they fare?

♦ Did the First World War enhance or interrupt the pursuit of liberty and equality on the home front?

Europe's Descent into War

Europe began its descent into war on June 28, 1914, in Sarajevo, Bosnia, when a Bosnian nationalist assassinated Archduke Franz Ferdinand, heir to the Austro-Hungarian throne. This act was meant to protest the Austro-Hungarian imperial presence in the Balkans and to encourage the Bosnians, Croatians, and other Balkan peoples to join the Serbs in establishing independent nations. Austria-Hungary responded to this provocation on July 28 by declaring war on Serbia, holding it responsible for the archduke's murder.

The conflict might have remained local if an intricate series of treaties had not divided Europe into two hostile camps. Germany, Austria-Hungary, and Italy, the so-called Triple Alliance, had promised to come to each other's aid if attacked. Italy would soon opt out of this alliance, to be replaced by the Ottoman Empire. Arrayed against the nations of the Triple Alliance were Britain, France, and Russia in the Triple Entente. Russia was obligated by another treaty to defend Serbia against Austria-Hungary, and consequently on July 30, it mobilized its armed forces to go to Serbia's aid. That brought Germany into the conflict to protect Austria-Hungary from Russian attack. On August 3, German troops struck not at Russia but at France, Russia's western ally. To reach France, German troops had marched through neutral Belgium. On August 4, Britain reacted by declaring war on Germany. Within the space of only a few weeks, Europe was engulfed in war.

Complicated alliances and defense treaties of the European nations undoubtedly hastened the rush toward war. But equally important was the competition among the larger powers to build the strongest economies, the largest armies and navies, and the grandest colonial empires. Britain and Germany, in particular, were engaged in a bitter struggle for European and world supremacy. Few Europeans had any idea that these military buildups might lead to a terrible war that would kill nearly an entire generation of young men and expose the barbarity lurking in their civilization. Historians now believe that several

CHRONOLOGY

1914	First World War breaks out (July–August)
1915	German submarine sinks *Lusitania* (May 7)
1916	Woodrow Wilson unveils peace initiative • Wilson reelected as "peace president"
1917	Germany resumes unrestricted submarine warfare (February) • Tsar Nicholas II overthrown in Russia (March) • U.S. enters the war (April 6) • Committee on Public Information established • Congress passes Selective Service Act, Espionage Act, Immigration Restriction Act • War Industries Board established • Lenin's Bolsheviks come to power in Russia (Nov.)
1918	Lenin signs treaty with Germany, pulls Russia out of war (March) • Germany launches offensive on western front (March–April) • Congress passes Sabotage Act and Sedition Act • French, British, and U.S. troops repel Germans, advance toward Germany (April–October) • Eugene V. Debs jailed for making antiwar speech • Germany signs armistice (Nov. 11)
1919	Treaty of Versailles signed (June 28) • Chicago race riot (July) • Wilson suffers stroke (October 2) • Police strike in Boston • 18th Amendment (Prohibition) ratified
1919–20	Steelworkers strike in Midwest • Red Scare prompts "Palmer raids" • Senate refuses to ratify Treaty of Versailles • Universal Negro Improvement Association grows under Marcus Garvey's leadership
1920	Anarchists Sacco and Vanzetti convicted of murder
1923	Marcus Garvey convicted of mail fraud
1924	Woodrow Wilson dies
1927	Sacco and Vanzetti executed

advisers close to the German emperor, Kaiser Wilhelm II, were actually eager to engage Russia and France in a fight for supremacy on the European continent. They expected that a European war would be swift and decisive—in Germany's favor. England and France also believed in their own superiority. Millions of young men, rich and poor, rushed to join the armies on both sides and share in the expected glory.

Victory was not swift. The two camps were evenly matched. Moreover, the first wartime use of machine guns and barbed wire made defense against attack easier than staging an offensive. (Both tanks and airplanes had been invented by this time, but military strategists on both sides were slow to put them to offensive use). On the western front, after the initial German attack narrowly failed to take Paris in 1914, the two opposing armies confronted each other along a battle line stretching from Belgium in the north to the Swiss border in the southeast. Troops dug trenches to protect themselves from artillery bombardment and poison gas attacks. Commanders on both sides mounted suicidal ground assaults on the enemy by send-

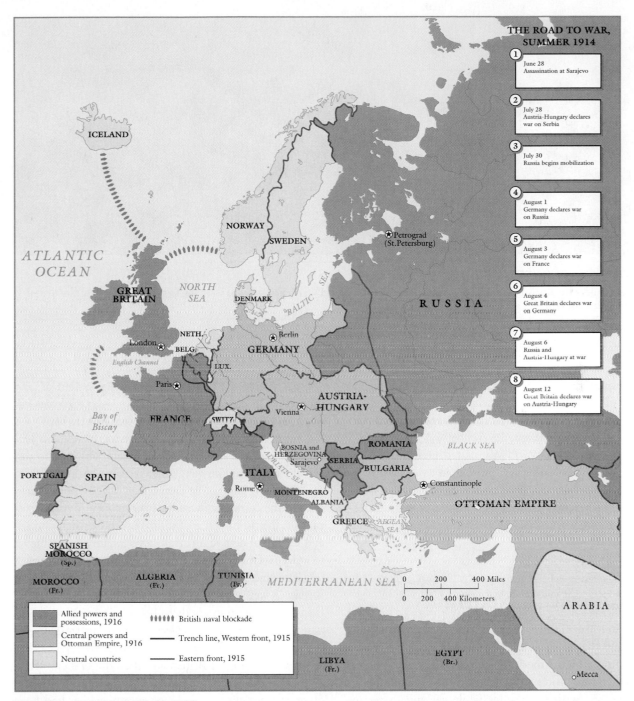

THE ROAD TO WAR, SUMMER 1914

1. June 28
   Assassination at Sarajevo

2. July 28
   Austria-Hungary declares war on Serbia

3. July 30
   Russia begins mobilization

4. August 1
   Germany declares war on Russia

5. August 3
   Germany declares war on France

6. August 4
   Great Britain declares war on Germany

7. August 6
   Russia and Austria-Hungary at war

8. August 12
   Great Britain declares war on Austria-Hungary

Legend:

- Allied powers and possessions, 1916
- Central powers and Ottoman Empire, 1916
- Neutral countries
- ♦♦♦♦♦♦ British naval blockade
- —— Trench line, Western front, 1915
- —— Eastern front, 1915

MAP 23.1 EUROPE GOES TO WAR

In the First World War, Great Britain, France, and Russia squared off against Germany, Austria-Hungary, and the Ottoman Empire. Most of the fighting occurred in Europe along the western front in France (purple line) or the eastern front in Russia (red line). This map also shows Britain's blockade of German ports. British armies based in Egypt (then a British colony) clashed with Ottoman armies in Arabia and other parts of the Ottoman Empire.

 View an animated version of this map or related maps at http://history.wadsworth.com/murrin_LEP4e.

ing tens of thousands of infantry, armed only with rifles, bayonets, and grenades, out of the trenches and directly into enemy fire. Barbed wire further retarded forward progress, enabling enemy artillery and machine guns to cut down appalling numbers of men. In 1916, during one

10-month German offensive at Verdun (France), 600,000 German troops died; 20,000 British troops were killed during only the first day of an Entente assault on the Somme River (also in France). Many of those who were not killed in combat succumbed to disease that spread rapidly in the

Imperial War Museum, London.

GASSED, **BY JOHN SINGER SARGENT**

An artist renders the horror of a poison gas attack in the First World War. The Germans were the first to use this new and brutal weapon, which contributed greatly to the terror of war.

cold, wet, and rat-infested trenches. In Eastern Europe, the armies of Germany and Austria-Hungary squared off against those of Russia and Serbia. Although that front did not employ trench warfare, the combat was no less lethal. By the time the First World War ended, an estimated 8.5 million soldiers had died and more than twice that number had been wounded. Total casualties, both military and civilian, had reached 37 million. Europe had lost a generation of young men, as well as its confidence, stability, and global supremacy.

American Neutrality

Soon after the fighting began, Woodrow Wilson told Americans that this was a European war; neither side was threatening a vital American interest. The United States would therefore proclaim its neutrality and maintain normal relations with both sides while seeking to secure peace. Normal relations meant that the United States would continue trading with both camps. Wilson's neutrality policy met with lively opposition, especially from Theodore Roosevelt, who was convinced that the United States should join the Entente to check German power and expansionism. Most Americans, however, applauded Wilson's determination to keep the country out of war.

Neutrality was easier to proclaim than to achieve, however. Many Americans, especially those with economic and political power, identified culturally more with Britain than with Germany. They shared with the English a language, a common ancestry, and a commitment to liberty.

Wilson revered the British parliamentary system of government. His closest foreign policy adviser, Colonel Edward M. House, was pro-British, as was Robert Lansing, a trusted counselor in the State Department. William Jennings Bryan, Wilson's secretary of state, objected to this pro-British tilt, but he was a lone voice in Wilson's Cabinet.

Germany had no such attraction for U.S. policy makers. On the contrary, Germany's acceptance of monarchical rule, the prominence of militarists in German politics, and its lack of democratic traditions inclined U.S. officials to judge Germany harshly.

The United States had strong economic ties to Great Britain as well. In 1914, the United States exported more than $800 million in goods to Britain and its allies, compared with $170 million to Germany and Austria-Hungary (which came to be known as the Central Powers). As soon as the war began, the British and then the French turned to the United States for food, clothing, munitions, and other war supplies. The U.S. economy, which had been languishing in 1914, enjoyed a boom as a result. Bankers began to issue loans to the Allied Powers, further knitting together the American and British economies and giving American investors a direct stake in an Allied victory. Moreover, the British navy had blockaded German ports, which damaged the United States' already limited trade with Germany. By 1916, U.S. exports to the Central Powers had plummeted to barely 1 million dollars, a fall of more than 99 percent in two years.

The British blockade of German ports clearly violated American neutrality. The Wilson administration protested the British navy's search and occasional seizure of American merchant ships, but it never retaliated by suspending loans or exports to Great Britain. To do so would have plunged the U.S. economy into a severe recession. In failing to protect its right to trade with Germany, however, the United States compromised its neutrality and allowed itself to be drawn into war.

Submarine Warfare

To combat British control of the seas and to check the flow of U.S. goods to the Allies, Germany unveiled a terrifying new weapon, the *Unterseeboot,* or U-boat, the first militarily effective submarine. Early in 1915, Germany announced its intent to use its U-boats to sink on sight enemy ships en route to the British Isles. On May 7, 1915, without warning, a German U-boat torpedoed the British passenger liner *Lusitania,* en route from New York to London. The ship sank in 22 minutes, killing 1,198 men, women, and children, 128 of them U.S. citizens. Americans were shocked by the sinking. Innocent civilians who had been given no warning of attack and no chance to surrender had been murdered in cold blood. The attack appeared to confirm what anti-German agitators were saying: that the Germans were by nature barbaric and uncivilized. The circumstances surrounding the sinking of the *Lusitania,* however, were more complicated than most Americans realized.

Before its sailing, the Germans had alleged that the *Lusitania* was secretly carrying a large store of munitions to Great Britain (a charge later proved true) and that it therefore was subject to U-boat attack. Germany had warned American passengers not to travel on British passenger ships that carried munitions. Moreover, Germany claimed, with some justification, that the purpose of the U-boat attacks—the disruption of Allied supply lines—was no different from Britain's purpose in blockading German ports. Because its surface ships were outnumbered by the British navy, Germany claimed it had no alternative but to choose the underwater strategy. If a submarine attack seemed more reprehensible than a conventional sea battle, the Germans argued, it was no more so than the British attempt to starve the German people into submission with a blockade.

American political leaders might have used the *Lusitania* incident to denounce both Germany's U-boat strategy and Britain's blockade as actions that violated the rights of citizens of neutral nations. Only Secretary of State Bryan had the courage to say so, however, and his stand proved so unpopular in Washington that he resigned from office; Wilson chose the pro-British Lansing to take his place. Wilson denounced the sinking of the *Lusitania* and demanded that Germany pledge never to launch another attack on the citizens of neutral nations, even when they were traveling in British or French ships. Germany acquiesced to Wilson's demand.

The resulting lull in submarine warfare was short-lived, however. In early 1916, the Allies began to arm their merchant vessels with guns and depth charges capable of destroying German U-boats. Considering this a provocation, Germany renewed its campaign of surprise submarine attacks. In March 1916, a German submarine torpedoed the French passenger liner *Sussex,* causing a heavy loss of life and injuring several Americans. Again Wilson demanded that Germany spare civilians from attack. In the so-called *Sussex* pledge, Germany once again relented but warned that it might resume unrestricted submarine warfare if the United States did not prevail on Great Britain to permit neutral ships to pass through the naval blockade.

The German submarine attacks strengthened the hand of Theodore Roosevelt and others who had been arguing that war with Germany was inevitable and that the United States must prepare itself to fight. By 1916, Wilson could no longer ignore these critics. Between January and September of that year, he sought and won congressional approval for bills to increase the size of the army and navy, tighten federal control over National Guard forces, and authorize the building of a merchant fleet. Although Wilson had conceded ground to the pro-war agitators, he did not share their belief that war with Germany was either inevitable or desirable. To the contrary, he accelerated his diplomatic initiatives to secure peace, and he dispatched Colonel House to London in January 1916 to draw up a peace plan with the British foreign secretary, Lord Grey. This initiative resulted in the House-Grey memorandum of February 22, 1916, in which Britain agreed to ask the United States to negotiate a settlement between the Allies and the Central Powers. The British believed that the terms of such a peace settlement would favor the Allies. They were furious when Wilson revealed that he wanted an impartial, honestly negotiated peace in which the claims of the Allies and Central Powers would be treated with equal respect and consideration. Britain now rejected U.S. peace overtures, and relations between the two countries grew unexpectedly tense.

The Peace Movement

Underlying Wilson's 1916 peace initiative was a vision of a new world order in which relations between nations would be governed by negotiation rather than war and in which justice would replace power as the fundamental principle of diplomacy. In a major foreign policy address on May 27, 1916, Wilson formally declared his support for what he would later call the League of Nations, an international parliament dedicated to the pursuit of peace, security, and justice for all the world's peoples.

Many Americans supported Wilson's efforts to commit national prestige to the cause of international peace rather than conquest and to keep the United States out of war. Carrie Chapman Catt, president of the National American Woman Suffrage Association, and Jane Addams, founder of the Women's Peace Party, actively opposed the war. In 1915, an international women's peace conference at The Hague (in the Netherlands) had drawn many participants from the United States. A substantial pacifist group emerged among the nation's Protestant clergy. Midwestern progressives such as Robert La Follette, Bryan, and George Norris urged that the United States steer clear of this European conflict, as did leading socialists such as Eugene V. Debs. In April 1916, many of the country's most prominent progressives and socialists joined hands in the American Union Against Militarism and pressured Wilson to continue pursuing the path of peace.

Wilson's peace campaign also attracted support from the country's sizable Irish and German ethnic populations, who wanted to block a formal military alliance with Great Britain. That many German ethnics, who continued to feel affection for their native land and culture, would oppose U.S. entry into the war is hardly surprising. And the Irish viewed England as an arrogant imperial power that kept Ireland subjugated. That view was confirmed when England crushed the Easter Rebellion that Irish nationalists had launched on Easter Monday 1916 to win their country's independence. The Irish in America, like those in Ireland, wanted to see Britain's strength sapped (and Ireland's prospects for freedom enhanced) by a long war.

Wilson's Vision: "Peace without Victory"

The 1916 presidential election revealed the breadth of peace sentiment. At the Democratic convention, Governor Martin Glynn of New York, the Irish American speaker who renominated Wilson for a second term, praised the president for keeping the United States out of war. His portrayal of Wilson as the "peace president" electrified the convention and made "He kept us out of war" a campaign slogan. The slogan proved particularly effective against Wilson's Republican opponent, Charles Evans Hughes, whose close ties to Theodore Roosevelt seemed to place him in the pro-war camp. Combining the promise of peace with a pledge to push ahead with progressive reform, Wilson won a narrow victory.

Emboldened by his electoral triumph, Wilson intensified his quest for peace. On December 16, 1916, he sent a peace note to the belligerent governments, entreating them to consider ending the conflict and, to that end, to state their terms for peace. Although Germany refused to specify its terms and Britain and France announced a set of conditions too extreme for Germany ever to accept, Wilson pressed ahead, initiating secret peace negotiations with both sides. To prepare the American people for what he hoped would be a new era of international relations, Wilson appeared before the Senate on January 22, 1917, to

ON A MISSION FOR PEACE

Members of the American Women's Peace Party pose on a ship taking them to The Hague (The Netherlands) for a 1915 meeting of the International Committee for Permanent Peace. These women were part of a large domestic movement that opposed U.S. involvement in the war. Jane Addams, one of the peace movement's leaders, is third from the right behind the banner.

outline his plans for peace. In his speech, he reaffirmed his commitment to the League of Nations, but for such a league to succeed, Wilson argued, it would have to be handed a sturdy peace settlement. This entailed a "peace without victory." Only a peace settlement that refused to crown a victor or humiliate a loser would ensure the equality of the combatants, and "only a peace between equals can last."

Wilson listed the crucial principles of a lasting peace: freedom of the seas; disarmament; and the right of every people to self-determination, democratic self-government, and security against aggression. He was proposing a revolutionary change in world order, one that would allow all of the world's peoples, regardless of their size or strength, to achieve political independence and to participate as equals in world affairs. These views, rarely expressed by the leader of a world power, stirred the despairing masses of Europe and elsewhere caught in deadly conflict.

German Escalation

Wilson's oratory came too late to serve the cause of peace. Sensing the imminent collapse of Russian forces on the eastern front, Germany had decided, in early 1917, to throw its full military might at France and Britain. On land it planned to launch a massive assault on the trenches, and at sea it prepared to unleash its submarines to attack all vessels heading for British ports. Germany knew that this last action would compel the United States to enter the war, but it was gambling on being able to strangle the British economy and leave France isolated before significant numbers of American troops could reach European shores.

On February 1, the United States broke off diplomatic relations with Germany. Wilson continued to hope for a negotiated settlement, however, until February 25, when the British intercepted and passed on to the president a telegram from Germany's foreign secretary, Arthur Zimmermann, to the German minister in Mexico. The infamous "Zimmermann telegram" instructed the minister to ask the Mexican government to attack the United States in the event of war between Germany and the United States. In return, Germany would pay the Mexicans a large fee and regain for them the "lost provinces" of Texas, New Mexico, and Arizona. Wilson, Congress, and the American public were outraged by the story.

In March, news arrived that Tsar Nicholas II's autocratic regime in Russia had collapsed and had been replaced by a liberal-democratic government under the leadership of Alexander Kerensky. As long as the tsar ruled Russia and stood to benefit from the Central Powers' defeat, Wilson could not honestly claim that America's going to war against Germany would bring democracy to Europe. The fall of the tsar and the need of Russia's fledgling democratic government for support gave Wilson the rationale he needed to justify American intervention.

Appearing before a joint session of Congress on April 2, Wilson declared that the United States must enter the war because "the world must be made safe for democracy." He continued:

> We shall fight for the things which we have always carried nearest our hearts—for democracy, for the right of those who submit to authority to have a voice in their own Governments, for the rights and liberties of small nations, for a universal dominion of right by such a concert of free peoples as shall bring peace and safety to all nations and make the world itself at last free. To such a task we dedicate our lives and our fortunes.

Inspired by his words, Congress broke into thunderous applause. On April 6, Congress voted to declare war by a vote of 373 to 50 in the House and 82 to 6 in the Senate.

The United States thus embarked on a grand experiment to reshape the world. Wilson had given millions of people around the world reason to hope, both that the terrible war would soon end and that their strivings for freedom and social justice would be realized. Although he was taking America to war on the side of the Allies, he stressed that America would fight as an "associated power," a phrase meant to underscore America's determination to keep its war aims separate from and more idealistic than those of the Allies.

Still, Wilson understood all too well the risks of his undertaking. A few days before his speech to Congress, he had confided to a journalist his worry that the American people, once at war, will "forget there ever was such a thing as tolerance. To fight you must be brutal and ruthless, and the spirit of ruthless brutality will enter into the very fibre of our national life, infecting Congress, the courts, the policeman on the beat, the man in the street."

🌎 American Intervention

The entry of the United States into the war gave the Allies the muscle they needed to defeat the Central Powers, but it came almost too late. Germany's resumption of unrestricted submarine warfare took a frightful toll on Allied shipping. From February through July 1917, German subs sank almost 4 million tons of shipping, more than one-third of Britain's entire merchant fleet. One of every four large freighters departing Britain in those months never returned; at one point, the British Isles were down to a mere four weeks of provisions. American intervention ended Britain's vulnerability in dramatic fashion. U.S. and British naval commanders now grouped merchant ships into convoys and provided them with warship escorts through the most dangerous stretches of the North Atlantic. Destroyers armed with depth charges were particularly effective as escorts. Their shallow draft made them invulnerable to torpedoes, and their great acceleration and speed allowed them to pursue slow-moving U-boats. The U.S. and British navies had begun to use sound waves (later called "sonar") to pinpoint the location of underwater craft, and this new technology increased the effectiveness of destroyer attacks. By the end of 1917, the tonnage of Allied shipping lost each month to U-boat attacks had declined by two-thirds, from almost 1 million tons in April to 350,000 tons in December. The increased flow of supplies stiffened the resolve of the exhausted British and French troops.

The French and British armies had bled themselves white by taking the offensive in 1916 and 1917 and had scarcely budged the trench lines. The Germans had been content in those years simply to hold their trench position in the West because they were engaged in a huge offensive against the Russians in the East. The Germans intended first to defeat Russia and then to shift their eastern armies to the West for a final assault on the weakened British and French lines. Their opportunity came in the winter and spring of 1918.

A second Russian revolution in November 1917 had overthrown Kerensky's liberal-democratic government and had brought to power a revolutionary socialist government under Vladimir Lenin and his Bolshevik Party. Lenin pulled Russia out of the war on the grounds that the war did not serve the best interests of the working classes, that it was a conflict between rival capitalist elites interested only in wealth and power (and indifferent to the slaughter of soldiers in the trenches). In March 1918, Lenin signed a treaty at Brest-Litovsk that added to Germany's territory and resources and enabled Germany to shift its eastern forces to the western front.

Russia's exit from the war hurt the Allies. Not only did it expose French and British troops to a much larger German force, but it also challenged the Allied claim that they were fighting a just war against German aggression. Lenin had published the texts of secret Allied treaties showing that Britain and France, like Germany, had plotted to enlarge their

nations and empires through war. The revelation that the Allies were fighting for land and riches rather than democratic principles outraged large numbers of people in France and Great Britain, demoralized Allied troops, and threw the French and British governments into disarray.

The treaties also embarrassed Wilson, who had brought America into the war to fight for democracy, not territory. Wilson quickly moved to restore the Allies' credibility by unveiling, in January 1918, a concrete program for peace. His Fourteen Points reaffirmed America's commitment to an international system governed by laws rather than by might and renounced territorial aggrandizement as a legitimate war aim. This document provided the ideological cement that held the Allies together at a critical moment. (The Fourteen Points are discussed more fully in the section "The Failure of the International Peace.")

In March and April 1918, Germany launched its huge offensive against British and French positions, sending Allied troops reeling. A ferocious assault against French lines on May 27 met with little resistance; German troops advanced 10 miles a day—a faster pace than any on the western front since the earliest days of the war—until they reached the Marne River, within striking distance of Paris. The French government prepared to evacuate the city. At this perilous moment, a large American army—fresh, well-equipped, and oblivious to the horrors of trench warfare—arrived to reinforce what remained of the French lines.

The Granger Collections, New York.

THE ROCK OF THE MARNE

Mal Thompson's painting shows infantry units of the U.S. 30th and 38th regiments from the Third Division of the American Expeditionary Force engaging German troops in France in July 1918. Although he shows them under fire, Thompson depicts the soldiers as focused, calm, and determined against a landscape desolated by war.

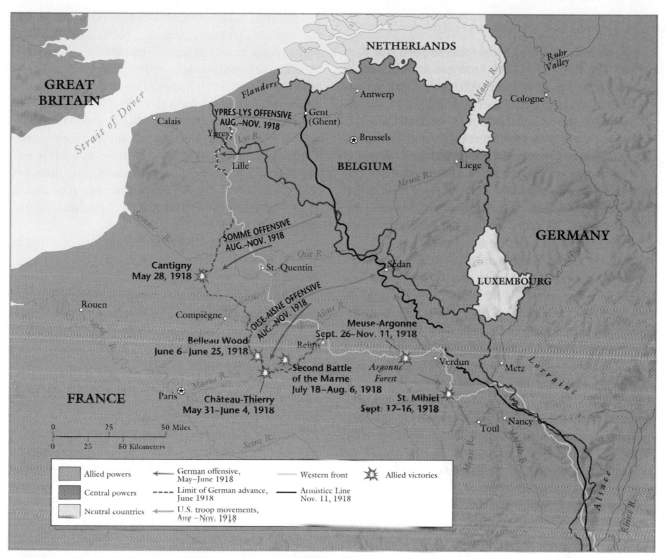

MAP 23.2 AMERICA IN THE FIRST WORLD WAR: WESTERN FRONT, 1918

In 1918, American forces joined the Allied forces in the climactic battles of the war. The red arrows show the major offensive by the Germans in the spring of 1918 and the blue arrows the decisive counteroffensive by the Allies in the fall of 1918. The fighting stopped along the black armistice line on November 11, 1918, after German capitulation.

In fact, these American troops, part of the American Expeditionary Force (AEF) commanded by General John J. Pershing, had begun landing in France almost a year earlier. During the intervening months, the United States had had to create a modern army from scratch, because its existing force was so small, ranking only 17th in the world. Men had to be drafted, trained, and supplied with food and equipment; ships for transporting them to Europe had to be found or built. In France, Pershing put his troops through additional training before committing them to battle. He was determined that the American soldiers—or "doughboys," as they were called—should acquit themselves well on the battlefield. The army he ordered into battle to counter the German spring offensive of 1918 fought well. Many American soldiers fell, but the German

offensive ground to a halt. Paris was saved, and Germany's best chance for victory slipped from its grasp.

Buttressed by this show of AEF strength, the Allied troops staged a major offensive of their own in late September. Millions of Allied troops (including more than a million from the AEF) advanced across the 200-mile-wide Argonne forest in France, cutting German supply lines. By late October, they had reached the German border. Faced with an invasion of their homeland and with rapidly mounting popular dissatisfaction with the war, German leaders asked for an armistice, to be followed by peace negotiations based on Wilson's Fourteen Points. Having forced the Germans to agree to numerous concessions, the Allies ended the war on November 11, 1918. The carnage was finally over.

Mobilizing for "Total" War

Compared to Europe, the United States suffered little from the war. The deaths of 112,000 American soldiers paled in comparison to European losses: 900,000 by Great Britain, 1.2 million by Austria-Hungary, 1.4 million by France, 1.7 million by Russia, and 2 million by Germany. The U.S. civilian population was spared most of the war's ravages— the destruction of homes and industries, the shortages of food and medicine, the spread of disease—that afflicted millions of Europeans. Only with the flu epidemic that swept across the Atlantic from Europe in 1919 to claim approximately 500,000 American lives did Americans briefly experience wholesale suffering and death.

Still, the war had a profound effect on American society. Every military engagement the United States had fought since the Civil War—the Indian wars, the Spanish-American War, the American-Filipino War, the Boxer Rebellion, the Latin American interventions—had been limited in scope. Even the troop mobilizations that seemed large at the time—the more than 100,000 needed to fight the Spanish and then the Filipinos—failed to tax severely American resources. The First World War was different. It was a "total" war to which every combatant had committed virtually all of its resources. The scale of the effort in the United States became apparent early in 1917 when Wilson asked Congress for a conscription law that would permit the federal government to raise a multimillion-man army. The United States would also have to devote much of its agricultural, transportation, industrial, and population resources to the war effort if it wished to end the European stalemate. Who would organize this massive effort? Who would pay for it? Would Americans accept the sacrifice and regimentation it would demand? These were vexing questions for a nation long committed to individual liberty, small government, and a weak military.

Organizing Industry

At first, Wilson pursued a decentralized approach to mobilization, delegating tasks to local defense councils throughout the country. When that effort failed, however, Wilson created several centralized federal agencies, each charged with supervising nationwide activity in its assigned economic sector.

The success of these agencies varied. The Food Administration, headed by mining engineer and executive Herbert Hoover (see Americans Abroad feature in this chapter), substantially increased production of basic foodstuffs and put in place an efficient distribution system that delivered food to millions of troops and European civilians. Treasury Secretary William McAdoo, as head of the U.S. Railroad Administration, also performed well in shifting the rail system from private to public control, coordinating dense train traffic, and making capital improvements that allowed goods to move rapidly to eastern ports, where they were loaded onto ships and sent to Europe. At the other extreme, the Aircraft Production Board and Emergency Fleet Corporation did a poor job of supplying the Allies with combat aircraft and merchant vessels. On balance, the U.S. economy performed wonders in supplying troops with uniforms, food, rifles, munitions, and other basic items; it failed badly, however, in producing more sophisticated weapons and machines such as artillery, aircraft, and ships.

At the time, many believed that the new government war agencies possessed awesome power over the nation's economy and thus represented a near revolution in government. Most such agencies, however, were more powerful on paper than in fact. Consider, for example, the War Industries Board (WIB), an administrative body established by Wilson in July 1917 to harness manufacturing might to military needs. The WIB floundered for its first nine months, lacking the statutory authority to force manufacturers and the military to adopt its plans. Only the appointment of Wall Street investment banker Bernard Baruch as WIB chairman in March 1918 turned the agency around. Rather than attempting to force manufacturers to do the government's bidding, Baruch permitted industrialists to charge high prices for their products. He won exemptions from antitrust laws for corporations that complied with his requests. In general, he made war production too lucrative an activity to resist; however, he did not hesitate to unleash his wrath on corporations that resisted WIB enticements.

Baruch's forceful leadership worked reasonably well throughout his nine months in office. War production increased, and manufacturers discovered the financial benefits of cooperation between the public and private sectors. But Baruch's approach created problems, too. His favoritism toward the large corporations hurt smaller competitors. Moreover, the cozy relationship between government and corporation that he encouraged violated the progressive pledge to protect the people against the "interests." Achieving cooperation by boosting corporate profits, finally, was a costly way for the government to do business. The costs of the war soared to $33 billion, a figure more than three times expectations.

Securing Workers, Keeping Labor Peace

The government worried as much about labor's cooperation as about industry's compliance, for the best-laid

Herbert C. Hoover: International Mining Engineer and Businessman

From the time that he graduated from Stanford in 1897 at the age of 22 until he returned to America after the First World War, Herbert Hoover largely lived abroad, chiefly in Australia, China, and England. No other president, with the possible exception of Thomas Jefferson, brought such an impressive international résumé to the White House. Unlike Jefferson, Hoover had gone abroad not for culture or diplomacy but to seek his fortune as a businessman. He would be enormously successful in this quest.

Soon after graduating from Stanford with a geology degree, Hoover was sent by his employer, Bewick, Moreing, and Company of London, to Australia to look for gold. Enterprising, hardworking, and bold, he quickly made a name for himself by persuading Bewick to purchase a mine, known as the Sons of Gwalia, that would yield an immense amount of gold. "Boy Hoover," "Boy Wonder," and "Chief," as he came to be known, had quickly made himself a fortune.

Bewick next sent Hoover to China, where he shifted from gold to coal exploration. When the Boxer Rebellion broke out in 1900 (see chapter 22), Hoover took charge of the colony of Europeans, Americans, and Christian Chinese at Tientsin, to which the Boxers had laid siege. Hoover played a critical role in keeping his colony fed, united, and in good spirits until the rebellion had dissipated.

In 1901, Hoover moved to London, which would remain his base until the First World War. Working first for Bewick and then on his own, Hoover built a multinational mining business that, by the First World War, was extracting minerals on every one of the world's continents. Increasingly, Hoover turned his attention to politics. Raised a Quaker, he had always possessed a strong commitment to public service. He was particularly intrigued with American progressives such as

Theodore Roosevelt, who were attempting to help the United States find a solution to the turmoil of industrialization.

Hoover's opportunity came in the First World War. When war broke out in 1914, he took charge of getting the many Americans stranded in London home. Then he headed up the Committee for Relief in Belgium, somehow getting both the Allies and the Central Powers to support his efforts to get food to the Belgian people and thereby save them from starvation. And, finally, he became head of Woodrow Wilson's Food Administration, charged with organizing the production and distribution of American foodstuffs to feed millions of Allied soldiers and European civilians. He performed brilliantly at this task, continuing his efforts into the postwar period to stop the spread of famine in Europe.

In 1920, Hoover returned to America for good, becoming President Harding's secretary of commerce (see chapter 23). But for the misfortune of becoming president in 1929 just before the Great Depression struck, Hoover might be celebrated today as one of the most versatile men ever to occupy the Oval Office.

© Corbis.

HERBERT HOOVER, LOU HENRY HOOVER, AND FRIENDS IN CHINA, 1900

This photograph was taken shortly after Hoover had helped secure the safety of the European-American colony in Tientsin during the Boxer Rebellion. Hoover is standing on the far right in the back row, and his wife, Lou Henry Hoover, is seated on the left in the first row. They are surrounded by friends who, like Hoover, had graduated from Stanford University.

THE MIGRATION OF THE NEGRO, PANEL 40: "THE MIGRANTS ARRIVED IN GREAT NUMBERS," BY JACOB LAWRENCE (1940–1941)

This panel illustrates the rural origins of the black migrants who came north during the First World War.

production plans could be disrupted by a labor shortage or an extended strike. War increased the demand for industrial labor while cutting the supply. European immigrants had long been the most important source of new labor for American industry, and during the war they stopped coming. Meanwhile, millions of workers already in America were conscripted into the military and thus lost to industry.

Manufacturers responded to the labor shortage by recruiting new sources of labor from the rural South; a half million African Americans migrated to northern cities between 1916 and 1920. Another half million white southerners followed the same path during that period. Hundreds of thousands of Mexicans fled their revolution-ridden homeland for jobs in the Southwest and Midwest. Approximately 40,000 northern women found work as streetcar conductors, railroad workers, metalworkers, munitions makers, and in other jobs customarily reserved for men. The number of female clerical workers doubled between 1910 and 1920, with many of these women finding work in the government war bureaucracies. Altogether, a million women toiled in war-related industries.

These workers alleviated but did not eliminate the nation's labor shortage. Unemployment, which had hovered around 8.5 percent in 1915, plunged to 1.2 percent in 1918. Workers were quick to recognize the benefits of the tight labor market. They quit jobs they did not like and took part in strikes and other collective actions in unprecedented numbers. From 1916 to 1920, more than 1 million workers went on strike every year.

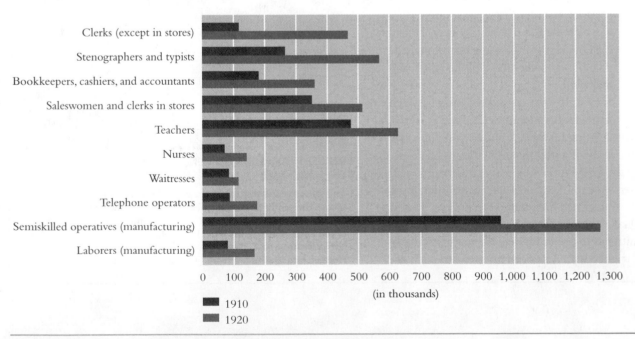

OCCUPATIONS WITH LARGEST INCREASE IN WOMEN, 1910–1920

Source: Joseph A. Hill, *Women in Gainful Occupations, 1870–1920*, U.S. Bureau of the Census, Monograph no. 9 (Washington, D.C.: Government Printing Office, 1929), p. 33.

Union membership almost doubled, from 2.6 million in 1915 to 5.1 million in 1920. Workers commonly sought higher wages and shorter hours through strikes and unionization. Wages rose an average of 137 percent from 1915 to 1920, although inflation largely negated these gains. The average workweek declined in that same period from 55 to 51 hours. Workers also struck in response to managerial attempts to speed up production and tighten discipline. As time passed, increasing numbers of workers began to wonder why the war for democracy in Europe had no counterpart in their factories at home. "Industrial democracy" became the battle cry of an awakened labor movement.

Wilson's willingness to include labor in his 1916 progressive coalition reflected his awareness of labor's potential power (see chapter 21). In 1918, he bestowed prestige on the newly formed National War Labor Board (NWLB)

by appointing former president William Howard Taft to be cochair alongside Samuel Gompers, president of the American Federation of Labor. The NWLB brought together representatives of labor, industry, and the public to resolve labor disputes.

Raising an Army

To raise an army, the Wilson administration committed itself to conscription—the drafting of most men of a certain age, irrespective of their family's wealth, ethnic background, or social standing. The Selective Service Act of May 1917 empowered the administration to do just that. By war's end, local Selective Service boards had registered 24 million young men age 18 and older and had drafted nearly 3 million of them into the military; another 2 million volunteered for service.

LINK TO THE PAST

"A Storm of Our People toward the North"

When jobs became available in the North during the First World War, African Americans from the South began journeying north in record numbers. Between 1916 and 1920, 500,000 made the journey, a population movement so large it became known as the Great Migration. That so many went north in such a brief period demonstrates how tough life was in the South for most African Americans and how ready they were to seize an opportunity to improve their situation. Many of the migrants were rural folk—tenant farmers, sharecroppers, and agricultural laborers—whose skills were not easily transferable to the urban and industrial economies of northern cities. They thus had to enter northern labor forces at the bottom—as unskilled industrial or service employees. But the Great Migration also counted educated African Americans in its ranks, as this excerpt from a letter sent to the *Chicago Defender*, a prominent black newspaper, demonstrates. The four letter writers were educated women from Florida who had been teachers in black schools and were now looking for jobs as domestic servants with well-off Chicago families. We do not know whether the *Chicago Defender* responded to this particular letter, but we do know that in general the newspaper played a key role in facilitating migration by providing important information to both southern migrants and northern employers.

We have several times read your noted newspaper and we are delighted with the same because it is a thorough Negro paper. There is a storm of our people toward the North and especially to your city. We have watched your want ad regularly and we are anxious for location with good families (white) where we can be cared for and do domestic work. We want to engage as cook, nurse, and maid. We have had some educational advantages, as we have taught in rural schools for few years but our pay so poor we could not continue. We can furnish testimonial of our honesty and integrity and moral standing. Will you please assist us in securing places as we are anxious to come but want jobs before we leave. Our chance here is so poor.

1. What, if anything, can we learn about these four potential migrants from this letter excerpt? In particular, how desperate were they to leave the South?
2. What steps had they taken to prepare for going north?
3. What risks were they willing to endure for the sake of gaining an opportunity for a better life?

For additional sources related to this feature, visit the *Liberty, Equality, Power* Web site at:

http://history.wadsworth.com/murrin_LEP4e

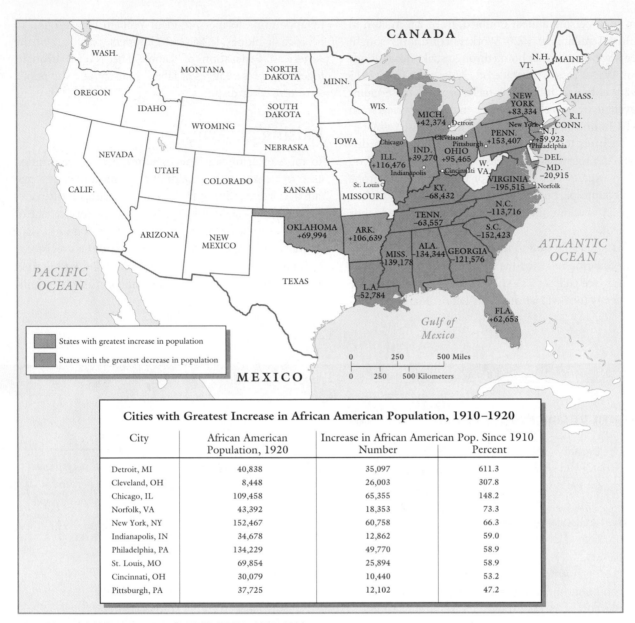

Cities with Greatest Increase in African American Population, 1910–1920			
City	African American Population, 1920	Increase in African American Pop. Since 1910 Number	Percent
Detroit, MI	40,838	35,097	611.3
Cleveland, OH	8,448	26,003	307.8
Chicago, IL	109,458	65,355	148.2
Norfolk, VA	43,392	18,353	73.3
New York, NY	152,467	60,758	66.3
Indianapolis, IN	34,678	12,862	59.0
Philadelphia, PA	134,229	49,770	58.9
St. Louis, MO	69,854	25,894	58.9
Cincinnati, OH	30,079	10,440	53.2
Pittsburgh, PA	37,725	12,102	47.2

MAP 23.3   AFRICAN AMERICAN MIGRATION, 1910–1920

Most southern states lost 50,000 to 200,000 African Americans each during the years of the Great Migration, while many northern states, in the industrial belt stretching from Illinois through New York, gained 40,000 to 150,000 apiece. The table inset on the map shows the cities posting the biggest gains.

Relatively few men resisted the draft, even among recently arrived immigrants. Foreign-born men constituted 18 percent of the armed forces—a percentage greater than their share of the total population. Almost 400,000 African Americans served, representing approximately 10 percent, the same as the percentage of African Americans in the total population.

The U.S. Army, under the command of Chief of Staff Peyton March and General John J. Pershing, faced the difficult task of fashioning these ethnically and racially diverse millions into a professional fighting force. Teaching raw

recruits to fight was hard enough, Pershing and March observed; the generals refused the task of teaching them to put aside their prejudices. Rather than integrate the armed forces, they segregated black soldiers from white. Virtually all African Americans were assigned to all-black units and barred from combat. Being stripped of a combat role was particularly galling to blacks, who, in previous wars, had proven themselves to be among the best American fighters. Pershing was fully aware of the African American contribution. He had commanded African American troops in the 10th Cavalry, the all-black regiment that had distinguished itself in the Spanish-American War (chapter 22). Pershing's military reputation had depended so heavily on the black troops who fought for him that he had acquired the nickname Black Jack.

For a time, the military justified its intensified discrimination against blacks by referring to the results of rudimentary IQ (intelligence quotient) tests administered by psychologists to two million AEF soldiers. These tests allegedly "proved" that native-born Americans and immigrants from the British Isles, Germany, and Scandinavia were well endowed with intelligence, whereas African Americans and immigrants from Southern and Eastern Europe were poorly endowed. The tests were scien tifically so ill-conceived, however, that their findings revealed nothing about the true distribution of intelligence in the population. Their most sensational revelation was that more than half of the soldiers in the AEF—white and black—were "morons," men who had failed to reach the mental age of 13. After trying to absorb the apparent news that most U.S. soldiers were feeble-minded, the military sensibly rejected the pseudo-science on which these intelligence findings were based. In 1919, it discontinued the IQ testing program.

National Archives.

WOMEN DOING "MEN'S" WORK

Labor shortages during the war allowed thousands of women to take industrial jobs customarily reserved for men. Here women operate pneumatic hammers at the Midvale Steel and Ordnance Company, Nicetown, Pennsylvania, 1918.

Given the racial and ethnic differences among American troops and the short time Pershing and his staff had to train recruits, the performance of the AEF was impressive. The United States increased the army from a mere 100,000 to 5 million in little more than a year. The Germans sank no troop ships, nor were any soldiers killed during the dangerous Atlantic crossing. In combat, U.S. troops became known for their sharpshooting skills.

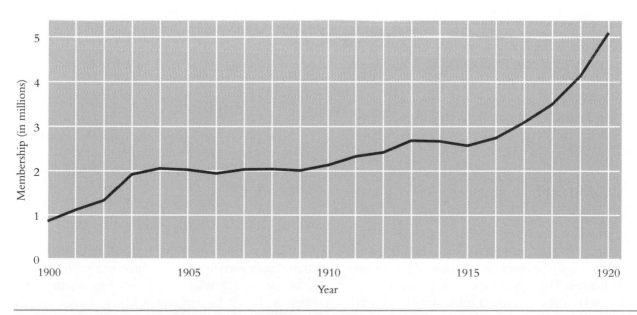

TOTAL MEMBERSHIP OF AMERICAN TRADE UNIONS, 1900–1920

Source: Leo Wolman, *The Growth of American Trade Unions, 1880–1923* (New York: National Bureau of Economic Research, 1924), p. 33.

RECRUITING POSTER, FIRST WORLD WAR, 1917
The government plastered public institutions with recruiting posters. This one represents navy work as glamorous, masculine, and brave, as a way of enticing more young men to join up.

The most decorated soldier in the AEF was Sergeant Alvin C. York of Tennessee, who captured 35 machine guns, took 132 prisoners, and killed 17 German soldiers with 17 bullets. York had learned his marksmanship hunting wild turkeys in the Tennessee hills. "Of course, it weren't no trouble nohow for me to hit them big [German] army targets," he later commented. "They were so much bigger than turkeys' heads." One of the most decorated AEF units was New York's 369th Regiment, a black unit recruited in Harlem. Bowing to pressure from civil rights groups to allow some black troops to fight, Pershing had offered the 369th to the French army. The 369th entered the French front line, served in the forward Allied trenches for 191 days (longer than any other U.S. regiment), and scored several major successes. In gratitude for its service, the French government decorated the entire unit with one of its highest honors—the *Croix de Guerre.*

Paying the Bills

The government incurred huge debts buying food, uniforms, munitions, weapons, vehicles, and sundry other items for the U.S. military. To help pay its bills, it sharply increased tax rates. The new taxes hit the wealthiest Americans the hardest: The richest were slapped with a 67 percent income tax and a 25 percent inheritance tax. Corporations were ordered to pay an "excess profits" tax. Proposed by the Wilson administration and backed by

Robert La Follette and other congressional progressives who feared that the "interests" would use the war to enrich themselves, these taxes were meant to ensure that all Americans would sacrifice something for the war.

Tax revenues, however, provided only about one-third of the $33 billion that the government ultimately spent on the war. The rest came from the sale of Liberty Bonds. These 30-year government bonds offered individual purchasers a return of 3.5 percent in annual interest. The government offered five bond issues between 1917 and 1920, and all quickly sold out, thanks, in no small measure, to a high-powered sales pitch, orchestrated by Treasury Secretary William G. McAdoo, that equated bond purchases with patriotic duty. McAdoo's agents blanketed the country with posters, sent bond "salesmen" into virtually every American community, enlisted Boy Scouts to go door-to-door, and staged rallies at which movie stars such as Mary Pickford, Douglas Fairbanks, and Charlie Chaplin stumped for the war.

Arousing Patriotic Ardor

The Treasury's bond campaign was only one aspect of an extraordinary government effort to arouse public support for the war. In 1917, Wilson set up a new agency, the Committee on Public Information (CPI), to popularize the war. Under the chairmanship of George Creel, a midwestern progressive and a muckraker, the CPI distributed 75

THE 369TH RETURNS TO NEW YORK

Denied the opportunity to fight in the U.S. Army, this unit fought for the French. For the length and distinction of its service in the front lines, this entire unit was awarded the *Croix de Guerre* by the French government.

National Archives.

million copies of pamphlets explaining U.S. war aims in several languages. It trained a force of 75,000 "Four-Minute Men" to deliver succinct, uplifting war speeches to numerous groups in their home cities and towns. It papered the walls of virtually every public institution (and many private ones) with posters, placed advertisements in mass circulation magazines, sponsored exhibitions, and peppered newspaper editors with thousands of press releases on the progress of the war.

Faithful to his muckraking past (see chapter 21), Creel wanted to give the people the "facts" of the war, believing that well-informed citizens would see the wisdom of Wilson's policies. He also saw his work as an opportunity to achieve the progressive goal of uniting all Americans into a single moral community. Americans everywhere learned that the United States had entered the war "to make the world safe for democracy," to help the world's weaker peoples achieve self-determination, and to bring a measure of justice into the conduct of international affairs. Americans were asked to affirm those ideals by doing everything they could to support the war.

This uplifting message affected the American people, although not necessarily in ways anticipated by CPI propagandists. It imparted to many a deep love of country and a sense of participation in a grand democratic experiment. Among others, particularly those experiencing poverty and discrimination, it sparked a new spirit of protest. Workers, women, European ethnics, and African Americans began demanding that America live up to its democratic ideals at home as well as abroad. Workers rallied

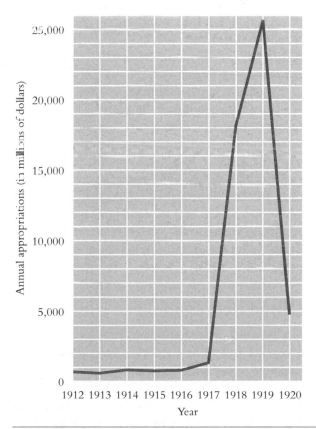

THE FIRST WORLD WAR AND THE FEDERAL BUDGET

Source: Data from *Statistical Abstract of the United States, 1919* (Washington, D.C.: Government Printing Office, 1920), p. 681.

to the cry of "industrial democracy." Women seized on the democratic fervor to bring their fight for suffrage to a successful conclusion (see chapter 21). African Americans began to dream that the war might deliver them from second-class citizenship. European ethnics believed that Wilson's support of their countrymen's rights abroad would improve their own chances for success in the United States.

Although the CPI had helped to unleash it, this new democratic enthusiasm troubled Creel and others in the Wilson administration. The United States, after all, was still deeply divided along class, ethnic, and racial lines. Workers and industrialists regarded each other with suspicion. Cultural differences compounded this class division, for the working class was overwhelmingly ethnic in composition, and the industrial and political elites consisted mainly of the native-born whose families had been "Americans" for generations. Progressives had fought hard to overcome these divisions. They had tamed the power of capitalists, improved the condition of workers, encouraged the Americanization of immigrants, and articulated a new, more inclusive idea of who could belong to the American nation. But their work was far from complete when the war broke out, and the war opened up new social and cultural divisions. German immigrants still formed the largest foreign-born population group—2.3 million. Another 2.3 million immigrants came from some part of the Austro-Hungarian Empire. And more than 1 million Americans—native-born and immigrants—supported the Socialist Party and the Industrial Workers of the World, both of which had opposed the war. The decision to authorize the CPI's massive unity campaign indicates that the progressives understood how widespread the discord was. Still, they had not anticipated that the promotion of democratic ideals at home would exacerbate, rather than lessen, the nation's social and cultural divisions.

Wartime Repression

By early 1918, the CPI's campaign had developed a darker, more coercive side. Inflammatory advertisements called on patriots to report on neighbors, coworkers, and ethnics whom they suspected of subverting the war effort. Propagandists called on all immigrants, especially those from Central, Southern, and Eastern Europe, to pledge themselves to "100 percent Americanism" and to repudiate all ties to their homeland, native language, and ethnic customs. The CPI aroused hostility toward Germans by spreading lurid tales of German atrocities and encouraging the public to see movies such as *The Prussian Cur* and *The Beast of Berlin*. The Justice Department arrested thou-

RENAMED GERMAN AMERICAN WORDS

Original German Name	Renamed "Patriotic" Name
hamburger	salisbury steak, liberty steak, liberty sandwich
sauerkraut	liberty cabbage
Hamburg Avenue, Brooklyn, New York	Wilson Avenue, Brooklyn, New York
Germantown, Nebraska	Garland, Nebraska
East Germantown, Indiana	Pershing, Indiana
Berlin, Iowa	Lincoln, Iowa
pinochle	liberty
German shepherd	Alsatian shepherd
Deutsches Hans of Indianapolis	Athenaeum of Indiana
Germania Maennerchor of Chicago	Lincoln Club
Kaiser Street	Maine Way

Source: From La Vern J. Rippley, *The German Americans* (Boston: Twayne, 1976), p. 186; and Robert H. Ferrell, *Woodrow Wilson and World War I, 1917–1921* (New York: Harper and Row, 1985), pp. 205–206.

sands of German and Austrian immigrants whom it suspected of subversive activities. Congress passed the Trading with the Enemy Act, which required foreign-language publications to submit all war-related stories to post office censors for approval.

German Americans became the objects of popular hatred. American patriots sought to expunge every trace of German influence from American culture. In Boston, performances of Beethoven's symphonies were banned, and the German-born conductor of the Boston Symphony Orchestra was forced to resign. Although Americans would not give up the German foods they had grown to love, they would no longer call them by their German names. Sauerkraut was rechristened "liberty cabbage," and hamburgers became "liberty sandwiches." Libraries removed works of German literature from their shelves, and Theodore Roosevelt and others urged school districts to prohibit the teaching of the German language. Patriotic school boards in Lima, Ohio, and elsewhere burned the German books in their districts.

German Americans risked being fired from work, losing their businesses, and being assaulted on the street. A St. Louis mob lynched an innocent German immigrant whom they suspected of subversion. After only 25 minutes of deliberation, a St. Louis jury acquitted the mob leaders, who had brazenly defended their crime as an act of patriotism. German Americans began hiding their ethnic identity, changing their names, speaking German only in the privacy of their homes, and celebrating their holidays only with trusted friends. This experience devastated the once-proud German American community; many would never

THE CAMPAIGN OF FEAR

By 1918, the government's appeal to Americans' best aspirations—to spread liberty and democracy—had been replaced by a determination to arouse fear of subversion and conquest. Here the German enemy is depicted as a terrifying brute who violates Lady Liberty and uses his *kultur* club to destroy civilization.

recover from the shame and vulnerability they experienced in those years.

The anti-German campaign escalated into a general anti-immigrant crusade. Congress passed the Immigration Restriction Act of 1917, over Wilson's veto, which declared that all adult immigrants who failed a reading test would be denied admission to the United States. The act also banned the immigration of laborers from India, Indochina, Afghanistan, Arabia, the East Indies, and several other countries within an Asiatic Barred Zone. This legislation marked the beginning of a movement in Congress that, four years later, would close the immigration door to virtually all transoceanic peoples. Congress also passed the 18th Amendment to the Constitution, which prohibited the manufacture and distribution of alcoholic beverages (see chapter 21). The crusade for prohibition was not new, but anti-immigrant feelings generated by the war gave it

added impetus. Prohibitionists pictured the nation's urban ethnic ghettos as scenes of drunkenness, immorality, and disloyalty. They also accused German American brewers of operating a "liquor trust" to sap people's will to fight. The states quickly ratified the 18th Amendment, and in 1919, Prohibition became the law of the land.

More and more, the Wilson administration relied on repression to achieve domestic unity. In the Espionage, Sabotage, and Sedition Acts passed in 1917 and 1918, Congress gave the administration sweeping powers to silence and even imprison dissenters. These acts went far beyond outlawing behavior that no nation at war could be expected to tolerate, such as spying for the enemy, sabotaging war production, and calling for the enemy's victory. Now citizens could be prosecuted for writing or uttering any statement that could be construed as profaning the flag, the Constitution, or the military. These acts constituted the most drastic restrictions of free speech at the national level since the Alien and Sedition Acts of 1798 (see chapter 8).

Government repression fell most heavily on the IWW and the Socialist Party. Both groups had opposed intervention before 1917. Although they subsequently muted their opposition, they continued to insist that the true enemies of American workers were to be found in the ranks of American employers, not in Germany or Austria-Hungary. The government responded by banning many socialist materials from the mails and by disrupting socialist and IWW meetings. By spring 1918, government agents had raided countless IWW offices and had arrested 2,000 IWW members, including its entire executive board. Many of those arrested would be sentenced to long jail terms. William Haywood, the IWW president, fled to Europe and then to the Soviet Union rather than go to jail. Eugene V. Debs, the head of the Socialist Party, received a 10-year jail term for making an antiwar speech in Canton, Ohio, in summer 1918.

This federal repression, carried out in an atmosphere of supercharged patriotism, encouraged local governments and private citizens to initiate their own antiradical crusades. In the mining town of Bisbee, Arizona, a sheriff with an eager force of 2,000 deputized citizens kidnapped 1,200 IWW members, herded them into cattle cars, and dumped them onto the New Mexico desert with little food or water. Vigilantes in Butte, Montana, chained an IWW organizer to a car and let his body scrape the pavement as they drove the vehicle through city streets. Next, they strung him up to a railroad trestle, castrated him, and left him to die. The 250,000 members of the American Protective League, most of them businessmen and professionals, routinely spied on fellow workers and neighbors. They opened mail and tapped phones and otherwise harassed those suspected of disloyalty. Attorney General Thomas Gregory publicly endorsed the group and sought federal funds to support its "police" work.

The spirit of coercion even infected institutions that had long prided themselves on tolerance. In July 1917, Columbia University fired two professors for speaking out against U.S. intervention in the war. The National Americanization Committee, which before 1917 had pioneered a humane approach to the problem of integrating immigrants into American life, now supported surveillance, internment, and deportation of aliens suspected of anti-American sentiments.

Wilson bore responsibility for this climate of repression. He did attempt to block certain pieces of repressive legislation; for example, he vetoed both the Immigration Restriction Act and the Volstead Act (the act passed to enforce Prohibition), only to be overridden by Congress. But Wilson did little to halt Attorney General Gregory's prosecution of radicals or Postmaster General Burleson's campaign to exclude Socialist Party publications from the mail. He ignored pleas from progressives that he intervene in the Debs case to prevent the ailing 62-year-old from going to jail. His acquiescence in these matters cost him dearly among progressives and socialists. Wilson believed,

however, that once the Allies, with U.S. support, won the war and arranged a just peace in accordance with the Fourteen Points, his administration's wartime actions would be forgiven and the progressive coalition would be restored.

The Failure of the International Peace

In the month following Germany's surrender on November 11, 1918, Wilson was confident about the prospects of achieving a just peace. Both Germany and the Allies had publicly accepted the Fourteen Points as the basis for negotiations. Wilson's international prestige was enormous. People throughout the world were inspired by his dream of a democratic, just, and harmonious world order free of poverty, ignorance, and war. Poles, Lithuanians, and other Eastern Europeans whose pursuit of nationhood had been frustrated for 100 years or more now believed that independence might be within their reach. Zionist Jews in Europe and the United States dared to dream of a Jewish homeland within their lifetimes. Countless African and Asian peoples imagined achieving their freedom from colonial domination.

New York Times, 1919.

"THE SAVIOR OF HUMANITY"
Wherever he went in Europe, Woodrow Wilson was greeted by huge crowds eager to thank him for ending Europe's terrible war and to endorse his vision of a peaceful, democratic world. Here millions of Italians greet Wilson's arrival in Milan.

To capitalize on his fame and to maximize the chances for a peace settlement based on his Fourteen Points, Wilson broke with diplomatic precedent and decided to head the American delegation to the Paris Peace Conference in January 1919. Enormous crowds of enthusiastic Europeans turned out to hail Wilson's arrival on the Continent in December. Some 2 million French citizens—the largest throng ever assembled on French soil—lined the parade route in Paris to catch a glimpse of "Wilson, *le juste* [the just]." In Rome, Milan, and La Scala, Italians acclaimed him "The Savior of Humanity" and "The Moses from Across the Atlantic."

In the Fourteen Points, Wilson had translated his principles for a new world order into specific proposals for international peace and justice. The first group of points called for all nations to abide by a code of conduct that embraced free trade, freedom of the seas, open diplomacy, disarmament, and the resolution of disputes through mediation. A second group, based on the principle of self-determination, proposed redrawing the map of Europe to give the subjugated peoples of the Austro-Hungarian, Ottoman, and Russian empires national sovereignty. The last point called for establishing the League of Nations, an assembly in which all nations would be represented and in which all international disputes would be given a fair hearing and an opportunity for peaceful solutions.

The Paris Peace Conference and the Treaty of Versailles

Although representatives of 27 nations began meeting in Paris on January 12, 1919, to discuss Wilson's Fourteen Points, negotiations were controlled by the "Big Four": Wilson, Prime Minister David Lloyd George of Great Britain, Premier Georges Clemenceau of France, and Prime Minister Vittorio Orlando of Italy. When Orlando quit the conference after a dispute with Wilson, the Big Four became the Big Three. Wilson quickly learned that his negotiating partners' support for the Fourteen Points was much weaker than he had believed. The cagey Clemenceau mused: "God gave us the Ten Commandments, and we broke them. Wilson gives us Fourteen Points. We shall see." Clemenceau and Lloyd George refused to include most of Wilson's points in the peace treaty. The points having to do with freedom of the seas and free trade were omitted, as were the proposals for open diplomacy and Allied disarmament. Wilson won partial endorsement of the principle of self-determination: Belgian sovereignty was restored, Poland's status as a nation was affirmed, and the new nations of Czechoslovakia, Yugoslavia, Finland, Lithuania, Latvia, and Estonia were created. In addition, some lands of the former Ottoman Empire—Armenia,

Palestine, Mesopotamia, and Syria—were to be placed under League of Nations' trusteeships with the understanding that they would someday gain their independence. Wilson failed in his efforts to block a British plan to transfer former German colonies in Asia to Japanese control, an Italian plan to annex territory inhabited by 200,000 Austrians, and a French plan to take from Germany its valuable Saar coal mines.

Nor could Wilson blunt the drive to punish Germany for its wartime aggression. In addition to awarding the Saar basin to France, the Allies gave portions of northern Germany to Denmark and portions of eastern Germany to Poland and Czechoslovakia. Germany was stripped of virtually its entire navy and air force, and forbidden to place soldiers or fortifications in western Germany along the Rhine. It was allowed to keep an army of only 100,000 men. In addition, Germany was forced to admit its responsibility for the war. In accepting this "war guilt," Germany was, in effect, agreeing to compensate the victors in cash (reparations) for the pain and suffering it had inflicted on them.

Lloyd George and Clemenceau brushed off the protests of those who viewed this desire to prostrate Germany as a cruel and vengeful act. That the German people, after their nation's 1918 defeat, had overthrown the monarch (Kaiser Wilhelm II) who had taken them to war, and had reconstituted their nation as a democratic republic—the

PRESIDENT WOODROW WILSON IN PARIS, 1919
Wilson arrives at the Paris Peace Conference to begin negotiations on the treaty that would formally end the First World War and establish the League of Nations as a first step to a new world order.

© UPI-Bettmann/Corbis.

first in their country's history—won them no leniency. On June 28, 1919, Great Britain, France, the United States, Germany, and other European nations signed the Treaty of Versailles. In 1921, an Allied commission notified the Germans that they were to pay the victors $33 billion, a sum well beyond the resources of a defeated and economically ruined Germany.

The League of Nations

The Allies' single-minded pursuit of self-interest disillusioned many liberals and socialists in the United States, but Wilson seemed undismayed. He had won approval of the most important of his Fourteen Points—that which called for the creation of the League of Nations. The League, whose structure and responsibilities were set forth in the Covenant attached to the peace treaty, would usher in Wilson's new world order. Drawing its membership from the signatories to the Treaty of Versailles (except, for the time being, Germany), the League would function as an international parliament and judiciary, establishing rules of international behavior and resolving disputes between nations through rational and peaceful means. A nine-member executive council—the United States,

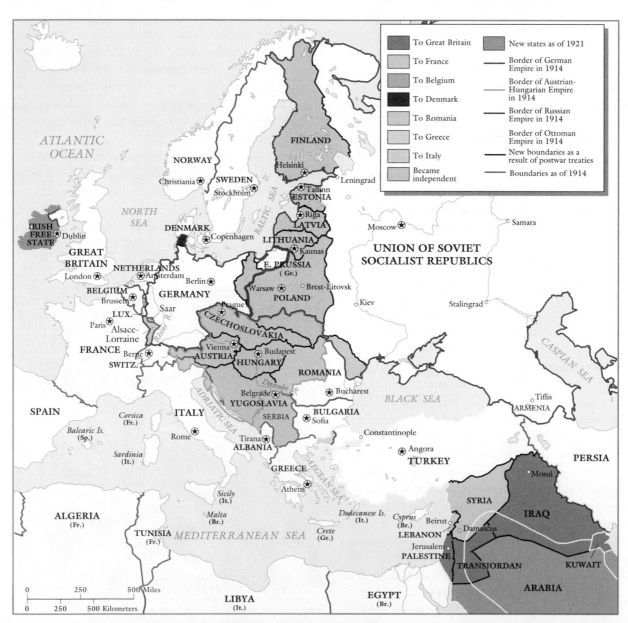

MAP 23.4 EUROPE AND THE NEAR EAST AFTER THE FIRST WORLD WAR

The First World War and the Treaty of Versailles changed the geography of Europe and the Near East. Nine nations in Europe, stretching from Yugoslavia in the south to Finland in the north, were created (or reformed) out of the defeated Austro-Hungarian and Ottoman Empires. In the Near East, meanwhile, Syria, Lebanon, Palestine, Transjordan, and Iraq were carved out of the Ottoman Empire, placed under British or French control, and promised eventual independence.

Britain, France, Italy, and Japan would have permanent seats on the council, while the other four seats would rotate among the smaller powers—was charged with administering decisions.

Wilson believed that the League would redeem the failures of the Paris Peace Conference. Under its auspices, free trade and freedom of the seas would be achieved, reparations against Germany would be reduced or eliminated, disarmament of the Allies would proceed, and the principle of self-determination would be extended to peoples outside Europe. Moreover, the Covenant (Article X) would endow the League with the power to punish aggressor nations through economic isolation and military retaliation.

Wilson versus Lodge: The Fight over Ratification

The League's success, however, depended on Wilson's ability to convince the U.S. Senate to ratify the Treaty of Versailles. Wilson knew that this would not be easy. The Republicans had gained a majority in the Senate in 1918, and two groups within their ranks were determined to frustrate Wilson's ambitions. One group was a caucus of 14 midwesterners and westerners known as the "irreconcilables." Most of them were conservative isolationists who wanted the United States to preserve its separation from Europe, but a few were prominent progressives—Robert La Follette, William Borah, and Hiram Johnson—who had voted against the declaration of war in 1917. The self-interest displayed by England and France at the peace conference convinced this progressive group that the Europeans were incapable of decent behavior in international matters.

Senator Henry Cabot Lodge of Massachusetts led the second opposition group. Its members rejected Wilson's belief that every group of people on earth had a right to form their own nation; that every state, regardless of its size, its economic condition, and the vigor and intelligence of its people, should have a voice in world affairs; and that disputes between nations could be settled in open, democratic forums. They subscribed instead to Theodore Roosevelt's vision of a world controlled by a few great nations, each militarily strong, secure in its own sphere of influence, and determined to avoid war through a carefully negotiated balance of power. These Republicans preferred to let Europe return to the power politics that had prevailed before the war rather than experiment with a new world order that might constrain and compromise U.S. power and autonomy.

This Republican critique was a cogent one that merited extended discussion. Particularly important were questions that Republicans raised about Article X, which

gave the League the right to undertake military actions against aggressor nations. Did Americans want to authorize an international organization to decide when the United States would go to war? Was this not a violation of the Constitution, which vested war-making power solely in the Congress? Even if the constitutional problem could be solved, how could the United States ensure that it would not be forced into a military action that might damage its national interest?

It soon became clear, however, that several Republicans, including Lodge, were as interested in humiliating Wilson as in developing an alternative approach to foreign policy. They accused Wilson of promoting socialism through his wartime expansion of government power. They were angry that he had failed to include any distinguished Republicans, such as Lodge, Elihu Root, or William Howard Taft, in the Paris peace delegation. And they were still bitter about the 1918 congressional elections, when Wilson had argued that a Republican victory would embarrass the nation abroad. Although Wilson's electioneering had failed to sway the voters (the Republicans won a majority in both Houses), his suggestion that a Republican victory would injure national honor had infuriated Theodore Roosevelt and his supporters. Roosevelt died in

REPUBLICAN ELDER STATESMEN

Henry Cabot Lodge is on the left; William Howard Taft is on the right. Lodge led the fight in the Senate against ratifying the Treaty of Versailles.

© Corbis.

1919, but his close friend Lodge kept his rage alive. "I never thought I could hate a man as much as I hate Wilson," Lodge conceded in a moment of candor.

As chairman of the Senate Foreign Relations Committee, charged with considering the treaty before reporting it to the Senate floor, Lodge did everything possible to obstruct ratification. He packed the committee with senators who were likely to oppose the treaty. He delayed action by reading every one of the treaty's 300 pages aloud and by subjecting it to endless criticism in six long weeks of public hearings. When his committee finally reported the treaty to the full Senate, it came encumbered with nearly 50 amendments whose adoption Lodge made a precondition of his support. Some of the amendments expressed reasonable concerns—namely, that participation in the League not diminish the role of Congress in determining foreign policy, compromise American sovereignty, or involve the United States in an unjust or ill-advised war. But many were meant only to complicate the task of ratification.

Despite Lodge's obstructionism, the treaty's chances for ratification by the required two-thirds majority of the Senate remained good. Many Republicans were prepared to vote for ratification if Wilson indicated his willingness to accept some of the proposed amendments. Wilson could have salvaged the treaty and, along with it, U.S. participation in the League of Nations, but Wilson refused to compromise with the Republicans and announced that he would carry his case directly to the American people instead. In September 1919, he undertook a whirlwind cross-country tour that covered more than 8,000 miles with 37 stops. He addressed as many crowds as he could reach, sometimes speaking for an hour at a time, four times a day.

On September 25, after giving a speech at Pueblo, Colorado, Wilson suffered excruciating headaches throughout the night. His physician ordered him back to Washington, where on October 2 he suffered a near-fatal stroke. Wilson hovered near death for two weeks and remained seriously disabled for another six. His condition improved somewhat in November, but his left side remained paralyzed, his speech was slurred, his energy level low, and his emotions unstable. Wilson's wife, Edith Bolling Wilson, and his doctor isolated him from Congress and the press, withholding news they thought might upset him and preventing the public from learning how much his body and mind had deteriorated.

Many historians believe that the stroke impaired Wilson's political judgment. He refused to consider any of the Republican amendments to the treaty, even after it had become clear that compromise offered the only chance of winning U.S. participation in the League of Nations. When Lodge presented an amended treaty for a ratification vote on November 19, Wilson ordered Senate Democrats to vote against it; 42 (of 47) Democratic senators complied, and with the aid of 13 Republican irreconcilables, the Lodge version was defeated. Only moments later, the unamended version of the treaty—Wilson's version—received only 38 votes.

The Treaty's Final Defeat

As the magnitude of the calamity became apparent, supporters of the League in Congress, the nation, and the world urged the Senate and the president to reconsider. Wilson would not budge. A bipartisan group of senators desperately tried to work out a compromise without con-

---

WOODROW WILSON'S FOURTEEN POINTS, 1918: RECORD OF IMPLEMENTATION

1. Open covenants of peace openly arrived at	Not fulfilled
2. Absolute freedom of navigation upon the seas in peace and war	Not fulfilled
3. Removal of all economic barriers to the equality of trade among nations	Not fulfilled
4. Reduction of armaments to the level needed only for domestic safety	Not fulfilled
5. Impartial adjustments of colonial claims	Not fulfilled
6. Evacuation of all Russian territory; Russia to be welcomed into the society of free nations	Not fulfilled
7. Evacuation and restoration of Belgium	Fulfilled
8. Evacuation and restoration of all French lands; return of Alsace-Lorraine to France	Fulfilled
9. Readjustment of Italy's frontiers along lines of Italian nationality	Compromised
10. Self-determination for the former subjects of the Austro-Hungarian Empire	Compromised
11. Evacuation of Romania, Serbia, and Montenegro; free access to the sea for Serbia	Compromised
12. Self-determination for the former subjects of the Ottoman Empire; secure sovereignty for Turkish portion	Compromised
13. Establishment of an independent Poland with free and secure access to the sea	Fulfilled
14. Establishment of the League of Nations to secure mutual guarantees of independence and territorial integrity	Compromised

Source: From G. M. Gathorne-Hardy, *The Fourteen Points and the Treaty of Versailles,* Oxford Pamphlets on World Affairs, no. 6 (1939), pp. 8–34; and Thomas G. Paterson et al., *American Foreign Policy: A History,* 2nd ed. (Lexington, Mass.: Heath, 1983), vol. 2, pp. 282–93.

sulting him. When that effort failed, the Senate put to a vote, one more time, the Lodge version of the treaty. Because 23 Democrats, most of them southerners, still refused to break with Wilson, this last-ditch effort at ratification failed on March 8, 1920, by a margin of seven votes. Wilson's dream of a new world order died that day. The crumpled figure in the White House seemed to bear little resemblance to the hero who, barely 15 months before, had been greeted in Europe as the world's savior. Wilson filled out his remaining 12 months in office as an invalid, presiding over the interment of progressivism. He died in 1924.

The judgment of history lies heavily on these events, for many believe that the flawed treaty and the failure of the League contributed to Adolf Hitler's rise in Germany and the outbreak of a second world war more devastating than the first. It is necessary to ask, then, whether American participation in the League would have significantly altered the course of world history.

The mere fact of U.S. membership in the League would not have magically solved Europe's postwar problems. The U.S. government was inexperienced in diplomacy and prone to mistakes. Its freedom to negotiate solutions to international disputes would have been limited by the large number of American voters who remained strongly opposed to U.S. entanglement in European affairs. Even if such opposition could have been overcome, the United States would still have confronted European countries determined to go their own way.

Nevertheless, one thing is clear: No stable international order could have arisen after the First World War without the full involvement of the United States. The League of Nations required American authority and prestige in order to operate effectively as an international parliament. We cannot know whether the League, with American involvement, would have offered the Germans a less humiliating peace, allowing them to rehabilitate their economy and salvage their national pride; nor whether an American-led League would have stopped Hitler's expansionism before it escalated into full-scale war in 1939. Still, it seems fair to suggest that American participation would have strengthened the League and improved its ability to bring a lasting peace to Europe.

◑ The Postwar Period: A Society in Convulsion

The end of the war brought no respite from the forces convulsing American society. Workers were determined to regain the purchasing power they had lost to inflation. Employers were determined to halt or reverse the wartime

gains labor had made. Radicals saw in this conflict between capital and labor the possibility of a socialist revolution. Conservatives were certain that the revolution had already begun. Returning white servicemen were nervous about regaining their civilian jobs and looked with hostility on the black, Hispanic, and female workers who had been recruited to take their places. Black veterans were in no mood to return to segregation and subordination. The federal government, meanwhile, uneasy over the centralization of power during the war, quickly dismantled such agencies as the War Industries Board and the National War Labor Board. By so doing, it deprived itself of mechanisms that might have enabled it to intervene in social conflicts and keep them from erupting into rage and violence.

Labor-Capital Conflict

Nowhere was the escalation of conflict more evident than in the workplace. In 1919, 4 million workers—one-fifth of the nation's manufacturing workforce—went on strike. In January 1919, a general strike paralyzed the city of Seattle when 60,000 workers walked off their jobs. By August,

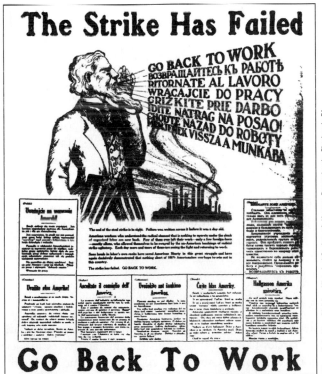

Library & Archives Division, Historical Society of Western Pennsylvania, Pittsburgh, PA.

THE 1919 STEEL STRIKE FAILS

The steel corporations were united in their opposition to the steelworkers' union and skillful in their use of media to demoralize the strikers. This poster reveals another reason for the strike's failure: a workforce so diverse that strike announcements had to be communicated in eight languages.

walkouts had been staged by 400,000 eastern and midwestern coal miners, 120,000 New England textile workers, and 50,000 New York City garment workers. Then came two strikes that turned public opinion sharply against labor. In September, Boston policemen walked off their jobs after the police commissioner refused to negotiate with their newly formed union. Rioting and looting soon broke out. Massachusetts Governor Calvin Coolidge, outraged by the policemen's betrayal of their sworn public duty, refused to negotiate with them, called out the National Guard to restore order, and fired the entire police force. His tough stand would bring him national fame and the Republican vice presidential nomination in 1920.

Hard on the heels of the policemen's strike came a strike by more than 300,000 steelworkers in the Midwest. No union had established a footing in the steel industry since the 1890s, when Andrew Carnegie had ousted the ironworkers' union from his Homestead, Pennsylvania,

mills. Most steelworkers labored long hours (the 12-hour shift was still standard) for low wages in dangerous workplaces. The organizers of the 1919 strike had somehow managed to persuade steelworkers with varied skill levels and ethnic backgrounds to put aside their differences and demand an eight-hour day and union recognition. When the employers rejected those demands, the workers walked off their jobs. The employers responded by procuring armed guards to beat up the strikers and by hiring nonunion labor to keep the plants running. In many areas, local and state police prohibited union meetings, ran strikers out of town, and opened fire on those who disobeyed orders. In Gary, Indiana, a confrontation between unionists and armed guards left 18 strikers dead. To arouse public support for their antiunion campaign, industry leaders portrayed the strike leaders as dangerous and violent radicals bent on the destruction of political liberty and economic freedom. They succeeded in arousing public opin-

HISTORY THROUGH FILM

Reds (1981)

Directed by Warren Beatty. Starring Warren Beatty (John Reed), Diane Keaton (Louise Bryant), Edward Herrmann (Max Eastman), Jerzy Kosinski (Grigory Zinoviev), Jack Nicholson (Eugene O'Neill), and Maureen Stapleton (Emma Goldman).

In this epic film, Warren Beatty, producer, director, and screenplay cowriter, attempts to integrate the history of the American Left in the early 20th century with a love story about two radicals of that era, John "Jack" Reed and Louise Bryant. Reed was a well-known radical journalist whose dispatches from Russia during its 1917 revolution were published as a book, *Ten Days That Shook the World,* that brought him fame and notoriety. Bryant never developed the public reputation that Reed enjoyed, but she was an integral member of the radical circles that gathered in apartments and cafés in New York's Bohemian Greenwich Village before and during the First World War.

At times, the love principals in this movie seem to resemble Warren Beatty and Diane Keaton more than they do the historical figures they are meant to represent. In general, however, the movie keeps love and politics in balance and thus successfully conveys an important and historically accurate message about the American Left, especially before the First World War: namely, that its participants wanted to revolutionize the personal as well as the political. Thus equality between men and women, women's right to enjoy the same sexual freedom as men, and marriage's impact on personal growth and adventure were issues debated with the same fervor as building a radical political party and accelerating the transition to socialism. (See chapter 20, The New Sexuality and the Rise of Feminism.)

Reds is also an exceptionally serious film about political parties and ideologies. The film follows the arc of John Reed's and Louise Bryant's lives from their prewar days as discontented members of the Portland, Oregon, social elite, through their flight to the freedom and radicalism of Greenwich Village, to the hardening of their radicalism as a

ion against the steelworkers, and the strike collapsed in January 1920.

Radicals and the Red Scare

The steel companies succeeded in putting down the strike by fanning the public's fear that revolutionary sentiment was spreading among workers. Radical sentiment was indeed on the rise. Mine workers and railroad workers had begun calling for the permanent nationalization of coal mines and railroads. Longshoremen in San Francisco and Seattle refused to load ships carrying supplies to the White Russians who had taken up arms against Lenin's Bolshevik government. Socialist trade unionists mounted the most serious challenge to Gompers's control of the AFL in 25 years. In 1920, nearly a million Americans voted for the Socialist presidential candidate Debs, who ran his campaign from the Atlanta Federal Penitentiary. Small groups

of anarchists contemplated, and occasionally carried out, bomb attacks on businessmen and public officials.

This radical surge did not mean, however, that leftists had fashioned themselves into a single movement or political party. On the contrary, the Russian Revolution had split the American Socialist Party. One faction, which would keep the name Socialist and would continue under Debs's leadership, insisted that radicals follow a democratic path to socialism. The other group, which would take the name Communist, wanted to establish a Lenin-style "dictatorship of the proletariat." Small groups of anarchists, some of whom advocated campaigns of terror to speed the revolution, represented yet a third radical tendency.

Few Americans noticed the disarray in the radical camp. Most assumed that radicalism was a single, coordinated movement bent on establishing a communist government on American soil. They saw the nation's immigrant communities as breeding grounds for Bolshevism.

Kobal Collection/Paramount

Jack Nicholson as Eugene O'Neill, Diane Keaton as Louise Bryant, and Warren Beatty as Jack Reed, together on the beaches of Provincetown, Massachusetts.

result of repression during the First World War at home and the Bolshevik triumph in November 1917. Beatty has recreated detailed and complex stories about internal fights within the Left both in the United States and Russia, through which he seeks to show how hopes for social transformation went awry. To give this film added historical weight, he introduces "witnesses," individuals who actually

knew the real Reed and Bryant and who appear on screen periodically to share their memories, both serious and whimsical, about the storied couple and the times in which they lived. *Reds* should be compared to *Wilson*, the movie featured in chapter 21, because the two films offer very different perspectives on the First World War era.

Beginning in 1919, this perceived "red scare" prompted government officials and private citizens to embark on yet another campaign of repression.

The postwar repression of radicalism closely resembled the wartime repression of dissent. Thirty states passed sedition laws to punish those who advocated revolution. Numerous public and private groups intensified Americanization campaigns designed to strip foreigners of their "subversive" ways and remake them into loyal citizens. Universities fired radical professors, and vigilante groups wrecked the offices of socialists and assaulted IWW agitators. A newly formed veterans' organization, the American Legion, took on the American Protective League's role of identifying seditious individuals and organizations and ensuring the public's devotion to "100 percent Americanism."

The Red Scare reached its climax on New Year's Day 1920, when federal agents broke into the homes and meeting places of thousands of suspected revolutionaries in 33 cities. Directed by Attorney General A. Mitchell Palmer, these widely publicized "Palmer raids" were meant to expose the extent of revolutionary activity. Palmer's agents uncovered three pistols, no rifles, and no explosives. Nevertheless, they arrested more than 4,000 people and kept many of them in jail for weeks without formally charging them with a crime. Finally, those who were not citizens (approximately 600) were deported and the rest were released.

Palmer's failure to expose a revolutionary plot blunted support for him in official circles, but, undeterred, Palmer now alleged that revolutionaries were planning a series of assaults on government officials and government buildings for May 1, 1920. When nothing happened on that date, his credibility suffered another serious blow.

As Palmer's exaggerations of the Red threat became known, many Americans began to reconsider their near-hysterical fear of dissent and subversion. Even so, the political atmosphere remained hostile to radicals, as the Sacco and Vanzetti case revealed. In May 1920, two Italian-born anarchists, Nicola Sacco and Bartolomeo Vanzetti, were arrested in Brockton, Massachusetts, and charged with armed robbery and murder. Both men proclaimed their innocence and insisted that they were being punished for their political beliefs. Their foreign accents and their defiant espousal of anarchist doctrines in the courtroom inclined many Americans, including the judge who presided at their trial, to view them harshly. Despite the weak case against them, they were convicted of first-degree murder and sentenced to death. Their lawyers attempted numerous appeals, all of which failed. Anger over the verdicts began to build among Italian Americans, radicals, and liberal intellectuals. Protests compelled the governor

THE PASSION OF SACCO AND VANZETTI,
BY BEN SHAHN

The 1920 trial and 1927 execution of Nicola Sacco and Bartolomeo Vanzetti became the passion of many immigrants, liberal intellectuals, and artists (such as Ben Shahn), who were convinced that the two anarchists had been unfairly tried and convicted.

of Massachusetts to appoint a commission to review the case, but no new trial was ordered. On August 23, 1927, Sacco and Vanzetti were executed, still insisting they were innocent.

Racial Conflict and the Rise of Black Nationalism

The more than 400,000 blacks who served in the armed forces believed that a victory for democracy abroad would help them achieve democracy for their people at home. At first, despite the discrimination they encountered in the military, they maintained their conviction that they would be treated as full-fledged citizens upon their return. Many began to talk about the birth of a New Negro—independent and proud. Thousands joined the NAACP at the forefront of the fight for racial equality. By 1918, 100,000 African Americans subscribed to the NAACP's magazine, the *Crisis,* whose editor, W. E. B. Du Bois, had urged them to support the war.

This wartime optimism made the postwar discrimination and hatred African Americans encountered difficult to endure. Many black workers who had found jobs in the North were fired to make way for returning white veterans. Returning black servicemen, meanwhile, had to scrounge for poorly paid jobs as unskilled laborers. In the South, lynch mobs targeted black veterans who now refused to tolerate the usual insults and indignities; 10 of the 70 blacks lynched in the South in 1919 were veterans.

The worst antiblack violence that year occurred in the North, however. Crowded conditions during the war had forced black and white ethnic city dwellers into uncomfortably close proximity. Many white ethnics regarded blacks with a mixture of fear and prejudice. They resented having to share neighborhoods, trolleys, parks, streets, and workplaces with blacks. Many also wanted African Americans barred from unions, seeing them as threats to their job security.

Racial tensions escalated into race riots. The deadliest explosion occurred in Chicago in July 1919, when a black teenager who had been swimming in Lake Michigan was killed by whites after coming too close to a whites-only beach. Rioting soon broke out, with white mobs invading black neighborhoods, torching homes and stores, and attacking innocent residents. Led by war veterans, some of whom were armed, blacks fought back, turning the border areas between white and black neighborhoods into battle zones. Fighting raged for five days, leaving 38 dead (23 black, 15 white) and more than 500 injured. Race rioting in other cities pushed the death total to 120 before summer's end.

The riots made it clear to blacks that the North was not the Promised Land. Confined to unskilled jobs and to segregated neighborhoods with substandard housing and exorbitant rents, black migrants in Chicago, New York, and other northern cities suffered economic hardship throughout the 1920s. The NAACP carried on its campaign for civil rights and racial equality, but many blacks no longer shared its belief that they would one day be accepted as first-class citizens. They turned instead to a leader from Jamaica, Marcus Garvey, who gave voice to

MARCUS GARVEY, BLACK NATIONALIST
This portrait was taken in 1924, after Garvey's conviction on mail fraud charges.

their bitterness. "The first dying that is to be done by the black man in the future," Garvey declared in 1918, "will be done to make himself free. And then when we are finished, if we have any charity to bestow, we may die for the white man. But as for me, I think I have stopped dying for him."

Garvey called on blacks to give up their hopes for integration and to set about forging a separate black nation. He reminded blacks that they possessed a rich culture stretching back over the centuries that would enable them to achieve greatness as a nation. Garvey's ambition was to build a black nation in Africa that would bring together all of the world's people of African descent. In the short term, he wanted to help American and Caribbean blacks to achieve economic and cultural independence.

Garvey's call for black separatism and self-sufficiency—or black nationalism, as it came to be known—elicited a favorable response among African Americans. In the early 1920s, the Universal Negro Improvement Association (UNIA), which Garvey had founded, enrolled millions of members in 700 branches in 38 states. His newspaper, the *Negro World,* reached a circulation of 200,000. The New York chapter of UNIA undertook an economic development program that included the establishment of grocery stores, restaurants, and factories. Garvey's most visible economic venture was the Black Star Line, a shipping company with three ships flying the UNIA flag from their masts.

This black nationalist movement did not endure for long. Garvey entered into bitter disputes with other black leaders, including W. E. B. Du Bois, who regarded him as a flamboyant, self-serving demagogue. Garvey sometimes showed poor judgment, as when he expressed support for the Ku Klux Klan on the grounds that it shared his pessimism about the possibility of racial integration. Inexperienced in economic matters, Garvey squandered UNIA money on abortive business ventures. The U.S. government regarded his rhetoric as inflammatory and sought to silence him. In 1923, he was convicted of mail fraud involving the sale of Black Star stocks and was sentenced to five years in jail. In 1927, he was deported to Jamaica and the UNIA folded. Nevertheless, Garvey's philosophy of black nationalism endured.

Conclusion

The resurgence of racism in 1919 and the consequent turn to black nationalism among African Americans were signs that the high hopes of the war years had been dashed. Industrial workers, immigrants, and radicals also found their pursuit of liberty and equality interrupted by the fear, intolerance, and repression unleashed by the war. They came to understand as well that Wilson's commitment to these ideals counted for less than did his administration's and Congress's determination to discipline a people whom they regarded as dangerously heterogeneous and unstable. Of the reform groups, only woman suffragists made enduring gains—especially the right to vote—but, for the feminists in their ranks, these steps forward failed to compensate for the collapse of the progressive movement and, with it, their program of achieving equal rights for women across the board.

A similar disappointment engulfed those who had embraced and fought for Wilson's dream of creating a new and democratic world order. The world in 1919 appeared as volatile as it had been in 1914. More and more Americans—perhaps even a majority—were coming to believe that U.S. intervention had been a mistake.

In other ways, the United States benefited a great deal from the war. By 1919, the American economy was by far the world's strongest. Many of the nation's leading corporations had improved productivity and management during the war. U.S. banks were poised to supplant those of London as the most influential in international finance. The nation's economic strength triggered an extraordinary burst of growth in the 1920s, and millions of Americans rushed to take advantage of the prosperity that this "people's capitalism" had put within their grasp. But even affluence failed to dissolve the class, ethnic, and racial tensions that the war had exposed. And the failure of the peace process added to Europe's problems, delayed the emergence of the United States as a leader in world affairs, and created the preconditions for another world war.

SUGGESTED READINGS

On America's neutrality and road to war, consult **Arthur S. Link**, *Woodrow Wilson: Revolution, War and Peace* (1979), and **John Milton Cooper Jr.**, *The Vanity of Power: American Isolationism and the First World War, 1914–1917* (1969). **Roland C. Marchand**, *The American Peace Movement and Social Reform, 1898–1918* (1972), reconstructs the large and influential antiwar movement, while **John W. Chambers**, *To Raise an Army: The Draft Comes to Modern America* (1987), analyzes American efforts to prepare for war by raising a multimillion-man fighting machine. **David Kennedy**, *Over Here: The First World War and American Society* (1980), is a superb account of the effects of war on American society. For details on industrial mobilization, consult **Robert D. Cuff**, *The War Industries Board: Business-Government Relations during World War I* (1973). **David Montgomery**, *The Fall of the House of Labor: The Workplace, the State, and American Labor Activism, 1865–1925* (1987), expertly reconstructs the escalation of labor-management tensions during the war, but it should be read alongside **Joseph A. McCartin**, *Labor's Great War: The Struggle for Industrial Democracy and the Origins of Modern Labor Relations, 1912–1921* (1997). On the migration of African Americans to northern industrial centers and the movement of women into war production see **Joe William Trotter Jr., ed.**, *The Great Migration in Historical Perspective: New Dimensions of Race, Class, and Gender* (1991), and **Maurine W. Greenwald**, *Women, War and Work* (1980). **Stephen Vaughn**, *Holding Fast the Inner Lines: Democracy, Nationalism, and the Committee on Public Information* (1980), is an important account of the CPI, the government's central propaganda agency. **Harry N. Scheiber**, *The Wilson Administration and Civil Liberties, 1917–1921* (1960), analyzes the repression of dissent. On Wilson, Versailles, and the League of Nations, consult **Thomas J. Knock**, *To End All Wars: Woodrow Wilson and the Quest for a New World Order* (1992), **Arno Mayer**, *The Politics and Diplomacy of*

Peacemaking: Containment and Counterrevolution at Versailles, 1918–1919 (1967), Lloyd C. Gardner, *Safe for Democracy: The Anglo-American Response to Revolution, 1913–1923* (1984), John Milton Cooper, Jr., *Breaking the Heart of the World: Woodrow Wilson and the Fight for the League of Nations* (2001), and Katherine A. S. Siegel, *Loans and Legitimacy: The Evolution of Soviet-American Relations, 1919–1933* (1996). On Republican opposition to the League of Nations, see William C. Widenor, *Henry Cabot Lodge and the Search for an American Foreign Policy* (1980). Nell Irvin Painter, *Standing at Armageddon: The United States, 1877–1919* (1987), offers a good overview of the class and racial divisions that convulsed American society in 1919. On the Red Scare, consult Robert K. Murray, *Red Scare: A Study in National Hysteria* (1955). William Tuttle, Jr., *Race Riot: Chicago in the Red Summer of 1919* (1970), examines race conflict after the First World War, while Judith Stein, *The World of Marcus Garvey: Race and Class in Modern Society* (1986), explores the emergence of Marcus Garvey and the Universal Negro Improvement Association.

 AMERICAN JOURNEY ONLINE AND INFOTRAC COLLEGE EDITION

Visit the source collections at www.ajaccess.wadsworth.com and infotrac.thomsonlearning.com and use the Search function with the following key terms to explore documents, images, audio and video clips, articles, and commentary related to the material in this chapter.

Woodrow Wilson	Red Scare
Lusitania	Sacco and Vanzetti
Fourteen Points	W. E. B. Du Bois
Treaty of Versailles	Marcus Garvey
League of Nations	black nationalism

GRADE AIDS

Visit the Liberty Equality Power Companion Web Site for resources specific to this textbook: http://history.wadsworth.com/murrin_LEP4e

The CD in the back of this book and the U.S. History Resource Center at http://history.wadsworth.com/u.s./ offer a variety of tools to help you succeed in this course, including access to quizzes; images; documents; interactive simulations, maps, and timelines; movie explorations; and a wealth of other sources.

Chapter 24

The 1920s

THE JAZZ AGE
This 1923 painting by William Patrick Roberts, entitled "The Dance Club" or "The Jazz Party," captures the dress, dancing, physical intimacy, and emotional intensity associated with modernist impulse of the 1920s.

CHAPTER OUTLINE

In 1920, Americans elected as president a man, Warren G. Harding, who could not have been more different from his predecessor Woodrow Wilson. A Republican, Harding presented himself as a common man with common desires. In his 1920 campaign, he called for a "return to normalcy." Although he died in office in 1923, his carefree spirit is thought to characterize the 1920s.

To many Americans, the decade was one of fun rather than reform, of good times rather than high ideals. It was, in the words of novelist F. Scott Fitzgerald, the "Jazz Age," a time when the search for personal gratification seemed to replace the quest for public welfare.

Despite Harding's call for a return to a familiar past, America seemed to be rushing headlong into the future. The word *modern* began appearing everywhere: modern times, modern women, modern technology, the modern home, modern marriage. Although the word was rarely defined, it connoted certain beliefs: that science was a better guide to life than religion; that people should be free to choose their own lifestyles; that sex should be a source of pleasure for women as well as men; that women and minorities should be equal to white men and enjoy the same rights.

Many other Americans, however, reaffirmed their belief that God's word transcended science; that people should obey the moral code set forth in the Bible; that women were not equal to men; and that blacks, Mexicans, and Eastern European immigrants were inferior to Anglo-Saxon whites. They made their voices heard in a resurgent Ku Klux Klan and the fundamentalist movement, and on issues such as evolution and immigration. In seeking to restore an older America, some in their ranks were prepared to deny individual Americans the liberty to choose their own ways of living and to insist that all people were not fundamentally equal.

Modernists and traditionalists confronted each other in party politics, in legislatures, in courtrooms, and in the press. Their battles belie the vision of the 1920s merely as a time for the pursuit of leisure. Nor were the 1920s free of the economic and social problems that had troubled Americans for decades.

CHAPTER FOCUS

♦ What were the achievements and limitations of "people's capitalism?"

♦ Why is the 1920s sometimes described as the "age of celebrity," and what caused this culture to arise?

♦ What were the key similarities and differences in the politics of the three Republican presidents of the 1920s: Harding, Coolidge, and Hoover?

♦ Who were the "traditionalists" of the 1920s, and what did they believe?

♦ How were the experiences of ethnic and racial communities in 1920s America similar to each other and how were they different?

Prosperity

On balance, the First World War had been good for the American economy. American industries had emerged intact, even strengthened, from the war. The war needs of the Allies had created an insatiable demand for American goods and capital. Manufacturers and bankers had exported so many goods and extended so many loans to the Allies that by war's end, the United States was the world's leading creditor nation. New York City challenged London as the hub of world finance. At home, the government had helped the large corporations and banks to consolidate their power. Corporate America had responded by raising productivity and efficiency to new heights through advances in technology and management.

Postwar economic turmoil and depression hampered these advances for a time. From 1919 to 1921, the country struggled to redirect industry from wartime to civilian production, a process slowed by the government's hasty withdrawal from its wartime role as economic regulator and stabilizer. Workers went on strike to protest wage reductions or increases in the workweek. Farmers were hit by a depression as the overseas demand for American foodstuffs fell from its 1918–19 peak. Disgruntled workers and farmers even joined forces to form statewide farmer-labor parties, which for a time threatened to disrupt the country's two-party system in the upper Midwest. In 1924, the two groups formed a national Farmer-Labor Party. Robert La Follette, their presidential candidate, received

CHRONOLOGY

1920	Prohibition goes into effect • Warren G. Harding defeats James M. Cox for presidency • Census reveals that most Americans live in urban areas • 8 million cars on road
1921	Sheppard-Towner Act passed
1922	United States, Britain, Japan, France, and Italy sign Five-Power Treaty, agreeing to reduce size of their navies
1923	Teapot Dome scandal lands Secretary of the Interior Albert Fall in jail • Harding dies in office; Calvin Coolidge becomes president
1924	Dawes Plan to restructure Germany's war debt put in effect • Coolidge defeats John W. Davis for presidency • Ku Klux Klan membership approaches 4 million • Johnson-Reed Act cuts immigration by 80 percent and discriminates against Asians and southern and eastern Europeans
1925	Scopes trial upholds right of Tennessee to bar teaching of evolution in public schools • *Survey Graphic* publishes a special issue announcing the Harlem Renaissance • F. Scott Fitzgerald publishes *The Great Gatsby* • U.S. withdraws Marines from Nicaragua
1926	Revenue Act cuts income and estate taxes • U.S. sends Marines back to Nicaragua to end civil war and protect U.S. property
1927	Coolidge vetoes McNary-Haugen bill, legislation meant to relieve agricultural distress • Babe Ruth hits 60 home runs • Charles Lindbergh flies across the Atlantic
1928	15 nations sign Kellogg-Briand pact, pledging to avoid war • Coolidge vetoes McNary-Haugen bill again • Herbert Hoover defeats Alfred E. Smith for presidency
1929	Union membership drops to 3 million • 27 million cars on road • William Faulkner publishes *The Sound and the Fury* • Josh Gibson joins the National Negro League
1930	Los Angeles's Mexican population reaches 100,000

an impressive 16 percent of the vote that year, but then the third-party movement fell apart.

Its collapse reflected a rising public awareness of how vigorous and productive the economy had become. Beginning in 1922, the nation embarked on a period of remarkable growth. From 1922 to 1929, the gross national product grew at an annual rate of 5.5 percent, rising from $149 billion to $227 billion. The unemployment rate never exceeded 5 percent—and real wages rose about 15 percent.

A Consumer Society

The variety of products being produced matched the rate of economic growth. In the 19th century, economic growth had rested primarily on the production of capital goods, such as factory machinery and railroad tracks. In the 1920s, however, growth rested more on consumer goods. Some products, such as cars and telephones, had been available since the early 1900s, but in the 1920s, their sales reached new levels. In 1920, just 12 years after Ford introduced the Model T, 8 million cars were on the road. By 1929, there were 27 million—one for every five Americans. Other consumer goods became available for the first time: tractors, washing machines, refrigerators, electric irons, radios, and vacuum cleaners. The term "consumer durable" was coined to describe such goods, which, unlike food, clothing, and other perishables, were meant to last. Even perishables took on new allure. Scientists had discovered the importance of vitamins in the diet and began urging Americans to consume more fresh fruits and vegetables. The agricultural economy of southern California grew rapidly as urban demand for the region's fresh fruits and vegetables skyrocketed. Improvements in refrigeration and in packaging, meanwhile, allowed fresh produce to travel long distances and extended its shelf life in grocery stores. And more stores were being operated by large grocery chains that could afford the latest refrigeration and packaging technology.

The public responded to these innovations with excitement. American industry had made fresh food and stylish clothes available to the masses. Refrigerators, vacuum cleaners, and washing machines would spare women the drudgery of housework. Radios would expand the public's cultural horizons. Cars, asphalt roads, service stations, hot dog stands, "tourist cabins" (the forerunners of motels), and traffic lights seemed to herald a wholly new automobile civilization. By the middle of the decade, the country possessed a network of paved roads. City dwellers now had easy access to rural areas and made a ritual of day-long excursions. Camping trips and long-distance

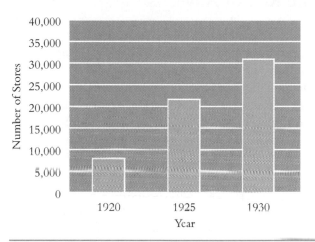

GROWTH OF SIX LEADING GROCERY CHAINS BY NUMBER OF STORES, 1920–1930

Source: From Godfrey M. Labhar, *Chain Stores in America, 1859–1962* (New York: Chain Store Publishing, 1963).

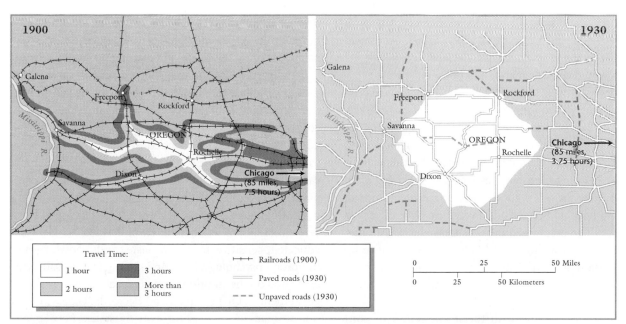

MAP 24.1 AUTOMOBILE CIVILIZATION: CARS, ROADS, AND THE EXPANSION OF TRAVEL HORIZONS IN OREGON, ILLINOIS

In 1900, someone wanting to travel outside Oregon, Illinois, could not get very far in an hour or two, unless his or her destination lay exactly on the major train line running through town. By 1930, the distances a person could travel and the variety of destinations a person could reach in two hours—signified on the right-hand map by the tan and yellow circles surrounding Oregon—had expanded enormously.

vacations became routine. Farmers and their families could now hop into their cars and head for the nearest town with its stores, movies, amusement parks, and sporting events. Suburbs proliferated, billed as the perfect mix of urban and rural life. Young men and women everywhere discovered that cars were a place where they could "make out," and even make love, without fear of reproach by prudish parents or prying neighbors.

In the 1920s, some Americans also discovered the benefits of owning stocks. The number of stockholders in AT&T, the nation's largest corporation, rose from 140,000 to 568,000. U.S. Steel stockholder numbers increased from 96,000 to 146,000. By 1929, as many as 7 million Americans owned stock, most of them people of middle-class means. This spread of stock ownership reflected the need for working capital among the nation's corporations. Because privately held wealth could not satisfy that need, corporations sought to sell their stocks and bonds to the general public. The New York Stock Exchange, first organized in 1792, assisted in processing complicated transactions.

A People's Capitalism

Capitalists boasted that they had created a "people's capitalism" in which virtually all Americans could participate. Now, everyone could own a piece of corporate America. Now, everyone could have a share of luxuries and amenities. Poverty, capitalists claimed, was banished and the gap between rich and poor all but closed. If every American could own a car and house, buy quality clothes, own stock, take vacations, and go to the movies, then economic inequality would cease to matter as a political issue.

Actually, although wages were rising, millions of Americans still earned too little to partake fully of the marketplace. The percentage of Americans owning stocks remained small. Social scientists Robert and Helen Lynd discovered, in their celebrated 1929 study of Muncie, Indiana, that working-class families who bought a car often lacked money for other goods. One housewife admitted, "We don't have no fancy clothes when we have the car to pay for. . . . The car is the only pleasure we have." Another declared, "I'll go without food before I'll see us give up the car." Many industrialists resisted pressure to increase wages, and workers lacked the organizational strength to force them to pay more.

One solution came with the introduction of consumer credit. Car dealers, home appliance salesmen, and other merchants began to offer installment plans that enabled consumers to purchase a product by making a down payment and promising to pay the rest in install-

ments. By 1930, 15 percent of all purchases—including 60 percent of all cars and 75 percent of all radios—were made on the installment plan.

Even so, many poor Americans benefited little from the consumer revolution. Middle-class Americans acquired a disproportionate share of consumer durables. They also could afford to purchase far more fresh fruits and vegetables and stocks than most working-class Americans.

The Rise of Advertising and Mass Marketing

But even middle-class consumers had to be wooed. How could they be persuaded to buy another car only a few years after they had bought their first one? General Motors had the answer. In 1926, it introduced the concept of the annual model change. GM cars took on a different look every year as GM engineers changed headlights and chassis colors, streamlined bodies, and added new features. The strategy worked. GM leaped past Ford and became the world's largest car manufacturer.

Henry Ford reluctantly introduced his Model A in 1927 to provide customers with a colorful alternative to the drab Model T. Having spent his lifetime selling a product renowned for its utility and reliability, Ford rejected the idea that sales could be increased by appealing to the intangible hopes and fears of consumers. He was wrong. The desire to be beautiful, handsome, or sexually attractive; to exercise power and control; to demonstrate competence and success; to escape anonymity, loneliness, and boredom; to experience pleasure—all such desires, once activated, could motivate a consumer to buy a new car even when the old one was still serviceable, or to spend money on goods that might have once seemed frivolous.

Arousing such desires required more than bright colors, sleek lines, and attractive packaging. It called for advertising campaigns intended to make a product seem to be the answer to the consumer's desires. To create those campaigns, corporations turned to a new kind of company: professional advertising firms. The new advertising entrepreneurs, people such as Edward Bernays, Doris Fleischmann, and Bruce Barton, tended to be well-educated, sensitive to public taste, and knowledgeable in human psychology. In their campaigns, these advertisers played on the emotions and vulnerabilities of their target audiences. One cosmetics ad decreed: "Unless you are one woman in a thousand, you must use powder and rouge. Modern living has robbed women of much of their natural color." A perfume manufacturer's ad pronounced: "The first duty of woman is to attract. . . . It does not matter how clever or independent you may be, if you fail to

Sunshine Mellows Heat Purifies

LUCKIES are always <u>kind</u> to your throat

The advice of your physician: Keep out of doors, in the open air, breathe deeply; take plenty of exercise in the mellow sunshine, and have a periodic check-up on the health of your body.

Everyone knows that sunshine mellows—that's why the "TOASTING" process includes the use of the Ultra Violet Rays. LUCKY STRIKE—made of the finest tobaccos—the Cream of the Crop—THEN—"IT'S TOASTED"—an extra, secret heating process. Harsh irritants present in all raw tobaccos are expelled by "TOASTING." These irritants are sold to others. They are **not** present in your LUCKY STRIKE. No wonder LUCKIES are always kind to your throat.

"It's toasted"
Your Throat Protection—against irritation—against cough

LUCKY STRIKE CIGARETTES

The Granger Collection, New York.

SELLING BEAUTY AND HEALTH

This advertisement hints at the negative health effects of smoking, but touts "Luckies" as a healthful cigarette more appropriate for the delicate bodies of beautiful women.

influence the men you meet, consciously or unconsciously, you are not fulfilling your fundamental duty as a woman." A mouthwash ad warned about one unsuspecting gentleman's bad breath—"the truth that his friends had been too delicate to mention," while a tobacco ad matter-of-factly declared: "Men at the top are apt to be pipe-smokers. . . . It's no coincidence—pipe-smoking is a calm and deliberate habit—restful, stimulating. His pipe helps a man think straight. A pipe is back of most big ideas."

Advertising professionals believed they were helping people to manage their lives in ways that would increase their satisfaction and pleasure. American consumers responded enthusiastically. Their interest in fashion, their eagerness to fill their homes with the latest products, their alacrity to take up the craze of the moment (the mah-jongg card game, crossword puzzles, miniature golf)—all evidenced Americans' preoccupation with self-improvement and personal pleasure. The most enthusiastic of all were middle-class Americans, who could afford to buy what the advertisers were selling. Many of them were newcomers to middle-class ranks, searching for ways to affirm—or even create—their new identity. The aforementioned ad for pipe tobacco, for example, was targeted at the new middle-class man, imagined by advertisers to be someone holding a salaried position in a corporate office or bank, or working as a commission salesman, or owning a small business.

As male wage earners moved into the new middle class, their wives were freed from the necessity of outside work. Advertisers appealed to the new middle-class woman, too, as she refocused her attention toward dressing in the latest fashion, managing the household, and raising the children. Vacuum cleaners and other consumer

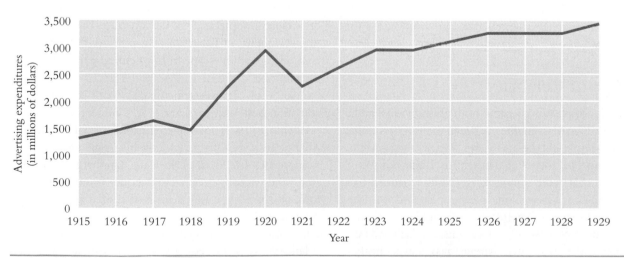

EXPENDITURES ON ADVERTISING, 1915–1929

Source: Data from *Historical Statistics of the United States, Colonial Times to 1970* (White Plains, N.Y.: Kraus International, 1989), p. 856.

durables would make her more efficient, and books on child-rearing, many imbued with a popularized Freudianism, would enable her to mold her children for future success in work and marriage. Cosmetics would aid women in their "first duty"—to be beautiful and sexual for their husbands and boyfriends.

Changing Attitudes toward Marriage and Sexuality

That husbands and wives were encouraged to pursue sexual satisfaction together was one sign of how prescriptions for married life had changed since the 19th century, when women were thought to lack sexual passion and men were tacitly expected to satisfy their drives through extramarital liaisons (see chapter 19). Modern husbands and wives were expected to share other leisure activities as well—dining out, playing cards with friends, going to the movies, attending concerts, and discussing the latest selection from the newly formed Book-of-the-Month Club. Husbands and wives now aspired to a new ideal—to be best friends, full partners in the pursuit of happiness.

The public pursuit of pleasure was also noticeable among young and single middle-class women. The so-called "flappers" of the 1920s set out to break the informal rules governing young women's lives: they donned short dresses, rolled their stockings down, wore red lipstick, and smoked in public. They took their inspiration from depictions of saucy, working-class women of the previous decade, whom moviemakers had popularized and refined. Flappers were signaling their desire for independence and equality, but they had little thought of achieving those goals through politics, as had their middle-class predecessors in the woman suffrage movement. Rather, they aimed to create a new female personality endowed with self-reliance, outspokenness, and a new appreciation for the pleasures of life.

An Age of Celebrity

The pursuit of pleasure became both an individual and a group endeavor. Mass marketers began to understand that much money could be made by staging mega-events, mostly connected to sports, that tens of thousands would attend and that radio announcers would broadcast to a "virtual" audience of millions. Newspapers and word-of-mouth would ensure that enthusiasts would discuss these events for days, even weeks and months. Baseball and boxing became the two sports where mass marketing had advanced the furthest. When Yankee Stadium opened in 1923, it dwarfed every other sport amphitheater in the country. Boxing matches began drawing audiences that would have been unimaginable 20 years earlier. To succeed on this scale, these sports required not just stirring athletic competitions but also individual athletes who seemed larger than life and whose exploits and character could be endlessly promoted. No sports figure achieved greater fame than did George Herman "Babe" Ruth, who overcame the hardships of a poor and orphaned youth to become the slugging star, the "Sultan of Swat," of the New York Yankees. In the 1920s, Ruth hit more home runs than baseball experts had thought humanly possible, culminating in 1927, when he hit a magical 60, a record that would last for 34 years and that would be surpassed only three times in the 20th century. A close second in popularity to Ruth was heavyweight prizefighter Jack Dempsey, whose combination of ruthlessness and efficiency in the ring with gentleness outside it enthralled millions.

Americans also drew their celebrities from the movies, where stars such as comedian Charles Chaplin and the exotically handsome Rudolph Valentino stirred laughter and sexual longings in audiences. These and other figures became so familiar on the silver screen that they created an insatiable appetite among movie fans for news about their private lives as well, an interest that the movie industry was only too eager to exploit.

The popular figures of the 1920s did not earn their status through their accomplishments in politics or war, but through their prowess at a game or their skill at acting in front of a camera. Historians have tended to criticize such celebrity worship, especially when the lionized individual seemed to possess no quality greater than the ability to hit a ball 400 feet or to smash an opponent's face. But such scholarly criticism perhaps has been too quick to overlook the human longing to experience the intensity of emotions associated with competition and triumph or to draw close to someone who demonstrates that the impossible—whether in the form of a physical feat, or a love relationship, or an escape from a confining life—could be accomplished.

Some of these sentiments can be discerned in the adulation bestowed on Charles A. Lindbergh, the young pilot who, in 1927, became the first individual to cross the Atlantic in a solo flight. Piloting his single-engine white monoplane, *The Spirit of St. Louis*, Lindbergh flew nonstop (and without sleep) for 34 hours from the time he took off from Long Island until he landed at Le Bourget Airport in Paris. Thousands of Parisians were waiting for him at the airfield and began charging his plane as soon as it landed. When he returned to New York, an estimated 4 million fans lined the parade route. This shy young man from Minnesota instantly became the most famous and

CHARLES A. LINDBERGH AND THE *SPIRIT OF ST. LOUIS*
Lindbergh poses before the plane that will carry him from Long Island to Paris in the first solo flight across the Atlantic.

From the Collections of the Library of Congress.

adored man in America, mobbed by crowds everywhere he went.

None of this fame could have happened without the new machinery of celebrity culture—aggressive journalists and radio commentators, promoters, and others who understood how fame could make a profit. It mattered, too, that Lindbergh performed his feat in an airplane, one of the newest and most exciting innovations of the time. But Lindbergh's celebrity involved more than hype and technology: He accomplished what others said could not be done, and he did it on his own in a time when corporations and other private institutions of power seemed to be shrinking the realm for individual initiative. Some of Lindbergh's popularity no doubt rested on his ability to demonstrate that an individual of conviction and

skill could still make a difference in an increasingly industrialized and bureaucratized world.

Celebrating Business Civilization

Industrialists, advertisers, and merchandisers in the 1920s began to claim that their accomplishments lay at the heart of American civilization. Business, they argued, made America great, and businessmen provided the nation with its wisest, most vigorous leadership. In 1924, President Calvin Coolidge declared that "the business of America is business." Even religion became a business. Bruce Barton, in his best-seller *The Man Nobody Knows* (1925), depicted Jesus as a business executive "who picked up twelve men from the bottom ranks of business and forged them into an organization that conquered the world." Elsewhere, Barton hailed Jesus as an early "national advertiser," and proclaimed that Peter and Paul were really not so different from Americans who sold vacuum cleaners.

Some corporate leaders adopted benevolent attitudes toward their employees. They set up workplace cafeterias, hired doctors and nurses to staff onsite medical clinics, and engaged psychologists to counsel troubled workers. They built ball fields and encouraged employees to join industry-sponsored leagues. They published employee newsletters and gave awards to employees who did their jobs well and with good spirit. Some employers set up profit-sharing plans and offered stock options to reward employees for their efforts. And some even gave employees a voice in determining working conditions.

WELFARE CAPITALISM AT WORK
Employees at the Cluett Peabody plant in Troy, New York, eat lunch in a spacious, well-lit, and clean cafeteria. By providing their workforces with first-rate facilities, large corporations hoped to secure the loyalty of their employees.

© Bettmann/Corbis.

The real purpose of these measures—collectively known as welfare capitalism—was to encourage employees to be loyal to their firm and to convince them—contrary to what labor union critics had been arguing—that industry did have the best interests of its employees at heart. Management had an understandable fear of union power, arising from the paralyzing strikes of 1919. As the decade proceeded and as prosperity rolled on, welfare capitalism reflected the confidence that capitalism had become more responsive to employee concerns and thus more humane.

Industrial Workers

Many industrial workers benefited from the nation's prosperity. Most of them enjoyed rising wages and a reasonably steady income. Skilled craftsmen in the older industries of construction, railroad transportation, and printing fared especially well. Their real wages rose by 30 to 50 percent over the decade. The several million workers employed in the large mass-production industries (such as automobile and electrical equipment manufacture) also did well. Their wages were relatively high, and they enjoyed good benefits—paid sick leave, paid vacations, life insurance, stock options, subsidized mortgages, and retirement pensions. Although all workers in companies with these programs were eligible for such benefits, skilled workers were in the best position to claim them.

Semiskilled and unskilled industrial workers had to contend with a labor surplus throughout the decade. As employers replaced workers with machines, the aggregate demand for industrial labor increased at a lower rate than it had in the preceding 20 years. Despite a weakening demand for labor, rural whites, rural blacks, and Mexicans continued their migration to the cities, stiffening the competition for factory jobs. Employers could hire and fire as they saw fit and could therefore keep wage increases lagging behind increases in productivity.

This softening demand for labor helps explain why many working-class families benefited little from the decade's prosperity or from its consumer revolution. An estimated 40 percent of workers remained mired in poverty, unable to afford a healthy diet or adequate housing, much less any of the more costly consumer goods. In 1930, for instance, only 25 to 40 percent of American households owned a washing machine, a vacuum cleaner, and a radio, and only 50 percent had a car.

The million or more workers who labored in the nation's two largest industries, coal and textiles, suffered the most during the 1920s. Throughout the decade, both industries experienced severe overcapacity. By 1926, only

half of the coal mined each year was being sold. Many New England textile cities experienced levels of unemployment that sometimes approached 50 percent. One reason was that many textile industrialists had shifted their operations to the South, where taxes and wages were lower. But the southern textile industry also suffered from excess capacity, exerting a downward pressure on prices and wages there as well. Plant managers pressured their workers to speed up production. Workers loathed the frequent "speed-ups" of machines and the "stretch-outs" in the number of spinning or weaving machines each worker was expected to tend. By the late 1920s, labor strife and calls for unionization were rising among disgruntled workers in both the South and the North.

Unionization of textiles and coal, and of more prosperous industries as well, would have brought workers a larger share of the decade's prosperity. Some labor leaders, such as Sidney Hillman of the Amalgamated Clothing Workers, argued that unionization would actually increase corporate profits by compelling employers to observe uniform wage and hour schedules that would restrain ruinous competition. Hillman pointed out—as Henry Ford had in the preceding decade—that rising wages would enable workers to purchase more consumer goods and thus increase corporate sales and revenues, but Hillman's views were ignored outside the garment industry.

Elsewhere, unions lost ground as business and government, backed by middle-class opinion, remained hos-

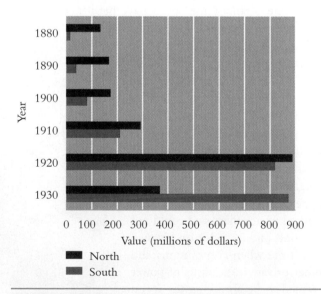

VALUE OF REGIONAL COTTON TEXTILE OUTPUT, 1880–1930

Source: Data from Nancy F. Kane, *Textiles in Transition: Technology, Wages, and Industry Relocation in the U.S. Textile Industry, 1880–1939* (New York: Greenwood Press, 1988), p. 29.

tile to labor organization. Employers attacked unions as un-American. A conservative Supreme Court whittled away at labor's legal protections. In 1921, it ruled that lower courts could issue injunctions against union members, prohibiting them from striking or picketing an employer. State courts also enforced what union members called "yellow dog" contracts, written pledges by which employees promised not to join a union while they were employed. Any employee who violated that pledge was subject to immediate dismissal.

These measures crippled efforts to organize trade unions. Membership fell from a high of 5 million in 1920 to less than 3 million in 1929, a mere 10 percent of the nation's industrial workforce. Other forces contributed to the decline, too. Many workers, especially those benefiting from welfare capitalist programs, decided they no longer needed trade unions. And the labor movement hurt itself by moving too slowly to open its ranks to semiskilled and unskilled factory workers.

Women and Work

Women workers experienced the same hardships as men in the industrial workforce and fewer of the benefits. They were largely excluded from the ranks of the skilled craftsmen and thus missed out on the substantial wage increases that the men in those positions enjoyed. Women also had trouble finding work in the automobile industry, the highest paying of the mass-production industries. They had better access to the electrical equipment and meat-packing industries, although they were often segregated in departments given over to "women's work." Where women were allowed to compete for the same jobs as men, they usually earned less. Thus, a female trimmer in a meat-packing plant typically made 37 cents per hour, only two-thirds what a male trimmer earned. The textile industry had long been a major source of employment for women, but, in the 1920s, women and men alike in this ailing manufacturing sector suffered high rates of unemployment and declining wages.

White-collar work established itself, in the 1920s, as a magnet for women. This sector enjoyed rapid growth in a decade in which corporations expanded and refined their managerial and accounting practices. Discrimination prevented women from becoming managers, accountants, or supervisors, but they did dominate the lower level ranks of secretaries, typists, filing clerks, bank tellers, and department store clerks. By the 1930s, 2 million women, or 20 percent of the female workforce, labored in these and related occupations. Initially, these positions had a glamour that factory work lacked. Work environments were cleaner and brighter, and women had the opportunity—indeed were expected—to dress well and fashionably. But wages were low and managerial authority was absolute. Unions had virtually no presence in white-collar places of employment, and workers had difficulty finding alternative ways of protesting unfair managers or difficult working conditions.

Women with ambitious work aspirations had to pursue the "female" professions, such as teaching, nursing,

NEW OCCUPATIONS FOR WOMEN

By the 1920s, employers preferred women for the telephone operator jobs that were proliferating. The fancy dresses and high heels worn by the women in this photograph underscore the white-collar status of this job.

© Corbis.

social work, and librarianship. Opportunities in several of these fields, especially teaching and social work, were growing, and women responded by enrolling in college in large numbers. The number of female college students increased by 50 percent during the 1920s. Some of these college graduates used their new skills in new fields, such as writing for women's magazines. A few, drawing strength from their feminist forebears during the Progressive Era, managed to crack such male bastions of work as mainstream journalism and university research and teaching (see the Americans Abroad feature for chapter 25). In every field of endeavor, even such new and exotic ones as airplane flying, at least one woman arose to demonstrate that her sex had the necessary talent and drive to match or exceed what men had done. Thus in 1932, Amelia Earhart became the first woman to fly the Atlantic solo, matching Lindbergh's feat and inspiring women everywhere. Even so, Earhart's feat failed to substantially improve opportunities for women who wanted to work as pilots in the airline industry. In this industry, as in most lines of work, gender prejudices remained too entrenched. And the women who had broken the gender line remained, by and large, solitary figures.

The Women's Movement Adrift

Many supporters of the 19th Amendment to the Constitution, which, in 1920, gave women the right to vote, expected it to transform American politics. Women voters would reverse the decline in voter participation, cleanse politics of corruption, and launch a variety of reform initiatives that would improve the quality of life for women and men alike. This female-inspired transformation, however, failed to materialize. Voter participation rates did not increase nor did American politics become imbued with female-inspired virtue and honesty. The women's movement, instead, seemed to succumb to the same exhaustion and frustration as had the more general progressive movement from which it had emerged 20 years earlier. Younger women searching for independence and equality (such as the flappers discussed earlier in this chapter) often turned away from reform altogether, preferring a lifestyle that emphasized private achievement and personal freedom to a political career devoted to improving the collective status of America's women. Those who continued to agitate for reform found progress more difficult to achieve once the conservative Republican administrations of Harding and Coolidge came to power.

Despite the difficult political environment in which they had to work, some female reformers made significant strides in the 1920s. In 1921, one group succeeded in getting Congress to pass the Sheppard-Towner Act, a major

social welfare program that provided federal funds for prenatal and child health care centers throughout the United States. It remained in effect until 1929. In 1923, Alice Paul, still head of the National Women's Party (NWP, see chapter 20), and her allies prevailed on Congress to consider an Equal Rights Amendment (ERA) to the Constitution, phrased as follows: "Men and women shall have equal rights throughout the United States and every place subject to its jurisdiction." And the National American Woman Suffrage Association, the major force behind the struggle for suffrage, transformed itself in 1920 into the League of Women Voters (LWV). During the next decade, the LWV launched numerous initiatives to encourage women to run for elective office, to educate voters about the issues before them, and to improve the condition of those Americans—the poor, female and child laborers, the mentally ill—who needed assistance.

Sometimes the women's movement was stymied not just by external opposition but also by internal division—as it was over the ERA. The NWP and other supporters of the ERA insisted that there could be no compromise with the proposition that women were the equals of men in every respect. But, the LWV countered, child-rearing and mothering duties did render women different from men in key respects and thus, in some instances, in need of special treatment by Congress and other lawmaking bodies.

The question of women's difference crystallized around the issue of protective labor legislation for women. Over the years, a series of state and federal laws had given women protections at the workplace—limitations on the hours of labor, prohibitions on overnight work, and other such measures—that men did not have. Many women reformers supported these measures, believing they were vital to protecting the masses of women workers from the worst forms of exploitation and thus enabling them to have enough time and energy to perform their vital roles as mothers and wives. Fearing that a successful ERA would render this protective legislation unconstitutional, the LWV and its allies opposed the ERA. But Alice Paul and her allies argued that female protective laws did not really benefit women. Instead, employers used these laws as an excuse to segregate women in stereotyped jobs that were mostly low status and low paying and thus to deny women the opportunities for advancement and fulfillment open to men.

This issue of whether women should be treated like men in all respects or offered some protections that no men enjoyed was a genuinely complicated one, and women activists would continue to argue about it with each other for decades. In the 1920s, however, their inability to speak with a single voice on this matter weakened their cause in the eyes of their adversaries.

The Politics of Business

Republican presidents governed the country from 1921 to 1933. In some respects, their administrations resembled those of the Gilded Age, a time of mediocre presidents, rampant corruption, and government bent on removing obstacles to capitalist development. In other respects, however, the state-building tradition of Theodore Roosevelt lived on, although in somewhat altered form.

Harding and the Politics of Personal Gain

Warren Gamaliel Harding defeated Democrat James M. Cox for the presidency in 1920. From modest origins as a newspaper editor in the small town of Marion, Ohio, Harding had risen to the U.S. Senate chiefly because the powerful Ohio Republican machine knew it could count on him to do its bidding. He gained the presidency for the same reason. The Republican Party bosses believed that almost anyone they nominated in 1920 could defeat the Democratic opponent. They chose Harding because they could control him. Harding's good looks and geniality made him a favorite with voters, and he swept into office with 61 percent of the popular vote, the greatest landslide since 1820.

To his credit, Harding released the aging Socialist Party leader Eugene V. Debs from jail and took other measures to cool the passions unleashed by the Red Scare. Aware of his own intellectual limitations, Harding included talented men in his cabinet. His choices of Herbert Hoover as secretary of commerce, Charles Evans Hughes as secretary of state, and Andrew Mellon as secretary of the treasury were particularly impressive appointments. Still, Harding lacked the will to alter his ingrained political habits. He had built his political career on a willingness to please the lobbyists who came to his Senate office asking for favors and deals. He had long followed Ohio boss Harry M. Daugherty's advice and would continue to do so with Daugherty as his attorney general. Harding apparently did not consider men such as Daugherty self-serving or corrupt. They were his friends; they had been with him since the beginning of his political career. He made sure the "boys" had jobs in his administration, and he continued to socialize with them. Many a night he could be found drinking (despite Prohibition), gambling, and womanizing with the "Ohio Gang" at its K Street hangout. Sometimes the gang even convened in the White House. Alice Roosevelt Longworth, Theodore Roosevelt's daughter, once came into the White House study and found the air "heavy with tobacco smoke," its tables cluttered with "bottles containing every imaginable brand of whiskey, . . . [and] cards and poker chips at hand."

The K Street house was more than a place to carouse. It was a place of business where the Ohio Gang became rich selling government appointments, judicial pardons, and police protection to bootleggers. By 1923, the corruption could no longer be concealed. Journalists and senators began to focus public attention on the actions of Secretary of the Interior Albert Fall, who had persuaded Harding to transfer control of large government oil reserves at Teapot Dome, Wyoming, and Elk Hills, California, from the navy to the Department of the Interior. Fall had immediately leased the deposits to two oil tycoons, Harry F. Sinclair and Edward L. Doheny, who pumped oil from the wells in exchange for providing the navy with a system of fuel tank reserves. Fall had issued the leases secretly, without allowing other oil corporations to compete for them, and he had accepted almost $400,000 from Sinclair and Doheny.

Fall would pay for this shady deal with a year in jail. He was not the only Harding appointee to do so. Charles R. Forbes, head of the Veterans' Bureau, would go to Leavenworth Prison for swindling the government out of $200 million in hospital supplies. The exposure of Forbes's theft prompted his lawyer, Charles Cramer, to commit suicide; Jesse Smith, Attorney General Daugherty's close friend and housemate, also killed himself, apparently to avoid being indicted and brought to trial. Daugherty managed to escape conviction and incarceration for bribery by burning incriminating documents held by his brother's Ohio bank. Still, Daugherty left government service in disgrace.

Brown Brothers.

WARREN G. HARDING, CAMPING PARTNER

This photo shows President Harding (on the right) participating in the kind of informal male gathering he so enjoyed. His "buddies" on this camping trip were Henry Ford (left) and Thomas Edison (center).

Harding initially kept himself blind to the widespread use of public office for private gain that characterized his administration but grew depressed when he finally realized what had been going on. In summer 1923, in poor spirits, he left Washington for a West Coast tour. He fell ill in Seattle and died from a heart attack in San Francisco. The train returning his body to Washington attracted crowds of grief-stricken mourners who little suspected the web of corruption and bribery in which Harding had been caught. Even as the revelations poured forth in 1924 and 1925, few Americans seemed bothered. Some of this insouciance reflected the carefree atmosphere of the 1920s, but much of it had to do with the character of the man who succeeded Harding.

Coolidge and Laissez-Faire Politics

Calvin Coolidge rarely smiled. At the many dinners he attended as vice president, he said hardly a word. Silence was his public creed, much to the chagrin of Washington's socialites. He was never enticed into carousing with the "boys," nor did he ever stand by as liquor was being served. He believed that the best government was the government that governed least, and that the welfare of the country hinged not on politicians but on the people—their willingness to work hard, to be honest, and to live within their means.

Born in Vermont and raised in Massachusetts, Calvin Coolidge gained national visibility in September 1919, when as governor of Massachusetts he took a firm stand against Boston's striking policemen (see chapter 23). His reputation as a man who battled labor radicals earned him a place on the 1920 national Republican ticket. His image as an ordinary man helped convince voters in 1920 that the Republican Party would return the country to its commonsensical ways after eight years of reckless reforms. Coolidge won his party's presidential nomination handily in 1924 and easily defeated his Democratic opponent, John W. Davis. Coolidge's popularity remained strong throughout his first full term, and he probably would have been renominated and reelected in 1928, but he chose not to run.

Coolidge took greatest pride in those measures that reduced the government's control over the economy. The Revenue Act of 1926 slashed the high income and estate taxes that progressives had pushed through Congress during the First World War. Coolidge curtailed the power of the Federal Trade Commission to regulate business affairs and endorsed Supreme Court decisions invalidating Progressive Era laws that had strengthened organized labor and protected children and women from employer exploitation.

Brown Brothers.

A STERN YANKEE

In sharp contrast to Harding, President Calvin Coolidge did not enjoy informality, banter, or carousing. Here he fishes alone and in formal attire.

Hoover and the Politics of Associationalism

Republicans in the 1920s did more than simply lift government restraints and regulations from the economy. Some, led by Secretary of Commerce Herbert Hoover, conceived of government as a dynamic, even progressive, economic force. Hoover did not want government to control industry, but he did want government to persuade private corporations to abandon their wasteful, selfish ways and turn to cooperation and public service. Hoover envisioned an economy built on the principle of association. Industrialists, wholesalers, retailers, operators of railroad and shipping lines, small businessmen, farmers, workers, doctors—each of these groups would form a trade association whose members would share economic information, discuss problems of production and distribution, and seek ways of achieving greater efficiency and profit. Hoover believed that the very act of associating in this way—an approach that historian Ellis Hawley has called "associationalism"—would convince participants of the superiority of cooperation over competition, of negotiation over conflict, of public service over selfishness.

A graduate of Stanford University, Hoover had worked first as a mining engineer and then as an executive in multinational mining corporations. During the war, he had directed the government's Food Administration (see chapter 23, especially the Americans Abroad feature on p. 709). From that experience, he had come to appreciate the role that government could play in coordinating the activities of thousands of producers and distributors scattered across the country.

Hoover's ambition as secretary of commerce was to make the department the grand orchestrator of economic cooperation. During his eight years in that post, from 1921 to 1929, he organized more than 250 conferences and brought together government officials, representatives of business, policy makers, and others who had a stake in strengthening the economy.

Hoover achieved some notable successes. He persuaded farmers to join together in marketing cooperatives, steel executives to abandon the 12-hour day for their employees, and some groups of bankers in the South to organize their institutions into regional associations with adequate resources and expertise. Hoover's dynamic conception of government did not endear him to Coolidge, who declared in 1927: "That man has offered me unsolicited advice for six years, all of it bad."

The Politics of Business Abroad

Republican domestic policy disagreements over whether to pursue laissez-faire or associationalism spilled over into foreign policy as well. Hoover had accepted the post of secretary of commerce thinking he would represent the United States in negotiations with foreign companies and governments. In fact, he intended to apply associationalism to international relations. He wanted the world's leading nations to meet regularly in conferences, to limit military buildups, and to foster an international environment in which capitalism could flourish. Aware that the United States must help create such an environment, Hoover hoped to persuade American bankers to adopt investment and loan policies that would aid European recovery. If they refused to do so, he was prepared to urge the government to take an activist, supervisory role in foreign investment.

In 1921 and 1922, Hoover helped to design the Washington Conference on the Limitation of Armaments. Although he did not serve as a negotiator at the conference —Secretary of State Charles Evans Hughes reserved that role for himself and his subordinates— Hoover did supply Hughes's team with a wealth of economic information. And he helped Hughes to use that information to design forceful, detailed proposals for disarmament. Those proposals gave U.S. negotiators a decided advantage

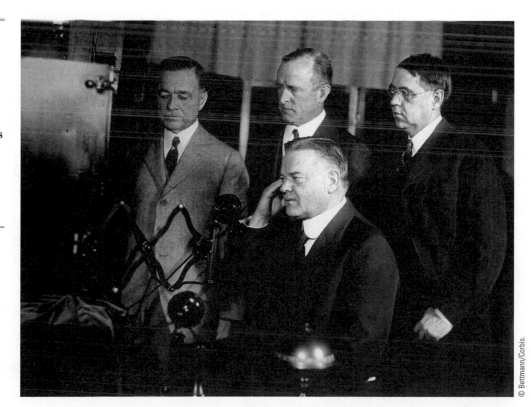

HERBERT HOOVER, SECRETARY OF COMMERCE

Hoover used his cabinet position to encourage innovation in American industry. In 1927, he participated in the nation's first television broadcast. Men in an ATT broadcast studio in New York speak and listen to Hoover and his associates in Washington.

© Bettmann/Corbis.

over their European and Asian counterparts and helped them win a stunning accord, the Five-Power Treaty, by which the United States, Britain, Japan, France, and Italy agreed to scrap more than 2 million tons of warships. Hughes also obtained pledges from all of the signatories that they would respect the "Open Door" in China, long a U.S. foreign policy objective (see chapter 22).

These triumphs redounded to Hughes's credit but not to Hoover's, and Hughes used it to consolidate his control over foreign policy. He rebuffed Hoover's efforts to put international economic affairs under the direction of the Commerce Department and rejected Hoover's suggestion to intervene in the international activities of U.S. banks.

Hughes was not entirely laissez faire in approach, as he demonstrated in his 1923 reaction to a crisis in Franco-German relations. The victorious Allies had imposed on Germany an obligation to pay $33 billion in war reparations (see chapter 23). In 1923, when the impoverished German government suspended its payments, France sent troops to occupy the Ruhr valley, whose industry was vital to the German economy. German workers retaliated by going on strike, and the crisis threatened to undermine Europe's precarious economic recovery. Hughes did not stand on the sidelines. He intensified American financial pressure on the French and compelled them to attend a U.S.-sponsored conference in 1924 to restructure Germany's debt obligation.

The conference produced the Dawes Plan (after the Chicago banker and chief negotiator, Charles G. Dawes), which reduced German reparations from $542 million to $250 million annually and called on U.S. and foreign banks to stimulate the German economy with a quick infusion of $200 million in loans. Within a matter of days, banker J. P. Morgan, Jr., raised more than $1 billion from American investors. Money poured into German financial markets, and the German economy appeared to stabilize.

The Dawes Plan won applause on both sides of the Atlantic, but soon the U.S. money flooding into Germany created its own problems. American investors were so eager to lend to Germany that their investments became speculative and unsound. At this point, a stronger U.S. government effort to direct loans to sound investments, a strategy that Hoover supported, might have helped. But neither Hughes nor his successor as secretary of state, Frank Kellogg, was interested in such initiatives, and neither was Secretary of the Treasury Mellon. The laissez-faire approach had reasserted itself, and Hoover's plan to involve the U.S. government directly in international economic matters had been rebuffed.

The Republicans' continued pursuit of disarmament and world peace seemed to diverge from their general re-

luctance to involve the U.S. government in foreign affairs. To follow up the success of the 1922 Five-Power treaty, Secretary of State Kellogg drew up a treaty with Aristide Briand, the French foreign minister, outlawing war as a tool of national policy. In 1928, representatives of the United States, France, and 13 other nations met in Paris to sign the Kellogg-Briand pact, an agreement that soon attracted the support of 48 other nations. Coolidge viewed Kellogg-Briand, however, not as a way of extending U.S. government power abroad but as a way of reducing further the size of the U.S. government at home. With the threat of war removed, the United States could scale back its military forces and eliminate much of the bureaucracy needed to support a large standing army and navy. Unfortunately, the pact contained no enforcement mechanism, thus rendering itself ineffective as a foreign policy tool.

The Republican administrations flexed U.S. power more effectively in Latin American affairs. U.S. investments in the region more than doubled from 1917 to 1929, and the U.S. government continued its policy of intervening in the internal affairs of Latin America to protect U.S. interests. Republican administrations did attempt initially to curtail American military involvement in the Caribbean. The Coolidge administration pulled American troops out of the Dominican Republic in 1924 and Nicaragua in 1925. In the case of Nicaragua, however, U.S. Marines returned in 1926 to end a war between liberal and conservative Nicaraguans and to protect American property; this time they stayed until 1934. U.S. troops, meanwhile, occupied Haiti continuously between 1919 and 1934, keeping in power governments friendly to U.S. interests. Opposition to such heavy-handed tactics continued to build in the United States, but they would not yield a significant change in U.S. policy until the 1930s (see chapter 25).

🌐 Farmers, Small-Town Protestants, and Moral Traditionalists

Although many Americans benefited from the prosperity of the 1920s, others did not. Overproduction was impoverishing substantial numbers of farmers. Beyond these economic hardships, many moral-traditionalist white Protestants, especially those in rural areas and small towns, believed that the country was being overrun by racially inferior and morally suspect foreigners.

Agricultural Depression

The 1920s brought hard times to the nation's farmers after the boom period of the war years. During the war, domes-

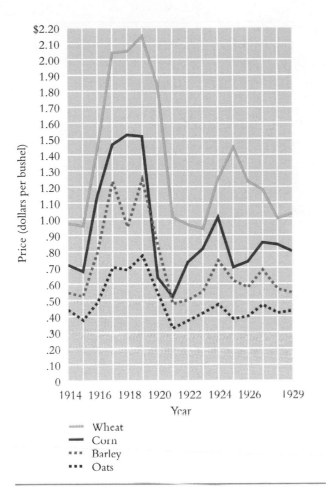

PRICE OF MAJOR CROPS, 1914–1929

Source: Data from *Historical Statistics of the United States, Colonial Times to 1970* (White Plains, N.Y.: Kraus International, 1989), pp. 511–12.

tic demand for farm products had risen steadily and foreign demand had exploded as the war disrupted agricultural production in France, Ukraine, and other European food-producing regions. Soon after the war, however, Europe's farmers quickly resumed their customary levels of production. Foreign demand for American foodstuffs fell precipitously, leaving U.S. farmers with an oversupply and depressed prices.

A rise in agricultural productivity made possible by the tractor also worsened the plight of many farmers. The number of tractors in use almost quadrupled in the 1920s, and 35 million new acres came under cultivation. Produce flooded the market. Prices fell even further, as did farm incomes. By 1929, the annual per capita income of rural Americans was only $223, one-quarter that of the nonfarm population. Hundreds of thousands had to sell their farms and either scrape together a living as tenants or abandon farming altogether. Many chose to abandon farm life, packed their belongings into jalopies or loaded them onto trains, and headed for the city.

Those who stayed on the land grew increasingly assertive in their demands. Early in the decade, radical farmers working through such organizations as the Nonpartisan League of North Dakota and farmer-labor parties in Minnesota, Wisconsin, and other midwestern states led the movement. By the second half of the decade, however, leadership had passed from farming radicals to farming moderates, and from small farmers in danger of dispossession to larger farmers and agribusinesses seeking to extend their holdings. By lobbying through such organizations as the Farm Bureau Federation, the more powerful agricultural interests brought pressure on Congress to set up economic controls that would protect them from failure. Their proposals, embodied in the McNary-Haugen Bill, called on the government to erect high tariffs on foreign produce and to purchase surplus U.S. crops. The government would then sell the surplus crops on the world market for whatever prices they fetched. Any money lost in international sales would be absorbed by the government rather than by the farmers. The McNary-Haugen Bill passed Congress in 1927 and in 1928, only to be vetoed by President Coolidge both times.

Cultural Dislocation

Added to the economic plight of the farmers was a sense of cultural dislocation among the majority who were white, Protestant, and of northwest European descent. These farmers had long perceived themselves as the backbone of the nation—hardworking, honest, God-fearing yeomen, guardians of independence and liberty.

The 1920 census challenged the validity of that view. For the first time, a slight majority of Americans now lived in urban areas. That finding in itself signified little because the census classified as "urban" those towns with a population as small as 2,500. But the census figures did reinforce the widespread perception that both the economic and cultural vitality of the nation had shifted from the countryside to the metropolis. Industry, the chief engine of prosperity, was an urban phenomenon. Commercialized leisure—the world of amusement parks, department stores, professional sports, movies, cabarets, and theaters—was to be enjoyed in cities; so too were flashy fashions and open sexuality. Catholics, Jews, and African Americans, who together outnumbered white Protestants in many cities, seemed to be the principal creators of this new world. They were also thought to be the purveyors of Bolshevism and other modes of radicalism. Cities, finally, were the home of secular intellectuals who had scrapped their belief in Scripture and in God and had embraced science as their new, unimpeachable authority.

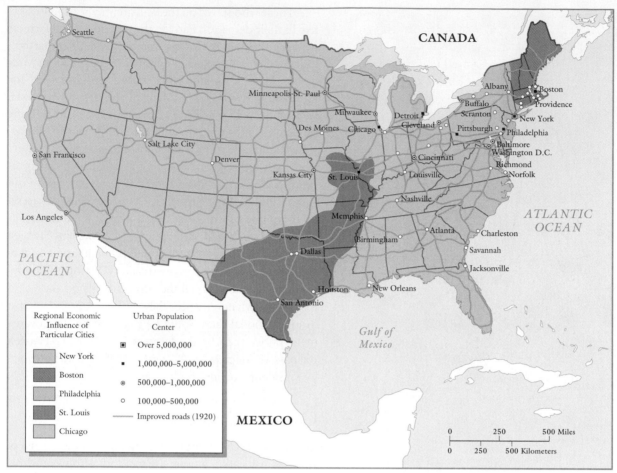

MAP 24.2   URBANIZATION, 1920

By 1920, New York City had surpassed 5 million people, and Boston, Philadelphia, Pittsburgh, Detroit, Chicago, and St. Louis had surpassed 1 million. Another 10 cities, from Los Angeles, California, to Buffalo, New York, had surpassed 500,000. This map, through its color coding, also shows the regions in which the country's five largest cities exercised economic influence.

All through the Progressive Era, rural white Americans had believed that the cities could be redeemed, that city dwellers could be reformed, that the Protestant values of rural America would triumph. War had crushed that confidence and had replaced it with the fear that urban culture and urban people would undermine all that "true" Americans held dear.

These fears grew even more intense with the changes brought by prosperity. Urban-industrial America increased in power and affluence and spread its consumer culture and its commodities to the countryside as never before. Even small towns now sported movie theaters and automobile dealerships. Radio waves carried news of city life into isolated farmhouses. The growth in the circulation of national magazines also broke down the wall separating country from city. Mail-order catalogs—Sears, Roebuck, and Company and others—invited farmers to fantasize that they too could fill their homes with refrigerators, RCA Victrolas, and Hoover vacuum cleaners.

Brown Brothers.

CONSUMER CULTURE PENETRATES THE COUNTRYSIDE

By the 1920s, cars, Coca-Cola, radios, and other commodities had found their way to the country's smallest towns. Here a farmer tunes his radio as he milks his cow.

Rural white Americans showed ambivalence toward this cultural invasion. On the one hand, most country dwellers were eager to participate in the consumer marketplace. On the other hand, many worried that doing so would expose the countryside to atheism, immorality, and radicalism. They expressed their determination to protect their imperiled way of life in their support for Prohibition, the Ku Klux Klan, immigration restriction, and religious fundamentalism.

Prohibition

The 18th Amendment to the Constitution, which prohibited the manufacture and sale of alcohol, went into effect in January 1920. Initially it drew support from a large and varied constituency that included farmers, middle-class city dwellers, feminists, and progressive reformers who loathed the powerful "liquor trust" and who saw firsthand the deleterious effects of drink on the urban poor. It soon

MUSICAL LINK TO THE PAST

Women Singers and the Birth of Modern Country Music

Composer: A. P. Carter (credited as writer but probably was not)

Title: "Single Girl, Married Girl" (1927)

Performers: The Carter Family

Plaintive and never preachy, "Single Girl, Married Girl" explores women's roles and marriage in ways rarely seen in the country music of the 1920s. As she did throughout her career, Sara Carter, a country music pioneer, sang simply and passionately about the lives of common people, in this case women: "Single girl, single girl, she goes to the store and buys . . . Married girl, married girl, she rocks the cradle and cries . . . Single girl, single girl, she's going where she please . . . Married girl, married girl, baby on her knees." Is Sara sad or angry about the plight of this "married girl" tied down by her baby, or is she just plainly stating how women's lives change when children arrive? In either case, Sara Carter, in this song, offers us a glimpse of how country women of the 1920s, often thought to be conservative in outlook, were themselves struggling to balance traditional female responsibilities (in this case, motherhood) with the freedoms that modern society seemed to be offering young women.

The national commercialization of country and blues music in the 1920s opened up new, but still limited, roles for women in the mass media. The Carter Family was by far the most successful of the initial female country groups, producing hit recordings that sold throughout the United States, England, and South Africa, among other places. The group consisted of Sara, who played autoharp and contributed lead vocals; her sister-in-law Maybelle on guitar; and her husband A. P., who occasionally sang with them, but whose most important job

was traveling in search of material for the group, which he often took unwarranted credit for, a common practice at the time. Victor Records's talent scout Ralph Peer discovered them at an open talent audition held in Bristol, Tennessee, on August 2, 1927. This recording, made at those sessions, provides us with a historic glimpse of the birth of modern country music.

The Carter women were relegated to the background in publicity concerning the group. Posters promised a "morally good" program in which a man (A. P.) appeared onstage, an important announcement because women performing popular music independently were viewed as morally suspect. Also, despite general agreement that Sara had a major hand in writing and arranging Carter Family material, her name rarely surfaced in the credits, where A.P.'s name typically dominated. Despite such caveats, the Carter Family represented an important example of the trend of women claiming new kinds of identities and expression in the modern mass media. Sara seemed to be an innovator in her personal life as well—her relatives described her as "very liberated" for a Southern woman in the 1920s and 1930s, wearing slacks, shooting big game, writing and arranging music, openly smoking, and divorcing A.P. in 1938.

---

1. Why do you think women performing music independently were frowned on and viewed by many as morally suspect during this period?

Listen to an audio recording of this music on the Musical Links to the Past CD.

became apparent, however, that Prohibition was doing as much to encourage law-breaking as abstinence. With only 1,500 federal agents to enforce the law, the government could not possibly police the drinking habits of 110 million people. With little fear of punishment, those who wanted to drink did so, either brewing liquor at home or buying it from speakeasies and bootleggers. Because the law prevented legitimate businesses from manufacturing liquor, organized crime added alcohol to its portfolio. Mobsters procured much of their liquor from Canadian manufacturers, smuggled it across the border, protected it in warehouses, and distributed it to speakeasies. Al Capone's Chicago-based mob alone employed 1,000 men to protect its liquor trafficking, which was so lucrative that Capone became the richest (and most feared) gangster in America. Blood flowed in the streets of Chicago and other northern cities as rival mobs fought one another to enlarge their share of the market.

These unexpected consequences caused many early advocates of Prohibition, especially in the cities, to withdraw their support. Not so for Prohibition's rural, white Protestant supporters, however. The violence spawned by liquor trafficking confirmed their view of alcohol as evil. The high-profile participation of Italian, Irish, and Jewish gangsters in the bootleg trade reinforced their belief that Catholics and Jews were threats to law and morality. Many rural white Protestants became more, not less, determined to rid the country of liquor once and for all; some among them resolved to rid the country of Jews and Catholics as well.

The Ku Klux Klan

The original Ku Klux Klan, formed in the South in the late 1860s, had died out with the defeat of Reconstruction and the reestablishment of white supremacy (see chapter 17). The new Klan was created in 1915 by William Simmons, a white southerner who had been inspired by D. W. Griffith's racist film, *Birth of a Nation,* in which the early Klan was depicted as having saved the nation from predatory blacks. By the 1920s, control of the Klan had passed from Simmons to a Texas dentist, Hiram Evans, and its ideological focus had expanded from a loathing of blacks to a hatred of Jews and Catholics as well. Evans's Klan propagated a nativist message that the country should contain—or better yet, eliminate—the influence of Jews and Catholics and restore "Anglo-Saxon" racial purity, Protestant supremacy, and traditional morality to national life. This message swelled Klan ranks and expanded its visibility and influence in the North and South alike. By 1924, as many as 4 million Americans are thought to have belonged to the Klan, including the half-million members of its female auxiliary, Women of the Ku Klux Klan. Not only was the Klan strong in states of the Old Confederacy such as Louisiana and Texas and in border states such as Oklahoma and Kansas, but it thrived, too, in such northern states as Indiana, Pennsylvania, Washington, and Oregon. It even drew significant membership from the cities of those states. Indiana, for example, was home to 500,000 Klansmen and women, many of them in the Indianapolis area. In 1924, Indiana voters elected a Klansman to the governorship and sent several other Klan members to the statehouse.

In some respects, the Klan resembled other fraternal organizations. It offered its members friendship networks, social services, and conviviality. Its rituals, regalia, and mock-medieval language (the Imperial Wizard, Exalted Cyclops, Grand Dragons, and such) gave initiates a sense of superiority, valor, and mystery similar to what other fraternal societies, from the Masons to the Knights of Columbus, imparted to their members.

But the Klan also thrived on hate. It spread lurid tales of financial extortion by Jewish bankers and sexual exploitation by Catholic priests. The accusations were sometimes general, as in the claim that an international con-

AL CAPONE, CHICAGO MOB LEADER
Capone, in the first row on the right, sits with his son, Sonny, and chats with Chicago Cubs player Gabby Hartnett at a charity baseball event in 1931. Capone's presence at this charity event was part of his campaign to build a favorable public reputation for himself. He never strayed far from his gangsters, however, several of whom are seated behind him in the second row.

From the Collections of the Library of Congress.

WOMEN OF THE KU KLUX KLAN
Women made up a substantial portion of the Klan's membership in the 1920s. Here a group marches in an "America First" parade in Binghamton, New York.

spiracy of Jewish bankers had caused the agricultural depression, or allegations that the pope had sent agents to the United States with instructions to destroy liberty and democracy. More common, and more incendiary, however, were the seemingly plausible, yet totally manufactured, tales of Jewish or Catholic depravity. Stories circulated of Jewish businessmen who had opened amusement parks and dance halls to which they lured innocent adolescents, tempting them with sexual transgression and profiting handsomely from their moral debasement. Likewise, Catholic priests and nuns were said to prey on Protestant girls and boys who had been forced into convents and Catholic orphanages. These outrageous stories sometimes provoked attacks on individual Jews and Catholics. More commonly, they prompted campaigns to boycott Jewish businesses and Catholic institutions, and to ruin reputations.

The emphasis on sexual exploitation in these stories reveals the anxiety Klan members felt about society's growing acceptance of sexual openness and sexual gratification. Many Klan supporters lived in towns suffused with these modern attitudes. That such attitudes might reflect the yearnings of Protestant children rather than the manipulation of deceitful Jews and Catholics was a truth some Protestant parents found difficult to accept.

Immigration Restriction

Although most white Protestants never joined the Klan, many of them did respond to the Klan's nativist argument that the country and its values would best be served by

limiting the entry of outsiders. That was the purpose of the Johnson-Reed Immigration Restriction Act of 1924.

By the early 1920s, most Americans believed that the country could no longer accommodate the million immigrants who had been arriving each year before the war and the more than 800,000 who arrived in 1921. Industrialists no longer needed unskilled European laborers to operate their factories, their places having been taken either by machines or by African American and Mexican workers. Most labor movement leaders were convinced that the influx of workers unfamiliar with English and with trade unions had weakened labor solidarity. Progressive reformers no longer believed that immigrants could be easily Americanized or that harmony between the native-born and the foreign-born could be readily achieved. Congress responded to constituents' concerns by passing an immigration restriction act in 1921. In 1924, the more comprehensive Johnson-Reed Act imposed a yearly quota of 165,000 immigrants from countries outside the Western Hemisphere, effectively reducing total immigration to only 20 percent of the prewar annual average.

The sponsors of the 1924 act believed that certain groups—British, Germans, and Scandinavians, in particular—were racially superior and that, consequently, these groups should be allowed to enter the United States in greater numbers; however, because the Constitution prohibited the enactment of explicitly racist laws, Congress had to achieve this racist aim through subterfuge. Lawmakers established a formula to determine the annual immigrant quota for each foreign country, which was to be

ANNUAL IMMIGRANT QUOTAS UNDER THE JOHNSON-REED ACT, 1925–1927

Northwest Europe and Scandinavia		Eastern and Southern Europe		Other Countries	
Country	*Quota*	*Country*	*Quota*	*Country*	*Quota*
Germany	51,227	Poland	5,982	Africa (other than Egypt)	1,100
Great Britain and Northern Ireland	34,007	Italy	3,845	Armenia	124
Irish Free State (Ireland)	28,567	Czechoslovakia	3,073	Australia	121
Sweden	9,561	Russia	2,248	Palestine	100
Norway	6,453	Yugoslavia	671	Syria	100
France	3,954	Romania	603	Turkey	100
Denmark	2,789	Portugal	503	New Zealand and Pacific Islands	100
Switzerland	2,081	Hungary	473	All others	1,900
Netherlands	1,648	Lithuania	344		
Austria	785	Latvia	142		
Belgium	512	Spain	131		
Finland	471	Estonia	124		
Free City of Danzig	228	Albania	100		
Iceland	100	Bulgaria	100		
Luxembourg	100	Greece	100		
Total (number)	142,483	Total (number)	18,439	Total (number)	3,745
Total (%)	86.5%	Total (%)	11.2%	Total (%)	2.3%

Note: Total annual immigrant quota was 164,667

Source: From *Statistical Abstract of the United States* (Washington, D.C.: Government Printing Office, 1929), p. 100.

computed at 2 percent of the total number of immigrants from that country already resident in the United States in the year 1890. In 1890, immigrant ranks had been dominated by the British, Germans, and Scandinavians, so the new quotas would thus allow for a relatively larger cohort of immigrants from those countries. Immigrant groups that were poorly represented in the 1890 population—Italians, Greeks, Poles, Slavs, and Eastern European Jews—were effectively locked out. The Johnson-Reed Act also reaffirmed the long-standing policy of excluding Chinese immigrants, and it added Japanese and other groups of East and South Asians to the list of groups that were altogether barred from entry. The act did not officially limit immigration from nations in the Western Hemisphere, chiefly because agribusiness interests in Texas and California had convinced Congress that cheap Mexican labor was indispensable to their industry's prosperity. Still, the establishment of a Border Patrol along the U.S.–Mexican border and the imposition of a $10 head tax on all prospective Mexican immigrants made entry into the United States more difficult than it had been.

The Johnson-Reed Act accomplished Congress's underlying goal. Annual immigration from transoceanic nations fell by 80 percent. The large number of available slots for English and German immigrants regularly went unfilled, while the smaller number of available slots for Italians, Poles, Russian Jews, and others prevented hundreds of thousands of them from entering the country. A "national origins" system put in place in 1927 further reduced the total annual quota to 150,000 and reserved more than 120,000 of these slots for immigrants from northwestern Europe. Except for minor modifications in 1952, the Johnson-Reed Act would dictate U.S. immigration policy until 1965.

Remarkably few Americans, outside of the ethnic groups being discriminated against, objected to these laws at the time they were passed—an indication of how broadly acceptable racism and nativism had become. In fact, racism and religious bigotry enjoyed a resurgence during the Jazz Age. The pseudoscience of eugenics, based on the idea that nations could improve the racial quality of their population by expanding its stronger racial strains and shrinking its weaker ones, found supporters not only in Congress but among prestigious scientists as well. Universities such as Harvard and Columbia set quotas similar to those of the Johnson-Reed Act to reduce the proportion of Jews among their undergraduates.

Fundamentalism versus Liberal Protestantism

Of all the movements protesting against the modern elements of urban life in the 1920s, Protestant fundamentalism was perhaps the most enduring. Fundamentalists regarded the Bible as God's word and thus the source of all "fundamental" truth. They believed that every event depicted in the Bible, from the creation of the world in six days to the resurrection of Christ, happened exactly as the Bible described it. For fundamentalists, God was a deity who intervened directly in the lives of individuals and communities and who made known both his pleasure and his wrath to those who acknowledged his divinity. Sin had to be actively purged, and salvation actively sought.

The rise of the fundamentalist movement from the 1870s through the 1920s roughly paralleled the rise of urban-industrial society. Fundamentalists recoiled from the "evils" of the city—from what they perceived as its poverty, its moral degeneracy, its irreligion, and its crass materialism. Fundamentalism took shape in reaction against two additional aspects of urban society: the growth of liberal Protestantism and the revelations of science.

Liberal Protestants believed that religion had to be adapted to the skeptical and scientific temper of the modern age. No biblical story in which a sea opens up, the sun stands still, or a woman springs forth from a man's rib could possibly be true. The Bible was to be mined for its ethical values rather than for its literal truth. Liberal Protestants removed God from his active role in history and refashioned him into a distant and benign deity who watched over the world but did not intervene to punish or to redeem. They turned religion away from the quest for salvation and toward the pursuit of good deeds, social conscience, and love for one's neighbor. Although those

with a liberal bent constituted only a minority of Protestants, they were articulate, visible, and influential in social reform movements. Fundamentalism arose in part to counter the "heretical" claims of the liberal Protestants.

Liberal Protestants and fundamentalists both understood that science was the source of most challenges to Christianity. Scientists believed that rational inquiry was a better guide to the past and to the future than prayer and revelation. Scientists even challenged the ideas that God had created the world and had fashioned humankind in his own image. These were assertions that many religious peoples, particularly fundamentalists, simply could not accept. Conflict was inevitable. It came in 1925, in Dayton, Tennessee.

The Scopes Trial

No aspect of science aroused more anger among fundamentalists than Charles Darwin's theory of evolution. There was no greater blasphemy than to suggest that man emerged from lower forms of life instead of being created by God. In Tennessee in 1925, fundamentalists succeeded in passing a law that forbade teaching "any theory that denies the story of the divine creation of man as taught in the Bible."

For Americans who accepted the authority of science, denying the truth of evolution was as ludicrous as insisting that the sun revolved around the earth. They ridiculed the fundamentalists, but they worried that the passage of the Tennessee law might signal the onset of a campaign to undermine First Amendment guarantees of free speech. The American Civil Liberties Union (ACLU), founded by liberals during the Red Scare of 1919 and 1920, began searching for a teacher who would be willing to challenge the constitutionality of the Tennessee law. They found their man in John T. Scopes, a 24-year-old biology teacher in Dayton, Tennessee. After confessing that he had taught evolution to his students, Scopes was arrested. The case quickly attracted national attention. William Jennings Bryan, the former Populist, progressive, and secretary of state, announced that he would help prosecute Scopes, and the famous liberal trial lawyer Clarence Darrow rushed to Dayton to lead Scopes's defense. That Bryan and Darrow had once been allies in the progressive movement only heightened the drama. A small army of journalists descended on Dayton, led by H. L. Mencken, a Baltimore-based journalist famous for his

Brown Brothers.

THE SCOPES TRIAL

Defense attorney Clarence Darrow (left) and prosecutor William Jennings Bryan take a break from their celebrated courtroom fight to enjoy each other's company. The two men had been allies in the Progressive era.

savage critiques of the alleged stupidity and prudishness of small-town Americans.

The trial dragged on, and most of the observers expected Scopes to be convicted. He was, but the hearing took an unexpected turn when Darrow persuaded the judge to let Bryan testify as an "expert on the Bible." Darrow knew that Bryan's testimony would have no bearing on the question of Scopes's innocence or guilt. The jury was not even allowed to hear it. His aim was to expose Bryan as a fool for believing that the Bible was a source of literal truth and thus to embarrass the fundamentalists. In a riveting confrontation, Darrow made Bryan's defense of the Bible look problematic and led Bryan to admit that the "truth" of the Bible was not always easy to determine. But Darrow could not shake Bryan's belief that the Bible was God's word and thus the source of all truth.

In his account of the trial, Mencken portrayed Bryan as a pathetic figure devastated by his humiliating experience on the witness stand, a view popularized in the 1960 movie *Inherit the Wind*. When Bryan died only a week after the trial ended, Mencken claimed that the trial had broken Bryan's heart.

Bryan deserved a better epitaph than the one Mencken had given him. Diabetes caused his death, not a broken heart. Nor was Bryan the innocent fool that Mencken made him out to be. He remembered when social conservatives had used Darwin's phrase "survival of the fittest" to prove that the wealthy and politically powerful were racially superior to the poor and powerless (see chapter 20). His rejection of Darwinism evidenced his democratic faith that all human beings were creatures of God and thus capable of striving for perfection and equality.

The public ridicule attendant on the Scopes trial took its toll on fundamentalists. Many of them retreated from politics and refocused their attention on purging sin from their own hearts rather than from the hearts of others.

HISTORY THROUGH FILM

The Jazz Singer (1927)

The Jazz Singer was a sensation when it opened because it was the first movie to use sound (although relatively few words of dialogue were actually spoken). It also starred Al Jolson, the era's most popular Broadway entertainer, and bravely explored an issue that the film industry usually avoided—the religious culture and generational dynamics of a "new immigrant" family.

The movie focuses on Jake Rabinowitz and his immigrant parents, who are Jewish and devout. Jake's father is a fifth-generation cantor whose job it is to fill his New York City synagogue with ancient and uplifting melodies on the Sabbath and Jewish holidays. Cantor Rabinowitz looks upon his work as sacred, and he expects Jake to take his place one day. But Jake has other ideas. He loves music but is drawn to the new rhythmic ragtime and sensual jazz melodies emerging from his American surroundings. In an early scene, we encounter Jake at a dance hall, absorbed in playing and singing ragtime tunes and forgetting that he should be at home preparing for Yom Kippur, the holiest day in the Jewish calendar. His distraught father finds him and whips him, and Jake, in anger and pain, runs away.

Directed by Alan Crosland. Starring Al Jolson (Jake Rabinowitz/Jack Robin), May McAvoy (Mary Dale), and Warner Oland (Cantor Rabinowitz).

Jake's break with his family allows him to pursue his passion for American song and to reinvent himself as Jack Robin, the jazz singer. A relationship with a prominent (and non-Jewish) stage actress, Mary Dale, brings him a starring role in a Broadway show. Jack hopes to use his return to New York to reconcile with his father. This eventually happens when Jake, on the eve of Yom Kippur once again, agrees to skip his show's premiere in order to take his ailing father's place as cantor in the synagogue. Jake's melodies soar to the heavens and reach his bedridden father who, thinking that his son has succeeded him as cantor and thus fulfilled his (the father's) deepest wish, peacefully and contentedly dies.

The movie ultimately rejects the father's insistence that Jake must choose between the Old World and the New, between Judaism and America. After Yom Kippur ends, Jake returns to his Broadway show and to his non-Jewish lover and, with his approving mother in the audience, delivers an outstanding performance that secures his reputation as the "Jazz Singer."

Watching the movie today raises questions about its optimistic belief that America permits resolution of even

In the end, the fundamentalists prevailed on three more states to prohibit the teaching of evolution, but the controversy had even more far-reaching effects. Worried about losing sales, publishers quietly removed references to Darwin from their science textbooks, a policy that would remain in force until the 1960s. In this respect, the fundamentalists had scored a significant victory.

● Ethnic and Racial Communities

The 1920s were a decade of change for ethnic and racial minorities. Government policy simultaneously discouraged the continued immigration of "new immigrants" from Southern and Eastern Europe and encouraged the migration of African Americans from the South to the North and of Mexicans across the Rio Grande and into the American Southwest. Some minorities benefited from the prosperity of the decade; others created and sustained vibrant subcultures. All, however, experienced a surge in religious and racial discrimination that made them uneasy in Jazz Age America.

European American Ethnics

European American ethnics—and especially the Southern and Eastern European majority among them—were concentrated in the cities of the Northeast and Midwest. Many were semiskilled and unskilled industrial laborers who suffered economic insecurity. In addition, they faced cultural discrimination. Catholics and Jews were targets of the Klan and its politics of hate. Catholics generally opposed Prohibition, viewing it as a crude attempt by Protestants to control their behavior. Southern and Eastern Europeans, particularly Jews and Italians, resented the most serious conflicts between immigrant parents and American-born children. Jake's blackface routine—his use of burnt cork to turn his face and neck black and thus to appear to audiences as a "black" performer—also draws attention. "Blacking up" was a performance style popular among white entertainers from the early 19th century to the early 20th century. These entertainers wanted both to appropriate and ridicule expressive aspects of black culture. What did it mean for someone like Jake, the child of Eastern European Jewish immigrants and thus himself vulnerable to being stigmatized as an outsider in America, to "black up"? Jake may have been expressing in part a desire to draw closer to rich elements in black musical culture—he did, after all, love jazz and aspire to be a jazz singer. But Jake may also have been signaling his desire to distance himself from African Americans by participating in a popular tradition of white American entertainment. Ironically, "blacking up" may have been a way for an entertainer to embrace not black but white America, and for someone like Jake to be accepted by non-Jewish white Americans as one of their own.

A German poster advertising *The Jazz Singer.* Al Jolson is shown in blackface.

immigration restriction and the implication that they were not worthy of having a chance to come to America. Many Italians were outraged by the execution of Nicola Sacco and Bartolomeo Vanzetti in 1927 (chapter 23). If the two men had been native-born white Protestants, Italians argued, their lives would have been spared.

Southern and Eastern Europeans everywhere endured intensive Americanization campaigns. State after state passed laws requiring public schools to instruct children in the essentials of citizenship. Several states, including Rhode Island, extended these laws to private schools as well, convinced that the children of immigrants who were attending Catholic parochial schools were spending too much time learning about their native religion, language, and country. An Oregon law tried to eliminate Catholic schools altogether by ordering all children aged 8 to 16 to enroll in public schools. But attending a public school was no guarantee of acceptance, either—a lesson learned by Jewish children who had excelled in their studies only to be barred from Harvard, Columbia, and other elite universities.

Southern and Eastern Europeans responded to these insults and attacks by strengthening the very institutions and customs Americanizers sought to undermine. Ethnic associations flourished in the 1920s—Catholic churches and Jewish synagogues, fraternal and mutual benefit societies, banks and charitable organizations, athletic leagues and youth groups. Children learned their native languages and customs at home and at church if not at school, and they joined with their parents to celebrate their ethnic heritage. Among Italians and French Canadians, saints' days were occasions for parades, speeches, band concerts, games, and feasts, all serving to solidify ethnic bonds and affirm ethnic identity.

Many of these immigrants and their children, however, also embraced the new consumer culture. They

DEMOCRATIC PRESIDENTIAL VOTING IN CHICAGO BY ETHNIC GROUPS, 1924 AND 1928

	Percent Democratic	
	1924	*1928*
Czechoslovaks	40%	73%
Poles	35	71
Lithuanians	48	77
Yugoslavs	20	54
Italians	31	63
Germans	14	58
Jews	19	60

Source: From John M. Allswang, *A House for All Peoples: Ethnic Politics in Chicago, 1890–1936* (Lexington: University Press of Kentucky), p. 42.

flocked to movies and amusement parks, to baseball games and boxing matches. Children usually entered more enthusiastically into the world of American mass culture than did their immigrant parents, a behavior that often set off family conflicts. The famed New York Yankee, Lou Gehrig, had to fight to convince his German-born mother that playing baseball was honorable work. But many ethnics found it possible to reconcile their own culture with American culture. Youngsters who went to the movies did so with friends from within their community. Ethnics also played baseball in leagues organized around churches or ethnic associations. In these early days of radio, ethnics living in large cities could always find programs in their native language and music from their native lands.

European American ethnics also resolved to develop sufficient political muscle to defeat the forces of nativism and to turn government policy in a more favorable direction. One sign of this determination was a sharp rise in the number of immigrants who became U.S. citizens. Immigrant Poles, Slavs, Italians, Lithuanians, and Hungarians who became naturalized citizens nearly doubled their numbers during the decade; the number of naturalized Greeks almost tripled. Armed with the vote, ethnics turned out on election day to defeat unsympathetic city councilmen, mayors, state representatives, and even an occasional governor. Their growing national strength first became apparent at the Democratic national convention of 1924, when urban-ethnic delegates almost won approval of planks calling for the repeal of Prohibition and condemnation of the Klan. After denying the presidential nomination to William G. McAdoo—Woodrow Wilson's treasury secretary, son-in-law, and heir apparent—they nearly secured it for their candidate, Alfred E. Smith, the Irish American governor of New York. McAdoo represented the rural and southern constituencies of the Democratic Party. His forces ended up battling Smith's urban-ethnic forces for 103 ballots, until the two men gave up and supporters from each camp switched their votes to a compromise candidate, the corporate lawyer John W. Davis.

The nomination fight devastated the Democratic Party in the short term, and popular Calvin Coolidge easily defeated the little-known Davis. This split between the party's rural Protestant and urban-ethnic constituencies would keep the Democrats from the White House for nearly a decade, but the convention upheaval of 1924 also marked an important milestone in the bid by European American ethnics for political power. They would achieve a second milestone at the Democratic national convention of 1928 when, after another bitter nomination struggle, they finally secured the presidential nomination for Al Smith. Never before had a major political party nomi-

National Portrait Gallery, Smithsonian Institution/Art Resource, NY.

ALFRED E. SMITH, NEW YORK DEMOCRAT

This portrait of Al Smith, the New York–born Irish American politician who became the first Catholic to be nominated for the presidency by either party, originally appeared in the *New Yorker* magazine in 1934. It suggests that his spirit was as buoyant and irrepressible as that of New York City. But there is a touch of sadness etched in his eyes and smile, a reflection perhaps of the defeats he had suffered, first in the 1928 presidential election and then in 1932, when the presidential nomination that he hoped would come his way again went instead to his successor as governor of New York, Franklin D. Roosevelt.

nated a Catholic for president. Herbert Hoover crushed Smith in the general election, as nativists stirred up anti-Catholic prejudice yet again and as large numbers of southern Democrats either stayed home or voted Republican. Even so, the campaign offered encouraging signs, none more so than Smith's beating Hoover in the nation's 12 largest cities. European American ethnics would yet have their day.

African Americans

Despite the urban race riots of 1919 (see chapter 23), African Americans continued to leave their rural homes for the industrial centers of the South and the North. In the 1920s alone, nearly a million blacks traveled North. In New York City and Chicago, their numbers grew so large—300,000 in New York and 234,000 in Chicago—

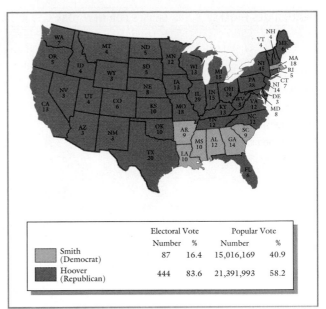

	Electoral Vote		Popular Vote	
	Number	%	Number	%
Smith (Democrat)	87	16.4	15,016,169	40.9
Hoover (Republican)	444	83.6	21,391,993	58.2

MAP 24.3   PRESIDENTIAL ELECTION, 1928

This map shows Hoover's landslide victory in 1928, as he carried all but eight states and won almost 84 percent of the electoral vote.

that they formed cities unto themselves. When word of New York City's urban black enclave reached the Caribbean, thousands of West Indian blacks set off for Harlem. Within these black metropolises emerged complex societies consisting of workers, businessmen, professionals, intellectuals, artists, and entertainers. Social differentiation intensified as various groups—long-resident northerners and newly arrived southerners, religious conservatives and cultural radicals, African Americans and African Caribbeans—found reason to disapprove of one another's ways. Still, the diversity and complexity of urban black America were thrilling, nowhere more so than in Harlem, the "Negro capital." Black writer James Weldon Johnson described Harlem in the 1920s:

> Throughout colored America Harlem is the recognized Negro capital. Indeed, it is Mecca for the sightseer, the pleasure-seeker, the curious, the adventurous, the enterprising, the ambitious, and the talented of the entire Negro world. . . . Not merely a colony or a community or a settlement—not at all a "quarter" or a slum or a fringe—[Harlem is] . . . a black city, located in the heart of white Manhattan, and containing more Negroes to the square mile than any other spot on earth. It strikes the uninformed observer as a phenomenon, a miracle straight out of the skies.

Not even the glamour of Harlem could erase the reality of racial discrimination, however. Most African Americans could find work only in New York City's least-desired and lowest-paying jobs. Because they could rent

DEATH RATES FROM SELECTED CAUSES FOR NEW YORK CITY RESIDENTS, 1925

Cause of Death	Total Population	African American Population
General death rate (per 1,000 population)	11.4	16.5
Pneumonia	132.8	282.4
Pulmonary tuberculosis	75.5	258.4
Infant mortality (per 1,000 live births)	64.6	118.4
Maternal mortality (per 1,000 total births)	5.3	10.2
Stillbirths (per 1,000 births)	47.6	82.7
Homicide	5.3	19.5
Suicide	14.8	9.7

Note: Rate is per 100,000 population, unless noted

Source: Cheryl Lynn Greenberg, *"Or Does It Explode?" Black Harlem in the Great Depression* (New York: Oxford University Press, 1991), p. 32.

apartments only in areas that real estate agents and banks had designated as "colored," African Americans suffered the highest rate of residential segregation of any minority group. Although Harlem had its fashionable districts where affluent blacks lived, most of the housing stock was poor and rents were high. Harlem became a black ghetto, an area set apart from the rest of the city by the skin color of its inhabitants, by its higher population density and poverty rate, by its higher incidence of infectious diseases, and by the lower life expectancy of its people.

Blacks did enjoy some important economic breakthroughs in the 1920s. Henry Ford, for example, hired large numbers of African Americans to work in his Detroit auto factories. Even here, however, a racist logic was operating, for Ford believed that black and white workers, divided along racial lines, would not challenge his authority. Until the 1940s, in fact, unions made less headway at Ford plants than at the plants of other major automobile manufacturers.

Racial divisions carried over from work to play. African Americans loved baseball as much as white Americans did, and Babe Ruth enjoyed a large black following. But black baseball players were themselves barred from playing in the lily-white major leagues. In response, they formed their own Negro Leagues in the United States and also played professional ball in Mexico and the Caribbean, where they earned extra income and escaped some of the prejudice that met them everywhere in America. Cuba, Puerto Rico, Mexico, and other countries in which African Americans played did not organize baseball along racial lines.

The greatest black baseball player was probably Josh Gibson, who joined the Homestead Grays of the National Negro League in 1929 at the age of 18. In his 17-year career, he compiled statistics that surpassed those of any professional ballplayer of his era, white or black, including those of the legendary Babe Ruth. Gibson slugged 962

JOSH GIBSON, NEGRO LEAGUES STAR

This photograph captures Gibson in 1944, near the end of his career, being tagged out at home plate by Ted Radcliffe in the 10th annual East-West All Star Game at Comiskey Park, Chicago.

© Bettmann/Corbis.

career home runs, hit 84 home runs in a single season, and compiled a .373 lifetime batting average. Because he died in 1947, at the age of 35, just months before the integration of major league baseball, Gibson never got the opportunity to test his skills against the best white ballplayers—and they never got a chance to play against him.

African Americans grew pessimistic about achieving racial equality. After Marcus Garvey's black nationalist movement collapsed in the mid-1920s (see chapter 23), no comparable organization arose to take its place. The NAACP continued to fight racial discrimination, and the Urban League carried on quiet negotiations with industrial elites to secure jobs for African Americans. Black socialists led by A. Philip Randolph built a strong all-black union, the Brotherhood of Sleeping Car Porters, but the victories were small and white allies were scarce. The political initiatives emerging among European American ethnics had few counterparts in the African American community.

In terms of black culture, however, the 1920s were vigorous and productive. Black musicians coming north to Chicago and New York brought with them their distinctive musical styles, most notably the blues and ragtime. Influenced by the harmonies and techniques of European classical music, which black musicians learned from their European American ethnic counterparts, these southern styles metamorphosed into jazz. Urban audiences, first black and then white, found this new music alluring. They responded to its melodies, its sensuality, its creativity, its savvy. In Chicago, Detroit, New York, New Orleans, and elsewhere, jazz musicians came together in cramped apartments, cabarets, and nightclubs to jam, compete, and entertain. Willie Smith, Charles P. Johnson, Count Basie, Fats Waller, Duke Ellington, and Louis Armstrong were among the most famous musicians of the day. By the late 1920s, they were being hailed in Europe as well.

Jazz seemed to express something quintessentially modern. Jazz musicians broke free of convention, improvised, and produced new sounds that gave rise to new sensations. Both blacks and whites found in jazz an escape from the routine, the predictability, and the conventions of their everyday lives.

The Harlem Renaissance

Paralleling the emergence of jazz was a black literary and artistic awakening known as the Harlem Renaissance. Black novelists, poets, painters, sculptors, and playwrights set about creating works rooted in their own culture instead of imitating the styles of white Europeans and Americans. The movement had begun during the war, when blacks sensed that they might at last be advancing to full equality. It was symbolized by the image of the "New Negro," a black man or woman who would no longer be deferential to whites but who would display his or her independence through talent and determination. The "New Negro" would be assertive in every field—at work, in politics, in the military, and in arts and letters. As racial discrimination intensified after the war, cultural activities took on special significance. The world of culture was one place where blacks could express their racial pride and demonstrate their talent.

Langston Hughes, a young black poet, said of the Harlem Renaissance: "We younger Negro artists who create now intend to express our individual dark-skinned selves without fear or shame. If white people are pleased, we are glad. If they are not, it doesn't matter. We know we are beautiful. And ugly, too." Writers Claude McKay, Jean Toomer, and Zora Neale Hurston; poet Countee Cullen; and painter Aaron Douglas were other prominent Renaissance participants. In 1925, *Survey Graphic*, a white liberal magazine, devoted an entire issue to "Harlem—the Mecca of the New Negro." Alain Locke, an art and literary critic and professor of philosophy at Howard University in Washington, D.C., edited both the issue and the book *The New Negro*, published later that year. Locke became the movement's leading visionary and philosopher.

But even these cultural advances failed to escape white prejudice. The most popular jazz nightclubs in Harlem, most of which were owned and operated by whites, often refused to admit black customers. The only African Americans permitted inside were the jazz musicians, singers and dancers, prostitutes, and kitchen help. Moreover, the musicians often had to perform what the white patrons wanted to hear. Duke Ellington, for example, was called on to play "jungle music," which for whites revealed the "true" African soul—sensual, innocent, primitive. Such pressures curtailed the artistic freedom of musicians and reinforced racist stereotypes of African Americans as inferior people who were closer to nature than the "more civilized" white audiences who came to hear their music.

Black artists and writers experienced similar pressures. Many of them depended for their sustenance on the support of wealthy white patrons. Those patrons were generous, but they wanted a return on their investment. Charlotte Mason, the New York City matron who supported Hughes and Hurston, for example, expected them to entertain her friends by demonstrating "authentic Negritude" in their work. Hurston accepted this role, but for Hughes it became intolerable. Both Hughes and Hurston paid a price for their patron's support, including the collapse of their once-close friendship with each other.

Mexican Americans

After the Johnson-Reed Act of 1924, Mexicans became the country's chief source of immigrant labor. A total of 500,000 Mexicans came to the United States in the 1920s. Some headed for the steel, auto, and meatpacking plants of the Midwest, but most settled in the Southwest, where they worked on the railroads and in construction, agriculture, and manufacturing. In Texas, three of every four construction workers and eight of every ten migrant farm workers were Mexicans. An official of the San Antonio Chamber of Commerce declared: "Mexican farm labor is rapidly proving the making of this State." In California, Mexican immigrants made up 75 percent of the state's agricultural workforce.

Mexican farm laborers in Texas worked long hours for little money. As a rule, they earned 50 cents to a dollar less per day than Anglo workers. They were usually barred from becoming machine operators or assuming other skilled positions. Forced to follow the crops, they had little

opportunity to develop settled homes and communities. Mexican farm workers depended for shelter on whatever facilities farm owners offered. Because farm owners rarely required the services of Mexican workers for more than several days or weeks, few were willing to spend the money required to provide decent homes and schools. Houses typically lacked even wooden floors or indoor plumbing. Mexican laborers found it difficult to protest these conditions because their knowledge of English was limited. Few owned cars or trucks that would have allowed them to escape a bad employer and search for a good one. Many were in debt to employers who had advanced them money and who threatened them with jail if they failed to fulfill the terms of their contract. Others feared deportation; they lacked visas, having slipped into the United States illegally rather than pay the immigrant tax or endure harassment from the Border Patrol.

Increasing numbers of Mexican immigrants, however, found their way to California, where, on the whole, wages exceeded those in Texas. Some escaped agricultural

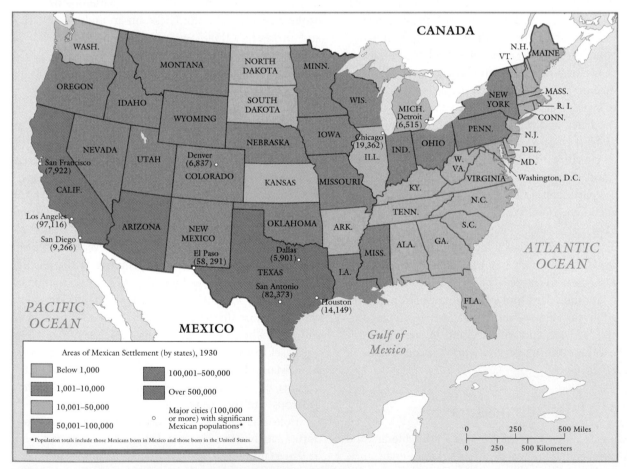

MAP 24.4   MEXICAN POPULATION IN THE UNITED STATES, 1930

By 1930, Mexican immigrants had established their pattern of settling primarily in the U.S. Southwest. Texas had the largest concentration of Mexican immigrants, followed by California and Arizona, and then by New Mexico and Colorado. Though Texas had a larger overall population, Los Angeles had surpassed San Antonio as the city with the largest single Mexican community in the United States.

labor altogether for construction and manufacturing jobs. Many Mexican men in Los Angeles, for example, worked in the city's large railroad yards, at the city's numerous construction sites, and as unskilled workers in local factories. Mexican women labored in the city's garment shops, fish canneries, and food processing plants. By 1930, Los Angeles had become the largest area of settlement for Mexicans in the United States.

The Los Angeles Mexican American community increased in complexity as it grew in size. By the mid-1920s, it included a growing professional class, a proud group of *californios* (Spanish-speakers who had been resident in California for generations), many musicians and entertainers, a small but energetic band of entrepreneurs and businessmen, conservative clerics and intellectuals who had fled or been expelled from revolutionary Mexico, and Mexican government officials who had been sent to counter the influence of the conservative exiles and to strengthen the ties of the immigrants to their homeland. This diverse mix created much internal conflict, but it also generated considerable cultural vitality. Los Angeles became the same kind of magnet for Mexican Americans that Harlem had become for African Americans.

Mexican musicians flocked to Los Angeles, as did Mexican playwrights. The city supported a vigorous Spanish-language theater. Mexican musicians performed on street corners, at ethnic festivals and weddings, at cabarets, and on the radio. Especially popular were folk ballads, called *corridos,* that spoke to the experiences of Mexican immigrants. Although different in form and melody from the African American blues, *corridos* resembled the blues in their emphasis on the suffering, hope, and frustrations of ordinary folk.

This flowering of Mexican American culture in Los Angeles could not erase the low wages, high rates of infant mortality, racial discrimination, and other hardships Mexicans faced; nor did it encourage Mexicans, in Los Angeles or elsewhere, to mobilize themselves as a political force. Unlike European immigrants, Mexican immigrants showed little interest in becoming American citizens and acquiring the vote. Yet the cultural vibrancy of the Mexican immigrant community did sustain many individuals who were struggling to survive in a strange, and often hostile, environment.

The "Lost Generation" and Disillusioned Intellectuals

Many native-born white artists and intellectuals also felt uneasy in America in the 1920s. Their unease arose not from poverty or discrimination but from alienation. They despaired of American culture and regarded the average American as anti-intellectual, small-minded, materialistic, and puritanical. The novelist Sinclair Lewis, for example, ridiculed small-town Americans in *Main Street* (1920), "sophisticated" city dwellers in *Babbitt* (1922), physicians in *Arrowsmith* (1925), and evangelicals in *Elmer Gantry* (1927).

Before the First World War, intellectuals and artists had been deeply engaged with "the people." Although they were critical of many aspects of American society, they believed they could help bring about a new politics and improve social conditions. Some of them joined the war effort on the side of the Allies before the United States had officially intervened. Ernest Hemingway, John Dos Passos, and e. e. cummings, among others, sailed to Europe and volunteered their services, usually as ambulance drivers carrying wounded Allied soldiers from the front.

America's intellectuals were shaken by the war's effect on American society. The wartime push for consensus created intolerance of radicals, immigrants, and blacks. Intellectuals had been further dismayed by Prohibition, the rebirth of the Ku Klux Klan, the rise of fundamentalism, and the execution of Sacco and Vanzetti. Not only had many Americans embraced conformity for themselves, but they seemed determined to force conformity on others. The

MEXICAN AMERICAN WOMEN WORKERS, 1920s
These women were employed at a tortilla factory in Los Angeles.

Security Pacific Collection/Los Angeles Public Library.

Josephine Baker: An African American Entertainer in Paris

In the 1920s, Paris became a magnet not only for white American artists and writers disillusioned with life in the United States but for black American artists and writers as well. African American writers Richard Wright and James Baldwin, for example, both made their home in Paris for lengthy periods of time, as did significant numbers of African American jazz musicians, who enthralled Parisian audiences with their work. Few did as much to establish Paris as a destination for African Americans, however, as Josephine Baker, the legendary dancer and entertainer.

Born in 1906 to a domestic worker and musician in St. Louis, Baker grew up poor, fatherless, and with few opportunities. Leaving home to join a band as a teenager, she eventually made her way to New York City and begged her way into the chorus line for one of the hottest shows of the 1920s, the all-black musical *Shuffle Along.* In 1925, Baker, already a hit on the line for her rollicking movements and comical nature, traveled to Paris for a better dance role in another all-black production, *La Revue Nègre.* Dancing her way into the famed Folies-Bergère with only feathers or, later, a ring of bananas garnishing her hips, Baker entranced French audiences with her slick movements as well as her black skin, beautiful body, outrageous wit, and promiscuity. A country exhausted by the First World War delighted in her energy, frivolity, and freedom of expression. Baker relished her reception among the French, who seemed to carry within them less racial prejudice and prudery than did American whites. Baker met European royalty and dignitaries, stayed in the finest hotels, and enjoyed interracial relationships without public censure or disapproval.

Returning to the United States in 1936, Baker expected the top billing that had been hers in France.

But she soon ran into the kind of racial prejudice that she had not known since her St. Louis youth. In New York, a hotel manager asked her to use the service or employee entrance so as not to offend white patrons. In the Ziegfeld Follies, a popular New York musical and comedy revue, she received second billing to entertainers Fanny Brice and Bob Hope, whom she regarded as her inferiors. Much of the white public, and a slice of the black public, too, regarded her as too outspoken, too haughty, and too exhibitionist. Baker moved back to France in 1936 and made it her lifelong home. In the 1940s, she involved herself in politics, first by joining the Resistance against the Nazis and then by emerging as an international crusader for racial equality. In America, she finally began to receive positive recognition for her talents as a performer and her courage in standing up for the rights of African Americans. But she never returned to live in the land of her birth; she died in France in 1975, an expatriate to the end.

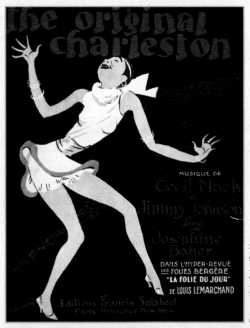

JOSEPHINE BAKER IN PARIS
This poster conveys the sexual power, allure, and whimsy of Baker's dance performances in Paris.

young critic Harold Stearns wrote in 1921 that "the most moving and pathetic fact in the social life of America today is emotional and aesthetic starvation." Before these words were published, Stearns had sailed for France. So many alienated young men like Stearns showed up in Paris that Gertrude Stein, an American writer whose Paris apartment became a gathering place for them, took to calling them the "Lost Generation."

Their indictment of America was often too harsh. Most of these writers possessed little knowledge of how most Americans lived. Few expressed sympathy for the plight of farmers or the working-class poor. Few knew much about the rich cultural heritage of immigrant communities. Still, they managed to convert their disillusionment into a rich literary sensibility. The finest works of the decade focused on the psychological toll of living in what the poet T. S. Eliot referred to as *The Waste Land* (1922). F. Scott Fitzgerald's novel *The Great Gatsby* (1925) told of a man destroyed by his desire to be accepted into a world of wealth, fancy cars, and fast women. In the novel *A Farewell to Arms* (1929), Ernest Hemingway wrote of an American soldier overwhelmed by the senselessness and brutality of war who deserts the army for the company of a woman he loves. Playwright Eugene O'Neill created characters haunted by despair, loneliness, and unfulfilled longing. Writers created innovations in style as well as in content. Sherwood Anderson, in his novel *Winesburg, Ohio* (1919), blended fiction and autobiography. John Dos Passos, in *Manhattan Transfer* (1925), mixed journalism with more traditional literary methods. Hemingway wrote

in an understated, laconic prose that somehow drew attention to his characters' rage and vulnerability.

White Southern writers found a tragic sensibility surviving from the South's defeat in the Civil War that spoke to their own loss of hope. One group of such writers, calling themselves the Agrarians, argued that the enduring agricultural character of their region offered a more hopeful path to the future than did the mass-production and mass-consumption regime that had overtaken the North. In 1929, William Faulkner published *The Sound and the Fury,* the first in a series of novels set in northern Mississippi's fictional Yoknapatawpha County. Faulkner explored the violence and terror that marked relationships among family members and townspeople, while maintaining compassion and understanding. Faulkner, Lewis, Hemingway, O'Neill, and Eliot would each receive the Nobel Prize for Literature.

Democracy on the Defensive

Disdain for the masses led many intellectuals to question democracy. If ordinary people were as stupid, prejudiced, and easily manipulated as they seemed, how could they be entrusted with the fate of the nation? Although few intellectuals were as frank as Mencken, who dismissed democracy as "the worship of jackals by jackasses," their distrust of democracy ran deep. Walter Lippmann, a former radical and progressive, declared that modern society had rendered democracy obsolete. In his view, average citizens, buffeted by propaganda emanating from powerful opinion makers, could no longer make the kind of informed, rational judgments needed to make democracy work. They were vulnerable to demagogues who played on their emotions and fears. Lippmann's solution, and that of many other political commentators, was to shift government power from the people to educated elites. Those elites, who would be appointed rather than elected, would conduct foreign and domestic policy in an informed, intelligent way. Only then, in Lippmann's view, could government be effective and just.

Mencken and Lippmann enjoyed especially strong influence and prestige among university students, whose ranks and political significance were growing. But their antidemocratic views did not go uncontested. The philosopher John Dewey, who taught at Columbia University but whose reputation and influence extended well beyond academia, was the most articulate spokesman for the "prodemocracy" position. He acknowledged that the concentration of power in a few giant organizations had eroded the authority of Congress, the presidency, and other democratic institutions, but democracy, he insisted, was not doomed. The people could reclaim their freedom by

The Granger Collection, New York.

THE GREAT GATSBY

F. Scott Fitzgerald emerged as a major American novelist with publication of *The Great Gatsby*. Like so much of the best 1920s fiction, *Gatsby* tells the story of a man's disillusionment and ruin.

762 CHAPTER 24 ■ The 1920s

making big business subject to government control. The government could use its power to democratize corporations and to regulate the communications industry to ensure that every citizen had access to the facts needed to make reasonable, informed political decisions.

Dewey's views attracted the support of a wide range of liberal intellectuals and reformers, including Robert and Helen Lynd; Rexford Tugwell, professor of economics at Columbia; and Felix Frankfurter, a rising star at Harvard's law school. Some of these activists had ties to labor leaders and to New York Governor Franklin D. Roosevelt. They formed the vanguard of a new liberal movement committed to taking up the work the progressives had left unfinished.

But these reformers were utterly without power, except in a few states. The Republican Party had driven reformers from its ranks. The Democratic Party was a fallen giant, crippled by a split between its principal constituencies—rural Protestants and urban ethnics—over Prohibition, immigration restriction, and the Ku Klux Klan. The labor movement was moribund. The Socialist Party had never recovered from the trauma of war and Bolshevism. La Follette's Farmer-Labor Party had stalled after a promising debut. John Dewey and his friends tried to launch yet another third party, but they failed to raise money or arouse mass support.

Reformers took little comfort in the presidential election of 1928. Hoover's smashing victory suggested that the trends of the 1920s—the dominance of the Republicans, the centrality of Prohibition to political debate, the paralysis of the Democrats, the growing economic might of capitalism, and the pervasive influence of the consumer culture—would continue unabated.

Conclusion

Signs abounded in the 1920s that Americans were creating a new and bountiful society. The increased accessibility of cars, radios, vacuum cleaners, and other consumer durables; rising real wages, low unemployment, and install-ment buying; the widening circle of stock owners; the spread of welfare capitalism—all these pointed to an economy that had become more prosperous, more consumer-oriented, even somewhat more egalitarian. Moves to greater equality within marriage and to enhanced liberty for single women suggested that economic change was propelling social change as well.

Even so, many working-class and rural Americans benefited little from the decade's prosperity. Moreover, the decade's social changes aroused resistance, especially from white farmers and small-town Americans who feared that the rapid growth of cities and the large urban settlements of European and Mexican Catholics, Jews, and African Americans were rendering their Protestant America unrecognizable.

In the Democratic Party, farmers, small-town Americans, and moral traditionalists fought bitterly against the growing power of urban, ethnic constituencies. Elsewhere, the traditionalists battled hard to protect religion's authority against the inroads of science and to purge the nation of "inferior" population streams. In the process they arrayed themselves against American traditions of liberty and equality, even as they posed as the defenders of the best that America had to offer.

Their resistance to change caused many of the nation's most talented artists and writers to turn away from their fellow Americans in disgust. Meanwhile, although ethnic and racial minorities experienced high levels of discrimination, they nevertheless found enough freedom to create vibrant ethnic and racial communities and to launch projects—as in the case of African Americans in Harlem and Mexican Americans in Los Angeles—of cultural renaissance.

The Republican Party, having largely shed its reputation for reform, took credit for engineering the new economy of consumer plenty. It looked forward to years of political dominance. A steep and unexpected economic depression, however, would soon dash that expectation, revive the Democratic Party, and destroy Republican political power for a generation.

SUGGESTED READINGS

William Leuchtenberg, *The Perils of Prosperity, 1914–1932* (1958), and **Ellis Hawley,** *The Great War and the Search for a Modern Order: A History of the American People and Their Institutions, 1917–1933* (1979), offer useful overviews of the 1920s that stress political and economic developments. For an overview more attentive to culture and society, see **Nathan Miller,** *A New World Coming: The 1920s and the Making of Modern America* (2003). Important works on the consumer revolution include **Warren I. Susman,** *Culture as History: The Transformation of American Society in the Twentieth Century* (1984), **Roland Marchand,** *Advertising the American Dream: Making Way for Modernity, 1920–1940* (1985), and **Kathy Lee Peiss,** *Hope in a Jar: The Making of America's Beauty Culture* (1998). **John D. Hicks,** *Republican Ascendancy, 1921–1933* (1960), still serves as a good introduction to national politics, but consult, too, **Thomas B. Silver,** *Coolidge and the Historians* (1982), **Ellis Hawley, ed.,** *Herbert Hoover as Secretary of Commerce: Studies in New Era Thought and Practice* (1974), and **John W. Dean,** *Warren G. Harding* (2004). For a penetrating look at U.S. imperialism in the Caribbean in the 1920s, see **Mary A. Renda,** *Taking Haiti: Military Occupation and the Culture of U.S. Imperialism* (2001).

On agricultural distress and protest, see **Theodore Saloutos and John D. Hicks,** *Twentieth Century Populism: Agricultural Discontent in the Middle West, 1900–1939* (1951). For an examination of the economic and social effects of Prohibition, see **Norman Clark,** *Deliver Us From Evil: An Interpretation of American Prohibition* (1976). **John Higham,** *Strangers in the Land: Patterns of American Nativism, 1865–1925* (1955), remains an excellent work on the spirit of intolerance that gripped America in the 1920s. On the 1920s resurgence of fundamentalist movements and such reactionary groups as the Ku Klux Klan, consult **Nancy MacLean,** *Behind the Mask of Chivalry: The Making of the Second Ku Klux Klan* (1994), and **Ferenc Morton Szasz,** *The Divided Mind of Protestant America, 1880–1930* (1982), which expertly analyzes the split in Protestant ranks between liberals and fundamentalists. **Irving Bernstein,** *The Lean Years: A History of the American Worker, 1920–1933* (1960), remains the most thorough examination of 1920s workers. On ethnic communities, Americanization, and political mobilization in the 1920s, see **Gary Gerstle,** *Working-Class Americanism: The Politics of Labor in a Textile City, 1914–1960* (1989), **George J. Sánchez,** *Becoming Mexican American: Ethnicity, Culture and Identity in Chicano Los Angeles, 1900–1945* (1993), and **Kristi Andersen,** *The Creation of a Democratic Majority, 1928–1936* (1979). On the Harlem Renaissance, see **Nathan Huggins,** *Harlem Renaissance* (1971). **Malcolm Cowley,** *Exiles Return* (1934), is a marvelous account of the writers and artists who comprised the "Lost Generation." For a provocative interpretation of the intertwined character of white and black literary cultures in 1920s New York, see **Ann Douglas,** *Terrible Honesty: Mongrel Manhattan in the 1920s* (1995).

 AMERICAN JOURNEY ONLINE AND INFOTRAC COLLEGE EDITION

Visit the source collections at www.ajaccess.wadsworth.com and infotrac.thomsonlearning.com and use the Search function with the following key terms to explore documents, images, audio and video clips, articles, and commentary related to the material in this chapter.

Warren G. Harding	Scopes Trial
Prohibition	Harlem Renaissance
Teapot Dome scandal	F. Scott Fitzgerald
Calvin Coolidge	Herbert Hoover
Dawes Plan	William Faulkner
Immigration Restriction Act	Johnson-Reed Act

GRADE AIDS

Visit the Liberty Equality Power Companion Web Site for resources specific to this textbook: http://history.wadsworth.com/murrin_LEP4e

 The CD in the back of this book and the U.S. History Resource Center at http://history.wadsworth.com/u.s./ offer a variety of tools to help you succeed in this course, including access to quizzes; images; documents; interactive simulations, maps, and timelines; movie explorations; and a wealth of other sources.

Chapter 25

The Great Depression and the New Deal, 1929–1939

VICTIMS OF THE DEPRESSION
This image evokes the hardship of the 1930s in the form of a strong,
able-bodied man in the prime of his life who is unable to find work and
must depend on charity.

CHAPTER OUTLINE

The Great Depression began on October 29, 1929—"Black Tuesday"—with a spectacular stock market crash. On that one day, stock values plummeted $14 billion. By the end of that year, stock prices had fallen 50 percent from their September highs. By 1932, the worst year of the depression, they had fallen another 30 percent. In three years, $74 billion of wealth had simply vanished. Meanwhile, the unemployment rate had soared to 25 percent.

Many Americans who lived through the Great Depression could never forget the scenes of misery they saw everywhere. In cities, the poor meekly awaited their turn for a piece of stale bread and thin gruel at ill-funded soup kitchens. Scavengers poked through garbage cans for food, scoured railroad tracks for coal that had fallen from trains, and sometimes ripped up railroad ties for fuel. Hundreds of thousands of Americans built makeshift shelters out of cardboard, scrap metal, and whatever else they could find in the city dump. They called their towns "Hoovervilles," after the president whom they despised for his apparent refusal to help them.

The Great Depression brought cultural crisis as well as economic crisis. In the 1920s, American business leaders had successfully redefined the national culture in business terms, as Americans' values became synonymous with the values of business: economic growth, freedom of enterprise, and acquisitiveness. But the swagger and bluster of American businessmen during the 1920s made them vulnerable to attack in the 1930s, as jobs, incomes, and growth all disappeared. With the prestige of business and business values

From the Collections of the Library of Congress.

UNEMPLOYED MEN IN NEW YORK CITY

These unemployed men bow their heads, trying to get warm from the fire in the barrel and to ignore the devastation that everywhere surrounds them. Such scenes and experiences help to explain why the Great Depression seared itself into the memories of those who lived through it.

in decline, how could Americans regain their hope and recover their confidence in the future? The first years of the 1930s held no convincing answers.

The gloom broke in early 1933 when Franklin Delano Roosevelt became president and unleashed the power of government to regulate capitalist enterprises, to restore the economy to health, and to guarantee the social welfare of Americans who were unable to help themselves. Roosevelt called his pro-government program a "new deal for the American people," and it would dominate national politics for the next 40 years. Hailed as a hero, Roosevelt became (and remains) the only president to serve more than two terms. In the short term, the New Deal failed to restore prosperity to America, but the "liberalism" it championed found acceptance among millions, who agreed with Roosevelt that only a large and powerful government could guarantee Americans their liberty.

C H A P T E R
F O C U S

♦ What caused the Crash of 1929, and why did the ensuing depression last so long?

♦ What were the First and Second New Deals? What were their similarities and differences? When and why did one give way to the other?

♦ Which groups in American society benefited most from the New Deal and which benefited least?

♦ In what ways did the Great Depression and New Deal shape American culture?

C H R O N O L O G Y

1929 Herbert Hoover assumes the presidency • Stock market crashes on "Black Tuesday"

1930 Tariff Act (Hawley-Smoot) raises tariffs

1931 More than 2,000 U.S. banks fail

1932 Unemployment rate reaches 25 percent • Reconstruction Finance Corporation established • Bonus Army marches on Washington • Roosevelt defeats Hoover for presidency

1933 Roosevelt assumes presidency • Hundred Days legislation defines First New Deal (March–June) • Roosevelt administration recognizes the Soviet Union • Good Neighbor Policy toward Latin America launched

1934 Father Charles Coughlin and Huey Long challenge conservatism of First New Deal • 2,000 strikes staged across country • Democrats overwhelm Republicans in off-year election • Radical political movements emerge in Wisconsin, Minnesota, Washington, and California • Indian Reorganization Act restores tribal land, provides funds, and grants limited right of self-government to American Indians • Reciprocal Trade Agreement lowers tariffs

1935 Committee for Industrial Organization (CIO) formed • Supreme Court declares NRA unconstitutional • Roosevelt unveils his Second New Deal • Congress passes Social Security Act • National Labor Relations Act (Wagner Act) guarantees workers' right to join unions • Holding Company Act breaks up utilities' near-monopoly • Congress passes Wealth Tax Act • Emergency Relief Administration Act passed; funds Works Progress Administration and other projects • Rural Electrification Administration established • Number of Mexican immigrants returning to Mexico reaches 500,000

1936 Roosevelt defeats Alf Landon for second term • Supreme Court declares AAA unconstitutional • Congress passes Soil Conservation and Domestic Allotment Act to replace AAA • Farm Security Administration established

1937 United Auto Workers defeat General Motors in sit-down strike • Roosevelt attempts to "pack" the Supreme Court • Supreme Court upholds constitutionality of Social Security and National Labor Relations acts • Severe recession hits

1938 Conservative opposition to New Deal does well in off-year election • *Superman* comic debuts

1939 75,000 gather to hear Marian Anderson sing at Lincoln Memorial

🌐 Causes of the Great Depression

America had experienced other depressions, or "panics," and no one would have been surprised if the boom of the 1920s had been followed by a one- or two-year economic downturn. No one was prepared, however, for the economic catastrophe of the 1930s.

Stock Market Speculation

In 1928 and 1929, the New York Stock Exchange had undergone a remarkable run-up in prices. In less than two years, the Dow Jones Industrial Average had doubled. Money had poured into the market, but many investors were buying on 10 percent "margin"—putting up only 10 percent of the price of a stock and borrowing the rest from brokers or banks. Few thought they would ever have to repay these loans with money out of their own pockets. Instead, investors expected to resell their shares within a few months at dramatically higher prices, pay back their loans from the proceeds, and still clear a handsome profit. And, for a while, that is exactly what they did. In 1928 alone, for example, RCA stock value increased 400 percent.

The possibility of making a fortune by investing only a few thousand dollars only intensified investors' greed. As speculation became rampant, money flowed indiscriminately into all kinds of risky enterprises. The stock market spiraled upward, out of control. When, in October 1929, confidence in future earnings finally faltered, creditors began demanding that investors who had bought stocks on margin repay their loans. The market crashed from its dizzying heights.

Still, the crash, by itself, fails to explain why the Great Depression lasted as long as it did. Poor decision making by the Federal Reserve Board, an ill-advised tariff that took effect soon after the depression hit, and a lopsided concentration of wealth in the hands of the rich deepened the economic collapse and made recovery more difficult.

Mistakes by the Federal Reserve Board

In 1930 and 1931, the Federal Reserve curtailed the amount of money in circulation and raised interest rates, thereby making credit more difficult for the public to secure. Although employing such a tight money policy during the boom years of 1928 or 1929 might have restrained the stock market and strengthened the economy, it was disastrous once the market had crashed. What the economy needed in 1930 and 1931 was an expanded money supply, lower interest rates, and easier credit. Such a course would have enabled debtors to pay their creditors. Instead, by choosing the opposite course, the Federal Reserve plunged an economy starved for credit deeper into depression. Higher interest rates also triggered an international crisis, as the banks of Germany and Austria, heavily dependent on U.S. loans, went bankrupt. The German-Austrian collapse, in turn, spread financial panic through Europe and ruined many U.S. manufacturers and banks specializing in European trade and investment.

An Ill-Advised Tariff

The Tariff Act of 1930, also known as the Hawley-Smoot Tariff Act, accelerated economic decline abroad and at home. Throughout the 1920s, agricultural interests had sought higher tariffs to protect American farmers against foreign competition. But Hawley-Smoot not only raised tariffs on 75 agricultural goods from 32 to 40 percent (the highest rate in American history), it also raised tariffs by a similar percentage on 925 manufactured products. Industrialists had convinced their supporters in the Republican-controlled Congress that such protection would give American industry much-needed assistance. The legislation was a disaster. Angry foreign governments retaliated by raising their own tariff rates to keep out American goods. International trade, already weakened by the tight credit policies of the Federal Reserve, took another blow at the very moment when it desperately needed a boost.

A Maldistribution of Wealth

A maldistribution in the nation's wealth that had developed in the 1920s also stymied economic recovery. Although average income rose in the 1920s, the incomes of the wealthiest families rose higher than the rest. Between 1918 and 1929, the share of the national income that went to the wealthiest 20 percent of the population rose by more than 10 percent, while the share that went to the poorest 60 percent fell by almost 13 percent. The Coolidge administration contributed to this maldistribution by lowering taxes on the wealthy, thereby increasing the proportion of the national wealth concentrated in their hands. The deepening inequality of income distribution slowed consumption and held back the growth of consumer-oriented industries (cars, household appliances, processed and packaged foods, recreation), the most dynamic elements of the U.S. economy. Even when the rich spent their money lavishly—building huge mansions, buying expensive cars, vacationing on the French Riviera—they still spent a smaller proportion of their total incomes on consumption than wage earners did. The average 1920s wage earner, for example, might spend one-quarter to one-half of his annual earnings to buy a car.

Putting more of the total increase in national income into the pockets of average Americans during the 1920s would have steadied the demand for consumer goods and kept the newer consumer industries correspondingly stronger. Such an economy might have recovered relatively quickly from the stock market crash of 1929. Instead, recovery from the Great Depression lagged until 1941, more than a decade later.

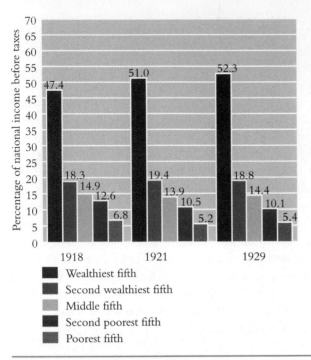

INCOME DISTRIBUTION BEFORE THE GREAT DEPRESSION

Source: From Gabriel Kolko, *Wealth and Power in America: An Analysis of Social Class and Income Distribution* (New York: Praeger, 1962), p. 14.

Hoover: The Fall of a Self-Made Man

In 1928, Herbert Hoover seemed to represent living proof that the American dream could be realized by anyone willing to work for it. A Stanford University geology major, a mining engineer, and a tireless and talented executive, Hoover rose quickly in corporate ranks. His government service had begun during the First World War, when he won an international reputation for his success in feeding millions of European soldiers and civilians. Then, in the 1920s, he became an active and influential secretary of commerce (see chapters 23 and 24). As the decade wound down, no American seemed better qualified to become president of the United States, an office that Hoover assumed in March 1929. Hoover was certain he could make prosperity a permanent feature of American life. "We in America today are nearer to the final triumph over poverty than ever before in the history of any land," he declared in August 1928. A little more than a year later, the Great Depression struck.

Hoover's Program

To cope with the crisis, Hoover first turned to the associational principles he had followed as secretary of commerce (see chapter 24). He encouraged organizations of farmers, industrialists, and bankers to share information, bolster one another's spirits, and devise policies to aid economic recovery. He urged farmers to restrict output, industrialists to hold wages at predepression levels, and bankers to help each other remain solvent. The federal government would provide them with information, strategies of mutual aid, occasional loans, and morale-boosting speeches.

Hoover turned to other aggressive policies once he realized that associationalism was failing. To ease the European crisis, Hoover secured a one-year moratorium on loan payments that European governments owed American banks. He steered through Congress the Glass-Steagall Act of 1932, which was intended to help American banks meet the demands of European depositors who wished to convert their dollars to gold. And to ease the crisis at home, he began to expand the government's economic role. The Reconstruction Finance Corporation (RFC), created in 1932, made $2 billion available in loans to ailing banks and to corporations willing to build low-cost housing, bridges, and other public works. The RFC was the biggest federal peacetime intervention in the economy up to that point in American history. The Home Loan Bank Board, set up that same year, offered funds to savings and loans, mortgage companies, and other financial institutions that lent money for home construction and mortgages.

Despite this new government activism, Hoover was uncomfortable with the idea that the government should be responsible for restoring the nation's economic welfare. When RFC expenditures, in 1932, created the largest peacetime deficit in U.S. history, Hoover tried to balance the federal budget. He supported the Revenue Act of 1932, which aimed to erase the deficit by raising taxes. He also insisted that the RFC issue loans only to relatively healthy institutions that were capable of repaying them and that it favor public works, such as toll bridges, that were likely to become self-financing. As a result of these constraints, the RFC spent considerably less than Congress had mandated.

Hoover was especially reluctant to engage the government in providing relief to unemployed and homeless Americans. To give money to the poor, he insisted, would destroy their desire to work, undermine their sense of self-worth, and erode their capacity for citizenship.

Hoover saw no similar peril in extending government assistance to ailing banks and businesses. Critics pointed to the seeming hypocrisy of Hoover's policies. For example, in 1930, Hoover refused a request of $25 million to help feed Arkansas farmers and their families but approved $45 million to feed the same farmers' livestock. In 1932, shortly after rejecting an urgent request from the city of

Chicago for aid to help pay its teachers and municipal workers, Hoover approved a $90 million loan to rescue that city's Central Republic Bank.

The Bonus Army

In spring 1932, a group of army veterans mounted a particularly emotional challenge to Hoover's policies. In 1924, Congress had authorized a $1,000 bonus for First World War veterans in the form of compensation certificates that would mature in 1945. Now the veterans were demanding that the government pay the bonus immediately. A group of Portland, Oregon, veterans, calling themselves the Bonus Expeditionary Force, hopped onto empty boxcars of freight trains heading east, determined to stage a march on Washington. As the impoverished "army" moved eastward, its ranks multiplied, so that by the time it reached Washington its numbers had swelled to 20,000, including wives and children. The so-called Bonus Army set up camp in the Anacostia Flats, southeast of the Capitol, and petitioned Congress for early payment of the promised bonus. The House of Representatives agreed, but the Senate turned them down. Hoover refused to meet with the veterans. In July, federal troops led by Army Chief of Staff Douglas MacArthur and 3rd Cavalry Commander George Patton attacked the veterans' Anacostia

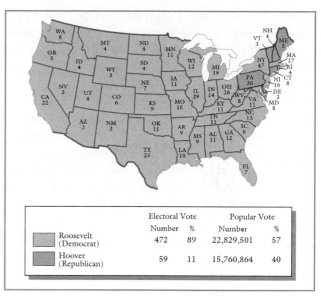

	Electoral Vote		Popular Vote	
	Number	%	Number	%
Roosevelt (Democrat)	472	89	22,829,501	57
Hoover (Republican)	59	11	15,760,864	40

MAP 25.1 PRESIDENTIAL ELECTION, 1932

The trauma of the Great Depression can be gauged by the shifting fortunes of President Herbert Hoover. In 1928, he had won 444 electoral votes and carried all but eight states (see Map 24.3, p. 755). In 1932, by contrast, he won only 59 electoral votes and carried only seven states. His Democratic opponent, Franklin D. Roosevelt, was the big winner.

THE BONUS ARMY'S ENCAMPMENT SET ABLAZE

U.S. troops under the command of General Douglas MacArthur torched the tents and shacks that housed thousands of First World War veterans who had come to Washington to demand financial assistance from the government.

encampment, set the tents and shacks ablaze, and dispersed the protestors. In the process, more than 100 veterans were wounded and one infant was killed.

News that veterans and their families had been attacked in the nation's capital served only to harden anti-Hoover opinion. In the 1932 elections, the discredited Republicans were voted out of office after having dominated national politics (excepting Woodrow Wilson's two terms) for 36 years. Hoover received only 39.6 percent of the popular vote and just 59 (of 531) electoral votes. Hoover left the presidency in 1933 a bewildered man, reviled by Americans for his seeming indifference to suffering and his ineptitude in dealing with the economy's collapse.

A Culture in Crisis

The economic crisis of the early 1930s expressed itself not just in politics but also in culture, especially in the literature and cinema of the time. Many writers who, in the 1920s, had castigated ordinary Americas for their small-mindedness and crass materialism now felt compelled to travel among them, learn about their condition, and seek signs of social renewal. But writers found mostly economic misery and a deep spiritual depression. Edmund Wilson, a leading literary critic, traveled the country in 1930 and 1931 and wrote numerous essays about how Americans had lost their way and knew not where to turn. When he reached San Diego, he got hold of the city's coroner reports on the numerous individuals who, in desperation, had taken their own lives. Wilson had believed that San Diego, that lovely outpost of the American frontier sitting astride the great and beckoning Pacific, would be a place where the American dream still thrived. But here, too, Wilson claimed, failure and death suffused life and snuffed out hope. He reported on the city's suicides in this fashion:

> They drive their cars into dark alleys, get into the back seat and shoot themselves; they hang themselves in hotel bedrooms, take overdoses of suphonal or barbital; they slip off to the municipal golf-links and there stab themselves with carving-knives; or they throw themselves into the bay, blue and placid, where gray battleships and cruisers guard the limits of their broad-belting nation.

A sense of aimlessness and hopelessness characterized one of the major literary works of the early 1930s, the Studs Lonigan trilogy (1932–35) written by the Chicago-born writer James T. Farrell. In another decade, one easily imagines that Farrell might have cast his scrappy Irish-American protagonist, Studs, as an American hero who, through pluck, guile, and force of character, rises from poverty to wealth, success, and influence. But Studs lacks the necessary focus and is too easily overcome by the harshness of his environment. He dies poor and alone, not even having reached the age of 30. The popular writer Nathaniel West, meanwhile, was publishing such novels as *Miss Lonelyhearts* (1933) and *A Cool Million* (1934), works similarly built around central characters succumbing to failure, drift, and even insanity.

One can detect parallel themes of despair in the period's cinema, especially in such movies as *Fugitive from a Chain Gang* (1932), in which an industrious and honorable man, James Allen, returns from Europe a war hero, only to sink into vagabondage. Caught by the police when he becomes an innocent accessory to a crime, Allen is sentenced to 10 years on a Georgia chain gang. Unable to tolerate the hardship and injustice of his punishment, Allen escapes from jail and uses his intelligence, determination, and good character to start a new life for himself under an alias. He finds satisfying work as an engineer and falls in love, but must abandon both once his true identity is revealed. His desire to stay out of prison condemns him to being a man always on the run, unable to prove his innocence or to earn a decent living or build enduring relationships. It is a powerful and utterly bleak cinematic work that was, nevertheless, popular with moviegoers and given an Academy Award for Best Picture.

Less bleak but still sobering were the gangster movies of the early 1930s, especially *Little Caesar* (1930) and *The Public Enemy* (1931), which told stories of hard-nosed, crooked, and violent men who made themselves into figures of wealth and influence by living outside the law and bending the social environment in which they lived to their will. These gangsters usually had to pay for their sins by dying or going to jail, but, before that happened, they were often portrayed sympathetically, as individuals who, against all odds, found a way to succeed. Moviegoers were gripped by the intensity, suspense, and violence of gangster–police confrontations in these films but they were drawn, too, to the gangsters themselves, modern-day outlaws who demonstrated how tough it was to succeed in America and how necessary it might be to break the rules.

The lawlessness that was so integral to the gangster movies also surfaced in the wild comedy of Groucho, Chico, Harpo, and Zeppo Marx, entertainers who, in the 1920s and 1930s, made the transition from vaudeville stage to silver screen. In their films, the Marx Brothers ridiculed figures of authority, broke every rule of etiquette, smacked around their antagonists (and each other), and deliberately and delightfully mangled the English language. Anarchy ruled their world. Many of the moviegoers who went to see the Marx Brothers on the big screen simply wanted to enjoy 90 minutes of side-splitting laughter, if only to escape for a time the harsh realities of their daily lives.

But some of the Marx Brothers movies carried a more serious political message, perhaps none more so than *Duck Soup* (1933), a withering political satire set in the fictional nation of Fredonia. Fredonia's dictatorial leaders are pompous and small-minded, its legal system is a fraud, and its citizens are clueless and easily misled; by the movie's end, the latter are called to arms through spectacularly ludicrous song and dance scenes, and then led off to fight a meaningless but deadly war. In one of the film's most famous and controversial lines, Rufus T. Firefly, leader of Fredonia (played by Groucho Marx), declares to his troops: "And remember while you're out there risking life and limb through shot and shell, we'll be in here thinking what a sucker you are."

The Marx Brothers frame their critique of politics and war in their customary comedic style; the movie contains some of the funniest scenes the Marx Brothers ever filmed. But *Duck Soup* also delivers the dispiriting message that people could not hope to better themselves through politics, for politics had been emptied of all meaning and

Margaret Mead: Studying the South Pacific

In the 1920s and 1930s, the practitioners of a relatively new intellectual discipline, cultural anthropology, began making research trips abroad an integral part of their work. Their ambition was to understand more about the diversity of the human experience and the power of culture to shape social life. These anthropologists rejected the notions that American culture was inherently superior to all others or that all the world's people should assimilate the values and beliefs that guided the West. Instead, these scholars delighted in the world's diversity and insisted on treating all cultures as fundamentally equal.

Few anthropologists were as influential in this quest as Margaret Mead. Born in Philadelphia in 1901, Mead received her B.A. from Barnard College in 1923 and then enrolled in Columbia University to study with the preeminent cultural anthropologist Franz Boas. Rather than travel to the American Southwest to conduct her initial field research, as most Boas students had done, Mead opted to study adolescents in the American Samoa of the South Pacific. This was a remarkable decision given that few young women in this era traveled such a long distance by themselves. In Samoa, Mead selected for study a T'au village on the least westernized Samoan island. Studying the transition of T'au children to adulthood, Mead discovered that young girls there did not experience as stormy an adolescence as did their counterparts in the United States and that this Samoan society, as a whole, seemed to be less convulsed by sexual anxiety than America. The book in which Mead published her findings, *Coming of Age in Samoa* (1928), became an overnight sensation and brought anthropology to the attention of the general American public. For Americans who were perturbed by what they perceived to be the limits of their own culture (see chapter 24),

Mead's work seemed to demonstrate that humans could develop alternative and more wholesome ways of living.

Mead's trip to Samoa was only the first of 24 expeditions to the South Pacific that she would undertake during her long and distinguished career. In the 1930s, she worked among no less than six different groups of Pacific Islanders: the Arapesh, Mundugumor, Chambri, Iatmul, Omaha, and Balinese. Everywhere she went, she explored how different cultures shaped gender roles, gender temperaments, sex, child rearing, and children's experience in particular ways. By the end of the 1930s, she had confirmed her initial claims and research about the variability of human experience and about how different societies assigned different roles and personalities to men and women, parents, and children. Culture, she insisted, mattered more than nature or biology in determining these roles and identities.

By the 1950s, Mead had become a public figure of great repute. In the 1960s, her arguments about the variability of human experience helped to propel a sexual revolution and the rebirth of feminism. In such ways did knowledge gained on faraway Pacific islands begin to shape American culture.

MARGARET MEAD

Mead in an intimate conversation with a Manus mother and child during a visit to the Admiralty Islands in 1953, one of Mead's many expeditions abroad to learn about peoples very different from those in America among whom she had grown up.

© Bettmann/Corbis.

honesty. This cinematic sentiment paralleled the conviction held by many Americans in 1932 and early 1933 that their own politicians, especially Hoover and the Republicans, had failed them in a time of need. In such ways did the political pessimism of the early 1930s seep into the era's culture.

The Democratic Roosevelt

Between 1933 and 1935, the mood of the country shifted sharply, and politics would, once again, generate hope rather than despair. This change was largely attributable to the personality and policies of Hoover's successor, Franklin D. Roosevelt, and to the social movements that emerged during his presidency.

An Early Life of Privilege

Roosevelt was born in 1882 into a patrician family descended, on his father's side, from Dutch gentry who in the 17th century had built large estates on the fertile land along the Hudson River. By the 1880s, the Hyde Park manor where Roosevelt grew up had been in the family for more than 200 years. His mother's family—the Delanos—traced its ancestry back to the Mayflower. Roosevelt's education at Groton, Harvard College, and Columbia Law School was typical of the path followed by the sons of America's elite.

The Roosevelt family was wealthy, although not spectacularly so by the standards of the late 19th century. His parents' net worth of more than $1 million was relatively small in comparison to the fortunes being amassed by the rising class of industrialists and railroad tycoons, many of whom commanded fortunes of $50 to $100 million or more. This widening gap in wealth disturbed families like the Roosevelts, who worried that the new industrial elite would dislodge them from their social position. Moreover, they took offense at the newcomers' vulgar displays of wealth, lack of taste and etiquette, indifference to the natural environment, and hostility toward those less fortunate than themselves. Theodore Roosevelt, an older cousin of Franklin Roosevelt, had called on the men of his gentry class to set a better example by devoting themselves to public service and the public good. Though young Franklin often said he wanted to follow in his famous cousin's footsteps, he showed little of Teddy's seriousness of purpose. He distinguished himself neither at school nor at law. Prior to the 1920s, he could point to few significant political achievements, and he owed his political ascent in the Democratic Party mostly to his famous name. He was charming and gregarious, and devoted a great deal of energy to sailing, partying, and enjoying the company of women other than his wife, Eleanor. Then, in 1921, at the age of 39, Roosevelt was both stricken and transformed by a devastating illness, polio, which paralyzed him from the waist down for the rest of his life.

During the two years that Roosevelt spent bedridden, he seemed to acquire a new determination and seriousness. He developed a compassion for those suffering misfortune that would later enable him to reach out to the millions caught in the Great Depression. Roosevelt's physical debilitation also transformed his relationship with Eleanor, with whom he had shared a testy and increasingly loveless marriage. Eleanor's dedication to nursing Franklin back to health forged a new bond between them. More conscious of his dependence on others, he now welcomed her as a partner in his career. Eleanor soon displayed a talent for political organization and public speaking that surprised those who knew her only as a shy, awkward woman. She was an indispensable player in the revival of Franklin's political fortunes, which began in 1928, with his election to the governorship of New York state. Eleanor would also become an active, eloquent First Lady, her husband's trusted ally, and an architect of American liberalism.

Roosevelt Liberalism

As governor of New York for four years (1929–33), Roosevelt had initiated various reform programs, and his success made him the front-runner for the 1932 Democratic presidential nomination. Even so, he had little assurance that he would be the party's choice. Since 1924, the Democrats had been sharply divided between southern and midwestern agrarians on the one hand and northeastern ethnics on the other. The agrarians favored government regulation—both of the nation's economy and of the private affairs of its citizens. Their support of government intervention in the pursuit of social justice marked them as economic progressives, while their advocacy of Prohibition revealed a cultural conservatism as well as a nativistic strain. By contrast, urban ethnics opposed Prohibition and other forms of government interference in the private lives of its citizens. Urban ethnics were divided over whether the government should regulate the economy, with former New York governor Al Smith increasingly committed to a laissez-faire policy and Senator Robert Wagner of New York and others supporting more federal control.

Roosevelt understood the need to carve out a middle ground. As governor of New York, and then as a presidential candidate in 1932, he surrounded himself with men and women who embraced the new reform movement called liberalism. Frances Perkins, Harry Hopkins, Raymond Moley, Rexford Tugwell, Adolph Berle, Samuel Rosenman—all were interventionist in economic matters and libertarian on questions of personal behavior. They shared with the agrarians and Wagner's supporters a desire to regulate capitalism, but they agreed with Al Smith that the government had no business telling people how to live their lives. Although it seemed unlikely at first, Roosevelt did manage to unite the party behind him at the 1932 Democratic Party convention. In his convention acceptance speech, he declared: "Ours must be the party of liberal thought, of planned action, of enlightened international outlook, and of the greatest good for the greatest number of citizens." He promised "a new deal for the American people."

The First New Deal, 1933–1935

By the time Roosevelt assumed office in March 1933, the economy lay in shambles. From 1929 to 1932, industrial production had fallen by 50 percent, while new investment had declined from $16 billion to less than $1 billion. In those same years, more than 100,000 businesses went bankrupt. The nation's banking system was on the verge of collapse. In 1931 alone, more than 2,000 banks had shut their doors. The unemployment rate was soaring.

Some Americans feared that the opportunity for reform had already passed.

Not Roosevelt. "This nation asks for action, and action now," Roosevelt declared in his inaugural address. Roosevelt was true to his word. In his first Hundred Days, from early March through early June 1933, Roosevelt persuaded Congress to pass 15 major pieces of legislation to help bankers, farmers, industrialists, workers, homeowners, the unemployed, and the hungry. He also prevailed on Congress to repeal Prohibition. Not all of the new laws helped to relieve distress and promote recovery, but, in the short term, that seemed to matter little. Roosevelt had brought excitement and hope to the nation. He was confident, decisive, and defiantly cheery. "The only thing we have to fear is fear itself," he declared.

Roosevelt used the radio to reach out to ordinary Americans. On the second Sunday after his inauguration, he launched a series of radio addresses known as "fireside chats," speaking in a plain, friendly, and direct voice to the forlorn and discouraged. In his first chat, he explained the banking crisis in simple terms but without condescension. "I want to take a few minutes to talk with the people of the United States about banking," he began. An estimated 20 million Americans listened.

To hear the president speaking warmly and conversationally—as though he were actually there in the room—was riveting. An estimated 500,000 Americans wrote letters to Roosevelt within days of his inaugural address.

LEGISLATION ENACTED DURING THE "HUNDRED DAYS," MARCH 9–JUNE 16, 1933

Date	Legislation	Purpose
March 9	Emergency Banking Act	Provide federal loans to private bankers
March 20	Economy Act	Balance the federal budget
March 22	Beer-Wine Revenue Act	Repeal Prohibition
March 31	Unemployment Relief Act	Create the Civilian Conservation Corps
May 12	Agricultural Adjustment Act	Establish a national agricultural policy
May 12	Emergency Farm Mortgage Act	Provide refinancing of farm mortgages
May 12	Federal Emergency Relief Act	Establish a national relief system, including the Civil Works Administration
May 18	Tennessee Valley Authority Act	Promote economic development of the Tennessee Valley
May 27	Securities Act	Regulate the purchase and sale of new securities
June 5	Gold Repeal Joint Resolution	Cancel the gold clause in public and private contracts
June 13	Home Owners Loan Act	Provide refinancing of home mortgages
June 16	National Industrial Recovery Act	Set up a national system of industrial self-government and establish the Public Works Administration
June 16	Glass-Steagall Banking Act	Create Federal Deposit Insurance Corporation; separate commercial and investment banking
June 16	Farm Credit Act	Reorganize agricultural credit programs
June 16	Railroad Coordination Act	Appoint federal coordinator of transportation

Source: Arthur M. Schlesinger, Jr., *The Coming of the New Deal* (Boston: Houghton Mifflin, 1959), pp. 20–21.

FRANKLIN D. ROOSEVELT

A smiling, confident Roosevelt delivering a speech. The man on the left in the first row behind Roosevelt is Interior Secretary Harold Ickes.

Millions more would write to him and to Eleanor Roosevelt over the next few years. Many of the letters were simply addressed to "Mr. or Mrs. Roosevelt, Washington, D.C." Democrats began to hang portraits of Franklin Roosevelt in their homes, often next to a picture of Jesus or the Madonna.

Roosevelt was never the benign father figure he made himself out to be. He skillfully crafted his public image. Compliant news photographers agreed not to show him in a wheelchair or struggling with the leg braces and cane he used to take even small steps. His political rhetoric sometimes promised more than he was prepared to deliver in actual legislation. This was not simply a strategy meant to confuse his opponents and to sustain his own appeal. Roosevelt was struggling to keep together a party that was divided over a variety of issues. At the same time, he was attempting to establish a strong government in a society that had long been hostile to that idea. In America, unlike Great Britain, for example, relatively few individuals were experienced in public service. This lack of administrative expertise created dilemmas for Roosevelt and other New

Dealers, who often found it difficult to translate ambitious social programs into effective social policy.

Saving the Banks

Roosevelt's first order of business was to save the nation's financial system. By inauguration day, several states had already shut their banks. Roosevelt immediately ordered all of the nation's banks closed—a bold move he brazenly called a "bank holiday." At his request, Congress rushed through the Emergency Banking Act (EBA), which made federal loans available to private bankers, and followed that with the Economy Act (EA), which committed the government to balancing the budget.

Both the EBA and the EA were fiscally conservative programs that Hoover had proposed. The EBA made it possible for private bankers to retain financial control of their institutions, and the EA announced the government's intention of pursuing a fiscally prudent course. Only after the financial crisis had eased did Roosevelt turn to the structural reform of banking. A second Glass-Steagall Act (1933) separated commercial banking from investment banking. It also created the Federal Deposit Insurance Corporation (FDIC), which assured depositors that the government would protect up to $5,000 of their savings. The Securities Act (1933) and the Securities Exchange Act (1934) imposed long-overdue regulation on the New York Stock Exchange, both by reining in buying on the margin and by establishing the Securities and Exchange Commission (SEC) to enforce federal law.

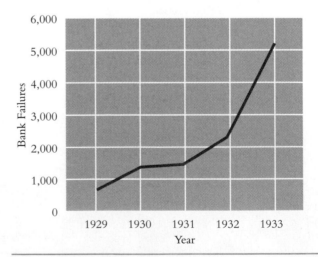

BANK FAILURES, 1929–1933

Source: From C. D. Bremer, *American Bank Failures* (New York: Columbia University Press, 1935), p. 42.

Economic Relief

Roosevelt understood the need to temper financial prudence with compassion. Congress responded swiftly in 1933 to Roosevelt's request to establish the Federal Emergency Relief Administration (FERA), granting it $500 million for relief to the poor. To head FERA, Roosevelt appointed a brash young reformer, Harry Hopkins, who disbursed $2 million during his first two hours on the job. Roosevelt next won congressional approval for the Civilian Conservation Corps (CCC), which put more than 2 million single young men to work planting trees, halting erosion, and otherwise improving the environment. The following winter, Roosevelt launched the Civil Works Administration (CWA), an ambitious work-relief program, also under Harry Hopkins's direction, which hired 4 million unemployed at $15 per week and put them to work on 400,000 small scale government projects. For middle-class Americans threatened with the loss of their homes, Roosevelt won Congressional approval for the Homeowners' Loan Corporation (1933) to refinance mortgages. These direct subsidies to millions of jobless and home-owning Americans lent credibility to Roosevelt's claim that the New Deal would set the country on a new course.

Agricultural Reform

In 1933, Roosevelt expected economic recovery to come not from relief, but through agricultural and industrial cooperation. He regarded the Agricultural Adjustment Act, passed in May, and the National Industrial Recovery Act (NIRA), passed in June, as the most important legislation of his Hundred Days. Both were based on the idea that curtailing production would trigger economic recovery. By shrinking the supply of agricultural and manufactured goods, Roosevelt's economists reasoned, they could restore the balance of normal market forces. As demand for scarce goods exceeded supply, prices would rise and revenues would climb. Farmers and industrialists, earning a profit once again, would increase their investment in new technology and hire more workers, and prosperity and full employment would be the final result.

To curtail farm production, the Agricultural Adjustment Administration (AAA), which was set up by the Agricultural Adjustment Act, began paying farmers to keep a portion of their land out of cultivation and to reduce the size of their herds. The program was controversial; many farmers were skeptical of a government offer to pay more money for working less land and husbanding

HELPING DUST BOWL VICTIMS

This poster by the artist and New Deal supporter Ben Shahn dramatizes the plight of the Dust Bowl's victims while expressing the belief that relief is forthcoming from a New Deal agency, the Resettlement Administration.

From the Collections of the Library of Congress.

fewer livestock, but few refused to accept payments. As one young Kansas farmer reported:

> There were mouthy individuals who seized every opportunity to run down the entire program . . . condemning it as useless, crooked, revolutionary, or dictatorial; but . . . when the first AAA payments were made available, shortly before Christmas, these same wordy critics made a beeline for the courthouse. They jostled and fell over each other in their mad scramble to be the first in line to receive allotment money.

The AAA had made no provision, however, for the countless tenant farmers and farm laborers who would be thrown out of work by the reduction in acreage. In the South, the victims were disproportionately black. A Georgia sharecropper wrote Harry Hopkins of his misery: "I have Bin farming all my life But the man I live with

Has Turned me loose taking my mule [and] all my feed. . . . I can't get a Job so Some one said Rite you." New Dealers within the Department of Agriculture, such as Rexford Tugwell and Jerome Frank, were sympathetic to the plight of sharecroppers, but they failed during the First New Deal to extend to them the government's helping hand.

The programs of the AAA also proved inadequate to Great Plains farmers, whose economic problems had been compounded by ecological crisis. Just as the depression rolled in, the rain stopped falling on the plains. The land, stripped of its native grasses by decades of excessive plowing, dried up and turned to dust. And then the dust began to blow, sometimes traveling 1,000 miles across open prairie. Dust became a fixed feature of daily life on the plains (which soon became known as the Dust Bowl), covering furniture, floors, and stoves, and penetrating people's hair and lungs. The worst dust storm occurred on April 14, 1935, when a great mass of dust, moving at speeds of 45 to 70 miles per hour, roared through Colorado, Kansas, and Oklahoma, blackening the sky, suffocating cattle, and dumping thousands of tons of topsoil and red clay on homes and streets.

The government responded to this calamity by establishing the Soil Conservation Service (SCS) in 1935. Rec-

FDR Library.

SEARCHING FOR A BETTER LIFE

Scenes like this one were common in the 1930s as farm families in Oklahoma and Texas who had lost their land began heading to California. Here a family's entire belongings are packed onto a truck, and the mother tends to her baby on an isolated road. The woman's fur collar suggests that this family had once known better times.

ognizing that the soil problems of the Great Plains could not be solved simply by taking land out of production, SCS experts urged plains farmers to plant soil-conserving grasses and legumes in place of wheat. They taught farmers how to plow along contour lines and how to build terraces—techniques that had been proven effective in slowing the runoff of rainwater and improving its absorption into the soil. Plains farmers were open to these suggestions, especially when the government offered to subsidize those willing to implement them. Bolstered by the new assistance, plains agriculture began to recover.

Still, the government offered little assistance to the rural poor—the tenant farmers and sharecroppers. Nearly 1 million had left their homes by 1935, and another 2.5 million would leave after 1935. Most headed west, piling their belongings onto their jalopies, snaking along Route 66 until they reached California. They became known as Okies, because many, although not all, had come from Oklahoma. Their dispossession and forced migration disturbed many Americans, for whom the plight of these once-sturdy yeomen became a symbol of how much had gone wrong with the American dream.

In 1936, the Supreme Court ruled that AAA-mandated limits on farm production constituted an illegal restraint of trade. Congress responded by passing the Soil Conservation and Domestic Allotment Act, which justified the removal of land from cultivation for reasons of conservation rather than economics. This new act also called on landowners to share their government subsidies with sharecroppers and tenant farmers, although many landowners managed to evade this and subsequent laws that required them to share federal funds.

The use of subsidies, begun by the AAA, did eventually bring stability and prosperity to agriculture, but at high cost. Agriculture became the most heavily subsidized sector of the U.S. economy, and the Department of Agriculture grew into one of the government's largest bureaucracies. The rural poor, black and white, never received a fair share of federal benefits. Beginning in the 1930s, and continuing in the 1940s and 1950s, they would be forced off the land and into the cities of the North and West.

Industrial Reform

American industry was so vast that Roosevelt's administration never contemplated paying individual manufacturers direct subsidies to reduce, or even halt, production. Instead, the government decided to limit production through persuasion and association—techniques that Hoover had also favored.

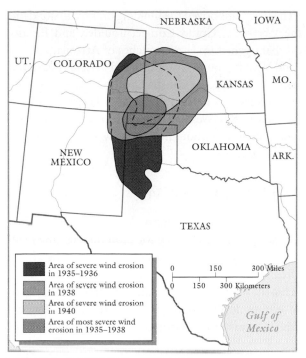

MAP 25.2 DUST BOWL, 1935–1940

This map shows the areas in six states—Texas, New Mexico, Oklahoma, Colorado, Kansas, and a bit of Nebraska—claimed by the Dust Bowl between 1935 and 1940. The light red color shows the area where the winds caused the worst damage.

To head the National Recovery Administration (NRA), authorized under the National Industrial Recovery Act, Roosevelt chose General Hugh Johnson, a participant in industrial planning experiments during the First World War. Johnson's first task was to persuade industrialists and businessmen to agree to raise employee wages to a minimum of 30 to 40 cents per hour and to limit employee hours to a maximum of 30 to 40 hours per week. The limitation on hours was meant to reduce the quantity of goods that any factory or business could produce.

Johnson launched a high-powered publicity campaign. He distributed NRA pamphlets and pins throughout the country. He used the radio to exhort all Americans to do their part. He staged an NRA celebration in Yankee Stadium and a parade down New York City's Fifth Avenue. He sent letters to millions of employers asking them to place a "blue eagle"—the logo of the NRA—on storefronts, at factory entrances, and on company stationery to signal their participation in the campaign to limit production and restore prosperity. Blue eagles soon sprouted everywhere, usually accompanied by the slogan "We Do Our Part."

Johnson understood, however, that his propaganda campaign could not by itself guarantee recovery. So he brought together the largest producers in every sector of manufacturing and asked each group (or conference) to work out a code of fair competition that would specify prices, wages, and hours throughout the sector. He also asked each conference to restrict production.

In summer and fall 1933, the NRA codes drawn up for steel, textiles, coal mining, rubber, garment manufacture, and other industries seemed to be working. The economy improved, and people began to hope for an end to the depression. But in winter and spring 1934, economic indicators plunged downward once again, and manufacturers began to evade the code provisions. Government

SELLING THE NRA THROUGH SEX AND SUNBURN

Americans were asked to display their support for the NRA by pasting eagles onto their factory entrances, storefronts, and even clothes. The young women in this photo dispensed with pasting, choosing instead to allow the sun to burn their bare backs around a stenciled blue eagle and NRA lettering, which were being applied by the woman in the white gown.

committees set up to enforce the codes were powerless to punish violators. By fall 1934, it was clear that the NRA had failed. When the Supreme Court declared the NRA codes unconstitutional in May 1935, the Roosevelt administration allowed the agency to die.

Rebuilding the Nation's Infrastructure

In addition to establishing the NRA, the National Industrial Recovery Act launched the Public Works Administration (PWA). The PWA had a $3.3 billion budget to sponsor internal improvements that would strengthen the nation's infrastructure of roads, bridges, sewage systems, hospitals, airports, and schools. The labor needed for these projects would shrink relief rolls and reduce unemployment, but the projects could be justified in terms that conservatives approved: economic investment rather than short-term relief.

The PWA authorized the building of three major dams in the West—the Grand Coulee, Boulder, and Bonneville—that opened up large stretches of Arizona, California, and Washington to industrial and agricultural development. It funded the construction of the Triborough Bridge in New York City and the 100-mile causeway linking Florida to Key West. It also appropriated money for the construction of thousands of new schools between 1933 and 1939.

The TVA Alternative

One piece of legislation passed during Roosevelt's First New Deal specified a strategy for economic recovery significantly different from the one promoted by the NIRA. The Tennessee Valley Authority Act (1933) called for the government—rather than private corporations—to promote economic development throughout the Tennessee Valley, a vast river basin winding through parts of

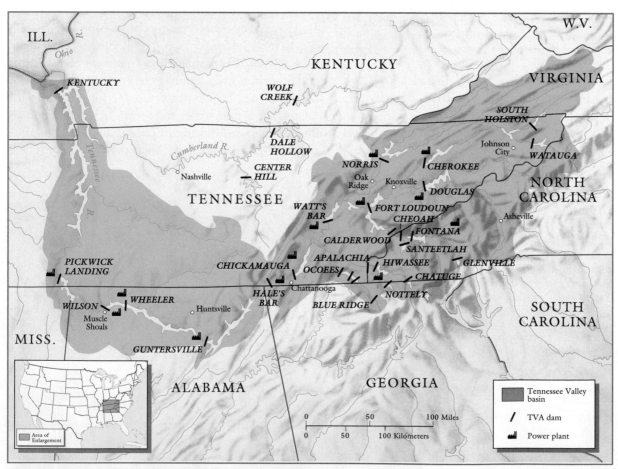

MAP 25.3   TENNESSEE VALLEY AUTHORITY

This map shows the vast scale of the TVA, and pinpoints the locations of 29 dams and 13 power plants that emerged from this project.

Kentucky, Tennessee, Mississippi, Alabama, Georgia, and North Carolina. The act created the Tennessee Valley Authority (TVA) to control flooding on the Tennessee River, harness its water power to generate electricity, develop local industry (such as fertilizer production), improve river navigability, and ease the poverty and isolation of the area's inhabitants. In some respects, the TVA's mandate resembled that of the PWA, but the TVA enjoyed even greater authority. The extent of its control over economic development reflected the influence of Rexford Tugwell and other New Dealers who were committed to a government-planned and government-operated economy. Although they rarely said so, these reformers were drawn to socialism.

The accomplishments of the TVA were many. It built, completed, or improved more than 20 dams, including the huge Wheeler Dam near Muscle Shoals in Alabama. At several of the dam sites, the TVA built hydroelectric generators and soon became the nation's largest producer of electricity. Its low rates compelled private utility companies to reduce their rates as well. The TVA also constructed waterways to bypass non-navigable stretches of the river, reduced the danger of flooding, and taught farmers how to prevent soil erosion and use fertilizers.

Although the TVA was one of the New Deal's most celebrated successes, it generated little support for more ambitious experiments in national planning. For the government to have assumed control of established industries and banks would have been quite a different matter from bringing prosperity to an impoverished region. Like Roosevelt, few members of Congress or the public favored the radical growth of governmental power that such programs would have entailed. Thus, the thought of replacing the NRA with a nationwide TVA, for instance, made little headway. The New Deal never embraced the idea of the federal government as a substitute for private enterprise.

The New Deal and Western Development

As the TVA showed, New Deal programs could make an enormous difference to a particular region's welfare. Other regional beneficiaries of the New Deal included the New York City area, which prospered from the close links of local politicians to the Roosevelt administration. The region that most benefited from the New Deal, however, was the West. Between 1933 and 1939, per capita payments for public works projects, welfare, and federal loans in the Rocky Mountain and Pacific Coast states outstripped those of any other region.

Central to this western focus was the program of dam building. Western real estate and agricultural interests

wanted to dam the West's major rivers to provide water and electricity for urban and agricultural development. But the costs were prohibitive, even to the largest capitalists, until the New Deal offered to defray the expenses with federal dollars. Western interests found a government ally in the Bureau of Reclamation, a hitherto small federal agency (in existence since 1902) that became, under the New Deal, a prime dispenser of funds for dam construction, reservoir creation, and the provision of water to western cities and farms. Drawing on PWA monies, the bureau oversaw the building of the Boulder Dam (later renamed Hoover Dam), which provided drinking water for southern California, irrigation water for California's Imperial Valley, and electricity for Los Angeles and southern Arizona. It also authorized the Central Valley Project and the All-American Canal, vast water-harnessing projects in central and southern California meant to provide irrigation, drinking water, and electricity to California farmers and

© Lester Lefkowitz/Corbis.

IMPROVING THE NATION'S INFRASTRUCTURE
The federal government built several major dams in the West to boost agricultural and industrial development. This is a photograph of the mammoth Boulder Dam (later renamed the Hoover Dam) on the Colorado River.

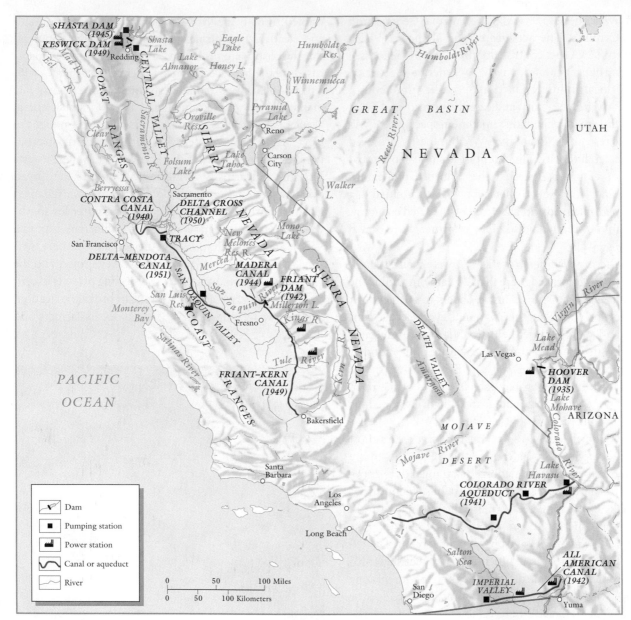

MAP 25.4 FEDERAL WATER PROJECTS IN CALIFORNIA BUILT OR FUNDED BY THE NEW DEAL

This map demonstrates how much California cities and agriculture benefited from water projects—dams, canals, aqueducts, pumping stations, and power plants—begun under the New Deal. The projects extended from the Shasta Dam in the northern part of the state to the All-American Canal that traversed the Imperial Valley south of San Diego, and included the Colorado River Aqueduct that would bring vital drinking water to Los Angeles.

towns. The greatest construction project of all was the Grand Coulee Dam on the Columbia River in Washington, which created a lake 150 miles long. Together with the Bonneville Dam (also on the Columbia), the Grand Coulee gave the Pacific Northwest the cheapest electricity in the country and created the potential for huge economic and population growth. Not surprisingly, these two dams also made Washington state the largest per capita recipient of New Deal aid.

These developments attracted less attention in the 1930s than the TVA because their benefits did not fully materialize until after the Second World War. Also, dam building in the West was not seen as a radical experiment in government planning and management. Unlike the TVA, the Bureau of Reclamation hired private contractors to do the work. Moreover, the benefits of these dams were intended to flow first to large agricultural and real estate interests, not to the poor; they were intended to aid private enterprise, rather than bypass it. In political terms, dam building in the West was more conservative than it was in the Tennessee Valley. Even so, this activity made the federal government a key architect of the modern American West.

Political Mobilization, Political Unrest, 1934–1935

Although Roosevelt and the New Dealers quickly dismantled the NRA in 1935, they could not stop the political forces it had set in motion. Ordinary Americans now believed they could make a difference. If the New Dealers could not achieve economic recovery, the people would find others who could.

Populist Critics of the New Deal

Some critics were disturbed by what they perceived as the conservative character of New Deal programs. Banking reforms, the AAA, and the NRA, they alleged, all seemed to favor large economic interests. Ordinary people had been ignored.

In the South and Midwest, millions listened regularly to the radio addresses of Louisiana Senator Huey Long, a former governor of that state and an accomplished orator. In attacks on New Deal programs, he alleged that "not a single thin dime of concentrated, bloated, pompous

HUEY LONG, POPULIST

A spellbinding speaker, Long influenced millions with his calls for redistributing America's wealth in a more equitable manner.

wealth, massed in the hands of a few people has been raked down to relieve the masses." Long offered a simple alternative: "Break up the swollen fortunes of America and . . . spread the wealth among all our people." He called for a redistribution of wealth that would guarantee each American family a $5,000 estate.

Long's rhetoric inspired hundreds of thousands of Americans to join the Share the Wealth clubs his supporters organized. Most came from middle-class ranks or from the ranks of skilled workers. Long's supporters worried that the big business orientation of New Deal programs would undermine their economic and social status. By 1935, Roosevelt regarded Long as the man most likely to unseat him in the presidential election of 1936. Before that campaign began, however, Long was murdered by an assassin.

Meanwhile, in the Midwest, Father Charles Coughlin, the "radio priest," delivered his stinging critique of the New Deal to a weekly radio audience of between 30 and 40 million listeners. Like Long, Coughlin appealed to anxious middle-class Americans and to privileged groups of workers who believed that middle-class status was slipping from their grasp. A devoted Roosevelt supporter at first—he had once called the New Deal "Christ's Deal"—Coughlin had become, by 1934, a harsh critic. He charged that the New Deal was run by bankers and the NRA simply aimed to resuscitate corporate profits without concern for the average working man. Coughlin called for a strong government to compel capital, labor, agriculture, professionals, and other interest groups to do its bidding. He founded the National Union of Social Justice (NUSJ) in 1934 as a precursor to a political party that would challenge the Democrats in 1936. Coughlin increasingly admired dictators such as Italy's Benito Mussolini who built their power and programs through decree rather than through democratic consent. If necessary, he admitted in 1936, he would "'dictate' to preserve democracy."

As Coughlin's disillusionment with the New Deal deepened, a strain of anti-Semitism became apparent in his radio talks, as in his accusation that Jewish bankers were masterminding a world conspiracy to dispossess the toiling masses. Although Coughlin was a compelling speaker, he failed to build the NUSJ into an effective political force. Its successor, the Union Party, attracted only a tiny percentage of voters in 1936. Embittered, Coughlin moved further to the political right. By 1939, his denunciations of democracy and Jews had become so extreme that some radio stations refused to carry his addresses. But millions of ordinary Americans continued to put their faith in the "radio priest."

Another popular figure was Francis E. Townsend, a California doctor who claimed that the way to end the depression was to give every senior citizen $200 per month

© UPI-Bettmann/Corbis.

with the stipulation that seniors would spend that money, thus putting more money in circulation and reviving economic demand. The Townsend Plan also made clear the need for some kind of pension program to ease the plight of the nation's elderly. While the Townsend movement did not last long, it did prod a nervous Roosevelt administration to make relief for the elderly—a program that Roosevelt would label Social Security—an important component of the New Deal.

Labor Protests

The attacks by Long, Coughlin, and Townsend on the New Deal deepened popular discontent and inspired other insurgent movements. The most important of them was the labor movement. Workers began joining unions in response to the National Industrial Recovery Act, and especially its Clause 7 (a), which granted workers the right to join labor unions of their own choosing, and obligated employers to recognize unions and bargain with them in good faith. Union members made quite modest demands at first: They wanted employers to observe the provisions of the NRA codes; they wanted to be treated fairly by their foremen; and they wanted employers to recognize and negotiate with their unions.

Few employers, however, were willing to grant their employees any say in their working conditions. Many ignored the NRA's wage and hour guidelines altogether and even used their influence over NRA code authorities to thwart worker requests for wage increases and union recognition. Workers flooded Washington with letters addressed to President Roosevelt, Labor Secretary Frances Perkins, and General Hugh Johnson, asking them to force employers to comply with the law. A Rhode Island textile worker who had been fired for joining a union asked why the NRA had neither responded to his complaint nor punished the company that had fired him. "If people can be arrested for violating certain laws," he wondered, "why can't this company?"

When their pleas went unanswered, workers began to take matters into their own hands. In 1934, they staged 2,000 strikes, some of which escalated into armed confrontations between workers and police. In Toledo, Ohio, in May, 10,000 workers surrounded the Electric Auto-Lite plant, declaring that they would block all exits and entrances until the

company agreed to shut down operations and negotiate a union contract. Two strikers were killed in an exchange of gunfire. In Minneapolis, unionized truck drivers and warehousemen fought police, private security forces, and the National Guard in a series of street battles from May through July that left four dead and hundreds wounded. In San Francisco in July, skirmishes between longshoremen and employers killed two and wounded scores of strikers. This violence provoked a general strike in San Francisco that shut down the city's transportation, construction, and service industries for two weeks. In September, 400,000 textile workers at mills from Maine to Alabama walked off their jobs. Attempts by employers to bring in replacement workers triggered violent confrontations that caused several deaths, hundreds of injuries, and millions of dollars in property damages.

Anger at the Polls

By late September, textile union leaders had lost their nerve and called off the strike, but workers took their anger to the polls. In Rhode Island, they broke the Republican Party's 30-year domination of state politics. In the South Carolina gubernatorial race, working-class voters rejected a conservative Democrat, Coleman Blease, and chose instead Olin T. Johnston, a former mill worker and an ardent New Dealer. In the country as a whole, Demo-

Detroit Industry, North Wall, 1932–1933. Diego Rivera. Gift of Edsel B. Ford. Photograph © 1991 The Detroit Institute of Arts.

MEN AT WORK

This picture depicts part of the mural that the Mexican artist Diego Rivera painted for the walls of the Detroit Art Museum in 1932–33. The mural conveys both the awesome size of Detroit's industrial plants and the centrality of workers to their operation. Rivera's work, like that of other 1930s artists, suggested that industrial workers stood at the very heart of American civilization and that they would play a key role in rehabilitating an economy devastated by depression.

crats won 70 percent of the contested seats in the Senate and House. The Democrats increased their majority, from 310 to 319 (out of 432) in the House, and from 60 to 69 (out of 96) in the Senate. No sitting president's party had ever done so well in an off-year election.

The victory was not an unqualified one for Roosevelt and the First New Deal, however. The 74th Congress would include the largest contingent of radicals ever sent to Washington: Tom Amlie of Wisconsin, Ernest Lundeen of Minnesota, Maury Maverick of Texas, Vito Marcantonio of New York, and some 30 others. Their support for the New Deal depended on whether Roosevelt delivered more relief, more income security, and more political power to farmers, workers, the unemployed, and the poor.

Radical Third Parties

Radical critics of the New Deal also made an impressive showing in state politics in 1934 and 1936. They were particularly strong in states gripped by labor unrest. In Wisconsin, for example, Philip La Follette, the son of Robert La Follette (see chapter 21), was elected governor in 1934 and 1936 as the candidate of the radical Wisconsin Progressive Party. In Minnesota, discontented agrarians and urban workers organized the Minnesota Farmer-Labor (MFL) Party and elected their candidate to the governorship in 1930, 1932, 1934, and 1936. In Washington, yet another radical third party, the Commonwealth Builders, elected both senators and almost half the state legislators in 1932 and 1934. And in California, the socialist and novelist Upton Sinclair and his organization, End Poverty in California (EPIC), came closer to winning the governorship than anyone had expected.

A widespread movement to form local labor parties offered further evidence of voter volatility, as did the growing appeal of the Communist Party. The American Communist Party (CP) had emerged in the early 1920s with the support of radicals who wanted to adopt the Soviet Union's path to socialism. The CP began to attract attention in the early 1930s, as its organizers spread out among the poorest and most vulnerable populations in America—homeless urban blacks in the North, black and white sharecroppers in the South, Chicano and Filipino agricultural workers in the West—and mobilized them in unions and unemployment leagues. CP members also played significant roles in strikes described earlier, and they were influential in the Minnesota Farmer-Labor Party and in Washington's Commonwealth Builders. Once they stopped preaching world revolution in 1935 and began calling instead for a "popular front" of democratic forces against fascism (a term used to describe the new kinds of dictatorships appearing in Hitler's Germany and Mussolini's Italy), their ranks grew even more. By 1938, approximately 80,000 Americans were thought to have been members of the Communist Party.

Although the Communist Party proclaimed its allegiance to democratic principles beginning in 1935, it nevertheless remained a dictatorial organization that took its orders from the Soviet Union. Many Americans feared the growing strength of the CP and began to call for its suppression. The CP, however, was never strong enough to gain power for itself. Its chief role in 1930s politics was to channel popular discontent into unions and political parties that would, in turn, force New Dealers to respond to the demands of the nation's dispossessed.

The Second New Deal, 1935–1937

The labor unrest of 1934 had taken Roosevelt by surprise. For a time, he kept his distance from the masses mobilizing in his name, but in spring 1935, with the 1936 presidential election looming, he decided to place himself at their head. He called for the "abolition of evil holding companies," attacked the wealthy for their profligate ways, and called for new programs to aid the poor and downtrodden. Rather than becoming a socialist, as his critics charged, Roosevelt sought to reinvigorate his appeal among poorer Americans and turn them away from radical solutions.

Philosophical Underpinnings

To point the New Deal in a more populist direction, Roosevelt turned increasingly to a relatively new economic theory, underconsumptionism. Advocates of this theory held that a chronic weakness in consumer demand had caused the Great Depression. The path to recovery lay, therefore, not in restricting production, as the architects of the First New Deal had tried to do, but in boosting consumer expenditures through government support for strong labor unions (to force up wages), higher social welfare expenditures (to put more money in the hands of the poor), and ambitious public works projects (to create hundreds of thousands of new jobs).

Underconsumptionists did not worry that new welfare and public works programs might strain the federal budget. If the government found itself short of revenue, it could always borrow additional funds from private sources. These reformers, in fact, viewed government borrowing as a crucial antidepression tool. Those who lent the government money would receive a return on their investment; those who received government assistance would have additional income to spend on consumer goods; and manufacturers would profit from increases in consumer spending. Government borrowing, in short, would stimulate the circulation of money through the economy and end the depression. This fiscal policy, a reversal of the conventional wisdom that government should always balance its budget, would in the 1940s come to be known as Keynesianism, after John Maynard Keynes, the British economist who had been its most forceful advocate.

Many politicians and economists rejected the notion that increased government spending and the deliberate buildup of federal deficits would lead to prosperity. Roosevelt was not easily convinced that he should put aside his concern for fiscal restraint and balanced budgets. But in 1935, as the nation entered its sixth year of the depression,

he was willing to give the new ideas a try. Reform-minded members of the 1934 Congress were eager for a new round of legislation directed more to the needs of ordinary Americans than to the needs of big business.

Legislation

Congress passed much of that legislation in January to June 1935—a period that came to be known as the Second New Deal. Two of the acts were of historic importance: the Social Security Act and the National Labor Relations Act. The Social Security Act, passed in May, required the states to set up welfare funds from which money would be disbursed to the elderly poor, the unemployed, unmarried mothers with dependent children, and the disabled. It also enrolled a majority of working Americans in a pension

HISTORY THROUGH FILM

Mr. Deeds Goes to Town (1936)

Mr. Deeds Goes to Town was one of several films made by Frank Capra, the most popular director of the 1930s, in which he charmed audiences with fables of simple, small-town heroes vanquishing the evil forces of wealth and decadence. The heroic ordinary American in *Mr. Deeds* is Longfellow Deeds from Mandrake Falls, Vermont, who goes to New York City to claim a fortune left to him by a deceased uncle. Deciding to give the fortune away, he becomes the laughingstock of slick city lawyers, hardboiled newspapermen and women, cynical literati, and self-styled aristocrats. He also becomes a hero to the unemployed and downtrodden to whom he wishes to give the money. By making the conflict between the wealthy and ordinary Americans central to this story, Capra illuminated convictions that were popular in 1930s politics, as expressed by the New Deal.

The movie delivers its serious message, however, in an entertaining and often hilarious style. Capra was a master

Directed by Frank Capra. Starring Gary Cooper (Longfellow Deeds), Jean Arthur (Babe Bennett), Lionel Stander (Cornelius Cobb), George Bancroft (McWade), and H. B. Warner (Judge Walker).

of what became known as "screwball" comedy. Longfellow Deeds slides down banisters, locks his bodyguards in a closet, uses the main hall of his inherited mansion as an echo chamber, punches a famous intellectual in the "kisser" (face), and turns his own trial for insanity into a delightful attack on the pretensions and peculiarities of corporate lawyers, judges, and psychiatrists. Central to the story, too, is an alternately amusing and serious love story between Deeds and a newspaperwoman, Babe Bennett (Jean Arthur). Bennett insinuates herself into Deeds's life by pretending to be a destitute woman without work, shelter, family, or friends. Deeds has long dreamed about rescuing a "lady in distress," and he falls for the beautiful Bennett. Bennett, in turn, uses her privileged access to Deeds to learn about his foibles and to mock them (and him) in newspaper stories written for a ruthless and scandal-hungry public. But Deeds's idealism, honesty, and virtue overwhelm Bennett's cynicism and cause her to fall in love

program that guaranteed them a steady income upon retirement. A federal system of employer and employee taxation was set up to fund the pensions. Despite limitations on coverage and inadequate pension levels, the Social Security Act of 1935 provided a sturdy foundation on which future presidents and congresses would erect the American welfare state.

Equally historic was the passage, in June, of the National Labor Relations Act (NLRA). This act delivered what the NRA had only promised: the right of every worker to join a union of his or her own choosing and the obligation of employers to bargain with that union in good faith. The NLRA, also called the Wagner Act after its Senate sponsor, Robert Wagner of New York, set up a National Labor Relations Board (NLRB) to supervise union elections and to investigate claims of unfair labor practices. The NLRB was to be staffed by federal appointees, who would have the power to impose fines on employers who violated the law. Union leaders hailed the act as their Magna Carta.

Congress also passed the Holding Company Act to break up the 13 utility companies that controlled 75 percent of the nation's electric power. It passed the Wealth Tax Act, which increased tax rates on the wealthy from 59 to 75 percent, and on corporations from 13.75 to 15 percent; and it passed the Banking Act, which strengthened the power of the Federal Reserve Board over its member banks. It created the Rural Electrification Administration (REA) to bring electric power to rural households. Finally, it passed the huge $5 billion Emergency Relief Appropriation Act. Roosevelt funneled part of this sum to the PWA and the CCC and used another part to create the National

with him. By movie's end, she has proclaimed her love and seems ready to return with Deeds to Mandrake Falls, where she will become his devoted wife and the nurturing mother of his children.

In Babe Bennett's conversion from tough reporter to female romantic, we can detect the gender conservatism of 1930s culture. The movie suggests that Bennett's early cruelty toward Deeds arose as a consequence of her inappropriate involvement in the rough, male realm of newspaper work. Only by abandoning this realm and returning to the "natural" female realm of hearth and home can she recover her true and soft womanly soul. Thus this movie is as rich a document for exploring attitudes toward male and female behavior as for examining relations between the rich and poor.

The Granger Collection

Gary Cooper as Longfellow Deeds (center of photo with hand on cheek) during his hilarious insanity trial. Cooper's bodyguard, Lionel Stander (Cobb) sits to the left of Cooper, and Cooper is looking at H. B. Warner (Judge Walker), who is presiding at the trial.

The Granger Collection.

WPA MURAL BY ANTON REFREGIER

The WPA funded a vast program of public art that employed thousands of artists and adorned public buildings with murals, paintings, and sculptures. This mural depicts an encounter between a Franciscan monk and Indians at a California mission during the era of Spanish rule.

SELECTED WPA PROJECTS IN NEW YORK CITY, 1938

Construction and Renovation	Education, Health, and Art	Research and Records
East River Drive	Adult education: homemaking, trade and technical skills, and art and culture	Sewage treatment, community health, labor relations, and employment trends surveys
Henry Hudson Parkway		
Bronx sewers	Children's education: remedial reading, lip reading, and field trips	Museum and library catalogs and exhibits
Glendale and Queens public libraries		Municipal office clerical support
King's County Hospital	Prisoners' vocational training, recreation, and nutrition	Government forms standardization
Williamsburg housing project	Dental clinics	
School buildings, prisons, and firehouses	Tuberculosis examination clinics	
Coney Island and Brighton Beach boardwalks	Syphilis and gonorrhea treatment clinics	
Orchard Beach	City hospital kitchen help, orderlies, laboratory technicians, nurses, doctors	
Swimming pools, playgrounds, parks, drinking fountains	Subsistence gardens	
	Sewing rooms	
	Central Park sculpture shop	

Source: John David Millet, *The Works Progress Administration in New York City* (Chicago: Public Administration Service, 1938), pp. 95–126.

Youth Administration (NYA), which provided work and guidance to the nation's youth.

Roosevelt directed most of the new relief money, however, to the Works Progress Administration (WPA) under the direction of Harry Hopkins, now known as the New Deal's "minister of relief." The WPA built or improved thousands of schools, playgrounds, airports, and hospitals. WPA crews raked leaves, cleaned streets, and landscaped cities. In the process, the WPA provided jobs to approximately 30 percent of the nation's jobless.

By the time the decade ended, the WPA, in association with an expanded Reconstruction Finance Corporation, the PWA, and other agencies, had built 500,000 miles of roads, 100,000 bridges, 100,000 public buildings, and 600 airports. The New Deal had transformed America's urban and rural landscapes. The awe generated by these public works projects helped Roosevelt retain popular support at a time when the success of the New Deal's economic policies was uncertain. The WPA also funded a vast program of public art, supporting the work of thousands of painters, architects, writers, playwrights, actors, and intellectuals. Beyond extending relief to struggling artists, it fostered the creation of art that spoke to the concerns of ordinary Americans, adorned public buildings with colorful murals, and boosted public morale.

Victory in 1936: The New Democratic Coalition

Roosevelt described his Second New Deal as a program to limit the power and privilege of the wealthy few and to increase the security and welfare of ordinary citizens. In his 1936 reelection campaign, he excoriated the corporations as "economic royalists" who had "concentrated into their own hands an almost complete control over other people's property, other people's money, other people's labor—other people's lives." He called on voters to strip the corporations of their power and "save a great and precious form of government for ourselves and the world." American voters responded by handing Roosevelt the greatest landslide victory in the history of American politics. He received 61 percent of the popular vote; Alf Landon of Kansas, his Republican opponent, received only 37 per-

cent. Only two states, Maine and Vermont, representing a mere eight electoral votes, went for Landon.

The 1936 election won the Democratic Party its reputation as the party of reform and the party of the "forgotten American." Of the 6 million Americans who went

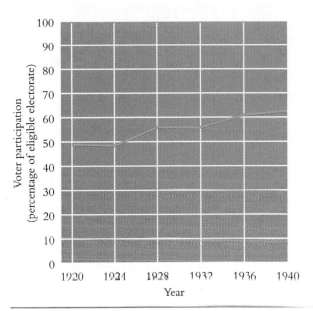

VOTER PARTICIPATION IN PRESIDENTIAL ELECTIONS, 1920–1940

Source: Data from *Historical Statistics of the United States, Colonial Times to 1970* (White Plains, N.Y.: Kraus International, 1989), p. 1071.

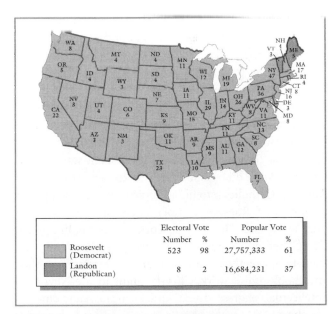

MAP 25.5 PRESIDENTIAL ELECTION, 1936

In 1936, Franklin D. Roosevelt's reelection numbers were overwhelming: 98 percent of the electoral vote, and more than 60 percent of the popular vote. No previous election in American history had been so one-sided.

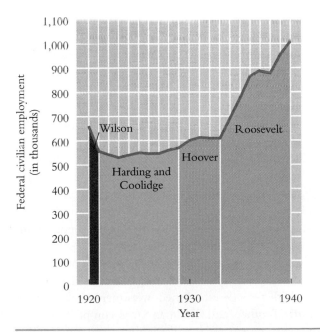

GROWTH IN FEDERAL CIVILIAN EMPLOYMENT, 1920–1940

Source: Data from *Historical Statistics of the United States, Colonial Times to 1970* (White Plains, N.Y.: Kraus International, 1989), p. 1102.

to the polls for the first time, many of them European ethnics, 5 million voted for Roosevelt. Among the poorest Americans, Roosevelt received 80 percent of the vote. Black voters in the North deserted the Republican Party—the "Party of Lincoln"—calculating that their interests would best be served by the "Party of the Common Man." Roosevelt also did well among white middle-class voters, many of whom stood to benefit from the Social Security Act. These constituencies would constitute the "Roosevelt coalition" for most of the next 40 years, helping to solidify the Democratic Party as the new majority party in American politics.

Rhetoric Versus Reality

Roosevelt's 1935–36 anticorporate rhetoric was more radical than the laws he supported. The Wealth Tax Act took considerably less out of wealthy incomes and estates than was advertised, and the utility companies that the Holding Company Act should have broken up remained largely intact. Moreover, Roosevelt promised more than he delivered to the nation's poor. Farm workers, for example, were not covered by the Social Security Act or by the National Labor Relations Act. Consequently, thousands of African American sharecroppers in the South, along with substantial numbers of Mexican American farm workers in the Southwest, missed out on their protections and benefits. The sharecroppers were shut out because southern Democrats would not have voted for an act that was meant to improve the economic or social condition of southern blacks. For the same reason, the New Deal made little effort to restore voting rights to southern blacks or to protect their basic civil rights. White supremacy lived on in New Deal democracy.

Roosevelt's 1935–36 populist stance also obscured the enthusiastic support that some capitalists were according the Second New Deal. In the West, Henry J. Kaiser headed a consortium of six companies that built the Hoover, Bonneville, and Grand Coulee dams; and in Texas, building contractors Herman and George Brown were bankrolling a group of elected officials that included a young Democratic congressman named Lyndon Johnson. In the Midwest and the East, Roosevelt's corporate supporters included real estate developers, mass merchandisers (such as Bambergers and Sears, Roebuck), clothing manufacturers, and the like. These firms, in turn, had financial connections with recently established investment banks such as Lehman Brothers and Goldman Sachs, competitors of the House of Morgan and its allies in the Republican banking establishment, and with consumer-oriented banks such as the Bank of America and the Bowery Savings Bank. They

tolerated strong labor unions, welfare programs, and high levels of government spending in the belief that these developments would strengthen consumer spending. But they had no intention of surrendering their wealth or power. The Democratic Party had become, in effect, the party of the masses and one section of big business. The conflicting interests of these two constituencies would create tensions within the Democratic Party throughout all of the years of its political domination.

Men, Women, and Reform

The academics, policy makers, and bureaucrats who designed and administered the rapidly growing roster of New Deal programs and agencies found 1936 and 1937 exciting years. Fired by idealism and dedication, they were confident they could make the New Deal work. They planned and won congressional approval for the Farm Security Administration (FSA), an agency designed to improve the economic lot of tenant farmers, sharecroppers, and farm laborers. They drafted and passed laws that outlawed child labor, set minimum wages and maximum hours for adult workers, and committed the federal government to building low-cost housing. They investigated and tried to regulate concentrations of corporate power.

Although they worked on behalf of "the people," the New Dealers constituted a new class of technocrats. The prospect of building a strong state committed to prosperity and justice fired their imaginations. They delighted in the intellectual challenge and the technical complexity of social policy. They did not welcome interference from those they regarded as less intelligent or motivated by outworn ideologies.

This was particularly true of the men. Many had earned advanced degrees in law and economics at elite universities such as Harvard, Columbia, and Wisconsin. Not all had been raised among wealth and privilege, however, as was generally the case with earlier generations of reformers. To his credit, Franklin Roosevelt was the first president since his cousin Theodore Roosevelt to welcome Jews and Catholics into his administration. Some became members of Roosevelt's inner circle of advisers—men such as Thomas "Tommy the Cork" Corcoran, Jim Farley, Ben Cohen, and Samuel Rosenman. These men had struggled to make their way, first on the streets and then in school and at work. They brought to the New Deal intellectual aggressiveness, quick minds, and mental toughness.

The profile of New Deal women was different. Although a few, notably Eleanor Roosevelt and Secretary of Labor Frances Perkins, were more visible than women in

RATES OF UNEMPLOYMENT IN SELECTED MALE AND FEMALE OCCUPATIONS, 1930		
Male Occupations	Percentage Male	Percentage Unemployed
Iron and steel	96%	13%
Forestry and fishing	99	10
Mining	99	18
Heavy manufacturing	86	13
Carpentry	100	19
Laborers (road and street)	100	13
Female Occupations	Percentage Female	Percentage Unemployed
Stenographers and typists	96%	5%
Laundresses	99	3
Trained nurses	98	4
Housekeepers	92	3
Telephone operators	95	3
Dressmakers	100	4

Source: U.S. Department of Commerce, Bureau of the Census, *Fifteenth Census of the United States, 1930, Population* (Washington, D.C.: Government Printing Office, 1931).

previous administrations had been, many of the female New Dealers worked in relative obscurity, in agencies such as the Women's Bureau or the Children's Bureau (both in the Department of Labor). Women who worked on major legislation, as did Mary Van Kleeck on the Social Security Act, or who directed major programs, as did Jane Hoey, chief of the Social Security's Bureau of Public Assistance, received less credit than men in comparable positions. Moreover, female New Dealers tended to be a generation older than their male colleagues and were more likely to be Protestant than Catholic or Jewish. Many of them had known each other since the days of Progressive-era reform and woman suffrage (see chapter 21).

The New Deal offered these female reformers little opportunity to advance the cause of women's equality. Demands for greater economic opportunity, sexual freedom, and full equality for women and men were put forward less often in the 1930s than they had been in the preceding two decades. One reason was that the women's movement had lost momentum after achieving the vote in 1920 (see chapter 24). Another was that prominent New Deal women, rather than vigorously pursuing a campaign for equal rights, chose to concentrate instead on "protective legislation"—laws that safeguarded female workers, whom they considered more fragile than men. Those who insisted that women needed special protections could not easily argue that women were the equal of men in all respects.

Even so, feminism was hemmed in on all sides by a male hostility that the depression had only intensified. Many American men had built their male identities on the

value of hard work and the ability to provide economic security for their families. For them, the loss of work unleashed feelings of inadequacy. Male vulnerability increased as unemployment rates of men—most of whom labored in blue-collar industries—tended to rise higher than those of women, many of whom worked in white-collar occupations less affected by job cutbacks. Many fathers and husbands resented wives and daughters who had taken over their breadwinning roles.

This male anxiety had political and social consequences. Several states passed laws outlawing the hiring of married women. New Deal relief agencies were reluctant to authorize aid for unemployed women. The labor movement made protection of the male wage earner one of its principal goals. The Social Security pension system left out waitresses, domestic servants, and other largely female occupations. Some commentators even proposed ludicrous gender remedies to the problem of unemployment. Norman Cousins of the *Saturday Evening Post*, for example, suggested that the depression could be ended simply by firing 10 million working women and giving their jobs to men. "Presto!" he declared. "No unemployment, no relief rolls. No Depression."

AP/Wide World Photos.

AN ACTIVIST FIRST LADY

No woman was more prominent in the 1930s than Eleanor Roosevelt. During the decade, she met with many different groups of Americans, including the miners depicted in this photo, seeking to learn more about their condition and the ways in which the New Deal could assist them.

Michael Barson Collection/Past Perfect.

MAN OF STEEL

The comic book *Superman* debuted in 1938, with the cover that appears in this reproduction. The character Superman partook of the New Deal's commitment to help ordinary Americans in need while offering men a fantasy about unconquerable male power.

Many artists introduced a strident masculinism into their painting and sculpture. Mighty *Superman,* the new comic-strip hero of 1938, reflected the spirit of the times. Superman was depicted as a working-class hero who, on several occasions, saved workers from coal mine explosions and other disasters caused by the greed and negligence of villainous employers.

Superman's greatest vulnerability, however, other than kryptonite, was his attraction to the sexy and aggressive *working* woman, Lois Lane. He could never resolve his dilemma by marrying Lois and tucking her away in a safe domestic sphere, because the continuation of the comic strip demanded that Superman be repeatedly exposed to kryptonite and female danger. But the producers of male and female images in other mass media, such as the movies, faced no such technical obstacles. Anxious men could take comfort from the conclusion of the movie *Woman of the Year,* in which Spencer Tracy persuades the

ambitious Katharine Hepburn to exchange her successful newspaper career for the bliss of motherhood and homemaking. From a thousand different points, 1930s politics and culture made it clear that a woman's proper place was in the home. Faced with such obstacles, it is not surprising that women activists failed to make feminism a major part of New Deal reform.

Labor in Politics and Culture

In 1935, John L. Lewis of the United Mine Workers, Sidney Hillman of the Amalgamated Clothing Workers, and the leaders of six other unions that had seceded from the American Federation of Labor (AFL) cobbled together a new labor organization: The Committee for Industrial Organization (CIO—later renamed the Congress of Industrial Organizations) aspired to organize millions of nonunion workers into unions that would strengthen labor's influence in politics. In 1936, Lewis and Hillman created a second organization, Labor's Non-Partisan League (LNPL), to develop a labor strategy for the 1936 elections. Although professing the league's nonpartisanship, Lewis intended from the start that the LNPL's role would be to channel labor's money, energy, and talent into Roosevelt's reelection campaign. Roosevelt welcomed the league's help, and labor would become one of the most important constituencies of the new Democratic coalition. The passage of the Wagner Act and the creation of the NLRB in 1935 enhanced the labor movement's status

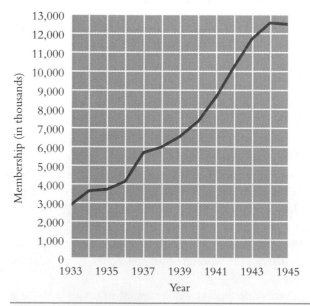

LABOR UNION MEMBERSHIP, 1933–1945

Source: From Christopher Tomlins, "AFL Unions in the 1930s," in Melvyn Dubofsky and Stephen Burwood, eds., *Labor* (New York: Garland, 1990), p. 1023.

and credibility. Membership in labor unions climbed steadily, and in short order, union members began flexing their new muscles.

In late 1936, the United Auto Workers (UAW) took on General Motors, widely regarded as the most powerful corporation in the world. Workers occupied key GM factories in Flint, Michigan, declaring that their sit-down strike would continue until GM agreed to recognize the UAW and negotiate a collective bargaining agreement. Frank Murphy, the pro-labor governor of Michigan, refused to use National Guard troops to evict the strikers, and Roosevelt declined to send federal troops. The 50-year-old practice of using soldiers to break strikes came to an end, and General Motors capitulated after a month of resistance. Soon, the U.S. Steel Corporation, which had defeated unionists in the bloody strike of 1919 (see chapter 23), announced that it was ready to negotiate a contract with the newly formed CIO steelworkers union.

The labor movement's public stature grew along with its size. Many writers and artists, funded through the WPA, depicted the labor movement as the voice of the people and the embodiment of the nation's values. Murals sprang up in post offices and other public buildings featuring portraits of blue-collar Americans at work. Broadway's most celebrated play in 1935 was Clifford Odets's *Waiting for Lefty,* a raw drama about taxi drivers who confront their bosses and organize an honest union. Audiences were so moved by the play that they often spontaneously joined in the final chorus of "Strike, Strike, Strike," the words that ended the play. *Pins and Needles,* a 1937 musical about the hopes and dreams of garment workers, performed by actual members of the International Ladies Garment Workers Union, became the longest-running play in Broadway history (until *Oklahoma!* broke its record of 1,108 performances in 1943).

Similarly, many of the most popular novels and movies of the 1930s celebrated the decency, honesty, and patriotism of ordinary Americans. In *Mr. Deeds Goes to Town* (1936) and *Mr. Smith Goes to Washington* (1939), Frank Capra delighted movie audiences with fables of simple, small-town heroes vanquishing the evil forces of wealth and decadence. Likewise, in *The Grapes of Wrath,* the best-selling novel of 1939, John Steinbeck told an epic tale of an Oklahoma family's fortitude in surviving eviction from their land, migrating westward, and suffering exploitation in the "promised land" of California. In 1940, John Ford turned Steinbeck's novel into one of that year's highest-grossing and most acclaimed movies. Moviegoers found special meaning in the declaration of one of the story's main characters, Ma Joad: "We'll go on forever . . . 'cause we're the people." In themselves and in one another, Americans seemed to discover the resolve they needed to rebuild a culture that had surrendered its identity to corporations and business.

John Steinbeck wrote about the Okie migrants to California as an outsider. But the Okies produced a writer and musician of their own who became, in the late 1930s, a popular folk singer. Born in 1913 in Okemah, Oklahoma, Woody Guthrie grew up in nearby Pampa, Texas. He wasn't born poor—his father was a small businessman and a local politician—but by the time he reached his 20s, Guthrie had known a great deal of hardship: his father's business failed, three family homes burned down, one sister died from burns, and then the drought and dust storms struck. In the 1930s, Guthrie joined the large migration of Okies to California. There, his musical gifts were discovered, chiefly because radio stations, in particular, were keen to put "singing cowboys" on the air. Guthrie had emerged from a country music tradition in Texas and Oklahoma and found an immediate audience among the many people from those states who had gone to California. But Guthrie quickly developed a far broader appeal as he cast himself as the bard of ordinary Americans everywhere. He loved America for the beauty of its landscape and its people, sentiments he expressed in one of his most

From the Collections of the Library of Congress

WOODY GUTHRIE

A bard from Okemah, Oklahoma, embraced by millions for his homespun melodies and lyrics and for his hopeful message that Americans could survive the Depression with their dignity and sense of humor intact.

popular songs, "This Land Is Your Land," which he wrote in 1940 in response to Irving Berlin's "God Bless America" (a song Guthrie did not like because he thought it comforted people with a false sense of complacency). Guthrie did not possess a refined singing voice, but his "hillbilly" lyrics, melodies, and humor were inventive and often inspiring. He would become a powerful influence on subsequent generations of musicians, including such major figures as Bob Dylan and Bruce Springsteen.

Most comfortable on the road and away from his family, Guthrie traveled ceaselessly in the 1930s, from Los Angeles to New York and from Texas to Washington state. The more he learned about the hardships of individual Americans, the angrier and more politically active he became. He drew close to the labor movement and to the Communist Party, and increasingly, in his writings and songs, he criticized the industrialists, financiers, and their political agents who, he believed, had brought the calamity of the Depression on America. But Guthrie always associated his criticism with the hope that the working people of America, if united, could take back their land—which is the message he meant to convey when he sang "This Land Is Your Land"—and restore its greatness. The optimism of his message underscored how much the cultural mood had changed since the early 1930s. In his focus on ordinary working Americans, in his hope for the future, and in his fusion of dissent and patriotism, Guthrie was emblematic of the dominant stream of culture and politics in the late 1930s.

America's Minorities and the New Deal

1930s reformers generally believed that issues of capitalism's viability, economic recovery, and the inequality of wealth and power outweighed problems of racial and ethnic discrimination; only in the case of American Indians did New Dealers pass legislation specifically designed to improve a minority's social and economic position. Because they were disproportionately poor, most minority groups did profit from the populist and pro-labor character of New Deal reforms, but the gains were distributed unevenly. Eastern and Southern European ethnics benefited the most, and African Americans and Mexican Americans advanced the least.

Eastern and Southern European Ethnics

Eastern and Southern European immigrants and their children had begun mobilizing politically in the 1920s in response to religious and racial discrimination (see chap-

ter 24). Roosevelt understood their political importance well, for he was a product of New York Democratic politics, where men such as Robert Wagner and Al Smith had begun to organize the "ethnic vote" even before 1920 (see chapter 21). He made sure that a significant portion of New Deal monies for welfare, building and road construction, and unemployment relief reached the urban areas where most European ethnics lived. As a result, Jewish and Catholic Americans, especially those descended from Eastern and Southern European immigrants, voted for Roosevelt in overwhelming numbers. The New Deal did not eliminate anti-Semitism and anti-Catholicism from American society, but it did allow millions of European ethnics to believe, for the first time, that they would overcome the second-class status they had long endured.

Eastern and Southern European ethnics also benefited from their strong working-class presence. Forming one of the largest groups in the mass-production industries of the Northeast, Midwest, and West, they formed a large part of the labor movement's new membership. Roosevelt accommodated himself to their wishes because he understood and feared the power they wielded through their labor organizations.

African Americans

The New Deal did more to reproduce patterns of racial discrimination than to advance the cause of racial equality. African Americans who belonged to CIO unions or who lived in northern cities benefited from New Deal programs, but most blacks lived in the rural South, where they were barred from voting, largely excluded from AAA programs, and denied federal protection in their efforts to form agricultural unions. The CCC ran separate camps for black and white youth. The TVA hired few blacks. Those enrolled in the CWA and other work-relief programs frequently received less pay than whites for doing the same jobs. Roosevelt consistently refused to support legislation to make lynching a federal crime.

This failure to push a strong civil-rights agenda did not mean that New Dealers were racist. Eleanor Roosevelt spoke out frequently against racial injustice. In 1939, she resigned from the Daughters of the American Revolution when the organization refused to allow black opera singer Marian Anderson to perform in its concert hall. She then pressured the federal government into granting Anderson permission to sing from the steps of the Lincoln Memorial. On Easter Sunday, 75,000 people gathered to hear Anderson and to demonstrate their support for racial equality. The president did not attend.

Roosevelt did eliminate segregationist practices in the federal government that had been in place since Woodrow

Wilson's presidency. He appointed Mary McLeod Bethune, Robert Weaver, William Hastie, and other African Americans to important second-level posts in his administration. Working closely with each other in what came to be known as the Black Cabinet, these officials fought hard to end discrimination in New Deal programs.

Roosevelt, however, refused to support the Black Cabinet if it meant alienating white southern senators who controlled key congressional committees. He believed that pushing for civil rights would cost him the support of the white South. Meanwhile, African Americans and their supporters were not yet strong enough as an electoral constituency or as a reform movement to force Roosevelt to accede to their wishes.

Mexican Americans

The Mexican American experience in the Great Depression was particularly harsh. In 1931, Hoover's secretary of labor, William N. Doak, announced a plan for repatriating illegal aliens (returning them to their land of origin) and giving their jobs to American citizens. The federal campaign quickly focused on Mexican immigrants in California and the Southwest. The U.S. Immigration Service staged a

---

MUSICAL LINK TO THE PAST

An African American Rhapsody

Songwriter: Duke Ellington

Title: "Creole Rhapsody Parts One and Two" (1931—the second recording)

Performers: Duke Ellington and His Orchestra

By 1931, Duke Ellington had established himself as the premier African American bandleader, his hit songs airing nightly courtesy of a live national radio hook-up (the first for any black act) emanating from Harlem's Cotton Club. But Ellington was not satisfied with popularity and fame. "I have always been a firm believer in musical experimentation," he proclaimed during this period. "To stand still musically is equivalent to losing ground." Ellington wished to be viewed as a serious artist and composer, and "Creole Rhapsody" represented one of his first major bids to cultivate this image. Most pop records seldom broke the three-minute barrier, but "Creole" lasted nine minutes, spanning two sides of a 78-RPM record. While jazz and blues artists generally composed within 8-, 12-, and 16-bar forms, Ellington experimented with different phrase lengths. In an era when blacks were primarily associated with "torrid" dance records, the shifting tempos of "Creole" marked it as a record for concentrated listening. Ellington also composed the solos to ensure that they jelled with his elaborate arrangement, which did away with musical improvisation, a trademark of jazz and blues performances. Ellington was more involved with recording technique than most artists, sometimes placing microphones far away from his players to achieve a more evocative sound.

"Creole Rhapsody" reached only minor hit status, but Ellington and his manager Irving Mills took advantage of the event of this unprecedented recording to bolster Ellington's image as a serious artist, a status that no other African Americans of his period had achieved in the segregated white-dominated popular music marketplace. In contrast to the denigrating stereotypes that accompanied the appearance of most blacks in the mass media, Ellington was respectfully portrayed in the manner of a classical conductor, usually clad in a tuxedo and tails, baton in his hand.

Not all contemporary observers endorsed the idea of Ellington as a major composer. The English critic Constant Lambert wrote in 1934 that "Ellington is definitely a *petit maitre*," a "small master" not capable of extended composition. Many music lovers, however, embraced "Creole Rhapsody." The New York School of Music named it the best composition of the year because "it portrayed Negro life as no other piece had." Ellington attempted to keep the critics, both the laudatory and castigating ones, at a distance and to keep searching for musical innovation. He almost never took a formal political stand or made a speech demanding civil rights for blacks during the 1930s, choosing to let his music and his reputation as an innovative band leader speak for themselves.

1. From listening to "Creole Rhapsody," can you discern what the New York School of Music meant in celebrating this composition as a unique portrait of Negro life?

Listen to an audio recording of this music on the Musical Links to the Past CD.

series of highly publicized raids, rounded up large numbers of Mexicans and Mexican Americans, and demanded that each detainee prove his or her legal status. Those who failed to produce the necessary documentation were deported. Local and state governments pressured many more Mexicans into leaving. The combined efforts of federal, state, and local governments created a climate of fear in Mexican communities that prompted 500,000 to return to Mexico by 1935. This total equaled the number of Mexicans who had come to the United States in the 1920s. Los Angeles lost one-third of its Mexican population. Included in repatriate ranks were a significant number of legal immigrants who were unable to produce their immigration papers, the American-born children of illegals, and some Mexican Americans who had lived in the Southwest for generations.

The advent of the New Deal in 1933 eased but did not eliminate pressure on Chicano communities. New Deal agencies made more money available for relief, thereby lightening the burden on state and local governments. But federal laws, more often than not, failed to dissuade local officials from continuing their campaign against Mexican immigrants. Where Mexicans gained access to relief rolls, they received payments lower than those given to "Anglos" (whites) or were compelled to accept tough agricultural jobs that paid less than living wages.

Life grew harder for immigrant Mexicans who stayed behind. The Mexican cultural renaissance that had arisen in 1920s Los Angeles (see chapter 24) stalled. Hounded by government officials, Mexicans everywhere sought to escape public attention and scrutiny. In Los Angeles, where their influence had been felt throughout the city in the 1920s, they retreated into the separate community of East Los Angeles. To many, they became the "invisible minority." Mexicans and Mexican Americans who lived in urban areas and worked in blue-collar industries, however, did benefit from New Deal programs. In Los Angeles, for example, Chicanos employed in canneries, in garment and furniture shops, and on the docks responded to the New Deal's pro-labor legislation by joining unions in large numbers and winning concessions from their employers. Most Chicanos, however, lived in rural areas and labored in agricultural jobs, and the New Deal offered them little help. The National Labor Relations Act did not protect their right to organize unions, and the Social Security Act excluded them from the new federal welfare system.

American Indians

From the 1880s until the early 1930s, federal policy had contributed to the elimination of American Indians as a distinctive population. The Dawes Act of 1887 (see chap-

INDIAN CHILDREN

An Arnold Rothstein photograph depicting three Indian children on the Mescalero Reservation in New Mexico in 1936.

From the Collections of the Library of Congress.

ter 19) had called for tribal lands to be broken up and allotted to individual owners in the hope that Indians would adopt the work habits of white farmers. But American Indians had proved stubbornly loyal to their languages, religions, and cultures. Few of them succeeded as farmers, and many lost land to white speculators. By 1933, nearly half the American Indians living on reservations whose land had been allotted were landless, and many who retained allotments held land that was largely desert or semidesert.

The shrinking land base in combination with a growing population deepened American Indian poverty. The assimilationist pressures on American Indians, meanwhile, reached a climax in the intolerant 1920s when the Bureau of Indian Affairs (BIA) outlawed Indian religious ceremonies, forced children from tribal communities into federal boarding schools, banned polygamy, and imposed limits on the length of men's hair.

Government officials working in the Hoover administration began to question this draconian policy, but its reversal had to await the New Deal and Roosevelt's appointment of John Collier as the commissioner of the BIA. Collier pressured the CCC, AAA, and other New Deal agencies to employ Indians on projects that improved reservation land and trained Indians in land conservation methods. He prevailed on Congress to pass the Pueblo Relief Act of 1933, which compensated Pueblos for land taken from them in the 1920s, and the Johnson-O'Malley Act of 1934, which funded states to provide for Indian health care, welfare, and education. As part of his campaign to make the BIA more responsive to American Indian needs, Collier increased the number of Indian employees of the BIA from a paltry few hundred in 1933 to a respectable 4,600 in 1940.

Collier also took steps to abolish federal boarding schools, encourage enrollment in local public schools, and establish community day schools. He insisted that American Indians be allowed to practice their traditional religions, and he created the Indian Arts and Crafts Board in 1935 to nurture traditional Indian artists and to help them market their works.

The centerpiece of Collier's reform strategy was the Indian Reorganization Act (also known as the Wheeler-Howard Act) of 1934, which revoked the allotment provisions of the Dawes Act. The IRA restored land to tribes, granted Indians the right to establish constitutions and bylaws for self-government, and provided support for new tribal corporations that would regulate the use of communal lands. This landmark act signaled the government's recognition that American Indian tribes possessed the right to chart their own political, cultural, and economic futures. It reflected Collier's commitment to "cultural pluralism," a doctrine that celebrated the diversity of peoples and cultures in American society and sought to protect that diversity against the pressures of assimilation. Collier hoped that the IRA would invigorate traditional Indian cultures and tribal societies and sustain both for generations. Cultural pluralism was not a popular creed in America during the depression years, which makes its acceptance as the rationale for the IRA all the more remarkable.

Collier encountered opposition everywhere: from Protestant missionaries and cultural conservatives who wanted to continue an assimilationist policy; from white farmers and businessmen who feared that the new legislation would restrict their access to Native American land; and even from a sizable number of Indian groups, some of which had embraced assimilation and others that viewed the IRA cynically, as one more attempt by the federal government to impose "the white man's will" on the Indian peoples. This opposition made the IRA a more modest bill than the one Collier had originally championed.

A vocal minority of Indians continued to oppose the act even after its passage. The Navajo, the nation's largest tribe, voted to reject its terms along with 76 other tribes. Still, 181 tribes, nearly 70 percent of the total, supported Collier's reform and began organizing new governments under the IRA. Although their quest for independence would suffer setbacks, as Congress and the BIA continued to interfere with their economic and political affairs, these tribes gained significant measures of freedom and autonomy during the New Deal.

The New Deal Abroad

When he first entered office, Roosevelt seemed to favor a nationalist approach to international relations. The United States, he believed, should pursue foreign policies to benefit its domestic affairs, without regard for the effects of those policies on world trade and international stability. Thus, in June 1933, Roosevelt abruptly pulled the United States out of the World Economic Conference in London, a meeting called by leading nations to strengthen the gold standard and thereby stabilize the value of their currencies. Roosevelt feared that the United States would be forced into an agreement designed to keep the gold content of the dollar high and U.S. commodity prices low, which would frustrate New Deal efforts to inflate the prices of agricultural and industrial goods.

Soon after his withdrawal from the London conference, however, Roosevelt put the United States on a more internationalist course. In November 1933, he became the first president to recognize the Soviet Union and to establish diplomatic ties with its Communist rulers. In December 1933, he inaugurated a Good Neighbor Policy toward Latin America by formally renouncing U.S. rights to intervene in the affairs of Latin American nations. To back up his pledge, Roosevelt ordered home the Marines stationed in Haiti and Nicaragua, scuttled the Platt Amendment that had given the United States control over the Cuban government since 1901, and granted Panama more political autonomy and a greater administrative role in operating the Panama Canal (see chapter 22).

None of this, however, meant that the United States had given up its influence over Latin America. When a 1934 revolution brought a radical government to power in Cuba, the United States ambassador there worked with conservative Cubans to replace it with a regime more favorable to U.S. interests. The United States did refrain from sending troops to Cuba. It also kept its troops at home in 1936 when a radical government in Mexico nationalized several U.S.-owned and British-owned petroleum companies. The United States merely demanded that the new Mexican government compensate the oil companies for their lost property—a demand that Mexico eventually met. Although the United States was still the dominant power in hemispheric affairs, its newfound restraint inspired Latin American hopes that a new era had dawned.

The Roosevelt administration's recognition of the Soviet Union and embrace of the Good Neighbor Policy can be seen as an international expression of the liberal principles that guided its domestic policies. These diplomatic initiatives, however, also reflected Roosevelt's interest in stimulating international trade. American businessmen wanted access to the Soviet Union's domestic market.

Latin America was already a major market for the United States, but one in need of greater stability. To win the support of American traders and investors, Roosevelt stressed how the Good Neighbor Policy would improve the region's business climate.

Roosevelt further expressed his interest in building international trade through his support for the Reciprocal Trade Agreement, passed by Congress in 1934. This act allowed his administration to lower U.S. tariffs by as much as 50 percent in exchange for similar reductions by other nations. By the end of 1935, the United States had negotiated reciprocal trade agreements with 14 countries. Roosevelt's emphasis on international trade—a move consonant with the Second New Deal's program of increasing the circulation of goods and money through the economy—further solidified support for the New Deal in parts of the business community, especially among those firms, such as United Fruit and Coca-Cola, with large overseas investments.

Actually increasing the volume of international trade was more difficult than passing legislation to encourage it. In Germany and Italy, belligerent nationalists Adolf Hitler and Benito Mussolini told their people that the solution to their ills lay not in foreign trade but in military strength and conquest. Throughout the world, similar appeals to national pride proved more popular than calls for tariff reductions and international trade. In the face of this historical current, the New Deal's internationalist economic policies made little headway.

Stalemate, 1937–1940

By 1937 and 1938, the New Deal had begun to lose momentum. One reason was an emerging split between working-class and middle-class Democrats. After the UAW's victory over General Motors in 1937, other workers began to imitate the successful tactics of the Flint, Michigan, militants. Sit-down strikes spread to many industries and regions, a development that many middle-class Americans found disturbing.

The Court-Packing Fiasco

The president's proposal on February 5, 1937, to alter the makeup of the Supreme Court exacerbated middle-class fears. Roosevelt asked Congress to give him the power to appoint one new Supreme Court justice for every member

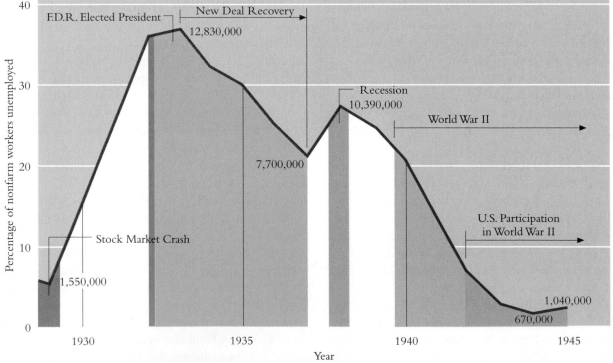

Unemployment, 1920–1945

UNEMPLOYMENT IN THE NONFARM LABOR FORCE, 1929–1945

Source: Data from *Historical Statistics of the United States, Colonial Times to 1970* (White Plains, N.Y.: Kraus International, 1989), p. 126.

of the court who was older than age 70 and who had served for at least 10 years. His stated reason was that the current justices were too old and feeble to handle the large volume of cases coming before them. But his real purpose was to prevent the conservative justices on the court—most of whom had been appointed by Republican presidents—from dismantling his New Deal. His proposal, if accepted, would have given him the authority to appoint six additional justices, thereby securing a pro–New Deal majority.

The president seemed genuinely surprised by the storm of indignation that greeted his "court-packing" proposal. Roosevelt's political acumen had apparently been dulled by his 1936 victory. His inflated sense of power infuriated many who had previously been New Deal enthusiasts. Although working-class support for Roosevelt remained strong, many middle-class voters turned away from the New Deal. In 1937 and 1938, a conservative opposition took shape, uniting Republicans, conservative Democrats (many of them southerners), and civil libertarians who were determined to protect private property and government integrity.

Ironically, Roosevelt's court-packing scheme may have been unnecessary. In March 1937, just one month after he proposed his plan, Supreme Court Justice Owen J. Roberts, a former opponent of New Deal programs, decided to support them. In April and May, the Court upheld the constitutionality of the Wagner Act and Social Security Act, both by a 5-to-4 margin. The principal reforms of the New Deal would endure. Roosevelt allowed his court-reform proposal to die in Congress that summer. Within three years, five of the aging justices had retired, giving Roosevelt the opportunity to fashion a court more to his liking. Nonetheless, Roosevelt's reputation had suffered.

The Recession of 1937–1938

Whatever hope Roosevelt may have had for a quick recovery from the court-packing fiasco was dashed by a sharp recession that struck the country in late 1937 and 1938. The New Deal programs of 1935 had stimulated the economy, prompting Roosevelt to scale back relief programs. Meanwhile, new payroll taxes took $2 billion from wage earners' salaries to finance the Social Security pension fund even though the government did not intend to begin paying benefits until 1941. Thus, the government substantially shrunk the volume of dollars it was putting into circulation. Starved for money, the economy and stock market crashed once again. Unemployment, which had fallen to 14 percent, shot back up to 20 percent. In the 1938 elections, voters vented their frustration by electing many

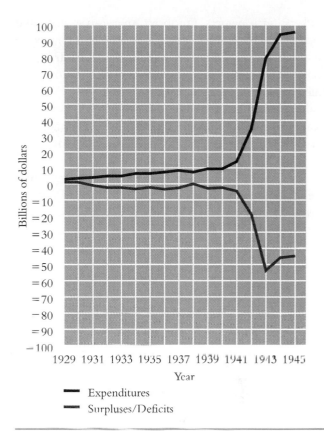

FEDERAL EXPENDITURES AND SURPLUSES/DEFICITS, 1929–1945

Source: Data from *Historical Statistics of the United States, Colonial Times to 1970* (White Plains, N.Y.: Kraus International, 1989), p. 1105.

conservative Democrats and Republicans who were opposed to the New Deal. These conservatives could not dismantle the New Deal reforms already in place, but they did block the passage of new programs.

Conclusion

Roosevelt first assumed the presidency in the same week that Adolf Hitler established a Nazi dictatorship in Germany. Some feared that Roosevelt, by accumulating more power into the hands of the federal government than had ever been held in peacetime, aspired to autocratic rule. Nothing of the sort happened. Roosevelt and the New Dealers not only strengthened democracy, they also inspired millions of Americans who had never before voted to go to the polls. Groups that had been marginalized—Eastern and Southern European ethnics, unskilled workers, American Indians—now believed that their political activism could make a difference.

Not everyone benefited to the same degree from the broadening of American democracy. Northern factory workers, farm owners, European American ethnics, and middle-class consumers (especially homeowners) were among the groups who benefited most. In contrast, the socialist and communist elements of the labor movement failed to achieve their radical demands. Southern industrial workers, black and white, benefited little from New Deal reforms; so did farm laborers. Feminists made no headway. African Americans and Mexican Americans gained meager influence over public policy.

Of course, New Deal reforms might not have mattered to any group if the Second World War had not rescued the New Deal economic program. With government war orders flooding factories from 1941 on, the economy grew vigorously, unemployment vanished, and prosperity finally returned. The architects of the Second New Deal,

who had argued that large government expenditures would stimulate consumer demand and trigger economic recovery, were vindicated.

The war also solidified the political reforms of the 1930s: an increased role for the government in regulating the economy and in ensuring the social welfare of those unable to help themselves; strong state support of unionization, agricultural subsidies, and progressive tax policies; and the use of government power and money to develop the West and Southwest. In sharp contrast to progressivism, the reforms of the New Deal endured. Voters returned Roosevelt to office for unprecedented third and fourth terms. And these same voters remained wedded for the next 40 years to Roosevelt's central idea: that a powerful state would enhance the pursuit of liberty and equality.

SUGGESTED READINGS

T. H. Watkins, *The Great Depression: America in the 1930s* (1993), provides a broad overview of society and politics during the 1930s. No work better conveys the tumult and drama of that era than **Arthur M. Schlesinger Jr.'s** three-volume *The Age of Roosevelt: The Crisis of the Old Order* (1957), *The Coming of the New Deal* (1958), and *The Politics of Upheaval* (1960). On Hoover's failure to restore prosperity and popular morale, see **David Burner,** *Herbert Hoover: A Public Life* (1979). The most complete biography of FDR, and one that is remarkably good at balancing Roosevelt's life and times, is **Kenneth S. Davis,** *FDR* (1972–1993), in four volumes. On Eleanor Roosevelt, see **Blanche Wiesen Cook,** *Eleanor Roosevelt,* vol. 1 (1992). On the New Deal, see **William E. Leuchtenberg,** *Franklin D. Roosevelt and the New Deal, 1932–1940* (1963), **Anthony J. Badger,** *The New Deal: The Depression Years, 1933–1940* (1989), and **Steve Fraser and Gary Gerstle, eds.,** *The Rise and Fall of the New Deal Order, 1930–1980* (1989). **Ellis Hawley,** *The New Deal and the Problem of Monopoly* (1966), is essential to understand the First New Deal's industrial policy, while **Steven Fraser,** *Labor Will Rule: Sidney Hillman and the Rise of American Labor* (1991), examines the role of the labor movement in national politics. **Michael Denning,** *The Cultural Front: The Laboring of American Culture in the Twentieth Century* (1996), is essential reading on the centrality of labor and the "common man" to literary and popular culture in the 1930s,

as is **Lary May,** *The Big Tomorrow: Hollywood and the Politics of the American Way* (2000). For the economic and cultural ties between the New Deal and the rebirth of the labor movement, see **Lizabeth Cohen,** *Making a New Deal: Industrial Workers in Chicago, 1919–1939* (1990). **Irving Howe and Lewis Coser,** *The American Communist Party: A Critical History, 1919–1957* (1957), is still the best single-volume history of the Communist Party during the 1930s. **Harvard Sitkoff,** *A New Deal for Blacks* (1978), is a wide-ranging examination of the place of African Americans in New Deal reform. **Abraham Hoffman,** *Unwanted Mexican Americans in the Great Depression: Repatriation Pressures, 1929–1939* (1974), analyzes the repatriation campaign, while the problems of illegal alienage created by that campaign are expertly analyzed in **Mae Ngai,** *Impossible Subjects: Illegal Aliens and the Making of Modern America* (2004). The importance of John Collier and the Indian Reorganization Act are treated well in **Lawrence C. Kelly,** *The Assault on Assimilation: John Collier and the Origins of Indian Policy Reform* (1983). **James T. Patterson,** *Congressional Conservatism and the New Deal* (1967), expertly analyzes the growing opposition to the New Deal in the late 1930s, while **Alan Brinkley,** *The End of Reform: New Deal Liberalism in Recession and War* (1995), provocatively examines the efforts of New Dealers to adjust their beliefs and programs as they lost support, momentum, and confidence in the late 1930s.

AMERICAN JOURNEY ONLINE

AND

INFOTRAC COLLEGE EDITION

Visit the source collections at www.ajaccess.wadsworth.com and infotrac.thomsonlearning.com and use the Search function with the following key terms to explore documents, images, audio and video clips, articles, and commentary related to the material in this chapter.

Black Tuesday	Tennessee Valley Authority
The Great Depression	National Recovery Administration
Herbert Hoover	John L. Lewis
Bonus Army	Works Progress Administration
Franklin D. Roosevelt	Eleanor Roosevelt
New Deal	

GRADE AIDS

Visit the Liberty Equality Power Companion Web Site for resources specific to this textbook: http://history.wadsworth.com/murrin_LEP4e

The CD in the back of this book and the U.S. History Resource Center at http://history.wadsworth.com/u.s./ offer a variety of tools to help you succeed in this course, including access to quizzes; images; documents; interactive simulations; maps, and timelines; movie explorations; and a wealth of other sources.

Chapter 26

America during the Second World War

"UNITED WE WIN"
Government posters during the Second World War attempted to mute class and racial divisions and offer images of Americans united against fascism.

The Second World War, a struggle of unprecedented destruction that brought death to some *60 million* people worldwide, transformed American life. During a decade-long process, the United States abandoned isolationism, moved toward military engagement on the side of the Allies, and emerged triumphant in a global war in which U.S. forces fought and died in North Africa, Europe, and Asia.

To succeed militarily, the United States greatly expanded the power of its national government. The mobilization for war finally brought the country out of the Great Depression and produced significant economic and social change. The nation's productive capacity—spurred by new technologies and by a new working relationship among government, business, labor, and scientific researchers—dwarfed that of every other nation and provided the economic basis for military victory.

At home, citizens reconsidered the meanings of liberty and equality. A massive propaganda effort to bolster popular support for wartime sacrifice presented the conflict as a struggle to protect and preserve "the American way of life." This message inevitably raised questions about how to define the American way. How would America, while striving for victory, reorder its economy, its culture, and the social patterns that had shaped racial, ethnic, and gender relationships during the 1930s? What processes of reconstruction, at home and abroad, might be required to build a prosperous and lasting peace?

CHAPTER FOCUS

♦ How did events in Asia and in Europe affect the domestic debate over isolationism versus intervention in the war?

♦ What central strategic issues arose in fighting the war in both Europe and Asia?

♦ How did mobilization for war produce economic and social changes in American life?

♦ What major institutions and policies shaped the reconstruction of the postwar world?

⟐ The Road to War: Aggression and Response

The road to the Second World War began at least two decades before it started. Resentments growing out of the First World War, together with the worldwide depression of the 1930s, set the stage for international political instability. In Japan, Italy, and Germany, economic collapse and rising unemployment created political conditions that nurtured ultranationalist movements promising recovery through military buildup and territorial expansion. Elsewhere in Europe and in the United States itself, economic problems made governments turn inward, concentrating on domestic ills and avoiding expensive foreign entanglements. As international economic and political conditions deteriorated, Americans debated how to respond to acts of aggression overseas.

The Rise of Aggressor States

War began first in Asia. On September 18, 1931, Japanese military forces seized Manchuria and created a puppet state called Manchukuo. This action violated the League of Nations charter, the Washington treaties, and the Kellogg-Briand Pact (see chapter 24). Japanese military leaders, who had urged their nation to create an Asian empire, won their gamble: The international community was too preoccupied with domestic economic problems to counter Japan's move. In the United States, the Hoover-Stimson Doctrine declared a policy of "nonrecognition" of Manchukuo, and the League of Nations also condemned Japan's action. These stands were not backed by military force, however, and Japan first ignored them and then withdrew from the League of Nations in 1935.

Meanwhile, ultranationalist states in Europe also sought to alleviate domestic ills through military aggression. Adolf Hitler's National Socialist (Nazi) Party came to power in Germany in 1933 and instituted a fascist regime, a one-party dictatorial state. Hitler denounced the Versailles peace settlement of 1919, blamed Germany's plight on a Jewish conspiracy, proclaimed the genetic superiority of the Aryan race of German-speaking peoples, and promised to build a new empire (the Third Reich). The regime renounced the League of Nations in 1933 and reinstituted compulsory military service. Nearly doubling Germany's military expenditures (a blatant violation of the Treaty of Versailles), Hitler sought to create an air force and an army that would outnumber those of France, Germany's major European rival. The fascist government of Italy, headed by Benito Mussolini, who had come to power in 1922, also

launched a military buildup and dreamed of an empire. In October 1935, Mussolini's armies invaded Ethiopia, an independent African kingdom that had never before succumbed to colonialist rule. Although Mussolini's forces met fierce Ethiopian resistance, Italy soon prevailed.

C H R O N O L O G Y

1931 Japanese forces seize Manchuria

1933 Hitler takes power in Germany

1936 Spanish Civil War begins • Germany and Italy agree to cooperate as the Axis Powers

1937 Neutrality Act broadens provisions of Neutrality Acts of 1935 and 1936 • Roosevelt makes "Quarantine" speech • Japan invades China

1938 France and Britain appease Hitler at Munich

1939 Hitler and Stalin sign Soviet–German nonaggression pact • Hitler invades Poland; war breaks out in Europe • Congress amends Neutrality Act to assist Allies

1940 Paris falls after German *blitzkreig* (June) • Battle of Britain carried to U.S. by radio broadcasts • Roosevelt makes "destroyers-for-bases" deal with Britain • Selective Service Act passed • Roosevelt wins third term

1941 Lend-Lease established • Roosevelt creates Fair Employment Practices Commission • Roosevelt and Churchill proclaim the Atlantic Charter • U.S. engages in undeclared naval war in North Atlantic • Congress narrowly repeals Neutrality Act • Japanese forces attack Pearl Harbor (December 7)

1942 Rio de Janeiro Conference (January) • President signs Executive Order 9066 for internment of Japanese Americans (February) • General MacArthur driven from Philippines (May) • U.S. victorious in Battle of Midway (June) • German army defeated at Battle of Stalingrad (August) • Operation TORCH begins (November)

1943 Axis armies in North Africa surrender (May) • Allies invade Sicily (July) and Italy (September) • "Zoot suit" incidents in Los Angeles; racial violence in Detroit • Allies begin drive toward Japan through South Pacific islands

1944 Allies land at Normandy (D-Day, June 6) • Allied armies reach Paris (August) • Allies turn back Germans at Battle of the Bulge (September) • Roosevelt reelected to fourth term • Bretton Woods Conference creates IMF and World Bank • Dumbarton Oaks Conference establishes plan for UN

1945 U.S. firebombs Japan • Yalta Conference (February) • Roosevelt dies; Truman becomes president (April) • Germany surrenders (May) • Hiroshima and Nagasaki hit with atomic bombs (August) • Japan surrenders (September) • United Nations established (December)

Isolationist Sentiment and American Neutrality

Many Americans wished to isolate their country from these foreign troubles. Many historians, writing after the First World War, had maintained that Woodrow Wilson manipulated the country into a war that had not been in the nation's best interests. Popular antiwar movies, such as *All Quiet on the Western Front* (1931) and *The Big Parade* (1925), portrayed the conflict as a selfish power game played by business and governmental elites, who used appeals to nationalism to dupe common people into serving as cannon fodder. Between 1934 and 1936, a Senate investigating committee headed by Republican Gerald P. Nye of North Dakota held well-publicized hearings on U.S. participation in the First World War. The Nye committee endorsed claims that the nation had been maneuvered into the war to preserve the profits of American bankers and munitions makers, who had developed a huge financial stake in an Anglo-French victory. By 1935, public opinion polls suggested that Americans overwhelmingly opposed involvement in foreign conflicts and feared being manipulated by what one writer called "merchants of death."

To prevent a repetition of the circumstances that had supposedly drawn the United States into the First World War, Congress enacted neutrality legislation to halt the growth of financial connections to warring countries. The Neutrality Acts of 1935 and 1936 mandated an arms embargo against belligerents, prohibited loans to them, and curtailed travel by Americans on ships belonging to nations at war. The Neutrality Act of 1937 further broadened the embargo to cover all trade with any belligerent, unless it paid in cash and carried the products away in its own ships. This "cash-and-carry" provision minimized damage to America's export sector while it reduced the risk that loans or the presence of American commerce in a war zone might entangle the United States in a conflict overseas.

The isolationist mood in the United States, matched by British policies of appeasing Hitler, encouraged Germany's expansionist designs. In March 1936, Nazi troops again violated the Versailles agreement by remilitarizing the Rhineland. A few months later, Hitler and Mussolini extended aid to General Francisco Franco, a fellow fascist who was seeking to overthrow Spain's republican government. By lending Franco sophisticated weaponry and soldiers, Italy and Germany used Spain's civil war as a training ground for fascist forces. Republicans in Spain appealed to antifascist nations for assistance, but only the Soviet Union responded. Britain, France, and the United States, fearing that the conflict would flare into world war if more nations took sides, adopted policies of noninvolvement.

The United States even extended its arms embargo to cover civil wars, a move that aided the well-armed fascist forces and crippled republican resistance.

Growing Interventionist Sentiment

Although the United States remained officially uninvolved, the Spanish Civil War precipitated a major debate over foreign policy. Many conservative groups in the United States applauded General Franco as a strong anticommunist whose fascist government would support religion and social stability in Spain. In contrast, the political left championed the cause of republican Spain and denounced the fascist repression sweeping Europe. Cadres of Americans, including the famed "Abraham Lincoln Brigade," crossed the Atlantic and joined Soviet-organized, international troops, which fought alongside republican forces from Spain. American peace groups, strong during the 1920s and early 1930s, split over how to avoid a wider war. Some continued to advocate neutrality and isolation, but others argued for a strong stand against fascist militarism and aggression. Increasingly, Americans separated into camps of isolationists and interventionists.

The administration of President Franklin Roosevelt, tilting cautiously toward interventionism, tried to influence the debate. In October 1937, Roosevelt called for international cooperation to "quarantine" aggressor nations, and he gingerly suggested some modification of America's neutrality legislation. Congress, however, remained adamant in maintaining the policy of noninvolvement.

The Mounting Crisis

As Americans debated strict neutrality versus cautious engagement, Japan attacked China. In summer 1937, after an exchange of gunfire between Japanese and Chinese troops at the Marco Polo Bridge southwest of Beijing, Japanese armies invaded and captured Shanghai, Nanjing, Shandong, and Beijing. Japan demanded that China become subservient politically and economically to Tokyo. It also announced a plan for an East Asian Co-Prosperity Sphere, a self-sufficient economic zone that would supposedly liberate peoples throughout Asia from Western colonialism. Toward the end of 1937, Japanese planes sank the American gunboat *Panay* as it evacuated American officials from Nanjing, but Japan's quick apology defused a potential crisis. Even so, the *Panay* incident and Japanese brutality in occupying Nanjing, where perhaps 300,000 Chinese were killed in an assault against civilians, alarmed Roosevelt. The president began to consult with Britain about planning for a possible war in Asia.

Further aggression heightened the sense of alarm among American interventionists, especially when the expansionist states began working together. In October 1936, Germany and Italy agreed to cooperate as the Axis Powers, and Japan joined them in alliance against the Soviet Union in November 1936. Italy followed Japan and Germany in withdrawing from the League of Nations. In March 1938, Hitler annexed Austria to the Third Reich and announced his intention to seize the Sudetenland, a portion of Czechoslovakia inhabited by 3.5 million people of German descent. In May, Roosevelt announced a program of naval rearmament that would increase the U.S. Navy beyond the treaty limits that Japan had already violated.

The Outbreak of War in Europe

French and British leaders, wishing to avoid a confrontation with Germany, met with Hitler in Munich in September 1938. They acquiesced to Germany's seizure of the Sudetenland in return for Hitler's promise to seek no more territory. Roosevelt expressed relief that the Munich Conference seemed to promise future peace in Europe.

The promise of peace did not last. In March 1939, Germans marched into Prague and, within a few months, annexed the rest of Czechoslovakia. In August 1939, Hitler secured Germany's eastern flank by signing a nonaggression pact with the Soviet Union. The most bitter of enemies, Stalin and Hitler nonetheless agreed to cooperate in carving up territory. In a secret protocol, they plotted to divide Poland and the Baltic states. By fall 1939, Germany was clearly preparing to attack Poland.

Britain and France were finally ready to draw the line. Both countries pledged to defend Poland, and on September 1, 1939, Hitler's invasion forced them into action. Two days after Hitler's armies stormed into Poland, Britain and France declared war on Germany. The Allies, however, were unable to mobilize in time to help the Poles. Outnumbered and outgunned, Polish forces fought valiantly but could not withstand Germany's unrelenting strikes on land and from the air. With Soviet troops moving in simultaneously from the east, Poland fell within weeks. Once the occupation of Poland was completed, Hitler's troops waited out the winter of 1939–40. Some observers dubbed this period a *sitzkrieg*, or "sitting war."

The lull proved only temporary. In April 1940, a German *blitzkrieg*, or "lightning war" of massed tank formations, motorized infantry and artillery, and air support, swiftly overran Denmark, Norway, the Netherlands, Belgium, Luxembourg, and France. The speed with which Hitler's well-trained army moved shocked Allied leaders in Paris and London. Britain barely managed to evacuate its troops, but not its equipment, from the French coastal town of Dunkirk, just before it fell to the German onslaught that began in late May. Early in June, Italy joined Germany by declaring war on the Allies. In June 1940, France fell, and Hitler installed a pro-Nazi government at Vichy in southern France. French officials were forced to surrender to Hitler in the same railway car used for the German surrender to France at the end of the First World War. In only six weeks, Hitler's army had seized complete control of Europe's Atlantic coastline, from the North Sea south to Spain, where Franco remained officially neutral but decidedly pro-Axis.

America's Response to War in Europe

In a somber, six-minute speech delivered on the day that Britain and France entered the war against Germany, President Roosevelt declared U.S. neutrality. But the tone of his speech was hardly neutral. Unlike Woodrow Wilson when the European war had broken out in 1914, Roosevelt did not urge Americans to be impartial. From 1939 to 1941, Roosevelt tried to mobilize public opinion against Congress's Neutrality Acts and in favor of what he called "measures short of war" that would bolster the Allied fight against the Axis.

At Roosevelt's urging, late in 1939, Congress did ease the Neutrality Act's ban on selling military armaments to either side by broadening the earlier "cash-and-carry" trade provision to allow arms sales to belligerents who could pay immediately and use their own ships for transport. Because Britain and France controlled the Atlantic sea lanes, they clearly benefited from this change in policy. Congress responded further to Roosevelt's requests, appropriating more funds for rearmament and passing the Selective Training and Service Act of 1940, the first peacetime draft in U.S. history. Abandoning any further pretense of neutrality, the United States began supplying war matériel directly to Great Britain. The appointment of two distinguished Republicans to the cabinet—Henry Stimson as secretary of war and Frank Knox as secretary of the navy—gave the new policies bipartisan overtones, if not fully bipartisan support.

Meanwhile, Hitler concentrated on Great Britain. From August through October 1940, Germany's *Luftwaffe* subjected British air bases to daily raids, coming close to knocking Britain's Royal Air Force (RAF) out of the war. Just as he was on the verge of success, however, Hitler lost patience with this strategy and ordered instead the bombing of London and other cities—first by day and then by night. In addition to giving the RAF time to recover, Ger-

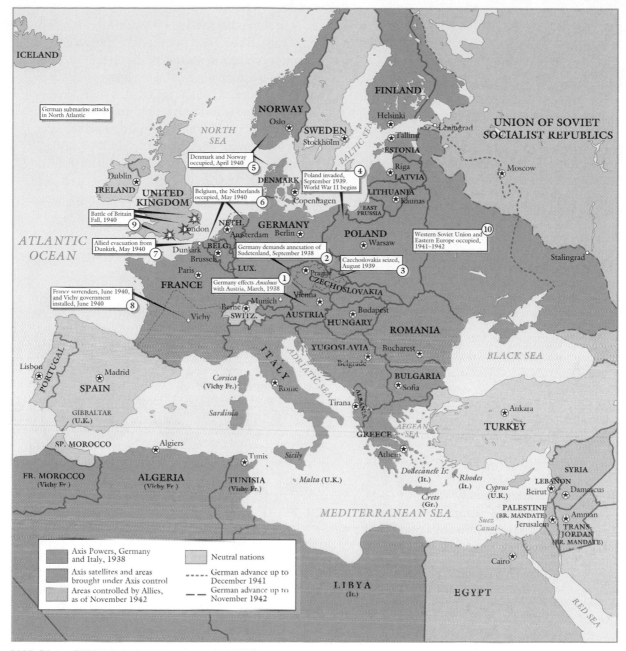

MAP 26.1 GERMAN EXPANSION AT ITS HEIGHT

This map shows the expansion of German power from 1938 through 1942. Which countries fell to German control? Why might Americans have differed over whether these moves by Germany represented a strategic threat to the United States?

many's nighttime bombings of Britain's cities aroused sympathy in the United States. The use of airpower against civilians in the Battle of Britain, as it was called, shocked Americans, who heard the news in dramatic radio broadcasts from London. As writer Archibald MacLeish phrased it, radio journalist Edward R. Murrow "skillfully burned the city of London in our homes and we felt the flames."

In September 1940, Roosevelt ignored any possible constitutional questions about the limits of his authority and transferred 50 First World War–era naval destroyers to

the British navy. In return, the United States gained the right to build eight naval bases in British territory in the Western Hemisphere. This "destroyers-for-bases" deal infuriated isolationist members of Congress. Even within the president's own party, opposition was strong. Democratic Senator Burton K. Wheeler of Montana distributed more than a million antiwar postcards, at government expense, an action that Secretary of War Stimson characterized as "very near the line of subversion . . . if not treason."

Margaret Bourke-White: Adventure as a Photojournalist

On July 22, 1941, Margaret Bourke-White (1904–1971) rushed into the streets of Moscow, quickly assembled her camera equipment, and captured photos of German bombs falling on the Soviet capital. She was the only foreign photographer in the Soviet Union at the time, and her spectacular photos soon splashed across the pages of *Life* magazine. The U.S. Army accredited her as a war correspondent, the first woman to be so designated. During the next four years, Bourke-White photographed the European theater. She saw action in North Africa, documented the Allied campaign in Italy, took aerial shots while flying in American bombers, and crossed into Germany with General George Patton's troops.

Born in the Bronx, New York, Bourke-White graduated from Cornell University in 1927 and quickly established her reputation in the new field of photojournalism. After accepting a position as associate editor of *Fortune* magazine in 1929, she became the first western photographer to receive a visa to enter the Soviet Union. During the early 1930s, she shot 3,000 photos of Russian life—dams, farms, factories, and people—and gained the confidence of the Soviet government. Her book *Eyes on Russia* (1931) became a landmark of photojournalism. She soon joined *Life* magazine, which published her picture of America's Fort Peck Dam on its very first cover. On assignment from *Life*, she had returned to the Soviet Union to do a follow-up to her earlier work when she found herself in the German bombing raid that began her career as one of the world's top war photographers.

Near the end of the Second World War, as Allied troops entered Germany, Bourke-White was among the first photographers to document the Nazi death camps. *Life* published her photos, bringing images of the horrors to the American public for the first time. Her book *The Living Dead of Buchenwald* became a classic. In the postwar era, Bourke-White continued to pursue international themes for *Life*. She covered India, Pakistan, South Africa, and the Korean War. Her many pictures of India's Mahatma Gandhi, including one taken just before he was assassinated, are among her most enduring images.

© Bettmann/Corbis.

MARGARET BOURKE-WHITE
Famed photographer pursues her high-flying career.

Resistance to Roosevelt's pro-Allied policy extended beyond Congress. The most formidable opposition came from the America First Committee, organized by General Robert E. Wood, head of Sears, Roebuck, and Company, the giant department store chain. Included among its members was the aviation hero Charles Lindbergh, who campaigned vigorously at mass rallies across the country against aid to the Allies. Although the people who tried to keep the United States out of the war were generally lumped together as isolationists, this single term obscures their diversity. Some pacifists, including members of religious groups committed to nonviolence, opposed all wars as immoral, even those against evil regimes. Some political progressives disliked fascism but feared even more the centralization of governmental power that conducting a war would require in the United States; they also distrusted the elites who dominated international decision making. Some conservatives sympathized with the anticommunism of fascist states and viewed Germany not as an enemy but as an anticommunist bulwark. Finally, some

Americans opposed Roosevelt's pro-Allied policies because they shared Hitler's anti-Semitic beliefs.

A strong current of anti-Jewish sentiment existed in the United States. An organization called the German American Bund, for example, defended Hitler's anti-Semitic policies and denounced Roosevelt's "Jew Deal," a reference to the presence of Jewish advisers in FDR's New Deal administration. In 1939, congressional leaders had quashed the Wagner-Rogers Bill, which would have boosted immigration quotas in order to allow for the entry of 20,000 Jewish children otherwise slated for Hitler's concentration camps. Bowing to anti-Semitic prejudices, the United States adopted a restrictive refugee policy that did not permit even the legal quota of Jewish immigrants from Eastern Europe to enter the country during the Second World War. The consequences of these policies became even more grave after June 1941, when Hitler established the death camps that would systematically exterminate millions of Jews, gypsies, homosexuals, and anyone else whom the Nazis deemed unfit for life in the Third Reich and its occupied territories.

To counteract the isolationists, those who favored supporting the Allies also organized. The Military Training Camps Association lobbied on behalf of the Selective Service Act. The Committee to Defend America by Aiding the Allies, headed by William Allen White, a well-known Republican newspaper editor, organized more than 300 local chapters in just a few weeks. Similar to the isolationists, interventionist organizations drew from a diverse group of supporters. All, however, sounded alarms about the dangerous possibility that fascist brutality, militarism, and racism might overrun Europe as Americans watched passively.

Roosevelt toned down his pro-Allied rhetoric as the presidential election of 1940 approached. The Republicans nominated Wendell Willkie, a lawyer and business executive with ties to the party's East Coast, internationalist wing. Democrats broke with the apparently settled tradition of limiting presidents to two terms and nominated Roosevelt for a third. To defuse the third-term issue and to differentiate his policies from Willkie's, the president played to the popular opposition to war. He promised not to send American boys to fight in "foreign wars." Once he had defeated Willkie and won an unprecedented third term in November 1940, however, Roosevelt unveiled his most ambitious plan yet to support Britain's war effort.

An "Arsenal of Democracy"

Britain was nearly out of money, so the president proposed an additional provision to the Neutrality Act. The United States would now loan, or "lend-lease," rather than sell, munitions to the Allies. By making the United States

ANTI-INTERVENTIONISTS PICKET THE WHITE HOUSE
Women rally in March 1941 against H.R. 1776, the Lend-Lease Act, which many isolationists feared would lead the United States into another world war.

a "great arsenal of democracy," FDR said, he would "keep war away from our country and our people." Isolationists rallied against the measure. During bitter debate over the Lend-Lease Act, Senator Wheeler evoked Roosevelt's unpopular destruction of farm surpluses during the early years of the New Deal by charging that the act would result in the "plowing under" of every fourth American boy. Nevertheless, Congress passed the symbolically numbered House Resolution 1776 on March 11, 1941. When Germany turned its attention away from Britain and suddenly attacked its recent ally the Soviet Union in June, Roosevelt extended lend-lease to Joseph Stalin's communist regime.

Wheeler continued his opposition. In September 1941, he chaired a special Senate committee investigating whether Hollywood movies were being used to sway people in a pro-war direction. Some isolationists, pointing out that many Hollywood producers were Jewish, expressed blatantly anti-Semitic views.

Still claiming to support a policy of nonbelligerence, Roosevelt next took steps to coordinate military strategy with Britain. In the event that the United States was drawn into a two-front war against both Germany and Japan, the president pledged to follow a Europe-first military strategy. To back up his promise, Roosevelt deployed thousands of

U.S. marines to Greenland and Iceland to relieve British troops, which had occupied these strategic Danish possessions after Germany's seizure of Denmark.

In August 1941, Roosevelt and British Prime Minister Winston Churchill met on the high seas off the coast of Newfoundland to work toward a formal wartime alliance. An eight-point declaration of common principles, called the Atlantic Charter, disavowed territorial expansion, endorsed free trade and self-determination, and pledged the postwar creation of a new world organization that would ensure "general security." Roosevelt agreed to Churchill's request that the U.S. Navy convoy American goods as far as Iceland. This step, aimed at ensuring the safe delivery of lend-lease supplies headed for Britain, inched the United States even closer to belligerence. Soon, in an undeclared naval war, Germany was using its formidable submarine "wolf packs" to attack U.S. ships.

By this time, Roosevelt and his advisers firmly believed that defeating Hitler would require U.S. entry into the war, but public support still lagged. The president urged Congress to repeal the Neutrality Act altogether to allow U.S. merchant ships to carry munitions directly to Britain. Privately, he may have hoped that Germany would commit some provocative act in the North Atlantic that would jar public opinion. The October 1941 sinking of the U.S. destroyer *Reuben James* did just that, and Congress repealed the Neutrality Act. The vote was so close and the debate so bitter, however, that Roosevelt knew he could not yet seek a formal declaration of war. By avoiding any further provocations at sea, Hitler made Roosevelt's task harder. In addition, since late June 1941, Hitler had been concentrating his attacks on the Soviet Union, a country for which Americans held far less sympathy than they did for Britain.

Pearl Harbor

As it turned out, Japan, rather than Germany, sparked America's formal entry into the war. In response to Japan's invasion of China in 1937, the United States sought to bolster China's defense by extending economic credits to China and halting sales of some U.S. equipment to Japan. In 1939, the United States abrogated its Treaty of Commerce and Navigation with Japan, an action that allowed for the possible future curtailment or even the outright prohibition of U.S. exports to the island nation.

These measures did little to deter Japanese aggression, and by 1940 Germany's successes in Europe had further raised the stakes in Asia. As the European war sapped their strength, France, Britain, and the Netherlands had more trouble maintaining links with their Southeast Asian colonies. Japan quickly mobilized to exploit the vacuum as Japanese expansionists called for the incorporation of Southeast Asia into their East Asian Co-Prosperity Sphere.

President Roosevelt hoped that a 1940 ban on the sale of aviation fuel and high-grade scrap iron to Japan would slow Japan's imminent military advance into Southeast Asia. Instead, this act intensified Japanese militancy. After joining the Axis alliance in September 1940, Japan pushed deeper into French Indochina to secure strategic positions and access to raw materials it could no longer buy from the United States. When Japan's occupation of Indochina went unopposed, its military forces prepared to launch attacks on Singapore, the Netherlands East Indies (Indonesia), and the Philippines. Roosevelt expanded the trade embargo against Japan, promised further assistance to China, and accelerated the U.S. military buildup in the Pacific.

In mid-1941, Roosevelt played his most important diplomatic card. He froze Japanese assets in the United States, effectively bringing under presidential control all commerce between the two countries, including trade in petroleum, which was vital to the Japanese economy. Faced with impending economic strangulation, Japanese leaders did not reassess their plan to create an empire. Instead, they began planning a preemptive attack on the United States.

On December 7, 1941, Japanese bombers swooped down without warning on Pearl Harbor, Hawaii, and destroyed much of the U.S. Pacific Fleet. Altogether, 19 ships were sunk or severely damaged; 188 aircraft were destroyed or disabled; and more than 2,200 Americans were killed. The attack could have been worse: The three American carriers and seven heavy cruisers were not in port at the time, and Japan's commander failed to destroy the navy's submarine base, fuel storage tanks, or repair facilities. The psychological effect galvanized the nation. Secretary of War Stimson remembered: "My first feeling was of relief that the indecision was over and that a crisis had come that would unite all our people." In a war message broadcast by radio on December 8, Roosevelt decried the attack and labeled December 7 "a date which will live in infamy," a phrase that served as a rallying cry throughout the war.

Japan's attack on Pearl Harbor was an act of desperation. The U.S. embargoes, especially on petroleum, had narrowed Japan's options. Negotiations between the two countries proved fruitless: Japan was unwilling to abandon its designs on China, the only concession that might have ended the embargoes. With limited supplies of raw materials, Japan had little hope of winning a prolonged war. Japanese military strategists decided to risk a surprise attack, gambling that a crippling blow might so weaken U.S. military power as to avoid a long war. "Sometimes a man has to jump with his eyes closed," remarked General Hideki Tojo, who became Japan's prime minister.

A few Americans charged that Roosevelt had intentionally provoked Japan in order to open a "back door" to war. They pointed out that the fleet at Pearl Harbor, the nation's principal Pacific base, lay vulnerable at its docks, not even in a state of full alert. In actuality, the American actions and inactions that led to Pearl Harbor were more confused than devious. Beginning in 1934, the United States had gradually enlarged its Pacific fleet, and Roosevelt had also increased the number of B-17 bombers based in the Philippines. The president hoped that the possibility of aerial attacks would intimidate Japan and slow its expansion. This strategy of deterrence failed. It may also have contributed to the lack of vigilance at Pearl Harbor. Intelligence experts, who had broken Japan's secret diplomatic code (the decrypted messages were called MAGIC), expected Japan to move toward Singapore or other British or Dutch possessions. MAGIC intercepts, along with visual sightings of Japanese transports, seemed to confirm preparations for a strike in Southeast Asia (a strike that did occur). American leaders doubted that Japan would risk a direct attack on the United States and gravely underestimated the skill of Japan's military planners.

On December 8, 1941, Congress declared war against Japan. The lone dissenting vote came from Representative Jeannette Rankin, a longtime peace activist from Montana. Japan's allies, Germany and Italy, declared war on the United States three days later. Hitler, whose eastern offensive had stalled within sight of Moscow, mistakenly assumed that war with Japan would keep the United States preoccupied in the Pacific. The three Axis Powers had not foreseen America's ability to mobilize swiftly and effectively in a unified war effort.

Fighting the War in Europe

The first few months after America's entry into the war proved discouraging. German forces controlled most of Europe from Norway to Greece and had pushed eastward into the Soviet Union. Now they rolled across North Africa, threatening the strategically important Suez Canal, which remained under British control. In the Atlantic,

IS THAT A WAR PLANT?
This photo from 1945 shows an aircraft plant bedecked with camouflage.

German submarines were endangering Allied supply lines, sinking 7 million tons of Allied shipping in the first 16 months after Pearl Harbor. Japan seemed unstoppable in the Pacific. Japanese forces overran Malaya, the Dutch East Indies, and the Philippines and drove against the British in Burma and the Australians in New Guinea. At home, Americans had been unprepared for war. Before Pearl Harbor, army morale was low, industrial production was still on a peacetime footing, and labor–management relations were contentious.

New government bureaucracies and technologies assisted rapid economic and military mobilization. Military priorities—acquiring naval bases, securing landing rights for aircraft, ensuring points for radio transmissions, and gaining access to raw materials—superseded all other demands. The newly formed Joint Chiefs of Staff, consisting of representatives from each of the armed services, became Roosevelt's major source of guidance on strategy. The War Department's new Pentagon complex dwarfed the State Department's cramped quarters. The giant five-story, five-sided building was completed in January 1943, after 16 months of around-the-clock work. In 1942, aircraft equipped with radar, a new technology developed in collaboration with Britain, proved effective against submarines. Although the army and navy engaged in months of bickering over who should conduct the antisubmarine warfare, the navy finally received official responsibility and performed well. During 1943, Germany's submarine capability faded "from menace to problem," in the words of Admiral Ernest King. Radar was one of the most important innovations of the war.

Code-breaking was another. In the 1920s, a private company had developed the complex ENIGMA encryption machine to encode radio messages. Realizing that radio communications would be essential to his war strategy, Hitler adapted the machine to military purposes. ENIGMA messages were considered unbreakable because the cipher keys changed once or twice a day, and the machine could be configured 150 million million million different ways for any message. Polish mathematicians, however, obtained an ENIGMA machine and made some key breakthroughs in the science of decryption. They escaped from Poland just as German armies overran the country. Their discoveries contributed to a massive Allied code-breaking operation that was established at Bletchley Park in England, an endeavor so secret that most records were destroyed after the war, and no open mention was allowed before 1974. At its height, Bletchley Park employed some 4,000 people, including many Americans. Gradually, cryptographers perfected decryption machines. Decoded German messages, called "Ultra" for "Ultra-secret," helped British defenses during the Battle of Britain and gave the Allies a crucial advantage in campaigns in North Africa and France. Throughout the war, the Germans never discovered that many of their radio communications were being forwarded to Allied commanders—occasionally even before they had made it to their German recipient. In the postwar world, the code-breaking technologies of Ultra would lead to the development of computer technology.

Campaigns in North Africa and Italy

Military strategy divided the Allied Powers, now consisting principally of the United States, Britain, and the Soviet Union. All agreed that the primary focus would be the European theater of the war, and Roosevelt and his military strategists immediately established a unified command with the British. The Soviet Union, facing 200 German divisions just west of Moscow and suffering hundreds of thousands of casualties, pleaded with Roosevelt and Churchill to open a second front in Western Europe, by an invasion across the English Channel into France, to relieve pressure on the USSR. Many of Roosevelt's advisers, including Stimson and General George C. Marshall, agreed. They feared that if German troops forced the Soviet Union out of the war, Germany could turn its full attention toward Britain.

Churchill, however, urged instead the invasion of French North Africa, which was under the control of Vichy France. Churchill's strategy sought to peck away at the edges of enemy power rather than strike at its heart. At a meeting between Roosevelt and Stalin at Casablanca,

Morocco, in January 1943, Roosevelt sided with Churchill, and the promised invasion of France was postponed. The risk of any cross-Channel assault was great, Roosevelt reasoned, and he wanted some rapid victories to build morale on the home front. To assuage Stalin's fears that his capitalist allies might sign a separate peace with Hitler, the two leaders announced that they would stay in the fight until Germany agreed to nothing less than unconditional surrender. Continuing disagreements over the timing of the cross-Channel invasion, however, still strained the alliance.

The North African operation, code-named TORCH, began with Anglo-American landings in Morocco and Algeria in November 1942. To ease resistance against this North African invasion, U.S. General Dwight D. Eisenhower struck a deal with French Admiral Jean Darlan, a Nazi sympathizer and the Vichy officer who controlled France's colonies in North Africa. Darlan agreed to break with the Vichy regime and stop resisting the Allied operation in return for Eisenhower's pledge that the United States would support his political aspirations. The deal outraged some Americans, who believed that it compromised the moral purpose of the war. Darlan's assassination in December 1942, called an "act of Providence" by one of Eisenhower's deputies, ended the embarrassment. Even so, the antagonism that Eisenhower's action had generated in the Free French movement, led by General Charles de Gaulle, had lasting consequences for postwar relations.

As TORCH progressed, assisted by Ultra intercepts, the Soviets suddenly turned the tide of battle at Stalingrad. They cut off and destroyed one German army in the city and sent other German armies reeling backward. Despite this defeat in the East, Hitler poured reinforcements into North Africa but could not stop either TORCH or the British, who were driving west from Egypt. About 200,000 Axis soldiers surrendered to the Allies in April and May 1943. In summer 1943, Allied troops followed up the successful North African campaign by overrunning the island of Sicily and fighting their way slowly north through Italy's mountains. Their successes boosted morale in the United States, but the Italian campaign drained badly needed resources for the upcoming cross-Channel invasion of France, while scarcely denting the German stranglehold on Europe.

Some American officials increasingly worried about the postwar implications of wartime strategy. Stimson, for example, warned that the peripheral campaigns through Africa and Italy might leave the Soviets dominating central Europe. Unless the western democracies confronted Germany in the heart of Europe, he argued, Germany would be left holding "the leg for Stalin to skin the deer

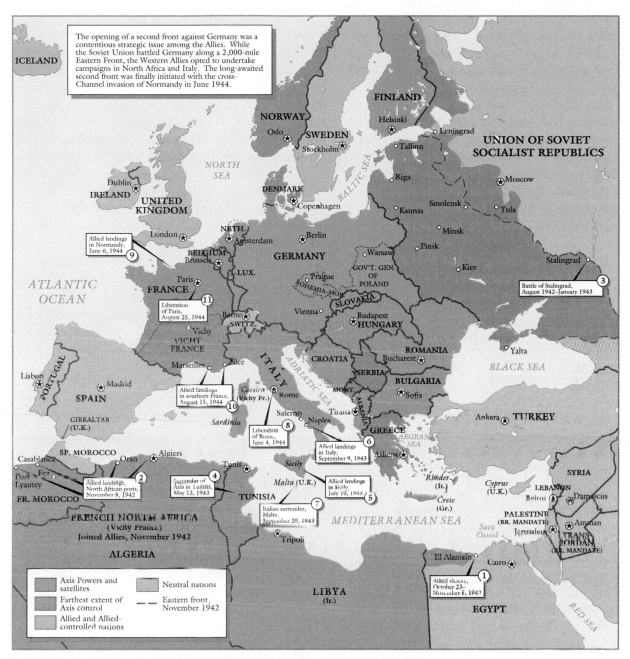

The opening of a second front against Germany was a contentious strategic issue among the Allies. While the Soviet Union battled Germany along a 2,000-mile Eastern Front, the Western Allies opted to undertake campaigns in North Africa and Italy. The long-awaited second front was finally initiated with the cross-Channel invasion of Normandy in June 1944.

MAP 26.2   ALLIED MILITARY STRATEGY IN NORTH AFRICA, ITALY, AND FRANCE

This map shows the European theater of war from 1942 through 1944. Note how the crucial Battle of Stalingrad and the North African campaign began a rollback of German power. Why did June 1944 appear to be a critical month for the Allied effort?

and I think that will be dangerous business for us at the end of the war." Acting on such advice, Roosevelt finally agreed to set a date for the cross-Channel invasion that Stalin had long been promised.

Operation OVERLORD

Operation OVERLORD, directed by Eisenhower, finally began on June 6, 1944, D-Day. During the months pre-

ceding D-Day, probably the largest invasion force in history had been assembled in England. Allied double agents and diversionary tactics had fooled the Germans into expecting a landing at the narrowest part of the English Channel rather than in the Normandy region. Just five months earlier, a new decoding machine had dramatically increased the number of Ultra intercepts, and Allied intelligence officers therefore had the advantage of knowing that their deception had worked. After several delays, because of the Channel's unpredictable weather, nervous commanders finally ordered the daring plan to begin. The night before, as naval guns pounded the Normandy shore, three divisions of paratroopers were dropped behind enemy lines to disrupt German communications. Then, at dawn, more than 4,000 Allied ships landed troops and supplies on Normandy's beaches. The first American troops to land at Omaha Beach met especially heavy German fire and took enormous casualties, but the waves of invading troops continued throughout the day and through the weeks that followed. Within three weeks, more than 1 million people had landed, secured the Normandy coast, and opened the long-awaited second front.

Just as the Battle of Stalingrad had reversed the tide of the war in the East, so Operation OVERLORD turned the tide in the West. Within three months, U.S., British, and Free French troops entered Paris. After repulsing a desperate German counteroffensive in Belgium, at the Battle of the Bulge in December and January, Allied armies swept eastward, crossed the Rhine, and headed toward Berlin.

The Allies disagreed on how to orchestrate the defeat of Germany. British strategists favored a swift drive, so as to meet up with Soviet armies in Berlin or even farther east. General Eisenhower favored a strategy that was militarily less risky and politically less provocative to the Soviets. He doubted that Allied troops could reach Berlin from the west before the Soviet armies arrived, and he knew that stopping short of Berlin would save lives among the troops under his command. He was also eager to end the war on a note of trust and believed that racing the Soviets to Berlin would undermine the basis for postwar Soviet–American cooperation. In the end, Eisenhower's views prevailed. The general moved cautiously along a broad front, halting his troops at the Elbe River, west of Berlin, and allowing Soviet troops to roll into the German capital. The Soviets, who suffered staggering casualties in taking Berlin, worked with the other Allies to establish joint administration of the city.

HISTORY THROUGH FILM

Saving Private Ryan (1998)

Directed by Steven Spielberg. Starring Tom Hanks (Captain John Miller), Matt Damon (Private James Ryan), Harve Presnell (General George Marshall).

Hollywood marked the 50th anniversary of the Allied effort in the Second World War with a series of films about "the good war." Although *Saving Private Ryan* invited comparison with *The Longest Day* (1962) because of its depiction of the D-Day invasion of Normandy, Steven Spielberg's battlefield sequences represented a considerable advance in the arts of waging war on film. His production team employed sophisticated computer graphics and nearly deafening Dolby sound to mount battle scenes so realistic that reviewers cautioned veterans susceptible to post-traumatic stress syndrome about watching the film.

The film also suggested the kind of family-centered melodrama that Spielberg had grafted onto the sci-fi genre in *E.T.: The Extra-Terrestrial* (1982). A heroic squad led by Captain John Miller is trying to locate a single U.S. soldier, Private James Ryan, whose mother has already lost her three other sons to the war. The film poses the question of whether such a family-related mission legitimates and sanctifies the sacrifices of the Second World War. *Private Ryan* answers "yes" to this question.

The major body of the film carefully justifies the rescue mission. Although Captain Miller wonders if his dangerous assignment is simply a public relations stunt, he quickly drops this idea and pursues his mission with the gallantry required of a Hollywood-commissioned officer. Later, his platoon members debate the morality of risking eight lives to save one, but the cause of Ryan's mother always seems overriding. General George Marshall cuts off debate over the appropriateness of the Ryan mission by invoking an earlier war leader, Abraham Lincoln, who once faced a similar dilemma. When Miller's troops finally locate Private Ryan, the film's audience discovers that he is the kind of clean-cut Iowa farm boy who

As the war in Europe drew to a close, the horrors perpetrated by the Third Reich became visible to the world. Hitler's campaign of extermination, now called the Holocaust, killed between 5 and 6 million Jews out of Europe's prewar population of 10 million; hundreds of thousands more from various other groups—especially gypsies, homosexuals, intellectuals, communists, and the physically and mentally challenged—were also murdered. Although only a military victory could close the German death camps, the Allies might have saved thousands of Jews by helping them escape and emigrate. Allied leaders, however, worried about how to deal with large numbers of Jewish refugees, and they also were reluctant to use scarce ships to transport Jews to neutral sanctuaries. In 1943, after Romania proposed permitting an evacuation of 70,000 Jews from its territory, for example, Allied leaders avoided any serious discussion of the plan. With few places to go, hundreds of thousands of people who might have been saved went to Nazi death camps.

The Allies would, in 1945 and 1946, bring 24 high German officials to trial at Nuremberg for "crimes against humanity." Large quantities of money, gold, and jewelry that Nazi leaders stole from victims of the Holocaust and deposited in Swiss banks, however, remained largely hidden from view for more than 50 years. Not until 1997 did Jewish groups and the U.S. government force an investigation of the Swiss banking industry's holdings of stolen "Nazi gold," an inquiry that finally prompted some restitution for victim's families.

With Hitler's suicide in April and Germany's surrender on May 8, 1945, the military foundations for peace in Europe were complete. Soviet armies controlled Eastern Europe; British and U.S. forces predominated in Italy and the rest of the Mediterranean; Germany and Austria fell under divided occupation. Governmental leaders now needed to work out a plan for transforming these military arrangements into a comprehensive political settlement for the postwar era. Meanwhile, the war in the Pacific was still far from over.

will stay with his would-be saviors rather than retreat to safety. Ryan survives, although most of his comrades perish. Captain Miller, dying, implores young Ryan to lead a "good" life, to justify the sacrifice of so many others.

The film *Private Ryan,* in contrast to its characters, takes few risks. It secures its emotional investment in the rescue effort by bracketing the Second World War segments with two brief framing sequences in which an aging Ryan, along with his own family, returns to Normandy and visits the grave of Captain Miller. In the final segment, Ryan's wife provides the final reassurance that the trauma of the Second World War served a good cause, because Private Ryan's own family life has justified Miller's sacrifice. "Tell me I've led a good life. Tell me I'm a good man," he implores his wife. After nearly three hours of this Spielberg epic, the question is rhetorical.

© AFP/Corbis.

Saving Private Ryan, **which garnered four Academy Award nominations, celebrated the heroism of what popular historians called America's "greatest generation."**

MAP 26.3 ALLIED ADVANCES AND COLLAPSE OF GERMAN POWER

This map depicts the final Allied advances and the end of the war in Germany. Through what countries did Soviet armies advance, and how might their advance have affected the postwar situation? How was Germany divided by occupying powers, and how might that division have affected postwar politics?

 View an animated version of this map or related maps at **http://history.wadsworth.com/murrin_LEP4e.**

The Pacific Theater

For six months after Pearl Harbor, nearly everything in the Pacific theater of the war went Japan's way. Britain's supposedly impregnable colony at Singapore fell easily. American naval garrisons in the Philippines and on Guam and Wake islands were overwhelmed, and American and Filipino armies were forced to surrender at Bataan and Corregidor in the Philippines. In one of the most notorious incidents of the war, the Bataan Death March, Japanese commanders forced many of their 70,000 American and Filipino captives to walk 60 miles with almost no food or water and then packed them tightly onto ships for transport to prison camps. Suffering from disease, hunger, and cruelty, more than 7,000 soldiers died in the forced march. Elsewhere, Japanese forces streamed southward to menace Australia. Then the tide turned.

Seizing the Initiative in the Pacific

When Japan finally suffered its first naval defeat at the Battle of the Coral Sea in May 1942, Japanese naval commanders decided to hit back hard. They amassed 200 ships and 600 planes to destroy what remained of the U.S. Pacific fleet and to take Midway Island, a strategic location for Hawaii's security. U.S. Naval Intelligence, however, was able to break enough of the Japanese code to warn Admiral Chester W. Nimitz of the plan. Surprising the Japanese navy, U.S. planes sank four Japanese carriers, destroyed a total of 322 planes, and preserved the American presence at Midway. The U.S. Navy's losses were substantial, but Japan's were so much greater that its offensive capabilities were crippled.

Two months later, American forces splashed ashore at Guadalcanal in the Solomon Islands and successfully relieved the pressure on Australia and its military supply lines. The bloody engagements in the Solomons continued for months on both land and sea, but they accomplished one major objective: seizing the initiative against Japan. This success, combined with the delay in opening received front in Europe, also affected grand strategy. received highest priority, the war in Europe was to have receiving roughly equal resources, but by 1943 the two theaters were

The bloody engagements in the Pacific dramatically illustrated that the conflict had become, in historian John Dower's phrase, a "war without mercy." It was one in which racial prejudice reinforced brutality. For Japan, the war was to establish forever the superiority of the divine Yamato race. Prisoners taken by the Japanese, mostly on the Asian mainland, were brutalized in unimaginable ways, and few survived. The Japanese army's Unit 731 tested bacteriological weapons in China and, like the Nazi doctors, conducted horrifying medical experiments on live subjects. American propaganda images also played on themes of racial superiority, portraying the Japanese as animalistic subhumans. American troops often rivaled Japan's forces in their disrespect for the enemy dead and sometimes killed Japanese soldiers rather than take prisoners. The longer the Pacific war lasted, the more it seemed to loosen the boundaries of acceptable violence against combatants and civilians alike.

China Policy

U.S. policy makers hoped that China would fight effectively against Japan and emerge from the war as a strong and united nation. Neither hope was realized.

General Joseph W. Stilwell, who had worked with the Chinese armies resisting the Japanese invasion in the late 1930s, undertook the job of turning China into an effective military force. Jiang Jieshi (formerly spelled Chiang Kai-shek) headed China's government and accepted the prickly Stilwell as his chief of staff, but friction between "Vinegar Joe" Stilwell and Jiang, fueled by disputes over military priorities, became so intense that in May 1943 Roosevelt bowed to Jiang's demand for Stilwell's dismissal. Meanwhile, Japan's advance into China continued, and in 1944 its forces captured seven of the principal U.S. air bases in China.

To complicate matters further, China was beset by civil war. Jiang's Nationalist government was incompetent, corrupt, and unpopular. It avoided engaging the Japanese invaders and still made extravagant demands for U.S. assistance. Meanwhile, a growing communist movement led by Mao Zedong was fighting effectively against the Japanese and enjoyed widespread support among Chinese peasants. Stilwell urged Roosevelt to cut off support to Jiang unless he fought with more determination. Roosevelt, however, feared that such actions would create even greater chaos and resisted strengthening Mao's position. He continued to provide moral support and matériel to Jiang's armies and even convinced Stalin to support Jiang rather than Mao. Moreover, pressed by a powerful "China lobby" in the United States, Roosevelt insisted that Jiang's China be permitted to stand alongside the major powers after victory had been won. By tying U.S. policy to Jiang's leadership and entertaining the pretense that China was a stable power, Roosevelt and the "China lobby" prepared the way for great difficulties in forging a China policy in the postwar period.

Pacific Strategy

In contrast to the war in Europe, there was no unified command to guide the war in the Pacific; consequently, military actions often emerged from compromise. General Douglas MacArthur, commander of the army in the South Pacific, favored an offensive launched from his headquarters in Australia through New Guinea and the Philippines and on to Japan. After Japan drove him out of the Philippines in May 1942, he had promised to return, and he was determined to keep his pledge. He argued that the United States needed to control the Philippines at war's end in order to preserve its strategic position in Asia. Admiral Nimitz disagreed. He favored a more direct route, advancing toward Japan via the smaller islands of the central Pacific and bypassing the Philippines. Unable to decide between the two strategies, the Joint Chiefs of Staff authorized both. Marked by fierce fighting and heavy casualties, both offensives moved forward. MacArthur took New Guinea,

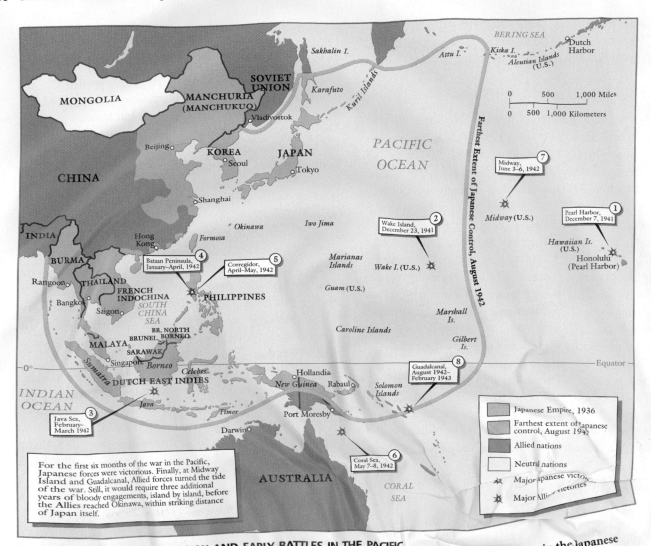

MAP 26.4 JAPANESE EXPANSION AND EARLY BATTLES IN THE PACIFIC
This map shows the expansion of Japanese power prior to the Battle of Midway. What countries were in the Japanese orbit? U.S. opinion polls from the late 1930s suggest that more Americans supported strong measures against this Japanese threat in Asia than against the German threat in Europe. What might be some explanations for this concern?

and Nimitz's forces liberated the Marshall Islands and the Marianas in 1943 and 1944. An effective radio communication system conducted by a Marine platoon of Navajo Indians made a unique contribution to success. On hundreds of Pacific beaches Navajo-speaking squads set up radio contact with headquarters and with supporting units. Navajo, a language unfamiliar to Japanese intelligence officers, provided a secure medium for sensitive communications. In late 1944, the fall of Saipan brought American bombers within range of Japan. The capture of the islands of Iwo Jima—18 square miles taken at the cost of 27,000 American casualties—and of Okinawa further shortened that distance during spring 1945. Okinawa illustrated the nearly unbelievable ferocity of the island campaigns: 120,000 Japanese soldiers died; 48,000 Americans. U.S. military planners extrapolated from these num-

bers when considering the dreaded prospect of an invasion of the home islands of Japan.

As the seaborne offensive proceeded, airpower also played a role. Before the war, Roosevelt had become convinced that aerial bombing offered almost magical military power. At one time, he even had hoped that the mere threat of bombing would be so frightening that airpower would be a deterrent to war rather than a means of conducting it. The effects of strategic bombing in Europe, however, had been ambiguous. The Nazi bombardment of British cities in 1940 and 1941 did heavy damage but only steeled British resolve, uniting the nation and boosting civilian morale. The Allies' strategic bombing of Germany, including the destruction of such large cities as Hamburg and Dresden, produced equally mixed results. Military historians continue to debate the relative merits of the

NAVAJO SIGNAL CORPS
Sending messages in their native language, which neither the Japanese nor the Germans could decipher, Navajo Indians in the Signal Corps made a unique contribution to preserving the secrecy of U.S. intelligence.

strategic bombing in Europe, wondering whether the gains against military targets really offset the huge civilian casualties and the unsustainable losses of American pilots and aircraft.

Still, Roosevelt continued to believe that strategic bombing might provide the crucial advantage in the Pacific. In February 1944, General Henry Harley ("Hap") Arnold, commander of the newly formed 20th Army Air Force, presented Roosevelt with a plan for a systematic campaign of firebombing against Japanese cities, "not only because they are greatly congested but because they contain numerous war industries." Roosevelt approved the plan. In the month before bombing began, the Office of War Information lifted its ban on atrocity stories about Japan's treatment of American prisoners. As grisly reports swept across the country, officials expected that the American public would become more accepting of killing Japanese civilians. Arnold's original air campaign, operating from bases in China, turned out to be cumbersome and ineffective. It was replaced by an even more lethal operation, run by General Curtis LeMay from Saipan.

The official position was that the incendiary raids on Japanese cities constituted "precision" rather than "area" bombing. In actuality, the success of a mission was measured in terms of the number of square miles it left scorched. Destroying Japan's industrial capacity by firebombing the workers who ran the factories and by systematically burning entire cities brought unprecedented civilian casualties. The number of Japanese civilians killed in the raids is estimated to have been greater than Japanese soldiers killed in battle. An attack on Tokyo on the night of March 9–10, 1945, inaugurated the new policy by leveling 16 square miles (one-fourth) of the city, destroying 267,000 buildings and inflicting 185,000 casualties. One by one, LeMay torched other cities. In his memoirs, LeMay summarized his strategy: "Bomb and burn them until they quit."

By the winter of 1944–45, a combined sea and air strategy had emerged: The United States would seek "unconditional surrender" by blockading Japan's seaports, continuing its bombardment of Japanese cities from the air, and perhaps invading Japan. Later critics of the policy of unconditional surrender have suggested that it may have hardened the determination with which Japan fought the war even after its ultimate defeat had become obvious. These critics have pointed out that many Japanese

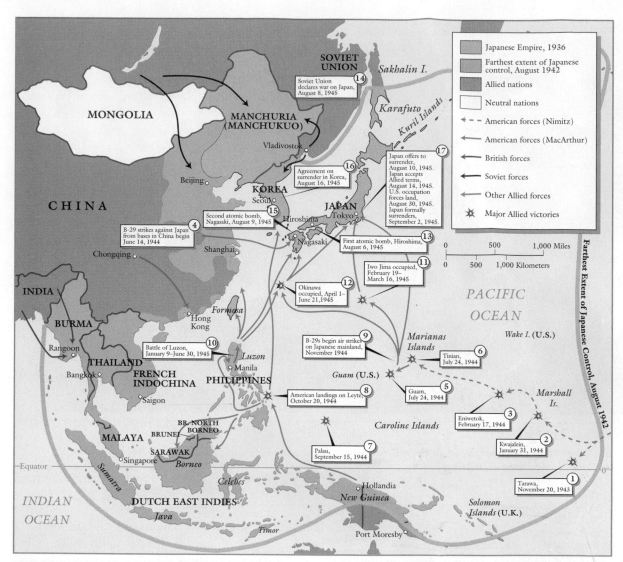

MAP 26.5 PACIFIC THEATER OFFENSIVE STRATEGY AND FINAL ASSAULT AGAINST JAPAN

This map suggests the complicated nature of devising a war strategy in the vast Pacific region. What tactics did the United States use to advance upon and finally prevail over the island nation of Japan?

assumed that unconditional surrender would mean the death of the emperor. Moreover, the policy prevented U.S. negotiators from vigorously pursuing peace feelers, which some Japanese leaders were trying to send through third parties. With the unconditional surrender policy in place and Japan's decision to fight even in the face of certain defeat, the strategy of American leaders seemed to require massive destruction to achieve victory.

A New President

On April 13, 1945, just one month before Germany's formal surrender and five months before Japan's, newspaper headlines across the country mourned, "President Roose-

velt Dead." FDR succumbed to a massive cerebral hemorrhage. Profound sorrow and shock spread through the armed forces, where many young men and women had hardly known any other president; through diplomatic conference halls, where Roosevelt's personal magnetism had often brought unity, if not clarity; and among factory workers, farmers, and bureaucrats, for whom Roosevelt had symbolized optimism and unity through depression and war. Roosevelt had also accumulated a host of critics and enemies. He had defeated Republican Thomas E. Dewey in the 1944 presidential election by the smallest popular vote margin in nearly 30 years. Still, FDR had been the most popular president in modern history, and he left an enduring imprint on American life. "He was

Commander-in- Chief, not only of the Armed Forces, but of our generation," wrote an editor of *Yank* magazine.

Compared with the legacy of Roosevelt, the stature of the new president, Harry S. Truman, seemed impossibly small. Born on a farm near Independence, Missouri, Harry Truman had served in France during the First World War. After the war, he went into politics, under the auspices of Thomas J. Pendergast's Democratic party machine in Kansas City, and was elected to the U.S. Senate in 1934. There, he made his reputation in the early years of the Second World War by fighting waste in spending programs and was chosen as Roosevelt's running mate in 1944. In contrast to Roosevelt, who was upper class, elite educated, and worldly, Truman was simply a "little man from Missouri." He prided himself on plain, direct talk. His critics considered him poorly prepared for the job of president. He had little background in international affairs. Moreover, because Roosevelt had not included him in high-level policy discussions, Truman knew little about any informal understandings Roosevelt may have made with foreign leaders. In fact, during the period between the inauguration following the 1944 election and the president's death, Truman had met with Roosevelt only three times.

Atomic Power and Japanese Surrender

At Los Alamos, New Mexico, scientists from all across the world had been secretly working on a new weapon. Advances in theoretical physics during the 1930s had suggested that splitting the atom (fission) would release a tremendous amount of energy that could fuel incredibly powerful bombs. Fearful that Germany was racing ahead of the United States in this area, Albert Einstein, a Jewish refugee from Germany, in 1939 had urged President Roosevelt to launch a secret program to build a bomb based on atomic research. The government subsequently enlisted top scientists in the Manhattan Project, the largest and most secretive military project yet undertaken. On July 16, 1945, after a succession of breakthroughs in physics research, the first atomic weapon was successfully tested at Trinity Site, near Alamogordo, New Mexico. The researchers notified Truman that the terrifying new weapon was ready.

Truman and his top policy makers assumed that the weapon should be put to immediate military use. They were eager to end the war, both because a possible land invasion of Japan might have cost so many American lives and because the Soviet Union was planning to enter the Pacific theater, and Truman wished to limit Soviet power

in that region. Secretary of War Stimson wrote: "It was our common objective, throughout the war, to be the first to produce an atomic weapon and use it. The possible atomic weapon was considered to be a new and tremendously powerful explosive, as legitimate as any other of the deadly explosive weapons of modern war." Churchill called the bomb a "miracle of deliverance" and a peace giver. Truman later claimed that he had never lost a night's sleep over its use because it saved lives.

Other advisers admitted to more qualms, and disagreement arose over where and how the bomb should be deployed. A commission of atomic scientists, headed by Jerome Franck, recommended a demonstration that would impress Japan with the bomb's power yet cause no loss of life. General George C. Marshall suggested using the bomb only on military installations or on some large manufacturing area where people would be warned away in advance. Most of Truman's advisers, however, agreed that simply demonstrating the bomb's power might not be enough. The purpose of the bomb, Stimson said, was to make "a profound psychological impression on as many inhabitants as possible."

In the context of the earlier aerial bombardment of Japanese cities, dropping atomic bombs on the previously unbombed cities of Hiroshima and Nagasaki on August 6 and 9, 1945, respectively, seemed simply an acceleration of existing policy rather than a departure from it. "Fat Man" and "Little Boy," as the two bombs were nicknamed, came to be viewed as merely bigger, more effective firebombs. Atomic weapons did, however, produce yet a new level of violence. Colonel Paul Tibbets, who piloted the plane that dropped the first bomb, reported that "the shimmering city became an ugly smudge . . . a pot of bubbling hot tar." Teams of U.S. observers who entered the two Japanese cities in the aftermath of their bombing were stunned at the immediate devastation, including the instantaneous incineration of both human beings and manmade structures, as well as the longer-lasting horror of radiation disease.

The mushroom clouds over Hiroshima and Nagasaki inaugurated a new "atomic age" in which dreams of peace were mingled with nightmares of Armageddon. But in those late summer days of 1945, most Americans sighed with relief. Although some of Japan's military leaders wanted to continue the fight, Emperor Hirohito summoned his cabinet and declared that, with the nation on the brink of destruction, "I cannot endure the thought of letting my people suffer any longer." News reports on August 15 proclaimed Japan's defeat. On September 2, dubbed V-J Day, Japan formally signed a surrender document aboard the battleship *Missouri* in Tokyo Bay.

© UPI-Bettmann/Corbis.

TOTAL WAR: DRESDEN AND HIROSHIMA

The effects of "total war" are graphically illustrated in these photographs—of the devastation of Dresden, Germany (top), by the British Bomber Command and the U.S. 8th Air Force on February 13 and 14, 1945, and that of Hiroshima, Japan (bottom), by the U.S. 509th Composite Group on August 6, 1945. In the initial attack on Dresden, 786 aircraft dropped 5,824,000 pounds (2,600 long tons) of bombs on the city, killing an estimated 60,000 people and injuring another 30,000. An area of more than 2.5 square miles in the city center was demolished, and some 37,000 buildings were destroyed. To critics, the bombing of Dresden, a target that many argued was of little strategic value, exemplified the excessive use of airpower.

In sobering comparison, Hiroshima was devastated by one bomb weighing only 10,000 pounds (4.4 long tons)—an atomic bomb—dropped from one aircraft. The single U-235 bomb killed 68,000 people outright, injured another 30,000, and left 10,000 missing. (These figures do not include those who later developed diseases from deadly gamma rays.) The bomb obliterated almost 5 square miles of the city's center and destroyed 40,653 buildings. Truman reported the strike as "an overwhelming success." Many hailed the atomic bomb as a necessary step toward military victory; others worried about the dawn of the "nuclear age."

The War at Home: The Economy

The success of the U.S. military effort in both Europe and Asia depended on economic mobilization at home. This effort ultimately brought the Great Depression of the 1930s to an end and transformed the nation's political economy—its government, its business and financial institutions, and its labor force.

Government's Role in the Economy

The federal bureaucracy nearly quadrupled in size during the war. New economic agencies proliferated. The most powerful of these, the War Production Board, oversaw the conversion and expansion of factories, allocated resources, and enforced production priorities and schedules. The War Labor Board had jurisdiction over labor–management disputes, and the War Manpower Commission allocated workers to various industries. The Office of Price Administration regulated prices to control inflation and rationed such scarce commodities as gasoline, rubber, steel, shoes, coffee, sugar, and meat. All of these agencies, and others, intruded into the workings of the market economy by placing government controls on economic decisions, both in business and in the home. Although most of the specific controls were abandoned after the war, the concept of greater governmental regulation of the economy survived.

From 1940 to 1945, the U.S. economy expanded rapidly, accelerating from a decade of sluggishness to one of full-speed, even force-fed production. In each year of the war, gross national product (GNP) rose by 15 percent or more. According to a War Production Board report, "A country that . . . could produce in 1944 $199,000,000,000 in goods and services was an invincible opponent." When Roosevelt called for the production of 60,000 planes, shortly after Pearl Harbor, skeptics jeered. Yet within the next few years the nation produced nearly 300,000 planes—in a dazzling range of designs. The Maritime Commission oversaw construction of more than 53 million tons of shipping, turning out ships faster than German submarines could sink them. The previously stagnant economy spewed out prodigious quantities of other supplies, including 2.5 million trucks and 50 million pairs of shoes. This was a "war of massed machines," as journalist Hanson Baldwin described it.

Striving to increase production, industry entered into a close relationship with Washington, D.C. to promote scientific and technological research and development (R&D). Government money subsidized new industries, such as electronics, and enabled others, such as rubber and chemicals, to transform their processes and products. Annual expenditures on R&D doubled prewar levels, with the government providing most of the funds. The newly established Office of Scientific Research and Development, headed by Vannevar Bush, entered into contracts for a variety of projects with universities and scientists. Under this program, radar and penicillin (both British breakthroughs), rocket engines, and other new products were rapidly perfected for wartime use. Refugees from Nazi tyranny brought added strength to the scientific and academic establishments, contributing to advances in physics, astronomy, psychiatry, and architecture. In the four decades after 1930, they won no fewer than 24 Nobel Prizes. The Manhattan Project was perhaps the most dramatic example of the new connections among science, national defense, and the federal government. The project employed nearly 130,000 people by mid-1944 and eventually cost more than $2 billion. Many of the émigré scientists who had fled the Nazis participated.

Business and Finance

To finance the war effort, government spending rose from $9 billion in 1940 to $98 billion in 1944. In 1941 the national debt stood at $48 billion; by V-J Day it was $280 billion. With few goods to buy, Americans invested in war bonds, turning their savings into tanks and planes. Although war bonds provided a relatively insignificant contribution to overall defense spending, they helped drive the level of personal saving up to 25 percent of consumer income. War bond purchases, which gave millions of Americans an even larger stake in victory, also became an important psychological motivator.

As production shifted from autos to tanks, from refrigerators to guns, many consumer goods became scarce. Essentials such as food, fabrics, and gasoline were rationed and, consequently, were shared more equitably than they had been before the war. Higher taxes on wealthier Americans tended to redistribute income and narrow the gap between the well-to-do and other people. War bonds, rationing, and progressive taxation encouraged a sense of shared sacrifice and helped ease the class tensions of the 1930s.

Even as the war fostered an increase in personal savings and some redistribution of income and wealth, many of the New Deal agencies most directly concerned with the interests of the poor were dismantled. A Republican surge in the off-year elections of 1942—the GOP gained 44 seats in the House and 7 in the Senate—helped strengthen a

National Archives.

RITA HAYWORTH SCRAPS HER BUMPERS

Movie stars aided the war effort by promoting the sale of war bonds and urging sacrifice. Here Hayworth urges Americans to scrap their unessential car parts.

course, became a matter of definition. Coca-Cola and Wrigley's chewing gum won precious sugar allotments by arguing that GIs overseas "needed" to enjoy these products. Both companies prospered. The Kaiser Corporation, whose spectacular growth in the 1930s had been spurred by federal dam contracts, now turned its attention to building ships, aircraft, and military vehicles, such as the famous "jeep." By 1943 the company was handling nearly one-third of the nation's military construction, establishing a new industrial base for southern California's previously agricultural economy. Federal subsidies, low-interest loans, and tax breaks enabled factories to expand and re-tool. A cost-plus formula built into government contracts guaranteed a profit for manufacturers.

The war concentrated power in the largest corporations. Roosevelt ordered his justice department to postpone enforcement of antitrust laws. Legal challenges that had been years in preparation, such as the case against America's great oil cartel, were tucked away. The renewal of some antitrust activity in 1944, when victory seemed assured, helped keep alive the concept of trust-busting but did little to curtail the growing power of giant enterprises. Congressional efforts to investigate alleged collusion in the awarding of government contracts and to increase assistance to small businesses similarly made little progress in Washington's crisis atmosphere. The top 100 companies, which had provided 30 percent of the nation's total manufacturing output in 1940, were providing 70 percent by 1943. Small businesses were left catering mainly to the civilian economy, which was plagued by erratic allocations, shortages, and stagnation.

The Workforce

During the first two years of military buildup, many workers who had been idled during the Great Depression found jobs. Employment in heavy industry invariably went to men, and most of the skilled jobs went to whites. Initially, administrators of newly established, government-sponsored vocational training centers focused their efforts on training white males. They refused to set up courses for women or, especially in the South, to admit minority workers. Employers, they said, would never hire from these groups. But as military service drained the supply of white male workers, women and minorities became more attractive candidates for production jobs. Soon, both private employers and government were encouraging women to go to work, southern African Americans to move to northern industrial cities, and Mexicans to enter the United States under the *bracero* guest farm-worker program. In response to labor shortages, the composition of the workforce changed dramatically.

conservative, anti–New Deal coalition in Congress. In 1943 Congress abolished the job-creation programs of the Works Progress Administration (WPA), the Civilian Conservation Corps (CCC), and the National Youth Administration (NYA) (see chapter 25). It also shut down the Rural Electrification Administration (REA) and Farm Security Administration (FSA), agencies that had assisted impoverished rural areas. The budget was drastically reduced for the National Recovery Planning Board, which was designed to introduce comprehensive national planning into America's market economy. As "dollar-a-year" business executives flocked to Washington, D.C., to run the new wartime bureaus, the Roosevelt administration adopted a more cooperative stance toward big business. Although many people in the business community never fully trusted Roosevelt, the war nevertheless nudged the president's New Deal to the right.

In win-the-war Washington, social programs withered as big businesses considered essential to victory flourished under government subsidies. What was essential, of

© Bettmann/Corbis.

WOMEN JOIN THE WAR EFFORT
Women employees at the Convair Company in California use a rivet gun and bucking bar, tools traditionally used only by men.

Hired for jobs never before open to them, women became welders, shipbuilders, lumberjacks, and miners. For the first time, women won places in prestigious symphony orchestras. As major league baseball languished from a lack of top flight players, female teams sprang up to give new life to the national pastime; the owner of the Chicago Cubs organized a woman's league in 1943 that eventually fielded 10 teams. Many employers hired married women, who before the war were often banned even from such traditionally female occupations as teaching. Minority women, who before the war had worked mostly on farms or as domestic servants, moved into clerical or secretarial jobs, where they had not previously been welcome. Although most workplaces continued to be largely segregated by sex—women working with other women and men working with other men—the range of jobs open to women grew wider.

The character of unpaid labor, long provided mostly by women, also underwent significant change. Volunteer activities such as Red Cross projects, civil defense work, and recycling drives claimed more and more of the time of women, children, and older people. Government propaganda exhorted homemakers: "Wear it out, use it up, make it do, or do without." "Work in a garden this summer." "Save waste fats for explosives." Most Depression-era Americans were already used to scarcity, but the war now equated a parsimonious lifestyle with patriotism rather than with poverty. Both in the home and in the factory, women's responsibilities and workloads increased.

The new labor market improved the general economic position of African Americans as many moved into labor-scarce cities and into jobs previously off limits to them. By executive order in June 1941, the president created the Fair Employment Practices Commission (FEPC), which tried to ban discrimination in hiring. In 1943 the government announced that it would not recognize as collective bargaining agents any unions that denied admittance to minorities. The War Labor Board outlawed the practice of paying different wages to whites and nonwhites doing the same job. Before the war, the African American population had been mainly southern, rural, and agricultural; within a few years, a substantial percentage of African Americans had become northern, urban, and industrial. Although employment discrimination was hardly eliminated, twice as many African Americans held skilled jobs at the end of the war as at the beginning.

For both men and women, the war brought higher wages and longer work hours. Although in 1943 the government insisted that labor unions limit demands for wage increases to 15 percent, overtime often raised paychecks far more. During the war, average weekly earnings rose nearly 70 percent. Income derived from farming, which had lagged through the many years of low prices and overproduction, doubled and then doubled again.

Labor Unions

The scarcity of labor during the war substantially strengthened the union movement. Union membership rose by 50 percent. Women and minority workers joined unions in unprecedented numbers (women accounted for 27 percent of total membership by 1944), but the main beneficiaries of labor's new power were the white males who still comprised the bulk of union workers.

Especially on the national level, the commitment of organized labor to female workers was weak. Not a single woman served on the executive boards of either the American Federation of Labor (AFL) or the Congress of Industrial Organizations (CIO). The International Brotherhood of Teamsters even required women to sign a statement that their union membership could be revoked when the war was over. Unions did fight for contracts stipulating equal pay for men and women in the same job, but these benefited women only as long as they held "male" jobs. The unions' primary purpose in advocating equal pay was to maintain wage levels for the men who would return to their jobs after the war. During the first year of peace, as employers trimmed their workforces, both business and

CHILDREN ENLIST IN THE WAR EFFORT

These children, flashing the "V-for-Victory" sign, stand atop a pile of scrap metal. Collecting scrap of all kinds for war production helped engage millions of Americans young and old on the home front.

unions gave special preference to returning veterans and worked to ease both women and minority workers out of their wartime jobs. During the war, women held 25 percent of all jobs in automobile factories; by mid-1946 they held only 7.5 percent of these positions. Unions based their policies on seniority and their wage demands on the goal of securing male workers a "family wage," one that would be sufficient to support an entire family.

Some union members feared that hiring traditionally lower-paid workers (women and minorities) would jeopardize whatever wage gains and recognition unions had obtained during the hard-fought labor struggles of the 1930s. Early in the war, most AFL affiliates in the aircraft and shipbuilding industries—sources of the highest-paid jobs—had refused to accept African Americans as members. They quarreled with the FEPC over this policy throughout the war, some even claiming that the effort to advance blacks was the work of subversive, pro-communist "agitators." As growing numbers of African Americans were hired, racial tensions in the workplace increased. In a Baltimore munitions factory, whites suspended work rather than integrate their washrooms and cafeterias. In Beaumont, Texas, martial law was declared to protect black workers from attacks by whites. All across the country—in a defense plant in Lockland, Ohio, at a

transit company in Philadelphia, at a shipbuilding company in Mobile—white workers walked off the job to protest the hiring of African Americans. Beyond suggesting deep-seated racism, such incidents dramatized the fear that management might use the war as an excuse to erode the power and size of unions.

The labor militancy of the 1930s, although muted by a wartime no-strike pledge, nonetheless persisted. Despite no-strike assurances, for example, the United Mine Workers union called a walkout in the bituminous coal fields in 1943. When the War Labor Board took a hard line against the union's demands, the strike was prolonged, prompting Secretary of the Interior Harold L. Ickes to blast both sides. He called the impasse "a black and stupid chapter in the history of the home front." In Detroit, disgruntled aircraft workers roamed the factory floors, cutting off the neckties of their supervisors; wildcat strikes erupted among St. Louis bus drivers, Detroit assembly-line employees for Dodge, and Philadelphia streetcar conductors. The increasingly conservative Congress responded by passing the Smith-Connally Act of 1943, which empowered the president to seize plants or mines if strikes interrupted war production. Even so, the war helped strengthen organized labor's place in American life. By the end of the war, union membership was at an all-time high.

Assessing Economic Change

Overall, the impact of the war on America's political economy was varied. During the conflict, the workplace became more inclusive than ever before in terms of gender and race, and so did labor unions. More people entered the paid labor force, and many of them earned more money than rationing restrictions on consumer goods allowed them to spend. In a remarkable and welcome change from the decade of the Great Depression, jobs were plentiful and savings piled up. Although some of these changes proved short-lived, the new precedents and expectations arising from the wartime experience could not be entirely effaced at war's end.

More than anything else, the institutional scale of American life was transformed. Big government, big business, and big labor all grew even bigger during the war years. Science and technology helped forge new links of mutual interest among these three sectors. The old America of small farms, small businesses, and small towns did not disappear, but urban-based, bureaucratized institutions, in both the public and private sectors, increasingly organized life in postwar America.

● The War at Home: Social Issues

Dramatic social changes accompanied the wartime mobilization. By the end of the war, 16 million Americans had served in the military. Ordered by military service or attracted by employment, many people moved away from the communities where they had grown up. The war demanded new sacrifices, and most Americans willingly obliged. Yet wartime ideals also highlighted everyday inequalities.

Wartime Propaganda

During the First World War, government propagandists had asked Americans to fight for a more democratic world and a permanent peace. Such idealistic goals had little appeal for the skeptical generation of the 1930s and 1940s, who had witnessed the failures of Woodrow Wilson's promises. Only 20 years after Wilson's "war to end all wars," Americans were now embroiled in another worldwide conflict. Sensitive to widespread cynicism about high-minded goals, the Roosevelt administration asked Americans to fight to preserve the "American way of life"—not to save the world.

Artist and illustrator Norman Rockwell and movie director Frank Capra, masters of nostalgia, became the

From the Collections of the Library of Congress.

"FREEDOM OF SPEECH"

Norman Rockwell's illustrations of Roosevelt's "Four Freedoms"—Freedom of Speech, Freedom of Worship, Freedom from Fear, and Freedom from Want—appeared in *The Saturday Evening Post* magazine in early 1943. These images seemed to reassure Americans that the war was a struggle to preserve and protect basic American liberties, not a crusade to change the world.

most celebrated and successful of the wartime image makers. Hollywood studios and directors eagerly answered the government's call by shaping inspiring and sentimental representations of American life. "The American film is our most important weapon," proclaimed one Hollywood producer. During the 1930s, Frank Capra had become the champion of the common man in box office winners such as *Mr. Deeds Comes to Town* (1936) and *Mr. Smith Goes to Washington* (1939). Now called to make a series of government films entitled *Why We Fight*, Capra set Rockwell-like characters in motion and contrasted their lives with harrowing portrayals of the mass obedience and militarism in Germany, Italy, and Japan. (In this, he used footage from the enemy's own propaganda films.) A hundred or so Hollywood personalities received commissions to make films for the army's Pictorial Division. Darryl Zanuck, head of Twentieth Century Fox, filmed Allied troops in North Africa and the Aleutian Islands. John Ford produced gripping combat documentaries on the Battle of Midway and Pearl Harbor.

Print advertising also contributed to the wartime propaganda effort. Roosevelt encouraged advertisers to sell the benefits of freedom. Most obliged, and "freedom" often appeared in the guise of new washing machines, ingenious kitchen appliances, improved automobiles, a wider range of lipstick hues, and automation in a hundred forms. As soon as the fighting ended, these wartime ads promised, American technological know-how would usher in a consumer's paradise. Ads sometimes suggested that Americans were fighting to restore the consumer society of the 1920s (see chapter 24).

The president initially resisted the creation of an official propaganda bureau, preferring to rely on a newly created Office of Facts and Figures (OFF) to disseminate information to the public. Poet Archibald MacLeish, who headed the OFF, however, acknowledged that his office most often resembled a "Tower of Babel" when it came to setting forth the aims and progress of the war. So, in spring 1942, Roosevelt created the Office of War Information (OWI) to coordinate policies related to propaganda and censorship. Democratic critics charged that the OWI was dominated by advertising professionals who dealt in slogans rather than substance. Republicans blasted it as a purveyor of crass political advertisements for causes favored by Roosevelt and New Deal Democrats. Despite such criticism, the OWI established branches throughout the world; published a magazine called *Victory;* and produced hundreds of films, posters, and radio broadcasts.

Gender Equality

Nostalgic portraits of an "American way of life" often clashed with the socioeconomic changes that wartime mobilization brought. Nowhere was this more apparent than in matters affecting the lives and status of women. As women took over jobs traditionally held by men, many people began to take more seriously the idea of gender equality. Some 350,000 women volunteered for military duty during the war; more than 1,000 women served as civilian pilots with the Women's Airforce Service Pilots (WASPs). Although they constituted only 2 percent of all military personnel, these women broke gender stereotypes. Not everyone approved. One member of Congress asked: "What has become of the manhood of America,

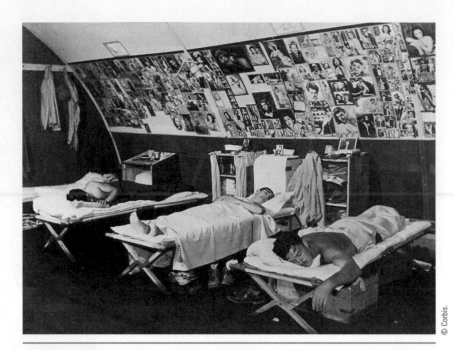

"PIN-UP GIRLS"
Male GIs often surrounded themselves with "pin-up girls," images very different from that of the home front "Rosie-the-Riveter."

that we have to call on our women?" Still, Congress eventually authorized a women's corps, with full status, for each branch of the military, a step that had been thwarted during the First World War.

The military service of women, together with their new importance in the labor market, strengthened arguments for laws guaranteeing equal treatment. Congress seriously considered, but did not pass, an Equal Rights Amendment (ERA) to the Constitution and a national equal-pay law. Women's organizations, however, disagreed over how to advance equality. Organizations representing middle-class women strongly backed passage of the ERA, but other groups, which were more responsive to the problems of women who worked outside their homes, opposed its passage. They saw it as a threat to the protective legislation, regulating hours and hazardous conditions, which women's rights crusaders had struggled to win earlier in the century. Should women continue to be accorded "protected" status in view of their vulnerability to exploitation in a male-directed workplace? Or should they fight for "equal" status?

Even as the war temporarily narrowed gender differences in employment, governmental policies and propaganda frequently framed changes in women's roles in highly traditional terms. Women's expanded participation in the workplace was often portrayed as a short-term sacrifice, necessary to preserve women's "special" responsibilities—hearth and home. A typical ad suggesting that women take on farm work declared: "A woman can do anything if she knows she looks beautiful doing it." Despite the acceptance of women into the armed services, most were assigned to stateside clerical and supply jobs; only a relatively few women served overseas. Day care programs for mothers working outside their homes received reluctant and inadequate funding. The 3,000 centers set up during the conflict filled only a fraction of the need and were swiftly shut down after the war. Social scientists and welfare experts, mostly male, blamed working mothers for an apparent rise in juvenile delinquency and in the divorce rate during the war years.

The war also widened the symbolic gap between "femininity" and "masculinity." Military culture often fostered a "pin-up" mentality toward women. Service publications contained pin-up sections, and tanks and planes were decorated with glossy images of female sexuality. Wartime fiction often associated manliness with brutality and casual sex. After the war, tough-guy fiction with a violent and misogynist edge, like Mickey Spillane's "Mike Hammer" series of detective novels, became one of the most successful genres of popular culture.

Racial Equality

Messages about race were as ambiguous as those related to gender; wartime culture both propelled yet firmly resisted change. Before the Second World War, America had been a sharply segregated society, with racial inequality enforced by law and custom. African Americans, disenfranchised in the South and only beginning to achieve voting power in the North, had only limited access to the political, legal, and economic systems. The fight against fascism, however, challenged this old order.

Nazism, based on the idea of racial inequality, exposed the racist underpinnings of much of 20th-century social science theory. "The Huns have wrecked the theories of the master race with which we were so contented so long," Frank Dixon, ex-governor of Alabama, remarked in 1944. The view that racial difference was not a function of biology but a function of culture—a view most American anthropologists had been advancing for a generation—gained wider popular acceptance during the war. The idea that a democracy could accommodate racial difference provided a basis for the postwar struggle against discrimination.

The northward migration of African Americans accelerated demands for equality. They found an outspoken advocate of civil rights within the White House. First Lady Eleanor Roosevelt repeatedly antagonized southern Democrats and members of her husband's administration (often including the president) by her support for civil rights and her participation in integrated social functions. The writer Clare Boothe Luce once remarked that Mrs. Roosevelt "enjoyed comforting the afflicted and afflicting the comfortable." Although the president often ignored her appeals for federal action against discrimination, her advocacy nevertheless dramatized the case for reform.

African Americans understood the irony of fighting overseas for a country that denied them equality at home. Many challenged the government to live up to its own rhetoric about freedom and democracy. The *Amsterdam News*, a Harlem newspaper, called for a "Double V" campaign—victory at home as well as abroad. In January 1941, even before the United States entered the war, the labor leader A. Philip Randolph promised to lead tens of thousands of frustrated black workers in a march on Washington to demand more defense jobs and integration of the military forces. With the support of major black organizations and other prestigious African American leaders, Randolph invited Roosevelt to address the planned gathering. The president, however, feared the event would embarrass his administration and urged that it be canceled. Randolph's persistence, however, forced Roosevelt to make concessions. In return for Randolph's canceling

A SEGREGATED MILITARY

This photo of an African American regiment eating in a mess hall during the Second World War illustrates racial segregation in the armed forces.

the march, the president created the FEPC. This initially seemed a victory for equal rights, but Roosevelt gave the agency little power over employers who continued to resist integrating their workforces. During the war, the agency lost as many antidiscrimination cases as it won. Still, it provided an important precedent for federal action in civil rights.

Roosevelt also let stand the policy of segregation in the armed forces. "A jim crow army cannot fight for a free world," proclaimed the National Association for the Advancement of Colored People (NAACP)'s newspaper *The Crisis*. Yet General Marshall, Secretary of War Stimson, and others remained opposed to change. The army and the Red Cross even went so far as to follow the scientifically absurd practice of segregating donated blood into "white plasma" and "black plasma." African Americans were relegated to inferior jobs in the military and excluded from combat status, practices that Roosevelt supported out of deference to his white southern constituency who feared that participation in combat might give African Americans new claims on full civil rights. Toward the end of the war, when manpower shortages forced the administration to put African American troops into combat, they performed with distinction.

Complaints about discrimination in the military reached a peak in July 1944 when an explosion at a naval ammunition depot at Port Chicago, near San Francisco, killed 300 stevedores, most of them black and untrained in the process of loading ammunition. When the navy assigned another group of black sailors to similar duty nearby, some of them refused, citing inadequate safety conditions. The resulting court-martial of 50 African American men was the largest mass trial in naval history. All of the sailors were found guilty of disobeying orders and received prison terms ranging from 8 to 15 years. After the war, the men were released on reduced sentences, but their convictions were not overturned, even after Congress requested a special naval review of the incident in 1994. In 1999, one of the men, Freddie Meeks, then 80, requested and received a presidential pardon.

Racial Tensions

In industrial cities, the wartime boom threw overcrowded, working-class neighborhoods into turmoil. Many of the residents of these neighborhoods came from European immigrant backgrounds or had migrated from rural areas in the United States. Wartime work provided their first real economic opportunity, and they viewed the minority newcomers as unwelcome rivals for jobs and housing. In 1943, for example, it was estimated that between 6,000 and 10,000 African Americans arrived in Los Angeles every month. Once there, their living options were effectively limited to a few overcrowded areas segregated by landlords' practices and by California's restrictive housing covenants—legal agreements prohibiting the sale of homes to certain religious or racial groups. One official reported: "You will see life as no human is expected to endure it. Conditions are pitiful, and health problems are prevalent." Under such conditions, racial tensions festered.

Around the country, public housing projects presented a particularly explosive dilemma to federal officials charged with administering the supply of desperately needed accommodations. Should they follow local practice and keep housing segregated, or should they integrate people of color into hostile white neighborhoods? Whites resisted the forced integration of public housing; nonwhites denounced the government for vacillating. In Buffalo, New York, threats of violence caused the cancellation of one housing project. In Detroit in June 1943, a full-scale race riot erupted when police escorted African American tenants into a new complex. Several cities that attempted integration had to call in federal troops to restore order.

Racial disturbances were not restricted to confrontations between whites and blacks. In Los Angeles, the so-called zoot suit incidents of 1943 pitted Anglos against Mexican Americans. Minor incidents between young Mexican American men wearing "zoot suits"—flamboyant outfits that featured oversized coats and trousers—and soldiers and sailors from nearby military bases escalated into virtual warfare between the zoot-suiters and local police. The Los Angeles City Council, recognizing that the zoot suit was becoming a symbol of rebellion for Mexican American youths, even tried to make it a crime to wear one. The Roosevelt administration feared that the zoot suit violence might have a negative effect on the Good Neighbor Policy in Latin America. The president's coordinator of inter-American affairs, therefore, implemented a series of programs to ameliorate conditions contributing to tension. He allocated federal money to train Spanish-speaking Americans for wartime jobs, to improve education in barrios, and to open up more spaces in colleges throughout the American Southwest.

American Indians constituted a significant group of new migrants to urban areas during the war. Although New Deal Indian policies (see chapter 25) had attempted to restore tribal communities and Indian traditions, the Second World War introduced powerful pressures for migration and assimilation. By the end of the war, approximately 25,000 Indian men and several hundred Indian women had served in the armed forces, where they were fully integrated with whites. Some 40,000 other Indians found war work in nearby cities, many leaving their reservation for the first time. For Indians, the white-dominated towns and cities tended to be strange and hostile places. Rapid City, South Dakota, for example, attracted more than 2,000 Sioux from the Pine Ridge Reservation; most settled in informal camps at the outskirts of the city. Especially in smaller towns near reservations—such as Gallup, New Mexico; Flagstaff, Arizona; or Billings, Montana— white residents constructed formalized systems of discrimination against the newcomers. Many Indians moved back and forth between city and reservation, holding their urban jobs for only a few months while seeking to live between two quite different worlds. Economic opportunities remained limited on most reservations.

For African Americans, Latinos, and Indians, fighting for the "American way of life" represented a commitment not to the past but to a more egalitarian future. Increasingly, Americans of all backgrounds were realizing that racial grievances had to be addressed. In Detroit, for example, the local chapter of the NAACP emerged from the wartime years with a strong base from which to fight for jobs and political power. The Committee (later, Congress)

LINK TO THE PAST

Civil Liberties in Wartime: *Korematsu* v. *United States*

Fred Korematsu, an American of Japanese background, was born in Oakland and had been a law-abiding citizen. In his early twenties, when the order to relocate Japanese Americans to internment camps was announced, he challenged the legality of the measure. The case was ultimately heard by the Supreme Court. In a controversial decision in December 1944, a divided court upheld the constitutionality of internment. The following selections suggest some of the arguments made in both the majority and minority opinions. Nearly 45 years later, after an examination of military records, Congress took a stand on the issue. Officially apologizing for internment, Congress stated that it was "not justified by military necessity, and . . . not driven by analysis of military conditions."

EXCLUSION OF THOSE of Japanese origin was deemed necessary because of the presence of an unascertained number of disloyal members of the group, most of whom we have no doubt were loyal to this country. It was because we could not reject the finding of the military authorities that it was impossible to bring about an immediate segregation of the disloyal from the loyal. . . .

Compulsory exclusion of large groups of citizens from their homes, except under circumstances of direct emergency and peril, is inconsistent with our basic governmental institutions. But when under conditions of modern warfare our shores are threatened by hostile forces, the power to protect must be commensurate with the threatened danger. . . . To cast this case into outlines of racial prejudice, without reference to the real military dangers which were presented, merely confuses the issue.

JUSTICE HUGO BLACK
from the majority opinion of the Supreme Court in *Korematsu* v. *U.S.* (1944), upholding the constitutionality of Executive Order 9066

WE MUST ACCORD great respect and consideration to the judgments of the military authorities who are on the scene and who have full knowledge of the military facts. . . . At the same time, however, it is essential that there be definite limits to military discretion, especially where martial law has not been declared. Individuals must not be left impoverished of their constitutional rights on a plea of military necessity that has neither substance nor support. . . .

In support of this blanket condemnation of all persons of Japanese descent, however, no reliable evidence is cited to show that such individuals were generally disloyal, or had . . . furnished reasonable ground for their exclusion as a group. . . . No adequate reason is given for the failure to treat these Japanese Americans on an individual basis by holding investigations and hearings to separate the loyal from the disloyal, as was done in the case of persons of German and Italian ancestry. . . . I dissent, therefore, from this legalization of racism.

JUSTICE FRANK MURPHY
from the dissenting opinion in *Korematsu* v. *U.S.*

1. Are there conditions that would constitutionally permit detention of citizens on the basis of their nationality or ethnic background?
2. What might explain Congress's later decision to issue an apology?

For additional sources related to this feature, visit the *Liberty, Equality, Power* Web site at:

http://history.wadsworth.com/murrin_LEP4e

on Racial Equality (CORE), an organization founded in 1942 and composed of whites and blacks who advocated nonviolent resistance to segregation, devised new strategies during the war. CORE activists staged sit-ins to integrate restaurants, theaters, and even prison dining halls in Washington, D.C. These same tactics would serve in the 1950s and 1960s to force the desegregation of interstate buses and public accommodations. As the Swedish sociologist Gunnar Myrdal predicted in his influential study of American racial issues, *An American Dilemma* (1944), "fundamental changes" would soon have to come throughout the nation. Prominent African American novelist Richard Wright wrote that America had to do something about its "white problem."

People of Japanese descent faced a unique situation. During the two months after the attack on Pearl Harbor, fear of sabotage by pro-Japanese residents engulfed West Coast communities. One military report concluded that a "large, unassimilated, tightly knit racial group, bound to an enemy nation by strong ties of race, culture, custom, and religion . . . constituted a menace" that justified extraordinary action. Despite lack of evidence of disloyalty, the president in February 1942 issued Executive Order 9066, directing the relocation and internment of first- and second-generation Japanese Americans (called Issei and Nisei, respectively) at inland camps. Curiously, in Hawaii, where the presumed danger of subversion might have been much greater, no such internment took place; there, people of Japanese ancestry constituted 37 percent of the population and were essential to the economy. Forced to abandon their possessions or sell them for a pittance, nearly 130,000 mainland Japanese Americans were confined in flimsy barracks, enclosed by barbed wire and under armed guard. Two-thirds of the detainees were native-born U.S. citizens. Many had been substantial landowners in California's agricultural industries.

Despite the internment, the courage and sacrifice of Japanese American soldiers became legendary. The 100th Battalion, composed of Nisei from Hawaii, was nearly wiped out; 57 percent of the famed 442nd Regimental Combat Team were killed or wounded in the mountains of Italy; and 6,000 members of the Military Intelligence Service provided invaluable service in the Pacific theater.

Racial hostilities reflected the underlying strains in America's social fabric, but other tensions pulled at Americans as well. Rifts developed between city dwellers and migrants from rural areas. Some Californians derided the "Okies," people who had fled the Dust Bowl in Oklahoma looking for agricultural work on the West Coast, as ignorant and unruly. In Chicago, migrants from Appalachia

INTERNMENT
Uniformed officials check the baggage of people of Japanese descent as they are being evacuated to internment camps.

FDR Library.

met similar derision. At the beginning of the war, more than one-third of white Americans were still either first- or second-generation immigrants. Many ethnic communities that had preserved the language and culture of their homelands felt the pressure to assimilate.

The symbol of the "melting pot," together with appeals to nationalism, grew more and more powerful in American culture. Wartime propaganda stressed the theme of national unity by calling the Second World War a "people's war," and it contrasted America's melting pot with German and Japanese obsessions about racial purity. Wartime movies, plays, and music reinforced a sense of national community by building on cultural nationalism and stressing historical themes. Many foreign-language broadcasts and publications ceased to exist during the war, and naturalization applications nearly doubled from what they had been only five years earlier.

The great movements of population during the war—rural to urban, south to north, east to west—helped erode distinctions based on geography, ethnicity, and race. Wartime demands for additional labor weakened the barriers to many occupations. As each of America's racial and ethnic minorities established records of distinguished military service, the claim of equality—"Americans All," in the words of a wartime slogan—took on greater moral force. The possibility for more equitable participation in the mainstream of American life, together with rhetoric extolling social solidarity and freedom, provided a foundation for the antidiscrimination movements of the decades ahead. The war for the American way of life, it turned out, carried many different meanings.

Shaping the Peace

The end of the war raised difficult questions about demobilization and peace. Truman built on Roosevelt's many wartime conferences and agreements to shape the framework of international relations for the next half-century. He participated in establishing the United Nations, creating new international economic institutions, and settling global political issues involving territory and governance.

International Organizations

In the Atlantic Charter of 1941 and at a conference in Moscow in October 1943, the Allies had already pledged to create an international organization to replace the defunct League of Nations. The new United Nations (UN) fulfilled Woodrow Wilson's vision of an international body to deter aggressor nations. At the Dumbarton Oaks Conference in Washington in August 1944 and at a subsequent

meeting in San Francisco in April 1945, the Allies worked out the organizational structure of the UN. It would have a General Assembly, in which each member nation would be represented and have one vote. It would also have a Security Council, whose makeup would include five permanent members—the United States, Great Britain, the Soviet Union, France, and China—and six rotating members. The Security Council would have primary responsibility for maintaining peace, but permanent members of the council enjoyed an absolute veto over any council decision. The inclusion of China in the Security Council was a victory for the United States, which hoped that Jiang's government could remain in power and would become an effective U.S. ally. A UN Secretariat would handle day-to-day business, and an Economic and Social Council would promote social and economic advancement throughout the world.

The U.S. Senate accepted the UN charter in July 1945 with only two dissenting votes. This resounding victory for internationalism contrasted sharply with the Senate's rejection of membership in the League of Nations after the First World War. Americans of an earlier generation had worried that internationalist policies might impinge on their country's ability to follow its own national interests. Following the Second World War, because U.S. power clearly dominated emerging organizations such as the UN, Americans thought it less likely that decisions of international bodies would impede their nation's foreign policies. In addition, Americans recognized that the war had partly resulted from the lack of a coordinated, international response to aggression during the 1930s and wanted to avoid the same situation again.

Eleanor Roosevelt, the former first lady and a domestic social activist, also played a prominent role in building the new postwar internationalist ethos. A delegate to the first meeting of the UN's General Assembly, she chaired the U.S. Commission on Human Rights and guided the drafting of a Universal Declaration of Human Rights, adopted by the UN in 1948. The Declaration set forth "inalienable" human rights and freedoms as cornerstones of international law.

Postwar economic settlements also illustrated a growing acceptance of other new international organizations. At the Bretton Woods (New Hampshire) Conference of 1944, assembled nations created the International Monetary Fund (IMF), which was designed to maintain stable exchange by ensuring that each nation's currency could be converted into any other national currency at a fixed rate. Exchange rates could be altered only with the agreement of the fund. (This international system of fixed exchange rates was replaced in 1971 by a system of floating rates.) The International Bank for Reconstruction and

Development, later renamed the World Bank, was also created at Bretton Woods to provide loans to war-battered countries and promote the resumption of world trade. In 1947 the General Agreement on Tariffs and Trade (GATT) created an institutional structure for breaking up closed trading blocs and implementing free and fair trade agreements. Policy makers hoped that these three institutions would preclude the currency devaluation and economic protectionism that had unsettled the world economy during the 1930s. American capital and American policies dominated the bodies, even though they were international bodies financed by member nations throughout the world. The Soviet Union, whose state-directed economy challenged the assumptions of western capitalism, did not participate.

Spheres of Interest and Postwar Settlements

Wartime conversations among Stalin, Churchill, and Roosevelt had often assumed that there would be special "spheres of influence," areas dominated by a single power, in the postwar world. As early as January 1942, the Soviet ambassador to the United States reported to Stalin that Roosevelt had tacitly assented to Soviet postwar control over the Baltic states of Lithuania, Latvia, and Estonia. The Soviets accepted British and U.S. dominance of Italy's post-fascist government. And in 1944 Stalin and Churchill agreed informally and secretly that Britain would continue its sway over Greece and that the Soviets could control Romania and Bulgaria.

Roosevelt had implied to Stalin that he understood the Soviet's need to create friendly states on its vulnerable western border, but, at the same time, he had talked about self-determination for small nations. For example, at the Tehran Conference of November 1943, held just one year before the 1944 presidential election, Roosevelt told Stalin that American voters of Polish, Latvian, Lithuanian, and Estonian descent expected their homelands to be independent after the war.

Precisely how Roosevelt intended to reconcile his contradictory positions on Soviet spheres of influence in the postwar world will never be known. Roosevelt, a master of finesse, probably believed that he could improvise a solution. As long as Soviet armies were essential to Germany's defeat—and the president also wanted the USSR to join the war against Japan—Roosevelt struck a tone of cooperation with Stalin. Flexibility, holding together unlikely coalitions, and taking contradictory positions simultaneously were Roosevelt's special strengths. On many critical international issues of the 1930s—the gold standard, tariff policy, and entry into the war—he had managed to straddle both sides of seemingly irreconcilable positions. On postwar issues, for which he seemed to have only vague policy ideas, Roosevelt likely thought he could perform a similar juggling act.

Roosevelt's contradictory policies toward a Soviet sphere of interest, however, bedeviled his successors. The military results of the war, particularly the USSR's powerful position in Eastern Europe, strongly influenced postwar territorial settlements. On issues of governance—particularly in Germany, Poland, and Korea—splits between U.S. and Soviet interests widened.

Germany, especially, became a focus and a symbol of bipolar tensions. Early in the war, both the United States and the Soviet Union had urged the dismemberment and deindustrialization of Nazi Germany after its defeat. Roosevelt endorsed a controversial plan proposed by Secretary of the Treasury Henry Morgenthau that would have turned Germany into a pastoral, agricultural country. At a conference held at Yalta, Ukraine, in early February 1945, the three Allied powers agreed to divide Germany into four zones of occupation (with France as the fourth occupying force). Later, as relations among the victors cooled, this temporary division of Germany permanently solidified into a Soviet-dominated zone in the East that faced off against the three other Allied zones in the West. Berlin, the German capital, also was divided, even though it lay totally within the Soviet zone. As fear of the Soviets began to replace earlier concerns of a revived Germany, Truman abandoned the Morgenthau plan in favor of efforts to rebuild the western zones of Germany.

Postwar rivalries for influence also focused on Poland. During the war, Poland had two governments: a government-in-exile based in London and a communist-backed one in Lublin. At the Yalta Conference, the Soviets agreed to permit free elections in postwar Poland and to create a government "responsible to the will of the people," but Stalin also believed that the other Allied leaders had tacitly accepted Soviet dominance over Poland. The agreement at Yalta was ambiguous at best, as many on the negotiating teams realized at the time. During Yalta, the war was still at a critical stage, and the western Allies chose to sacrifice clarity over the Polish issue in order to encourage cooperation with the Soviets. After Yalta, the Soviets assumed that Poland was to be in their sphere of influence, but many Americans charged the Soviets with bad faith for failing to hold free elections and for not relinquishing control.

In Asia, military realities likewise influenced postwar settlements. Roosevelt had long wanted to bring the USSR into the war against Japan to relieve pressure on U.S. forces in the Pacific. At Tehran in November 1943 and again at

Yalta, Stalin pledged to send troops to Asia as soon as Germany was defeated, but when U.S. policy makers learned that the atomic bomb was ready for use against Japan, they became eager to limit Soviet involvement in the Pacific theater. The first atomic bomb fell on Hiroshima just one day before the Soviets were to enter the war against Japan, and the United States took sole charge of the occupation and postwar reorganization of Japan. The Soviet Union and the United States split Korea, which had been controlled by Japan, into separate zones of occupation. Here, as in Germany, these zones later emerged as two antagonistic states (see chapter 27).

The fate of the European colonies seized by Japan in Southeast Asia was another issue that remained unresolved in the planning for peace. During the war, the United States had declared itself in favor of decolonization. Although the United States would have preferred to see the former British and French colonies become independent nations, with governments friendly to the West and especially to American interests, U.S. policy makers worried about the pro-communist politics of many anticolonial nationalist movements. After the war, as the United States developed an anticommunist foreign policy, it moved to support British and French efforts to reassemble their colonial empires. Long struggles would ensue over the independence and political orientation of postwar governments throughout the colonized world.

In its own colony of the Philippines, the United States honored a long-standing pledge to grant independence. A friendly government that agreed to respect U.S. economic interests and military bases took power in 1946 and enlisted American advisers to help suppress leftist rebels. The Mariana, Caroline, and Marshall Islands, all of which had been captured by Japan during the war, were designated Trust Territories of the Pacific by the United Nations and placed under U.S. administration in 1947.

Although the countries of Latin America had been only indirectly involved in military conflict or peace negotiations, the Second World War directly affected U.S. relations with them. During the 1930s the Roosevelt administration had sought to curb Nazi influence in Latin America. The Good Neighbor Policy, building on a 1928 pledge to carry out no more military interventions in the hemisphere, had helped improve U.S.–Latin American relations. The Office of Inter-American Affairs (OIAA), created in 1937, further expanded cultural and economic ties. Just weeks after the German invasion of Poland in 1939, at a Pan American Conference in Panama City, Latin American leaders showed that the hemisphere was nearly united behind the Allies. The conferees strengthened hemispheric economic cooperation and declared a 300-mile-wide band of neutrality in waters around the hemisphere (excepting

Canada). After U.S. entry into the war, at a January 1942 conference in Rio de Janeiro, all of the Latin American countries except Chile and Argentina broke off diplomatic ties with the Axis governments. When naval warfare in the Atlantic severed commercial connections between Latin America and Europe, Latin American countries became critical suppliers of raw materials to the United States, to the benefit of all.

Wartime conferences and settlements avoided clear decisions about creating a Jewish homeland in the Middle East, a proposal that England had supported, but not effected, after the First World War. The Second World War prompted survivors of the Holocaust and Jews from around the world to take direct action. Zionism, the movement to found a Jewish state in Palestine, their ancient homeland, attracted thousands of people, who began to carve out the new nation of Israel. Middle Eastern affairs, which had seldom concerned U.S. policy makers before 1941, would take on greater urgency after 1948, when the Truman administration formally recognized Israel as a sovereign state.

Conclusion

The world changed dramatically during the era of the Second World War. Wartime mobilization ended the Great Depression and shifted the New Deal's focus away from domestic social issues and toward international concerns. It brought victory over dictatorial, brutal regimes. As Europe lay in ruins, with at least 22 million people displaced from their homes, the United States emerged as the world's preeminent power, owning two-thirds of the world's gold reserves and controlling more than half of its manufacturing capacity.

At home, the war transformed the nation's economic structure. During the war emergency, a powerful national government, concerned with preserving national security, assumed nearly complete power over the nation's economy. New, cooperative ties were forged among government, business, labor, and scientific researchers. All sectors worked together to provide the seemingly miraculous growth in productivity that ultimately won the war.

The early 1940s sharpened debates over liberty and equality. Many Americans saw the Second World War as a struggle to protect and preserve the power and liberties they already enjoyed. Others, inspired by a struggle against racism and injustice abroad, insisted that a war for freedom should help secure equal rights at home.

News of Japan's surrender prompted joyous celebrations throughout the country, but questions remained about postwar policies. International conferences established a structure for the United Nations and for new, global economic institutions. Still, Americans remained uncertain about postwar reconstruction of former enemies and about future relations with wartime allies, particularly the Soviet Union. Domestically, the wrenching dislocations of war—psychic, demographic, and economic—took their toll. Postwar adjustments would be difficult for all Americans. And, of course, the nation now faced the future without the charismatic leadership of Franklin D. Roosevelt, the only president that many Americans had ever known.

For the next 50 years, veterans of the Second World War remained relatively quiet about their combat experiences. "The reason they don't talk," a former tank commander commented, "is they couldn't get the picture over to somebody that wasn't there. He would think that you're making that story up." After the 50th anniversary of the war's end, however, with remaining veterans reaching old age, Americans suddenly rediscovered what journalist Tom Brokaw called the "greatest generation." Books about the war dominated bestseller lists during the late 1990s; Steven Spielberg's film *Saving Private Ryan* packed theaters; and Congress approved construction of a huge memorial on the grounds of the National Mall in Washington, D.C. The Second World War, through these popular representations, continued to stand as a powerful symbol of honor, unity, and common sacrifice.

SUGGESTED READINGS

On the United States and the coming of World War II, see **Robert Dallek, *Franklin D. Roosevelt and American Foreign Policy, 1932–1945*** (1979), and **Waldo H. Heinrichs, *Threshold of War: Franklin D. Roosevelt and American Entry into World War II*** (1988). For the war's military aspects, see **Gerhard L. Weinberg, *A World at Arms: A Global History of World War II*** (1994), and **Gerald F. Linderman, *The World within War: America's Combat Experience in World War II*** (1997). Few narrative histories can match the dramatic narrative sweep of **Stephen Ambrose's many works, such as *D-Day: June 6, 1944: The Climactic Battle of World War II*** (1994) and ***Band of Brothers: E Company, 506th Regiment, 101st Airborne from Normandy to Hitler's Eagle's Nest*** (2001). **Michael Beschloss, *The Conquerors: Roosevelt, Truman and the Destruction of Hitler's Germany, 1941–1945*** (2002) is also highly readable. The decision to drop atomic bombs on Japan is adroitly analyzed in **J. Samuel Walker, *Prompt and Utter Destruction: Truman and the Use of the Atomic Bombs against Japan*** (1997).

For overviews of America's wartime experience, **William L. O'Neill, *A Democracy at War: American's Fight at Home and Abroad in World War II*** (1993), and **Michael C. C. Adams, *The Best War Ever: America and World War II*** (1994) present contrasting perspectives.

On the home front, see the superb overview by **John Morton Blum, *V Was for Victory: Politics and American Culture during World War II*** (1976). It may be supplemented by essays from **Lewis A. Erenberg and Susan E. Hirsch, eds., *The War in American Culture: Society and Consciousness during World War II*** (1996), and **Thomas Patrick Doherty, *Projections of War: Hollywood, American Culture, and World War II*** (1993). **Richard W. Steele, *Free Speech and the Good War*** (1999) examines governmental efforts to regulate dissent. **Karen Anderson, *Wartime Women: Sex Roles, Family Relations, and the Status of Women during World War II*** (1981) surveys women's roles during the war. **Ronald Takaki, *Double Victory: A Multicultural History of America in World War II*** (2000) is a good synthesis of issues related to race and ethnicity.

AMERICAN JOURNEY ONLINE
AND
INFOTRAC COLLEGE EDITION

Visit the source collections at www.ajaccess.wadsworth.com and infotrac.thomsonlearning.com and use the Search function with the following key terms to explore documents, images, audio and video clips, articles, and commentary related to the material in this chapter.

Adolph Hitler	Dwight D. Eisenhower
Joseph Stalin	Navajo Signal Corps
Neutrality Act	Harry S. Truman
Franklin D. Roosevelt	Hiroshima
Lend-Lease	Women in World War II
Pearl Harbor	Japanese Internment

GRADE AIDS

Visit the Liberty Equality Power Companion Web site for resources specific to this textbook: http://history.wadsworth.com/murrin_LEP4e

The CD in the back of this book and the U.S. History Resource Center at http://history.wadsworth.com/u.s./ offer a variety of tools to help you succeed in this course, including access to quizzes; images; documents; interactive simulations, maps, and timelines, movie explorations; and a wealth of other sources.

The Age of Containment, 1946–1954

HOLLYWOOD IN THE SERVICE OF THE ANTICOMMUNIST CRUSADE
Fears about communist infiltration of the motion picture industry prompted Hollywood studios to display their anticommunist credentials by blacklisting left-leaning employees and by making films such as RKO's *I Married a Communist*. These anticommunist films, with their simplistic political messages, generally bombed at the box office. This particular film did better when rereleased as *The Woman on Pier 13*.

CHAPTER OUTLINE

The Second World War, heralded as an effort to preserve and protect the fabric of American life, had ended up transforming it. The fight against fascism brought foreign policy issues to the center of U.S. politics, and the international turmoil of the postwar period kept them there. As the Second World War gave way to a "Cold War" between the United States and the Soviet Union, American policy makers adopted global policies to "contain" the Soviet Union and to enhance America's economic and military security. Preoccupation with national security abroad also raised calls for limiting dissent at home. Americans debated how the fight against communism overseas might affect their own liberties.

The Cold War years from 1946 to 1954 raised questions about governmental power. Should the activist, New Deal–style national government be scaled back? What role should Washington, D.C., play in planning the postwar economy? What should be government's relationship to social policy making, especially efforts to achieve equality? These broad issues first emerged during the 1945–53 presidency of Democrat Harry Truman as he struggled to define his Fair Deal programs.

CHAPTER FOCUS

♦ What were the principal elements of the foreign policy called containment, and what major conflicts shaped the Cold War?
♦ How did the foreign policy of containment affect domestic policy and American life?
♦ What was the Fair Deal, and how did it affect American politics?
♦ How did social changes such as population growth and movement to the suburbs affect Americans?

☛ Creating a National Security State, 1945–1949

The wartime alliance between the United States and the Soviet Union had been little more than a marriage of convenience. Defeat of the Axis powers had required the two nations to cooperate, but collaboration scarcely lasted beyond victory. Especially after President Franklin Roosevelt's death in April 1945, relations between the United States and the Soviet Union steadily degenerated into a Cold War of suspicion and tension.

Onset of the Cold War

Historians have discussed the origins of the Cold War from many different perspectives. The traditional interpretation, which gained new power after the collapse of the Soviet Union in 1991, focuses on Soviet expansionism, stressing a historic Russian appetite for new territory, or an ideological zeal to spread international communism, or some interplay between the two. According to this view, the United States needed to take as hard a line as possible. Other historians—generally called *revisionists*—argue that the Soviet Union's obsession with securing its borders was an understandable response to the invasion of its territory during both world wars. The United States, in this view, should have tried to reassure the Soviets by seeking accommodation, instead of pursuing policies that intensified Soviet fears. Still other scholars maintain that assigning blame obscures the clash of deep-seated rival interests that made postwar tensions between the two superpowers inevitable.

In any view, Harry Truman's role proved important. His brusque manner, in sharp contrast to Franklin Roosevelt's urbanity, brought a harsher tone to U.S.–Soviet meetings. Truman initially hoped that he could somehow cut a deal with Soviet Premier Joseph Stalin, much like his old mentor, "Boss" Tom Pendergast, struck bargains with rogue politicians back in Kansas City. "I like Stalin," Truman once wrote his wife. "[He] knows what he wants and will compromise when he can't get it." However, as disagreements between the two former allies mounted, Truman came to rely on his more hard-line advisers.

The atomic bomb provided an immediate source of friction. At the Potsdam Conference of July 1945, Truman had casually remarked to Stalin, "We have a new weapon of unusual destructive force." Calmly, Stalin had replied that he hoped the United States would make "good use" of it against Japan. Less calmly, Stalin immediately ordered a crash program to develop nuclear weapons of his own. After atomic bombs hit Japan, Stalin reportedly told his

scientists that "the equilibrium has been destroyed. Provide the bomb. It will remove a great danger from us." Truman hoped that the bomb would scare the Soviets, and it did. Stalin grew even more concerned about the Soviet Union's future security. Historians still debate whether "wearing the bomb ostentatiously on our hip," as Secretary of War Henry Stimson put it, frightened the Soviets into more cautious behavior or made them more fearful and aggressive.

In 1946 Truman authorized Bernard Baruch, a presidential adviser and special representative to the United Nations, to offer a proposal for the international control of atomic power. The Baruch Plan called for full disclosure by all UN member nations of nuclear research and materials, creation of an international authority to ensure compliance, and destruction of all U.S. atomic weapons once these first steps were completed. Andrei A. Gromyko, the Soviet ambassador to the UN, argued that the Baruch plan would require other nations to halt their atomic research and disclose their secrets to the UN (dominated by the United States) before the United States was required to do anything. Gromyko countered by proposing that the United States unilaterally destroy its atomic weapons first, with international disclosure and control to follow. The United States refused. Both sides used this deadlock to justify a stepped-up arms race.

Other sources of Soviet-American friction involved U.S. loan policies and the Soviet sphere of influence in Eastern Europe. Truman abruptly suspended lend-lease assistance to the Soviet Union in early September 1945, partly to pressure Moscow into holding elections in Poland. Subsequently, Truman's administration similarly linked extension of U.S. reconstruction loans to its goal of rolling back Soviet power in Eastern Europe. This linkage strategy never worked. Lack of capital and signs of Western hostility provided the Soviets with excuses for tightening their grip on Eastern Europe, a course of action that further discouraged the United States from extending economic assistance to countries dominated by Moscow. The Soviet sphere of influence in Eastern Europe, which Stalin called defensive and Truman labeled proof of communist expansionism, solidified. By 1946, the former allies were well on their way to becoming bitter adversaries.

From 1947 on, Harry Truman placed his personal stamp on the presidency by focusing on "national security," a relatively new and emotionally powerful term, and on an international fight against the spread of communism. His policy initiatives, in both foreign and domestic affairs, extended the reach and power of the executive branch of government.

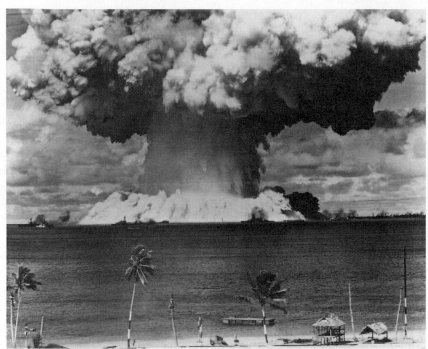

The Granger Collection, New York.

TESTING THE ATOMIC BOMB AT BIKINI ATOLL
This atomic test, one of 23 detonations at Bikini Atoll in the Marshall Islands during the late 1940s, raised a column of water 5,000 feet high. Although Bikini islanders were evacuated from the blast sites, the radiation still affected nearby people, including U.S. service personnel, and the area's ecology for years to come. As nuclear-related imagery spread through Cold War culture, new "bikini" swimsuits for "bombshell" women became a fashion rage.

Containment Abroad: The Truman Doctrine

In March 1947, the president announced what became known as the Truman Doctrine. He was addressing Congress concerning the civil war in Greece, a conflict in which communist-led insurgents were trying to topple a corrupt but pro-Western government. Historically, Greece had fallen within Great Britain's sphere of influence. Britain, however, was badly weakened by the Second World War and could no longer maintain its formerly strong presence there or in the Middle East. Truman's advisers claimed that a leftist victory in Greece would open neighboring Turkey, which they considered especially critical to U.S. interests, to Soviet subversion. Truman's policy makers doubted they enjoyed broad support, either among the public or in Congress, for a U.S. foreign aid program to Greece and Turkey. The president consequently made his case to Congress in especially dramatic terms. U.S. security interests, he said, were now worldwide, and the fate of "free peoples" everywhere, not simply the future of Greece and Turkey, hung in the balance. Unless the United States aided countries "who are resisting attempted subversion by armed minorities or by outside pressures," totalitarian communism would spread around the world and threaten the security of the United States.

Although the Truman Doctrine's global vision of national security encountered skepticism, the president got his request. Henry Wallace, the president's most visible Democratic critic, chided Truman for exaggerating the Soviet threat. Conservative Republicans looked suspiciously at the increase of executive power and the vast expenditures the Truman Doctrine seemed to imply. If Truman wanted to win support for his position, Republican Senator Arthur Vandenberg had already advised, he would need to "scare hell" out of people, something that Truman proved quite willing to do. With backing from both Republicans and Democrats, Congress passed Truman's request for $400 million in assistance to Greece and Turkey, most of it in military aid, in spring 1947. This vote signaled broad, bipartisan support for a national security policy that came to be called "containment."

The term containment had appeared in a 1947 article in the influential journal *Foreign Affairs*. The author, writing under the pseudonym "X," was George Kennan, the State Department's leading expert on Soviet affairs. Kennan argued that the "main element" in any U.S. policy "must be that of a long-term, patient but firm and vigilant containment of Russian expansive tendencies." Although Kennan later insisted that he had meant containment to be a series of discrete responses to specific moves by the Soviets and had never proposed an open-ended crusade, his broad prose lent itself to different interpretations. Whatever Kennan's precise intent, his "X" article quickly became associated with the alarmist tone of the Truman Doctrine.

Containment thus became the catchphrase for a global, anticommunist, national security policy. In the popular view, containment linked all leftist insurgencies, wherever they occurred, to a totalitarian movement controlled from Moscow that directly threatened, by its ideas as much as by military might, the United States. Although foreign policy debates regularly included sharp disagreements over precisely *how* to pursue the goal of containment, few Americans dared to question the basic premise that their country needed a global and activist foreign policy.

Truman's Loyalty Program

Nine days after proclaiming the Truman Doctrine, the president issued Executive Order 9835, which brought the containment of communism to the home front. Truman's order called for a system of loyalty boards empowered to determine if there were "reasonable grounds" for believing that any government employee belonged to an organization or held political ideas that might pose a "security risk" to the United States. People judged to be security risks would lose their government jobs. The Truman loyalty program also authorized the attorney general's office to identify organizations it considered subversive, and in December 1947 the first Attorney General's List was released.

The Truman administration's domestic loyalty program rested on its assessment of the extent of Soviet espionage activity in the United States, an issue that has generated great controversy over the years. Although few people ever doubted that Soviets were carrying out operations in the United States during the 1940s, sharp disagreement has persisted regarding their scope and success. Were Soviet agents operating only at the fringes, or had they penetrated the top levels of the U.S. government? Were they obtaining easily available information or stealing vital national secrets? Did the administration exaggerate, underestimate, or accurately assess the situation?

Such debates now take place in light of recently declassified evidence about Soviet activities in the United States. As early as 1943, a super-secret Army counterintelligence unit had begun intercepting transmissions between Moscow and the United States in 1943. Called the "Venona files" and finally released to the public in 1995, these intercepted messages suggested that the USSR gave financial support to America's Communist Party; had informants in wartime governmental agencies, including the Office of War Information (OWI) and the intelligence-gathering agency, the Office of Strategic Services (OSS); and began obtaining secret information about U.S. atomic work in 1944. The issue of Soviet espionage, in short, was a legitimate national security concern, but historians remain divided over the significance and reliability of specific pieces of the Venona evidence and over the extent of Truman's knowledge about the intercepts.

The president justified his loyalty program by claiming that the government faced relatively few security risks but that their potential to do harm demanded a response that was unprecedented in peacetime. Truman's position, however, failed to satisfy a wide range of critics. Some Republicans charged that hundreds, perhaps even thousands, of Communist Party members had been infiltrating the federal bureaucracy since the New Deal and stronger measures were required. On the other hand, the president's program worried civil liberties groups, who insisted that a limited internal security threat logically demanded an equally limited governmental response. Should not, for example, civil libertarians asked, any loyalty investigation distinguish between an atomic scientist with suspicious ties to the Soviet embassy and a clerical worker in the Interior Department with leftist political leanings? Truman's approach angered both fervent anticommunists, who accused the president of doing too little to fight the Red Menace at home, and civil libertarians, who charged him with going too far.

The National Security Act, the Marshall Plan, and the Berlin Crisis

The Truman Doctrine and the loyalty program only began the administration's national security initiatives. The National Security Act of 1947 created several new bureaucracies. It began the process that transformed the old Navy and War departments into a new Department of Defense, finally established in 1949. It instituted another new arm of the executive branch, the National Security Council, with broad authority over planning foreign policy.

It established the Air Force as a separate service equal to the Army and Navy. And it created the Central Intelligence Agency (CIA) to gather information and to undertake covert activities in support of the nation's newly defined security interests.

The CIA proved to be the most flexible arm of the national security bureaucracy. During the Second World War, the OSS had provided valuable intelligence and conducted espionage, but it was disbanded when the war was over because Americans generally opposed having a permanent secret agency devoted to spying in peacetime. Cold War fears about the spread of communism in Europe, however, had created pressure to reinstitute an intelligence agency, the CIA. Shrouded from public scrutiny, the new agency used its secret funds to gather information on Soviet activities and to encourage anticommunist activities around the globe. Between 1949 and 1952, the CIA's office for covert operations expanded its overseas stations from 7 to 47. The CIA cultivated ties with anti-Soviet groups in Eastern Europe and within the Soviet Union. It helped finance pro-U.S. labor unions in Western Europe to curtail the influence of leftist organizations. It orchestrated covert campaigns to prevent the Italian Communist Party from winning an electoral victory in 1948 and to bolster anticommunist parties in France, Japan, and elsewhere. From the beginning, the Truman administration encouraged the CIA to use its national security mandate broadly and aggressively.

Truman's White House also linked economic policies in Western Europe to the doctrine of containment. Concerned that the region's severe economic problems might embolden communist movements, Secretary of State George Marshall sought to strengthen the economies of Western Europe. Shortly after Congress approved funding for the Truman Doctrine, the secretary proposed the Marshall Plan. Under his plan, funds provided by the United States would enable governments in Western Europe to work together to design and carry out a broad program of postwar economic reconstruction. Between 1946 and 1951, the United States provided nearly $13 billion in assistance to 17 Western European nations. The Soviets were also invited to participate in the Marshall Plan, but American policy makers correctly anticipated that Moscow would avoid any program whose major goal was rebuilding capitalism in Europe. Instead, Stalin responded to the Marshall Plan by further consolidating the Soviets' sphere of influence in Eastern Europe.

The Marshall Plan proved a stunning success. When conservatives called it a "giveaway" program, the administration emphasized how it opened up both markets and investment opportunities in Western Europe to American

Courtesy of the George C. Marshall Research Library, Lexington, Virginia.

MARSHALL PLAN

This poster, by an artist from the Netherlands, was the winning entry in a contest run in Marshall Plan countries. It suggests how the plan encouraged a united Europe to transcend the divisions that had led to two World Wars.

businesses. Moreover, within its first few years the Marshall Plan helped stabilize the European economy by quadrupling industrial production. Improved standards of living enhanced political stability and, along with the CIA's covert activities, helped undermine the appeal of communist parties in Western Europe.

American policy makers believed that to revitalize Europe under the Marshall Plan they must first restore the economy of Germany, which was still divided into zones of occupation. In June 1948 the United States, Great Britain, and France announced a plan for currency reform that would be the first step in merging their sectors of occupation into a federal German republic. Soviet leaders were alarmed by the prospect of a revitalized German state under Western auspices. Having twice been invaded by Germany during the preceding 35 years, they wanted Germany reunited but weak. Hoping to sidetrack Western plans for Germany, in June 1948 the Soviets cut off all highways, railroads, and water routes linking West Berlin, which was located within their zone, to West Germany.

This Soviet blockade of Berlin failed. American and British pilots, in what became known as the Berlin Airlift, made 250,000 flights, 'round-the-clock, to deliver a total of 2 million tons of supplies to the city's beleaguered residents. Truman, hinting at a military response, reinstated the draft and sent two squadrons of B-29 bombers to Britain. Conceding defeat, Stalin abandoned the blockade in May 1949. The Soviets then created the German Democratic Republic out of their East German sector. West Berlin survived as an enclave tied to the West. The "two Germanys" and the divided city of Berlin stood as symbols of Cold War divisions.

The Election of 1948

Concerns about national security helped Harry Truman win the 1948 presidential election, a victory that capped a remarkable political comeback. Truman had been losing the support of left-leaning Democrats, led by his Secretary of Commerce Henry A. Wallace, who thought his containment policies too militant. In September 1946, after Wallace criticized Truman's policies toward the Soviet Union, Truman had ousted him from the cabinet. Two months later, in the off-year national election of 1946, voters had given the Republicans control of Congress for the first time since 1928. Although Truman's standing in opinion polls had risen slowly in 1947 and 1948, most political

pundits thought he had little chance to win the presidency in his own right in 1948. Truman waged a vigorous campaign against challenges from the left by a new Progressive Party, which nominated Wallace, and from the right by both the Republican nominee Thomas E. Dewey and the southern segregationist Strom Thurmond, the candidate of the States' Rights Party, or "Dixiecrats." Truman called the Republican-controlled Congress into special session, presented it with domestic policy proposals that were anathema to the GOP, and then denounced the "Republican Eightieth Congress, that do-nothing, good-for-nothing, worst Congress."

Thomas Dewey, who had been defeated by Franklin Roosevelt four years earlier, proved a cautious, lackluster campaigner in 1948. Even Republicans complained about his bland speeches and empty platitudes. A pro-Democratic newspaper caricatured Dewey's standard speech as four "historic sentences: Agriculture is important. Our rivers are full of fish. You cannot have freedom without liberty. The future lies ahead." When Dewey's campaign train, called "The Victory Special," reached Kansas City, Truman's old political base, Dewey was so confident of victory that he booked the hotel suite the president used whenever he was in town.

By contrast, Truman conducted an old-style, energetic campaign. He moved from town to town, stopping to denounce Dewey and Henry Wallace from the back of a railroad car. Dewey was plotting "a real hatchet job on the New Deal," he charged, and the Republican Party was controlled by a cabal of "cunning men" who were planning

WHISTLESTOP CAMPAIGN, 1948
Truman addressed cheering crowds from the back of a train, as captured in this photograph from Chillicothe, Ohio. How and why have electioneering techniques changed since 1948?

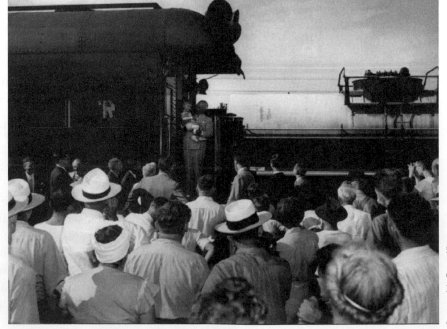

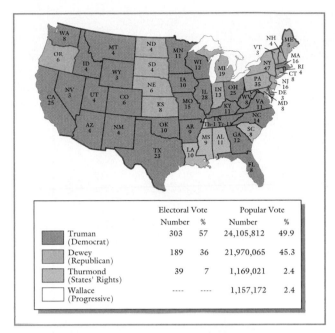

MAP 27.1 PRESIDENTIAL ELECTION, 1948
This electoral map helps show how, in this close election, Truman won the presidency with less than 50 percent of the popular vote.

	Electoral Vote		Popular Vote	
	Number	%	Number	%
Truman (Democrat)	303	57	24,105,812	49.9
Dewey (Republican)	189	36	21,970,065	45.3
Thurmond (States' Rights)	39	7	1,169,021	2.4
Wallace (Progressive)	----	----	1,157,172	2.4

"a return of the Wall Street economic dictatorship." "Give 'em hell, Harry!" shouted enthusiastic crowds. In November, Truman won only 49.6 percent of the popular vote but gained a solid majority in the electoral college. He, and not Thomas Dewey, would be moving back into the presidential suite in Kansas City—and into the White House in Washington, D.C.

Truman's victory now seems less surprising to historians than it did to political analysts in 1948. Despite Republican electoral gains in the congressional elections of 1946, the Democratic Party was hardly enfeebled. The Democrats running for Congress in 1948, who identified themselves with Franklin Roosevelt rather than with his successor, generally polled a higher percentage of the popular vote in their districts than did Truman. Still, voter loyalty to the memory of Roosevelt and to his New Deal coalition—labor union members, farmers, people of color, and social justice activists—helped Truman.

Truman also attracted a constituency of his own by virtue of his anticommunist policies. In this sense, Truman's presidency established a pattern that would persist for several decades: If Democratic candidates could avoid appearing "soft" or "weak" on national security issues, they stood a good chance of being elected president. The candidacies of both George McGovern in 1972 and Jimmy Carter in 1980 faltered on the issue of national security. Conversely, Harry Truman stood tough in 1948. His hardline national security credentials proved especially effec-

tive against Henry Wallace. After the election, Wallace's Progressive Party, which had challenged Truman's national security policies and had promised to revive the New Deal at home, lay in shambles. Hampered by his refusal to reject support from the Communist Party, Wallace failed to win a single electoral vote and received less than 3 percent of the popular tally.

The Korean War Era, 1949–1952

To carry out the containment policy, the Truman administration marshaled the nation's economic and military resources and deepened its focus on national security issues. A series of Cold War crises in 1949 and the outbreak of war on the Korean peninsula heightened anticommunist fervor.

NATO, China, and the Bomb

Building on the Truman Doctrine, the Marshall Plan, the Berlin Airlift, and the 1949 creation of the Federal Republic of Germany (West Germany), the United States set about creating a worldwide system of military alliances. In April 1949 the United States, Canada, and 10 European nations formed the North Atlantic Treaty Organization (NATO). Members of NATO pledged that an attack against one would automatically be considered an attack against all and agreed to cooperate on economic and political, as well as military, matters. Some U.S. leaders worried about the implications of NATO. Republican Senator Robert Taft of Ohio declared that it was a provocation to the Soviet Union and an "entangling alliance" that defied common sense, violated the traditional U.S. foreign policy of nonentanglement, and threatened constitutional government by eclipsing Congress's power to declare war. The nation's use of military force, Taft warned, could be dictated by a response to events in other countries rather than shaped through its own policy-making processes. Even so, the NATO concept prevailed, and the United States expanded the idea of pursuing containment through such mutual security pacts during the 1950s.

Meanwhile, events in China aggravated Cold War tensions. Between 1945 and 1948, the United States had extended to Jiang Jieshi's government $1 billion in military aid and another billion in economic assistance. Jiang, however, steadily lost ground to the communist forces of Mao Zedong, who promised land reform and commanded wide support among China's peasantry. Although experienced U.S. diplomats privately predicted that Jiang's downfall was inevitable, the Truman administration continued

The cold war split Europe into two opposing alliances. Germany was divided into two countries: The Federal Republic of Germany (West Germany) and the German Democratic Republic (East Germany). Berlin, the former capital of Germany, was also divided. In 1949 NATO was formed, and in 1955 the Warsaw Pact came into existence.

THE DIVISION OF BERLIN

American Zone
British Zone
French Zone
Soviet Zone

(The American, British, and French zones were consolidated as West Berlin)

NATO Countries
Warsaw Pact Countries
Nonaligned Countries

MAP 27.2 DIVIDED GERMANY AND THE NATO ALLIANCE

This map shows the geopolitics of the Cold War. Which countries aligned with the United States through NATO? Which aligned with the Soviet Union through the Warsaw Pact? Note how Berlin became a divided city, although it was located within East Germany.

to publicly portray Jiang as a respected leader of "free China" and to prop up his regime.

In 1949, when Mao's armies forced Jiang off the mainland to the island of Formosa (Taiwan), many Americans wondered how communist forces could have triumphed. Republican opponents charged the Truman administration with a "sellout." Financed by conservative business leaders, the still powerful "China lobby" excoriated Tru-

man and his new secretary of state, Dean Acheson, for being soft on communism. Despite evidence of friction between Stalin and Mao, the detractors spoke of a global communist conspiracy directed from Moscow. Tainted by the "loss" of China, several State Department officials who had criticized Jiang or merely predicted his downfall were dismissed and discredited, depriving Washington of its most knowledgeable experts on China and Southeast Asia.

Meanwhile, responding to the criticism, Acheson and Truman escalated their anticommunist rhetoric. For more than 20 years, even after friction between China and the Soviet Union became evident, the United States refused to recognize or deal with Mao's "Red China." Jiang's anticommunist island of Taiwan, like Berlin, became a powerful symbol of the Cold War.

The communist threat seemed even more alarming when, in September 1949, the Soviets exploded a crude atomic device, marking the end of the U.S. nuclear monopoly. Already besieged by critics who saw a world filled with Soviet gains and American defeats, Truman issued reassuring public statements but privately took the advice of hard-line advisers and authorized the development of a new bomb based on the still unproven concept of nuclear fusion. The decision to build this "hydrogen bomb" wedded the doctrine of containment to the creation of ever more deadly nuclear technology.

NSC-68

Prompted by events of 1949, the Truman administration reviewed its foreign policy assumptions. George Kennan, worried that a simplistic and increasingly militaristic version of his containment concept was emerging, resigned from the State Department's policy planning staff. As a result, the task of conducting this review fell to Paul Nitze, a hard-liner who produced a top-secret policy paper officially identified as National Security Council document 68 (NSC-68). It provided a blueprint for both the rhetoric and the substance of future Cold War foreign policy.

NSC-68 opened with a melodramatic account of a global ideological clash between "freedom," spread by U.S. power, and "slavery," promoted by the Soviet Union as the center of "international communism." Warning against any negotiations with the Soviets, the report urged a full-scale offensive to enlarge U.S. power. It endorsed the more vigorous use of covert action, economic pressure, propaganda campaigns, and a massive military buildup. Because Americans might oppose larger military spending and budget deficits, the report warned, U.S. actions should be labeled as "defensive" and be presented as a stimulus to the economy rather than as a drain on national resources. Although NSC-68 remained classified for more than two decades, the early 1950s public heard its message well. Secretary of State Dean Acheson stumped the country preaching its tenets and elaborating on its portrayal of the Cold War as a global showdown between good and evil.

The Korean War

The dire warnings of NSC-68 seemed to be confirmed in June 1950 when communist North Korea attacked South Korea. The Truman administration portrayed the move as a simple case of Soviet-inspired aggression against a free state. An assistant secretary of state remarked that the relationship of the Soviet Union to North Korea was "the same as that between Walt Disney and Donald Duck." Truman again invoked the policy of containment: "If aggression is successful in Korea, we can expect it to spread through Asia and Europe to this hemisphere."

The Korean situation, however, was partly a civil war. Korea had been occupied by Japan between 1905 and 1945, and after Japan's defeat in the Second World War, Koreans had expected to establish their own independent state. Instead, the postwar Soviet and U.S. zones of occupation became separate political entities. Against the desires of both North and South Koreans, Korea became two states, split at the 38th parallel. The Soviet Union supported a North Korean communist government under the oppressive dictatorship of Kim Il-sung. The United States backed Syngman Rhee, who held a Ph.D. from Princeton University, to head the unsteady and autocratic government in South Korea. Despite being split along an arbitrary line, Korea remained a single society, divided by political factions and religious differences as much as by geography.

Both Korean leaders hoped that the patronage of a superpower might help bolster their control and advance their respective notions of how Korean society should be organized. Rhee's regime, protective of upper-class landholders, generated opposition in South Korea, a movement that Kim's communist dictatorship encouraged. As discontent spread in South Korea, Kim moved troops across the 38th parallel on June 25, 1950, to attempt unification. Earlier, he had consulted both Soviet and Chinese leaders about his plans and received their support, after assuring them that a U.S. military response was highly unlikely. Under attack, Rhee appealed to the United States to protect his government.

The fighting in Korea escalated into an international conflict. The Soviets, uninformed about the precise details of Kim's plans, were boycotting the UN on the day the invasion was launched. Consequently, they were not present to veto a U.S. proposal to send a peacekeeping force to Korea. Under UN auspices, the United States rushed assistance to Rhee, who moved to eliminate disloyal South Korean civilians as well as to repel the invading North Koreans.

U.S. goals in Korea were unclear. Should the United States seek to contain communism by driving the North Koreans back over the 38th parallel? Or should it try to reunify the country under Rhee's leadership? At first, that decision could be postponed because the war was going so badly. North Korean troops pushed their Soviet-made

Courtesy of the Truman Library.

REFUGEES MOVE SOUTH

The Korean War disrupted life on the peninsula. Here, refugees flee their homes after receiving evacuation orders from the South Korean army.

tanks rapidly southward; within three months, they took Seoul, the capital of South Korea, and reached the southern tip of the Korean peninsula. American troops seemed unprepared and, unaccustomed to the unusually hot Korean weather during these first months, many fell sick. Fearing the worst, U.S. generals laid contingency plans for a large-scale American evacuation from Pusan. American firepower, however, gradually took its toll on the elite troops who had spearheaded North Korea's rapid move southward. North Korea had to send fresh, untrained recruits to replace seasoned fighters. As supply lines stretched out, the North Korean effort became more vulnerable.

General Douglas MacArthur devised a plan that most other commanders considered crazy: an amphibious landing behind enemy lines at Inchon. MacArthur, now 70 years old, remained as bold and egotistical as he had been both during the Second World War and as head of the occupation government of Japan. Those stunned by his invasion proposal were even more astounded by its results.

On September 15, 1950, the Marines successfully landed 13,000 troops at Inchon, suffered only 21 deaths, and moved back into Seoul within 11 days.

The price of recovering the military offensive was devastation on the ground. The Korean War was called a "limited" war because the United States did not employ atomic weapons, but intense American bombing preceded every military move. The number of estimated dead and wounded reached perhaps one-tenth of Korea's total population. As armies contested for control of Seoul, the city became rubble, with only the Capitol building and a train station left standing.

As MacArthur's troops drove northward, Truman faced a crucial decision. MacArthur, emboldened by success, urged moving beyond containment to an all-out war of "liberation" and reunification. Other advisers warned Truman that China would retaliate if U.S. forces approached its border. Truman allowed MacArthur to carry the war into North Korea but ordered him to avoid antagonizing China.

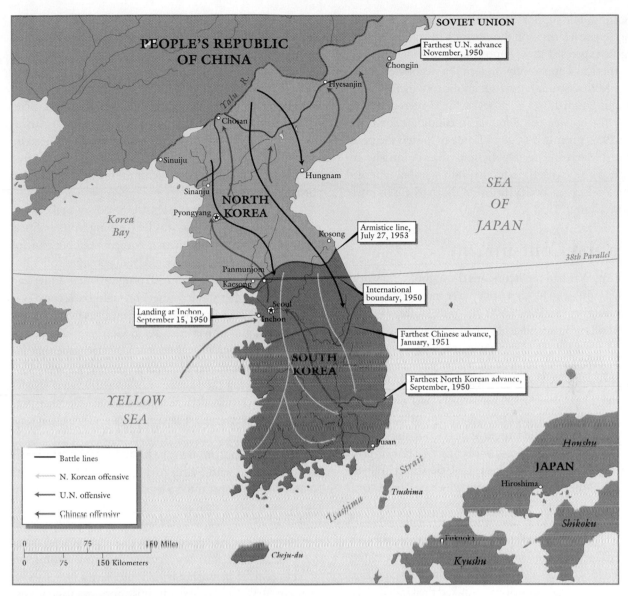

MAP 27.3 KOREAN WAR

This map shows the lines of battle and the armistice line that still divides the two Koreas. Note the advances made first by North Korea and then by UN (United States–led) troops.

 View an animated version of this map or related maps at **http://history.wadsworth.com/murrin_LEP4e.**

MacArthur pushed too far. Downplaying encounters between his troops and Chinese "volunteers," he continued to advance toward the Yalu River on the Chinese–Korean border. China responded by sending troops into North Korea and driving MacArthur back across the 38th parallel. With China now in the war, Truman again faced the question of military goals. When MacArthur's troops regained the initiative, Truman ordered his general to negotiate a truce at the 38th parallel. MacArthur, challenging the president, argued instead for all-out victory over North Korea—and over China, too. Truman thereupon relieved MacArthur of his command in April 1951, pointing out that the Constitution specified that military officers must obey the orders of the president, the commander-in-chief.

MacArthur returned home as a war hero. New York City greeted him with a ticker-tape parade that drew a crowd nearly twice as large as the one that had greeted General Dwight Eisenhower at the end of the Second World War. One poll reported that less than 30 percent of the U.S. public supported Truman's actions. The China lobby portrayed MacArthur as a martyr to Truman's "no-win" containment policy. For a brief but intense moment, MacArthur seemed a genuine presidential possibility for 1952. This outpouring of admiration, however, reflected MacArthur's personal charisma rather than any significant public support for a full-scale land war in Asia. During Senate hearings on the general's dismissal, military strategists expressed their opposition to a wider war, and most Americans apparently preferred a negotiated settlement in Korea. Truman now set about convincing North Korea and South Korea to meet at the conference table. Dwight Eisenhower, the Republican candidate for president in 1952, promised to go to Korea to hasten the peace process, if elected. The negotiations that eventually reestablished the borderline at the 38th parallel emerged as a major foreign policy task for the new Eisenhower administration in 1953.

Korea and Containment

The Korean War had repercussions throughout the world. It focused American foreign policy ever more narrowly on anticommunism and justified the global offensive that NSC-68 had recommended. The United States announced a plan to rearm West Germany, scarcely five years after Germany's defeat, and increased NATO's military forces. In 1951 the United States signed a formal peace treaty with Japan, and a Japanese-American security pact granted the United States bases on Okinawa and permission to station U.S. troops in Japan. The United States also acquired bases in Saudi Arabia and Morocco, bolstering its strategic position in the oil-rich Middle East. In 1950 direct military aid to Latin American governments, which had been voted down in the past, slid through Congress. In French Indochina, Truman provided assistance to strengthen French efforts against a communist-led independence movement. In the Philippines, the United States stepped up military assistance to suppress the leftist Huk rebels. And in 1951 the ANZUS collective security pact linked the United States strategically to Australia and New Zealand. Throughout the world, economic pressure, CIA covert activities, and propaganda campaigns helped forge anticommunist alliances. Truman's global "Campaign of Truth," an intensive informational and psychological offensive, used mass media and cultural exchanges to counter Soviet propaganda.

While the Truman administration fortified America's strategic position throughout the world, U.S. military budgets increased in order to fund ongoing weapons research and production. The Atomic Energy Commission had been created in 1946 to succeed the Manhattan Project in overseeing development of nuclear power; aviation had received special government funding for the first time in the 1946 budget; the army had joined with aircraft manufacturers in an effort to develop surface-to-surface missiles. To coordinate global strategy with the development of long-range weapons, a new "think tank"—RAND, an acronym for Research and Development—was created. Expensive contracts for manufacturing military materials worried cost-conscious members of Congress, but the prospect that the contracts would create new jobs in their home districts muted their opposition. The Cold War, especially after Korea, thus intensified what historian Michael Sherry has called "the militarization of American life": a steady military buildup and an intermingling of military and economic policies, all justified by an emphasis on anticommunism at home and abroad.

Fearful of communist gains, U.S. policy makers opposed any movement that was left-leaning in its political orientation. The U.S. occupation government in Japan, for example, increasingly restricted the activities of labor unions, suspended an antitrust program that American officials had earlier implemented, brought back conservative wartime leaders, and barred communists from government offices and universities. As in Germany, the United States tried to contain communism by strengthening industrial elites and promoting economic growth. U.S. purchases during the Korean conflict stimulated Japan's economy and provided the foundation for the pro-capitalist, anticommunist Japanese government that succeeded the American occupation in 1952.

In Africa, anticommunism brought the United States into an alliance with South Africa. In 1948 the all-white Nationalist Party instituted a legal system based on elaborate rules of racial separation and subordination of blacks (called *apartheid*). Some State Department officials warned that supporting apartheid in South Africa would damage U.S. prestige, but the Truman administration decided to cement an alliance with South Africa nonetheless. That country, the Truman administration reasoned, possessed important raw materials (especially uranium for bombs and manganese for steel) and a large labor force. Moreover, South Africa's Nationalist Party was militantly anticommunist.

From 1947 to the early 1950s, U.S. citizens often felt embattled and insecure. Stalin in the Soviet Union and Mao in China, both ambitious dictators, denounced the United States and promoted communism in other countries. The American policy of containment invoked the rhetoric of defensiveness: the term "national security" replaced "national interest"; the War Department became the Department of Defense. Yet the United States, a regional power before the Second World War, was anything but passive. It moved rapidly during the early Cold War era to stake out a global military and strategic presence. The Truman administration extended U.S. power into the former British sphere of influence of Iran, Greece, and

Edward Lansdale:
Psy-ops in the Cold War

EDWARD LANSDALE

America's best known super-spy stands here (second from left) with CIA director Allen Dulles (left) and Generals Charles P. Cabell and Nathan Twining.

Edward G. Lansdale (1908–1987) was one of America's most influential spies during the early Cold War. He introduced a strategy of psychological operations, or "psy-ops." Born in Detroit in 1908, Lansdale learned techniques of psychological persuasion as a young advertising executive and, during the Second World War, in the famed Office of Strategic Services (OSS). At the end of the war, Lansdale was sent to the Philippines, America's former colony, to rebuild security services. Returning there a few years later as the CIA's chief operative, he helped design the Philippine government's campaign, including psy-ops, against an uprising led by a communist-oriented peasant army called the Huks.

Lansdale had formed a close friendship with Ramón Magsaysay, who became president of the Philippines after an electoral battle marked by an influx of U.S. money. Lansdale's advertising expertise was also evident in the slogan "Magsaysay is my guy" and in an electoral theme song called the "Magsaysay Mambo." Lansdale tramped through the countryside, learning folktales and collecting songs. He later wrote that he came to understand that "the Huk battleground was a haunted place filled with ghosts and eerie creatures." He sought to design psy-ops to simulate vampire-like figures, malevolent eyes, and other supernatural events that he felt would strike fear into the Huk rebels. The anti-Huk campaign also featured intensive bombing and huge shipments of military equipment from the United States.

With Magsaysay's military victory over the Huks, Landale's reputation as a skilled anticommunist operative soared. In 1954, he worked with a team that went to Saigon, Vietnam, to mount a campaign modeled on the one in the Philippines. In Southeast Asia, he orchestrated a strategy that included distribution of documents purporting to show that communist forces under Ho Chi Minh were slaying civilian opponents, sabotage in North Vietnam, training a new South Vietnamese army, and helping to rig an election that installed Ngo Dinh Diem as president of South Vietnam. U.S. involvement in the South Vietnamese government of Diem steadily expanded.

Throughout the late 1950s and 1960s, Lansdale served in various posts in the U.S. government, once trying to organize a plan of psychological warfare against Fidel Castro in Cuba and returning again to Vietnam in 1965. In 1963, he received a Distinguished Service Medal for his work, which was becoming known as "counter-insurgency."

Lansdale's legacy of using secret psychological operations and daring, even ruthless, tactics in foreign nations attracted both defenders and critics. Some admirers have called him America's "greatest spy." To others, his assumption that the United States could manipulate other people's culture for political ends projected a hubris that could easily veer into disaster. Upon his death, Lansdale left an impressive, well-documented collection of songs, which he had taped in the Philippines and Vietnam, and had gathered from U.S. soldiers serving in Southeast Asia. Edward Lansdale will remain an enigmatic figure—part spy, part ethnomusicologist.

Turkey; initiated the Marshall Plan and NATO; and transformed former enemies—Italy, Germany, and Japan—into anti-Soviet states. Furthermore, the United States assumed control of hundreds of Pacific islands, launched research to develop the hydrogen bomb, winked at anticommunist ally South Africa's apartheid policies, solidified its sphere of influence in Latin America, acquired bases around the world, and devised a master plan for using military, economic, and covert action to fight any group that opposed U.S. interests. Beginning with the Truman Doctrine of 1947, the United States reinvented itself as a global superpower.

Containment at Home

Although containment abroad generally gained bipartisan support, Harry Truman's national security policies at home became increasingly divisive. An emotional debate over alleged communist influences in the United States raged from the late 1940s through the early 1950s. Taking their cue from Truman's anticommunist rhetoric, conservatives leveled more strident allegations of internal communist subversion, even charging Truman's own administration with harboring people who were disloyal or soft on communism. Civil libertarians, on the other side, complained that a witch-hunt was being conducted against people whose only sins were dissent or support for leftist, or pro-labor, political agendas. Many people, even devoted anticommunists, began to worry that irresponsible smear campaigns and wild goose chases after unlikely offenders only hampered the search for authentic Soviet agents. The search for supposed subversives affected many aspects of postwar life. Many politicians, professional organizations, labor unions, business corporations, and individual citizens found it prudent to join in the "red-baiting" to demonstrate their anticommunist credentials. A particularly aggressive group of anticommunists emerged in Congress.

Anticommunism and the Labor Movement

An unprecedented wave of labor strikes had swept across the country after the end of the Second World War. Militant workers had struck for increased wages and for a greater voice in workplace routines and production decisions. Strikes had brought both the auto industry and the electronics industry to a standstill. In Stamford, Connecticut, and Lancaster, Pennsylvania, general strikes had led to massive work stoppages that later spread to Rochester,

STEELWORKERS' STRIKE
Striking steelworkers picket their employer in 1946. During that year, strikes affected millions of American workers.

New York; Pittsburgh, Pennsylvania; Oakland, California; and other large cities. By 1947 labor militancy had begun to subside as Truman took a hard line. He warned oil refinery strikers to "cut out all the foolishness." He threatened to seize mines and railroads shut down by work stoppages, and ordered the strikers to return to their jobs.

The labor unrest of the immediate postwar years made unions a prominent target for anticommunist legislators. In 1947 congressional opponents of organized labor effectively tapped anticommunist sentiment to help pass the Labor-Management Relations Act, popularly known as the Taft-Hartley Act. The law negated some of the gains unions had made during the 1930s by limiting a union's power to conduct boycotts, to compel employers to accept "closed shops" in which only union members could be hired, and to conduct a strike that the president judged against the national interest. In addition, as a means of curtailing "wildcat" strikes, the law strengthened the power of union leaders to discipline their own members. Finally, Taft-Hartley required that these same union officials sign affidavits stating that they did not belong to the Communist Party or to any other "subversive" organization. A union that refused to comply was effectively denied protection under national labor laws when engaged in conflict with management. Truman vetoed Taft-Hartley, but Congress swiftly overrode him.

The issue of communists in the labor movement not only concerned Congress but, especially after Taft-Hartley, affected union politics as well. Anticommunist unionists had long charged that some communist organizers, despite their energetic work in grassroots campaigns, were more loyal to the Communist Party than to their unions or to the nation. Differences over whether labor should endorse the Democratic Party or Henry Wallace's third-party effort in 1948 also heightened tensions within many unions. In the years following Truman's victory, the Congress of Industrial Organizations (CIO) expelled 13 unions—and a full third of its membership—for allegedly following Communist Party policies. Meanwhile, as red-hunters searched for subversives in the workplace, many workers found their jobs at risk because of their political ideas. Businesses that were hostile to worker demands often employed anticommunism as a tactic to lessen labor's power. By the end of the Truman era, some type of loyalty-security check had been conducted on about 20 percent of the American workforce, more than 13 million people.

HUAC and the Loyalty Program

Anticommunists also scrutinized the entertainment industry. In 1947, only three days after the unveiling of the Truman Doctrine, the House Un-American Activities Committee (popularly known as HUAC) opened hearings to expose alleged communist infiltration in Hollywood. Basking in the glare of newsreel cameras, committee members seized on the refusal of 10 screenwriters, producers, and directors who had been or still were members of the Communist Party to testify about their own political affiliations and those of other members of the film community. Known as "the Hollywood Ten," this group claimed that the First Amendment shielded their political activities from HUAC's scrutiny. After the federal courts upheld HUAC's power and denied the Hollywood Ten's First Amendment claim, members of the group went to prison for contempt of Congress.

Meanwhile, studio heads secretly drew up a blacklist of alleged subversives who could no longer work in the entertainment industry. Industry leaders denied the existence of such a list, but their disavowals were unconvincing. The actor John Wayne later explained, "The only thing our side did that was anywhere near blacklisting was just running a lot of people out of the business." By the mid-1950s hundreds of people in Hollywood and in the fledgling television industry—technicians who worked behind the scenes as well as performers who appeared in front of them—were unable to find jobs until they agreed to appear before HUAC and other investigative bodies. There, they were required to name people whom they had seen at some "communist meeting" some time in the past. Some well-known celebrities, such as writer Lillian Hellman, invoked the Fifth Amendment and refused to answer any questions. Others, such as Hollywood director Elia Kazan,

cooperated with the interrogation. Compliance or resistance to naming names created a split in the entertainment industry that lasted for decades.

Ronald Reagan and Richard Nixon, two future Republican presidents, first attracted the political spotlight through the HUAC hearings. Reagan, who was president of the Screen Actors Guild and also a secret informant for the FBI (identified as "T-10"), decried the communist presence in Hollywood. Nixon, then an obscure member of Congress from California, began his political ascent in 1948 when he associated himself with Whittaker Chambers, a journalist who had once been active in communist circles. Appearing before HUAC, Chambers charged Alger Hiss, a prominent New Deal Democrat who had a long career in government, with having links to the Communist Party and with divulging classified information to Soviet agents during the late 1930s.

The Hiss-Chambers-Nixon affair set off a raging controversy. Hiss maintained that he had been framed in an elaborate FBI plot and alleged that the Bureau had even rigged his typewriter so it would appear to be the source of incriminating evidence. Although the passage of time legally shielded Hiss from prosecution for any acts of espionage that might have occurred during the 1930s, he was charged with committing perjury in his Congressional testimony. Nixon and his supporters considered the exposure of Hiss, who had been one of Franklin Roosevelt's advisers during the Yalta Conference (see chapter 26), proof that the search for Soviet subversion required greater vigor than the Truman administration could provide. To HUAC's critics, however, the Hollywood Ten and Hiss cases suggested the consequences of overzealous witch-hunting. Debates over whether the Hiss case was an example of high-level espionage or anticommunist hysteria would continue for decades.

During the mid-1990s, the availability of long-classified documents, such as those in the Venona files, tilted the debate against Hiss. He died in 1996, at the age of 92, still maintaining his innocence and still attracting his defenders. Even so, a growing number of historians came to agree that the evidence suggested that Hiss (along with several other high-ranking public officials and certain lower-level government employees with ties to the American Communist Party) had passed some information to agents of the Soviet Union during the 1930s and 1940s. The precise circumstances surrounding each individual case, however, remained hotly contested.

Meanwhile, as controversy swirled around the Hiss episode, the Truman administration continued to pursue its own anticommunist policies. Under the president's loyalty program, hundreds of government employees were dismissed. Truman's attorney general Tom Clark (whom

Truman appointed to the Supreme Court in 1949) allowed J. Edgar Hoover, head of the FBI, to assume broad, discretionary power to uncover subversion. He authorized Hoover to draw up his own list of alleged subversives and to detain them, without any legal hearing, in the event of a national security emergency. Clark's successor, Howard McGrath, proclaimed that communist subversives, each carrying "the germs of death for society," were lurking "in factories, offices, butcher stores, on street corners, in private business."

At the same time, the FBI was also accumulating dossiers on a wide range of artists and intellectuals. The Bureau compiled secret files on prominent people who had no ties to the Communist Party, such as writers Ernest Hemingway and John Steinbeck. African American artists and writers became special targets. Richard Wright (author of the novel *Native Son*), W. E. B. Du Bois (the nation's most celebrated African American historian and intellectual), and Paul Robeson (one of America's best-known entertainer-activists) were singled out by State Department and immigration officials because of their ties to the American Communist Party and their identification with anti-imperialist and antiracist struggles throughout the world. The Communist Party, after all, had been one of the few institutions in American life to adopt an uncompromising stance against racial discrimination.

In 1952, Congress's concern that subversives might immigrate to the United States produced the McCarran-Walter Act. This law placed greater barriers to immigration from areas outside northern and western Europe and on the entry of people who immigration officials suspected might bring in dangerous ideas.

HISTORY THROUGH FILM

High Noon (1952)

During the first two-thirds of the 20th century, Hollywood made more movies in the western genre than in any other. Featuring story lines and visual images about the conquest of the nation's 19th-century frontier, the western linked viewers to a triumphant past. The messages and imagery of the western resonated particularly powerfully during the difficult Cold War years, and no other western of that era gained as much popular and critical acclaim—and created more controversy—as *High Noon*.

A number of fabled Hollywood figures contributed to the movie. Producer Stanley Kramer and screenwriter Carl Forman liked projects that touched on contested social and political issues, a preference that contributed to Forman's being blacklisted, as *High Noon* neared completion, for refusing to testify before Congress about his alleged ties to the Communist Party. Director Fred Zinnemann seemed attracted to filmic characters who faced grave moral crises. Although Montana-born actor Gary Cooper had broken into films as a cowboy actor, he had become, as a result

Directed by Fred Zinnemann. Starring Gary Cooper (Will Kane), Grace Kelly (Amy Fowler Kane), Katy Jurado (Helen Ramirez).

of nonwesterns such as *Sergeant York* (1939), Hollywood's iconic "everyman." Here, Cooper plays the aging Will Kane, whose hopes of retiring as marshal of Hadleyville and settling down with his young bride (Grace Kelly) are interrupted by news that a vicious outlaw who had once run the town, Frank Miller, is returning from prison on the noon train. Will Marshal Kane strap back on his gun to defend the town, or will he respect his wife's Quaker faith and abandon his violent ways?

Although the rules of the western genre require Kane to pursue his duty, *High Noon* greatly complicates his course. Kane had earlier "tamed" Hadleyville by vanquishing Miller, yet the townspeople now refuse, for various reasons, to help him defend their community. They simply want Kane to leave and let them cut a deal with Miller. As images of clocks ticking toward high noon fill the screen, Kane grimly prepares for a showdown with Miller and his gang.

Most viewers saw *High Noon* as a statement about the Cold War but differed on its precise message. Some fervent

Targeting Difference

The crusade against communist influence in American life also focused on homosexuals. During the Second World War, with the disruption of many traditional social patterns, more visible and assertive gay and lesbian subcultures had begun to emerge, even within the armed forces. After the war, Dr. Alfred Kinsey's research on sexual behavior—the first volume, on male sexuality, was published in 1948—claimed that homosexual behavior could be found throughout American society. At about the same time, gays formed the Mattachine Society (in 1950) and lesbians founded the Daughters of Bilitis (in 1955), organizations that began to push for recognition of legal rights for homosexuals.

The Kinsey Report's implicit claim that homosexuality was simply another form of sexuality that should be tolerated, together with the discreet militancy among gays and lesbians, produced a backlash that became connected to the broader antisubversion crusade. The fact that several founders of the Mattachine Society had also been members of the Communist Party, coupled with the claim that homosexuals could be blackmailed by Soviet agents more easily than heterosexuals, helped link homosexuality with subversion.

A connection between antihomosexual and anticommunist rhetoric developed. Radical political ideas and homosexuality were both portrayed as "diseases" that could be spread throughout the body politic by people who often looked no different from "ordinary" Americans. As a report from the U.S. Senate put it, "one homosexual can pollute a Government office" in much the same way as could a person with subversive ideas. According to this logic,

anticommunists (including the western star John Wayne) condemned the movie as writer Carl Forman's allegory on how Hollywood had failed to stand up for him and other embattled radicals. Other commentators, by contrast, viewed *High Noon* as a broader morality tale about international affairs. In a symbolic affirmation of the Cold War policy of confronting, rather than negotiating with, communist aggressors, Kane (with crucial help from his Quaker wife) ultimately guns down the Miller gang. Then, in a scene that prompted widely different readings, he throws down his marshal's badge and leaves town with his bride.

High Noon, which gained four Academy Awards and inspired the long-running TV show "Gunsmoke," showed how Hollywood could adapt its version of western history to Cold War concerns. Still re-run frequently on television, this 1952 film can offer a historical lens for viewing domestic and foreign policy issues during the age of containment.

© Sunset Boulevard/Corbis Sygma.

Gary Cooper as Marshal Will Kane.

homosexuality was an acceptable basis for denying people government employment.

The "Great Fear"

Truman's final years as president unfolded in an atmosphere of public anxiety that historian David Caute has called the "Great Fear." Foreign policy events of 1949 and 1950, especially the Soviets' nuclear tests, highlighted the issue of whether spy rings were at work in the U.S. government, and stories circulated about Soviet agents having stolen U.S. nuclear secrets. How had the Soviets so quickly developed atomic weaponry? In early 1950, Great Britain released evidence that a spy ring had long been operating in the United States. Shortly afterward, the U.S. Justice Department arrested several alleged members of this ring, including two members of the American Communist Party, Julius and Ethel Rosenberg.

The Rosenberg case became a key symbol of Cold War politics. The trial, the verdicts of guilty, the sentences of death at Sing Sing prison, the numerous legal appeals, the worldwide protests, and the executions in 1953—all provoked intense controversy. Were the Rosenbergs guilty of having been involved in the theft of important nuclear secrets? And if so, were their death sentences on the charge of espionage the constitutionally appropriate punishment? To their supporters, the Rosenbergs (who steadfastly maintained their innocence) had fallen victim to anticommunist hysteria. Many believed that the government seemed less interested in conducting a fair trial than in finding scapegoats. To others, the evidence showed that information had been channeled to the Soviets. Documents released during the 1990s convinced most historians that Julius Rosenberg had been engaged in espionage (although the usefulness of his information is still at issue) and that Ethel Rosenberg, although not directly involved, may have known of his activities. Yet, as a report by the Commission on Protecting and Reducing Government Secrecy noted in 1997, the government declined to prosecute "a fair number of Americans who almost certainly were atomic spies." In some instances, it seems, officials feared a court trial could have compromised ongoing intelligence projects; in other cases, they worried that a formal legal proceeding could have revealed illegal activities by Hoover's FBI and likely ended in a failed prosecution. Of those prosecuted for dealing with the Soviets, only Julius and Ethel Rosenberg were charged with a crime that carried the death penalty.

The courts' response to the anticommunist effort sparked controversy. During the 1949 prosecution of leaders of the American Communist Party, the trial judge accepted the Justice Department's claim that, by definition,

From the Collections of the Library of Congress.

IT'S OKAY—WE'RE HUNTING COMMUNISTS
This 1947 "Herblock" (Herbert Block) cartoon presents a critical view of the impact of HUAC's communist-hunting.

the American Communist Party was simply the arm of an international conspiracy. Its Marxist ideology and its theoretical publications, even in the absence of any proof of subversive *acts,* justified convicting the party's leaders of sedition. In contrast, civil libertarians insisted that the government lacked evidence that communist publications and speeches, by themselves, posed any "clear and present danger" to national security. In this view, the abstract political beliefs of any group, including the Communist Party, should enjoy the protection of the First Amendment, and only people's actions could be put on trial. When the convictions of the Communist Party leaders were appealed to the Supreme Court, in the landmark case of *Dennis* v. *U.S.* (1951), the High Court modified the "clear and present danger" doctrine and upheld the broad definition of sedition used by the lower courts. The defendants, a majority of the Justices declared, had been constitutionally convicted.

By 1950, the anticommunist Truman administration had become a target of even more zealous red-hunters. In Congress, Republicans and conservative Democrats condemned the administration's handling of anticommunist initiatives and introduced their own legislation, the McCarran Internal Security Act of 1950. It authorized the detention, during any national emergency, of alleged subversives in special camps, and created the Subversive Activities Control Board (SACB) to investigate organizations suspected of being affiliated with the Communist Party and to administer the registration of organizations allegedly controlled by communists.

The Truman administration responded ambiguously to the McCarran Act. Although the president vetoed the law, a futile gesture that Congress quickly overrode, his administration allowed the FBI's J. Edgar Hoover to devise a secret detention program that offered even fewer legal safeguards than the McCarran Act. No national emergency ever triggered the detention procedures proposed in either of these plans, but their existence demonstrates the breadth of anticommunist sentiment. Yet, despite his administration's anticommunist initiatives, Truman could never defuse the charges that were leveled at his administration.

McCarthyism

Republican Senator Joseph McCarthy of Wisconsin became Truman's prime accuser. Charging in 1950 that hundreds, and later dozens, of communists were at work in Truman's State Department, McCarthy put the administration on the defensive. This allegation supposedly explained foreign policy "losses" such as China. The nation was in a precarious position, according to McCarthy, "not because our only powerful potential enemy has sent men to invade our shores, but rather because of the traitorous actions of those who have been treated so well by this Nation." Among those people, McCarthy named Secretary of State Dean Acheson and his predecessor, General George C. Marshall. He produced no credible evidence to support his case.

Although McCarthy rarely tried to substantiate his charges, he lacked neither imagination nor targets. McCarthy and his imitators took aim at former members of the American Communist Party and at people associated with "communist front" organizations, political groups supposedly being manipulated by communists. In most of the cases McCarthy cited, the affiliations had been perfectly legal. He also made vague charges against the entertainment industry and academic institutions.

McCarthy seemed unstoppable. In summer 1950, a subcommittee of the Senate Foreign Relations Committee, after examining State Department files in search of the damning material, concluded that McCarthy's charges amounted to "the most nefarious campaign of half-truths and untruths in the history of this republic." McCarthy simply charged that the files had been "raped," and he

broadened his mudslinging to include Millard Tydings, the distinguished Democratic senator from Maryland who had chaired the subcommittee and who had called McCarthy's charges "an effort to inflame the American people with a wave of hysteria and fear on an unbelievable scale." In the November 1950 elections, Tydings was defeated, in part because of a fabricated photograph that linked him to communist activities.

Despite McCarthy's recklessness, influential people tolerated, even supported, him. Conservative, anticommunist leaders of the Roman Catholic Church endorsed McCarthy, who was a Catholic. Leading Republicans—including Senator Robert Taft, chair of the GOP policy committee in the Senate, and Kenneth Wherry, the Republican minority leader in the Senate—welcomed McCarthy's attacks on their Democratic rivals. Wherry, cheering McCarthy on, called for rooting out "the alien-minded radicals and moral perverts" in the Truman administration. As head of a special Senate Subcommittee on Investigations, popularly known as the "McCarthy committee," McCarthy enjoyed broad subpoena power and legal immunity from libel suits. He bullied hostile witnesses and encouraged sympathetic "experts" to offer exaggerated estimates of a vast Red Menace. Although most historians agree that his Cold War contemporaries overestimated his political power and personal appeal, the senator personified the form of demagoguery, "McCarthyism," that continues to bear his name.

Meanwhile, growing concern about national security subtly altered the nation's constitutional structure. Except for the 22nd and the 23rd Amendments (adopted in 1951 and 1961, respectively), which barred future presidents from serving more than two terms and allowed the District of Columbia a vote in presidential elections, the written Constitution was not formally modified during the Cold War years. But legislative enactments, especially the National Security Act of 1947, and the growing power of the executive branch of government, particularly of agencies such as the CIA and the FBI, brought significant informal changes to the nation's unwritten constitution. As the Truman administration sought to contain communism and conduct a global foreign policy, older ideas about a government of limited powers gave way to the idea that sweeping congressional legislation and broad executive-branch action were necessary to safeguard the nation's security. During the 1960s, when Lyndon Johnson waged an undeclared war in Southeast Asia, and the 1970s, when Richard Nixon used claims of national security to cover up his own administration's illegal actions, the view of expansive government power that emerged during the early Cold War era would come under intense scrutiny.

◈ Truman's Fair Deal

Even as the Truman administration confronted the Cold War, it also fashioned a domestic policy that sought to reconstruct the domestic legacy of Franklin Roosevelt's New Deal. Many of FDR's supporters still endorsed the idea of a "Second Bill of Rights," which Roosevelt had announced in 1944. According to this vision, all Americans had the "right" to a wide range of substantive liberties, including employment, food and shelter, education, and health care. Whenever people could not obtain these "rights," the national government was responsible for providing access to them. Such a commitment would require ongoing economic and social planning—and government spending—for the general welfare. In post–Second World War Europe, the idea of a "welfare state" that undertook economic planning in order to guarantee certain substantive rights was winning wide acceptance.

Talk about government planning and increased spending, however, proved highly controversial in the United States. Even before the Second World War, the New Deal's pace of domestic legislation had begun to slow, and throughout the war, critics had assailed economic planning as meddlesome interference in private decision making. Government programs that expanded the New Deal, Republicans charged, threatened unconstitutional intru-

LINK TO THE PAST

Senator Joseph McCarthy Interrogates Composer Aaron Copland

To further his anticommunist crusade, Senator Joseph McCarthy subpoenaed a wide range of Americans, including people from the artistic and musical communities, before his subcommittee. He and other senators then grilled these people, in secret sessions, about whether their past political affiliations marked them as communists or communist sympathizers. The transcripts of these sessions remained secret until 2003 but are now available on the Internet.

In this excerpt from a 1953 session, McCarthy (identified as "The CHAIRMAN") and Senator Karl Mundt are quizzing the famed musician Aaron Copland about his past relationships with the composer Hanns Eisler, a German communist, and with U.S. political organizations that supported labor leader Harry Bridges and Earl Browder, one-time head of the American Communist Party.

The McCarthy subcommittee found Copland to be a difficult witness. He avoided admitting any wrongdoing and worked at deflecting questions from the senators. Preferring witnesses who could be easily bullied, McCarthy never recalled Copland as he had threatened to do.

THE CHAIRMAN: *Do you feel now that your name was misused by various organizations or do you want further time to check into it?*

Mr. COPLAND: I would like further time to check into it. It is also well known that if they got your name in connection with one thing, they didn't hesitate to use it in connection with another. I would also like to say that my connection, insofar as it would show, was the direct outcome of the feelings of a musician. I was not moved by the Communist element, whatever it may have been. I was moved by specific causes to which I lent my name.

Musicians make music out of feelings aroused out of public events.

Senator MUNDT: I can't follow this line of argument. I don't see how that line of reasoning makes sense with a hatchet man like Bridges.

Mr. COPLAND: A musician, when he writes his notes he makes his music out of emotions and you can't make your music unless you are moved by events. If I sponsored a committee in relation to Bridges, I may have been misled, not through Communist leanings. If I had them, there was something about his situation that moved me.

Senator MUNDT: That would be true of anybody—any human beings, I think, not only musicians. Emotions are part of everyone's personality. That certainly stretches a point. We are all governed by the same rules of caution. When you get to Browder and Bridges, I think musicians have to go by the same code as governs other citizens.

Mr. COPLAND: We are assuming—I would like to see what it was I was supposed to have signed. I would have to know the circumstances to make any kind of sensible case.

sion into people's private affairs and posed a threat to individual initiative and responsibility.

During Truman's presidency, opposition to innovations in social policy making hardened. The National Association of Manufacturers (NAM) warned that new domestic programs would destroy the private free-enterprise system. Southern Democrats in Congress joined Republicans in blocking programs that might weaken white supremacy in their region. Even before Truman succeeded Roosevelt, these conservative forces had succeeded in abolishing several New Deal agencies that might have contributed to economic planning after the war and had flatly rejected FDR's Second Bill of Rights.

The Employment Act of 1946 and the Promise of Economic Growth

Faced with intense opposition to Roosevelt's old agenda, Truman needed a fresh approach to domestic policy making. The 1946 debate over the Full Employment Bill helped identify one. The Full Employment Bill, as initially conceived, would have increased government spending and empowered Washington to ensure employment for all citizens seeking work. To the bill's opponents, the phrase "full employment" and a significantly larger role for government resembled the European welfare state, even socialism.

The CHAIRMAN: Do you say now that your activities as a musician had to do with your connection with Bridges and Browder?

Mr. COPLAND: I would say that anything I signed was because of the human cause behind it that interested me—

The CHAIRMAN: Were you a good friend of Hanns Eisler?

Mr. COPLAND: No, I knew him slightly. I was not a good friend of his.

The CHAIRMAN: Did you meet him socially?

Mr. COPLAND: Yes.

The CHAIRMAN: Roughly, how many times?

Mr. COPLAND: Roughly, this is a guess, two or three times.

The CHAIRMAN: Did you agree with the statement by Eisler that "Revolutionary music is now more powerful than ever. Its political and artistic importance is growing daily."

Mr. COPLAND: That is a vague statement. I don't know what he means by "revolutionary music."

The CHAIRMAN: Do you agree with him that there is a political importance in music?

Mr. COPLAND: I certainly would not. What the Soviet government has been trying to do in forcing their composers to write along lines favorable to themselves is absolutely wrong. It is one of the basic reasons why I could have no sympathy with such an attitude.

The CHAIRMAN: Would you say a good musician who is a Communist could be important in influencing people in favor of the Communist cause?

Mr. COPLAND: Perhaps in some indirect way.

The CHAIRMAN: One final question. Quoting Hanns Eisler, is this a correct description of you by Eisler?:

I am extremely pleased to report a considerable shift to the left among the American artistic intelligentsia. I don't think it would be an exaggeration to state that the best people in the musical world of America (with very few exceptions) share at present extremely progressive ideas.

Their names? They are Aaron Copland.

Would you say that is a correct description of you?

Mr. COPLAND: No, I would not. I would say he is using knowledge of my liberal feelings in the arts and in general to typify me as a help to his own cause.

1. How does Copland invoke his status as a musician to deflect inquiries from members of the subcommittee?
2. What other rhetorical techniques does Copland use to hold his questioners at bay?
3. How might this inquiry raise questions about the relationship between art and politics?

For a link to a complete transcript of the once-secret hearings, visit the *Liberty, Equality, Power* Web site at:

http://history.wadsworth.com/murrin_LEP4e

As the effort to enact this part of the bill stalled, a scaled-down vision of domestic policymaking gradually emerged. The law that Congress finally passed, renamed the Employment Act of 1946, called for "maximum" (rather than full) employment and specifically acknowledged that private enterprise, not government, bore primary responsibility for economic decision making. Recognizing that the national government could play an ongoing role in economic management, however, the act created a new executive branch body, the Council of Economic Advisers, to help formulate long-range policy recommendations. The measure signaled that government would assume some yet to be defined responsibility for the performance of the economy.

A crucial factor in the gradual acceptance of Washington's new role was a growing faith that *advice* from economic experts, as an alternative to government *planning*, could guarantee a constantly expanding economy. An influential group of theorists, many of them disciples of the British economist John Maynard Keynes, insisted that the United States no longer needed to endure the boom-and-bust cycles that had long afflicted its economy. Instead of holding the economy hostage to the largely uncoordinated decisions of private individuals and business firms, economists with new theoretical expertise could advise the government on coherent policies most likely to produce uninterrupted economic growth. If the economy lagged, for example, government might help encourage growth by boosting its own spending.

The promise of economic growth as a permanent condition dazzled postwar leaders. Corporate executives, many of whom had feared that the end of the war would intensify labor unrest and trigger recession, viewed economic growth as a guarantee of social stability. The Truman administration embraced the idea that the government should encourage economic growth by updating, through measures such as the Employment Act of 1946, the cooperative relationship with both big business and organized labor that the Roosevelt administration had pursued during the Second World War. The president's advisers claimed that such cooperation would actually ease domestic policy making. Economic growth would produce increased tax revenues and, in turn, finance Washington's domestic programs. "With economic expansion, every problem is capable of solution," insisted George Soule, a celebrant of economic growth. Walter Heller, another leader of the postwar generation of economists, likened the promise of sustained growth to finding both the rainbow and its proverbial pot of gold. Using the relatively new measure of gross national product (GNP), postwar experts could actually calculate the nation's growing economic bounty. Developed in 1939, GNP—defined

as the total dollar value of all goods and services produced in the nation during a given year—became the standard gauge of economic health.

Truman and his advisers soon began preaching the gospel of economic growth. This economic faith nicely complemented their foreign policy programs. Sharp increases in military spending stimulated the sluggish postwar economy without raising the opposition that costly domestic measures would have sparked. Rearmament and the Keynsian-style stimulus dovetailed in a policy that some historians now call "military Keynsianism." As *U.S. News and World Report* put it at the time, "government planners figure that they have found the magic formula for almost endless good times. [The] Cold War is an automatic pump primer." Cold War assistance programs, such as the Marshall Plan, also helped create markets and investment opportunities overseas. As Western Europe made its postwar recovery, sales of American products, such as Coca-Cola, soared. Economic growth at home was linked to development in the world at large—and to the all-pervasive concern with national security.

Shaping the Fair Deal

In his inaugural address of 1949, Truman unveiled a domestic agenda he had outlined during his 1948 presidential campaign: the "Fair Deal." He called for the extension of popular New Deal programs such as Social Security and minimum wage laws; enactment of long-stalled, Democratic-sponsored civil rights and national health care legislation; federal aid for education; and repeal of the Taft-Hartley Act of 1947. Charles Brannan, Truman's secretary of agriculture, proposed an ambitious new plan for supporting farm prices by means of additional governmental subsidies, and the president urged substantial spending on public housing projects. The assumption on which Truman built his Fair Deal—that enlarged domestic programs could be financed from economic growth—would dominate political discussions for years to come. Through the magic of constant economic growth, all Americans would enjoy progressively bigger pieces of an always expanding economic pie.

Two prominent government programs, both of which predated Truman's administration, illustrate the approach to domestic policy making that dominated the Fair Deal years. The first, the so-called GI Bill (officially entitled the Serviceman's Readjustment Act of 1944), had always enjoyed strong support in Congress. After the First World War, Congress had voted veterans cash pensions or bonuses. This time, Congress worked out a comprehensive set of benefits for the several million men and 40,000 women who had served in the armed forces. The GI Bill

GI JOES STORM CAMPUS, 1946

Men who had served in the Second World War, aided by the GI Bill, flooded colleges after war's end. This picture from the University of Minnesota shows the surge in male students along with the attire and the slightly older average age of college students in the late 1940s.

Courtesy of the Minnesota Historical Society.

encompassed several different programs, including immediate financial assistance for college and job-training programs for veterans of the Second World War. By 1947, the year of peak veteran enrollment, about half of the entire college and university population was receiving government assistance. In other provisions, veterans received preferential treatment when applying for government jobs; generous terms on loans when purchasing homes or businesses; and, eventually, comprehensive medical care in veterans' hospitals. The Veterans' Readjustment Assistance Act of 1952, popularly known as the GI Bill of Rights, extended these programs to veterans of the Korean War. In essence, although the Truman administration did not enact FDR's Second Bill of Rights in its entirety, the Fair Deal did grant many of its social and economic protections to veterans.

Social Security, the most popular part of Roosevelt's New Deal, expanded under Truman's Fair Deal. When conservatives attacked Social Security as an unwarranted extension of federal power, the Truman administration noted that the program included needed support for the disabled and the blind and that older people had earned the "income security" through years of work and monetary contributions withheld from their paychecks. Under the Social Security Act of 1950, the level of benefits increased significantly; the retirement portions of the program expanded; and coverage was extended to more than 10 million people, including agricultural workers. As subsequent debate would highlight, however, no new financing system accompanied this expansion—a consequence of a widespread faith that sustained growth could under-

write the cost of domestic programs and a belief that politically divisive adjustments could be postponed for a later day.

The more expansive (and expensive) Fair Deal proposals either failed or were scaled back. For instance, Truman's plan for a comprehensive national health insurance program ran into strong opposition. The American Medical Association (AMA) and the American Hospital Association (AHA) blocked any government intervention in the traditional fee-for-service medical system and steered Congress toward a less controversial alternative—federal financing of new hospitals under the Hill-Burton Act. Opinion polls suggested that most voters, many of whom were enrolling in private health insurance plans such as Blue Cross and Blue Shield, were either apathetic or confused about Truman's national health proposals.

Continued shortage of affordable housing in urban areas after the war stirred greater support for home-building programs, another part of Truman's Fair Deal. Private construction firms and real estate agents welcomed extension of federal home loan guarantees, such as those established under the GI Bill and through the Federal Housing Administration (FHA), but they lobbied against publicly financed housing projects. Yet even conservatives such as Senator Taft recognized the housing shortage and supported the Housing Act of 1949. This law promised "a decent home and a suitable living environment for every American family." It authorized construction of 810,000 public housing units (cutting back Truman's goal of 1.05 million). The same law also provided federal funds for "urban renewal" zones, areas to be

KIDS LINE UP FOR SHOTS
Polio was one of the most feared diseases of the Cold War period because it crippled young children. Its postwar history illustrated differences between the Canadian and U.S. medical systems. The Canadian government, with its national health care system, was heavily involved in funding research, testing new medicines, and ultimately distributing the new vaccine. In the United States, a nongovernmental organization called the March of Dimes—famous for its effective solicitation of small donations—took the lead. Dr. Jonas Salk, cooperating with Canadian researchers, developed an effective vaccine that was approved in 1954.

© Bettmann/Corbis.

cleared of rundown dwellings and rebuilt with new construction. The Housing Act of 1949 set forth bold goals but provided only modest funding for its public housing component.

Fair Deal policy making ultimately focused on specific groups, such as veterans and older Americans, rather than on more extensive programs such as a national health care plan and a large-scale commitment to government-built, affordable housing projects. Opponents of economic planning and greater government spending considered the broader proposals of the Fair Deal—such as health care—to be "welfare," and the Truman administration found it easier to defend more narrowly targeted programs that could be hailed as economic security measures for specific groups. This approach to social policy making under the Fair Deal significantly narrowed the approach of Roosevelt's Second Bill of Rights, which had envisioned an array of constitutionally guaranteed entitlements for all citizens, even as it embraced the idea that government should play an active role in social and economic betterment.

Civil Rights

Truman, while modifying the New Deal's domestic policy assumptions, actually broadened its commitment to civil rights. In fact, he supported the fight against racial discrimination more strongly than any previous president.

During his 1948 presidential campaign, Truman had made a special appeal to African American voters. He had strongly endorsed proposals advanced by a civil rights committee he established in 1946. The committee's report, entitled "To Secure These Rights," called for federal legislation against lynching; a special civil rights division within the Department of Justice; antidiscrimination initiatives in employment, housing, and public facilities; and desegregation of the military. Although these proposals prompted many white southern Democrats to bolt to the short-lived Dixiecrat Party in the 1948 election, they won Truman significant support from African Americans.

The Dixiecrat Party episode of 1948, a reaction to Truman's stance on civil rights, portended significant political change among southern whites, who had been voting overwhelmingly Democratic since the late 19th century. Strom Thurmond, the Dixiecrats' presidential candidate, denounced Truman for offering a "civil wrongs" program and charged that "radicals, subversives, and reds" had captured the Democratic Party. Although Thurmond claimed that southerners did not oppose the concept of civil rights measures, he maintained that the Constitution required that they come from state governments and not from Washington, D.C. Other white southern Democrats pledged to fight any federal effort to end the pattern of legally enforced racial segregation. Thurmond carried four states in 1948, and his candidacy showed that the race issue was powerful enough to lead lifelong southern Democrats to abandon their party in national presidential elections.

Despite discord within Democratic ranks, Truman generally supported the civil rights movement. When successive Congresses failed to enact any civil rights legislation—including a law against lynching and a ban on the poll taxes that prevented most southern blacks from voting—the movement turned to a sympathetic White House and to the federal courts. After the labor leader A. Philip Randolph threatened to organize protests against continued segregation in the military, Truman issued an executive order calling for desegregation of the armed forces, a move that began to be implemented toward the end of the Korean War. Truman also endorsed the efforts of the Fair Employment Practices Commission (FEPC) to end racial discrimination in federal hiring.

Members of Truman's administration also spoke candidly of how segregation tarnished America's image abroad. "Communist propaganda twisted and distorted our civil-rights problems," argued one Democratic Senator, and created an "enormous but little understood worldwide impact." In a world "which is 90 percent colored," said Truman, racial discrimination issued an invitation to communism. Cold War anxiety prompted the government to spy on some African American leaders with links to communism, but it also made segregation into a foreign policy liability by highlighting the limits of America's claim to represent liberty and equality.

Meanwhile, Truman's Justice Department regularly appeared in court on behalf of litigants who contested government-backed public school segregation and "restrictive covenants" (legal agreements that prevented racial or religious minorities from acquiring real estate). In 1946, the Supreme Court declared restrictive covenants illegal and began chipping away at the "separate but equal" principle used since *Plessy* v. *Ferguson* (1896) to justify segregated schools. In 1950, the Court ruled that under the 14th Amendment racial segregation in state-financed graduate and law schools was unconstitutional. In light of these decisions, all of the traditional legal arguments used since *Plessy* to legitimate racial segregation in public schools seemed open to a successful challenge. The challenge would finally come in 1954 (see chapter 28).

In summary, the years immediately after the Second World War marked a turning point in domestic policy making. The New Deal's hope for comprehensive socioeconomic planning gave way to the Fair Deal's view that the nation could expect uninterrupted economic growth. Henceforth, Washington could reap, through taxation, its own steady share of a growing economy and so finance programs targeted to assist specific groups, such as military veterans and older people. As one supporter of this new approach argued, postwar policy makers were sophisticated enough to embrace "partial remedies," such as the GI Bill, rather than to wait for fanciful "cure-alls," such as FDR's Second Bill of Rights.

🌐 A Changing Culture

The postwar years brought dramatic changes in the daily life of most Americans. Encouraged by the advertising industry, most people seemed, at one level, to automatically view anything new as "progress." Yet, at another level, the pace and scope of change during these years brought a feeling of uneasiness into American life.

Jackie Robinson and the Baseball "Color Line"

The interplay between embracing and resisting change could be seen in the integration of organized baseball during the 1940s and 1950s. In 1947, major league baseball's

policy of racial segregation finally cracked when Jackie Robinson, who had played in the Negro National League, became the Brooklyn Dodgers' first baseman. Certain players, including several on Robinson's own club, had talked about a boycott. Baseball's leadership, needing new sources of players and aware of the steady stream of African American fans coming out to the parks, threatened to suspend any player who refused to play with Robinson. (Baseball's moguls, though, did relatively little to protect Robinson. He was ordered to endure, without protest, racist insults, flying spikes, and brush-back pitches during his rookie season.)

The pressure to integrate the national pastime became inexorable. Several months after Robinson's debut, the Cleveland Indians signed center fielder Larry Doby, and other African American stars quickly began leaving the Negro leagues for the American and National circuits. Eventually, the talents of Robinson—named Rookie of the Year in 1947 and the National League's Most Valuable Player in 1949—and other African American players

JACKIE ROBINSON

In 1947 Jackie Robinson joined the Brooklyn Dodgers and became the first African American since the 19th century to play major league baseball. He had served as a lieutenant in the Army during the Second World War. Racial integration of the national pastime of baseball became a powerful symbol of progress in race relations.

carried the day. By 1960 every major league team fielded African American players, and some began extensive recruiting in Puerto Rico and elsewhere in the Caribbean. During the 50th anniversary of Robinson's debut, major league baseball staged elaborate memorial ceremonies for Robinson, who had died in 1972, and congratulated the sport for having led the fight against racial prejudice during the Cold War years.

During the late 1940s and early 1950s, however, baseball's leaders had also worked to limit the participation of African Americans. Several teams waited for years before fielding any black players, claiming they could find no talented prospects. More commonly, teams restricted the number of nonwhite players they would take on and

kept their managers, coaches, and front-office personnel solidly white. Even Jackie Robinson, a successful entrepreneur outside of baseball, never received an offer to return to the game in a management capacity after he retired as a player.

Suburban Development

In suburbia, too, change was both celebrated and feared. Suburban living had long been a feature of the "American dream." The new Long Island, New York, suburb of Levittown, which welcomed its first residents in October 1947, seemed to make that dream a reality, at affordable prices, for middle-income families.

M U S I C A L   L I N K   T O   T H E   P A S T

Big Band to Bebop

Songwriter: Charlie Parker
Title: "Koko" (1946)
Performers: Charlie Parker's Ri Bop Boys

The big band jazz craze of the late 1930s and 1940s drove the American record industry to new levels of profit. But it also inspired major corporate record companies to adopt conservative musical policies. By the early 1940s, most big band recordings adhered to strict formulas based on previous sales successes, which produced a lot of dull recordings. Because of this, it was left to independently owned, smaller companies to search out and present the next generation of innovative artists. Charlie "Bird" Parker, the most important artist to emerge from these labels in the mid-1940s, introduced a new kind of jazz called "bebop" with his recording of "Koko." Black bebop musicians such as Parker and Dizzy Gillespie broke the old big band formulas by performing at a faster, near anarchic tempo with more notes per bar, playing songs that extended beyond the usual three-minute commercial barrier, disdaining formal arrangements, reducing the number of players in ensembles, and stressing individual expression through extended solos. As can be heard on "Koko," the music was also fun and exciting, requiring a technical proficiency beyond the reach of most big band musicians.

Many in the jazz world resisted bebop. Artists like Parker and Gillespie refused to play dance music or entertain audiences as previous jazz figures did. They emphasized their own musical advancement and played a harsh, challenging, and intellectual music that some-

times was not immediately enjoyable. Some historians have argued that bebop, with its anti-commercial and anti-assimilationist attitude, symbolized the increasing rebellion and resistance by black Americans during the postwar years that eventually led to the civil rights movement of the 1950s and 1960s.

Bebop's initial recordings were on small record labels such as Savoy (owned by an electronics retailer who released music as a sideline) and Dial (opened by a Hollywood record store entrepreneur to give beboppers wider exposure). Independent labels have played a significant role in introducing trailblazing American musical movements in the face of short-term corporate thinking and musical conservatism. Other examples include 1950s rock and roll (spearheaded by labels such as Sun and Chess) and hip-hop (labels included Tommy Boy and Sugar Hill).

1. Could a similar argument concerning big band music in the 1940s be made for hip-hop music in the 21st century?
2. Has the widespread popularity of hip-hop and its dominance of the best-seller charts induced major record companies to adopt a conservative, formulaic approach toward the hip-hop records they release? Can this historical pattern be found in other styles of American popular music during the 20th century?

Listen to an audio recording of this music on the Musical Links to the Past CD.

SUBURBIA

Builder William Levitt's opening of Levittown, New York, in the late 1940s set a pattern for mass-produced homes in suburban developments. Assistance from governmental financing programs, such as the GI Bill, and the benefits of standardized production methods brought the cost of such homes within the reach of millions of buyers and hastened the flight, particularly of whites, out of central cities and older suburbs.

Nearly everything about Levittown seemed unprecedented. A construction company that had mass-produced military barracks during the Second World War, Levitt & Sons bragged that it was completing a five-room bungalow every 15 minutes. Architectural critics sneered at these "little boxes," but potential buyers stood in long lines hoping to purchase one. By 1950, Levittown consisted of more than 10,000 homes and 40,000 residents, and bulldozers and construction crews were sweeping into other suburban developments across the country. One-quarter of all the houses that existed in 1960 were built after 1949.

To help buyers purchase these homes, the government offered an extensive set of programs. The Federal Housing Administration (FHA), established during the New Deal, helped private lenders extend credit to mass-production builders, who in turn sold houses on generous financing terms. Typically, people who bought FHA-financed homes needed only 5 percent of the purchase price as a down payment; they could finance the rest with a long-term, government-insured mortgage. Millions of war veterans enjoyed even more favorable terms under the GI loan program operated by the Veterans Administration. These government programs made it cheaper to buy a new house in the average suburb than to rent a comfortable apartment in most cities. Moreover, families could deduct from their federal income tax the interest they paid on their mortgages. This deduction could be seen as a disguised form of governmental subsidy for the building and lending industries and for homeowners. Because construction never caught up with demand during the 1950s, many suburbanites could sell their first house at a profit and move up to a more spacious, more expensive dwelling.

The new suburban areas promised greater privacy and more amenities than crowded city neighborhoods or even older suburbs. Builders, quick to recognize the appeal of new housing developments, soon began to offer larger homes, including the sprawling, one-level "ranch" model. The joys of "easy and better" living often came with the house. A Levitt home, for example, contained an automatic washer and a built-in television set. Even the television, by being attached to the house itself, qualified as a "structural" component and could be financed under federally guaranteed loan programs.

The new postwar suburbs enjoyed a reputation for being ideal places in which to raise children, and many more families were having babies. After the war, a complex set of factors, including early marriages and rising incomes, helped produce a "baby boom" that would last well into the 1950s. With houses generally occupying only about 15 percent of suburban lots, large lawns served as private playgrounds. Nearby schools were as new as the rest of the neighborhood, and suburban school boards used their well-equipped, up-to-date buildings to attract both skilled teachers and middle-income families.

In many respects, the new suburban lifestyle epitomized an optimistic spirit of new possibilities, confidence in the future, and acceptance of change. In other respects, though, it represented an effort to create a material and

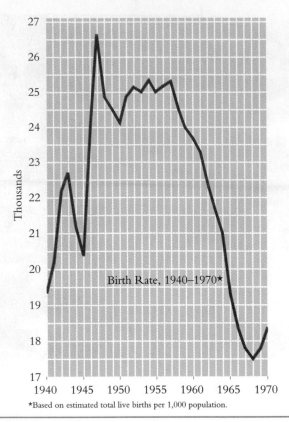

Thousands

Birth Rate, 1940–1970★

*Based on estimated total live births per 1,000 population.

THE BABY BOOM

psychological refuge. Most obviously, buying a new suburban home seemed a way of cushioning the impact of the social and demographic changes ushered in by the war. As African American families left the rural South in search of work in northern cities, "white flight" to suburbia quickened. Although Jackie Robinson, Larry Doby, and other talented athletes could find a place in professional baseball during the 1940s, not a single black person could buy a home in Long Island's Levittown until well into the 1960s.

Government and private housing policies helped structure and maintain the segregationist pattern of white suburbs and increasingly nonwhite urban neighborhoods. Federal laws allowed local groups to veto public housing projects in their communities. Although land and building costs would have been cheaper in the suburbs, public housing projects were concentrated on relatively expensive, high-density urban sites. More important, the lending industry channeled government loan guarantees away from most urban neighborhoods, and private lenders generally denied credit to nonwhites seeking new suburban housing.

No one in the postwar housing industry admitted intentional complicity in these discriminatory patterns. William Levitt could identify his private housing projects with the public crusade against communism. "No man who owns his house and lot can be a Communist," he remarked in 1948. "He has too much to do." Levitt held himself blameless, however, for racial issues. He could help solve the nation's housing problem—and perhaps even the problem of domestic communism—but he insisted that his "private" construction choices had nothing to do with the public issue of race.

Similarly, the architects of this new suburbia saw nothing problematic with postwar gender patterns. William Levitt's confident identification of home ownership with men unconsciously reflected the fact that the lending industry generally would not extend loan guarantees to women. Single women simply could not obtain FHA-backed loans, a policy that the agency justified on the grounds that men were the family breadwinners and that women rarely made enough money to qualify as good credit risks. As a result, home ownership in the new suburbs was invariably limited to white males, with wives as co-owners at best.

Allure and Danger: Women on Film

As postwar suburbs boomed, initially symbolizing promise and affluence, movie moguls found that older urban areas provided rich sites for popular drama. During the 1940s and 1950s, Hollywood released a cycle of motion pictures that came to be called *film noir*. Nearly always filmed in black and white and often set at night in large cities, these movies peeked into the dark corners of postwar America and hinted at deep-seated anxieties and fears.

Many film noir pictures populated their dark cities with alluring femmes fatales: beautiful but dangerous women who challenged the prevailing order. The femme fatale represented the opposite of the nurturing, faithful wife and mother. Usually unmarried and childless, she posed a threat to both men and other women. In *The File on Thelma Jordan* (1949), for instance, the title character, played by Barbara Stanwyck, cynically destroys the marriage of a young, weak-willed district attorney. She initiates an illicit affair with him not because of love, or even lust, but as part of a complicated plot to manipulate the criminal justice system. The postwar era's most prominent female stars—such as Stanwyck, Joan Crawford, Rita Hayworth, and Lana Turner—achieved both popular and critical acclaim playing such roles. Film noir features developed a loyal audience among female viewers, suggesting that women, as well as men, were drawn to the image of independent women.

The fear of communism during the years from 1946 to 1953 accentuated pressures for conformity and often made it difficult to advocate significant change. Yet grow-

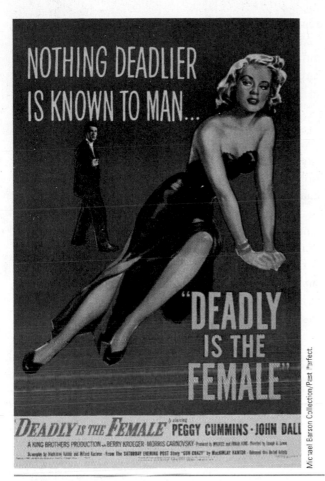

DEADLY IS THE FEMALE

Also called *Gun Crazy* (1949), this film noir played on fears of social breakdown and inspired the later movie *Bonnie and Clyde* (1967).

ing prosperity, new expectations stemming from the war, and demographic shifts, inevitably transformed many social and cultural patterns. The everyday lives of Americans—racial patterns and living arrangements and social expectations—were inexorably changing.

From Truman to Eisenhower

Harry Truman declined to run for another term in the presidential election of 1952. The Democrats were on the defensive, and denunciations of communism and Truman provided the focus of the Republican campaign.

The Election of 1952

Adlai Stevenson of Illinois, the Democratic presidential candidate in 1952, warned that "Soviet secret agents and their dupes" had "burrowed like moles" into governments throughout the world. "We cannot let our guard drop for even a moment." Stevenson approved of the prosecution of the Communist Party's leaders and the dismissal of schoolteachers who were party members. A strong anti-communist stance, however, could not save Stevenson or the Democratic Party.

The Republicans assailed the unpopular Truman presidency and Stevenson. Their vice presidential nominee, Senator Richard Nixon of California, called Stevenson "Adlai the appeaser" and claimed he held a Ph.D. from "Dean Acheson's Cowardly College of Communist Containment." Republicans criticized Truman's handling of the Korean War and highlighted revelations about favoritism and kickbacks on government contracts in his administration. The GOP's successful election formula could be reduced to a simple equation, "K1C2": "Korea, corruption, and communism."

A Soldier-President

For their presidential candidate, Republicans turned to a hero of the Second World War, General Dwight David Eisenhower, popularly known as "Ike." Eisenhower had never sought elective office, but nearly a half-century of military service had made him a skilled politician. Ike grew up in Kansas; won an appointment to, and graduated from, West Point; rose through the army ranks under the patronage of General George Marshall; and directed the Normandy invasion of 1944 as supreme Allied commander. He served as army chief of staff from 1945 to 1948 and, after an interim period as president of Columbia University, returned to active duty as the commander of NATO, a post he held until May 1952.

Eisenhower seemed an attractive political leader. Although his partisan affiliations had always been so vague that some Democrats had courted him in 1948, he finally declared himself a Republican. Initially reluctant to seek the presidency in 1952, he became convinced that Robert Taft, his main GOP rival, leaned too far to the right on domestic issues and lacked a firm commitment to containment policies overseas. Perceived as a middle-of-the-road candidate, Ike appeared able to lead the nation during a cold war as firmly as he had during a hot one. Adlai Stevenson grumbled that the press had embraced the old war hero even before knowing "what his party platform would be" or "what would be the issues of the campaign."

The first military leader to gain the presidency since Ulysses S. Grant (1869–1877), Eisenhower achieved a great personal victory in 1952. The Eisenhower-Nixon ticket received almost 7 million more popular votes than the

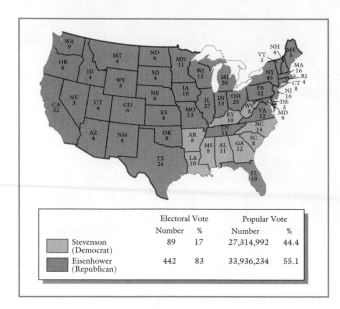

MAP 27.4 PRESIDENTIAL ELECTION, 1952

In this overwhelming victory for Eisenhower, Stevenson carried only a few states. Note that the so-called "solid South" was still solidly Democratic. This trend would shift substantially over the next two decades.

Democrats and won in the electoral college by a margin of 442 to 89. The Republican Party made more modest gains. The GOP gained a single-vote majority in the Senate and enjoyed only an eight-vote margin in the House of Representatives. The electoral coalition Franklin Roosevelt had put together during the 1930s still survived, even though it showed signs of fraying, especially in the South. There,

many of the white southern votes that had gone to the Dixiecrats in 1948 began moving toward the Republicans, and Eisenhower carried four states in the Democratic Party's once "solid South."

Conclusion

Efforts at containing communism dominated both domestic and foreign policy during the years after the Second World War. As worsening relations between the United States and the Soviet Union developed into the Cold War, the Truman administration pursued policies that expanded the power of the government, particularly the executive branch, to counter the threat. The militarization of foreign policy intensified when the United States went to war in Korea in 1950. At home, anticommunism focused on containing both the activities and ideas of alleged subversives. These initiatives raised difficult issues about how to protect legitimate national security interests while still safeguarding constitutional liberties.

Within this Cold War climate, struggles to achieve greater equality still emerged. Truman's Fair Deal promised that new economic wisdom would be able to guarantee economic growth and thereby provide the tax revenues to expand domestic programs. Truman also pressed for national measures against racial discrimination.

The election of Dwight D. Eisenhower in 1952 gave the Republicans the presidency for the first time in 20 years. Eisenhower's broad personal appeal, however, did not signal an imminent end to the power of the Democratic coalition that had held sway since the 1930s.

SUGGESTED READINGS

David Reynolds, *One World Divisible: A Global History since 1945* (2001) provides an international context for the emerging Cold War, while **Walter LaFeber,** *America, Russia, and the Cold War, 1945–2002* (9th rev. ed., 2002) offers an expert interpretive synthesis of U.S. policies. **Melvyn Leffler,** *The Specter of Communism* (1994) is a brief, critical account of the onset of the Cold War. **Leffler's** *A Preponderance of Power: National Security, the Truman Administration, and the Cold War* (1992) offers more detail, as does **Michael J. Hogan,** *A Cross of Iron: Harry S. Truman and the Origins of the National Security State, 1945–1954* (1998), and **Arnold A. Offner,** *Another Such Victory: President Truman and the Cold War, 1945–1953* (2002). **John Lewis Gaddis,** *We Now Know: Rethinking Cold War History* (1997) and his many other books present a less critical view. The most thorough and scholarly biography of

Harry Truman remains **Alonso L. Hamby,** *Man of the People: A Life of Harry S. Truman* (1995).

On the Korean War, **William Stueck,** *The Korean War: An International History* (1995) provides an overview, while **Bruce Cumings's many books, including** *Korea: The Unknown War* (coauthored with Jon Halliday) (1988), provide a more critical view. Postwar reconstruction of former enemies is expertly treated in **John Dower,** *Embracing Defeat: Japan in the Wake of World War II* (2000), and **Marc Trachtenberg,** *A Constructed Peace: The Making of the European Settlement, 1945–1963* (1999).

On communism and anticommunism in America during this period, **Allen Weinstein and Alexander Vassiliev,** *The Haunted Wood: Soviet Espionage in America, the Stalin Era* (1999) examines Soviet espionage. **Stanley I. Kutler,** *American*

Inquisition: Justice and Injustice in the Cold War (1982) and **Ellen Schrecker,** *The Age of McCarthyism* (2001) stress the excesses of anticommunist crusading.

The effect of the Cold War and containment on American culture is the subject of many excellent studies. **Michael S. Sherry,** *In the Shadow of War: The United States Since the 1930s* (1995), a broad synthesis, and **Stephen Whitfield,** *The Culture of the Cold War* (rev. ed., 1996) are good places to begin. **Tom Englehardt,** *The End of Victory Culture and the Disillusioning of a Generation* (1995) provides an influential interpretation. **Paul Boyer,** *By the Bomb's Early Light* (1985) and **Alan Nadel,** *Containment Culture: American Narrative, Postmodernism, and the Nuclear Age* (1995) examine diverse cultural effects of the atomic age. **Lary May,** *The Big Tomorrow: Hollywood and the Politics of the American Way* (2000) examines Hollywood film culture. **Jessica Wang,** *American Science in an Age of Anxiety: Scientists, Anticommunism, and the Cold War* (1999) stresses FBI pressure on scientists to support the Cold War. **Lizabeth Cohen,** *A Consumer's Republic: Mass Consumption In Postwar America* (2003) critically highlights the convergence of a number of important Cold War–era social and political forces.

 AMERICAN JOURNEY ONLINE AND INFOTRAC COLLEGE EDITION

Visit the source collections at www.ajaccess.wadsworth.com and infotrac.thomsonlearning.com and use the Search function with the following key terms to explore documents, images, audio and video clips, articles, and commentary related to the material in this chapter.

Harry S. Truman
GI Bill
House Un-American Activities
    Committee (HUAC)
George Kennan (Mr. X)
Containment
Jackie Robinson
NSC-68
Alger Hiss
North Atlantic Treaty
    Organization (NATO)

General Douglas MacArthur
Dwight D. Eisenhower
Cold War
Korean War
National Security Act
Marshall Plan
A. Philip Randolph
Joseph McCarthy

GRADE AIDS

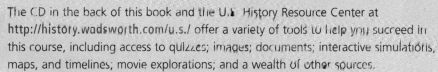

Visit the Liberty Equality Power Companion Web Site for resources specific to this textbook: http://history.wadsworth.com/murrin_LEP4e

The CD in the back of this book and the U.S. History Resource Center at http://history.wadsworth.com/u.s./ offer a variety of tools to help you succeed in this course, including access to quizzes; images; documents; interactive simulations, maps, and timelines; movie explorations; and a wealth of other sources.

Chapter 28

Affluence and Its Discontents, 1953–1963

THE QUEEN OF ABUNDANCE
The double-store, frost-free refrigerator offered consumers an elegant display case for the new prepackaged and frozen food products that became available during the 1950s. Advertisements such as this one proclaimed that Americans had become a "people of plenty."

CHAPTER OUTLINE

W ith the end of the fighting in Korea in 1953, Cold War tensions somewhat abated. The new president, Dwight ("Ike") Eisenhower (1953–61), lowered the pitch of anticommunist rhetoric. Yet he and his successor, John F. Kennedy (1961–63), continued to conduct a global anticommunist foreign policy and took it in new directions.

At home, Eisenhower and Kennedy pushed, cautiously, to extend some of the programs initiated during the Roosevelt and Truman eras. The economic growth of the late 1950s and early 1960s encouraged talk about an age of "affluence." It also generated apprehension about conformity, cultural tastes of young people, and the impact of commercial mass culture. At the same time, a movement to end racial discrimination and concern about the distribution of the nation's economic bounty renewed debates over the use of governmental power and the meanings of liberty and equality.

CHAPTER FOCUS

♦ How did the Eisenhower administration reorient the foreign policy of containment?
♦ How could economic prosperity be seen as both an opportunity and a problem during the 1950s?
♦ How did the fight against discrimination raise new political issues during the 1950s and early 1960s?

♦ How did the Eisenhower and Kennedy administrations respond to these issues?

♦ What foreign and domestic policies did Kennedy champion during his brief presidency?

♦ Why does Kennedy's presidency loom so large in popular memory?

Foreign Policy, 1953–1960

By 1953 the strident anticommunist rhetoric associated with McCarthyism and the Korean War era was beginning to subside. The dominant assumption of Cold War policy—that the United States must protect the "free world" and fight communism everywhere—remained unchanged, but the focus and tactics shifted. Bipolar confrontations between the United States and the Soviet Union over European issues gave way to greater reliance on nuclear deterrence and to more subtle and complex power plays in the "Third World": the Middle East, Asia, Latin America, and Africa.

Eisenhower Takes Command

Eisenhower honored a campaign pledge to travel to Korea as a means of ending U.S. military involvement there. Negotiations reached an apparent impasse, however, over whether North Korean and Chinese prisoners of war (POWs) wishing to remain in South Korea could forcibly be returned to North Korea and China. Hoping to end the stalemate, Eisenhower began to ruminate, in vague language heard in China and North Korea, about the use of nuclear weapons if diplomacy failed. Talks resumed, and on July 27, 1953, both sides signed a truce that established a special commission of neutral nations to handle the POW issue. (The POWs themselves were subsequently allowed to determine whether they wished to be repatriated.) A conflict in which more than 2 million Asians, mostly noncombatants, and 53,000 Americans died finally ended. A formal peace treaty remained unsigned, however, and the 38th parallel between North and South Korea became one of the most heavily militarized borders in the world.

At home, Ike gradually wrested control of the national security issue from Senator Joseph McCarthy and other extreme anticommunists. Congress did exceed the wishes of the Eisenhower administration when it passed the Communist Control Act of 1954, which barred the Communist Party from entering candidates in elections and extended the registration requirements established by the McCarran Act of 1950. But with a Republican president in the White House, most members of the GOP began to reject the McCarthyite style of anticommunism.

CHRONOLOGY

1953 Korean War ends • Julius and Ethel Rosenberg executed • *Playboy* magazine debuts

1954 Joseph McCarthy censured by U.S. Senate • Communist Control Act passed • *Brown v. Board of Education of Topeka* decision • SEATO formed • Arbenz government overthrown in Guatemala • Elvis Presley releases first record on Sun label • Geneva Peace Accords in Southeast Asia signed

1955 Montgomery bus boycott begins • *National Review* founded • *Brown II* decision

1956 Suez Crisis • Anti-Soviet uprisings occur in Poland and Hungary • Federal Highway Act passed • Eisenhower reelected

1957 Eisenhower sends troops to Lebanon • Eisenhower sends troops to Little Rock, Arkansas • Congress passes Civil Rights Act, first civil rights legislation in 80 years • Soviets launch *Sputnik* • Gaither Report urges more defense spending

1958 National Defense Education Act passed by Congress • *The Affluent Society* published

1959 Khrushchev visits United States

1960 Civil Rights Act passed • U-2 incident ends Paris summit • Kennedy elected president • Sit-in demonstrations begin

1961 Bay of Pigs invasion fails • Berlin Wall erected • Freedom rides begin in the South • Kennedy announces Alliance for Progress

1962 Cuban Missile Crisis • Kennedy sends troops to University of Mississippi to enforce integration

1963 Civil rights activists undertake march on Washington • Betty Friedan's *The Feminine Mystique* published • Kennedy assassinated (November 22); Lyndon Johnson becomes president

The erratic McCarthy careened completely out of control when he claimed that the U.S. Army was harboring subversives within its ranks. During spring 1954, a Senate committee conducted a televised investigation of his fantastic charge, and these Army–McCarthy Hearings brought him down. Under the glare of TV lights, McCarthy appeared as a crude, desperate bully who hurled slanders in every direction. In December 1954, a majority of the Senate, including colleagues who had once supported him, voted to censure him for conduct "unbecoming" a member. McCarthyism began to recede to the fringes of American politics. McCarthy faded from the limelight and died in obscurity in 1957, still holding onto a seat in the Senate.

Meanwhile, the Eisenhower administration expanded its own national security agenda. Compared to McCarthy's bombast, Eisenhower's low-key approach seemed eminently reasonable and moderate. The demonstrated unreliability of anticommunist zealots such as McCarthy strengthened the position of the White House when it successfully claimed a constitutional privilege to withhold from Congress classified information on national security matters. Relatively free from congressional and judicial oversight, the Eisenhower administration extended Truman's earlier programs of domestic surveillance, wiretapping, and covert action overseas. The president also backed a secret program to develop new aerial surveillance capabilities; by 1956, he enjoyed, courtesy of intelligence photographs taken from the new "U-2 spy planes," a clear view of the Soviet military arsenal.

Historians increasingly see Eisenhower as a skilled leader who could aggressively use the power of the presidency while often seeming to be doing very little. Eisenhower, in the words of one scholar, conducted a "hidden hand presidency." Mindful of how the ebullient Truman had become personally linked to popular controversies, Ike generally stayed in the background and projected an air of calm steadiness. In foreign policy, Eisenhower usually allowed John Foster Dulles, his secretary of state from 1953 to 1959, to take center stage; he encouraged the belief that George Humphrey, his secretary of the treasury, and Sherman Adams, his chief of staff, handled domestic issues.

The New Look and Summitry

Eisenhower quietly worked to reorient the nation's anticommunist foreign policy. The change of leadership in Moscow, following the 1953 death of Joseph Stalin, helped Ike make significant adjustments to U.S. policy. Nikita Khrushchev, who eventually emerged as the dominant Soviet leader, denounced Stalin's murderous despotism and talked of "peaceful coexistence" with capitalist nations. Seeking to free up resources to produce more consumer goods, Khrushchev began reducing Soviet armed forces.

U.S. military policy also underwent review. In December 1953, Admiral Arthur Radford, head of the Joint Chiefs of Staff, urged a reduction of the military budget and a fresh approach to defense strategy. Radford's "New Look" reflected Eisenhower's belief that unchecked military expenditures might eventually impede economic growth. The new strategy would look less to costly ground forces and more to airpower, advanced nuclear capabilities, and covert action.

The Eisenhower administration's doctrine of "massive retaliation" gambled that the threat of unleashing U.S. nuclear weaponry would check Soviet expansion. John Foster Dulles warned that Washington would not hesitate to launch an all-out nuclear attack on the Soviet Union if Moscow's actions, anywhere in the world, threatened

U.S. security. To make the U.S. nuclear umbrella more effective worldwide, Eisenhower expanded NATO to include West Germany in 1955 and added two other mutual defense pacts with noncommunist nations in Central and Southeast Asia. The Southeast Asia Treaty Organization (SEATO), formed in 1954, linked the United States to Australia, France, Great Britain, New Zealand, Pakistan, the Philippines, and Thailand. The weakly bonded Central Treaty Organization (CENTO), formed in 1959, included Pakistan, Iran, Turkey, Iraq, and Britain.

The Eisenhower administration elevated psychological warfare and "informational" programs into major Cold War weapons. The government-run Voice of America extended the geographic reach of its radio broadcasts and programmed in more languages. Washington also secretly funded Radio Free Europe, Radio Liberty (beamed to the Soviet Union), and Radio Asia. In 1953, Eisenhower persuaded Congress to create the United States Information Agency (USIA) to coordinate anticommunist informational and propaganda campaigns.

The United States and the Soviet Union, hoping to improve relations, began holding high-level "summit" meetings. In May 1955, an agreement was reached to end the postwar occupation of Austria and to transform it into a neutral country. Two months later, the United States, the Soviet Union, Britain, and France met in Geneva, Switzerland. Making little progress on arms reduction, the future of Germany, and other matters, this summit conference nonetheless inaugurated new cultural exchanges. Cold War tensions eased somewhat, and all sides hailed the conciliatory "spirit of Geneva." In fall 1959, to heal differences that had developed over Berlin, Khrushchev toured the United States, met with Eisenhower, and paid well-publicized visits to farmers in Iowa and Disneyland in California. Although a 1960 Paris summit meeting fell apart after the Soviets shot down a U-2 spy plane over their territory, the tone of cold-war rhetoric had grown less strident by the end of Eisenhower's presidency.

The superpowers also began to consider arms limitation. Eisenhower's "Open Skies" initiative of 1955 proposed that the two nations use reconnaissance flights over each other's territory to verify disarmament efforts. The Soviets balked, but some progress was made in limiting atomic tests. Responding to worries about the health hazards of atomic fallout, both countries slowed aboveground testing and discussed a broader test-ban agreement. For many Americans, efforts to curtail nuclear testing came too late. Government documents declassified in the 1980s confirmed what antinuclear activists had long suspected: People who had lived "downwind" from rural nuclear test sites during the 1940s and 1950s had suffered an unusual number of atomic-related illnesses. In the

Willis Conover: Fighting the Cold War with Jazz

Willis Conover (1921–1996) was known as the most famous American that few other Americans had ever heard about. His radio program, *Music USA: The Jazz Hour*, went out over the U.S. government–run Voice of America radio station, which could not be heard within the United States. It attracted some 30 million regular listeners in Eastern Europe and the Soviet Union and perhaps 100 million fans throughout Asia, Africa, and Latin America.

Proclaiming jazz as "the music of freedom," Conover, literally, *was* America's voice during the height of the Cold War. Six nights a week for two hours each, Conover's program would, in the words of his *New York Times* obituary, "bombard Budapest with Billy Taylor, strafe Poland with Oscar Peterson and drop John Coltrane on Moscow." Conover may have been more effective in generating admiration for the United States, especially among young people, and in fomenting dissent against disapproving communist regimes than most other weapons in America's Cold War arsenal.

Born in Buffalo, New York, Conover developed an interest in radio as a young man and became a popular local disc jockey in Washington, D.C., where he hosted the city's only jazz program. After Duke Ellington toured the Soviet Union in 1954, to wildly enthusiastic audiences, the Voice of America decided that a regular slot devoted to jazz would attract listeners. Conover broadcast his first program in 1955. For the next 40 years, *The Jazz Hour*, one of Voice of America's most popular programs, ran in a prime evening spot between two news broadcasts. During the late 1950s, it claimed more than 1,400 fan clubs in almost every country in the world.

Although some members of Congress charged that jazz was "pure noise" and complained that the U.S. government should not spend money broadcasting something so trivial, officials who were fighting the Cold War knew the cultural value of jazz. It was genuinely *American* music; it symbolized individuality and free expression; and its global popularity (which greatly exceeded its recognition at home) seemed boundless. *Look* magazine proclaimed the usefulness of jazz as a Cold War weapon in these words: "Jazz is a door opener everywhere, a Pandora's box full of friendliness that totalitarians won't easily be able to close." Conover, opening his program each night with "Take the 'A' Train," brought American jazz to the world and nurtured an international fascination with American culture.

CONOVER SPINS JAZZ, 1959

From his Voice of America studio in Washington, D.C., Willis Conover brought the sounds of jazz greats such as Miles Davis and Duke Ellington to the world.

© AP/Wide World Photo.

1990s, new revelations showed that the government had covertly conducted experiments with radioactive materials on unsuspecting American citizens.

Meanwhile, events in Eastern Europe during the middle of the 1950s underscored the danger of being drawn into a military confrontation with Moscow. The Soviet-dominated "satellite countries" were chafing under managed economies and police-state control. Seizing on the post-Stalinist atmosphere, insurgents in Poland staged a three-day rebellion in June 1956 and forced the Soviets to accept Wladyslaw Gomulka, an old foe of Stalin, as head of state. Hungarians then rallied in support of Imre Nagy,

another anti-Stalinist communist, who pledged to create a multiparty democracy. The Soviets sought an accommodation that would preserve Moscow's power while allowing minimal political change, but armed rebellion spread throughout Hungary.

The Hungarian revolutionaries appealed for American assistance. They took hope from Secretary of State Dulles's talk about an anticommunist policy aimed at "liberation" rather than merely containment. The United States, however, could hardly launch military operations so close to the Soviet Union. Soviet armies crushed the Hungarian uprising and killed thousands of dissidents, including Nagy. U.S. policy makers came to recognize that advocating freedom from communist rule might make good political rhetoric at home but could lead to tragedy abroad.

Covert Action and Economic Leverage

Increasingly, the U.S. battle against communism shifted its focus from Europe to the Third World. Covert action and economic leverage replaced overt military confrontation as the primary tools. These tactics proved both less expensive and less visible than military deployment, and therefore less likely to provoke public controversy at home or a military showdown with the Soviets overseas.

The CIA played a leading role in the new policy. In 1953, it helped bring about the election of Ramón Magsaysay, a strong anticommunist, as president of the Philippines. That same year, the CIA facilitated a coup that overthrew Mohammed Mossadegh's legitimate, although left-leaning, government in Iran and restored Shah Reza Pahlavi to power. The increasingly dictatorial Shah remained a firm ally of the United States and a friend of American oil interests in Iran until his ouster by Muslim fundamentalists in 1979. In 1954, the CIA, working closely with the United Fruit Company, secretly helped topple President Jacobo Arbenz Guzmán's elected government in Guatemala. Officials of the Eisenhower administration and officers of the fruit company saw Arbenz as a communist because he sought to nationalize and redistribute large tracts of land, including some owned by United Fruit. These successful covert actions gained the CIA, headed by Allen Dulles, brother of the U.S. secretary of state, even greater influence and power. In 1954, the National Security Council widened the CIA's mandate, and by 1960 it had approximately 15,000 agents (compared to about 6,000 when Eisenhower took office) deployed around the world.

Eisenhower also employed economic strategies—trade and aid—to fight communism and win influence for the United States in the Third World. These strategies aimed at opening new opportunities for American enterprises overseas, discouraging other countries from adopting state-directed economic systems, and encouraging trade expansion. U.S. policy makers came to identify "freedom" with the "free market" and thus regarded efforts of Third World nations to break old colonial bonds by creating government-controlled economies and nationalizing local industries as a threat to liberty. New governmental assistance programs offered economic aid to friendly nations, and military aid rose sharply as well. Under the Mutual Security Program and the Military Assistance Program,

the United States spent $3 billion annually and trained 225,000 representatives from nations around the world in anticommunism and domestic police tactics. The buildup of military allies in Third World nations strengthened the anticommunist resources of the United States but also contributed to the development of dictatorships in foreign nations.

America and the Third World

In pursuing its policies, the Eisenhower administration employed a broad definition of what counted as anticommunism. In many countries, groups seeking to change labor laws and land ownership patterns that might benefit large numbers of people had allied with communist movements. Economic elites and dictators could hope to win U.S. support against these internal political opponents simply by whispering the word communist.

Latin America

In Latin America, the White House talked about expanding freedom but regularly backed dictatorial regimes that welcomed U.S. investment and rejected leftist movements. Eisenhower awarded the Legion of Merit to unpopular dictators in Peru and Venezuela and privately confessed his admiration for the anticommunism of Paraguay's General Alfredo Stroessner, a tyrant who sheltered ex-Nazis and ran his country as a private fiefdom. Vice President Richard Nixon toasted Cuba's Fulgencio Batista, a corrupt despot beholden to illegal gambling syndicates in the United States, as "Cuba's Abraham Lincoln." The CIA secretly trained Batista's security forces. Surveying Eisenhower-era policies, America's disgruntled ambassador to democratic Costa Rica complained that Secretary of State Dulles had advised foreign service officers to "do nothing to offend the dictators; they are the only people we can depend on."

Such policies offended many Latin Americans. "Yankeephobia" spread, and events in Cuba dramatized the growth of anti-American sentiments. After a leftist movement led by Fidel Castro overthrew Batista in 1959, tried to curtail Cuba's dependence on the United States, and adopted policies that prompted many middle-class Cubans to flee to the United States, the Eisenhower administration imposed an economic boycott on the island. Castro turned to the Soviet Union for economic aid, declared himself a communist, further tightened his political grip over Cuba, and pledged to support Cuban-style insurgencies throughout Latin America. The CIA began formulating an invasion to unseat Castro, and the Eisenhower administration ordered a review of the U.S. policies that were generating ill will throughout Latin America. This review recommended greater emphasis on encouraging democratic political processes, protection of human rights, and economic growth in Latin America.

Nasserism and the Suez Crisis of 1956

In the Middle East, distrust of nationalism and neutralism shaped U.S. policy. In 1954, when Colonel Gamal Abdel Nasser overthrew the corrupt monarchy of King Farouk and seized control of Egypt, he also promised to rescue other Arab nations from European domination and guide them toward "positive neutralism." Denouncing Israel and accepting aid from both the United States and the Soviet Union, Nasser boosted Egypt's economic and military power. He also purchased advanced weapons from communist Czechoslovakia and extended diplomatic recognition to communist China. Those actions prompted the United States to cancel loans that were to finance the huge Aswan Dam, a project designed to improve agriculture along the Nile River and provide hydroelectric power for new industries. Nasser responded in July 1956 by nationalizing the British-controlled Suez Canal, arguing that canal tolls would provide substitute financing for the dam. The Suez was still of economic and symbolic importance to Britain, and its forces, joined by those of France and Israel, attacked Egypt in October and seized control of the the waterway.

Eisenhower distrusted Nasser, but he opposed Britain's blatant attempt to retain its imperial position. The Soviets were, at that same time, crushing the Hungarian revolt, and Eisenhower could not effectively criticize the Soviets for maintaining a sphere of influence in Eastern Europe when Britain was using military force in the Middle East. Denouncing the Anglo-French-Israeli action, Ike threatened to use America's economic might to destabilize Britain's currency unless the invasion ended. Eventually, a plan supported by the United States and the United Nations allowed Egypt to regain the Suez Canal, but America lost prestige and power in the area as the Soviet Union took over financing of the Aswan Dam and strengthened its ties with Nasser.

Egypt's new links to the Soviets increased the Eisenhower administration's fear that "Nasserism" might spread throughout the energy-rich Middle East. In spring 1957, Congress endorsed the "Eisenhower Doctrine," the president's pledge to defend Middle Eastern countries "against overt armed aggression from any nation controlled by international communism." Although Moscow's machinations only began to account for the spread of Nasser-style nationalism and civil unrest in the area, anticommunist rhetoric did provide a handy justification for backing governments that supported America's need for petroleum and natural gas. Elites in Lebanon and Jordan, fearful of more Nasser-style revolts, after military coups toppled the monarchy in oil-rich Iraq and threatened that of Jordan, asked the United States and Britain for help. In the spirit of the Eisenhower doctrine (which was never formally invoked), Ike sent U.S. marines to Lebanon to protect an anti-Nasser government in Beirut and supported Britain's simultaneous move to help King Hussein retain his throne in Jordan. These actions furthered the U.S. policy of supporting friendly, conservative governments in the Middle East but also intensified Arab nationalism and fostered anti-Americanism.

The Eisenhower administration tried to derail left-leaning political movements elsewhere in the world. In 1958, the president approved a CIA plan to help unseat Achmed Sukarno, leader of Indonesia, who drew support from that nation's large Communist Party. When civil war broke out, the CIA furnished planes, pilots, and encouragement to the rebels. But after the rebellion collapsed, the United States abandoned its Indonesian allies, and Sukarno tightened his grip on power. Other CIA activities included various schemes to assassinate Fidel Castro (which failed) and Patrice Lumumba, a popular black nationalist in the Congo. (Assassins did get Lumumba in 1961, and scholars still debate the CIA's role in his death.)

Vietnam

Eisenhower's strategy of thwarting communism and neutralism in the Third World set the stage for steadily increasing U.S. involvement in Indochina. There, communist-nationalist forces led by Ho Chi Minh (born Nguyen Tat Thanh) sought independence from France. Ho Chi Minh had studied in the Soviet Union and in France before returning to Indochina in 1941 to fight against the Japanese armies that had overrun this French colony. When Japan withdrew at war's end, Ho Chi Minh had vainly appealed to the United States to support independence for Indochina. Despite wartime criticism of colonialism, U.S. leaders supported the return of French rule. In 1946, Ho Chi Minh and his Vietminh forces went to war against France and its ally, Bao Dai. Despite U.S. willingness to finance French military operations, a stunning Vietminh victory, orchestrated by General Nguyen Giap at Dien Bien Phu in 1954, convinced Paris to abandon Indochina. The Geneva Peace Accords of 1954, which the United States refused to sign, removed French forces and divided Indochina into three new countries: Laos, Cambodia, and Vietnam. The

MAP 28.1   ISRAEL, THE MIDDLE EAST, AND THE SUEZ CRISIS, 1956

The creation of Israel and the Suez Crisis of 1956 shaped international politics in the Middle East in the postwar era.
This map helps suggest some reasons why the establishment of Israel sharpened Arab nationalism and why the Suez Canal
was considered to be such an important strategic location.

accords split Vietnam into two jurisdictions—North Vietnam and South Vietnam—until an election could unify the country under a single government.

Eisenhower's advisers expected that Ho Chi Minh would win any electoral contest and feared that a communist-nationalist victory in Vietnam could set off a geopolitical chain reaction. Using familiar Cold War language, the Eisenhower administration insisted that "the loss of any of the countries of Southeast Asia to Communist aggression" would ultimately "endanger the stability and security" of Europe and Japan, a formulation known

as the "domino theory." As a communist government took control of North Vietnam, Eisenhower supported a non-communist one in South Vietnam and ordered covert operations and economic programs to prevent Ho Chi Minh from becoming the head of a unified Vietnam.

Colonel Edward Lansdale, who had directed the CIA's campaign against a leftist insurgency in the Philippines from 1950 to 1953, arrived in Saigon, capital of South Vietnam, in 1954. Lansdale masterminded the creation of a pro-U.S. government in South Vietnam under Ngo Dinh Diem, an anticommunist Catholic who had been educated in the United States. At first, Lansdale seemed to be succeeding. Diem's government, with U.S. concurrence, renounced the Geneva Peace Accords and refused to hold elections to create a unified government for Vietnam. It extended its authority over South Vietnam, redistributed land formerly owned by the French, augmented its military, and even launched an industrialization program.

Diem's authoritarian policies, however, alienated much of South Vietnam's predominantly Buddhist population, and his narrowing circle of political allies became notoriously corrupt. With encouragement and matériel from North Vietnam, Vietminh supporters in the South spearheaded opposition to Diem. As time passed, Diem grew more and more isolated from his own people and increasingly dependent on U.S. support. As early as 1955, France had warned the United States of Diem's liabilities, but the Eisenhower administration could see no alternative. By 1960, the United States had sent billions of American dollars and 900 advisers to prop up Diem's government.

Opposition to Diem coalesced in the National Liberation Front (NLF). Formed in December 1960, the NLF included groups that resented Diem's dependence on the United States, communists who demanded more extensive land reform, and politicians who decried Diem's corruption and cronyism. North Vietnam began sending more supplies and, then, thousands of troops to the South to support the NLF.

Eisenhower's policy in Indochina lacked clarity. Although Ike had once said that U.S. military involvement would be a "tragedy" (and had refused direct military intervention to help the French in 1954), he committed more aid and national prestige to South Vietnam and tied America's honor to Diem's diminishing political fortunes. The decision of whether these commitments would lead to military action by the United States would fall to Ike's successors.

In his farewell address of 1961, the former general warned that the greatest danger to the United States was not communism but the nation's own "military-industrial complex." Despite Eisenhower's desire to limit militarism and reduce Cold War rivalries, he had directed a resolutely anticommunist foreign policy that helped fuel the nuclear arms race and accelerate superpower contests in the Third World.

L I N K   T O   T H E   P A S T

A Warning about the Future: President Dwight Eisenhower's Farewell Address, 1961

Eisenhower raised the stakes in the Cold War arms race with the Soviet Union: new missiles for the delivery of increasingly powerful nuclear bombs, new aerial surveillance techniques, and vast tracking centers to coordinate the nation's defenses. Yet he left office warning Americans about the growth in what he called the "military-industrial complex."

WE ANNUALLY SPEND on military security more than the net income of all United States corporations.

This conjunction of an immense military establishment and a large arms industry is new in the American experience. The total influence—economic, political, even spiritual—is felt in every city, every State house, every office of the Federal government. We recognize the imperative need for this development. Yet we must not fail to comprehend its grave implications. . . .

In the councils of government, we must guard against the acquisition of unwarranted influence, whether sought or unsought, by the military-industrial complex. The potential for the disastrous rise of misplaced power exists and will persist.

We must never let the weight of this combination endanger our liberties or democratic processes. . . . I confess that I lay down my official responsibilities in this field with a definite sense of disappointment.

PRESIDENT DWIGHT D. EISENHOWER

Farewell address, 1961

1. What did Eisenhower mean by the "military-industrial complex"?
2. Why did he think it threatened American democracy?
3. How might his warnings be evaluated today?

For additional sources related to this feature, visit the *Liberty, Equality, Power* Web site at:

http://history.wadsworth.com/murrin_LEP4e

Affluence—A "People of Plenty"

In 1940, the United States had still teetered on the brink of economic depression. Only a decade and a half later, the nation's GNP had soared to more than five times that of Great Britain and more than ten times that of Japan. The output of corporations such as General Motors surpassed the GNP of many nations. Writing in 1954, historian David Potter called Americans a "people of plenty."

Economic Growth

The 1950s marked the midpoint of a period of generally steady economic growth that began during the Second World War and continued until the early 1970s. Corporations turned out vast quantities of consumer goods and enjoyed rising profits. Investments and business ventures overseas boosted corporate profits at home. The domestic economy intersected with an international marketplace dominated by U.S.-based firms. The label "Made in America" symbolized both the quality of particular products and the economic power of the nation at large. National security policies helped maintain this economic growth by keeping raw materials and energy flowing from the Third World. Abundant supplies of inexpensive oil and natural

THE "MRS. AMERICA" GAS KITCHEN

In 1959, the American National Exhibition in Moscow featured a "typical housewife" working in this RCA/Whirlpool "Mrs. America" gas kitchen, a symbol of the streamlined material progress of the postwar United States.

THE TYPICAL HOUSEWIFE

This photograph depicts a different view of the "typical housewife" in her kitchen.

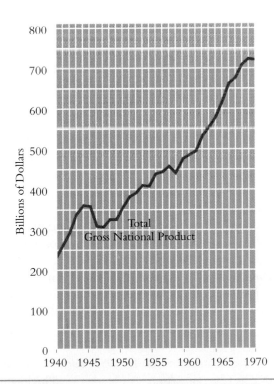

STEADY GROWTH OF GROSS NATIONAL PRODUCT, 1940–1970

gas lowered production costs and allowed industries to replace domestic coal with less costly, and less polluting, energy sources from abroad.

Newer industries, such as chemicals and electronics, became particularly dominant in the world market. The Corning Glass Company reported that most of its sales in the mid-1950s came from products that had been unknown in 1940. General Electric proclaimed that "progress is our most important product." Government spending on national security pumped money into the general economy and stimulated specific industries. In 1955, military expenditures accounted for about 10 percent of the GNP. The fact that national security had become big business was dramatized by President Eisenhower's selection of Charles Wilson of General Motors in 1953 and Neil McElroy of Procter & Gamble in 1957 to head the Department of Defense.

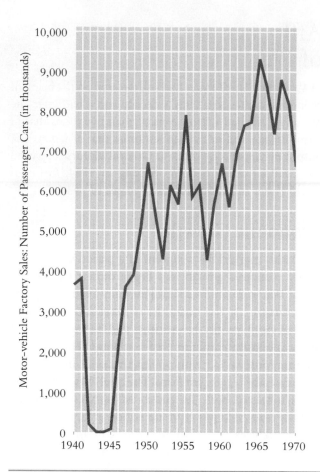

AUTO SALES, 1940–1970

YOU'LL HAVE PLENTY TO SHOW OFF *in the high-spirited performance of your* **NEW CHEVROLET.** *With its radical new Turbo-Thrust V8* and new action in all engines, it's so quick, agile and eager that once you take the wheel, you'll never want to leave it. You've got your hands on something really special!*

Your pride can't help showing just a bit when you slide behind the wheel of this new Chevrolet. You couldn't be sitting prettier—and you know it.

You're in charge of one of the year's most looked at, most longed for cars. Chevy's crisply sculptured contours and downright luxurious interiors are enough to make anybody feel like a celebrity.

Move your foot a fraction on the gas pedal and you feel the instant, silken response of a unique new kind of V8. You ride smoothly and serenely—cushioned by deep coil springs at every wheel. You can even have a real air ride*, if you wish.

See your Chevrolet dealer. . . . Chevrolet Division of General Motors, Detroit 2, Mich. **Optional at extra cost.*

AUTOMOBILES SYMBOLIZE A NEW LIFESTYLE

This ad for a 1958 pink convertible shows off not only the nation's new economic productivity and consumer lifestyle but also suggests the dominant ideal of family "togetherness."

The new suburbs and their residents exemplified the consumer abundance that many Americans thought characterized their age. Because these outlying areas lacked adequate mass transit, life revolved around the automobile. Initially, if the male breadwinner needed the family car to commute to work, his wife had to spend her day near home. As the opportunities for car buying expanded during the mid-1950s, however, the two-car family and the new suburban shopping malls became tangible symbols of economic growth.

Economic growth, according to celebrants of the 1950s, had made the United States the envy of the world. Widespread ownership of kitchen appliances, television sets, and automobiles supported the claim that Americans were a people of plenty. Worries about the limits of capitalism, widely expressed during the 1930s, all but disappeared. Capitalism worked, and it worked spectacularly well. Only a new vocabulary of superlatives, it seemed, could describe its wonders. In 1955, *Fortune* magazine hailed "The Changing American Market" and highlighted "The Rich Middle-Income Class" and "The Wonderful Ordinary Luxury Market." Harvard's celebrated economist John Kenneth Galbraith had simply entitled his 1952 study *American Capitalism;* his follow-up book, which topped the best-seller lists for nearly six months, bore a more grandiose title, *The Affluent Society* (1958).

Although Galbraith's second study took a more critical view than his first, the word *affluence* fit nicely with the dominant vision that celebrated constant economic growth. This term also directed attention away from the economic inequalities that still persisted. Talking about affluence, for example, meant that one could avoid using the word *wealth,* which might suggest its opposite, *poverty,* a term seldom used in economic analyses of the mid-1950s. By shifting the focus from what people *actually owned*—their accumulated wealth—to their affluence—what they could, with the aid

© Joe Munroe/Photo Researchers.

TURNING DESERTS INTO CROP LAND
California's 153-mile-long Friant-Kern Canal, one of many projects of the Army Corps of Engineers, allowed farmers to cultivate water-intensive fruit and other crops. Huge irrigation projects, financed by the federal government, turned dry western lands into farming areas but also carried long-term environmental implications for water table and soil quality.

of generous credit terms, *consume*—observers could easily conclude that the entire "American way of life" was constantly improving. The most buoyant observers even detected a leveling out of living standards between the top and the bottom levels of this consumer society. The gulf was no longer between people with cars and people without them, they declared, but between people with Cadillacs and Lincolns and those with Chevrolets and Fords. "Luxury has reached the masses," proclaimed *Fortune.*

Some economists promised that greater government expenditures would generate even faster growth, but Eisenhower clung to his fiscal conservatism. Fearing that increased spending would fuel an inflationary spiral of rising prices and destabilize the economy, his administration kept nonmilitary expenditures under tight control. Even the Pentagon's budget was reduced, and the federal government ran a balanced budget during the late 1950s.

Highways and Waterways

Ike never watched domestic affairs as closely as foreign policy, but he did sketch a broad policy outline. After due deliberation, Eisenhower endorsed several costly new programs. He supported the Highway Act of 1956, citing national security considerations as justification. (In a military emergency, supplies and personnel could, supposedly, speed along the new superhighways.) Financed by a national tax on gasoline and other highway-related prod-

ucts, the act funded construction of a national system of limited-access expressways. Touted as the largest public works project in the history of the world, the interstate highway program delighted the oil, concrete, and tire industries; provided steady work for construction firms; and boosted the interstate trucking business.

The highway-building program confirmed the victory of automotive travel over competing modes of transit. By the mid-1950s, Detroit's chrome-encrusted cars rivaled suburban homes and shopping malls as emblems of American abundance. With autos built overseas considered either luxuries or curiosities, a car buyer needed no reminder to "buy American." Motor City's auto industry touted its annual model changes and the increasingly larger engines in its cars. The emphasis was on speed and power. Automakers helped support other domestic industries such as steel. In 1956, the U.S. steel industry could boast of being far more efficient than its fledgling Japanese rival.

The Eisenhower administration also supported costly water-diversion projects in the West. The Army Corps of Engineers and the Bureau of Reclamation—federal agencies with powerful supporters in business and Congress—spent billions of dollars on dams, irrigation canals, and reservoirs. Irrigation turned desert into crop land, and elaborate pumping systems even allowed rivers to flow uphill. No society in the history of the world had ever devoted a similar portion of its national treasury to water projects. By 1960, the western states had access to trillions of gallons of water per year, and the basis for new economic growth in Texas, California, and Arizona was established.

These water projects came at a price. Technologically complicated and costly, they needed similarly complex and expensive bureaucracies to sustain them. As a consequence, local communities lost power to the government agencies and private entrepreneurs, whose decisions came to shape the water-dependent economy of the postwar West. Increasingly, large corporate-style operations pushed out smaller farmers and ranchers. In addition, American Indians found portions of their tribal lands being flooded for large water reservoirs or being purchased by agribusinesses or large ranching interests.

These vast projects also produced ecological problems. Plans to divert surface waters, to tap into groundwater tables, and to dot the West with dams and reservoirs took a toll on the environment, altering critical habitats and contributing to the buildup of salt by-products in the water and the soil. Some scientists began to warn about the accompanying overuse of pesticides such as DDT.

Labor–Management Accord

Most corporate leaders, supportive of the kind of government involvement required to build highways and water projects, were learning to live with labor unions as well. The auto industry, where management and labor leaders had negotiated a mutually acceptable work contract in 1950, led the way.

Closer cooperation with corporate management, some labor leaders reasoned, could guarantee employment stability and political influence for their unions. Taking their cue from the United Auto Workers, one of the most militant Congress of Industrial Organizations (CIO) unions during the 1930s, labor dropped the demand for greater union involvement in "management prerogatives," such as organization of the daily work routine, introduction of new technologies, and investment priorities. Union leaders agreed to confine aggressive bargaining to issues that immediately affected worker paychecks.

Moreover, union leaders guaranteed management that rank-and-file workers would abide by their union contracts and disavow the wildcat tactics that had been used during the 1930s and 1940s. To police this new labor–management détente, both sides looked to the federal government's National Labor Relations Board (NLRB). Meanwhile, in 1955, the American Federation of Labor (AFL) and the CIO, which had long differed on labor-organizing strategy, merged—another sign of declining militancy within the labor movement. The 1950s thus ended the fierce

labor–capital conflicts that had marked the 1930s and had continued through the 1940s.

Business leaders regarded this labor–management accord as a substantial victory. *Fortune* magazine noted that General Motors had paid a price in terms of more costly employee benefit packages and higher wages, but that "it got a bargain" in terms of labor peace. To safeguard their control over decision making, corporations expanded their supervisory staffs, a practice that drove up consumer prices and curtailed worker participation in planning the work process. This accord may also have helped divide industrial workers from one another, because those who worked in the more prosperous sectors of the economy, such as the auto industry, could bargain more effectively than those who worked in peripheral areas.

Many nonunionized businesses expanded benefits for their workers. Companies such as Sears and Eastman Kodak encouraged a cooperative corporate culture by offering health and pension plans, profit-sharing arrangements, and social programs. Some created private recreational parks for the exclusive use of their employees. Satisfying workers' needs, executives reasoned, would reduce the appeal of both unionization and governmental welfare measures.

During the 1950s and early 1960s, real wages (what workers make after paychecks are adjusted for inflation) steadily rose, and jobs were plentiful. The rate of industrial accidents dropped; fringe benefits (what workers receive in terms of health insurance, paid vacation time, and pension plans) invariably improved; and job security was generally high.

Political Pluralism

Many observers credited affluence with enriching the nation's political structure. Galbraith, for example, suggested that labor unions, consumer lobbies, farm organizations, and other groups could exert effective "countervailing power" against giant corporations. Only a few mavericks, such as the sociologist C. Wright Mills, disagreed. Mills saw corporate leaders as members of a small "power elite" that dominated American policy making. He claimed that this elite had made all of the crucial decisions on foreign and domestic issues during the decade since the Second World War. In the vaunted affluent society, he charged, work was becoming more regimented and jobs were bringing little satisfaction. Although Mills anticipated and inspired critics of the 1960s and early 1970s, most contemporaries dismissed his power-elite thesis as a simplistic conspiracy theory. To those who subscribed to the dominant view, called "pluralism," no single group could hope to dominate the political process.

According to pluralist accounts, policy making proceeded from wide participation in public debate by a broad range of different interest groups. Short-term conflicts over specific issues would never disappear, but the pluralist vision insisted that affluence was moderating political passions and fostering procedures by which different interests could eventually frame a consensus. As a professor at Harvard Law School put it, constant economic growth meant that "in any conflict of interest," it was "always possible to work out a solution" because affluence guaranteed that all interests would be "better off than before." Pluralists praised postwar leaders for finding inclusive and "realistic" solutions to difficult problems.

A Religious People

The celebration of political pluralism dovetailed with an exaltation of religion's role in American life. Congress, as part of the crusade against "atheistic communism," emphasized religious values. Its members funded construction of a nondenominational prayer room on Capitol Hill; added the phrase "under God" to the Pledge of Allegiance; and declared the phrase "In God We Trust," which had been emblazoned on U.S. currency for nearly a century, the official national motto.

This emphasis on a pluralistic, transdenominational religious faith was not simply a by-product of anticommunism. Intense religious commitments, most analysts insisted, no longer divided people as much as in the past. President Eisenhower urged people to practice their own religious creed, whatever it might be. "Our government makes no sense," he declared, "unless it is founded in a deeply felt religious faith—and I don't care what it is." Tommy Sands, a young pop singer, advised his teenage fans that "all religions are the greatest."

Religious leaders echoed this theme. Will Herberg's *Protestant-Catholic-Jew* (1955) argued that these three faiths were really "'saying the same thing' in affirming the 'spiritual ideals' and 'moral values' of the American Way of Life." Rabbi Morris Kretzer, head of the Jewish Chaplain's Organization, reassured Protestants and Catholics that they and their Jewish neighbors shared "the same rich heritage of the Old Testament . . . the sanctity of the Ten Commandments, the wisdom of the prophets, and the brotherhood of man." A 1954 survey indicated that more than 95 percent of the population identified with one of the three major faiths, and religious commentators increasingly talked about the "Judeo-Christian tradition."

Some religious leaders even became pop culture celebrities. Norman Vincent Peale, a Protestant minister who linked religious faith with peace of mind, sold millions of books declaring that belief in a Higher Power could reinvigorate daily life "with health, happiness, and goodness." His book *The Power of Positive Thinking* (1952) remained a best seller throughout the 1950s. The Catholic Bishop Fulton J. Sheen hosted an Emmy-winning, prime-time television program called *Life Is Worth Living*. Oral Roberts and Billy Graham—two younger, highly charismatic television ministers—began to spread their fiery brand of Protestant evangelism during the 1950s.

Peale, Sheen, Roberts, and Graham identified with conservative, anticommunist causes, but an emphasis on religious faith was hardly limited to the political right. Dorothy Day, who had been involved in grassroots activism since the early 1930s, continued to crusade for world peace and for a program aimed at redistributing wealth at home through the pages of the *Catholic Worker*. Church leaders and laypeople from all three major denominations supported the antidiscrimination cause and played important roles in the civil rights movement. Even so, the surge of religious faith during the 1950s remained closely identified with the culture of affluence.

Discontents of Affluence

Alongside the celebrations of economic affluence, political pluralism, and religious commitment, the 1950s still produced an immense body of literature that looked critically at conformity, youth, mass culture, discrimination, and inequality.

Conformity in an Affluent Society

In *The Organization Man* (1956), sociologist William H. Whyte, Jr., indicted corporate business for contributing to one of the problems of affluence: conformity. Criticizing the social, cultural, and psychological (although not the economic) impact of large corporations, Whyte saw middle-class corporate employees accepting the values of their employers at the expense of their own individuality. The security of knowing what the corporate hierarchy wanted—and when it wanted it—outweighed the organization man's concerns about loss of individuality, Whyte argued.

In *The Lonely Crowd* (1950), David Riesman, another sociologist, offered an even broader analysis. He wrote of a shift from an "inner-directed" society, in which people looked to themselves and to their immediate families for a sense of identity and self-worth, to an "other-directed" society, in which people looked to peer groups for approval and measured their worth against mass-mediated models. A nation of other-directed citizens emphasized "adjustment" to the expectations of others rather than the individual "autonomy" displayed by an

SPLIT-LEVEL LIVING

This 1960 cartoon, by the *Washington Post*'s "Herblock" (Herbert Block), illustrates the growing critique of Eisenhower-era social policy. While suburbanites enjoy new affluence in a split-level home, public services and distressed people remain underfunded.

From the Collections of the Library of Congress.

inner-directed citizenry. Riesman subsequently conceded that his autonomy-to-adjustment thesis might be overly broad but still insisted that it correctly identified a growing trend toward conformity in American life.

To illustrate the subtle manner in which children were taught conformist values, Riesman pointed to *Tootle, the Engine,* a popular children's book. When Tootle showed a preference for frolicking in the fields beside the tracks, people exerted peer pressure as a means of getting him to conform. If Tootle stayed on tracks laid down by others, they assured him, he would grow up to be a powerful and fast-moving streamliner. This message of adjusting to peer expectations in this "modern cautionary tale," Riesman argued, contrasted vividly with the conflict-filled fairy tales, such as *Little Red Riding Hood,* on which earlier generations of young people had been reared.

The critique of conformity reached its broadest audience through the best-selling books of journalist Vance Packard. *The Hidden Persuaders* (1957) argued that adver-

tising—especially through calculated, subtle appeals to the insecurities of consumers—produced conformity. The book, Packard claimed, could help its readers "to achieve a creative life in these conforming times" when so many people "are left only with the roles of being consumers or spectators."

Critics such as Whyte, Riesman, and Packard focused on the lives of middle-class men, but other writers such as Betty Friedan claimed to find an analogous psychological malaise among many women. Business corporations, for instance, expected that the wives of their male executives would help their husbands deal with the demands of corporate life, including the need for frequent moves to new locations. The organization man, it was said, should recognize that his ascent up the economic ladder could depend on how well his wife conformed to her informal duties in the corporate world.

Restive Youth

Concerns about young people, including their taste in culture, also intensified during the 1950s. Many criminologists attributed an alleged rise in juvenile delinquency to the burgeoning sales of comic books. Psychologist Frederick Wertham, in *The Seduction of the Innocent* (1954), blamed comics, especially those displaying sex and violence, for "mass-conditioning" children and for stimulating juvenile unrest. Responding to local legislation and to calls for federal regulation, the comic book industry quickly embraced self-censorship. Publishers who adhered to new, industry-developed guidelines for the portrayal of violence and deviant behavior could display a seal of approval on their comics. With this response, the great comic book scare faded away.

Critics of the youth culture, however, easily found other worrisome signs. In 1954, Elvis Presley, a former truck driver from Memphis, Tennessee, rocked the pop music establishment with a string of hits on the tiny Sun record label. In contrast to the people running the major record distributors, Sun's Sam Phillips correctly viewed rock as more than a passing fad. Presley's sensual, electric stage presence thrilled his young admirers. Presley ("The King") and other youthful rock stars—such as Buddy Holly from West Texas, Richard Valenzuela (Richie Valens) from East Los Angeles, and Frankie Lymon from Spanish Harlem—crossed cultural and ethnic barriers and shaped new musical forms from older ones, especially African American rhythm and blues (R & B) and the "hillbilly" music of southern whites.

The first rock 'n' rollers inspired millions of fans and thousands of imitators. They sang about the joys of "hav-

ELVIS PRESLEY
A former truck driver from Memphis, "Elvis the Pelvis" drew upon blues, gospel, hillbilly, and pop music traditions to become the premier rock 'n' roll star of the 1950s.

ing a ball tonight", the pain of the "summertime blues"; the torment of being "a teenager in love"; and the hope of deliverance, through the power of rock, from "the days of old." Songs such as "Roll Over Beethoven" by Chuck Berry (a black singer-songwriter who merged southern hillbilly music with the blues of his native St. Louis) became powerful teen anthems.

Guardians of older, family-oriented forms of commercial culture found rock 'n' roll far more frightening than comic books. They denounced its sparse lyrics, pulsating guitars, and screeching saxophones as an assault on the very idea of music. Religious groups condemned it as the sound of the devil; red-hunters detected a communist plan to corrupt youth; and segregationists saw it as part of a sinister plot by integrationists. The dangers of rock 'n' roll seemed abundantly evident in *The Blackboard Jungle* (1955), a hit movie about a racially mixed gang of high school students who terrorized teachers and mocked adult authority, which featured "Rock Around the Clock" on its soundtrack.

Rock 'n' roll music often spoke to the concerns of its young fans. The satirical "Charlie Brown" contrasted pieties about staying in school with the bleak educational opportunities open to many students. Chuck Berry sang of alienated teenagers riding around "with no particular place to go." This kind of implied social criticism, which older listeners invariably failed to decode, anticipated the more overtly rebellious rock music of the 1960s.

Rock music and the larger youth culture of the 1950s, however, gradually merged into the era's mass-consumption economy. Sun Records, lacking capital to distribute its music to a rapidly expanding market, sold Presley's contract to RCA and watched its other stars drift away. The major record labels and Top-40 radio stations quickly identified middle-class teenagers, whose average weekly income/allowance reached $10 by 1958, as a market worth targeting. Chuck Berry's "Sweet Little Sixteen" portrayed an affluent teenager eagerly chasing after the latest fashions, the next rock 'n' roll concert, and "about half a million famed autographs." By 1960, record companies and disc jockeys were promoting performers such as the Beach Boys and songs that exalted the pursuit of "fun, fun, fun" with the help of clothes, cars, and rock 'n' roll records. Rock music—and the product-centered culture of youth—could easily embrace the ethic of a people of plenty.

The Mass Culture Debate

The criticism of conformity and of youth culture was part of a broader phenomenon becoming known as the mass culture debate. Much of the anxiety about the decline of individualism and the rise of rock 'n' roll could be traced to fears that "hidden persuaders" could apparently use the cultural marketplace to reach millions of people with standardized imagery and messages.

Cosmopolitan cultural critics, most of whom admired elite, European culture, decried mass-marketed products. They worried that the "bad"—such as rock music and Mickey Spillane's best-selling "Mike Hammer" detective novels—was driving anything "good" from the cultural marketplace and preventing people from distinguishing between them. In addition, by treating millions of consumers in the same manner, mass culture threatened to obscure meaningful differences under a blur of pleasant, superficial imagery. In a classic study of a small town in upstate New York, a team of sociologists articulated another common complaint: The presence of mass media was "so overwhelming that little scope is left for the expression of local cultural forms" in many parts of American life.

Television provided a prominent target. Evolving out of the structure of network radio, the television industry was dominated by three major corporations (NBC, CBS, and ABC) and sustained by advertisers, euphemistically called sponsors. Picturing millions of seemingly passive viewers gathered around "the boob tube," critics decried both the quality of mass-produced programming and its presumed impact on the public. Network television responded to pressure from advertisers and avoided controversial programs in favor of shows that, according to TV's critics, encouraged retreat into unrealities such as a mythical Old West. Television networks in 1958 were broadcasting 25 westerns during their prime-time hours. Newton Minow, appointed to head the Federal Communications Commission (FCC) in 1961, denounced TV as a "vast wasteland" and hinted that only federal regulation might improve network programming.

Critics also noted how television seemed to be transforming the fabric of everyday life. Architects were calling for the rearrangement of living space within middle-class homes so that the television set, serving as an electronic substitute for the traditional fireplace hearth, could become the focal point for family life. New products—such as the frozen TV dinner, the TV tray, the recliner chair, and the influential magazine *TV Guide*—became extensions of television culture. The TV set itself, initially encased in a substantial wooden cabinet, became an important symbol of postwar affluence.

The mass culture they decried, these critics recognized, remained embedded within the economic system they generally celebrated. Was it really possible to eliminate the curse of mass culture while still enjoying the benefits of affluence and liberty? If, for example, Congress were encouraged (as it had been during the comic book scare) to legislate against "dangerous" cultural products, censorship might end up curtailing free expression. If local communities were to step in (as some had done in the case of comics), the result might be even worse. The prospect of southern segregationists confiscating civil rights literature or of local censorship boards banning movies produced in Hollywood or books published in New York City hardly appealed to these cosmopolitan, elite-educated critics. Their critique of mass culture, in short, seemed to generate few solutions. More important, it did nothing to halt the flood of products, especially TV programs, aimed at an ever-expanding audience of eager consumers.

Meanwhile, amid the concern about mass culture, other questions about the direction of postwar life emerged. Americans were adjusting to new gender patterns and remained especially divided over issues related to racial discrimination and to government's role in confronting it.

Changing Gender Patterns

The 1950s significantly altered how and where people lived and worked. Women, in particular, found their lives changing.

The New Suburbs and Gender Ideals

In middle-class homes, especially those located in the new suburbs, wives and mothers discovered how consumer technology kept them busy. Shiny appliances and "modern conveniences"—such as automatic clothes washers, more powerful vacuum cleaners, and home freezers—eased old burdens but created new ones. Contrary to what advertisers promised, women could devote as much of their day to household tasks during the 1950s as had their grandmothers in the early 1900s. The time that women spent on domestic duties was not reduced but reallocated to new activities that involved the household gadgets that accompanied affluence.

Daily life in the new suburbs was structured by a broad pattern of "separate spheres": a public sphere of work and politics dominated by men and a private sphere of housework and child care reserved for women. Because few businesses located in these suburbs, men began spending a good portion of their day commuting from home to work. Women who wanted to hold a job outside their homes found nearby employment opportunities about as scarce as child-care facilities. Consequently, mothers spent a great deal of time taking care of their baby-boom children. In contrast to the urban neighborhoods or the rural communities where many suburban housewives had grown up, suburbs of the 1950s contained few older relatives or younger single women who could help with household and child-care duties.

Without mothers and grandmothers living close by, suburban women turned elsewhere for child-rearing advice. Local Parents and Teachers Associations (PTAs), connected to neighborhood schools, offered the chance to exchange information, as did women's organizations such as the La Leche League. Increasingly, though, both parents consulted child-care manuals. Dr. Benjamin Spock's *Baby and Child Care,* first published in 1946, sold millions of copies. Like earlier advice books, Spock's assigned virtually all child-care duties to women and underscored their nurturing role by stressing the need to constantly oversee a child's psychological growth. The future of the family and the nation itself, Spock implied, depended on how well mothers handled the daily traumas of childhood. Other manuals picked up where Dr. Spock left off and counseled mothers on the care and feeding of teenagers. The alarmist tone of many of these books reflected—and helped generate—widespread concern over juvenile delinquency.

The ideal mother, according to most experts, did not work outside the home and devoted herself to rearing her own segment of the baby-boom generation and thereby fighting broader social dislocation. Delinquent children, according to a study of the early 1950s, sprang from a "family atmosphere not conducive to development of emotionally well-integrated, happy youngsters, conditioned to obey legitimate authority." It was up to parents, especially mothers, to rear good children. Women who sought careers outside of the home and marriage risked being labeled as lost, maladjusted, guilt-ridden, man-hating, or all of the above.

Versions of this message appeared nearly everywhere. Even the nation's prestigious women's colleges assumed a student would quickly pursue a man and a marriage rather than a career in the workplace. In his 1955 commencement address at Smith College, Adlai Stevenson, the Democratic Party's urbane presidential candidate in 1952 and 1956, told female graduates that it was the duty of each to keep her husband "truly purposeful, to keep him whole." Popular magazines, psychology literature, and pop-culture imagery suggested that understanding, supportive wives and mothers could help ensure social stability.

Some portraits of family life, however, were beginning to paint a more complicated view of gender arrangements. Most men told researchers that they preferred an active partner to a "submissive, stay-at-home" wife. Popular television shows, such as "Father Knows Best" or "Leave It to Beaver," suggested the hope that middle-class fathers would become more involved in family life than their own fathers had been. Experts on gender relationships still envisioned suburban men earning their family's entire income but increasingly urged them to be "real fathers" at home. Parenting literature emphasized "family togetherness," and institutions such as the Young Men's Christian Association (YMCA) began to offer courses on how to achieve it.

This call for family togetherness was partly a response to what some cultural historians have seen as an incipient "male revolt" against "family values." Hugh Hefner's *Playboy* magazine, which debuted in 1953, epitomized this trend. It saw men who neglected their own happiness in order to support a wife and children as suckers rather than saints. *Playboy*'s first issue proclaimed: "We aren't a 'family magazine.'" Hefner told women to pass it "along to the man in your life and get back to your *Ladies Home Companion*." In his version of the good life, the man rented a "pad" rather than owned a home; drove a sports car rather than a sedan or a station wagon; and courted the Playmate of the Month rather than the Mother of the Year.

Women's Changing Roles

Despite media images that depicted "the average woman" as a homebound wife and mother, economic realities were propelling more women into the job market. Female employment outside the home rose steadily during the late 1940s and throughout the 1950s. More married women were entering the labor force, many of them as part-time workers in the expanding clerical and "service" sectors. In 1948, about 25 percent of married mothers had jobs outside the home; at the end of the 1950s, nearly 40 percent did. With the introduction of a new, reliable oral contraception method in 1960—the birth control pill—women could enjoy greater control over family planning and career decisions. By 1964, one-quarter of the couples who used contraception relied on the pill.

Although more women were seeking jobs outside their homes, employment opportunities remained largely limited to well-defined, gender-segregated areas. Virtually all of the nation's nurses, telephone operators, secretaries, and elementary school teachers were women. Historically, pay scales in these areas lagged behind those paid to men in comparable fields, labor unions were rare, and chances for advancement were very limited. As the number of low-paid jobs for women expanded during the 1950s, better-paid professional opportunities actually narrowed. Medical and law schools and many professional societies admitted few, if any, women. When Sandra Day (who would later become Justice Sandra Day O'Connor of the U.S. Supreme Court) graduated with honors from a prestigious law school during the 1950s, not a single firm would extend her a job offer. The number of women on college faculties shrank back even from the low levels of the 1920s and 1930s.

Although employers still invoked the "family wage" ideal as a justification for disparities in pay and opportunity based on gender, more women were struggling to support a family on their own paychecks. This was especially true for women of color. By 1960, slightly more than 20 percent of black families were headed by women. Recognizing that images of domesticity hardly fit the lives of African American women, a large percentage of whom had always worked outside the home, *Ebony* magazine celebrated black women who combined success in parenting and at work. One story, for example, highlighted the only female African American mechanic at American Airlines; many others featured educators and prominent entertainers.

Mass-circulation magazines also carried mixed messages about domesticity. Although many social commentators labeled the pursuit of activities outside the home as "unnatural," any magazine that sought a broad readership invariably looked more favorably at women who were participating in public life, whether in politics or in the job market. Women's magazines, although deferential to the dominant ideal of domesticity, also published articles about the difficulty of staying at home and raising children and often featured stories on prominent career women. The 1950s, in short, saw growing diversity in both the social roles that women were assuming and the way mass culture represented them.

🌎 The Fight against Discrimination, 1953–1960

When Dwight Eisenhower took office, the Supreme Court was slated to rehear a legal challenge to racially segregated educational systems. The National Association for the Advancement of Colored People (NAACP) and its constitutional strategist, Thurgood Marshall, spearheaded the challenge. Before the rehearing took place, Eisenhower appointed Earl Warren, a former Republican governor of California, as Chief Justice. Under Warren, the Supreme Court would play an important role in the widening struggle against discrimination.

The *Brown* Cases, 1954–1955

What has become popularly known as "the *Brown* decision" actually included a series of Supreme Court cases on the constitutionality of segregated schools. In 1954, Chief Justice Warren wrote a unanimous opinion (in *Brown* v. *Board of Education of Topeka*), which declared that state-mandated segregation of public schools violated the constitutional right of African American students to equal protection of the law. A companion case decided the same day (*Bolling* v. *Sharpe*) outlawed segregation in the District of Columbia's school system. Although these decisions technically applied only to educational facilities, they implied that all segregated public facilities, not simply schools, were open to constitutional challenge. In 1955, though, yet another Supreme Court decision, known as *Brown II*, decreed that school desegregation would not go into effect immediately; the process only needed to move forward "with all deliberate speed."

Carrying out the broader implications of these cases tested the nation's political institutions. The crusade against racial discrimination had long focused on the 16 states that the Census Bureau officially called "the South," but demographic changes meant that national leaders could no longer treat the issue as if it were simply a regional one.

© UPI-Bettmann/Corbis.

SEGREGATION

Dressed in his Air Force uniform, a young man from New York City is faced with a "colored waiting room" in an Atlanta bus terminal in 1956. Before the civil rights revolution of the 1960s, southern states maintained legally enforced segregation in most public facilities, a practice popularly called "Jim Crow" (see chapter 18).

During the 1950s, the South inexorably became more like the rest of the country. New cultural forces, such as network television, were linking the once insular South more closely to broader ideas and practices. Economic forces were also at work. Machines were displacing the region's predominantly black field workers, and the absence of strong labor unions and the presence of favorable tax laws were attracting national chain stores and northern-based businesses.

At the same time, the racial composition of cities in the West, Midwest, and Northeast was becoming more like that of the South. In 1940, more than three-quarters of the nation's African Americans lived in the South. Accelerating the pattern begun during the Second World War, African Americans left the rural South and settled in Los Angeles, Chicago, New York, Cleveland, and other big cities during the late 1940s and early 1950s. This demographic shift was accompanied by "white flight" to suburban areas and by new political initiatives. With African American voters becoming increasingly important in the North, for example, urban representatives, especially Democrats, supported federal efforts to end racial discrimination. Fewer African Americans voted Republican, as the GOP continued to gain ground among white voters in what had long been the Democratic Party's "solid South." Most important, African Americans mounted a new attack on segregation and racial discrimination in the South.

The battle in the South increasingly affected national politics. Southern segregationists pledged "massive resistance" to the *Brown* decisions. When the Supreme Court's "all deliberate speed" approach in *Brown II* seemed to give segregationists time to maneuver, their lawyers went to court with traditional delaying tactics and newly invented ones. In 1956, 100 members of the U.S. House and Senate signed a "Southern Manifesto" that denounced the Court's antisegregationist rulings as a "clear abuse of judicial power" and promised support for any state that intended "to resist forced integration by any lawful means."

Defiance went beyond the courtroom. White vigilantes unfurled the banners and donned the robes of the Ku Klux Klan; new racist organizations, such as the White Citizens Council, appeared on the southern scene. As a result, people fighting discrimination constantly risked injury and death; even those who were only indirectly connected to the struggle could fall victim to racist violence. In August 1955, two white Mississippians murdered 14-year-old Emmett Till, a visitor from Chicago, because they thought he had acted "disrespectful" to a white woman. Mamie Till Bradley demanded that her son's murder not remain a private incident; she insisted that his maimed corpse be displayed publicly for "the whole world to see" and that his killers be punished. When their case came to trial, an all-white Mississippi jury quickly found the two men—who would subsequently confess their part in the murder to a magazine reporter—not guilty.

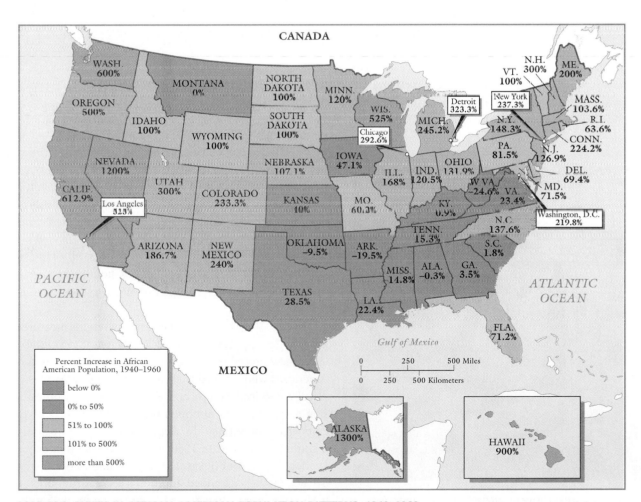

MAP 28.2 SHIFTS IN AFRICAN AMERICAN POPULATION PATTERNS, 1940–1960

During and after the Second World War, large numbers of African Americans left the rural South and migrated to new locations. Which states had the largest percentage of out-migration? Which saw the greatest percentage of population increase? How might this migration have affected American life?

View an animated version of this map or related maps at **http://history.wadsworth.com/murrin_LEP4e**.

The Montgomery Bus Boycott and Martin Luther King, Jr.

In response to the uncertainty of judicial remedies, African Americans began supplementing legal maneuvering with aggressive campaigns of direct action. One of the first occurred, even before the *Brown* cases, in Baton Rouge, Louisiana. In 1953, a brief boycott of the local bus system ended after white officials agreed, while formally maintaining a token segregation system, to grant more seats to black riders. Two years later, activists in Montgomery, Alabama, raised the ante when Rosa Parks, an active member of the local NAACP chapter, was arrested for defying a local segregation ordinance. Montgomery's black community quickly demanded complete desegregation, began a boycott of public transportation, and organized a system of private carpools as alternative transit. Joining with Rosa Parks, many African American women spearheaded this broad-based effort. The resulting financial losses eventually convinced the city of the desirability of ending its separatist transit policy, and the U.S. Supreme Court weighed in by declaring the segregation of Montgomery's buses to be unconstitutional. Events in Montgomery during 1955 and 1956 showed other southern black communities that they could also mobilize against racial discrimination.

AP/Gene Herrick/Wide World Photos.

ROSA PARKS IGNITES DESEGREGATION CAMPAIGN
Rosa Parks's refusal to sit at the back of a segregated bus in 1955 sparked a campaign to integrate public transportation in Montgomery, Alabama. Here, Rosa Parks is fingerprinted by a law enforcement officer.

The Montgomery boycott vaulted Dr. Martin Luther King, Jr., one of its leaders, into the national spotlight. Born, raised, and educated in Atlanta, Georgia, with a doctorate in theology from Boston University, King and other black ministers followed up the victory in Montgomery by forming the Southern Christian Leadership Conference (SCLC). In addition to demanding desegregation of public facilities, the SCLC launched an effort to register African American voters throughout the South. More activist than the NAACP, the SCLC embodied Dr. King's broad vision of using passive civil disobedience to obtain social change. According to King, civil disobedience would dramatize, through both words and deeds, the moral evil of racial discrimination. The ultimate goal of the civil rights crusade was to bring "redemption and reconciliation" to American society. Aided by the national media, especially network television, King's powerful presence and religiously rooted rhetoric carried the antidiscrimination message out of the South to most parts of the nation and, eventually, to a wider world.

The Domestic and International Politics of Civil Rights

Political institutions in Washington, D.C., responded slowly. The Supreme Court lent its support at crucial times, as during the Montgomery bus boycott, but it always lacked the power to mandate the sweeping institutional changes needed to translate its expanded definition of civil rights into enforceable practices. Congress, with the ability to enact legislation, remained deeply divided on racial issues. With southern segregationists, all of them members of the Democratic majority, holding key posts on Capitol Hill, antidiscrimination measures faced formidable obstacles.

Even so, Congress passed its first civil rights measures in more than 80 years. The Civil Rights Act of 1957 established new procedures for expediting lawsuits by African Americans who claimed that their right to vote had been illegally abridged. It also created a permanent Commission on Civil Rights, although this was an advisory body empowered only to study alleged violations and recommend new remedies. In 1960, with the crucial support of Lyndon Johnson of Texas, the Democratic leader in the Senate, another act added additional federal support for blacks who were being barred from voting in the South. These civil rights initiatives, which became law against fierce opposition from southern Democrats, dramatized the difficulty of getting even relatively limited antidiscrimination measures through Congress.

President Eisenhower, who held the office with the power to enforce legislation and court orders, initially appeared reluctant to tackle racial discrimination head on. Ike supported the Civil Rights Act of 1957 but held back when some Republicans urged a dramatic presidential step—perhaps issuing an executive order barring racial discrimination on construction projects financed by federal funds. Always the gradualist, Eisenhower regarded the fight against discrimination as primarily a local matter, and he publicly doubted that the power of Washington could do much to change the attitudes of people opposed to the integration of public facilities or job sites.

In 1957, however, Eisenhower was forced to use the full power of his office to enforce a federal court order that mandated the desegregation of Central High School in Little Rock, Arkansas. Orval Faubus, the state's segregationist governor, promised his white supporters he would prevent black students from entering the school building. Ike allowed Faubus time to play to the white supremacist galleries of Arkansas, and the governor eventually deployed his state's National Guard to block the desegregation. Responding to this direct challenge to a court decision, Eisenhower put the Arkansas National Guard under federal control and augmented it with members of the U.S. Army. Black students, escorted by armed troops, finally entered Central High. The primary issue at stake, in Eisenhower's view, was a state's blatant defiance of the law of the land rather than school desegregation.

The confrontation in Little Rock underscored, as Eisenhower also recognized, the international dimension of civil-rights politics in the United States. Washington often found itself on the defensive when foreign critics pointed to the U.S. record on civil rights. The Soviet Union delighted in telling people around the world, particularly those in the Third World, how racial discrimination showed "the façade of the so-called 'American democracy.'" Secretary of State Dulles suggested that racial conflict at home was "not helpful to the influence of the United States abroad." When the U.S. Supreme Court, in *Cooper* v. *Aaron* (1958), unanimously invalidated an Arkansas law intended to block further integrationist efforts, newspapers around the world highlighted the decision. Events in Arkansas reaffirmed the image, carried throughout the world by the Eisenhower administration's informational campaign, of the United States as a powerful nation that supported liberty and equality.

Ike's initial indecision during the situation at Little Rock also suggested, however, how his grasp of domestic issues seemed to slip during his second term as president. In the election of 1956, he had achieved another landslide victory over Democrat Adlai Stevenson, but Ike's contin-

ued personal popularity did relatively little for his party. The Republicans failed to win back control of Congress from the Democrats. In fact, in this presidential election and in the off-year races of 1958, the GOP lost congressional seats as well as state legislatures and governors' mansions to the Democrats. After the 1958 elections, the Democrats outnumbered Republicans by nearly 2-to-1 margins in both the Senate and in the House. Meanwhile, Eisenhower, who had suffered a mild heart attack before the 1956 election, seemed progressively enfeebled, physically as well as politically. He appeared especially unsteady in his approach to racial issues.

American Indian Policy

The Eisenhower administration struggled with its policy toward American Indians. It attempted to implement two programs, "termination" and "relocation," that had been developed before it took office. The first called for Washington to terminate the status of Indians as "wards of the United States" and to grant them all the "rights and privileges pertaining to American citizenship." The long-term goals of termination, to be pursued on a tribe-by-tribe basis, were to abolish reservations, liquidate assets of the tribes, and curtail the services offered by the Bureau of Indian Affairs (BIA). In 1954, one year after this general policy had received congressional approval, six bills of termination were enacted. Immediately at stake were the legal status of more than 8,000 American Indians and more than 1 million acres of tribal land.

Under the relocation program, which had begun in 1951, Indians were encouraged to leave rural reservations and seek jobs in urban areas. In 1954, the BIA intensified its relocation efforts, with Minneapolis, St. Louis, Dallas, and several other cities joining Denver, Salt Lake City, and Los Angeles as relocation sites. This program, like termination, assumed that American Indians could rather easily become assimilated into urban life.

The initiatives quickly failed. As several more termination bills were enacted during the Eisenhower years, almost 12,000 people lost their status as tribal members, and the bonds of communal life for many Indians grew weaker. At the same time, more than 1 million acres of tribal lands, which often fell into the hands of real estate speculators, were lost. Indians from terminated tribes also lost both their exemption from state taxation and the social services provided by the BIA. They gained little in return. Most terminated Indians saw their economic prospects grow dimmer. Relocation went no better. Most of the relocated Indians found only low-paying, dead-end jobs and racial discrimination. In some cities, Indian

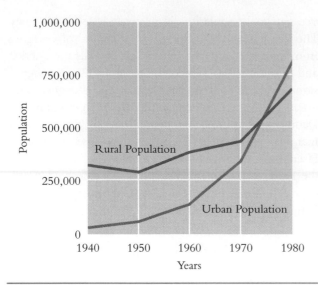

TOTAL URBAN AND RURAL INDIAN POPULATION IN THE UNITED STATES, 1940–1980

children who had left reservations found it difficult even to enter racially *segregated,* let alone integrated, public schools. Despite its problems, the relocation program nevertheless continued throughout the Eisenhower years.

Both Indians and their supporters soon mobilized against the termination and relocation policies. By 1957, the BIA had scaled back its initial timetable for liquidating every tribe within five years, and in 1960 the party platforms of both the Republicans and Democrats repudiated the policy entirely. In 1962, the policy was itself terminated. The relocation program continued, however, and by 1967 almost one-half of the nation's Indians lived in relocation cities. This policy neither touched the deep-rooted problems that many Indians confronted, including a life expectancy only two-thirds that of whites, nor provided significantly better opportunities for employment or education.

The Growth of Spanish-Speaking Populations

Millions of Spanish-speaking people, many of whom had recently arrived in the United States, also highlighted discrimination issues. Despite facing discriminatory practices in the job and housing markets in the United States, Puerto Ricans began moving in large numbers from their island commonwealth to the mainland during the 1950s. By 1960, New York City's Puerto Rican population was nearly 100 times greater than it had been before the Second World War. Chicago, Boston, and Hartford, Connecticut, also became the U.S. destinations for many Puerto Ricans during the 1950s. The government of Puerto Rico

encouraged this immigration as a way of easing population pressures but also urged the migrants to maintain cultural ties with the island. Although U.S. citizens, most of the newcomers spoke only Spanish, and the formation of social and cultural clubs helped link them with the Puerto Rican towns they had left behind and buffer the cultural impact of moving to the mainland. At the same time, Puerto Ricans began to organize against the discrimination they faced in the United States. The Puerto Rican–Hispanic Leadership Forum, organized in 1957, presaged the emergence of groups that looked more to social and economic conditions—and, ultimately, greater political clout—in the United States than to cultural affinities with Puerto Rico.

Meanwhile, large numbers of Spanish-speaking people from Mexico were moving to California and the Southwest, where they settled in long-established Mexican American communities. Beginning with the Second World War and continuing until 1967, the U.S. government sponsored the *bracero* (or farmhand) program, which brought nearly 5 million Mexicans northward, theoretically on short-term contracts, to fill agricultural jobs. Many *braceros* and their families remained in the United States after their contracts expired. Joining them were legal immigrants from Mexico and growing numbers of people who filtered across the border. These undocumented immigrants became the target of an ongoing government dragnet, begun in 1950 and intensified by the Eisenhower administration, called "Operation Wetback." ("Wetback" was a term of derision that implied people of Mexican ancestry had reached the United States by swimming across the Rio Grande River.) During a five-year period, the government claimed to have rounded up and deported to Mexico nearly 4 million people, allegedly all illegal immigrants. The operation helped stigmatize even citizens of Mexican heritage and justify discriminatory treatment by the government and employers.

People in long-established Mexican American communities mobilized to fight such discrimination. Labor organizers sought higher wages and better working conditions in the factories and fields, although the FBI labeled many of these efforts as "communist-inspired" and harassed unions—such as the United Cannery, Agricultural, Packing and Allied Workers of America (UCAPAWA)—that had large Mexican American memberships. A lengthy mining strike in New Mexico became the subject of the 1954 motion picture *Salt of the Earth.* Middle-class organizations, such as the League of United Latin American Citizens (LULAC) and the Unity League, sought to desegregate schools, public facilities, and housing in Southern California and throughout the Southwest. In 1940, Mexican Americans had been the most rural of all the major ethnic groups; by 1950, in contrast, more than 65 percent of Mexican Americans were living in urban areas, a figure that would climb to 85 percent by 1970. As a result of this fundamental demographic shift, Mexican Americans began to become an important political force in many southwestern cities.

Urban-Suburban Issues

The growth of suburban areas during the 1950s created new urban issues, many of them related to race. Throughout the 1950s, both public and private institutions were shifting resources away from cities, especially away from neighborhoods in which Latinos and African Americans had settled. Adopting a policy called "red-lining," many banks and loan institutions denied funds for home-buying and business expansion in areas that were labeled "decaying" or "marginal" because they contained aging buildings, dense populations, and growing numbers of people who were not of European descent. The Federal Housing Administration (FHA) and other government agencies channeled most lending toward the suburbs. In 1960, for example, the FHA failed to put up a single dollar for home loans in Camden or Paterson, New Jersey, cities in which minority populations were growing, while it poured millions of dollars into surrounding, largely all-white suburbs.

"Urban renewal" programs, authorized by the Housing Act of 1949 (see chapter 27), often amounted to "urban removal." Although the law called for "a feasible method for the temporary relocation" of persons displaced by urban renewal projects, developers could generally ignore the housing needs of the people they displaced. During the 1950s, Robert Moses, who directed New York City's vast construction projects, effectively concealed the number of people dislocated by his urban renewal and highway building programs. In New York and other cities, office buildings and freeways replaced the living units that people with low-income jobs could afford.

Plans for new, federally built public housing quickly faltered. Although suburban areas, where land was abundant and relatively inexpensive, seemed the obvious place to locate affordable housing, middle-income homeowners used zoning laws to freeze out government-sponsored housing projects. Consequently, officials turned toward urban sites, where population density was high and land was expensive. At the same time, private housing interests lobbied to limit the number of public units actually constructed and to ensure that they would offer tenants few amenities. Originally conceived as a temporary alternative for families who would rather quickly move to their own homes, publicly built facilities became stigmatized as "the

projects," housing of last resort for people with chronically low incomes and meager prospects for rapid economic advancement.

By the end of the 1950s, the urban policies of both the Truman and Eisenhower eras seemed spectacular failures. Urban renewal projects not only disrupted urban housing patterns but also helped disperse industries that had long provided entry-level jobs for unskilled workers. Both major presidential candidates in 1960 pledged to create a new cabinet office for urban affairs and to expand Washington's role in addressing the dilemma of suburban growth and urban decay.

Debating the Role of Government

Controversy over urban-suburban issues was tied to larger debates of the late 1950s over how Washington might deal with a wide range of domestic issues. Although Eisenhower sometimes hinted that he favored rolling back the New and Fair Deals, he lacked both the will and the political support to do so. Actually, Eisenhower presided over a modest expansion of earlier Democratic initiatives: an expanded Social Security system, a higher minimum wage, better unemployment benefits, and a new Department of Health, Education, and Welfare (HEW). Still, as his stance on urban and racial issues most dramatically showed, he hesitated to enlarge governmental power. Eisenhower liked to call his stance one of "moderate Republicanism."

The New Conservatives

Eisenhower's centrist position on most domestic issues angered a growing group of people, who became known as the "new conservatives." Eisenhower was popular—and the first Republican president since Herbert Hoover—but did his administration really represent the conservative principles for which the GOP was supposed to stand?

Not to Arizona's Barry Goldwater. Ruggedly handsome and militantly anticommunist, Goldwater won election to the U.S. Senate in 1952 and emerged as the spokesperson for those Republicans who viewed Eisenhower's policies as insufficiently conservative. *The Conscience of a Conservative* (1960) summarized Goldwater's critique of postwar policies. By refusing to take stronger military measures against the Soviet Union and by not making "victory the goal of American policy," Eisenhower had likely endangered national security. Goldwater decried almost all domestic programs, including federal civil rights legislation, as grave threats to individual liberty.

The Eisenhower administration, he charged, was simply aping the Democratic Party's "New Deal antics" in its own domestic policy making.

While Goldwater was pressing the GOP to reject Eisenhower's moderate Republicanism, others, particularly the publisher William F. Buckley, Jr., were trying to frame a new conservative message. Buckley, a devout Roman Catholic, first gained national attention while still in his twenties. In his *God and Man at Yale* (1952), Buckley attacked what he saw as a "collectivist" and antireligious tilt in American higher education and defended capitalism and Christianity. In 1955, Buckley helped found the *National Review*, a weekly magazine that attracted a talented group of writers. It avoided positions, particularly the anti-Semitism of some old-line conservatives and the hysterical anticommunism of groups such as the John Birch Society, that could be seen as extremist. Although this new conservatism began amid considerable doubts about its immediate prospects, it sought a long-term strategy for building a right-of-center political and cultural movement. To that end, conservatives established Young Americans for Freedom (YAF) in 1960, several years before similar college-based youth organizations emerged on the political left.

Advocates of a More Active Government

While the new conservative movement was criticizing the Eisenhower administration for failing to repudiate policies of the Roosevelt and Truman years, a more eclectic group was pressing Washington to expand these earlier efforts. After Eisenhower suffered a second heart attack and a mild stroke during his second term, these critics talked about the need for more vigorous presidential leadership. They were especially disturbed at Eisenhower's reluctance to use Washington's power to attack racial discrimination. In addition, many economists, pointing to a severe economic downturn in 1958–59 when unemployment rose precipitously, ridiculed Eisenhower's commitment to a balanced budget. Even after conditions improved, economists such as John Kenneth Galbraith urged deficit spending by Washington, which Eisenhower stoutly resisted, as a spur to even greater economic expansion.

Other critics, although avoiding the strident anticommunism of conservatives such as Goldwater, dissected Eisenhower's national security policies. The 1957 Gaither Report, prepared by foreign policy analysts with close ties to defense industries, claimed that the Soviet Union's GNP was growing even more quickly than that of the United States and that much of this expansion came in its military

sector. The Gaither Report urged an immediate increase of about 25 percent in the Pentagon's budget and longer-term programs for building fallout shelters, developing intercontinental ballistic missiles (ICBMs), and expanding conventional military forces. Another report, written by a young political scientist named Henry Kissinger and issued by the Rockefeller Foundation, claimed that Eisenhower's New Look undermined national security by relying too heavily on massive nuclear retaliation and by downplaying non-nuclear options. It, too, called for greater spending on defense.

Eisenhower, who remained far more attentive to foreign policy than domestic issues, reacted cautiously. Although he agreed to accelerate the development of ICBMs, he opposed a crash effort to build fallout shelters or one to create the capability for fighting limited, non-nuclear wars around the globe. In fact, he reduced the size of several army and air force units and kept his defense budget well below the levels his critics were proposing. Eisenhower felt confident in pursuing this course because super-secret U-2 surveillance flights over the USSR revealed that the Soviets were lagging behind, rather than outpacing, the United States in military capability.

Concerns about national security and calls for greater government spending also surfaced in the continuing controversy over education. Throughout the 1950s, some critics complained that schools were emphasizing "life adjustment" skills—getting along with others and adapting to social change—instead of teaching traditional academic subjects. Rudolf Flesch's best-selling *Why Johnny Can't Read* anticipated books that asked why Johnny and his classmates couldn't add or subtract well either and why they lagged behind their counterparts in the Soviet Union in science. Washington's help in funding K–12 instruction seemed an obvious way to upgrade educational performance. Simultaneously, the nation's leading research universities were seeking greater federal aid for higher education; in summer 1957, a committee of prominent scientists implored the Defense Department to expand its support for basic scientific research. "Research is a requisite for survival" in the nuclear age, it declared. The case for increased spending on all levels of education suddenly gained new intensity when, in October 1957, the Soviets launched the world's first artificial satellite, a 22-inch sphere called *Sputnik.*

In 1958, using the magical phrase "national security," school administrators and university researchers obtained the federal dollars they had been seeking. The National Defense Education Act funneled money to college-level programs in science, engineering, foreign languages, and the social sciences. This act marked a milestone in the long battle to overcome congressional opposition, especially

COLD WAR COMPETITION REACHES INTO SPACE

This "Space Race" card game was manufactured after the Soviet Union orbited its first *Sputnik* satellite in 1957. The fear that the Soviets were ahead of the United States in space technology prompted the nation to undertake a crash program of upgrading mathematics and science education and to accelerate its own space program, run by the newly created National Aeronautics and Space Administration (NASA). A fascination with space technology permeated popular culture in the late 1950s, but the cost implications of this initiative worried Eisenhower.

from southern representatives who feared that federal aid might bring pressures for racial integration, to educational spending by Washington. The Soviets' apparent superiority in satellite technology, seemingly confirmed by the launch of a second and much larger *Sputnik*, fueled a research-and-development (R&D) effort, overseen by a new National Aeronautics and Space Administration (NASA), to harness American educational and technological know-how so that outer space might be used for the benefit of "all mankind."

An effort to gain increased federal spending for social welfare programs also took root during the last years of Eisenhower's presidency. Galbraith's *The Affluent Society,* for instance, saw a dangerous tilt in the "social balance," away from "public goods." Affluent families could travel in shiny new automobiles, but they needed to pass through shabby cities, motor along litter-filled roadsides, and speed by unsightly billboards. The researcher who developed a new carburetor is well rewarded, but anyone "who dreams up a new public service is [labeled] a wastrel," Galbraith's book sardonically noted.

Galbraith's analysis seemed mild in comparison to the jeremiads of Michael Harrington. In 1959, *Commentary,* one of several national magazines beginning to feature social criticism, published an article in which Harrington claimed that the problem of economic inequality remained as urgent as it had been during the 1930s. At least one-third of the nation's people—living in rural areas, small towns, and cities—barely subsisted in a land of supposed abundance. Avoiding the usual trappings of economic analysis, Harrington crafted dramatic stories about how poverty continued to ravage the bodies and spirits of people whose lives had been largely untouched by the economic growth of the 1940s and 1950s.

During the early 1960s, when addressing social and economic issues became a priority in Washington, critics such as Galbraith and Harrington became political celebrities. Their critiques, however, grew out of the political culture of the late 1950s. The Kennedy presidency of 1961–63 would in fact be rooted in the calls for more active foreign and domestic policies that had emerged during the Eisenhower years.

☄ The Kennedy Years: Foreign Policy

A wealthy, politically ambitious father had groomed John Fitzgerald Kennedy for the White House. After graduation from Harvard in 1940, the young Kennedy pursued both private passions (especially for Hollywood movie stars) and public service. After winning military honors while serving in the navy during the Second World War, Kennedy entered Democratic party politics. In 1946, he won election from Massachusetts to the House of Representatives; six years later, he captured a seat in the Senate. Kennedy became better known for his social life than for his command of legislative details, but he eventually gained a national political reputation, largely on the basis of his charm and youthful image. His 1953 marriage to Jacqueline Bouvier added yet another dash of glamour. A favorite of the media, Jackie won plaudits for her tastes in culture, her stylish dress, and her fluency in several foreign languages. After John Kennedy narrowly missed winning the vice presidential nomination in 1956, he immediately took aim at the top spot on the 1960 Democratic ticket.

The Election of 1960

Kennedy, often accompanied by Jackie and by his brothers (Robert and Ted), barnstormed across the country. This early presidential campaigning, along with a talented staff and his family's vast wealth, helped Kennedy overwhelm his primary Democratic challengers, Senators Hubert Humphrey of Minnesota and Lyndon Johnson. By pledging to separate his Catholic religion from his politics and by confronting those who appealed to anti-Catholic prejudice, Kennedy tried to defuse the religious issue that had doomed the candidacy of Al Smith in 1928 (see chapter 24).

Vice President Richard Nixon, obliged to seek the White House on Eisenhower's record even though Ike seemed lukewarm to a Nixon candidacy, remained on the defensive throughout the 1960 campaign. Nixon seemed notably off-balance during the first of several televised debates in which the cool, tanned Kennedy emerged, according to surveys of TV viewers, with a clear victory over the pale, nervous Nixon. (People who only listened on radio generally gave Nixon much higher marks.) Despite chronic and severe health problems, which Kennedy's entourage effectively concealed, JFK projected the image of a vigorous, energetic leader.

Kennedy's 1960 campaign highlighted issues from the 1950s that, taken together, became his "New Frontier" agenda. Although Senator Kennedy's civil rights record had been mixed, candidate Kennedy declared that his White House would press for new congressional legislation. In an important symbolic act, he dispatched aides to Georgia to assist Martin Luther King, Jr., who was facing a jail sentence for a minor traffic violation. Kennedy further promised to use the president's executive authority, which Eisenhower had refused to do, against racial discrimination. Kennedy also endorsed the kind of social programs that Eisenhower's critics had been advocating. These included federal spending to rebuild rural communities, to increase educational opportunities, and to improve urban conditions.

Kennedy highlighted two other central issues of the late 1950s: promoting greater economic growth and conducting a more aggressive foreign policy. Dismissing Eisenhower's cautious policies as timid and ineffectual, Kennedy embraced advisers who spoke of stimulating the economy by means of tax cuts and deficit spending measures. On foreign policy, he criticized Eisenhower for failing to rid the hemisphere of Castro in Cuba and for allowing a "missile gap" to develop in the arms race with the Soviet Union. By spending more on defense than Eisenhower, Kennedy claimed, he would create a "flexible response" against communism, especially in the Third World. Adlai Stevenson, in his 1956 presidential campaign against Eisenhower, had claimed that Americans could no longer "drift, we must go forward." Reworking this phrase, Kennedy proclaimed that "the American people are tired of the drift in our national course . . . and that they are ready to move again."

The 1960 election defied easy analysis. Kennedy defeated Nixon by only about 100,000 popular votes, and his victory in the electoral vote rested on razor-thin margins in several states, including Illinois. Many Republicans urged Nixon to challenge Kennedy's triumph in Illinois as fraudulent, but the vice president chose to accept the disputed result. Anti-Catholic sentiment, especially in the South, resurfaced, and Kennedy won a smaller percentage of the popular vote than most of the Democrats who had competed for lesser offices in 1960. His election owed a great debt to his vice presidential running mate, Lyndon Johnson, whose regional appeal helped the Democratic ticket carry the Deep South and Johnson's home state of Texas. Democrats remained the majority party, but this did not translate into a groundswell of support for Kennedy and his New Frontier in 1960.

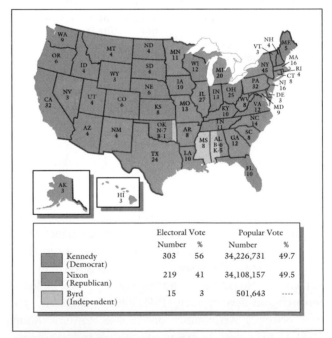

	Electoral Vote		Popular Vote	
	Number	%	Number	%
Kennedy (Democrat)	303	56	34,226,731	49.7
Nixon (Republican)	219	41	34,108,157	49.5
Byrd (Independent)	15	3	501,643	----

MAP 28.3 PRESIDENTIAL ELECTION, 1960

In one of the closest elections in American history in terms of the popular vote, Kennedy only narrowly out-polled Nixon. Kennedy's more commanding victory in the electoral vote produced some discussion about the consequences if the electoral college one day produced a president who had failed to carry the popular vote, a situation that did indeed occur in the election of 2000.

From the outset, JFK and Jackie riveted media attention on the White House. They hobnobbed with movie stars, and the new president welcomed prominent intellectuals to the administration. The Kennedy inaugural featured designer clothing, an appearance by the aged poet Robert Frost, and an oft-quoted speech in which JFK challenged people to "ask not what your country can do for you; ask what you can do for your country." The "best and the brightest," the name given to the hard-driving people who joined Kennedy's administration, promised to launch exciting and difficult crusades, even one to the frontier of outer space. Many of the administration's initiatives, including space exploration, drew from ideas developed during the 1950s.

Kennedy's Foreign Policy Goals

Kennedy promised vigorous action in foreign policy. Although Secretary of Defense Robert McNamara quickly found that the alleged "missile gap" did not exist, Kennedy raised the defense budget anyway. The White House strongly supported military assistance programs, propaganda agencies, and covert action plans. In one of his most popular initiatives, the president created the Peace Corps, a new program that sent Americans, especially young people, to nations around the world to work on development projects that might undercut communism's appeal.

Eisenhower's last-minute effort to reorient U.S. Latin American policy away from reliance on dictators and toward support of more broadly based socioeconomic programs was elaborated on and repackaged as Kennedy's "Alliance for Progress." Proposed in spring 1961 in hopes of checking the spread of anti-Americanism and Castro-like insurgencies, the Alliance offered $20 billion in loans over a 10-year period to Latin American countries that would undertake land reform and other economic development measures. The Alliance, which underestimated obstacles to rapid social and economic change in Latin America, rapidly failed.

Cuba and Berlin

The worst fiasco of the Kennedy presidency, a daring but ill-conceived CIA mission against Cuba, also had its roots in the Eisenhower administration. The CIA, looking back on earlier covert actions against anti-American governments in Iran and Guatemala, had been planning a secret, Eisenhower-endorsed invasion to oust Fidel Castro. Kennedy, overriding the doubts of some of his advisers, reaffirmed the operation. On April 17, 1961, however, when U.S.-backed and trained forces (mainly anticommunist Cuban exiles) landed at the Bahia de Cochinas (the Bay of Pigs) on the southern coast of Cuba, the expected popular uprising did not occur. Forces loyal to Castro quickly surrounded and imprisoned the invaders. Kennedy refused to provide the air support that the Cuban exiles had expected and, initially, tried to deny any U.S. involvement in the invasion. The CIA's role quickly became public, however, and anti-Yankee sentiment mounted throughout Latin America. Castro tightened his grip over Cuban life and strengthened his ties to the Soviet Union.

Kennedy responded to the Bay of Pigs by admitting error and by devising new anti-Castro strategies. "I have made a tragic mistake," Kennedy told one adviser. "Not only were our facts in error, but our policy was wrong." Stung by the failed invasion, the White House continued to target Castro with a covert program, "Operation Mongoose," which included efforts to destabilize Cuba's economy and several failed plots against Castro. During one of the attempts to kill the Cuban leader, the CIA worked directly with U.S. organized crime figures, who wanted revenge for Castro's closure of their casinos in Havana.

Another dramatic confrontation loomed in Berlin. In June 1961, Nikita Khrushchev and Kennedy met in Vienna, Austria, where the Soviets proposed ending the Western presence in Berlin and reuniting the city as part of East Germany. Khrushchev's offer responded to the steady flow of immigrants from East Germany into West Berlin, a migration that was both embarrassing and economically draining to the German communist regime. Kennedy refused to abandon West Berlin, and the East German government continued to press Khrushchev for help. In August 1961, the communist regime began to erect first a barbed-wire fence and then a concrete wall to separate East from West Berlin. East Germans attempting to escape into the West were shot down. The Berlin Wall became a symbol of communist repression. Kennedy's assertion, *"Ich bin ein Berliner"* ("I am a Berliner"), delivered in front of the wall to a cheering crowd of West Berliners, provided a memorable image of JFK's presidency.

Superpower confrontation escalated to a potentially lethal level during the Cuban Missile Crisis of October 1962. The Soviet Union, fulfilling a request from Castro, began sending sophisticated weapons to the island nation. After spy-plane flights showed missile-launching sites in Cuba, the Kennedy administration announced it would not allow the Soviet Union to place nuclear warheads so close to American soil. It demanded that the Soviets dismantle the missile silos and turn back supply ships, perhaps containing warheads, then heading for Cuba. After tense strategy sessions with his top advisers, Kennedy rejected a military strike against Cuba that might have taken the United States and the Soviet Union to war. Instead, he ordered the U.S. Navy to "quarantine" the island. The

Strategic Air Command went on full alert for a possible nuclear conflict. Meanwhile, both sides engaged in secret diplomatic maneuvers to forestall such a catastrophe.

Complicated moves by both governments finally yielded a peaceful resolution. On October 28, 1962, Khrushchev ordered the Soviet missiles in Cuba dismantled and the supply ships brought home; Kennedy promised not to invade Cuba and secretly assured Khrushchev that he would complete the previously ordered withdrawal of U.S. Jupiter missiles from Turkey. When some Soviet archives were opened in the mid-1990s, Americans learned that the confrontation had been even more perilous than they had imagined. Unknown to Kennedy's circle in 1962, the Soviets had already placed tactical nuclear weapons in Cuba that could have been launched against U.S. targets.

THE CUBAN MISSILE CRISIS
During the Cuban Missile Crisis of October 1962, these Cuban refugees, like most people, were riveted to their television sets to obtain the latest update from President Kennedy. This confrontation seemed to place the fate of the world at stake.

© UPI-Bettmann/Corbis.

The Cuban Missile Crisis, which underscored the risk of being drawn into nuclear conflict, made the superpowers more cautious. Secretary of Defense McNamara later recalled leaving a presidential conference during the 13-day crisis, looking up at the sky, and wondering if the world would still be there 24 hours later. To prevent a future confrontation or an accident involving nuclear weapons, a direct phone line was established between Moscow and Washington, D.C.

Southeast Asia and "Flexible Response"

In Southeast Asia, Kennedy continued Eisenhower's policy of creating a viable, noncommunist state in South Vietnam. After the Bay of Pigs fiasco, in which the attempt to overthrow an already established communist government had failed, Kennedy decided that the United States must defeat communist-led "wars of national liberation" before they ever succeeded.

Kennedy saw Vietnam as a test case for "flexible response," a new policy that proposed using a variety of different methods to combat communist movements around the globe. Elite U.S. troops, the Green Berets, were trained in "counterinsurgency" tactics to use against procommunist guerrillas; cadres of social scientists, charged with "nation building," were sent to advise on social and economic change; and Michigan State University dispatched experts to revamp South Vietnam's police forces. When these efforts brought only greater corruption and a sense of isolation to the Diem government, the CIA gave disgruntled military officers the green light to orchestrate its overthrow. Just weeks before Kennedy would be assassinated, Diem—once hailed by Eisenhower and Kennedy as the founding father of South Vietnam—was run out of his presidential palace and murdered. This coup, which brought a military regime to power in Saigon, seemed to breed even greater political instability throughout South Vietnam. The NLF and North Vietnam, in turn, ratcheted up their own military pressure on the South.

🌐 The Kennedy Years: Domestic Policy

Despite campaign promises to increase federal spending in hopes of stimulating faster economic growth, Kennedy seemed reluctant to jettison Eisenhower's cautious fiscal policies. JFK feared angering fiscal conservatives and business leaders by running federal budget deficits greater than those of the Eisenhower years. Relations with corporate leaders nevertheless turned ugly in 1962, when Kennedy publicly clashed with the president of U.S. Steel over that company's decision to raise prices beyond the guidelines suggested by the administration.

Policy Making under Kennedy

In 1962, the White House asked Congress to lower tax rates as a means of promoting economic growth. The economy had rebounded from its downturn of 1957–58, but Kennedy wanted even faster growth. Lower tax rates for everyone and special deductions for corporations that invested in new plants and equipment, his economic brainstrust argued, would spur new investment in facilities and jobs. Despite opposition from those Democrats who thought these changes would unfairly benefit corporations and the wealthy, the tax bill seemed headed for passage in fall 1963.

On social welfare, the Kennedy administration advanced policies initiated by the Fair Deal of the 1940s—namely, a higher minimum wage and urban rebuilding programs. It also supported the Area Redevelopment Bill of 1961, which called for directing federal grants and loans

to areas (such as Appalachia) that had been bypassed by the economic growth of the postwar years. This marked the cautious beginning of the ambitious "war on poverty" that Lyndon Johnson would wage during the mid-1960s. Meanwhile, under the programs begun during the 1940s, bulldozers continued to raze large parts of urban America; construction projects aimed to benefit middle- and upper-income people continued to replace low-income housing.

The Civil Rights Movement, 1960–1963

Although JFK had talked about new civil rights legislation, he tried to placate the segregationist wing of his party by not pressing for congressional action early in his presidency. (Initially, the Kennedy administration assigned the fight against organized crime greater priority than the one against racial discrimination.) The president and his brother, Robert, whom he had appointed attorney general, listened sympathetically when J. Edgar Hoover, director of the FBI, warned of links between Martin Luther King, Jr., and members of the Communist Party. To monitor King's activities and gather information that Hoover might use

BERNICE JOHNSON REAGON

During the civil rights crusade, "freedom songs" fostered solidarity. The singers pictured here include Bernice Johnson Reagon, a member of the Freedom Singers during the civil rights movement and, later, founder of the all-woman a cappella singing group, Sweet Honey in the Rock.

to smear him, the FBI intensified surveillance and illegally wiretapped King's private conversations.

Events, however, forced the Kennedy administration to devise legislative initiatives. In early 1960, African American students at North Carolina A & T College in Greensboro sat down at a drugstore lunch counter and asked to be served in the same manner as white customers. It was the beginning of the "sit-in" movement, a new phase in the civil rights movement in which young activists challenged local segregation laws by demanding equal access to hitherto racially separated places. All across the South, demonstrators staged nonviolent sit-in demonstrations at restaurants, bus and train stations, and other public facilities.

The courage and commitment of these demonstrators reenergized the antidiscrimination movement. With songs such as "We Shall Overcome" and "Oh, Freedom" inspiring solidarity, young people pledged their talents, their resources—indeed, their lives—to the civil rights struggle. In 1961, interracial activists from the Congress of Racial Equality (CORE) and the Student Nonviolent Coordinating Committee (SNCC), a student group that emerged from the sit-in movement, risked racist retaliation by conducting "freedom rides" across the South. The freedom riders were challenging the Kennedy administration to enforce a series of federal court decisions that had declared state laws requiring segregation on interstate buses (and in bus stations) to be unconstitutional.

This grassroots activism prompted a response from the Kennedy administration. It first dispatched U.S. marshals to protect the freedom riders. In 1962 and again the following year, it called on National Guard troops and federal marshals to prevent segregationist mobs from blocking court-ordered integration at several educational institutions in the Deep South, including the universities of Mississippi and Alabama. In November 1962 Kennedy issued a long-promised executive order that banned racial discrimination in federally financed housing. The following February, in hopes of curtailing future confrontations, he sent Congress a limited civil rights bill that called faster trial procedures in cases involving challenges racial discrimination in voting practices.

Events in the South, however, continued to outpace the Kennedy administration's policies. In 1963, racial conflict convulsed Birmingham, Alabama. White police officers unleashed dogs and high-pressure water hoses on African Americans, including children, who were seeking to desegregate that city. Four young girls were later murdered (and 20 people injured) when racists bombed Birmingham's Sixteenth Street Baptist Church, a center of the civil rights campaign. When thousands of blacks took to the streets in protest—and two more children were killed, this time by police officers—the Kennedy administration decided it had to staunch the bloodletting.

The determination of civil rights activists to defy racist violence created a real-life drama that played to the entire world. The major television networks carried vivid images of the struggle, and Kennedy made an emotional plea on TV for a national commitment to the battle against discrimination. Recent events had raised "a moral issue . . . as old as Scriptures and . . . as clear as the Constitution." The time for "patience" and "delay," he declared, had passed. Racial violence was also "retarding our Nation's economic and social progress and weakening the respect with which the rest of the world regards us," the President insisted. Against the backdrop of a televised battle line that seemed to stretch across the South, the issue of civil rights dominated national politics during the last six months of Kennedy's presidency.

AP/Wide World Photos.

RACIAL CONFLICT IN BIRMINGHAM

Images such as this 1963 photograph of a confrontation in Birmingham, Alabama, in which segregationists turned dogs on youthful demonstrators, helped rally public support for civil rights legislation. Events in Birmingham, however, also presaged the increasingly violent clashes that would punctuate the efforts to end racial discrimination.

Kennedy still hoped to control the direction and pace of change. The White House crafted additional legislation designed to dampen the enthusiasm for civil rights demonstrations without further inflaming white segregationists. It supported a ban on racial discrimination in all public facilities and housing and new measures to protect the voting rights of African Americans in the South. When the administration recognized that its legislative proposals would not derail a "March on Washington for Jobs and Freedom," planned for the late summer of 1963, it belatedly endorsed the event.

On August 28, 1963, an integrated group of more than 200,000 people marched through the nation's capital to the Lincoln Memorial. There, Martin Luther King, Jr., delivered his famous "I Have a Dream" speech. A broad coalition of civil rights and labor organizations sponsored the march. Speakers generally applauded Kennedy's latest initiatives but also urged a broader agenda. Demands included a higher minimum wage and a federal program to guarantee new jobs. Well-organized and smoothly run, this one-day demonstration received overwhelmingly favorable coverage from the national media and put even greater political pressure on the White House and Congress to lend their assistance.

Women's Issues

The seeds of a resurgent women's movement were also being sown, although more quietly, during the Kennedy years. Kennedy's own call for people to enter public service in organizations such as the Peace Corps helped raise young women's expectations for lives that included more than marriage and child rearing.

All across the political spectrum, women were speaking out on contemporary issues. The energy of women such as Phyllis Schlafly, whose book *A Choice, Not an Echo* (1964) became one of the leading manifestos on the political right, helped fuel the new conservatism. African American activists such as Bernice Johnson Reagon (whose work with the Freedom Singers combined music and social activism) and Fannie Lou Hamer (who spearheaded the organization of a racially integrated Freedom Democratic Party in Mississippi) fought discrimination based on both race and gender.

Similarly, Chicana farm workers became key figures in the union activism that led to the organization of the United Farm Workers of America. Women also played an important role in protests, through the Committee for a Sane Nuclear Policy (Sane) and the Women's Strike for Peace, against the U.S.–Soviet arms race. During Kennedy's final year in office, 1963, Betty Friedan published *The Feminine Mystique.* Widely credited with helping to

spark a new phase of the feminist movement, Friedan's book drew on her own social criticism from the late 1950s and articulated the dissatisfactions that many middle-class women felt about the narrow confines of domestic life and the lack of public roles available to them.

To address women's concerns, Kennedy appointed the Presidential Commission on the Status of Women, chaired by Eleanor Roosevelt. Negotiating differences between moderate and more militant members, the commission issued a report that documented discrimination against women in employment opportunities and wages. Kennedy responded with a presidential order designed to eliminate gender discrimination within the federal civil service system. His administration also supported the Equal Pay Act of 1963, which made it a federal crime for employers to pay lower wages to women who were doing the same work as men.

The Assassination of John F. Kennedy

By fall 1963, the Kennedy administration, although still worried about its ability to push legislation through a recalcitrant Congress, was preparing new initiatives on civil rights and economic opportunity. Then, on November 22, 1963, John F. Kennedy was shot down as his presidential motorcade moved through Dallas, Texas. Vice President Lyndon Johnson, who had accompanied Kennedy to Texas, took the oath of office and hurried back to Washington. The Dallas police quickly arrested Lee Harvey Oswald and pegged him as JFK's assassin. Oswald had ties to the Marcello crime family; had once lived in the Soviet Union; and had a bizarre set of political affiliations, including shadowy ones with groups interested in Cuba. Oswald, who declared his innocence, never faced trial. Jack Ruby, whose Dallas nightclub catered to powerful crime figures, killed Oswald on national television, while the alleged gunman was in police custody. A lengthy investigation by a special commission headed by Chief Justice Earl Warren concluded that both Oswald and Ruby had acted alone.

The Warren Commission's "lone gunman" report has come under increasing scrutiny. In 1978, a special panel of the House of Representatives speculated that Kennedy might have been the victim of a wider plot, perhaps involving organized crime, but produced little supporting evidence. Other theories of a conspiracy, including ones that pointed toward the CIA and high governmental officials, sprang up. Oliver Stone's *JFK* (1991) refocused attention on the flaws in the Warren Commission's report and prompted Congress to create the Assassinations

Records Review Board. It tried to preserve all existing evidence about Kennedy's death, such as the famous Zapruder home movie of the assassination, from destruction. Meanwhile, competing theories about the number of shots, the trajectory of the bullets, the nature of Kennedy's wounds, and the identity of his assassins have continued to circulate.

More than 40 years after Kennedy's assassination, his life also remains a topic of sharp historical debate and tabloid-style speculation. Researchers have provided new details about his poor health, his reliance on exotic medications, and his dalliances with women—all of which were kept from the public at the time. They disagree on how such revelations might affect an evaluation of his character and his presidency. In particular, historians sharply disagree over JFK's possible course in Vietnam,

had he won the 1964 election. Kennedy's persistent Cold War rhetoric suggests the depth of his commitment to preventing a communist military victory in South Vietnam. Yet JFK had already, in the Bay of Pigs episode, changed a policy he saw as flawed, and he might have exhibited more flexibility in Southeast Asia than his successor. The popular interest in John F. Kennedy and his presidency has grown more intense with the passage of time.

Conclusion

Beginning in 1953, fears of communist expansionism and internal subversion began to subside. Tensions with the Soviet Union slowly eased, especially after Kennedy found himself on the brink of nuclear war over the issue of

H I S T O R Y   T H R O U G H   F I L M

JFK (1991)

JFK addresses two issues that have intrigued the historical profession and the general public: (1) Who killed John F. Kennedy? and (2) How might the course of U.S. history, especially the nation's involvement in Vietnam, have been different if Kennedy's presidency had not ended in November 1963?

This movie restages the 1967 criminal prosecution by Jim Garrison, the district attorney of New Orleans, against Clay Shaw, a local business leader. It uses this real-life episode as the vehicle for speculating that a shadowy conspiracy—involving government officials, military officers, and business executives—ordered Kennedy's assassination because they feared he would soon withdraw U.S. troops from Vietnam.

To dramatize these claims, *JFK* employs cinematic techniques unavailable in print histories. When Garrison is showing jurors the famous Zapruder film, the home movie that provides the only visual record of Kennedy's shooting, for example, *JFK* inserts simulated, black-and-white images of sharpshooters catching the president in

Directed by Oliver Stone. Starring Kevin Costner (Jim Garrison), Tommy Lee Jones (Clay Shaw), Donald Sutherland ("Mr. X"), and Joe Pesci (David Ferrie).

a deadly cross-fire. Later, it shows a mysterious figure planting the "magic bullet," which the Warren Commission later claimed came from the rifle of Lee Harvey Oswald, on a hospital gurney.

The film is vintage Oliver Stone. The most prolific filmmaker-historian of the past 20 years, Stone has persistently delighted in disrupting clearly delineated narratives about recent events. His historical movies—*JFK*, *Platoon* (1986), *Born on the Fourth of July* (1989), *The Doors* (1991), and *Nixon* (1995)—all feature stories that abound in disjuncture and uncertainty. When Jim Garrison decides that he will defy the "lone-gunman theory," the official story of the Kennedy assassination, he warns his staff, ". . . we're through the looking glass . . . white is black, and black is white."

Like Stone's equally controversial *Natural Born Killers* (1994), *JFK* focuses less on telling a coherent tale than using a motion picture to ponder the relationship between visual imagery and popular perceptions. The opening of *JFK* bombards the screen with quick-moving, seemingly disconnected images. Viewers, as if they themselves have

Soviet weapons in Cuba in 1962. Even so, the United States remained committed to staunchly anticommunist foreign policies that featured the continued buildup of nuclear weapons, new forms of economic pressure, and expanded covert activities. Developments in the Third World, particularly in Cuba and Southeast Asia, became of growing concern to U.S. policy makers.

At home, the years between 1953 and 1963 were ones of generally steady economic growth. A cornucopia of new consumer products encouraged talk about an age of affluence but also produced apprehension about conformity, the problems of youth, and the impact of mass culture. At the same time, the millions of people who were missing out on this period's general affluence and those who faced racial and ethnic discrimination saw their causes move to the center of public debates over the meaning of

liberty and equality. The Eisenhower administration, some of its critics charged, seemed too reluctant to use the power of government to fight discrimination or to push economic programs designed to spread the benefits of affluence more widely. The political initiatives of the early 1960s, associated with Kennedy's New Frontier, grew out of the criticism of the 1950s. More quietly, in both the political and cultural arenas, a new conservative movement was also taking shape.

Although Kennedy preferred to focus on foreign policy rather than domestic issues, the press of events, particularly in the South, gradually forced his administration to consider how government power might be used to address the issues of liberty and equality at home. When Kennedy was killed in November 1963, a new kind of insurgent politics, growing out of the battle against racial

gone "through the looking glass," must struggle with the visual pieces contained in the cinematic puzzle that is *JFK*.

The movie, in this sense, is more interested in posing, rather than settling, historical questions. Viewers might compare and contrast how Kennedy's death is explained through performances of two veteran character actors, Donald Sutherland and Joe Pesci. Sutherland's "Mr. X," a fictive operative who works in the national security bureaucracy, tells Garrison that the assassination of a president was only one event in a history of "dirty tricks" by agents of the military-industrial complex. During a scene shot against the familiar iconography of the nation's capital—which seems adapted from Frank Capra's classic *Mr. Smith Goes to Washington* (1939)—Sutherland calmly offers Garrison (and film viewers) a logically ordered, tightly packaged explanation. In contrast, Joe Pesci's frenetic David Ferrie, a lowly foot soldier who traveled in the organized crime and Cuban-exile circles that some investigators have seen as involved in events leading up to November 22, 1963, warns Garrison that he will find no simple answers to his inquiry into Kennedy's death.

JFK did raise enough questions to prompt a massive, congressionally ordered project to declassify and save all government documents that might relate to Kennedy's assassination. These traditional sources, however, seem to have brought historians no closer to solving the puzzle of Kennedy's death. As Pesci's character warns in *JFK*, "It's a mystery, inside a riddle, wrapped in an enigma."

Kevin Costner portrays New Orleans District Attorney Jim Garrison in *JFK*.

discrimination in the Deep South, was poised to transform political life.

In the post-Kennedy era, debate would become riveted on questions related to the government's exercise of power: Was the United States spreading liberty in Vietnam? Was it sufficiently active in pursuing equality for racial minorities and the poor? The troubled presidencies of Kennedy's successors, Lyndon Johnson and Richard Nixon, would turn on these questions.

SUGGESTED READINGS

James T. Patterson, *Grand Expectations: The United States, 1945–1974* (1996) provides an overview of the period. For accounts of presidential leadership, begin with **Fred I. Greenstein**, *The Hidden-Hand Presidency: Eisenhower as Leader* (rev. ed., 1994). **Chester Pach, Jr. and Elmo Richardson**, *The Presidency of Dwight D. Eisenhower* (1991) presents a fine, brief history. On John Kennedy, see **Robert Dallek**, *An Unfinished Life: John F. Kennedy, 1917–1963* (2003); **Richard Reeves**, *President Kennedy: Profile of Power* (1994); and **Seymour Hersh**, *The Dark Side of Camelot* (1997).

There are many studies of Eisenhower's foreign policy, but a good sense of the issues and scholarly debates can be gleaned from **Robert R. Bowie and Richard H. Immerman**, *Waging Peace: How Eisenhower Shaped an Enduring Cold War Strategy* (2000). **John Prados**, *Presidents' Secret Wars: CIA and Pentagon Covert Operations from World War II through the Persian Gulf* (1996), and **Zachary Karabell**, *Architects of Intervention: The United States, the Third World, and the Cold War, 1946–1962* (1999) put an important aspect of policy in a broad perspective. **Walter L. Hixson**, *Parting the Curtain: Propaganda, Culture, and the Cold War, 1945–1961* (1997) argues that cultural initiatives provided powerful weapons in the Cold War. **Lawrence Freedman**, *Kennedy's Wars: Berlin, Cuba, Laos, and Vietnam* (2000) illuminates the major international crises of the Kennedy years.

For events on the home front, **James B. Gilbert**, *A Cycle of Outrage: America's Reaction to the Juvenile Delinquent in the 1950s* (1986) discusses cultural fears; **Karal Ann Marling**, *As Seen on TV: The Visual Culture of Everyday Life in the 1950s* (1994) stresses the new emphasis on visuality; and **James B. Gilbert**, *Redeeming Culture: American Religion in an Age of Science* (1997) examines another aspect of America's changing culture. **W. T. Lhamon, Jr.**, *Deliberate Speed: The Origins of a Cultural Style in the American 1950s* (1990) advances a provocative interpretation. The highly readable examination of the struggle against racial discrimination by **Taylor Branch**, *Parting the Waters: America in the King Years, 1954–1963* (1988) may be augmented by **Mary L. Dudziak**, *Cold War Civil Rights: Race and the Image of American Democracy* (2000), which places concerns over civil rights in an international context; by **James Patterson**, *Brown v. Board of Education: A Civil Rights Milestone and Its Troubled Legacy* (2001); and by **David L. Chappell**, *A Stone of Hope: Prophetic Religion and the Death of Jim Crow* (2004).

On women and families during the 1950s, **Elaine Tyler May**, *Homeward Bound: American Families in the Cold War Era* (rev. ed., 1999) stresses the new emphasis on family life, while **Leila J. Rupp**, *Survival in the Doldrums: The American Women's Rights Movement, 1945 to the 1960s* (1987); **Joanne Meyerowitz, ed.**, *Not June Cleaver: Women and Gender in Postwar America, 1945–1960* (1994); and **Stephanie Coontz**, *The Way We Never Were: American Families and the Nostalgia Trip* (1992) work against that grain.

AMERICAN JOURNEY ONLINE
AND
INFOTRAC COLLEGE EDITION

Visit the source collections at www.ajaccess.wadsworth.com and infotrac.thomsonlearning.com and use the Search function with the following key terms to explore documents, images, audio and video clips, articles, and commentary related to the material in this chapter.

Dwight D. Eisenhower	*Sputnik*
U-2 plane	Highway Act of 1956
Eisenhower Doctrine	Consumerism
Dr. Benjamin Spock	Elvis Presley
Baby Boom	Chuck Berry
Brown v. *Board of Education*	Rock 'n' roll
Rosa Parks	John F. Kennedy
Civil Rights Act of 1957	Bay of Pigs
Montgomery Bus Boycott	Cuban Missile Crisis
Martin Luther King, Jr.	Student Nonviolent Coordinating
Little Rock Central High	Committee (SNCC)
School	Betty Friedan
Termination and relocation	*The Feminine Mystique*
policies (Native Americans)	Kennedy assassination

GRADE AIDS

Visit the Liberty Equality Power Companion Web Site for resources specific to this textbook: http://history.wadsworth.com/murrin_LEP4e

The CD in the back of this book and the U.S. History Resource Center at http://history.wadsworth.com/u.s./ offer a variety of tools to help you succeed in this course, including access to quizzes; images; documents; interactive simulations, maps, and timelines; movie explorations; and a wealth of other sources.

America during Its Longest War, 1963–1974

THE VIETNAM WAR MEMORIAL
This memorial, a kind of wailing wall that bears the names of all Americans who were killed in action in Vietnam, was dedicated on the Mall in Washington, D.C., in 1982.

CHAPTER OUTLINE

Lyndon Baines Johnson promised that his presidency would finish what John F. Kennedy's New Frontier had begun. "Let us continue," he said in his first presidential address. That phrase, which recalled Kennedy's own "Let us begin," did characterize Johnson's first months in office. Ultimately though, Johnson's troubled presidency bore little resemblance to John Kennedy's thousand days of "Camelot."

In Southeast Asia, Johnson faced a crucial decision: Should the United States introduce its own forces and weaponry in hopes of propping up its South Vietnamese ally? If Johnson did order direct U.S. military involvement, what would result? At home, Johnson enthusiastically mobilized the federal government's power in order to promote equality. But could federal action produce the Great Society that Johnson envisioned?

Many Americans, particularly young people, came to oppose Lyndon Johnson's policies. With a war overseas and opposition at home, the late 1960s and early 1970s became a time of increasingly sharp political and cultural polarization. Richard Nixon's presidency both suffered from—and contributed to—these divisions. By the end of America's longest war and the Watergate crisis that caused Nixon's resignation, the nation's political culture and social fabric differed significantly from what Johnson had inherited from Kennedy in 1963.

CHAPTER FOCUS

◆ What were the goals of the Great Society? Why did it produce so much controversy?

◆ Why did the United States become involved in the war in Vietnam? How did the war affect the U.S. economy and its social fabric?

◆ In addition to the war in Vietnam, what were the other sources of domestic dissent, especially among young people, during the 1960s?

♦ What new domestic and foreign policies did the Nixon administration initiate? How successful were these policies?

♦ What controversies, beyond the illegal break-in at Democratic Party headquarters, were involved in the Watergate episode? How did Watergate ultimately force Nixon's resignation from the presidency?

The Great Society

Lyndon Johnson lacked Kennedy's charisma but held substantial political assets of his own. As a member of the House of Representatives during the late 1930s and early 1940s and as majority leader of the U.S. Senate during the 1950s, the gangling Texan became the consummate legislative horse trader. He drove himself to a nearly fatal heart attack tending to details and courting Senate colleagues. Few issues, Johnson believed, defied consensus. Nearly everyone could be flattered, cajoled, even threatened into lending him their support. In the end, he claimed, everyone would benefit. During LBJ's time in Congress, his wealthy Texas benefactors gained valuable oil and gas concessions and lucrative construction contracts, while Johnson acquired a personal fortune. Cities such as Dallas and Houston and much of the Southwest also benefited from Johnson's skill in gaining federal funding for new building projects.

Kennedy's death gave Johnson the opportunity to fulfill his dream of transforming the nation in much the same way that he had changed his own region. Confident of using the tactics of his congressional days to build a national consensus for expanding Washington's reach, Johnson immediately went to work. He began by urging Congress to honor JFK's memory by passing legislation that Kennedy's administration had proposed.

Closing the New Frontier

More knowledgeable in the ways of Congress than Kennedy, Johnson quickly achieved the major domestic goals of JFK's New Frontier. Working behind the scenes, he secured passage of Kennedy's proposed $10 billion tax cut, a measure intended to stimulate the economy by making more money available for business investment. Although economists still differ on how much this tax measure contributed to the boom of the mid-1960s, it *appeared* to work. The GNP rose 7 percent in 1964 and 8 percent the following year, unemployment dropped, and inflation remained low.

Johnson also built on Kennedy-era plans for helping people in economic distress. In his January 1964 State of

CHRONOLOGY

1963 Johnson assumes presidency and pledges to continue Kennedy's initiatives

1964 Congress passes Kennedy's tax bill, the Civil Rights Act of 1964, and the Economic Opportunity Act • Gulf of Tonkin Resolution gives Johnson authority to conduct undeclared war • Johnson defeats Barry Goldwater in presidential election

1965 Johnson announces plans for the Great Society • Malcolm X assassinated • U.S. intervenes in Dominican Republic • Johnson announces significant U.S. troop deployments in Vietnam • Congress passes Voting Rights Act • Violence rocks Los Angeles and other urban areas

1966 Black Power movement emerges • *Miranda* v. *Arizona* decision guarantees rights of criminal suspects • Ronald Reagan elected governor of California • U.S. begins massive air strikes in North Vietnam

1967 Large antiwar demonstrations begin • Beatles release *Sgt. Pepper's Lonely Hearts Club Band*

1968 Tet offensive (January) • Martin Luther King, Jr. assassinated (April) • Robert Kennedy assassinated (June) • Violence at Democratic national convention in Chicago • Civil Rights Act of 1968 passed • Vietnam peace talks begin in Paris • Richard Nixon elected president

1969 Nixon announces "Vietnamization" policy • News of My Lai massacre become public

1970 U.S. troops enter Cambodia • Student demonstrators killed at Kent State and Jackson State • First Earth Day observed • Environmental Protection Act passed • Clean Air Act passed

1971 "Pentagon Papers" published; White House "plumbers" formed • Military court convicts Lieutenant Calley for My Lai incident

1972 Nixon crushes McGovern in presidential election

1973 Paris peace accords signed • *Roe* v. *Wade* upholds women's right to abortion • Nixon's Watergate troubles begin to escalate

1974 House votes impeachment, and Nixon resigns • Ford assumes presidency

1975 Saigon falls to North Vietnamese forces

the Union address, Johnson declared "an unconditional war on poverty in America." Constantly prodded by Johnson, Congress created the Office of Economic Opportunity (OEO) to coordinate a multipart program. First headed by R. Sargent Shriver, brother-in-law of John Kennedy, the OEO was charged with "eliminat[ing] the paradox of poverty in the midst of plenty . . . by opening to everyone the opportunity to live in decency and in dignity." The Economic Opportunity Act of 1964, in addition to establishing the OEO, mandated loans for rural and small-business development; established a work-training

THE PRESENCE OF LYNDON B. JOHNSON
As both senator and president, Lyndon Johnson employed body language—the "Johnson treatment"—as a favored means of lining up support for his policies.

program called the Jobs Corps; created Volunteers in Service to America (VISTA), a domestic version of the Peace Corps; provided low-wage jobs for young people, primarily in urban areas; began a work-study plan to assist college students; and, most ambitiously, authorized the creation of additional federally funded social programs to be planned in concert with local community groups.

In addition, Johnson secured new civil rights legislation. Initially distrusted by many in the civil rights movement, Johnson took special pride in helping to push a beefed-up version of Kennedy's bill through Congress. Championing the measure as a memorial to Kennedy, he nevertheless recognized that southern segregationists in the Democratic Party would try to block—or at least dilute—it. Consequently, he successfully sought Republican support. The Civil Rights Act of 1964, passed in July after lengthy delaying tactics by southerners and modifications by Republicans, strengthened federal remedies, monitored by a new Equal Employment Opportunity Commission (EEOC), against job discrimination. The law also prohibited racial discrimination in all public accommodations connected to interstate commerce, such as hotels and restaurants. Moreover, Title VII, a provision added during congressional debate, barred discrimination based on sex and was extremely important to the reviving women's movement.

Despite helping generate grassroots pressure for this legislation, local civil rights organizers were reminded that they could not always influence decisions at the national level. During the same summer that Lyndon Johnson was pressing Congress to pass the Civil Rights Act of 1964, a coalition of civil rights groups was enlisting young volunteers for a voter registration campaign in Mississippi—an operation they called "Freedom Summer." During that tension-filled time, segregationists murdered six civil rights workers, but others pressed forward, only to see their local work frustrated by the national Democratic Party. Pressured by Johnson, who used the FBI to gather information on the dissidents, the 1964 Democratic Convention voted to seat Mississippi's "regular" all-white delegates rather than members of the alternative (and racially diverse) "Freedom Democratic Party."

This rebuff prompted activists such as Fannie Lou Hamer of the Freedom Democratic Party to recall earlier suspicions about Lyndon Johnson and the national Democratic Party. Although LBJ seemed more committed to civil rights than John Kennedy had been, would Johnson—and

Hubert Humphrey, his hand-picked vice presidential running mate—continue to press for legislation after the election? This question became all the more important as Johnson appeared increasingly more likely to win the 1964 presidential race.

The Election of 1964

The Republicans nominated Senator Barry Goldwater of Arizona, the hero of militant conservatives, to oppose Johnson. Strategists for Goldwater, who had captured his party's nomination through a grassroots organizing effort, predicted that a campaign based on new-conservative principles would attract the millions of voters who rejected Democratic policies and those of Eisenhower's moderate Republicanism. Goldwater denounced Johnson's foreign policy for tolerating communist expansion and his domestic agenda, including civil rights legislation, for destroying individual liberties. Only one of eight Republican senators who had voted against the Civil Rights Act of 1964, Goldwater criticized the measure as an unconstitutional extension of national power into areas reserved for state legislatures and private citizens.

Goldwater's penchant for blurting out ill-considered pronouncements on controversial issues helped the Democrats picture him as fanatical, unpredictable, and reactionary. Goldwater suggested that people who feared nuclear war were "silly and sissified." U.S. weapons were so accurate, he once quipped, that the Pentagon could target the men's room in the Kremlin. He wondered, out loud, if Social Security might become a voluntary program. His proclamation, at the 1964 Republican convention, that "extremism in the pursuit of liberty is no vice" and "moderation in the pursuit of justice is no virtue," fed fears that Goldwater might be an "extremist." Generally on the defensive throughout the presidential campaign, Goldwater could never clearly articulate his conservative principles and political vision.

Even many Republicans came to doubt Goldwater's candidacy, and he led the GOP to a spectacular defeat in November. Johnson carried 44 states and won more than 60 percent of the popular vote; Democrats also gained 38 new seats in Congress. Most political pundits immediately declared the 1964 election a triumph for Johnson's expansive view of domestic policy making.

In retrospect, however, the election signaled important political changes that would soon rebound against Johnson and, in time, against the Democratic Party. During the Democratic primaries, for example, Alabama's segregationist governor, George Wallace, had run strongly against the president in several northern states. Widely known for opposing civil rights legislation, Wallace broadened his platform and denounced any "meddling" by Washington in local affairs. The 1964 election was the last in which the Democratic Party would capture the White House by proposing, as it had since the New Deal, new

LBJ'S 1964 CAMPAIGN AGAINST BARRY GOLDWATER

In this television ad from the 1964 campaign, Lyndon Johnson's supporters exploited Republican Barry Goldwater's image as a far-right extremist who might take the nation into a nuclear war.

domestic programming that significantly expanded the power of the national government.

Goldwater's defeat invigorated rather than discouraged his supporters. His youthful staff pioneered several innovative campaign tactics, such as direct mail fundraising. By refining these techniques during future campaigns, conservative strategists helped make the 1964 election the beginning, not the end, of the Republican Party's movement to the right. Moreover, Goldwater's stand against the Civil Rights Act of 1964 helped him carry five southern states. These victories—along with Wallace's earlier appeal to "white backlash" voters—convinced most Republicans that opposition to new civil rights measures could woo southern whites who had once been solidly Democratic. In time, Goldwater gained recognition for his role in helping to refashion American conservatism.

The Goldwater campaign propelled an attractive group of conservatives into national politics. Ronald Reagan, an actor and corporate spokesperson, proved such an effective campaigner in 1964 that conservative Republicans began grooming him for a political career. Younger conservatives such as William Rehnquist also entered the national arena as part of the Goldwater movement. In the immediate aftermath of Goldwater's defeat, however, the prospect that President Ronald Reagan would one day nominate William Rehnquist to be Chief Justice of the United States seemed beyond any conservative's wildest dream (see chapter 31).

Lyndon Johnson's Great Society

Lyndon Johnson hoped to capitalize quickly on his electoral victory. Enjoying broad support in Congress, he announced plans for a "Great Society," an array of federal programs designed to "enrich and elevate our national life" by building a country that was wealthy "in mind and spirit." Some of the programs fulfilled the dreams of Johnson's Democratic predecessors. Nationally funded medical coverage for the elderly (Medicare) and for low-income citizens (Medicaid) culminated efforts begun during the New and Fair Deals. Similarly, an addition to the president's cabinet, the Department of Housing and Urban Development (HUD), built on earlier plans for coordinating urban revitalization programs. And the Voting Rights Act of 1965, which mandated federal oversight of local elections in the South, promised to strengthen the ongoing effort to end racial discrimination in political life.

Other initiatives rested on the prosperity of the 1960s. Franklin Roosevelt had to confront the Great Depression, and Harry Truman had to cope with the economic uncertainties of the postwar years. Johnson, in contrast, launched his Great Society during an economic boom.

Even a costly war in Southeast Asia could not dampen his faith that continued economic growth would support his bold expansion of national power.

The array of Johnson-sponsored initiatives that rolled through Congress heartened his supporters and appalled his conservative critics. The "Model Cities Program" offered smaller-scale alternatives to existing, and inequitable, urban renewal efforts; rent supplements went to help low-income families improve their living conditions; an expanded Food Stamp program hoped to boost nutritional levels; and Head Start was created to help children climb the educational ladder more quickly. Other new, federally financed educational programs would upgrade classroom instruction, especially in low-income neighborhoods, and the Legal Services program was designed to provide advice and access to the court system for those who could not afford private attorneys. These measures were intended to support a broad range of social services, funded by federal tax dollars, to help people fight their own way out of economic distress. This service-based approach to social policy, Johnson insisted, would give people a "hand up" rather than a "handout."

The Great Society's Community Action Program (CAP) went much further by promising greater political power to grassroots activists. It authorized citizens, working through neighborhood organizations, to design community-based projects that could be financed from Washington. By promoting "maximum feasible participation" by ordinary citizens rather than social planners, CAP was designed to spark the kind of local democracy that could revitalize American politics.

Evaluating the Great Society

Why did the Great Society become so controversial? Most obviously, the dramatic extension of Washington's influence rekindled old debates about the use, as both a matter of constitutional law and pragmatic policy making, of national power. In addition, Johnson's extravagant rhetoric, such as that promising an "unconditional" victory over poverty, raised expectations that could not be met during a single presidency. Most important, the expectation that economic growth would generate the tax revenues to finance new social programs collapsed as both the U.S. and international economies began to sputter during the late 1960s. Facing new financial worries of their own, many people who had initially been inclined to support the Great Society became receptive to the argument, popularized by George Wallace and the Goldwater campaign, that bureaucrats in Washington were taking their hard-earned dollars and redirecting them toward unproductive social experiments. Worsening economic conditions, exacerbated by the escalating cost of the war in Vietnam, made greater federal expenditures on domestic programs a highly controversial policy.

Observers still disagree on the impact of Johnson's Great Society programs. Charles Murray's influential book *Losing Ground* (1984) charged that massive government expenditures, associated with Johnson's initiatives, encouraged antisocial behavior. Lured by welfare payments, this study argued, people abandoned the goals of marrying, settling down, and seeking jobs that would raise their income. In this view, the money appropriated for Great Society programs also created government deficits that slowed economic growth. Had this ill-advised spending not undermined personal initiative and the nation's economic structure, continued growth would have guaranteed virtually everyone a middle-class lifestyle. This conservative argument portrayed the Great Society as the cause of, not the remedy for, economic distress.

Others vigorously rejected this view. They found scant evidence for the proposition that millions of people preferred welfare to meaningful work. Moreover, spending for the military sector outstripped that for social programming and seemed the principal cause of the burgeoning government deficit. Funds actually spent on Great Society programs, these observers have noted, neither matched Johnson's promises nor reached the lavish total claimed in critical studies such as *Losing Ground*.

Most antipoverty activists continued to fault the Great Society for not seriously challenging the prevailing distribution of political and economic power. The Johnson administration, they argued, remained closely wedded to large-scale bureaucratic solutions, by people connected to Washington elites, for problems that had many local variations. The White House quickly jettisoned the CAP model of grassroots participation. Moreover, the Great Society, which assumed that economic growth would continue to finance federal initiatives, never even considered measures that might seek to redistribute income and wealth. Its promises were never implemented, this critique alleged, and the proposed War on Poverty became only a series of small skirmishes.

Although historians disagree on the Great Society's impact, there is broad agreement that Johnson's domestic program brought the kind of federal support for domestic social programs that recalled the New Deal of the 1930s. Washington's financial outlay, although never what Johnson had seemed to promise, increased more than 10 percent in every year of his presidency. In 1960, federal spending on social welfare constituted 28 percent of total government outlays; by 1970, this figure had risen to more than 40 percent. Moreover, Great Society programs such as Medicaid, legal services, and job training permitted many low-income families to have some of the services, such as medical care, that more affluent Americans had long taken for granted.

The Great Society, by extending national power, inflamed political passions. When trying to promote equality, could social policy makers make the distinction, which was becoming increasingly important in political rhetoric, between people who really merited assistance—those seeking a "hand up"—and people merely seeking a "handout"? Partisan controversy over social spending policies, reinvigorated by the Great Society, would shape political life during the years that followed Lyndon Johnson's presidency.

🌏 Escalation in Vietnam

Johnson's divisive crusade to build a Great Society at home had its counterpart abroad. The pledge to protect South Vietnam demanded ever more of the nation's energy, its resources, and its military personnel. Johnson's foreign policy alienated many Americans, especially among the young, divided the entire nation, and eventually contributed to economic disarray.

The Gulf of Tonkin Resolution

Immediately after John Kennedy's assassination in November 1963, Johnson had avoided widening the war in Vietnam. He did not wish, however, to be seen as "soft" on communism. Seeing no alternative to backing the South Vietnamese government in Saigon, Johnson accepted the recommendation of his military advisers that the United States could beat back enemy offensives in South Vietnam by ordering air strikes against North Vietnam. He prepared a congressional resolution authorizing such an escalation of hostilities.

Events in the Gulf of Tonkin, off the coast of North Vietnam, provided the rationale for taking this resolution to Capitol Hill. On August 1, 1964, the U.S. destroyer *Maddox*, while conducting an intelligence-gathering mission, exchanged fire with North Vietnamese torpedo boats. Three days later, the *Maddox* returned with the *Turner Joy* and, during severe weather, reported what could have been evidence of a failed torpedo attack. Although the *Maddox*'s commander radioed that the episode needed further analysis, Johnson immediately claimed that North Vietnam had engaged in "unprovoked aggression" against U.S. forces. Congress overwhelmingly authorized Johnson to take "all necessary measures to repel armed attack." (A later study concluded that there had never been a North Vietnamese attack.) Johnson treated this Gulf of Tonkin

Resolution as tantamount to a congressional declaration of war and cited it as legal authorization for subsequent military action in Vietnam.

Despite Johnson's aggressive response to events in the Gulf of Tonkin, the president still positioned himself as a cautious moderate during the presidential campaign of 1964. When Republican candidate Barry Goldwater urged stronger measures against North Vietnam and hinted at possible use of tactical nuclear weapons, Johnson's campaign managers portrayed Goldwater as a threat to the survival of civilization. Johnson promised not to commit American troops to a land war in Asia.

Soon after the election, however, Johnson again escalated the war. The 1963 coup against Diem (see chapter 28) had left a political vacuum in South Vietnam. The incompetence of South Vietnam's military-led government was sparking growing popular discontent, and South Vietnamese soldiers were deserting at an alarming rate. In January 1965, this military regime fell, and factionalism stalled the emergence of a stable alternative.

Lacking an effective ally in South Vietnam, Johnson puzzled over his options. Did the nation's long-standing Cold War policy of containing communism mean that the conflict in Vietnam required full-fledged American involvement? What kind of backlash might a South Vietnamese defeat produce in the United States and around the world? Would a U.S. escalation against North Vietnam lead to confrontation with its communist allies, China and the Soviet Union?

Johnson's aides offered conflicting advice. National Security Adviser McGeorge Bundy predicted inevitable defeat unless the United States greatly increased its military role. Walt Rostow, a specialist in issues of economic development, assured Johnson that a broad-based effort would bring victory. Once the enemy recognized Johnson's determination to remain in Vietnam, he advised, they would give up their plans to overrun the South. Undersecretary of State George Ball, by contrast, warned that U.S. troops could not save South Vietnam. "The South Vietnamese are losing the war," he wrote, and "no one has demonstrated that a white ground force of whatever size can win a guerrilla war . . . in jungle terrain in the midst of a population that refuses cooperation to the white forces." Senate Majority Leader Mike Mansfield urged the president to devise a plan for reuniting Vietnam as a neutral country. The Joint Chiefs of Staff, afflicted by interservice rivalries, provided differing military assessments and no clear guidance.

Although privately doubting the chance for success, Johnson worried more about the political and diplomatic costs of a U.S. pullout. He feared that domestic criticism of any communist victory in South Vietnam would endanger his Great Society programs. Moreover, he accepted the familiar Cold War proposition that a U.S. withdrawal from a confrontation such as the one in South Vietnam would set off a "domino effect." It would encourage communist-leaning insurgencies in Latin America, increase pressure on West Berlin, and damage U.S. credibility around the world. Both Eisenhower and Kennedy had staked American prestige on the preservation of a noncommunist South Vietnam. Johnson either had to abandon that commitment or chart an uncertain course by ordering a massive infusion of U.S. troops into the Vietnam conflict.

Ultimately, Johnson decided he had no choice but to extend U.S. involvement. He ordered a sustained campaign of bombing in North Vietnam, code-named "Rolling Thunder." He also deployed U.S. ground forces to regain lost territory in the South, expanded covert operations, and stepped up economic aid to the beleaguered Saigon government. Only six months after the 1964 election, with his advisers still divided, Johnson committed the United States to war against not only the NLF but North Vietnam as well.

The War Widens

The war grew more intense throughout 1965. Trying to break the enemy's will, U.S. military commanders mounted an effort to inflict more casualties. Accordingly, the administration authorized the use of napalm, a chemical that charred both foliage and people, and allowed the Air Force to bomb new targets. Additional U.S. combat troops arrived to secure enclaves in the South against further enemy incursions. Every escalation seemed to require a further one. When North Vietnam rejected a Johnson "peace plan" that it viewed as a surrender, the United States again stepped up its military involvement. North Vietnam's leader, Ho Chi Minh, who was also playing a game of escalation and attrition, became convinced that Johnson commanded meager public and congressional support for continuing the costly war.

In April 1965, Johnson brought his Cold War, anti-communist crusade closer to home. Responding to exaggerated reports of a communist threat to the Dominican Republic, Johnson sent American troops to unseat a left-leaning elected president and to install a government favorable to U.S. interests in the Caribbean nation. This U.S. incursion violated a long-standing "good neighbor" pledge not to intervene militarily in the Western Hemisphere. Although the action raised criticism throughout Latin America, the successful overthrow of a leftist government in the Dominican Republic steeled the administration's determination to hold the line against communism in Vietnam.

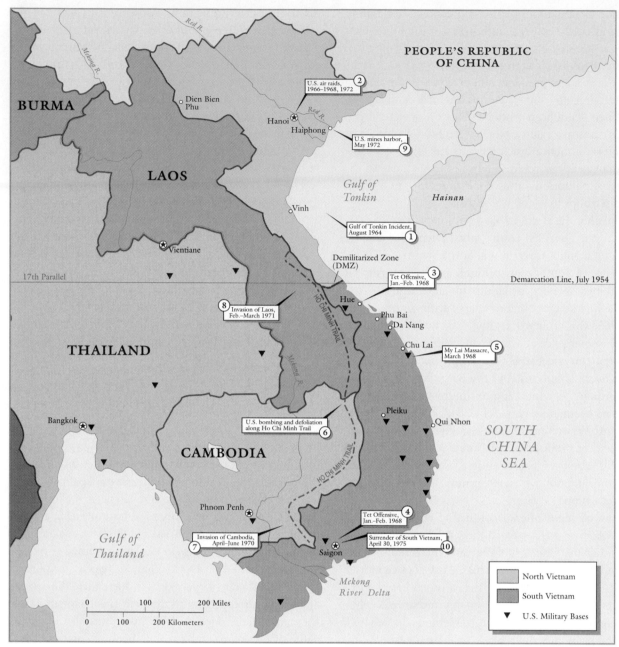

MAP 29.1 VIETNAM WAR

The war in Vietnam spread into neighboring countries as the North Vietnamese ran supplies southward along a network called the Ho Chi Minh Trail, and the United States tried to disrupt their efforts. Unlike the Korean War (see map on p. 847), this guerrilla-style war had few conventional "fronts" of fighting.

 View an animated version of this map or related maps at http://history.wadsworth.com/murrin_LEP4e.

Later that spring, as the fifth government since Diem's death was taking office in Saigon, U.S. strategists were still wondering how to prop up South Vietnam. General William Westmoreland, who directed the U.S. effort in Vietnam, recommended moving his troops out of their enclaves and sending them on "search and destroy" missions against communist forces. In July 1965, Johnson publicly agreed to order 50,000 additional military personnel to Vietnam, privately pledged to send an additional 50,000, and left open the possibility of sending even more. He also approved saturation bombing of the South Vietnamese countryside and intensified bombing of the North.

Some advisers urged Johnson to admit candidly the greatly expanded scope of the U.S. effort. They recommended either an outright declaration of war or at least legislation that would formally put the United States on a wartime footing so that the president could wield the economic and informational controls that previous administrations had used during conflicts of this magnitude. But Johnson feared such action would provoke the Soviet Union or China. He also worried about arousing greater protests from Congress and the public. Rather than risk a debate that might reveal his shallow political support, Johnson decided to stress the administration's negotiation efforts and to pretend that the war was not really a war. As the president talked about seeing "light at the end of the tunnel," the public remained in the dark about exactly what its government was doing and why.

Over the next three years, the U.S. involvement steadily increased. The number of U.S. troops in Vietnam grew to 535,000. Operation RANCHHAND scorched South Vietnam's croplands and defoliated half its forests in an effort to eliminate the natural cover for enemy troop movements. Approximately 1.5 million tons of bombs—more than all the tonnage dropped during the Second World War—leveled North Vietnamese cities and pummeled the villages and inhabitants of "free-fire zones" (designated areas in which anything could become a target) in the South. Still, Johnson carefully avoided bombing close to the Chinese border or doing anything else that might provoke either Chinese or Soviet entry into the war.

Despite the escalating violence, Vietnam remained a "limited" war; the U.S. strategy was to contain the other side by waging a war of attrition. The weekly body count of enemy dead remained the measure by which the Johnson administration gauged progress. Estimates that a kill ratio of 10 to 1 would force the North and NLF to pull back encouraged the military to unleash more firepower and further inflate enemy casualty figures. Johnson, whose notorious temper flared at the first sound of bad news, welcomed these statistics as a sign that "victory was around the corner." But North Vietnam, assisted by the Soviet Union and China, could match every U.S. escalation and could limit its losses by concealing troops under the jungle foliage that remained. The North Vietnamese funneled supplies into South Vietnam through a shifting network of paths called the Ho Chi Minh Trail. The war had reached a stalemate, but few members of Johnson's administration would admit it.

The destruction wreaked by the U.S. effort gave North Vietnamese leaders a decided propaganda advantage. Critics around the world condemned the escalating ferocity of U.S. attacks. The Soviet Union and China in-

AP/Wide World Photos.

AN IMAGE THAT SHOCKED

This 1968 photo, widely reproduced because of the absence of formal governmental censorship during the Vietnam conflict, shows a South Vietnamese military officer summarily executing a suspected Viet Cong leader on the streets of Saigon. The prevalence of images such as this one complicated the U.S. government's attempt to portray its support of South Vietnam as a fight for freedom and the rule of law.

creased aid to Ho Chi Minh and helped foment anti-Americanism elsewhere. In Western Europe, for example, demonstrations against the American war became prominent features of political life. Both at home and abroad, Johnson administration officials were hounded by protesters almost everywhere they went.

Meanwhile, the government in Saigon was still reeling. The devastation of the countryside, the economic destabilization caused by the flood of U.S. dollars, and the corruption in its politics took their toll. So-called pacification and strategic hamlet programs, which brought Vietnamese farmers together in tightly guarded villages, sounded viable in Washington but created greater chaos by uprooting one in four South Vietnamese from their villages and ancestral lands. Buddhist priests persistently demonstrated against foreign influence. When, in 1967, Generals Nguyen Van Thieu and Nguyen Cao Ky, who had headed the government in Saigon since 1965, tried to legitimate their regime by holding elections, the narrow margin of their victory only highlighted their precarious position.

The Media and the War

Johnson lectured the American public about upholding national honor and diplomatic commitments, but antiwar criticism continued to mount. In most previous wars, Washington had restricted journalistic coverage. Because the Vietnam War was undeclared, Johnson had to resort to informal, although initially effective, ways of managing information. With television reports making Vietnam into a "living room war"—one that citizens could watch in their own homes—Johnson kept three sets playing in his office in order to monitor what viewers were seeing. Sometimes he would phone network executives and castigate them for their broadcasts—the "Johnson treatment," some called it. After one report, Frank Stanton of CBS reportedly received this call: "Frank, are you trying to f—— me? . . . This is your president, and yesterday your boys shat on the American flag." Increasingly sensitive to criticism, Johnson equated any question or doubt about his policy with a lack of patriotism.

Antiwar activists were equally disturbed by what they regarded as the media's uncritical reporting on the war. Most journalists, they claimed, relied on official handouts for their stories, spent their time in Saigon's best hotels, and kowtowed to the White House. Especially in the early years, few reporters filed critical stories. Although the press corps did not invite the American public to cheer on the military effort, as it had during the two world wars, neither did its coverage help to encourage dissent.

In time, however, the tone of news coverage began to change. Images of unrelenting destruction on the nightly TV news and in magazine photos inevitably eroded enthusiasm for the war. In addition, a few journalists forthrightly expressed their opposition. Harrison Salisbury of the *New York Times* sent reports from Vietnam that detailed the destructive power of U.S. bombing missions. Gloria Emerson's grim reports portrayed the war as a class-based effort in which poor and disproportionately nonwhite troops fought and died so that rich men, with draft-exempt "fortunate sons," might reap war-related profits.

As the war dragged on, the media began to talk about a "war at home," one between "hawks" and "doves." Johnson insisted that he was merely following the containment policy favored by Eisenhower and Kennedy. Secretary of State Dean Rusk spoke of the dangers of "appeasement." But influential politicians—including J. William Fulbright of Arkansas, chair of the powerful Senate Foreign Relations Committee—warned of misplaced priorities and of an "arrogance of power." Meanwhile, antiwar protestors began to challenge the structure of American politics and culture.

🌏 The War at Home

Millions came to oppose the war in Southeast Asia, and support eroded for the Great Society at home. By 1968, tensions escalated into confrontation and violence.

A New Left

During the early 1960s, small groups of people, many of them college students, came to reject the policies of the postwar years. In 1962, two years after conservative activists had formed Young Americans for Freedom (YAF), insurgents on the left established an organization they dubbed Students for a Democratic Society (SDS). While YAF worked quietly to build a "New Right," SDS captured the media's attention with its more flamboyant attempt to create a "New Left." Although SDS endorsed familiar political causes, especially the fight against racial discrimination, its "Port Huron Statement" of 1962 also spoke of novel, more spiritual and personal issues. SDS pledged to attack the "loneliness, estrangement, isolation" of postwar society.

The SDS became one part of a New Left. This movement tried to distance its politics from those of the Democratic Party and that of the "old" communist-inspired Left. Charging that the dominant culture valued bureaucratic

The Granger Collection, New York.

ANTIWAR DEMONSTRATION IN WASHINGTON, D.C.
Mass rallies against U.S. involvement in the Vietnam War became an important part of antiwar politics during the late 1960s and early 1970s.

Responses to the question: "Do you think that the United States made a mistake in sending troops to fight there?"

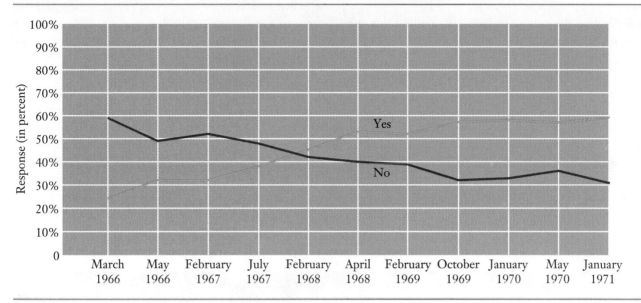

AMERICAN ATTITUDES TOWARD THE VIETNAM WAR

expertise over citizen engagement and economic growth over meaningful work, this New Left embraced an alternative socioeconomic vision. In politics, it called for "participatory democracy," grassroots activities, and institutions responsive to the wishes of local communities rather than the dictates of national elites. "We felt that we were different, and that we were going to do things differently," recalled one early SDS member. "It felt like the dawn of a new age."

During the early 1960s, the antidiscrimination movement in the Deep South inspired many young, white college students from the North. Risking racist violence, they went to the South and helped local political activists. Some remained there, working for civil rights; others returned to the North and joined neighborhood-based political projects. The New Left also tried to organize college campuses, mobilizing students on behalf of civil rights and against both the war in Southeast Asia and socioeconomic deprivation at home.

Even students not formally aligned with this New Left often saw colleges and universities as part of a vast "establishment" that blindly opposed change. On campus, young people had increasingly been complaining that required academic courses ignored relevant issues of the day and that college administrators imposed archaic restrictions, such as sex-segregated living arrangements and required dorm hours, from an authoritarian past when colleges acted *in loco parentis* (in place of parents). Giant universities, sustained by funds from government and corpora-

tions, seemed oblivious to the social and moral implications of their war-related research, dissenting students also claimed. During the "Berkeley student revolt" of 1964 and 1965, students and sympathetic faculty members protested restrictions on political organizing on campus and then began speaking out against the Vietnam War and racial discrimination. Although the long-running drama at Berkeley, which disrupted classes and polarized the university, was hardly the only or even the first example of student dissent, it came to symbolize the turmoil that the media called "the war on campus."

By 1966, the Vietnam issue convulsed many campuses. A young man's draft card signified a highly personal connection to U.S. involvement in Southeast Asia. Local draft boards usually granted an educational deferment to male students, but these always expired at graduation and could occasionally be revoked or denied. The burning of draft cards, as a symbolic protest against both the war and universal military service for men, became a central feature of antiwar demonstrations.

Bitter strife rocked many campuses after 1965. At "teach-ins," supporters and opponents of the war argued their positions. These debates soon gave way to less-structured demonstrations. As antiwar sentiment grew, students who supported the war began claiming that *their* rights were being restricted. Conservatives such as Ronald Reagan called on college administrators to return "civility" to the campus life and added opposition to student protests to their expanding political agenda.

The Counterculture

Accompanying the spread of New Left politics was the rise of a much-publicized "counterculture." Seen most broadly, this alternative culture helped support several ongoing causes—including the cooperative movement, environmentalism, and the fight against restrictions on lifestyle choices (see chapter 30)—but the mass media of the 1960s invariably highlighted only the most visible trappings of this insurgency. It focused on those individuals whose colorful, experimental approach to daily life defied traditional attitudes on matters such as clothing, hair style, and sexuality. The media liked to portray these people, caricatured as "hippies," as the vanguard of a suppos-edly massive "youth revolt." It detailed their association with drugs such as marijuana and LSD; communal living arrangements, especially rural communes; and new forms of music such as the folk-rock of the Byrds and the acid-rock of the Grateful Dead.

The media hailed young people linked to cultural innovation, particularly musicians, not simply as cultural symbols but, even if they shunned the role, as generational prophets. The reclusive singer-songwriter Bob Dylan, who had helped spur the revival of acoustic folk music during the early 1960s, became one such figure after his music "went electric" in 1965. Reworking idioms used by African American blues artists such as Muddy Waters, Dylan's "Like a Rolling Stone" (1965) exploded onto both the

---

M U S I C A L   L I N K   T O   T H E   P A S T

The Folk-Rock Moment

Songwriter: Bob Dylan
Title: "Subterranean Homesick Blues"
(1965)

From 1962 to 1964, Bob Dylan led the American folk music revival with Woody Guthrie–inspired original protest songs such as "Blowin' in the Wind," which Peter, Paul, and Mary made into a number-one single in 1963. Very rarely, if ever, in American popular music had songs that were so political become so popular. However, by 1965, Dylan decided to employ a more aggressive rock 'n' roll sound with electric guitar and drums, instead of the more rustic-sounding acoustic guitar. When he first "plugged in" publicly at the 1965 Newport Folk Festival, it was one of the iconic moments in American popular music history, both for the quality and intensity of Dylan's new songwriting style and because of the vehement negative response of the folk music community that had lauded him in years past. For the next year, audiences around the world booed when Dylan arrived on stage with an electric band.

"Subterranean Homesick Blues" was one of the first examples of Dylan's revamped musical direction. For many in his old audience, the electric amplification was perhaps less alarming than his new lyrical style. He dropped the relatively straightforward protest songs, which he then referred to as "finger-pointing songs," for a more free-form approach that used "chains of flashing images" in a manner reminiscent of 1950s Beat Generation writers Allen Ginsberg and Jack Kerouac. The words did not always immediately make sense, but many of the phrases burned into the national lexicon and consciousness ("don't follow leaders, watch the parking meters"; "you don't need a weatherman to know which way the wind blows"). Dylan's 1964–1966 compositions combined alienation with a sense of humor and questioned American values ("please her, please him, buy gifts / don't steal, don't lift / twenty years of schooling and they put you on the day shift!"). As Paul Williams, Dylan's most perceptive critic, has written: "Some reacted by calling Dylan a 'sell-out,' not realizing, at least at first, that he was now making the most anti-establishment, revolutionary music of his or anyone's career." A new style of American songwriting had been born and would soon sweep the world.

---

1. Why do you think that important stylistic turning points in music history (such as Dylan's embrace of a rock sound, or the arrival of the waltz in the 1850s or hip-hop in the 1980s) have often engendered fierce resistance from certain elements of the public? Why, at these times, do people view music as something threatening, something more than just a source of entertainment?

2. Do you think that Dylan's new songwriting style had an influence on hip-hop music of the 1980s, such as "The Message" (see Chapter 31)?

Listen to an audio recording of this music on the Musical Links to the Past CD.

Top-40 charts of AM radio and the freewheeling playlists of the new, alternative FM stations. Rock-music writers and sociologists took up "Dylanology," a hybrid journalistic-academic enterprise that combed Dylan's lyrics and eclectic musical tastes in search of clues to broader values of the counterculture. New publications, including the long-running magazine *Rolling Stone,* dispatched youthful journalists to report on—and also participate in—this new cultural "scene."

Images and products from the counterculture soon found a ready market. Recognizing the appeal of bands such as San Francisco's Grateful Dead and the Jefferson Airplane, the culture industry welcomed them to a world in which rock 'n' roll was really "here to pay." The Rolling Stones cashed in with their ode to a "Street Fighting Man" (1968) and their pledge of "Sympathy for the Devil" (1968). The Beatles made even more money and attracted critical acclaim with their albums *Sgt. Pepper's Lonely Hearts Club Band* (1967) and *The Beatles* (popularly known as *The White Album*) (1968).

Hollywood increasingly abandoned its traditional, all-ages market in favor of attracting a youth-dominated audience. Building on a trend evident in movies of the 1950s, such as *Rebel without a Cause,* the film industry targeted younger viewers with movies such as *The Graduate* (1967) and *Bonnie and Clyde* (1967) and followed up with a brief cycle of films, including *Easy Rider* (1969) and *Wild in the Streets* (1968), which portrayed adult authority figures as vampire-like ravagers of the young. Films from this "new Hollywood" often featured graphic images of sexuality and violence. Almost any consumer product could be linked to an advertising campaign that suggested rebellious young people. Fully embracing imagery connected to the counterculture, automobile manufacturers eagerly used the notion of youthful dissent to entice car buyers of almost any age. A true rebel, Detroit suggested, could combat conformity by rejecting the bulky, family-oriented automobile of the 1950s for something like the Ford Mustang, a car as sleek and stylish as youthful clothing fashions. In a series of famous TV spots, young women in brightly colored miniskirts hailed "the Dodge Rebellion," and General Motors proudly announced the death of "your father's Oldsmobile."

Media coverage of the counterculture sparked lively, increasingly bitter debates. Conservative commentators, along with supporters of President Johnson, charged the media with spreading dangerous, antisocial images. In this view, a focus on demonstrations in which young radicals and countercultural musicians joined with older opponents of the Vietnam War exaggerated the strength of the antiwar movement. Conversely, some veterans of the early New Left claimed that media attention on the coun-

terculture actually undercut their search for a new kind of politics.

A 1967 march on the Pentagon helped polarize this debate. Rejecting political speeches and draft-card burning as too tame, some of the marchers chanted mystical incantations and claimed they would levitate the Pentagon. In a similar vein, Abbie Hoffman, self-proclaimed leader of a nonexistent Youth International Party (the "Yippies"), facetiously urged "loot-ins at department stores to strike at the property fetish that underlies genocidal war" in Vietnam. The Pentagon march generated eye-catching TV footage and won novelist Norman Mailer a National Book Award for *Armies of the Night,* his personal account of this event. But the march's relationship to deepening antiwar sentiment seemed less certain. Could such a youth-dominated spectacle effectively convey the passionate moral stance of the variety of people who were coming, often for very different reasons, to oppose the war? Might not media images of colorful quipsters such as Hoffman help fuel cultural polarization rather than political action? Was the media's appetite for spectacular demonstrations and new celebrities helping to trivialize issues and pit cultural and political dissenters against one another?

From Civil Rights to Black Power

Meanwhile, sharp debate over the role of the media and its relationship to the political and cultural insurgencies began splintering the campaign against racial discrimination as well. Early on, leaders in the fight against discrimination, notably Dr. Martin Luther King, Jr., had recognized the value of media coverage. During King's 1965 drive to win easier access to the ballot box for African Americans, television pictures of the violence in Selma, Alabama, helped galvanize support for federal legislation. At one point, ABC television interrupted the anti-Nazi film *Judgment at Nuremberg* to show white Alabama state troopers beating peaceful, mostly African American, civil rights marchers. President Johnson used television to dramatize his support for voting-rights legislation and to promise that "we shall overcome" the nation's "crippling legacy of bigotry and injustice."

At the same time, the media became the forum for bitter arguments about what was increasingly being called a "racial crisis." Conservatives such as Goldwater and Reagan insisted that subversive agitators were provoking conflict and violence and that only a firm commitment to law and order would ease racial tensions. Social activists replied that racism, lack of educational and employment opportunities, and inadequate government remedies were producing the frustration and despair that burst forth in

Cassius Clay / Muhammad Ali: Champion of the Whole World

More than 3 billion people, from around the globe, were watching television on a summer night in 1996. Speculation centered on which American—ideally, one instantly recognizable throughout the world—would light the ceremonial fire for the Olympic Games in Atlanta. Might it be former president Jimmy Carter, a Georgia native whose personal, post-presidential diplomatic career had made him an international celebrity? The slightly stooped and graying middle-aged man who shuffled forward to light the flame, however, was better known to the world than any former U.S. president.

Muhammad Ali (born Cassius Marcellus Clay, Jr. in Louisville, Kentucky, 1942), who won an Olympic boxing championship in 1960, came to dominate what one TV network calls "the wide world of sports." After his Olympic triumph, Clay turned professional and gained the heavyweight championship in 1964. His first title defense attracted only several thousand people to a makeshift arena in Maine. When Ali concluded his career in 1978, however, he had fought before adoring crowds all over the world. Governments rather than sports promoters, Ali once bragged, negotiated his fights.

Once heavyweight champion, the twenty-two-year-old fighter set out to establish a global presence that transcended sports. He declared himself a member of the Muslim faith; officially changed his name; and pro-

claimed that, as a world champion, he would "meet the people I am champion of." In 1967, Ali became the most prominent opponent of U.S. involvement in Vietnam by refusing induction into the military. Temporarily stripped of his boxing honors in the United States, Ali traveled widely, especially to Africa and the Middle East, and became as well known abroad as at home. Eventually returning to the ring, Ali staged his most memorable (and physically damaging) bouts in Zaire and the Philippines. Despite increasing physical ailments—the harsh legacy of his profession—Ali has continued to travel abroad and to reconfirm his reputation as one of the best-known Americans of his generation.

© Bettmann/Corbis.

ALI VISITS EGYPT, 1964

In this photo, taken during Ali's trip to the Middle East at the invitation of the Arab Boxing Union, Ali kisses a bust of President Gamal Abdel Nasser.

sporadic racial violence. This debate intensified in 1965 in the wake of a devastating racial conflict in Los Angeles. A confrontation between a white highway patrol officer and a black motorist escalated into six days of urban violence, centered in the largely African American community of Watts in south-central Los Angeles. Thirty-four people died; hundreds of businesses and homes were burned; the National Guard patrolled the streets; and television cameras framed the conflagration as an ongoing media spectacle. Violence erupted in many other U.S. cities during the remainder of the 1960s.

A new "Black Power" movement was emerging, heralded by a charismatic minister named Malcolm X. A member of the Nation of Islam, a North American–based

group popularly known as the "Black Muslims," Malcolm X initially denounced the civil rights movement. He saw Dr. King's gradualist, nonviolent approach to political change as irrelevant to the social and economic problems of most African Americans and proclaimed that integration was unworkable. Although he never called for violent confrontation, he did endorse self-defense "by any means necessary." Malcolm X, a growing group of followers argued, was simply "telling it like it is."

Malcolm X offered more than angry rhetoric. He called for a renewal of pride in African American cultural practices and for economic reconstruction. In order to revitalize institutions of culture, he urged African Americans to "recapture our heritage and identity" and "launch a cultural revolution to unbrainwash an entire people." Seeking a broad movement, Malcolm X eventually broke from the Nation of Islam, established his own Organization of Afro-American Unity, and explored alliances with other insurgent groups. Murdered in 1965 by enemies from the Nation of Islam, Malcolm X remained a powerful symbol of militant politics and renewed pride in African American culture.

A new generation assumed the mantle of Malcolm X. Disdaining the integrationist agenda, the youthful militants embraced the word *black* and a political-cultural agenda based on their racial identity. As "Black Power" replaced the old civil rights call for "Freedom Now," advocates soon caught the media's attention and began to gain support within African American communities. "Black Is Beautiful" became a watchword. James Brown, the "Godfather of Soul," captured this new cultural spirit with his 1965 hit song, "Papa's Got a Brand New Bag," which renounced old rules and restrictions. Later, his "Say It Loud, I'm Black and Proud" encapsulated the cultural message of the Black Power movement.

The Black Power insurgency challenged the civil rights movement philosophically and tactically. Frustrated by the slow pace of change, some younger African Americans— including Stokely Carmichael, who became head of the Student Nonviolent Coordinating Committee (SNCC) in 1966, and members of the Black Panther Party—criticized the gradualist approach of older organizations such as King's Southern Christian Leadership Conference (SCLC). A Black Panther manifesto called for community "self-defense" groups as protection against police harassment, the release from jail of all African American prisoners (on the assumption that none had received fair trials in racist courts), and guaranteed employment for all citizens. Although opinion surveys suggested that most African Americans still supported an integrationist agenda, the new modes of challenging discrimination upset the established black–white civil rights alliance.

Within this context, Congress passed the Civil Rights Act of 1968. One provision of this omnibus law, popularly known as the Fair Housing Act, sought to eliminate racial discrimination in the real estate market. But in response

© UPI-Bettmann/Corbis.

VIOLENCE IN DETROIT, 1967

Outbreaks of violence, rooted in economic inequality and racial tension, swept through many U.S. cities between 1965 and 1969. The 1967 violence in Detroit, which federal troops had to quell, left many African American neighborhoods in ruin.

to charges that antidiscrimination efforts could invade the rights of landlords and realtors, the act provided exemptions that enfeebled its enforcement provisions. Moreover, another section in the law declared it a crime to cross state lines in order to incite a "riot." Its supporters hailed this provision as an effort to reestablish "law and order," while critics countered that it unconstitutionally invoked the power of the federal government against political activists, especially those supportive of the Black Power movement.

1968: The Violence Overseas

In 1968, several violent events abroad worsened political polarization in the United States. The first came in Vietnam. At the end of January, during a supposed truce in observance of Tet, the Vietnamese lunar new year celebration, troops of the National Liberation Front (NLF) and North Vietnamese forces mounted surprise attacks throughout South Vietnam. After sweeping through eight provincial capitals, they even seized the grounds of the U.S. embassy in Saigon for a few hours. Militarily, this so-called Tet offensive ended with the NLF and the North suffering heavy casualties and gaining relatively little territory. Supporters of the war blamed the media for exaggerating the effect of the early attacks and ignoring the heavy losses to the NLF and North Vietnamese and thereby turning a "victory" into a "defeat." Critics countered that the

Tet offensive had caught the U.S. military off guard and ill prepared to take advantage of enemy losses.

Tet turned out to be a serious psychological defeat for the United States because it undercut President Johnson's claims about an imminent South Vietnamese–United States victory. When General Westmoreland asked for 206,000 additional U.S. troops, most of Johnson's advisers, led by his new secretary of defense, Clark Clifford, insisted that South Vietnamese troops assume more of the military burden. Johnson accepted their argument, realizing that such a large increase in U.S. forces, even if troops could have been spared from other duties, would have fanned antiwar opposition at home. In a way, the events of Tet contributed to the beginning of a policy that would become known as the "Vietnamization" of the war.

The Tet offensive also destroyed much of whatever political support Johnson still commanded among antiwar Democrats and threw his strategic planners into confusion. Faced with revolt in his own party, led by Senator Eugene McCarthy of Minnesota, Johnson suddenly declared on March 31, 1968, that he would not run for reelection. He halted the bombing of North Vietnam and

HISTORY THROUGH FILM

Malcolm X (1992)

Directed by Spike Lee. Starring Denzel Washington (Malcolm X), Angela Bassett (Betty Shabbaz), Al Freeman, Jr. (Elijah Muhammad).

Spike Lee, the U.S. film industry's best-known African American director, campaigned actively to make a movie about *Malcolm X*. For nearly 25 years, Hollywood moguls had been trying to portray the charismatic leader who was gunned down in 1965 and whose *Autobiography,* published in 1963, had become a literary classic. Delays in obtaining financing, crafting a script, and finding a director always stymied production plans.

Lee, who had denounced the Hollywood establishment for passing over his celebrated (and controversial) *Do the Right Thing* (1989) for an Academy Award nomination, insisted that only he could do justice to the story of Malcolm X. Initially buoyed by a $34 million budget, Lee encountered problems of his own, including his insistence on releasing a movie that ran for more than three hours. Lee called *Malcolm X* "my interpretation of the man. It is nobody else's."

The finished film displays Lee's desire to show the presence of the past in the present. Produced by Lee's own independent production—whose name, "Forty Acres and a Mule," recalls the land-distribution program advanced by advocates of Radical Reconstruction after the Civil War—the movie argues for the continuing relevance of Malcolm X's ideas and initiatives.

The famous segments that begin and end the film feature a collage of iconic images. Against the backdrop of the Warner Brothers logo, the soundtrack features the voice of Malcolm X decrying American history as the continuing story of racist actions. Malcolm's accusations continue as a giant American flag, perhaps a reference to the popular film *Patton* (1970), appears on screen. Then, the image of the flag is cut into pieces by jagged images from the homemade videotape of the 1991 incident in which Los Angeles police officers beat an African American named Rodney King. Next, the flag begins to burn until, revealed behind it, a giant "X," adorned with remnants of the flag, dominates the film frame. The ending uses substantial archival footage of Malcolm, along with images of South African freedom fighter Nelson Mandela, while the soundtrack features the voice of Ozzie Davis, the celebrated African American actor, giving a eulogy to Malcolm X.

The body of the film, borrowing its organizational structure from Malcolm's *Autobiography,* breaks into three parts. The movie first traces how the young Malcolm, born Malcolm Little and later known as "Detroit Red," financed a gaudy lifestyle through small-time criminal schemes. The second part covers how, following his imprisonment and his embrace of the Nation of Islam (a group popularly known as the "Black Muslims"), the flamboyant hustler became the almost ascetic rebel, Malcolm X. The final portion of the film, which takes roughly 90 minutes, races through the rest of his private and public life.

promised to devote his remaining time in office to seeking an end to the war. McCarthy, campaigning on a peace platform, continued his electoral bid against Johnson's vice president and party stalwart, Hubert H. Humphrey.

1968: The Violence At Home

One former supporter who rejoiced at Johnson's withdrawal was Martin Luther King, Jr. He hoped that the Democratic Party would now turn to an antiwar candidate, preferably Senator Robert Kennedy of New York, JFK's younger brother, who might embrace King's new program for confronting economic inequality at home. But on April 4, 1968, during a trip to Memphis, Tennessee, in support of a strike by African American sanitation workers, King was assassinated. Allegedly, a lone gunman named James Earl Ray pulled the trigger. Ray quickly pleaded guilty and received a 99-year sentence. Subsequently, though, he recanted, insisting that he was a pawn in a larger racist conspiracy and unsuccessfully lobbying for a jury trial. When he died in 1998, Ray still insisted on his innocence, a claim roundly rejected by most legal observers.

Denzel Washington stars as Malcolm X.

© Corbis.

Released near Thanksgiving, the film opened to packed houses and took in considerably more money than Oliver Stone's *JFK* had garnered when it had debuted during the same time period only one year earlier. Despite a multimedia publicity blitz, *Malcolm X*'s box-office revenues steadily declined. Reviewers and industry spokespeople reported that the lengthy, episodic movie seemed to tax the patience and attention span of most filmgoers.

Watching *Malcolm X* on video or DVD, however, can allow a viewer to concentrate on its many stunning sequences, speeding by ones that seem to drag, and returning to scenes that may seem unclear at first viewing. *Malcolm X* remains a fascinating cinematic history of the creation of the Black Power movement and, more generally, of the social turmoil that engulfed the nation during its longest war.

As news of King's murder spread, violence swept through urban neighborhoods around the country. More than 100 cities and towns witnessed outbreaks; 39 people died; 75,000 regular and National Guard troops were called to duty. When President Johnson proclaimed Sunday, April 7, as a day of national mourning for the slain civil rights leader, parts of the nation's capital city, not far from the White House, remained ablaze.

Meanwhile, Robert Kennedy had joined the race for the 1968 Democratic presidential nomination. Campaigning at a feverish pace, Kennedy battled Eugene McCarthy in a series of primaries, hoping to gain a majority of those convention delegates who were not already pledged to Hubert Humphrey by the party's old-line bosses such as Richard J. Daley, mayor of Chicago. Then, on June 5, only minutes after winning California's primary, Kennedy fell victim to an assassin's bullets. Los Angeles police immediately arrested Sirhan Sirhan, a Palestinian immigrant, who was later convicted of the killing. Kennedy's nationally televised funeral was a disturbing reminder of King's recent murder and the assassination of his own brother five years earlier.

The violence of 1968 continued. During the Republican national convention in Miami, as presidential candidate Richard Nixon was promising to restore "law and order," racial violence, during which four people died, wracked that city. Later that summer, in Chicago, thousands of antiwar demonstrators converged on the

L I N K   T O   T H E   P A S T

Singing for Freedom: "We Shall Overcome"

Music provided a mobilizing force wherever people gathered to protest racial discrimination during the 1960s. Singing in large groups and small ones, activists built a powerful sense of community and purpose. "We Shall Overcome" became perhaps the most famous and most frequently used of the many civil rights songs. Its lyrics derived from the gospel song "I'll Overcome Some Day" (1900), and portions of the melody came from the pre–Civil War spiritual, "No More Auction Block for Me."

1. *We shall overcome*
    We shall overcome
    We shall overcome some day

CHORUS: Oh, deep in my heart
              I do believe
              We shall overcome
              Some day

2. *We'll walk hand in hand*
    We'll walk hand in hand
    We'll walk hand in hand some day

CHORUS

3. *We shall all be free*
    We shall all be free
    We shall all be free some day

CHORUS

4. *We are not afraid*
    We are not afraid
    We are not afraid some day

CHORUS

5. *We are not alone*
    We are not alone
    We are not alone
    We are not alone some day

CHORUS

6. *The whole wide world around*
    The whole wide world around
    The whole wide world around
        some day

CHORUS

1. How does the structure of this song contribute to its usefulness in civil rights demonstrations? Why did it adapt well to group singing?
2. Although this song was closely associated with the struggle to end racial discrimination, it can have larger meanings as well. In what contexts have you encountered this song?
3. How do the messages of this song compare to the views associated with the culture of the Black Power movement?

For additional sources related to this feature, visit the CD accompanying this text or the *Liberty, Equality, Power* Web site at:

http://history.wadsworth.com/murrin_LEP4e

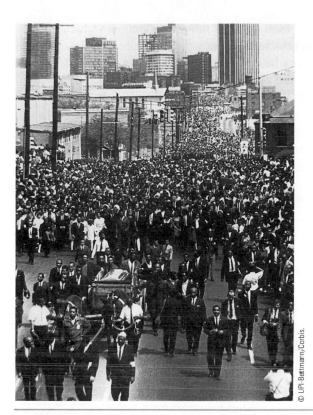

MARTIN LUTHER KING, JR.'S FUNERAL CORTEGE
Martin Luther King, Jr.'s assassination in 1968 sparked both violent protests and solemn mourning for the slain civil rights leader. Thousands of his grieving supporters followed the cart, drawn by mules, which carried King's body through the streets of his native Atlanta.

Democratic Party's convention to protest the nomination of Humphrey, who was still supporting Johnson's policy in Vietnam. Responding to acts of provocation by youthful demonstrators, who seemed to welcome confrontation, some police officers struck back with indiscriminate attacks on antiwar forces and some members of the media. Although an official report later talked about a "police riot," opinion polls showed that most Americans supported the use of force in Chicago. Hubert Humphrey easily captured the Democratic presidential nomination, but differing views of Johnson's Vietnam policy and the violence in Chicago left his party bitterly divided.

The Election of 1968

Both Humphrey and Nixon faced a serious challenge from the political right, spearheaded by Alabama's George Wallace, a southern Democrat who ran for president as a third-party candidate in 1968. A grassroots campaign eventually placed his American Independent Party on the presidential ballot in every state. Because Wallace's opposition to civil rights efforts was well established, he could

concentrate his fire on other controversial targets, particularly the counterculture and the antiwar movement. He bragged that if any "hippie" ever blocked his motorcade, "it'll be the last car he'll ever lay down in front of." Moreover, Wallace recognized that many voters were turning against Great Society programs and seeing themselves as victims of an aloof, "tax-and-spend" bureaucracy in Washington.

Wallace's candidacy hoped to tap the polarization of 1968. If neither major-party candidate won a majority of the electoral votes, the presidential election would rest with the House of Representatives, and Wallace might act as a power broker. (A president had last been selected by the House in 1824.) Hoping to court voters who wanted a U.S. victory in Vietnam, Wallace chose a militant hawk, the retired Air Force General Curtis LeMay, as his running mate. LeMay almost immediately self-destructed when he complained that too many Americans had a "phobia" about using nuclear weapons. Critical pundits lampooned Wallace and LeMay as the "Bombsey Twins."

Nixon narrowly prevailed in November. Although the former vice president won 56 percent of the electoral vote in 1968, he outpolled Humphrey in the popular vote by less than 1 percent. Humphrey had benefited when

ROBERT F. KENNEDY'S FUNERAL
An elaborately staged funeral also followed the 1968 assassination of Robert Kennedy. The shootings of the two beloved leaders—King and Kennedy—prompted widespread concern about the stability of America's social and political fabric and added to the tensions of this tumultuous year.

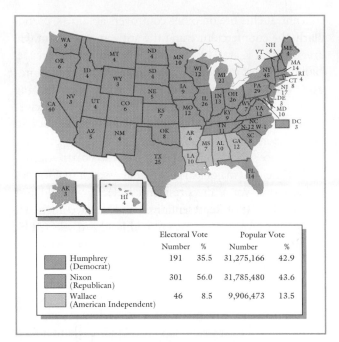

MAP 29.2 PRESIDENTIAL ELECTION, 1968
George Wallace's independent, third-party candidacy influenced the election of 1968. Compare this map with ones of earlier and later election years to see how the southern states gradually left the Democratic column and, in time, became a base of Republican power.

Johnson ordered a pause in the bombing of North Vietnam and pledged to begin peace talks in Paris, and he had helped his own cause with a belated decision to distance himself from the president's overall policy in Vietnam. Still, Humphrey carried only Texas in the South, losing the grip that the Democratic Party had held on that region since Reconstruction. George Wallace picked up 46 electoral votes, all from the Deep South, and 13.5 percent of the popular vote nationwide. Nixon won five key southern states and attracted, all across the country, those whom he called "the forgotten Americans, the nonshouters, the nondemonstrators." Hinting at a plan for ending the war in Vietnam, Nixon predicted he would restore tranquility to the domestic front, but his policies proved every bit as divisive as those of Lyndon Johnson.

🌐 The Nixon Years, 1969–1974

Raised in a modest Quaker home in southern California, Richard Nixon graduated from Whittier College, a small Quaker school. Three years of legal studies at Duke University, a hitch in the navy during the Second World War, and a job in Franklin Roosevelt's wartime bureaucracy

gave Nixon a taste of new, cosmopolitan worlds. After the war, however, he returned to a small-town California law practice before beginning a meteoric political career that took him to the House of Representatives in 1946, the Senate in 1950, and the vice presidency in 1952.

Nixon seemed to thrive on seeking out enemies, at home and abroad, and on confronting a constant series of personal challenges. He entitled an early memoir of his political life *Six Crises*. Devastated by his narrow loss to Kennedy in 1960, Nixon seemed crushed politically when, in 1962, he failed to win the California governorship. At a post-election press conference, Nixon angrily denounced the press for distorting his record and announced his retirement from politics. Although Barry Goldwater's 1964 defeat and Johnson's problems had revived Nixon's political fortunes, during his turbulent presidency (1969–74), he frequently seemed preoccupied with settling old scores and with confronting new enemies.

The Economy

Nixon's presidency coincided with a series of economic problems that had been unthinkable only a decade earlier. No simple cause can account for these difficulties, but most analyses begin with the war in Vietnam. This expensive military commitment, along with fundamental changes in the international economy, brought an end to the economic growth of the previous two decades.

Lyndon Johnson, determined to stave off defeat in Indochina without cutting Great Society programs, had concealed the rising costs of the war from the country and even from his own advisers. Johnson bequeathed Nixon a deteriorating (although still favorable) balance of trade and rising inflation rate. Between 1960 and 1965, consumer prices had risen an average of only about 1 percent per year; by 1968, the rate exceeded 4 percent.

Nixon hoped to check inflation by cutting government expenditures. He recovered some costs by reducing U.S. troop levels and expanding the use of bombing, but this strategy still drained economic resources. Moreover, although Nixon spoke about slashing domestic spending, many programs still enjoyed support in the Democratic-controlled Congress and among voters. During Nixon's first years in office, the percentage of federal funds that went to domestic programs increased steadily.

Meanwhile, unemployment soared, topping 6 percent by 1971. According to conventional wisdom, expressed in a technical economic concept called "the Phillips curve," when unemployment rises, prices should remain constant or even decline. Yet *both* unemployment and inflation were rising. Economists coined the term *stagflation* to describe this puzzling, unprecedented convergence of economic stagnation and price inflation. Along with stagflation, U.S. exports were becoming less competitive in international markets, and in 1971, for the first time in the 20th century, the United States ran a trade deficit, importing more products than it exported.

Long identified as an opponent of government regulation of the economy but now fearful of the political consequences of stagflation and the trade deficit, Nixon needed a quick cure for the nation's economic ills. In a reversal that one media commentator likened to a religious conversion, Nixon suddenly proclaimed himself a believer in governmental remedies. Hoping to relieve inflationary pressures before the 1972 election, he announced a "new economic policy" in August 1971. It mandated a 90-day freeze on any increase in wages and prices, to be followed by government monitoring to detect "excessive" increases in either.

To try to reverse the trade deficit, Nixon also revised the United States' relationship to the world monetary structure. Dating from the 1944 Bretton Woods agreement (see chapter 26), the value of the U.S. dollar had been tied to the value of gold at $35 for every ounce. This meant that the United States, in order to provide an anchor for world currencies, would exchange its dollars for gold at that rate if any other nation's central bank requested it to do so. Other countries had fixed their own exchange rates against the dollar. But U.S. trade deficits

undermined the value of the American dollar, enabling foreign banks to exchange U.S. dollars for gold at highly favorable rates.

In response to this situation, in August 1971, the Nixon administration abandoned the fixed gold-to-dollar ratio. It announced that the U.S. dollar would be free to "float" in value against the prevailing market price of gold and against all other currencies. In 1973, Nixon devalued the dollar, thereby reducing the price of American goods overseas in hopes of making them more competitive on the world market. The strategy fundamentally altered the international economic order but had little immediate impact on the deterioration of U.S. trade balances. Over the next decade, U.S. exports more than tripled in value, but imports more than quadrupled.

Social Policy

At the urging of Daniel Patrick Moynihan, a maverick Democrat who advised Nixon on domestic issues, the president pondered a drastic revision in welfare policy. Moynihan insisted that Nixon, while remaining identified as a conservative Republican, could radically change political life. After heated debates within his inner circle, Nixon unveiled his Family Assistance Plan (FAP). A complex package of different programs, FAP would replace most welfare measures, including the controversial Aid to Families with

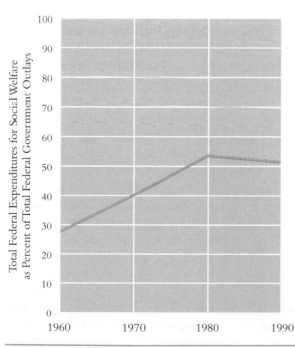

As a Percentage of Total Spending

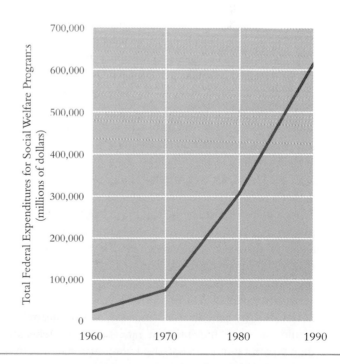

Total Expenditures

SOCIAL WELFARE SPENDING, 1960–1990

Dependent Children (AFDC), with a guaranteed annual income for all families. AFDC provided government payments to cover basic costs of care for low-income children who had lost the support of a bread-winning parent. By 1970, half of all persons in families headed by women were receiving AFDC payments.

Under Nixon's proposal, the government would guarantee a family of four an annual payment of $1,600, with the possibility of further assistance based on how much income the family earned. In one bold stroke, FAP would supplant existing welfare arrangements, which provided services and assistance *only* to those with special circumstances (such as low-income mothers with small children or people who were unemployed) with a new system of government aid for *all* low-income families. Even a family with an annual income of nearly twice the $1,600 level, according to one projection, would still benefit from Nixon's plan because of the tax refund and food stamp provisions included in the FAP proposal.

FAP attracted tepid support. Conservatives blasted it, claiming that income supplements for families that had a regularly employed, although low-paid, wage earner would be too costly. In contrast, proponents of more generous government assistance programs saw a guaranteed income of $1,600 as too miserly. The House of Representatives approved a modified version of FAP in 1970, but a Senate alliance that included people both to the right and to the left of Nixon blocked its passage. Beset by economic problems and the lingering war in Vietnam, Nixon simply abandoned FAP, and the nation's welfare system would not be comprehensively overhauled until the 1990s.

Some changes in domestic programs were enacted, however. In a significant move, Congress passed the president's revenue-sharing plan, part of his "new federalism," which returned a certain percentage of federal tax dollars to state and local governments in the form of "block grants." Instead of Washington specifying how these funds could be used, the block grant concept allowed state and local governments, within broad limits, to spend the funds as they saw fit.

The Democratic-controlled Congress also stitched together a revised social support network in the early 1970s. This patchwork arrangement included rent subsidies for people at the lowest income levels and Supplementary Security Insurance (SSI) payments to those who were elderly, blind, or disabled. The Medicare and Medicaid programs, established under Johnson's Great Society, gradually expanded during Nixon's presidency. In 1972, Social Security benefits were "indexed," which meant they would rise with the inflation rate. Less comprehensive than Nixon's FAP proposal, these congressional initiatives substantially extended the nation's income-support programs, albeit only for specific groups, especially older Americans. Between 1970 and 1980, the federal government's spending for social welfare rose from 40.1 percent of total government outlays to slightly more than 53 percent.

Environmentalism

A relatively new phenomenon, environmentalism became a significant force during Nixon's presidency; its roots reached back to the earlier conservation and preservation movements. During the first four decades of the 20th century, the conservation movement had begun to promote the "wise use" of water, forests, and farmlands by urging government to promote scientific resource management and to designate areas as national parks and forests (see chapter 21). A preservation movement—spearheaded by the Sierra Club, the Audubon Society, the Wilderness Society, and local advocacy groups—had been primarily concerned with the aesthetics of nature and had worked to preserve the natural environment in a state as pristine as possible. Lyndon's Johnson's Great Society proved to be particularly supportive of preservationism. Landmark legislation of the 1960s—the Wilderness Act of 1964, the National Wild and Scenic Rivers Act of 1968, and the National Trails Act of 1968—set aside new areas, protecting them from development. Lady Bird Johnson, the president's wife, championed a Commission on Natural Beauty that spurred the nation's growing interest in its natural habitat.

By 1970, the conservation and preservation movements had merged into a broader environmental crusade that focused on improving people's health and on maintaining an ecological balance. Accounts such as Rachel Carson's *Silent Spring* (1962) raised concern that the pesticides used in agriculture, especially DDT, threatened bird populations. Air pollution in cities such as Los Angeles became so bad that the simple act of breathing became equivalent to smoking several packs of cigarettes per day. Industrial processes polluted water systems, and atomic weapons testing and the proliferation of nuclear power plants prompted fear of overexposure to cancer-causing, radioactive materials. In response to all of these concerns, environmentalists tried to focus national attention on toxic chemicals and the adverse impact of industrial development on air, water, and soil quality. The Environmental Defense Fund, a private organization formed in 1967, took the crusade against DDT and other dangerous toxins to the courts. And in an event linked to the counterculture, environmental activists came together in 1970 for Earth Day. This one-day "happening"—which featured art, music, and countercultural theatre—aimed to raise awareness about environmental degradation and popularize the science of ecology, an area of biology concerned with the interrelationship between living organisms and their physical environments.

The Nixon administration, although not a sponsor of Earth Day, did take environmental issues seriously. The president established the Environmental Protection Agency (EPA) and signed major pieces of environmental legislation: the Resources Recovery Act of 1970 (dealing with waste management), the Clean Air Act of 1970, the Water Pollution Control Act of 1972, the Pesticides Control Act of 1972, and the Endangered Species Act of 1973. During Nixon's presidency, national parks and wilderness areas were further expanded, and a new law required that "environmental impact statements" be prepared in advance of any major government project.

The new environmental standards brought both unanticipated problems and significant improvements. The Clean Air Act's requirement for higher smokestacks for factories, for example, moved pollutants higher into the atmosphere, where they produced a dangerous by-product, "acid rain." Still, the act's restrictions on auto and smokestack emissions cleared smog out of city skies and benefited people with respiratory ailments. It reduced six major airborne pollutants by one-third in a single decade. Lead emissions into the atmosphere declined by 95 percent.

Controversies over Rights

New legislation on social and environmental concerns came against the backdrop of debate over how to define the federal government's responsibility to protect constitutional rights. The struggle to define these rights embroiled the U.S. Supreme Court in controversy.

A majority of the Justices, who supported the Great Society's political vision, sought to bring an expanding list of rights under constitutional protection. As this group charted the Court's path through the 1960s, two Eisenhower appointees, Chief Justice Earl Warren and Associate Justice William Brennan, often led the way. Although nearly all of the Warren Court's decisions involving the issue of rights drew critical fire, perhaps the most emotional cases raised claims by people accused of violent crime. *Miranda* v. *Arizona* (1966) held that the Constitution required police officers to advise anyone arrested for a felony offense of their constitutional rights to remain silent and to consult an attorney, including one provided to indigents by the government. Defenders of the decision, which inspired the famous "Miranda warning," saw it as the logical extension of settled judicial precedents; the Court's critics, in contrast, accused the Court's majority of

simply inventing rights not found in the Constitution. Amid rising public concern over crime, political conservatives made *Miranda* a symbol of the judicial "coddling" of criminals and the Warren Court's supposed disregard for constitutional law.

Richard Nixon campaigned for president as an opponent of the Warren Court and promised to appoint federal judges who would "apply" rather than "make" the law. Before the 1968 election, Chief Justice Warren announced his resignation, but Lyndon Johnson's plan to elevate his close confidante, Associate Justice Abe Fortas, stalled. Consequently, the victorious Nixon could appoint a Republican loyalist, Warren Burger, as Chief Justice. Subsequently, Nixon appointed three other Republicans—Harry Blackmun, William Rehnquist, and Lewis Powell—to the High Court.

This new Burger Court soon faced difficult rights-related cases of its own. Lawyers sympathetic to the Great Society vision advanced the controversial argument that access to adequate economic assistance from the federal government was a constitutionally protected right, one every bit as fundamental as, say, that of voting. The Supreme Court, however, rejected this claim when deciding *Dandridge* v. *Williams* (1970). A majority of Justices held that state laws capping the amount paid to welfare recipients did not violate the constitutional requirement of equal protection of the law. It drew a sharp distinction between the government's responsibility to protect the traditional liberties of all citizens, such as the right to vote and freedom of speech, and its discretionary ability to make distinctions in the administration of social-spending programs such as AFDC. In short, the Court flatly rejected the idea that welfare was a national right.

Other rights-related disputes involved health and safety. A vigorous consumer movement, initially drawing inspiration from Carson's *Silent Spring* and Ralph Nader's exposé about auto safety (*Unsafe at Any Speed*, 1965), joined with environmentalists in seeking to protect the right to safety in the workplace, the right to safe consumer products, and the right to a healthy environment. Their effort, overcoming strong opposition from many business groups, found expression in such legislation as the Occupational Safety Act of 1973, stronger consumer protection laws, and measures to protect the environment. The Burger Court invariably supported the constitutionality of health and safety laws.

At the same time, a newly energized women's rights movement pushed another set of issues. The National Organization for Women (NOW), founded in 1966, backed an Equal Rights Amendment (ERA) that would explicitly guarantee women the same legal rights as men. Easily passed by Congress in 1972 and quickly ratified by

MARCH FOR WOMEN'S RIGHTS

Demonstrations such as this one down New York City's Fifth Avenue in 1971 became a familiar part of politics during the 1960s and early 1970s. Modeled on earlier civil-rights and antiwar rallies, these marches helped focus attention on the issue of gender equality.

more than half the states, the ERA suddenly became controversial. Conservative women's groups, such as Phyllis Schlafly's "Stop ERA," charged that this change in the Constitution would undermine traditional "family values" and expose women to new hazards. Anti-ERA rallies featured children carrying signs such as "Please Don't Send My Mommy to War." As a result of such opposition, the ERA, which once seemed assured of passage, failed to attain approval from the three-quarters of states needed for ratification. Ultimately, women's groups abandoned the ERA effort in favor of using the courts to adjudicate equal rights claims on a case-by-case, issue-by-issue basis.

One of these issues, whether a woman could claim a constitutional right to terminate a pregnancy, became far more controversial than the ERA. In *Roe* v. *Wade* (1973), the Supreme Court narrowly ruled that a state law making abortion a criminal offense violated a woman's right to privacy. The *Roe* decision outraged conservatives. Rallying under the "Right to Life" banner and focusing on the rights of the unborn fetus, antiabortion groups denounced *Roe* v. *Wade*. In 1976, they succeeded in persuading Congress to ban the use of federal funds to finance abortions for women with low incomes. Standing behind the right to privacy—and behind the right of a woman to have access to a safe, medically supervised abortion—feminist groups made the issue of individual choice in reproductive decisions a principal rallying point. Invoking rights-based arguments of their own, antiabortion forces provided new support for the steadily expanding conservative wing of the Republican Party.

Richard Nixon had promised an administration that, in contrast to Lyndon Johnson's, would "bring us together."

Instead, divisions over economic policy, government spending programs, and the meaning of basic constitutional rights made Nixon's presidency a time of increasing, rather than decreasing, polarization.

🌐 Foreign Policy under Nixon and Kissinger

Even as it wrestled with divisive domestic concerns, the Nixon administration was far more preoccupied with international affairs. Henry Kissinger, a political scientist from Harvard, became Nixon's national security adviser and turned the National Security Council (NSC) into the most powerful shaper of U.S. foreign policy within the government. In 1973, Nixon appointed Kissinger as Secretary of State, a position he held until 1977. Working with Nixon, Kissinger orchestrated a grand strategy for foreign policy: détente with the Soviet Union, normalization of relations with China, and disengagement from direct military involvement in Southeast Asia and other parts of the world.

Détente

Although Nixon had built his political career on hard-line anticommunism, the Nixon-Kissinger team worked to ease tensions with the two major communist nations: the Soviet Union and China. Kissinger surmised that, as both nations began to seek favor with the United States, they might reduce their support for North Vietnam, facilitating

America's ability to withdraw from the war that was dividing the nation.

Arms-control talks took top priority in U.S.–Soviet relations. In 1969, the two superpowers opened the Strategic Arms Limitation Talks (SALT), and after several years of high-level diplomacy they signed an agreement (SALT I) that limited further development of both antiballistic missiles (ABMs) and offensive intercontinental ballistic missiles (ICBMs). SALT I's impact on the arms race was negligible because it said nothing about the number of nuclear warheads that one missile might carry. Still, the very fact that the two superpowers could conclude any pact on arms control signaled improving relations between Washington and Moscow. Moreover, to increase the possibility for new arms agreements, the Nixon administration offered the Soviets greater access to U.S. trade and technology for their faltering economy.

Nixon's overtures toward the People's Republic of China brought an even more dramatic break with the Cold War past. Supported by the China lobby, Nixon had been one of the most vocal critics of the communist regime established in China in 1949. Now, tentative conversations secretly arranged through embassies in Poland led to a slight easing of U.S. trade restrictions against China in early 1971 and then to an invitation from China for Americans to compete in a table tennis match. This much-celebrated ping-pong exhibition presaged more significant exchanges. In 1972, Nixon visited China, posing for photos with Mao Zedong and strolling along the Great Wall. Relations between the two countries remained difficult, especially over the status of Taiwan, which the United States still recognized as the legitimate government of China. A few months after Nixon's visit, however, the United Nations admitted the People's Republic as the representative of China, and in 1973 the United States and China exchanged informal diplomatic missions.

Vietnamization

In Vietnam, Nixon and Kissinger decided to start the withdrawal of U.S. ground forces (the policy called "Vietnamization") while stepping up the air war and intensifying diplomatic efforts to reach a settlement. In July 1969, the president announced the "Nixon Doctrine," which pledged that the United States would provide military assistance to anticommunist governments in Asia but would require them to provide their own combat forces. The goal of Vietnamization was the gradual removal of U.S. ground troops without accepting compromise or defeat. While officially adhering to Johnson's 1968 bombing halt over the North, Nixon and Kissinger accelerated both the ground and air wars by launching new offensives in South

Vietnam and by approving a military incursion into Cambodia, an ostensibly neutral country. The Cambodian decision underscored Kissinger's crucial role in shaping foreign policy; both Secretary of State William Rogers and Secretary of Defense Melvin Laird had counseled against such a drastic step.

The move into Cambodia set off a new wave of protest at home. Many campuses exploded in anger, and bomb threats led some colleges to close early for the 1970 summer recess. White police officers fatally shot two students at the all-black Jackson State College in Mississippi, and National Guard troops at Kent State University in Ohio fired on demonstrators and killed four students. As growing numbers of protestors took to the streets, business and political leaders became alarmed by how war-related passions were polarizing the country.

The continuing controversy over the "My Lai" incident was also spreading disillusionment about the war.

JACKSON STATE

In 1970, the violence associated with America's longest war came home. In May, police gunfire killed 2 students and wounded 15 others at Jackson State University in Mississippi. This picture was taken through a bullet-riddled window in a women's dorm.

© UPI-Bettmann/Corbis.

Shortly after the 1968 Tet episode, troops led by U.S. Lieutenant William Calley had entered the small hamlet of My Lai and shot more than 200 people, mostly women and children. This massacre of South Vietnamese civilians became public in 1969 and sparked new discussions about U.S policy. In 1971, a military court convicted Calley and, in a controversial decision, sentenced him to life imprisonment. The military was using Calley, many argued, as a scapegoat for a failed strategy that emphasized body counts. In 1974, Nixon pardoned Calley.

Meanwhile, the Nixon administration was conducting a widening war in Cambodia and Laos. Although it denied waging any such campaign, large areas of those agricultural countries were ravaged by U.S. bombing. As the number of Cambodian refugees swelled and food supplies dwindled, the communist guerrilla force in Cambodia—the Khmer Rouge—grew into a well-disciplined army. The Khmer Rouge eventually came to power and, in a murderous attempt to eliminate potential dissent, turned Cambodia into a "killing field." It murdered more than 1 million Cambodians. While Nixon continued to talk about U.S. troop withdrawals and peace negotiations with North Vietnam proceeded in Paris, the Vietnam War actually broadened into a conflict that destabilized all of Indochina.

Even greater violence was yet to come. In spring 1972, a North Vietnamese offensive approached within 30 miles of Saigon, and U.S. generals warned of imminent defeat. Nixon responded by resuming the bombing of North Vietnam and by mining its harbors. Just weeks before the November 1972 election, Kissinger again promised peace and announced a cease-fire. After the election, however, the United States unleashed even greater firepower. During the so-called Christmas bombing of December 1972, the heaviest bombardment in history, B-52 planes pounded military and civilian targets in North Vietnam around the clock.

By this time, however, much of the media, Congress, and the public had lost the desire to continue the bloodshed. Many were sickened by the violence in Asia and apprehensive about how the Nixon administration seemed to be expanding its power in the attempt to control dissent at home. Others simply decided that the United States should abandon a conflict that it seemed unable to conclude. Perhaps most important, sagging morale among troops in the field began to undermine the U.S. military's role in Indochina. Many soldiers questioned the larger purpose of their sacrifices, some refused to engage the enemy, and a few openly defied their own superiors. At home, Vietnam Veterans against the War (VVAW), a new organization, joined the antiwar coalition. During one dramatic demonstration, several thousand highly decorated combat vets returned their war medals. Testifying before Congress, a VVAW leader and later senator, John Kerry, wondered, "How do you ask a man to be the last man to die in Vietnam? How do you ask a man to be the last man to die for a mistake?"

Running out of options, Nixon proceeded with full-scale Vietnamization. In January 1973, North Vietnam and the United States signed peace accords, in Paris, which provided for the withdrawal of U.S. troops from South Vietnam. As American ground forces departed, the South Vietnamese government, headed by Nguyen Van Thieu, continued to fight, although it was growing increasingly demoralized and ineffectual.

In spring 1975, nearly two years after the Paris accords, South Vietnam's army could no longer withstand the forces of North Vietnam's skilled general Nguyen Giap. Thieu's government in Saigon collapsed, North Vietnamese armies entered South Vietnam's capital, soon to be renamed Ho Chi Minh City, while U.S. helicopters scrambled to airlift the last remaining officials out of the besieged U.S. embassy. America's longest war ended in defeat.

The Aftermath of War

Between 1960 and 1973, approximately 3.5 million American men and women served in Vietnam: 58,000 died, 150,000 were wounded, and 2,000 remained missing. In the aftermath of this costly, divisive war, Americans struggled to understand why their country failed to prevail over a small, barely industrialized nation. Those still supporting the war argued that it had been lost on the home front. They blamed an irresponsible media, a disloyal antiwar movement, and a Congress beset by a "failure of will." The war, they insisted, had been for a laudable cause; politicians, setting unrealistic limits on the military, had denied the country the means to attain victory. By contrast, those who had opposed the war stressed the overextension of American power, the misguided belief in U.S. omnipotence, the deceitfulness of governmental leaders, and the incompetence of bureaucratic processes. For them, the war had been waged in the wrong place for the wrong reasons. The human costs to the United States, and to the people of Indochina, outweighed any possible gain.

Regardless of their position on the war, most Americans seemed to agree on one proposition: There must be "no more Vietnams." The United States should not undertake another military involvement that lacked clear and compelling political objectives, demonstrable public support, and the provision of adequate means to accomplish the goal. Eventually, the people who wanted to aggressively reassert U.S. power in the world criticized this widely held position as "the Vietnam Syndrome."

Expanding the Nixon Doctrine

Although the Nixon Doctrine initially applied to the Vietnamization of the war in Indochina, Richard Nixon and Henry Kissinger extended its premise to other areas of the world. In molding foreign policy, Kissinger relied increasingly on pro-U.S. anticommunist allies to police their own regional spheres. Kissinger made it clear that the United States would not dispatch troops to oppose revolutionary insurgencies but would generously aid anticommunist regimes or factions willing to fight their own battles.

During the early 1970s, U.S. Cold War strategy came to rely on supporting staunchly anticommunist regional powers. These included nations such as Iran under Shah Reza Pahlavi, South Africa with its apartheid regime, and Brazil with its repressive military dictatorship. All of these countries built large military establishments trained by the United States. U.S. military assistance, together with covert CIA operations, also incubated and protected anticommunist dictatorships in South Korea, the Philippines, and much of Latin America. U.S. arms sales to the rest of the world skyrocketed from $1.8 billion in 1970 to $15.2 billion six years later. In one of its most controversial foreign policies, the Nixon administration employed covert action against the elected socialist government of Salvador Allende Gossens in Chile in 1970. After Allende took office, Kissinger gave top priority to encouraging destabilization of his government, and in 1973 Allende was overthrown by the Chilean military, who immediately suspended democratic rule and announced that Allende had committed suicide.

Critics charged that the United States, in the name of anticommunism, too often wedded its diplomatic fortunes to questionable covert actions and unpopular military governments. In 1975, Senator Frank Church conducted widely watched Senate hearings into possible abuses by the CIA (including the action in Chile). Supporters of the Nixon Doctrine, however, applauded the administration's systematic support of anticommunist allies. In many circles, Nixon received high marks for a pragmatic foreign policy that combined détente toward the communist giants with containment directed toward the spread of revolutionary regimes.

The Wars of Watergate

Nixon's presidency ultimately collapsed as a result of fateful decisions made in the president's Oval Office. Nixon arrived at the White House inclined to see nearly every person and institution in Washington as his enemy. He pressed the Internal Revenue Service (IRS) to harass prominent Democrats with expensive audits and suspected the IRS of disloyalty when it seemed to be moving too slowly on his request. Nixon's enmity focused on antiwar activists and old political opponents, but likely allies, such as J. Edgar Hoover, the staunchly conservative director of the FBI, could also come under suspicion. Isolated behind a close-knit group of advisers, Nixon ultimately created his own secret intelligence unit, which set up shop in the White House.

This group quickly acted on the president's behalf. During summer 1971, Daniel Ellsberg, a dissident member of the national security bureaucracy, leaked to the press a top-secret history of U.S. involvement in the Vietnam War, subsequently known as the "Pentagon Papers." Nixon responded by seeking, unsuccessfully, a court injunction to stop publication of the study and, more ominously, by unleashing his secret intelligence unit, now dubbed "the plumbers," to stop information leaks to the media. Looking for something that might discredit Ellsberg, the plumbers burglarized his psychiatrist's office. Thus began a series of "dirty tricks" and outright crimes, often financed by funds illegally solicited for Nixon's 1972 reelection campaign, which would culminate in the constitutional crisis known as "Watergate."

The Election of 1972

Nixon's political strategists worried that economic troubles and the war in Vietnam might deny the president another term. Creating a campaign organization separate from that of the Republican Party, with the ironic acronym of CREEP (Committee to Re-elect the President), they secretly raised millions of dollars, much of it from illegal contributions.

As the 1972 campaign proceeded, Nixon's chances of reelection dramatically improved. An assassin's bullet crippled George Wallace. Senator Edmund Muskie of Maine, initially Nixon's leading Democratic challenger, made a series of blunders (some of them, perhaps, precipitated by Republican "dirty tricksters") that derailed his campaign. Eventually, Senator George McGovern of South Dakota, an outspoken opponent of the Vietnam War but a lackluster campaigner, won the Democratic nomination.

McGovern never seriously challenged Nixon. He called for higher taxes on the wealthy, a guaranteed minimum income for all Americans, amnesty for Vietnam War draft resisters, and the decriminalization of marijuana—positions that angered many old-line Democrats. In foreign policy, McGovern called for deep cuts in defense spending and for vigorous efforts to achieve peace in Vietnam—proposals that Nixon successfully portrayed as signs of weakness.

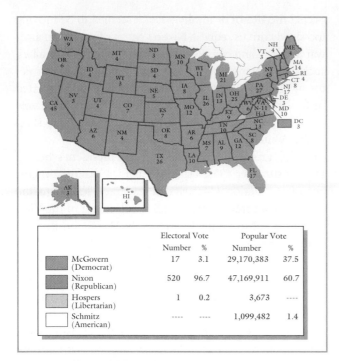

MAP 29.3 PRESIDENTIAL ELECTION, 1972

This map shows what is commonly called a landslide election. Less than two years later, however, Nixon would resign from the presidency to avoid facing impeachment charges connected to his role in the Watergate burglary and other "dirty tricks" associated with his presidency.

Nixon Pursued

In achieving victory, however, the president's supporters left a trail of crime and corruption that cut short Nixon's second term. In June 1972, a surveillance team with links to both CREEP and the White House had been arrested while fine-tuning some eavesdropping equipment it had installed earlier in the Democratic Party's headquarters in Washington's Watergate office complex. In public, Nixon's spokespeople dismissed the Watergate break-in as an insignificant "third-rate burglary"; privately, the president and his inner circle immediately launched a cover-up.

They paid hush money to the Watergate burglars and had the CIA falsely warn the FBI that any investigation into the break-in would jeopardize national security. Nixon succeeded in containing the political damage through the 1972 election, but events soon overtook him.

While reporters from the *Washington Post* pursued the taint of scandal around the White House, Congress and the federal judiciary sought evidence of legal violations during the 1972 campaign. In January 1973, Judge John Sirica, a Republican appointee who was presiding over the trial of the Watergate burglars, refused to accept their claim that neither CREEP nor the White House been involved in the break-in. While Sirica pushed for more information, Senate leaders convened a special Watergate Committee, headed by North Carolina's conservative Democratic Senator Sam Ervin, to investigate events surrounding November's election. Meanwhile, federal prosecutors uncovered evidence that seemed to link key administration and White House figures, including John Mitchell, Nixon's former attorney general and later the head of CREEP, to illegal activities.

Nixon's difficulties grew steadily worse during 1973. Under unyielding pressure from Judge Sirica, one of the Watergate burglars finally broke his silence. In May, he joined other witnesses who testified before the Senate's Watergate Committee about various illegal activities committed by CREEP and the White House. Senator Ervin called Nixon's closest aides before the committee, and the hearings became the biggest political soap opera since the Army-McCarthy hearings of 1954. Testimony from John Dean, who had been Nixon's chief legal counsel, linked the president to an attempt to cover up Watergate and to other illegal activities. The president steadfastly denied Dean's charges. (In 2003, a former Nixon aide admitted to having heard Nixon approve the initial break-in at Democratic headquarters, a claim that still lacks any corroboration.)

Along the way, though, Senate investigators discovered that a voice-activated taping machine had recorded every conversation held in Nixon's Oval Office. The "White House Tapes" made it possible to determine whether the president or Dean, Nixon's primary accuser, was lying. Nixon claimed "executive privilege" to keep the tapes from being released to other branches of government, but Judge Sirica, Archibald Cox (who had been appointed as a special, independent prosecutor in the Watergate case), and Congress all moved to gain access to the tapes.

If Nixon's own problems were not damaging enough, his vice president, the combative Spiro Agnew, resigned in October 1973 after pleading "no contest" to income-tax evasion. Agnew's fiery speeches had contributed to the cultural polarization of the time. "The mature and sensitive people of this country," he had proclaimed at a 1969

Nixon won an easy victory in November. McGovern lost traditional Democrats without attracting a significant number of new or disaffected voters. The president received the electoral college ballots of all but one state and the District of Columbia, won more than 60 percent of the popular vote, and carried virtually every traditionally Democratic voting group except African Americans. His margin of victory was one of the largest in U.S. history, only slightly below that of Johnson's 1964 landslide. Although the 26th Amendment, ratified one year before the election, had lowered the voting age to 18, relatively few of the newly enfranchised voters cast ballots.

dinner speech to fellow Republicans, "must realize that their freedom of protest is being exploited by avowed anarchists and communists who detest everything about this country and want to destroy it." Four years later, Agnew accepted a plea-bargain arrangement to avoid prosecution for having accepted illegal kickbacks while he was in Maryland politics. Acting under the 25th Amendment (ratified in 1967), Nixon appointed—and both houses of Congress confirmed—Representative Gerald Ford of Michigan, a Republican Party stalwart, as the new vice president.

Nixon's Final Days

During summer 1974, watchdogs of the nation's legal-constitutional system closed in on Nixon, and his attempts to sidetrack these pursuers only rebounded against him. During the previous autumn, for example, Nixon had clumsily orchestrated the firing of Archibald Cox, hoping to prevent him from gaining access to the White House tapes. When this rash action raised a public outcry—the affair came to be known as Nixon's "Saturday Night Massacre"—the president was obliged to appoint another, equally tenacious independent prosecutor, Leon Jaworski. Similarly, Nixon's own release of edited, and occasionally garbled, transcripts of a series of Watergate-related conversations merely prompted new demands for the original tape recordings. Finally, by proclaiming that he would obey only a "definitive" Supreme Court decision, Nixon all but invited the justices to deliver a unanimous ruling on the question of the tapes. On July 24, 1974, the Court did just that in the case of *U.S. v. Nixon.* All of the justices agreed that Nixon's claim of "executive privilege" over the tapes could not justify his refusal to release evidence needed in a criminal investigation. The Judiciary Committee of the House of Representatives prepared for a vote on impeachment.

By this time, the Nixon presidency had effectively come to an end. Only a few loyalists remained to defend Nixon. After nearly a full week of televised deliberations, a majority of the House Judiciary Committee voted three formal articles of impeachment against the president for obstruction of justice, violation of constitutional liberties, and refusal to produce evidence requested during the impeachment process. Nixon boasted that he would fight these accusations before the Senate, the body authorized by the Constitution (Article I, Section 3) to render a verdict of guilty or innocent after the House votes impeachment.

Nixon's aides, however, were already orchestrating his departure. One of his own attorneys had discovered that a tape Nixon had been withholding contained the long-sought "smoking gun." It confirmed that during a 1972

conversation, Nixon had agreed to a plan by which the CIA would advance the fraudulent claim of national security in order to stop the FBI from investigating the Watergate burglary. At this point, Nixon's own secretary of defense ordered military commanders to ignore any order from the president, the constitutional commander-in-chief, unless the secretary had countersigned it. Abandoned by almost every prominent Republican and confronted by a Senate prepared to vote him guilty on the impeachment charges, Nixon went on television on August 8, 1974, to announce his resignation. On August 9, Gerald Ford became the nation's 38th president.

In 1974, most people told pollsters that Watergate was one of the most grave crises in the history of the republic and that the Nixon administration had posed a serious threat to constitutional government. As time passed, though, the Watergate illegalities and Nixon's forced resignation faded from popular memory. Opinion polls conducted on the 20th anniversary of Nixon's resignation suggested that most Americans only dimly recalled the Watergate episode.

One reason for this may be that although nearly a dozen members of the Nixon administration—including its chief law enforcement officer, John Mitchell—were convicted of criminal activities, the president avoided prosecution. Only one month after Nixon's resignation, Gerald Ford granted Nixon an unconditional presidential pardon. The nation was spared the spectacle of witnessing a former president undergoing a lengthy, perhaps divisive trial; but it was also denied an authoritative accounting, in a court of law, of the full range of Nixon's misdeeds. Although his self-serving memoirs failed to remove the cloud from him or his presidency, Nixon eventually did regain some stature by writing a series of popular "how-to" books on the conduct of U.S. foreign policy. Every president who followed him in office attended Nixon's 1994 funeral.

Another reason for the fading memory of the underside of Nixon's presidency may be the media's penchant for linking the Watergate label to nearly every political scandal of the post-Nixon era. The suffix *-gate* became attached to grave constitutional episodes (such as Ronald Reagan's "Iran-Contragate" affair) and to the most trivial of political events (such as the brief "Nannygate" flap that doomed an attorney-general nomination in 1993). And in light of the impeachment trial of President Bill Clinton in 1998, the Watergate events of 1973 and 1974 could seem, to many people, as just another example of partisan political warfare rather than as a uniquely serious constitutional crisis.

Finally, what historian Stanley Kutler calls the "wars of Watergate" increasingly seem only one part of the upheaval that surrounded the conflict in Vietnam. In this sense, the Watergate episode tends to blend into a broader picture of political, social, economic, and cultural turmoil that accompanied U.S. involvement in the nation's longest war.

Conclusion

The power of the national government grew steadily during the 1960s. Lyndon Johnson's Great Society provided a blueprint for expanding domestic programs and waging a War on Poverty. Johnson's escalation of the war in Vietnam, a struggle that consumed more of the nation's wealth and energy, eventually dominated his presidency.

This growth of governmental power prompted divisive debates that polarized the country. During Johnson's term, both the war effort and the economy faltered, top leaders became discredited, and his presidency collapsed. Johnson's Republican successor, Richard Nixon, let loose an abuse of power that ultimately drove him from office in disgrace. The hopes of the early 1960s—that the U.S. government could promote liberty and equality both in America and throughout the rest of the world—ended in frustration.

The era of America's longest war was a time of high political passions, of generational and racial conflict, of differing definitions of patriotism. It saw the slow convergence of an antiwar movement, along with the emergence of youthful dissent, of Black Power, of "women's liberation," and of contests over what constituted the basic rights of Americans. Different groups invoked different explanations of the failures of both the Great Society and the war effort, and the divisions from these years shaped the fault lines of politics for years to come. Most Americans became much more skeptical, many even cynical, about further enlarging the power of the federal government in the name of expanding liberty and equality.

SUGGESTED READINGS

On Lyndon Johnson, see **Robert J. Dallek**, *Flawed Giant: Lyndon Johnson and His Times, 1961–1973* (1998). **Irving Bernstein**, *Guns or Butter: The Presidency of Lyndon Johnson* (1996) is a detailed synthesis.

The many outstanding overviews of U.S. involvement in Vietnam include **George Herring**, *America's Longest War: The United States and Vietnam, 1950–1975* (rev. ed., 2001); **Robert D. Schulzinger**, *A Time for War: The United States and Vietnam, 1941–1975* (1997); **Robert J. McMahon**, *The Limits of Empire: The United States and Southeast Asia Since World War II* (1999); **David Kaiser**, *American Tragedy: Kennedy, Johnson, and the Origins of the Vietnam War* (2000); and **Fredrik Logevall**, *The Origins of the Vietnam War* (2001). **Christian G. Appy**, *Working-Class War: American Combat Soldiers and Vietnam* (1993) focuses on soldiers, and his *Patriots: The Vietnam War Remembered from All Sides* (2003) provides a wider range of perspectives.

The social and cultural ferment of the 1960s can be surveyed, from diverse vantage points, in **David W. Levy**, *The Debate over Vietnam* (rev. ed., 1994); **Lynn Spigel and Michael Curtain**, *The Revolution Wasn't Televised: Sixties Television and Social Conflict* (1997); **Maurice Isserman and Michael Kazin**, *America Divided: The Civil War of the 1960s* (1999); and **Edward K. Spann and David L. Anderson, eds.,** *Democracy's Children: The Young Rebels of the 1960s and the Power of Ideals* (2003). On the civil rights movement, **Taylor Branch** continues his multivolume history with *Pillar of Fire: America in the King Years, 1963–1965* (1998), while **William L. Van Deburg,** *New Day in Babylon: The Black Power Movement and American Culture, 1965–1975* (1992) examines the emergence of the Black Power movement.

Different sides of the women's movement emerge from **Sara Evans**, *Personal Politics: The Roots of Women's Liberation in the Civil Rights Movement and the New Left* (1979); **Alice Echols**, *Daring to Be Bad: Radical Feminism in America, 1967–75* (1990); and **Susan Hartman**, *The Other Feminists: Activists in the Liberal Establishment* (1999). The background to the influential *The Feminine Mystique* (1963) emerges in **Daniel Horowitz**, *Betty Friedan and the Making of the Feminine Mystique: The American Left, the Cold War, and Modern Feminism* (1998).

For a series of very useful, encyclopedia-style sketches, see **David R. Farber and Beth Bailey, eds.,** *The Columbia Guide to America in the 1960s* (2001).

AMERICAN JOURNEY ONLINE
AND
 INFOTRAC COLLEGE EDITION

Visit the source collections at www.ajaccess.wadsworth.com and
infotrac.thomsonlearning.com and use the Search function with
the following key terms to explore documents, images, audio
and video clips, articles, and commentary related to the material
in this chapter.

Vietnam War	Sierra Club
The Great Society	Audobon Society
Lyndon B. Johnson	Rachel Carson
Civil Rights Act of 1964	*Silent Spring*
Gulf of Tonkin Resolution	Environmental Protection Agency
Malcolm X	Détente
Black Power movement	Vietnamization
Voting Rights Act	Kent State
Antiwar demonstrations	Jackson State
The Beatles	Equal Rights Amendment (ERA)
Tet Offensive	*Roe* v. *Wade*
Civil Rights Act of 1968	Watergate
Richard M. Nixon	Gerald R. Ford
Environmentalism	

GRADE AIDS

Visit the Liberty Equality Power Companion Web Site for resources specific to
this textbook: http://history.wadsworth.com/murrin LEP4e

The CD in the back of this book and the U.S. History Resource Center at
http://history.wadsworth.com/u.s./ offer a variety of tools to help you succeed in
this course, including access to quizzes; images; documents; interactive simulations,
maps, and timelines; movie explorations; and a wealth of other sources.

Chapter 30

Economic and Social Change in the Late 20th Century

21ST-CENTURY LOS ANGELES
Billboards such as these, one in English and the other in Chinese, showed how the advertising industry, like other American institutions, adjusted to the growing linguistic diversity.

CHAPTER OUTLINE

The period after 1970 marked a watershed in American life. Although the 1960s—a time of political assassinations, a lengthy foreign war, and domestic turmoil—had once seemed a period peculiar for its upheavals, the decades that followed brought even more far-reaching, although less violent, changes. Increasing immigration, urbanization, and movement of people southward and westward altered the demographics of American life. The continuing transformation from manufacturing to postindustrial employment swept through the economy. A digital revolution transfigured systems of information and entertainment. Social movements associated with women's rights, gay pride, racial and ethnic identity, and the New Right affected both politics and how people defined themselves as Americans.

CHAPTER FOCUS

- What major demographic trends characterized the last three decades of the 20th century, and how did they change American life?
- What were the most important technological and economic changes? How did these create both new problems and new possibilities?
- How did new forms of media change the ways in which people received information and entertainment?
- How have the various social movements of the post-1960s era affected social life, culture, and the ways in which people see their own personal identities?

A Changing People

America's population changed dramatically during the closing decades of the 20th century, becoming older, more urban, and more ethnically and racially diverse. Moreover, the nation's center of power continued shifting away from the Northeast and toward the South and West.

An Aging Population

After about 1970, the birthrate slowed significantly. During the 1950s, the height of the baby boom, the population had grown by 1.8 percent per year; during the 1970s and 1980s, even with a new wave of immigration and longer life expectancy, the growth rate slowed to about 1 percent per year. Birthrates sank to their lowest levels in U.S. history, except for the Great Depression decade of the 1930s. Most young people were delaying marriage until well into their twenties, and the percentage of never-married men and women in their mid-thirties more than tripled between 1970 and 2000. By 2002, the median age of first marriage for women was higher than at any time since statistics began to be collected in the late 19th century.

As a result of a declining birthrate, a rising life expectancy, and the aging of the huge baby boom generation, the median age of the population rose steadily. In 1970, at the height of student protest, the median age of Americans was 28; by 2000 it had risen to 35. Advertising agencies and television programs turned to midlife appeals. As aging baby boomers pondered retirement, policy makers worried that the projected Social Security and Medicare payouts would bequeath a staggering economic burden to the smaller post–baby boom generation of workers. Trend-watchers of the 1960s had talked of a "youth revolt"; at the beginning of the 21st century, they pondered the "graying of America."

The Rise of the Sunbelt

Not only did population growth slow, but the regional pattern of population distribution began to shift political and economic power. Historically, the country's development and its European settlers had generally proceeded from east to west. The nation's political capital was in the East, and so were its financial, industrial, and cultural centers. After 1970, however, 90 percent of the nation's population growth occurred in the South and the West. The 1980 census reported for the first time that more Americans lived in the South and the West than in the North and the East. Nevada, California, Florida, Arizona, and Alaska (after 1959) became the fastest-growing states, and by 2000 more than 1 in 10 Americans lived in California.

CHRONOLOGY

1965	Congress passes Immigration Act of 1965
1968	Indian Bill of Rights enacted by Congress
1969	The Stonewall Inn raid inaugurates new phase in gay and lesbian activism
1970	Congressional Black Caucus organized
1973	*Roe v. Wade* decision upholds women's right to abortion
1975	National Conservative Action Political Committee formed
1980	Microsoft licenses its first personal computer software
1981	MTV and CNN debut
1985	Supreme Court rules that home taping of TV programs does not violate copyright law
1986	Immigration Reform and Control Act toughens laws against employing undocumented immigrants • Supreme Court holds that sexual harassment qualifies as discrimination
1987	Alan Bloom's *Closing of the American Mind* published
1988	Congress enacts Indian Gaming Regulation Act • Fox television network debuts
1990	Immigration Act revises conditions for admittance • Census designates "Asian or Pacific Islanders" as single, pan-Asian category
1991	Clarence Thomas confirmation hearings highlight issue of sexual harassment • Catch-phrase "surfing the Internet" is coined
1993	Cesar Chavez dies • Number of Internet sites passes the 100,000 mark
1995	Million Man March takes place in Washington, D.C. • Dial-in Internet services begin • O. J. Simpson acquitted of murder
1996	Opponents of affirmative action pass Proposition 209 in California
1997	Golfer Tiger Woods wins Masters
1998	E-commerce begins in earnest • Daimler buys out Chrysler Motors
1999	E-commerce and dot-com stocks surge
2000	Last census of 20th century conducted • Many dot-com enterprises collapse
2001	People classified as "non-Hispanic whites" no longer a majority of California's population • America Online merges with Time-Warner

During the 1990s, Nevada enlarged its population by an astonishing 66 percent.

This population shift tilted the regional balance of national political power. In both 1990 and 2000, California gained eight seats in the House of Representatives, Florida added six, New York lost five, and several other northeastern states lost two or three. The focus of presidential

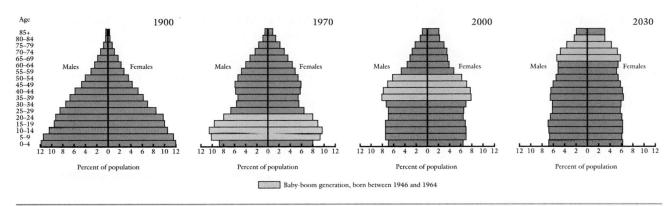

Age
85+
80–84
75–79
70–74
65–69
60–64
55–59
50–54
45–49
40–44
35–39
30–34
25–29
20–24
15–19
10–14
5–9
0–4

| 1900 | 1970 | 2000 | 2030 |

Males   Females

12 10 8 6 4 2 0 2 4 6 8 10 12

Percent of population

Baby-boom generation, born between 1946 and 1964

THE AGING OF AMERICA

Source: U.S. Census Bureau. Adapted from C. L. Himes, "Elderly Americans," *Population Bulletin 2002*, 56(4): p. 4.

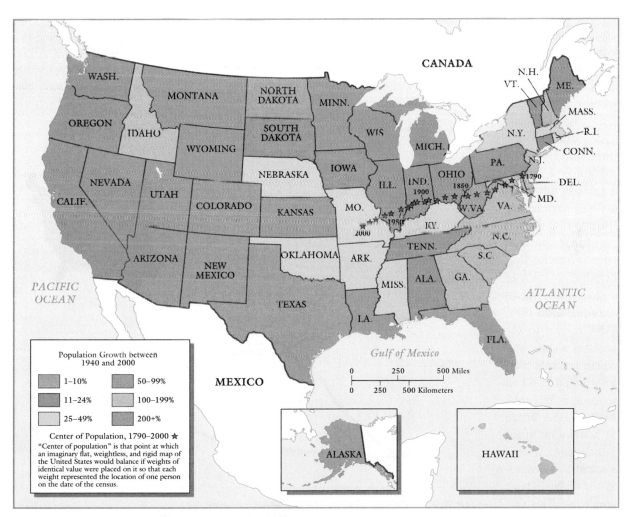

Population Growth between 1940 and 2000

- 1–10%
- 11–24%
- 25–49%
- 50–99%
- 100–199%
- 200+%

Center of Population, 1790–2000 ★

"Center of population" is that point at which an imaginary flat, weightless, and rigid map of the United States would balance if weights of identical value were placed on it so that each weight represented the location of one person on the date of the census.

MAP 30.1   POPULATION SHIFTS TOWARD THE SUNBELT

In the era after the Second World War, Americans gravitated toward the South and West. Which states grew the fastest? What might be some of the causes and consequences of such populations shifts?

 View an animated version of this map or related maps at http://history.wadsworth.com/murrin_LEP4e.

politics shifted from the northeastern states to Florida, Texas, and California.

Many reasons accounted for this demographic shift. One was the availability of affordable air-conditioning for homes and offices. Another was the expansion of tourism and the proliferation of new retirement communities in Nevada, California, Arizona, and Florida. Also, lower labor costs and the absence of strong unions prompted manufacturers to build new plants and relocate old ones in the Sunbelt. High-tech industries, initially tied to Cold War military-industrial spending and to the computer revolution, flourished in the Sunbelt. Santa Clara County, a once rural area near San Francisco, exemplified the trend. Experiencing spectacular growth in its new semiconductor industry and network of electronics-related suppliers, this locale came to be called Silicon Valley. It doubled its population each decade after 1940 and boasted one of the highest median family incomes in the country.

Government spending on the space program also helped shift research and technology to the Sunbelt. After the Soviet Union launched its Sputnik satellites in 1957, the United States stepped up its own space program under the newly formed National Aeronautics and Space Administration (NASA). In 1961, President Kennedy announced plans for the Apollo program, promising a manned mission to the moon by 1970. In July 1969, astronaut Neil Armstrong stepped from a spacecraft onto the lunar surface, planted the American flag, and gathered 47 pounds of rocks for later study. Apollo flights continued until 1972, when NASA turned to the development of a space station, an earth-orbiting platform from which to conduct experiments and research. In the 1980s, NASA began launching a series of "space shuttles," manned craft that served as scientific laboratories and could be flown back to Earth for reuse. This progression of ever more complicated initiatives in space technology, directed from NASA installations in Texas

and Florida, spurred economic development in the Sunbelt states.

New Immigration

Another reason for the sharp rise in the Sunbelt's population was a dramatic increase in immigration. Before 1960, most immigrants had come from Europe and entered the country through the cities of the Northeast. By 2000, however, only 5 million of America's foreign-born population had come from Europe while 26 million had arrived from countries in Asia, Africa, Oceania, and Latin America. These new first- and second-generation immigrants rapidly changed the face of America.

The largest number of non-European immigrants came from Mexico. Many Americans of Mexican ancestry, of course, were hardly recent arrivals; perhaps 80,000 Mexicans were living in the Southwest when the United States annexed northern Mexico in 1848. Immigration into the United States, however, became increasingly significant during the 20th century, spurred by the Mexican Revolution after 1910 (see chapter 24) and responding to U.S. labor shortages during the two world wars and

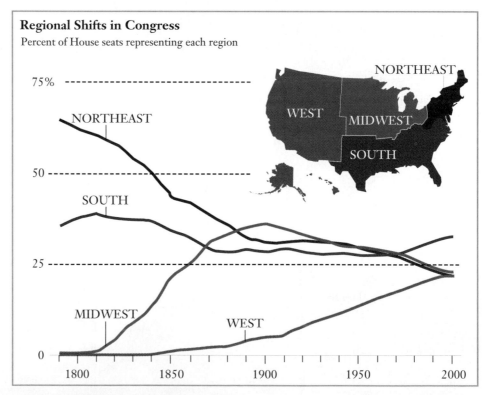

Regional Shifts in Congress
Percent of House seats representing each region

MAP 30.2 REGIONAL SHIFTS IN CONGRESS
This map and chart show the changing regional balance in the House of Representatives. Which regions have gained and lost the most political power? Which region is now strongest in the House?

Source: Clerk of the House.

the Korean conflict. In every decade after the Second World War, both legal and undocumented immigration from Mexico rose substantially. Many migrants came as seasonal agricultural workers; many others formed permanent communities. Ninety percent of all Mexican Americans lived in the Southwest, primarily Texas and California.

Although Mexican Americans constituted the majority of the Spanish-speaking population, Puerto Ricans were more numerous on the East Coast. The United States had annexed Puerto Rico after the Spanish-American War of 1898 (see chapter 22) and in 1917 had granted U.S. citizenship to its inhabitants. Puerto Ricans, therefore, were not really immigrants but could come and go freely from island to mainland. Before the Second World War, the Puerto Rican population in the United States was small and centered in New York City. After the war, however, ingress rose significantly (see chapter 28). Sizable Puerto Rican communities developed in Chicago and in industrial cities in New England and Ohio. U.S. economic problems during the 1970s decreased migration from Puerto Rico and increased the number of people who returned to the island, but trends reversed after the 1980s. By 2000, the Puerto Rican population on the U.S. mainland had grown to about 3 million, compared to a population of nearly 4 million in Puerto Rico.

Cubans began immigrating in large numbers as a result of Fidel Castro's revolution. In 1962, the U.S. Congress designated Cubans fleeing from Castro's regime as refugees eligible for admittance. Although initially these immigrants came largely from the middle and upper classes, during the next 30 years, more than 800,000 Cubans from every strata of society came to the United States. They gradually spread northward into many major American cities, but their greatest impact came in South Florida. Sociologists called Miami a "true ethnic enclave," a community that provided cradle-to-grave Cuban-owned services for residents of Cuban origin. An agreement with Castro in 1995 brought the first U.S. restrictions on the flow of immigrants from Cuba. By 2000, however, about half of all Miamians were of Cuban descent.

At the turn of the 21st century, the number of Spanish-speaking people in the United States totaled more than in all but four countries of Latin America, and 16 million Americans had been born in a Latin American country. Los Angeles was the second largest "Mexican city," after Mexico City; its Salvadoran population was about the same as that of San Salvador. More Puerto Ricans lived in New York City than in San Juan, and the Big Apple's Dominican population equaled that of Santo Domingo. The most popular name for baby boys in California and Texas was José.

LITTLE HAVANA
Vibrant ethnic neighborhoods, such as Miami's "Little Havana," reflected the nation's new, multicultural composition at the end of the 20th century.

Postwar changes in official U.S. immigration policy not only facilitated this growth of Latin American–born populations but also contributed to a rapid increase in people born in Asia (more than 8 million in 2000) and in Africa (nearly 1 million in 2000). Several immigration acts were the most important in establishing new rules for entry.

The Immigration Act of 1965, one of the least controversial but ultimately most important pieces of President Lyndon Johnson's Great Society legislation, sharply altered national immigration policy. Since the 1920s, rates of immigration had been determined by quotas based on national origins (see chapter 24). The 1965 act ended these quotas. Instead, the law placed a ceiling of 20,000 immigrants for every country, gave preference to those with close family ties in the United States, and accorded priority to people with special skills and those classified as "refugees." Although largely unforeseen at the time, this legislation laid the basis not only for a resumption of high-volume immigration but also for a substantial shift in region of origin. Under this new act, large numbers of people immigrated from areas such as Korea, China, the

Philippines, the Dominican Republic, Colombia, and the Middle East.

In the aftermath of the Vietnam War, Presidents Gerald Ford and Jimmy Carter facilitated the admittance of many Vietnamese, Cambodians, Laotians, and Hmong (an ethnically distinct people who inhabited lands extending across the borders of these three Asian countries). Their goal was to permit resettlement of people who had assisted the United States during the war and whose families were consequently in peril.

In response to the growing number of refugees seeking admission to the United States, Congress passed the Refugee Act of 1980. It specified that political refugees, "those fleeing overt persecution," could be admitted but that people seeking simply to improve their economic lot could be denied entry. In practice, the terms "political" and "economic" tended to be interpreted so that people leaving communist regimes were admitted but those fleeing right-wing dictatorships were turned away or deported. For example, Cubans and Soviet Jews were admitted, but Haitians were often denied immigrant status. (The number of undocumented Haitians entering the United States, however, rose rapidly.) Many Guatemalans and Salvadorans, hoping to escape repressive military governments backed by the United States during the 1980s, stood little chance of being admitted as legal immigrants. Thousands of immigrants from all over Central America, however, entered illegally to look for work. Some were helped during the 1980s by a church-based "sanctuary movement" that opposed U.S. policies in Central America. Most, however, made their way alone across the increasingly porous border into the United States.

Immigration policy became a major political issue during the mid-1980s, and Congress passed a law designed

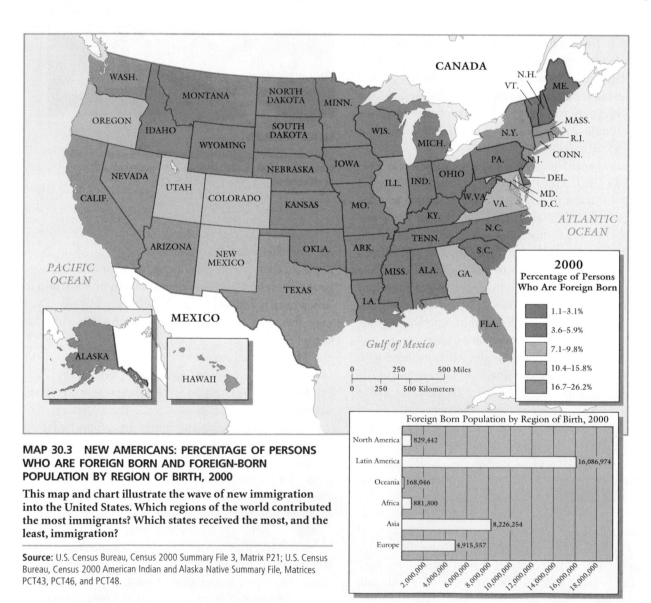

MAP 30.3   NEW AMERICANS: PERCENTAGE OF PERSONS WHO ARE FOREIGN BORN AND FOREIGN-BORN POPULATION BY REGION OF BIRTH, 2000

This map and chart illustrate the wave of new immigration into the United States. Which regions of the world contributed the most immigrants? Which states received the most, and the least, immigration?

Source: U.S. Census Bureau, Census 2000 Summary File 3, Matrix P21; U.S. Census Bureau, Census 2000 American Indian and Alaska Native Summary File, Matrices PCT43, PCT46, and PCT48.

to tighten enforcement procedures. The Immigration Reform and Control Act of 1986 imposed stricter penalties on businesses employing undocumented workers and granted residency to people who were able to prove that they had been living in the United States since 1982. Although this measure may have temporarily reduced the number of undocumented immigrants entering the country, its effectiveness soon dwindled, and illegal immigration continued to soar.

The booming economy of the 1990s acted as a magnet for new immigrants and, with prosperity and labor shortages, fear of newcomers abated along with political pressures for stronger controls. Old sources of illegal immigration from Latin America and new ones, especially from Asia, continued to transform the American population. Another Immigration Act in 1990 raised the number of immigrants legally admitted on the basis of special job skills or the investment capital they could bring into the United States.

California was the state perhaps most changed by the new immigration of the late 20th century: It became a microcosm of world cultures. Fewer than half of Los Angeles schoolchildren were proficient in English, and some 80 different languages were spoken in L.A. homes. In 1980, 8 of every 10 Californians had been classified as non-Hispanic whites. In 2001, however, this group no longer constituted a majority; in fact, there was no ethnic majority at all. Like the wave of immigration that had peaked shortly after 1900, the immigration of the late 20th century roused not only ethnic rivalries and tensions but also hope and cooperation.

Urbanization and Suburbanization

Urban-suburban demographics, too, were in a state of flux. At the end of the 20th century, more than 80 percent of Americans lived in metropolitan areas. With the overall population growing, the relationship between central city and adjacent suburbs changed. The suburbs melded into "urban corridors," metropolitan strips often running between older cities, as between Los Angeles and San Diego, Washington and Baltimore, Seattle and Tacoma. Suburbs also sprouted "edge cities," shopping and business centers such as the Galleria area west of Houston, the Perimeter

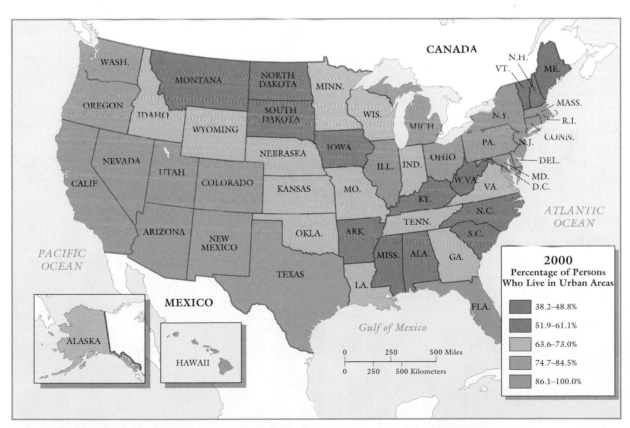

MAP 30.4   URBANIZATION: PERCENTAGE OF PERSONS WHO LIVE IN URBAN AREAS IN 2000
More and more Americans moved to cities in the postwar period. Which states had the most urban dwellers? Which states were the most rural? What might be some economic and political consequences of an urban/rural division?

Source: U.S. Census Bureau, Census 2000 Summary File 1, Matrices P1 and P2.

Center south of Atlanta, and Tysons Corner near Washington, D.C. Outlying areas continued to compete with inner cities for businesses, jobs, and residents.

Meanwhile, central cities transformed. As retail shopping shifted to suburban malls, cities became primarily financial, administrative, and entertainment centers. During the 1970s and 1980s, the percentage of upper- and middle-income residents within city boundaries fell, and tax bases declined at the same time that an influx of low-income populations placed greater demands on public services. Most large cities faced rising rates of homelessness and crime and the deterioration of their schools and urban infrastructures, especially their sewer and water systems.

During the mid-1970s, New York City's South Bronx symbolized urban decay. During a four-year period, 40,000 acts of arson reduced block after block of deterio-

rated apartment buildings to charred rubble. During the 1977 World Series, an ABC sportscaster noted the plumes of smoke drifting toward Yankee Stadium and reported, "There it is again, ladies and gentlemen. The Bronx is burning." During the 1980s, the national government did little to address urban problems. Big-city mayors complained about the decline of federal funding, which decreased from $64 per urban resident in 1980 to less than $30 per resident by 1993.

URBAN CORRIDORS

These official California road maps from the 1940s and the 1990s show urbanization and the development of urban corridors in the Los Angeles area.

California Department of Transportation.

During the 1990s, however, many central cities underwent a stunning revival. A building boom brought new office towers, residential buildings, and sports and arts complexes to downtowns across the country. This urban renaissance sprang from many sources. A vibrant national economy and improved air and water quality helped. Innovative urban design skillfully integrated diverse architectural styles with new green spaces and revitalized river and lakefronts. Community development corporations (CDCs), grassroots agencies first seen during the 1960s, helped low-income neighborhoods finance affordable housing, child care facilities, and employment opportunities. The Community Reinvestment Act, which obliged banks to invest in low-income neighborhoods, stimulated economic activity. Innovative retailers moved in and found new markets.

Cities also became safer and more convenient. Community policing, a trend toward harsher sentencing, and an aging population lowered urban crime rates during the 1990s. Moreover, as sprawling suburban developments continued to ring most American cities, frustrated commuters increasingly clogged freeways. The congestion, in turn, assisted urban revival. In Atlanta and Houston, cities with perhaps the worst traffic problems, approximately 22 percent of household budgets were spent on transportation. Some people found that they could save both time and money by moving from the suburbs to new downtown townhouses and condominiums.

In addition, new immigrants repopulated many once-declining neighborhoods. African newcomers in the South Bronx, Salvadorans and Vietnamese in Los Angeles, Cubans in Miami, all refurbished property and revived urban life. Rates of home ownership climbed. Along with these diverse new populations came new flavors and rhythms, making many American cities exciting, transnational spaces that paralleled the growing globalization of the world. Urban culture flourished, as artists celebrated the noise, power, and ethnic diversity of cities. The population growth of urban corridors continued to outpace that of traditional cities, and sprawl, traffic congestion, and affordable housing remained major challenges. Still, the decline and rebirth of America's cities provided a major theme of American life during the last 30 years of the 20th century.

Economic Transformations

An American adult of the early 21st century would likely awake to a digital alarm clock, pop breakfast into a microwave oven, work at a desktop computer, and relax with a movie or television program taped earlier off-air, while the children amused themselves at a computerized game or surfed the Internet. None of these products or activities existed in the early 1960s. The pace of technological change, after about 1970, had brought an astonishing transformation in production processes, the structure of the labor force, and consumer products.

New Technologies

The most noteworthy technological advances occurred in biotechnology, high-performance computing, and communications systems. After one of the most important research projects of the late 20th century, scientists announced in June 2000 that they had successfully mapped the entire human genetic code. This Human Genome Project deepened scientists' understanding of genetic engineering and promised to pave the way for new techniques of gene transfer, embryo manipulation, tissue regeneration, and even cloning. Such biotechnology promised new approaches to the treatment of cancer and genetically inherited diseases. Genetic manipulation in plants led to new experiments affecting farming, waste conversion, and toxic cleanup. At the same time, biotechnology advances contributed to fears about a decline in biodiversity, the variety of biological organisms on the planet. New ethical questions also arose about the role of science in manipulating genetic codes and reproduction. Large food producers heralded the use of genetically modified crops as an extension of the earlier "green revolution," which had boosted agricultural yields through new seed strains and fertilizer. Consumers around the world, however, remained wary of genetically modified foods. Research on fetal stem cells, which could be used to regenerate human tissue, raised a debate over the definition of life and provoked a highly politicized controversy that generally followed the battle lines over the issue of abortion.

The computer revolution, which began after the Second World War, entered a new phase during the 1970s, when the availability of microchips boosted the hardware capability and reduced the size and cost of individual computers. Sales of home units soared, initially led by a fledgling company, Apple, and by its formidable rival, IBM. High-performance computers with powerful memory capabilities and "parallel processors," which allow many operations to run simultaneously, began to transform both industry and information systems. Computerized factories and robotics heightened efficiency by lowering labor costs, making production schedules more flexible, and rendering obsolete the giant warehouses that had once held goods until they were shipped. "Artificial intelligence" (AI) capabilities emerged, along with voice interaction between people and machines.

Norman Borlaug: The "Green Revolution"

Raised on the rich farmlands of the upper Midwest, Norman Borlaug initially took agricultural bounty for granted. While a student at the University of Minnesota during the Great Depression and the Dust Bowl of the 1930s, however, Borlaug first confronted problems related to farm production. He received his Ph.D. in plant pathology in 1942 and soon launched a career devoted to helping people outside of the United States grow enough food to avoid famine.

Working with both U.S. charitable foundations and foreign governments, Borlaug traveled widely to develop new crop strains that could both survive and thrive in hostile environments. A varsity wrestler in college, Borlaug became almost as famous for his own physical labor in the fields of Africa and Asia as for the new varieties of wheat and rye he pioneered. By the 1960s, he had helped develop new strains of the basic grains, particularly wheat, and initiated the process called the "green revolution" in agriculture. Borlaug's scientifically produced seeds were not only hardier than older stains but also produced far greater yields.

Borlaug's work helped reverse the long-term trend in which population growth outpaced the food supply. The green revolution took hold almost everywhere in the world except sub-Saharan Africa. In the 1970s, Borlaug received the Nobel Peace Prize, largely for his contributions to ending famine in India and Pakistan during the 1960s.

The green revolution produced controversy as well as celebration. Some critics worried about the long-term ecological and social effects of the new agricultural system, which often relied on application of fertilizer and intensive irrigation. Responding to his critics and lured out of retirement by President Jimmy Carter, Borlaug continued to insist that his basic techniques, refined to meet new situations, would allow safe and abundant food production almost anywhere in the world.

At the beginning of the 21st century, as he neared the age of 90, Borlaug was still teaching college classes in agronomy and traveling the world on behalf of implementing the agricultural changes he had helped introduce. His admirers claimed that he had saved more lives, by preventing famine, than any other person of the 20th century.

© Ted Streshinsky/Corbis.

BORLAUG AT HIS FIELD STATION
In Sonora, Mexico, Borlaug established a major research center for advancing the "green revolution."

Enhanced by new communications technologies, such as fiber-optic networks and satellite transmission, the computer revolution fueled an "information revolution." Libraries replaced card catalogs with computer networks that could link users to specialized national and international databases. Electronic mail, fax transmissions, voice mail, and the World Wide Web rapidly came to supplement posted mail and telephone conversations. Cellular phones, including ones that transmitted visual images, became widespread. The variety of ways in which people could speedily communicate with other people or with information-bearing machines changed patterns of work and human interaction. "Telecommuting" from home became common, as electronic networks made it possible for people to go into work through an Internet connection rather than a door.

Big Business

Computerized communications helped transform ways of doing business by enabling the growth of nimble financial systems and far-flung business outsourcing and franchising. Although buying on credit had been widespread in the United States since the 1920s, bank-issued credit cards

LATTES IN SHANGHAI

American chain businesses spread throughout the world, part of the controversial process known as globalization.

(and later debit cards), efficiently organized through new computer systems, became more common than cash or checks. By 1990, 4,000 bankcard issuers served 75 million cardholding customers. Private debt and personal bankruptcies also soared, and the rate of personal savings in the United States fell to the lowest in the industrialized world. Other innovations in electronic banking—automated teller machines (ATMs), automatic depositing, debit cards, and electronic bill payment—moved Americans closer to a cashless economy where electronic codes substituted for currency. Congressional deregulation of financial industries during the 1980s and 1990s permitted banking institutions and brokerage houses to offer similar financial services and accelerated competition and innovation among financial giants that sold stocks, lent money, and offered insurance.

The boom in franchises and "chain" stores also transformed how consumer products were bought and sold. McDonald's and Holiday Inn had pioneered nationwide standardization in the fast-food and travel industries during the late 1950s. Other chains soon copied their models. Starbucks elevated a simple beverage into a pricey set of designer commodities, including an apparently endless variety of coffee-based drinks. Sam Walton's successful Wal-Mart chain, which symbolized the transformation engulfing the entire retailing industry, became the country's largest private employer. In 2003, one of every 123 workers and nearly one of every 20 workers in the retail sector worked for Wal-Mart. Books, videotapes, records, electronics equipment, shoes, groceries, travel accommodations, and just about every other consumer item became available in nationwide or regional chains that brought a greater array of merchandise and lower prices but often crushed local, independent retailers in thousands of mid-size and small towns.

American chain businesses expanded overseas as well as at home. Especially after the collapse of communist regimes in the Soviet Union and Eastern Europe at the end of the 1980s, chains rushed to supply consumers with long-denied, American-style goods and services. McDonald's opened to great fanfare in Moscow and Budapest, while the Hilton chain quickly opened new hotels in Eastern European capitals. Pepsi and Coke carried their "cola wars" into foreign markets. Starbucks created a controversy when it opened a branch in Beijing's imposing Forbidden City.

Amazon.com led another branch of innovation—e-commerce, or the practice of buying over the Internet. At the end of the 1990s, a wave of new "dot-com" businesses promised to move more and more purchasing to the Internet, and the extravagant claims of their often-youthful entrepreneurs fueled a short-term bubble in dot-com stocks. During 2000, however, stock prices for these enterprises collapsed as dramatically as they had risen. Many of the new companies folded, even though Internet retailing continued to expand. Buying and selling on the Web, often within a globalized market, became an important new feature of consumer culture, and Amazon and eBay, the online auction site, survived the dot-com crash and became models for doing business in cyberspace.

Production, as well as consumption, inexorably turned global. U.S. automakers, for example, increasingly moved their assembly work and parts procurement outside of the United States; by 1990, more than 50 percent of the sticker price on most "American" models went to foreign businesses and workers. Moreover, the trend toward privatization (the sale of government-owned industries to private business) in many economies worldwide provided firms based in the United States with new opportunities for overseas acquisitions. Foreign interests also purchased many U.S. companies and real estate holdings. In the early 1990s, RCA, Doubleday, Mack Truck, Goodyear, and Pillsbury were just some of the traditionally American brands owned by foreign-based corporations. In the late 1990s, German automaker Daimler took over the venerable Chrysler Corporation. Even the entertainment industry, which the United States had dominated for decades, attracted significant foreign investment. A Japanese conglomerate, for example, owned Columbia Pictures during the early 1990s, and Mexico's Televiso took over U.S.-owned Univision. So many industrial giants had become global by the early 21st century that it was often difficult to define what constituted an American company or a foreign one. Drinking the most prominent brands of "Mexican" beer, after a 1997 deal, actually meant drinking a product of Anheuser-Busch. The task of assembling a Honda may have employed more U.S. workers than assembling a Pontiac.

Postindustrial Restructuring

New technologies and economic globalization helped change the American business structure and the workforce. In the 1970s, citing pressure from international competition and declining profits, many companies began cutting back their workforce and trimming their management staff, a move known as "downsizing." More than a dozen major steel plants closed, and the auto industry laid off thousands of workers. In the 1980s and 1990s, the steel and auto industries regained profitability, and other sectors took their turn at downsizing. Business restructuring, together with the government's deregulation of major industries, touched off another merger boom. During the prosperity of the late 1990s, huge mergers, with acquisitions totaling more than $1.6 trillion per year, brought a concentration in corporate power unseen since the 1890s. The 2001 merger of America Online (AOL) with Time Warner, a company that had earlier acquired CNN, exemplified the new environment in which bigger promised to be better.

Meanwhile, the kinds of jobs Americans held shifted. As employment slots in traditional manufacturing and extractive sectors (such as mining) decreased, jobs in ser-

vice, high technology, and information and entertainment sectors increased. Computing and other high-tech sectors offered high salaries, but most jobs in the expanding service sector—clerks, servers, cleaners—were often low paying, part time, and nonunionized. Wal-Mart's enormous workforce, for example, was not unionized, earned an average of $7 to $8 per hour in 2003, and had limited health benefits. Moreover, manufacturers wanting to lower costs to attract the huge Wal-Mart contracts moved their plants into labor environments abroad, where wages were cheap. Such moves further contributed to the decline of relatively better-paid manufacturing jobs in the United States.

Labor union membership, traditionally highest in the manufacturing occupations that were coming to constitute a decreasing proportion of jobs in the restructuring economy, dropped dramatically. In the 1950s, 35 percent of American workers belonged to a union. By 2003, the figure stood at only 13 percent. While union membership rolls and labor's political clout steadily slipped, the union movement struggled to make inroads into new sectors of the economy. Some union locals around the country, for example, launched organizing drives in occupations held predominantly by women, such as clerical, restaurant, and hotel work. Businesses adamantly fought unionization, claiming that it would raise labor costs.

Efforts to organize agricultural workers, who were largely of Mexican and Filipino descent, also dramatized the difficulties of expanding the union movement into new, nonunionized sectors. Cesar Chavez, a charismatic leader who emulated the nonviolent tactics of Martin Luther King, Jr., vaulted the United Farm Workers (UFW)

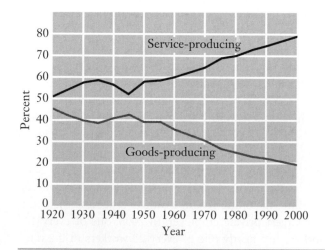

GROWTH OF SERVICE SECTOR JOBS, 1920–2000

Source: U.S. Census Bureau.

into public attention during the early 1970s. As union president, Chavez undertook a series of personal hunger strikes and instituted several well-publicized consumer boycotts of lettuce and grapes as means of pressuring growers to bargain with the UFW. He also established close ties with liberal Democrats in California and nationally and won several major contract victories. During the later 1970s and the 1980s, however, the UFW steadily lost ground. Strong stands by growers against union organizing and the continued influx of new immigrants eager for work undercut the UFW's efforts. When Chavez died in April 1993, his union was struggling to rebuild its membership and regain bargaining power.

The major growth for organized labor came among government employees and workers in the health care industry. These gains, however, failed to offset union membership losses in the shrinking industrial sector.

As early as the 1980s, critical economists warned that the shift to a "postindustrial" economy was "de-skilling" the labor force and putting people out of work because the jobs for which they were trained no longer existed. Might a globalized economy erode the living standards in America? Critics expressed alarm over statistical evidence that more than half of the new jobs created in the U.S. economy during the 1980s paid less than $7,000 per year. Moreover, the firms that provided temporary workers to other businesses already were becoming among the largest employers in the country. Some analysts warned that the widening gulf between highly paid, highly skilled positions and minimum-wage jobs augmented economic inequality and might ultimately undermine the middle-class nature of American society. In response, the labor movement tried to make limitations on part-time work and improvement in real wages the centerpieces of new organizing efforts.

Other economists hailed the new work environment. They acknowledged that internationalization and corporate downsizing might temporarily mean lost jobs for some people but insisted that gains in productivity would eventually translate into lower consumer prices and rising living standards. Real wages did begin to rise in the 1990s, but this trend reversed as the economy softened after 2000, and the gap between the highest and lowest income levels grew steadily wider.

Still, the celebrants of change pointed to many success stories, especially in high-tech industries, where innovation paved a broad avenue of upward economic mobility for those with computer-age skills. In 1980, for example, a small company called Microsoft, headed by a young engineer named Bill Gates, licensed the software for a computer operating system called MS-DOS to IBM and to

hundreds of companies, such as Dell, who were manufacturing clones of IBM personal computers (PCs). MS-DOS became the standard operating system for PCs and, together with a succession of other software products, transformed Microsoft into one of America's most profitable corporations. In 1995, Bill Gates, with his boyish grin and shrewd business instincts, became the richest person in the world. Business analysts marveled at the meteoric growth of a company whose product had only been invented in 1980; one comic suggested that MS-DOS stood for "Microsoft Seeks Dominion Over Society." The Microsoft story clearly was exceptional, but new high-tech businesses turned many computer mavens into millionaires and created more new jobs than the workforce could fill during the 1990s. A sharp economic downturn after 2001 cooled high-tech growth and led to controversy about the industry's continued potential to create well-paying jobs in the United States.

The revolutionary changes in technology and the economy had profound effects on the lives of Americans. Skilled workers of earlier generations had tended to stick to one profession or place of employment throughout their working life, but by the end of the 20th century, even middle-income workers were likely to switch occupations several times before retiring. The need for training and retraining programs that served all ages of people transformed ideas about education and work.

Media and Culture

New technologies significantly altered the nation's culture as well. By the early 21st century, virtually every home, apartment, and college dorm room had at least one television and VCR or DVD player, and about 80 percent had a personal computer. More than one-third of the population used a computer in their daily work, and most schoolchildren used one in the classroom. People looked to the Internet for access to newspapers, magazines, books, music, movies, and artistic creations. E-mail replaced "snail mail" (via the U.S. Postal Service) and the telephone as the easiest way for computer users to contact friends and to conduct business.

The omnipresent video screen, which became ever more portable, seemed the preeminent symbol of contemporary culture. Visitors to museums and historical sites obtained information through interactive monitors. Television sets replaced last year's magazines in doctors' waiting rooms and auto repair shops. Sports bars lined their walls with video screens, enabling patrons to simultaneously follow their favorite teams, glance at other sporting events, and compete in trivia contests. A special airport channel offered travelers news updates and weather reports.

The Video Revolution

The narrowly targeted TV programming found in airports highlighted the increasingly fragmented nature of cultural production, especially in television. At the beginning of the 1970s, TV broadcasters still expected a hit program to draw more viewers in a single evening than a hit motion picture attracted over an entire year. The three networks could promise advertisers that a rough cross section of the American public would be watching their nighttime sales pitches.

During the 1980s, however, the networks increasingly embraced a strategy called "narrowcasting." CBS replaced several highly watched programs, such as "The Beverly Hillbillies," with shows that were considered particularly attractive to urban and suburban viewers under the age of 50. This practice, the network calculated, would help advertisers reach the viewers who were most likely to spend money on their products and services. CBS also introduced "edgier" programming. "All in the Family," a sitcom about intergenerational conflict within a blue-collar family, made its bigoted protagonist, Archie Bunker, a lightning rod for issues involving race and gender. Although "The Mary Tyler Moore Show" rarely took overtly feminist positions, it did address the personal politics of working women. Other CBS shows, such as "M*A*S*H," also merged comedy and social commentary.

With CBS leading the way, the entire industry prospered between the mid-1970s and mid-1980s. ABC found its niche among high-school and college-age viewers. Aware that young people generally controlled at least one of the family's television sets, ABC emphasized sex-and-action programs ("Charlie's Angels"), mildly risqué sitcoms ("Three's Company"), and shows about teen life ("Happy Days"). NBC brought the barbed humor of the 1960s counterculture to network television by nurturing "Saturday Night Live." All three networks did so well during this time that media analysts likened owning one of their local, affiliated stations to operating a press that could print money. At the end of the 1970s, 9 of every 10 television sets were tuned to a network program during prime-time viewing hours.

By the late 1980s, however, network programmers were struggling to satisfy an increasingly diverse and segmented audience. NBC claimed two now-classic hits, "The Cosby Show" (featuring an affluent African American family) and "Cheers" (set in a Boston tavern where "everybody knows your name"), but its other prime-time programs garnered disappointing ratings. Facing a similar situation, the other two networks joined NBC in slashing budgets and staff, especially in their news divisions. Meanwhile, local stations, which had been limping along without a network tie, suddenly thrived. These independents programmed Hollywood films, sporting events, and reruns of cancelled, prime-time shows now being "syndicated" to individual stations. Although the number of daily newspapers was steadily shrinking, several hundred independent television stations debuted during the 1980s.

Capitalizing on the rise of these independents, the Fox television network went on the air in 1988. Using a pattern that was later imitated by the WB and UPN networks, Fox offered a limited schedule to previously nonaffiliated stations. Fox's first big hit, "The Simpsons," an animated send-up of the standard family sitcom, became a pop cultural phenomenon and mass-marketing bonanza, especially among younger and college-educated viewers. Fox gradually expanded its nightly offerings and in 1993 outbid CBS for the rights to carry professional football games.

© Archive Photos/Fotos International.

THE SIMPSONS

Homer and Marge Simpson, with their three children, Bart, Lisa, and Maggie, parodied the traditional family comedy and other television conventions. Initially assailed by conservative critics, "The Simpsons" gained cult status to become the longest-running sitcom in television history.

WB, UPN, and Fox featured programs—such as "Buffy the Vampire Slayer," "That 70s Show," and "Malcolm in the Middle"—for audiences that contained more minority, young, and urban viewers than those of the three older networks.

New technologies, which promised viewers greater choice, challenged all six networks. At the simplest level, the remote control, an innovation of the 1960s that finally caught on during the 1980s, created a television aesthetic, called "zapping" or "channel surfing," in which viewers flipped from program to program, usually during commercial breaks. The mass marketing of videocassette recorders (VCRs) and the introduction of other copying technologies allowed viewers even greater control over their TV-viewing habits.

The primary challenge to the networks came from cable television (CATV). By 2000, nearly 75 percent of the nation's homes received CATV. Designing programming for specific audiences, CATV accelerated the fragmentation of TV's viewership. Atlanta's Ted Turner, one of the first entrepreneurs to recognize CATV's potential, introduced the Cable News Network (CNN), several movie channels, and an all-cartoon network before his communication empire merged with that of Time-Warner. Companies selling direct satellite transmission challenged both the networks and CATV, but the lack of a standard reception format slowed the expansion of this competing medium. By 2000, the percentage of television viewers watching network programs during the evening hours had fallen from 90 percent to less than 60 percent, and the corporations that owned them, particularly NBC and Fox, had expanded into the CATV industry. At the 2003 Emmy awards ceremony, CATV shows, for the first time, won more awards than those carried on the networks.

The "New Hollywood"

New technologies and changing business practices transformed how works of popular culture, particularly motion pictures from a "New Hollywood," were produced,

---

M U S I C A L   L I N K   T O   T H E   P A S T

Not for Women Only

Songwriter: Joni Mitchell
Title: "Hejira" (1976)

With the notable exception of the African American blues queens of the 1920s, women had surprisingly little voice in the popular music of 20th-century America. Ella Fitzgerald, Billie Holiday, and Barbra Streisand gained considerable fame, but how many women wrote songs that detailed their inner lives? How many women were known for their expertise on an instrument? How many supervised studio production and arrangement, or worked in the upper echelon of record companies? Exceedingly few.

With a string of ground-breaking, best-selling albums in the 1970s, Joni Mitchell led the movement of women who brought their own personal voice to the popular music business. With her unique tunings and playing style on the acoustic guitar, she had an immediately recognizable sound. She produced most of her own recordings, enjoying full control in the studio.

"Hejira," like many of Mitchell's other songs, yearningly explored the benefits, adventures, and struggles of living as an independent woman, enjoying a career, and leading a nonconventional life, with no children and no settling down. Like many women of her time, she found that asserting her autonomy and bypassing traditional domestic roles did not always represent an easy task, personally or professionally: "I'm porous with travel fever / But you know I'm so glad to be on my own / Still sometimes the slightest touch of a stranger / Can set up a trembling in my bones." But her songs were not dependent on the lyrics for their impact: her melodies and harmonic structures were consistently more sophisticated than her singer/songwriter competition in the 1970s and beyond.

Throughout her career, Joni Mitchell stubbornly resisted being pigeonholed as a "women's artist." In 1991, she said: "For a while it was assumed that I was writing women's songs. Then men began to notice that they saw themselves in the songs, too. A good piece of art should be androgynous. I'm not a feminist. That's too divisional for me."

For additional sources related to this feature, visit the CD accompanying this text or the *Liberty, Equality, Power* Web site at:

http://history.wadsworth.com/murrin_LEP4e

distributed, and ultimately consumed. With movie attendance in 1980 about the same as it had been in 1960, Hollywood studios began raising ticket prices; betting on a few blockbuster films, such as the highly profitable "Star Wars" series (1977–); and hoping for a surprise hit, such as *My Big Fat Greek Wedding* (2002). Yet for every blockbuster or unexpected success, there was a super-expensive flop such as *Gigli* (2003) or a box-office disappointment such as *Eyes Wide Shut* (1999).

Volatility in the movie market encouraged most filmmakers to play it safe. Many movie-makers recycled titles and special effects that had made money in the past. They transferred television staples such as *How the Grinch Stole Christmas* (2000) to the big screen and produced sequels for any movie, such as *The Matrix* (1999), which even approached blockbuster status. In addition, Hollywood expanded the older practice of targeting younger viewers with movies such as *Ferris Bueller's Day Off* (1986) and the "American Pie" series (2000–). Meanwhile, celebratory

stories that tapped themes of popular history, such as *Braveheart* (1995) and *Titanic* (1997), impressed both ticket buyers and the industry insiders who selected Hollywood's Academy Award winners.

At the same time, however, relatively small-scale movies, which often looked to foreign models, began to flourish. Woody Allen became one of the first U.S. filmmakers to specialize in movies, such as *Crimes and Misdemeanors* (1989), that borrowed techniques and themes from European cinema. The actor (and sometimes director-producer) Robert Redford launched the Sundance Film Institute in the hopes of encouraging "offbeat" screenwriting and direction. The annual Sundance Film Festival, held in Park City, Utah, began attracting Hollywood moguls who sought the next "small" movie, such as *The Blair Witch Project* (1999), which might find a large audience. The CATV lineup included several outlets, including a Sundance channel, for independent films, and the Landmark movie chain successfully featured theatrical films that

HISTORY THROUGH FILM

Star Wars (1977)

The series of *Star Wars* movies, which began in 1977, eventually gained a vast, almost cult-like following. Not only did the initial *Star Wars* break all previous box-office records, but it also launched literally thousands of merchandising tie-ins. The marketing campaign began in the era of low-tech products, such as Luke Skywalker lunch boxes, and extended into the age of interactive computer games and screen savers. The film's creator, George Lucas, earned even more money from licensing images from *Star Wars* to marketers than he made from the unprecedented box-office receipts for the 1977 movie.

Star Wars, which took three years and a then-astronomical sum of $30 million to produce, immediately generated a similarly outsized popular response. Within three years, it returned a nearly 2,000 percent profit. It also gained 10 Academy Award nominations, 7 Oscars, and 3 Grammies. The movie financed Lucas's own private media empire, Lucasfilm Ltd.; introduced six-track Dolby

Directed by George Lucas. Starring Mark Hamill (Luke Skywalker), Alec Guinness (Obi-Wan Kenobi), Harrison Ford (Han Solo), Carrie Fisher (Princess Leia), and James Earl Jones (Voice of Darth Vader).

stereo to motion-picture theaters; helped make viewers in their teens and early twenties Hollywood's primary target audience; and pioneered breakthroughs in the use of computer-assisted graphics and computer-controlled camera work. The economics of movie making increasingly turned less on producing a steady supply of successful films than on releasing a few "blockbusters" modeled on *Star Wars.* These films were designed to attract huge initial audiences, to create the expectation of sequels, to sustain a variety of ancillary products, to boost sales in foreign markets, and to sell briskly in VCR and DVD formats.

In one sense, *Star Wars* tells an upbeat, allegorical story that responds to the cynicism and divisions of the Vietnam era. Young Luke Skywalker, aided by the wizened Obi-Wan Kenobi and the independent Han Solo, joins the fight to defeat the evil "Empire" and to rescue Princess Leia from the villainous Darth Vader. The movie embellishes this sparse tale with elaborate imagery borrowed from a wide

seemed unlikely prospects for the multiplex mall theaters. In time, movies that did especially well at Landmark theaters might earn a run on the mall circuit, a trend that encouraged the major studios to create special divisions, such as Paramount Classics, which financed and distributed so-called independent films. The Internet first welcomed filmmakers who were experimenting with digital technology; by 2004, digital movies that dispensed with traditional film stock regularly played in commercial movie theaters.

The New Hollywood became increasingly intertwined with the changing television establishment, once its feared rival, and with the emerging VCR and DVD industries. Hollywood gained badly needed revenue by licensing its theatrical films to broadcast and cable TV and, later, for VCR and DVD distribution. Film fans could easily convert their own home, upgraded with ever-larger video screens and new technologies, into a movie palace. During the 1980s and early 1990s, before a few video-store chains cornered the market, the United States claimed more video-rental outlets than movie theaters. During the same period, sales of VCRs soared, but digital video discs (DVDs) eventually won out. DVD technology gave viewers improved visual imagery; bonus attractions, such as footage cut from the theatrical release; wide-screen prints; and the kind of expert commentary hitherto only available at a film school. The DVD version of *Something About Mary* (1998), a lightweight comedy, featured nearly six hours of extra material and commentary. As Hollywood studios discovered that DVD sales easily matched theatrical receipts, they sought movies, such as action films with elaborate special effects, that promised to sell well on DVD.

The Changing Media Environment

CATV, VCRs, and ultimately digital technology also transformed the pop music industry. The Music Television channel (MTV), initially offering a 24-hour supply of rock

range of Hollywood genres, including science fiction, combat films, westerns, and the Saturday morning serials of the 1930s and 1940s.

The film's major event, the triumph of individual effort and resourcefulness—not sophisticated technology—over an evil enemy, arguably attempts to replace the traumatic history of U.S. involvement in Southeast Asia with a heroic folktale. Similarly, the alliance between youthful Skywalker and aging Obi-Wan Kenobi seems a parable about the need to repudiate the "generation gap" that had emerged during the cultural conflict of the 1960s.

Seen another way, though, the market logic that shaped a film product such as *Star Wars* focused less and less on crafting a story, even the kind of political-historical allegory found in Cold War–era movies such as *High Noon* (1952). Instead, a successful blockbuster primarily needed to create opportunities for inserting eye-filling special effects (often portraying considerable violence and mayhem) and

Star Wars' **C-3PO and R2-D2, a droid and a robot with personalities, generated considerable nonfilm revenue from product tie-ins.**

Kobal Collection/Lucasfilm/20th Century Fox.

for devising imagery (such as cute robots and cuddly creatures) that could be remarketed in various offscreen forms. In this sense, spectacles such as *Star Wars* merit attention less as representations of specific episodes in the past than as historical events in their own right.

videos, debuted in 1981. Critics immediately charged it with portraying women as sex objects and with excluding artists of color. Eventually, however, MTV defused complaints, especially after featuring Michael Jackson's 29-minute video based on his hit single "Thriller" (1983). By 2004, MTV and other CATV channels regularly programmed videos that represented the increasingly multiethnic nature of the music industry.

Performers such as Madonna used MTV to forge a new relationship between music and visual imagery, the "MTV aesthetic." This fast-paced visual style fed off its musical soundtrack; played with traditional ideas about time and space; recycled images from movies and TV programs; and often carried a sharp, satirical edge. The MTV aesthetic crossed over among video, television, and motion pictures. In the 1990s, MTV abandoned its all-video format and developed a wide range of youth-oriented programming. Its cult classic, "The Real World," anticipated the run of controversial "reality" shows such as "Survivor" on network and cable television.

Entertainment conglomerates such as Sony began marketing musical packages in a variety of different, constantly updated formats. The 45-rpm record and the longplay album (LP), which had propelled the musical revolutions of the 1950s and 1960s, all but disappeared. Digital compact discs (CDs) changed not only the technology through which pop music was delivered but also the nature of the product and the listening experience. The classic LPs of the late 1960s and early 1970s, such as The Beatles' *Abbey Road* (1969) or Willie Nelson's *The Red-Headed Stranger* (1975), had ideally featured 10 to 12 songs, split between the two sides and organized around a core theme or concept. The turn-of-the-21st-century CD, able to hold 15 or 20 minutes more music than an LP, was rarely structured thematically and often contained a hodgepodge of songs, several casually tossed in as "bonus tracks." Thematic coherence became increasingly irrelevant with the introduction of players that could shuffle back and forth between the tracks on a hundred different CDs. Listeners could program their machine according to their own whims or simply let songs play randomly.

The Internet also promised to change how people obtained and listened to music. First, it allowed access to commercial and noncommercial radio stations far beyond the range of any radio. More important, the Internet and digital technology permitted people to obtain, preserve, and exchange music in entirely new ways. Celebrants of the Internet proclaimed that they would break the hold of the commercial music companies and make a wide array of sounds instantly available to consumers. In reply, the music industry and various artists complained that people were using the Internet to "pirate" copyrighted material.

Although the U.S. Supreme Court, in 1986, had endorsed the home copying of television programs on VCRs, experts in copyright law joined the various interested parties in debating how this decision affected the downloading of music from the Internet. After years of indecisive legal sparring, while revenues from CD sales slumped and file-swapping soared, the music industry tried a carrot-and-stick approach. In 2003, it began selling songs online and filed an unprecedented number of lawsuits, for copyright infringement, against ordinary people who were sharing music files from their personal computers. Corporate executives seemed determined to bury the claim that the Internet provided a medium in which ordinary people could freely distribute music.

The New Mass Culture Debate

New trends in mass commercial culture generated other controversies. In 1975, the Federal Communications Commission (FCC) ordered the television networks to dedicate the first 60 minutes of prime time each evening to "family" programming free of violence or "mature" themes. Eventually, the courts struck down this family-hour requirement as a violation of the First Amendment's guarantee of free speech. Demands that Congress regulate rock lyrics and album covers also ran afoul of complaints that this kind of legislation would amount to unconstitutional censorship. Eventually, TV programmers and record companies, pressed by private organizations and the threat of new governmental action, adopted "warning labels," similar to the ones pioneered by the movie industry during the 1960s, that supposedly informed parents about products with violent and sexually explicit imagery.

Meanwhile, popular reviewers and university professors were paying serious attention to works of commercial culture. Unlike the critics of the 1950s, who had dismissed mass culture as trivial and condemned its effect on daily life, these writers often seemed to be unabashed fans of the cultural products they were studying. Instead of critically comparing mass culture to "high" culture (the "classical" works of Western civilization), this new generation jettisoned the distinction between lowbrow and highbrow. The music of The Beatles could be studied along with that of Beethoven; moreover, the lyrics of Chuck Berry and Bob Dylan merited academic analysis. Academics similarly pondered the meaning of the MTV aesthetic and wrote scholarly studies about pop celebrities such as Madonna, Nirvana's Kurt Cobain, and Britney Spears.

These analysts, who gravitated to the new academic field of "cultural studies," looked at how people merged the products of commercial culture into their daily lives. Again rejecting the cultural criticism of the 1950s—which had seen consumers as cultural dupes who passively soaked up worthless products—they stressed people's creative interaction with commercial culture. Scholarly studies of "Star Trek," for example, examined how loyal fans had kept this popular 1960s television series alive in syndication and had subsequently prompted a succession of motion pictures and new TV programs. Moreover, through self-produced magazines (called "fanzines"), conventions, and the Internet, these Trekkies created a grassroots subculture that used "Star Trek" as the launching pad for discussions of social and political issues, especially ones that touched on race, gender, and sexuality.

Academics associated with cultural studies tended to embrace multiculturalism. They urged new attention to works produced by women, political outsiders, and non-Western writers and artists. They also encouraged students to see traditional texts, such as those attributed to Shakespeare, in light of their political and historical contexts rather than as timeless works. Traditionalists condemned this "cultural turn" as a legacy of the counterculture of the 1960s and blamed it for eroding settled ideas of artistic quality and value.

☙ Social Activism

The activism associated with the 1960s became embedded in most areas of American life and rippled through the decades that followed. After 1970, an ever-increasing amount of activity aimed at advancing particular social, political, and cultural agendas. By the early 21st century, virtually every public forum, from neighborhood newspapers to the streets of the nation's capital, featured the influence, and the clash, of activists who claimed to represent some particular constituency or goal.

Mounting a mass demonstration, reminiscent of those against the Vietnam War, remained one tool of advocacy and protest. The nation's capital still provided a stage for rallies aimed at attracting the attention of national lawmakers and the media. Both anti-abortion and pro-choice forces, for example, intermittently sponsored demonstrations in Washington, D.C. In October 1995, the Million Man March sought to mobilize African American men behind a campaign of social reconstruction in their own communities; two years later, an evangelical men's group called the Promise Keepers filled Washington's Mall.

Increasingly, though, activists focused on smaller, more targeted demonstrations. During the 1980s, the Clamshell Alliance conducted a campaign of civil disobedience against a nuclear reactor being built in Seabrook, New Hampshire, and a broad coalition of West Coast activists waged a lengthy, unsuccessful struggle to close the University of California's Lawrence Livermore National Laboratory, which was developing nuclear weapons. In many cities, women's groups staged annual Take Back the Night rallies to protest the rising tide of sexual assaults. Beginning in the late 1990s, people representing workers' rights and environmental causes mobilized to disrupt meetings, in both the United States and overseas, of the World Trade Organization (WTO).

The media seldom covered demonstrations, unless they sparked violent conflict, as did some of those against the WTO. In 1991, for example, 30,000 Korean Americans staged a march for racial peace in Los Angeles. Although it was the largest demonstration ever conducted by any Asian American group, even the local media ignored it. Similarly, few people learned from newspapers and television that 75,000 California high school students staged a walkout in 1994 to denounce a state measure aimed at curtailing education, welfare, and medical care for undocumented immigrants. Even the 24/7 cable news operations, such as CNN and Fox, failed to track protests in the way that major networks had done during the civil-rights and Vietnam-war eras. Only C-Span, a niche network devoted to public-affairs programming, provided regular coverage of events of social protest.

Women's Issues

In this new environment, women's groups puzzled over how to rally new supporters and re-energize their core constituencies. Struggles over gender-related issues had emerged within the civil-rights and antiwar movements of the 1960s. Initially, most men attracted to these causes saw no contradiction between women's second-class status and their own egalitarian pronouncements. Male leaders of these movements often expected women to be available for secretarial services or sexual liaisons and complained that issues of gender equality interfered with the fight to redirect racial and foreign policies. Spread of the birth control pill, introduced in 1960, simultaneously gave women greater control over reproductive choices and complicated the meaning of "sexual freedom."

The new feminism that emerged during the last decades of the 20th century encompassed a wide range of movements. The National Organization for Women (NOW) became generally identified with the rights-based agenda of the mainstream of the Democratic Party. African American women often formed separate organizations that looked at issues of cultural and ethnic identity; Chicana groups coalesced within the UFW movement and many Mexican American organizations; lesbians organized their own groups, often allying with an emerging gay rights movement; and many feminist organizations based in the United States began exploring the possibility of joining with groups in other nations, an effort that viewed women's issues as international in scope.

Beginning in the 1970s, women promoted "consciousness-raising" sessions to discuss issues and share perspectives. Consciousness-raising produced a growing conviction that women's concerns about *political* empowerment were inseparable from *personal* power relationships involving housework, child-rearing, sexuality, and economic independence. Although this post-1960s generation of feminists still pursued traditional public issues, such as fighting discrimination in the workplace, "the personal is political" became its watchword.

Economic self-sufficiency remained a pressing issue. An increase in Aid to Families with Dependent Children (AFDC) payments and an expansion of the Food Stamp program had boosted the average social welfare "package" for single mothers with children during the 1960s, but the economic dislocations of the following decades inexorably undercut the value, measured in constant dollars, of these benefits. In 1972, a family of four, headed by a woman, received governmental benefits that, on average, totaled about $577 per month. Two decades later, the monthly value (in real dollars) of the same benefits had fallen to about $430. Homeless shelters, which once catered almost exclusively to single men, increasingly tried to meet the needs of women and children. Activists tried to highlight

LINK TO THE PAST

Cultural Disagreements: Equality for Women?

The changing role of women in America dramatically altered family and civic life during this era. Many of the cultural and political disputes of these years revolved around issues related to gender. Advocates of "full equality" for women, such as the National Organization for Women (NOW), clashed with New Right activists, who opposed gender equality as an affront to the "natural" order.

T*he purpose of NOW is to take action to bring women into full participation in the mainstream of American society now, exercising all the privileges and responsibilities thereof in truly equal partnership with men. . . . We reject the current assumptions that a man must carry the sole burden of supporting himself, his wife, and family, and that a woman is automatically entitled to lifelong support by a man upon her marriage, or that marriage, home and family are primarily woman's world and responsibility. . . . We believe that a true partnership between the sexes demands a different concept of marriage, an equitable sharing of the responsibilities of home and children and of the economic burdens of their support. . . .*

We will strive to ensure that no party, candidate, president, senator, governor, congressman, or any public official who betrays or ignores the principle of full equality between the sexes is elected or appointed to office.

NATIONAL ORGANIZATION FOR WOMEN (NOW)
Statement of Purpose, 1966

I *believe that at the foundation of the women's liberation movement there is a minority core of women who were once bored with life, whose real problems are spiritual problems. Many women have never accepted their God-given roles. . . . God Almighty created men and women biologically different and with differing needs and roles.*

He made men and women to complement each other and to love each other. Not all the women involved in the feminist movement are radicals. Some are misinformed, and some are lonely. . . . I believe that women deserve more than equal rights. . . . Men and women have differing strengths. . . . Because a woman is weaker does not mean that she is less important.

JERRY FALWELL
calling for a "moral majority" in his 1980 book,
Listen America!

1. Different assumptions about gender roles led to public policy disputes, especially in areas related to military service, families and reproduction, and labor rights. What specific social and political issues seem to be grounded in the contest over women's rights?

For additional sources related to this feature, visit the CD accompanying this text or the *Liberty, Equality, Power* Web site at:

http://history.wadsworth.com/murrin_LEP4e

the feminization of poverty and to urge greater public assistance for the growing number of children reared in low-income, female-headed families. Proposals for reshaping the pattern of governmental support increasingly sought to limit so-called entitlements and to emphasize moving women, even those with young children, into the workforce.

The job market, however, was laced with inequalities. Women constituted 30 percent of the labor force in 1950 and more than 45 percent in 2001. Although women increasingly entered the professions and gained unionized positions (by 2000 nearly 45 percent of union members were women, compared with 18 percent in 1960), the average female worker still made less than 70 cents for every dollar earned by the average male worker. "Glass ceilings" limited women's chances for promotion, and child-care expenses often fell disproportionately on women who worked outside the home.

With so many issues to address—and with agendas often varying along lines of class, race, ethnicity, and religion—the women's movement remained highly diverse. Women from different backgrounds increasingly cooperated to build new institutions and networks that addressed a wide range of economic, social, and cultural matters. Their efforts included battered-women's shelters, health and birthing clinics specializing in women's medicine, rape crisis centers, economic development counseling for women-owned businesses, union organizing efforts led by women, organizations of women in specific businesses or professions, women's studies programs in colleges and universities, and academic journals devoted to research on women's issues.

Pressure for gender equity also affected existing institutions. Country clubs and service organizations, such as Rotary International, faced pressure to admit women, and most began to do so. Many of the Protestant denominations, after some hesitation, accepted women into the ministry. Reform Judaism placed women in its pulpits. Educational institutions began to adopt "gender-fair" hiring practices and academic curricula. American women by the beginning of the 21st century lived in an environment significantly different from that of their mothers.

Sexual harassment, one of the most publicized of the new concerns, became a highly charged issue. To a few activists, such as Camille Paglia, a focus on sexuality—or on the related issue of pornography—tended to identify feminism with a puritanical spirit that the women's movement of the 1960s had pledged to end. Most women's groups, however, pressed government and private employers to regulate sexually charged behavior that they saw demeaning women and exploiting their lack of power vis-à-vis male supervisors and coworkers. In 1986, the U.S.

Supreme Court ruled that sexual harassment constituted a form of discrimination covered under the 1964 Civil Rights Act.

In 1991, the issue gained national attention when Anita Hill, an African American law professor, accused Clarence Thomas, an African American nominee for the Supreme Court, of having sexually harassed her when both had worked for the federal government. Feminists denounced the all-male Senate Judiciary Committee, which was responsible for considering Thomas's nomination, for its apparent inability to understand the issue of sexual harassment. Although the Senate narrowly approved Thomas for the Supreme Court, women's groups gained new converts. Political observers credited the Thomas-Hill hearings with mobilizing female voters and electing four women as U.S. Senators in 1992. The numbers of women in public office continued to rise slowly, as the political gender gap—a difference in the way men and women voted—became a feature of most electoral contests.

Sexual harassment also became a controversial issue within the U.S. military, which began to recruit women more actively. The service academies accepted female cadets, and women found places within the military hierarchy. Soon, however, revelations about harassment and even sexual assaults against female naval officers by their male comrades revealed problems. Attempts by navy officials to cover up sexual harassment during the 1991 "Tailhook" convention provoked outrage, and several high-ranking officers were forced to step down. More than a decade later, an investigation revealed both widespread evidence of harassment, including sexual assaults, at the Air Force Academy and apparent indifference among the institution's male-dominated leadership.

Sexual Politics

The politics of sexuality entered an entirely new phase with the emergence of public issues involving gays and lesbians. Some homosexuals, especially gay men affiliated with the left-leaning Mattachine Society and lesbians who organized the Daughters of Bilitis, had already begun to claim a right to nondiscriminatory treatment during the 1950s (see chapter 27). Insurgency spread during the 1960s. In 1969, New York City police raided the Stonewall Inn, a bar in Greenwich Village. Patrons resisted arrest, and the confrontation pitted the bar's largely homosexual patrons, who claimed to be the victims of police harassment, against law enforcement officials.

"Stonewall" marked an important turning point in sexual politics. Borrowing ideas and rhetoric from the civil-rights movement, New York City's Gay Liberation Front (GLF) provided a model for similar groups across the country. During the decades after the Stonewall episode, thousands of gay and lesbian advocacy groups sprang up, and many individuals "came out of the closet," proudly proclaiming their sexual orientation. During the 1990s, a group called Act Up introduced a new style of in-your-face protests that challenged what it saw as systematic discrimination against homosexuals.

Newspapers, theaters, nightspots, and religious groups identifying themselves with homosexual communities became part of daily life, particularly in larger cities. Specific forms of popular entertainment, such as the disco club scene of the late 1970s and early 1980s, became identified with the gay and lesbian subcultures, which benefited significantly from a general relaxation of legal and cultural controls over the portrayal and practice of explicit sexuality.

Homosexuals joined with civil-liberties groups in demanding that state and local governments enact laws pro-

hibiting discrimination against gays and lesbians in housing and jobs. They also demanded that the police treat attacks on homosexuals no less seriously than they handled other forms of violent crime. In addition, gay and lesbian activists joined with heterosexual supporters in insisting that private associations, such as church groups, drop discriminatory bylaws and practices. As gays and lesbians gained a voice in public and private life, however, their activism met determined opposition from cultural conservatives.

One issue, with international implications, initially overrode all others: acquired immune deficiency syndrome (AIDS), a generally fatal and contagious disease that attacks the body's immune system. First identified in the early 1980s, AIDS became an intensely contested medical and political issue. Before the emergence of AIDS, the medical establishment argued that improvements in vaccination, sanitation, and drug treatment would limit the

AIDS "ACT UP" CAMPAIGN
Health care issues increasingly galvanized grassroots activists in the late 20th century. In 1989, members of Act Up, a group that represented militant homosexuals, protested what they saw as the federal government's inattention to the issue of AIDS during the 1980s.

spread of any viral infection. Epidemiologists soon identified the AIDS virus, human immunodeficiency virus (HIV), as a grave threat for which medicine offered little in the way of prevention or cure. The disease could be transmitted through the careless use of intravenous drugs, tainted blood supplies, and unprotected heterosexual intercourse.

At first, the incidence of AIDS in the United States was primarily limited to gay men. AIDS activists charged that, as a consequence of this association, cultural and social conservatives placed a low priority on medical efforts to understand its causes, to check its spread, or to devise a cure. The resultant controversy over the level of medical funding galvanized gay and lesbian activists to voice their concern with ever-greater force. With the development of drugs that could combat AIDS, most public figures, even many who did not support other concerns involving gays and lesbians, came to support anti-AIDS efforts both at home and overseas, particularly in Africa. "AIDS has taught us both the power of science and its limitations," concluded one prominent physician.

Gay rights remained a rallying cry for activists—and a challenge to their conservative opponents. In response to legal tests, in 2003 a divided U.S. Supreme Court declared that state laws criminalizing sodomy were in violation of the Constitution. Even supporters of these anti-sodomy measures, enforceable only by the kind of intrusive policing that most Americans opposed, recognized their largely symbolic character, but the Supreme Court's opinion contained the hint that it might deploy the same reasoning to strike down bans against same-sex marriages. When a Canadian province and, in 2003, Vermont formally authorized homosexual unions, conservative activists in the United States rallied around a constitutional amendment that would protect the "sanctity of marriage."

🌐 Race, Ethnicity, and Social Activism

The emphasis on group identity as the fulcrum for social activism became especially strong among various racial and ethnic communities. In movements that recalled, and extended, the activism of the 1960s, groups emphasized pride in their distinctive traditions and declared that cultural differences should be affirmed rather than feared, celebrated rather than merely tolerated. Especially with the influx of new immigrants (by 2000, 1 of every 10 Americans was foreign born), identity politics and multiculturalism took on growing importance.

African American Activism

African Americans had developed a strong sense of cultural identity during the civil-rights and black power struggles of the 1960s (see chapters 28 and 29). As battles against discrimination and for cultural pride continued, controversies over future directions also emerged.

Activism often looked inward to stress pride in distinctively African American cultural practices. A variant of this impulse, popularly known as "Malcolmania," accelerated with the appearance of Spike Lee's film *Malcolm X* (1991). The emphasis on racial pride also showed in rap and hip-hop music and in the hundreds of schools established in order to offer students an "Afrocentric" curriculum. More broadly, the Black Entertainment Television network (BET) aimed its programming specifically to African American viewers but also attracted a multicultural audience, especially for its musical and comedy offerings.

Similarly, academics such as Henry Lewis Gates, Jr., who became head of Harvard's Afro-American Studies Department in 1991, made attention to the black experience part of a larger push toward multiculturalism. Gates and a colleague published *Africana: The Encyclopedia of the African and African American Experience* (1999). This project, which had been started by W. E. B. DuBois, brought together more than 200 contributors, who offered the latest scholarly perspective on thousands of issues and individuals. African American culture, in the view of Gates and other academics, was not "a thing apart, separate from the whole, having no influence on the shape and shaping of American culture." Gates and other supporters of multiculturalism insisted that African American authors, such as Toni Morrison (who won the Nobel Prize for Literature in 1993) and Alice Walker, be viewed as writers who take "the blackness of the culture for granted" and use this as "a springboard to write about those human emotions that we share with everyone else, and that we have always shared with each other." The cultural works of African Americans, in short, could simultaneously be seen as unique and different, *and also* be viewed in relationship to broader cultural traditions.

People of African descent expressed a broad spectrum of views on most public issues. The clash between Clarence Thomas and Anita Hill, for instance, split African Americans, just as it divided others. Many black feminists saw Hill's testimony against Thomas as evidence of pervasive sexism within African American life, but others focused on the racial implications of this episode. No nominee of European descent, they argued, would have ever faced the kind of personal scrutiny that Thomas confronted.

Opinion polls suggested that African Americans tended to see protecting Thomas's position as a successful male professional as more important than attacking his conservative politics or pressing the gender issues raised by Hill and her supporters.

The story of sports star and media personality O. J. Simpson, who starred in the longest-running legal spectacle in U.S. history, sparked another emotional, and longer-lasting, debate about the relationship between racial identity and law. In 1995, authorities in Los Angeles prosecuted Simpson for two brutal murders, including that of his former wife. His defense team successfully focused the trial on alleged misconduct by purportedly racist officers within the L.A. police department, and a largely black jury declared Simpson not guilty. Polls indicated that African Americans overwhelmingly supported this verdict and that members of other ethnic groups rejected it. (A subsequent civil trial for monetary damages, a judicial proceeding in which the laws of evidence and burden of proof differ from those in a criminal prosecution, resulted in another jury, largely white, finding Simpson monetarily liable for the murders.) The Simpson episode, which resurfaced whenever a prominent African American (such as basketball player Kobe Bryant in 2004) faced legal liability, continued to mark a significant gulf stemming from distrust of the police and the legal system in African American communities. Efforts to develop "community policing" and more racially diverse police forces failed to erase this kind of distrust.

Issues of equal treatment in the legal and criminal justice systems remained part of the agenda for African American activists. A post-Simpson investigation of the L.A. police department featured allegations that that some of its officers regularly manufactured evidence against people who were African American. Differences in the sentencing of convicted felons, in most parts of the country, raised a broader concern. In general, it appeared, courts imposed harsher sentences for crimes involving crack cocaine, a drug consumed in African American neighborhoods, than for those involving the more expensive varieties of cocaine favored by white, suburban drug users. The fact that, by the late 1990s, more African American men sat in jails and prisons than attended colleges and universities, activists claimed, could partly be explained by sentencing disparities such as the one involving different kinds of cocaine. In addition, statistical evidence also indicated that African Americans convicted of potential capital crimes were more likely to receive the death penalty than were prison inmates from other ethnic and racial backgrounds.

"Racial profiling," a practice that could touch anyone of African descent, also remained a prominent issue. Repeated studies suggested that police detained African Americans as criminal suspects and stopped black motor-ists far more often than members of any other ethnic group. Activists called this practice DWB, or "driving while black." (In Hispanic communities, DWB came to stand for "driving while brown.") Some police officials explained such statistics as merely reflecting probabilities based on crime data, but most recognized that the practice raised legitimate questions about equal protection and hardly engendered respect for the criminal justice system. Even if someone of non-European descent were released immediately, critics of policing practices argued that the mere fact of having been detained represented a serious, race-related affront to a person's dignity. Profiling seemed a symbolic reminder of the days of slavery and legally sanctioned discrimination.

Other practices that symbolized racism of the past also became the target of activists. At the beginning of the 1990s, several southern states and many institutions, such as colleges and private clubs, still flew the flag of the Confederacy. The battle over the flags, and over other memorials relating to the Civil War, could become highly charged. Groups that defended symbols of the Confederacy argued that they merely honored the people who had supported the southern cause in the mid-19th century, not the system of chattel slavery. Civil libertarians wondered how campaigns to remove symbolic forms that carried multiple meanings could be squared with the First Amendment's guarantee of free speech. Activists, however, countered that the cause of the Confederacy could not be separated from that of preserving slavery and that the Confederate flag had long provided a powerful symbol of racist resistance to efforts to attack racial discrimination during the civil-rights era of the 1950s and 1960s.

By the beginning of the 21st century, many African American activists no longer worked from outside of the country's dominant institutions. In 1970, 13 African American members of Congress established the Congressional Black Caucus (CBC) as a means of providing a common front on a wide range of foreign and domestic issues. By 2004, nearly 40 members of the House, all Democrats, supported the CBC. It issued a hypothetical "Alternative Budget," which targeted far more money toward social initiatives than the ones being passed by Congress; campaigned on behalf of better relations with African nations and other countries with large populations of African descent, such as Cuba and Haiti; and took stands on issues, such as racial profiling and drug sentencing, that particularly affected African Americans.

American Indian Activism

American Indians conducted their activism along two broad fronts. Indians had, of course, long-standing identities based on their tribal affiliation, and many issues, par-

CONGRESSIONAL BLACK CAUCUS

The Congressional Black Caucus frequently took collective stands on issues they felt would be of special importance to African Americans.

century, the federal government officially recognized more than 550 separate tribes and bands; another 150 were seeking such recognition; and 30 others had secured recognition from individual states. Tribes were not always geographical entities. Three-quarters of American Indians lived in urban areas, and about half of the people residing on reservations did not officially identify themselves as Indians.

Following the suggestion of American Indian lawyers and tapping the expertise of the Native American Rights Fund (NARF), tribes aggressively used the legal system. They pressed demands that derived from old treaties with the U.S. government and from the unique legal status of tribal nations. Some tribal representatives sought recognition of specific fishing and agricultural rights, a campaign that often provoked resentment among non-Indians, who argued that these special claims, based on federal authority, should not take precedence over state and local laws. At the same time, American Indians also sued to protect tribal water rights and traditional religious ceremonies (some of which included the ritualistic use of drugs such as peyote) and to secure repatriation of Indian skeletal remains that were being displayed or stored in museums across the country. (At one point, the Smithsonian Institution was housing the remains of more than 18,000 Indians, supposedly for historical and scientific purposes.) Pressure from American Indian rights groups led Congress to pass the Native American Graves Protection and Repatriation Act (1990), which required universities and museums to return human remains and sacred objects to any tribe that requested them.

Tribes also sued to obtain Las Vegas–style gaming privileges. Claiming exemption from state gambling laws, American Indians opened bingo halls and, then, full-blown casinos. In 1988, the U.S. Supreme Court ruled that states could not prohibit gaming operations on tribal land within their borders, and Congress responded with the Indian Gaming Regulatory Act, which gave a federal seal of approval to casino operations. As gambling emerged as one of the most lucrative sectors of the nation's entertainment business, American Indian–owned casinos became a major part of this phenomenon. In states such as Connecticut and Minnesota, American Indian gaming establishments employed growing numbers of Indians and non-Indians alike.

ticularly those involving land and treaty disputes, turned on specific, tribal-based claims. Other questions, which seemed to require strategies that extended beyond a single tribe, became identified as "pan-Indian" in nature. In 1969, people from several tribes began a two-year sit-in, designed to dramatize a history of broken treaty promises, at the former federal prison on Alcatraz Island in San Francisco harbor. Expanding on this tactic, the American Indian Movement (AIM), created by young activists from several Northern Plains tribes, adopted a similarly confrontational approach. Violent clashes, with both federal officials and older American Indian leaders, eventually erupted in early 1973 on the Pine Ridge Reservation in South Dakota. In response, federal officials targeted members of AIM for illegal surveillance and for controversial criminal prosecutions.

Meanwhile, important legal and social changes were taking place. The omnibus Civil Rights Act of 1968 contained several sections that became known as the "Indian Bill of Rights." In these sections, Congress finally extended most of the provisions of the constitutional Bill of Rights to American Indians on reservations while still upholding the legitimacy of tribal laws. Federal legislation and several Supreme Court decisions in the 1970s subsequently reinforced the principle of "tribal self-determination." In 1978, Congress passed the Tribally Controlled College Assistance Act, which supported educational institutions that would build job skills and preserve tribal cultures. Tribal identification itself required legal action. By the early 21st

© Gary A. Conner/PhotoEdit.

GAMING AT MYSTIC LAKE CASINO IN MINNESOTA

By the mid-1990s, legal gambling had become one of the nation's leading economic enterprises. Native Americans saw casinos as an important way to generate jobs and capital on Indian reservations.

The competition to establish casinos in prime locations prompted intertribal political and legal conflict.

Ironically, the glitzy, tribal-owned casinos existed alongside tribal powwows and other efforts to nurture older cultural practices. The Mashantucket Pequot tribe in Connecticut earmarked some of the profits from its lucrative Foxwoods casino to finance one of the nation's largest powwows, which offered nearly $1 million in prizes for entrants in its American Indian dance contests.

Powwows were only one part of the attempt to build a stronger sense of identity through the promotion of cultural practices viewed as traditional. To forestall the disappearance of native languages, American Indian activists urged bilingualism and the renewed attention to tribal rituals. By 2000, only about 175 native languages were spoken at all; of these, less than two dozen were used between parents and children. Indian groups denounced the use of stereotypical nicknames, such as "Chiefs" and "Redskins," and Indian-related logos in amateur and professional sports. The federal government assisted this cultural-pride movement by appropriating funds for two National Museums of the American Indian, one in New York and another in the nation's capitol. The National Park Service changed the name of "Custer Battlefield" in Montana to

Bill Pugliano/Gamma-Liaison Network.

LOS ANGELES POWWOW

Tribal dancers participate in a powwow in Los Angeles. Many Native Americans in the late 20th century embraced the rediscovery of traditional ways.

"Little Bighorn Battlefield," shifting the site's historical emphasis and redesigning its exhibits to help celebrate American Indian culture. Activists also forged links with aboriginal peoples throughout the Americas and the South Pacific to draw international attention to the problems facing aboriginal peoples around the globe.

Activism in Spanish-Speaking Communities

Spanish-speaking Americans, who constituted the fastest-growing ethnic group in the United States, highlighted the complexity of ethnic identity. Many Spanish-speaking people, especially in the Southwest, prefer the umbrella term "Latino," whereas others, particularly in Florida, use the term "Hispanic." At the same time, people whom the U.S. Census began (in 1980) labeling Hispanic more frequently identified themselves according to the Spanish-speaking country or commonwealth from which they or their ancestors had immigrated.

Beneath these general designations and a common Spanish language lay great diversity. The Cuban Americans who came to South Florida during the 1960s, for example, generally enjoyed greater access to education and higher incomes than did most Latinos who came later, even from Cuba. The initial wave of Cuban immigrants also tended to be more politically conservative than other Latinos; they generally voted Republican and espoused a hard-line stance against the communist government of Cuba's Fidel Castro. Émigrés from Puerto Rico focused some of their political energy on the persistent "status" question—that is, whether Puerto Rico should hope for independence, strive for statehood, or retain a commonwealth connection to the mainland. Immigrants from the Dominican Republic and Central America (both legal and undocumented) were among the most recent and economically deprived newcomers.

Mexican Americans, members of the oldest and most numerous Spanish-speaking group in the United States, could tap a long tradition of social activism. The 1960s saw an emerging spirit of *Chicanismo,* a populistic pride in a heritage that could be traced back to the ancient civilizations of Middle America. Young activists made "Chicano/a," once terms of derision that older Mexican Americans had generally avoided, a rallying cry. In cities in the Southwest, advocates of *Chicanismo,* although still a minority force in Mexican American politics, gained considerable cultural influence. Attempts by the police to crack down on Chicano activism during the 1970s backfired, especially in Los Angeles, and increasing numbers of young Mexican Americans identified with the new spirit of insurgency.

Beginning in the 1970s, cities and towns in the Southwest with large Mexican American populations experienced considerable cultural ferment and political-social change. Members of La Raza Unida, a movement founded in 1967, began to win local elections. At the same time, Mexican American communities experienced a cultural flowering. Although Catholic priests generally avoided militancy, many of them opened their churches to groups devoted to ethnic dancing, mural painting, poetry, and literature. Spanish language newspapers and journals, too, reinforced the growing sense of pride. Mexican Americans pushed for programs in Chicano/a Studies at colleges and universities.

Developments in San Antonio, a city with a large Mexican American population, suggested the potential fruits

MURAL ART IN CHICAGO

Themes in Mexican history and culture, inspired by the great Mexican muralists, appeared in Mexican American communities throughout the country.

of grassroots political organizing. In the 1970s, Ernesto Cortes, Jr., took the lead in founding Communities Organized for Public Service (COPS), a group that focused on achieving concrete, tangible changes that touched the everyday lives of ordinary citizens. In San Antonio this strategy meant that Mexican American activists worked with Anglo business leaders and with Democratic politicians such as Henry Cisneros, who became the city's mayor in 1981. COPS brought many Mexican Americans, particularly women, into the public arena for the first time.

By the early 21st century, Mexican American activism was becoming increasingly diverse. La Raza Unida continued its activities but never became a national force. Instead, the Mexican American Legal Defense and Educational Fund (MALDEF), established in 1968 with funding from the Ford Foundation, emerged as the most visible national group, one ready to lobby or litigate on behalf of Mexican Americans. At the local level, organizations formed on the model of COPS, such as United Neighborhood Organization (UNO) in Los Angeles, continued to work on community concerns. The booming U.S. economy of the 1990s offered expanding employment and educational opportunities, especially for women. Yet most new jobs, Mexican American advocacy groups complained, offered low wages and few benefits. Mexican Americans often spearheaded labor-organizing efforts, particularly in the rapidly expanding service sector of the economy. Women continued to join organizations such as the National Network of Hispanic Women, which represented Chicanas who had been successful in professional and business life. Conservatives such as Linda Chavez— a Republican activist who moved among the worlds of business, politics, and public policy—joined Democrats such as Henry Cisneros as symbols of Mexican American mobility.

Social activism among Puerto Ricans in the United States emerged more slowly than among Mexican Americans. Much of the effort during the 1960s went toward strengthening existing community-based institutions and building new ones. New York City's Puerto Rican Day Parade, an important focus of cultural pride that had begun during the 1950s, became the city's largest ethnic celebration. Despite the formation of activist groups, such as the Young Lords, however, the social programs of the Great Society often bypassed Puerto Ricans. A 1976 report by the U.S. Commission on Civil Rights concluded that Puerto Ricans remained "the last in line" for government-funded benefits and opportunity programs. By the 1980s, activists were focusing on legal and political issues. The Puerto Rican Legal Defense and Education Fund and allied groups obtained courtroom victories that helped

Puerto Ricans surmount obstacles to the ballot box and to political office. Puerto Rican voters provided important support for insurgent, grassroots politics in Chicago and in many cities on the East Coast.

Even after leaving the Caribbean, Puerto Ricans continued to address issues there as well. In 2000, the Puerto Rican Legal Defense and Education Fund joined other groups to organize a well-publicized, ultimately successful campaign to stop the U.S. Navy from using the small island of Vieques as a target range, thereby creating health and ecological hazards for Puerto Rico.

Americans of Cuban origin increasingly wrestled with how much energy they should devote to affairs in their homeland. Although Cuban Americans became active in southern Florida politics and civic affairs, critics noted the persistent "exile mentality" that revolved around anti-Castro activities. The issue of how to focus activism emerged most vividly in 2000 over a familial struggle involving a young Cuban boy whom U.S. authorities had picked up in the Atlantic after his mother, fleeing from the island, had drowned. Although most people in Miami's Little Havana seemed to rally behind the effort of the boy's U.S. relatives to contest the federal government's decision to return him to his father in Cuba, some Cuban Americans argued that this media-saturated spectacle misrepresented a diverse community whose involvement in American life increasingly overshadowed the one-time obsession with the fate of Castro's regime.

Asian American Activism

People with diverse ancestral roots in Asia increasingly adopted the term "Asian American" as a way of signifying a new identity consciousness. During the 1970s, Asian American studies programs took shape at colleges and universities on the West Coast. By the early 1980s, political activists were gaining influence, especially within the Democratic Party, and more Asian American politicians won election to public office during the late 1980s and 1990s. Meanwhile, older Japanese Americans finally began to talk about what had long been unspoken—their experiences in internment camps during the Second World War (see chapter 26). Talk eventually turned to political agitation, and in 1988, Congress issued a formal apology and voted a reparations payment of $20,000 to every living Japanese American who had been confined in the camps.

The new Asian American vision encouraged Americans of Chinese, Japanese, Korean, Filipino, and other backgrounds to join together in a single pan-Asian movement. Organizations such as the Asian Pacific Planning

Council (APPCON), founded in 1976, lobbied to obtain government funding for projects that benefited Asian American communities. The Asian Law Caucus, founded in the early 1970s by opponents of U.S. intervention in Vietnam, and the Committee Against Anti-Asian Violence, created a decade later in response to a wave of racist attacks, mobilized to fight a wide range of legal battles. Beginning in 1997, the National Asian Pacific American Network Council, the first civil-rights group to be formed by Asian Americans, began to lobby on issues related to immigration and education.

Emphasizing this broad, pan-Asian identity, however, raised questions of inclusion and exclusion. Filipino American activists, members of the second largest Asian American group in the United States in 1990, often resisted the Asian American label because they believed that Chinese Americans or Japanese Americans dominated groups such as APPCON. Many people of Filipino descent focused on specific goals, particularly an effort to obtain citizenship and veteran's benefits for former soldiers of the Second World War who had fought against Japan in the Philippines. Similarly, Hmong groups often pursued matters specific to their own particular concerns. In 2000, for instance, they and their allies succeeded in obtaining the Hmong Veterans Naturalization Act, which allowed Hmong immigrants (and their spouses and widows) to use an interpreter when taking the test to obtain U.S. citizenship. At the same time, as new arrivals continued to come from Asia, groups such as Filipinos for Affirma-

tive Action agreed to cooperate with other organizations in opposing efforts to deny social services to legal immigrants.

As a result of pressure from different ethnic groups, the federal government finally decided to designate "Asian or Pacific Islanders" (API) as a single pan-ethnic category in the censuses of 1990 and 2000. It also provided, however, nine specifically enumerated subcategories (such as Hawaiian or Filipino) and allowed other API groups (such as Hmong or Samoan) to write in their respective ethnic identifications.

Socioeconomic differences also made it difficult to frame a single Asian American agenda. Although in the late 1980s and early 1990s many Asian American groups showed remarkable upward mobility, demonstrating both economic and educational achievement, others such as Hmong immigrants and Chinese American garment workers struggled to find jobs that paid more than the minimum wage. Thus, the term Asian American—which, by the beginning of the 21st century, applied to more than 10 million people and dozens of different ethnicities—both reflected, and was challenged by, the new emphasis on ethnic identity.

The Dilemmas of Antidiscrimination Efforts

How might governmental power best advance the cause of equality? Between the end of the Second World War and about 1970, the antidiscrimination movement had demanded that the government not categorize individuals according to group identities based on race or ethnicity. On matters such as education, housing, or employment, the law must remain "color-blind" and treat people equally. The courts stood increasingly ready to strike down discriminatory laws and practices and to guarantee at least formal equality for all individuals.

Gradually, ideas about the relationship between group identities and moves toward greater equality began to change. By the 1970s, the new social-activist agenda envisioned that governmental power could do more than simply eliminate discriminatory barriers to *individual* opportunity. Social justice, according to this view, required government to take "affirmative action" so that *groups* that had historically faced discrimination could begin to receive an equitable share of the nation's jobs, public spending, and educational programs. It was not enough, in short, that individual members of ethnic minorities theoretically be permitted to compete for jobs and educational opportunities; rather, government needed to make sure

VIETNAMESE AMERICAN BUSINESSES IN LOS ANGELES
New Asian immigrants, especially from Southeast Asia, established a growing economic presence in many U.S. cities and helped revitalize older urban neighborhoods.

© Nik Wheeler/Corbis.

that a representative number of people from different groups had a reasonable chance of acceptance. Affirmative action, supporters argued, would help compensate for past discrimination and for hidden prejudices that continued to thwart members of particular ethnic groups.

Affirmative action sparked controversy. Some people, generally in the Republican ranks, saw affirmative action as a dangerous form of "interest-group politics." Any program that appeared to "set aside" jobs or openings in educational institutions for certain racial or ethnic groups, they charged, smacked of racist "quotas." Moreover, was not affirmative action *on behalf of* some groups inevitably also "reverse discrimination" *against* others? The claim of reverse discrimination became particularly emotional when members of one ethnic group received jobs or entry to educational institutions despite lower scores on admissions exams. Even some beneficiaries of compensatory programs began to claim that the derogatory label of "affirmative action hire" demeaned their individual talents and accomplishments.

Courts struggled to square affirmative action programs with legal precedents, from the civil-rights era, against discrimination. They tended to strike down, as unconstitutional, any affirmative action plan that seemed to contain inflexible quotas and to uphold less rigid ones designed to remedy "past patterns" of discrimination and to make ethnicity only one of several criteria for making hiring or educational decisions.

A drive to eliminate or radically scale back affirmative action plans gained momentum during the 1990s. In 1996, after a hotly contested referendum campaign, voters in California passed Proposition 209, which aimed at ending most affirmative action measures in California by abolishing racial or gender preference in state hiring, contracting, and college admissions. The number of African Americans and Latinos admitted to the state's most prestigious law and medical schools temporarily dropped as most of those who were admitted chose to go elsewhere. Proponents of affirmative action challenged Proposition 209 as discriminatory. New programs that boosted ethnic

AP/Wide World Photos.

RACIAL TENSION IN BROOKLYN, 1990

In 1990, African American demonstrators staged a four-month boycott of a Brooklyn grocery store, owned by Korean Americans, after a black customer allegedly was assaulted by the store's employees. Tensions among racial and ethnic groups were part of the new diversity during the late 20th century.

diversity were subsequently devised, in California and elsewhere. These emphasized income or high school ranking, rather than race or ethnicity, in the design of affirmative action programs.

Ironically, the debates over identity politics and affirmative action coincided with a rise in racial and ethnic intermarriage—a trend that might, in time, change the entire basis of discussion about equality. The 2000 census suggested that growing numbers of people identified themselves as "mixed race" and could, or would, not claim a single ethnic-racial identity. In 1997, the media hailed Eldrick ("Tiger") Woods as the first African American golfer to win the prestigious Masters tournament, but Woods, whose mother was from Thailand, fiercely resisted the label. In an official statement, Woods said he was "equally proud" to be "both African American and Asian!" But he hoped that he could also "be just a golfer and a human being."

The New Right

Beginning in the mid-1970s, a diverse coalition called the "New Right" began to mobilize. By the early 21st century, its vision of conservatism eventually captured the imagination of millions.

Several different constituencies made up the New Right. Older activists, who had rallied around William F. Buckley's *National Review* during the 1950s and Barry Goldwater during the mid-1960s, contributed continuity

ANTI-ABORTION PROTEST, 1989
Legalized abortions became a major political issue after the 1973 Supreme Court decision in *Roe* v. *Wade*. Here, on the 16th anniversary of *Roe*, protesters assemble in front of the Supreme Court building.

(see chapter 28). Espousing anticommunism and denouncing domestic spending programs, they also spoke out on a widening range of social and cultural issues. Phyllis Schlafly assumed a prominent role in successfully mobilizing opposition to ratification of the Equal Rights Amendment, and Buckley's broad-ranging *Firing Line* became one of public television's most successful programs during the 1970s and 1980s.

New Conservative Institutions

These established activists teamed up with a group of intellectuals called the "neoconservatives" or "neocons." The first neoconservatives, writers such as Norman Podhoretz and Gertrude Himmelfarb, had been anticommunist liberals during the 1950s and early 1960s. Unsettled by the insurgencies of the 1960s, they saw the Democratic Party abandoning an anticommunist foreign policy and catering to social activists. Most neocons supported Democrat Hubert Humphrey over Republican Richard Nixon in 1968, but some began moving steadily rightward during the 1970s and embraced the Republicans during the 1980s.

The neoconservatives of this era remained true to their political and cultural roots. Their lively essays, written for established organs of conservatism such as *National Review* and the *Wall Street Journal* and for neoconservative publications such as *Commentary* and the *New Criterion*, denounced any movement associated with the 1960s, including affirmative action. Neoconservatives offered intellectual sustenance to a new generation of conservative thinkers, who worked to reinvigorate the nation's anticommunist foreign policy and celebrate its capitalist economic system.

A new militancy among conservative business leaders also helped build the New Right. Denouncing the Great Society and even criticizing Richard Nixon's Republican administration, some business spokespeople claimed that health and safety regulations and environmental legislation endangered "economic freedom." They urged rededication to the idea of limited government. Generous funding by corporations and philanthropic organizations helped staff conservative research institutions (such as the American Enterprise Institute and The Heritage Foundation) and finance new lobbying organizations (such as the Committee on the Present Danger). Conservatism also gained considerable ground on college campuses, which had been incubators of the New Left and the counterculture during the 1960s.

The New Religious Right

The New Right of the 1970s also attracted important grass-roots support from Protestants in fundamentalist and evangelical churches. (Fundamentalists preach the necessity of fidelity to a strict moral code, of an individual commitment to Christ, and of a faith in the literal truth of the Bible. Evangelicals generally espouse the same doctrinal tenets as fundamentalists but place more emphasis on converting non-Christians and less on defending the literal truth of the Bible.) Since the 1920s, fundamentalist and evangelical Protestants had generally stayed clear of partisan politics, but the Supreme Court's abortion decision in *Roe* v. *Wade* (1973) mobilized their leaders. They joined with anti-abortion Catholics in opposing the *Roe* ruling. Reverend Jerry Falwell of the Thomas Road Baptist Church and the *Old Time Gospel Hour* television ministry declared that *Roe* showed that it was time to fight back on the political front because "liberals have been imposing morality on us for the last fifty years." Leaders of the New Religious Right, particularly in the South, also embarked on a lengthy legal battle to prevent the Internal Revenue Service from denying tax-exempt status to private Christian colleges and academies that opposed racial integration.

This chart shows the self-described religious affiliations of the American people compiled through sampling techniques.

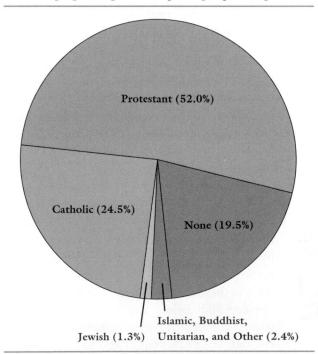

Protestant (52.0%)

Catholic (24.5%)

None (19.5%)

Jewish (1.3%)   Islamic, Buddhist, Unitarian, and Other (2.4%)

RELIGION IN AMERICA, 2001

Source: Data adapted from *The American Religious Identification Survey,* Graduate Center, City University of New York.

This wing of the New Right sought to redefine the relationship between religious and political action. During the 1950s, many mainstream religious leaders had supported the civil-rights crusade, and some joined in the antiwar movement of the 1960s. Those associated with the New Right went further in insisting that religious values should actively shape day-to-day political policy making. The insistence on a clear separation between church and state, a guiding principle of American constitutionalism during the era of Earl Warren's Supreme Court, struck the New Right as a violation of the right to the "free exercise of religion" that the First Amendment guaranteed. Going beyond this claim, some activists on the New Right declared that churches could provide the kind of divinely inspired assistance to people in need that secular institutions, such as social welfare agencies, could never dispense. Challenging older constitutional precedents against state aid to religious institutions, they urged that government, at all levels, should use tax monies to help fund church-centered education and "faith-based" social programming.

The New Right's Agenda

Political developments also contributed to the emergence of the New Right. Many on the right ultimately judged Richard Nixon to be more of an Eisenhower-style moderate than a Goldwater-style conservative, and the end of Nixon's presidency in 1974 intensified the desire to identify a "real" conservative leader. This search became a crusade after Nixon's successor, Gerald Ford, selected the old enemy of Goldwater Republicans, Nelson Rockefeller, as his vice president. "I could hardly have been more upset if Ford had selected Teddy Kennedy," one outraged conservative fumed.

It soon became apparent that opposition to a wide range of federal social programs and to cultural change could energize millions of voters. In 1975, New Right activists formed the National Conservative Political Action Committee (NCPAC), the first of many similar organizations, including the Conservative Caucus, The Committee for the Survival of a Free Congress, and Jerry Falwell's Moral Majority. Although these organizations initially focused on lobbying in Washington and backing conservative Republican candidates, they also looked to broader cultural and social goals. As one architect of this new coalition put it, they fervently believed that "God's truth ought to be manifest politically."

Increasingly, the New Right mobilized behind a defense of "family values." Its leaders opposed what they called "degenerate lifestyles," particularly those espoused

CONCLUSION ■ **969**

by feminists and homosexuals. Jerry Falwell's *Listen America!* (1980) suggested that the nation's military establishment was "under the complete control of avid supporters of the women's liberation movement." Because homosexuality was "one of the gravest sins condemned in the Scriptures," argued Paul Weyrich of NCPAC, the issue of gay and lesbian rights was not a matter of private lifestyles but a "question of morality which . . . affects the society as a whole." American institutions, particularly the male-headed nuclear family, needed protection. More broadly, parents needed to protect their children from educational "experiments." School boards and liberal educators, the New Right argued, were not only challenging Biblical precepts by teaching evolution but were also advancing dangerous new ideas such as multiculturalism and feminism. These activists saw educational bureaucrats forcing students to accept values that violated the religious and cultural values of their churches and families.

The New Right also condemned innovations associated with the 1960s in college curricula and in cultural life. Colleges were contributing to "the closing of the American mind" (the title of a best-selling 1987 book by Allan Bloom) by exposing students only to what was trendy and "politically correct" (or PC). The new attention to multicultural works, educational traditionalists charged, would soon debase intellectual life. In the broader public realm, the government-funded National Endowment for the Humanities (NEH) and the National Endowment for the Arts (NEA) came under fire for backing projects that focused on diversity and on politically sensitive cultural productions. The New Right, led by educational activists such as William Bennett and Lynn Cheney, championed what they called traditional cultural values and crusaded against multiculturalism. Their broad campaign won an important legal victory in 1998 when the U.S. Supreme Court ruled that the NEA's denial of a governmental grant, which had been supported by a preliminary review panel, to a controversial "performance artist" did not violate First Amendment guarantees of free speech.

The New Right adeptly publicized its positions. Well-funded conservative organizations sponsored academic conferences, popular gatherings, and radio and television programs. The religious wing of the New Right embraced the electronic media. Pat Robertson capitalized on the expansion of CATV to build a multimedia empire that, at one time, even included its own 24/7 Christian Broadcasting Network. Sexual and financial scandals overtook some religious broadcasters, but Robertson's "700 Club," a program that continually adapted his conservative evangelical style to new TV formats, flourished.

More important, conservative broadcasters, such as Rush Limbaugh, used the talk-radio genre, at both the local and national levels, to spread the New Right's message. Other conservative activists used television and, later, eagerly embraced the Internet. By the early 21st century, the fast-growing Fox News Channel (FNC), while proclaiming its news to be more "fair" and "balanced" than arch-rival CNN, also cultivated a conservative audience with commentators, such as Bill O'Reilly, who highlighted New Right perspectives.

The New Right, much like other activist groups, hardly moved in lockstep. More traditional members of the New Right coalition, such as the journalist and sometimes presidential candidate Patrick Buchanan, saw a new generation of neocons hijacking their cause and urging a "radical" turn in U.S. foreign policy during the 1990s. Buchanan and his followers denounced the free trade policies and the global military strategy that other conservatives promoted.

While remaining a coalition of disparate parts, the New Right became a powerful force in both American politics and culture. It successfully challenged the once-dominant political agenda of the Democratic Party, propelled the mainstream of the Republican Party decidedly rightward, established a strong foothold in public-policy and media discussions, and succeeded in remapping the nation's cultural and informational landscape.

Conclusion

Sweeping changes occurred in demographics, economics, culture, and society during the last quarter of the 20th century. The nation aged, and more of its people gravitated to the Sunbelt. Sprawling urban corridors and edge cities challenged older central cities as sites for commercial, as well as residential, development. Rapid technological change fueled the growth of globalized industries, restructuring the labor force to fit a postindustrial economy.

The most prominent development in American popular culture was the proliferation of the video screen. Television, motion pictures, and the Internet increasingly targeted specific audiences, and the fragmented nature of cultural reception was exemplified by the rise of new, particularistic media ventures.

Meanwhile, American society also seemed to fragment into specialized identifications. Social activism often organized around sexual, ethnic, and racial identities. Multiculturalists celebrated this fragmentation, while another activist movement, the New Right, argued that identity politics was dividing the nation. The New Right's stress on limiting the power of government and promoting conservative values increasingly set the terms for political debate during the 1980s and 1990s, reconfiguring dis-

cussions about whether government power advanced, or worked against, greater liberty and equality in American life.

SUGGESTED READINGS

The economic ferment of the late 20th and early 21st centuries may be surveyed, from differing perspectives, in **Daniel Yergin, *The Commanding Heights: The Battle between Government and the Marketplace That Is Remaking the Modern World*** (1998); **Robert N. McCauley, Judith Ruud, and Frank Iacano,** eds., *Dodging Bullets: Changing U.S. Corporate Structure in the 1980s and 1990s* (1999); **Randall E. Stross, *Eboys: the First Inside Account of Venture Capitalists at Work*** (2001); **Jeffrey A. Frankel and Peter R. Orszas, eds., *American Economic Policy in the 1990s*** (2002); **Kevin Phillips, *Wealth and Democracy: A Political History of the American Rich*** (2003); and **Paul Krugman, *The Great Unraveling: Losing Our Way in the New Century*** (2003).

An overview of major social issues can be gleaned, again from very different viewpoints, in studies such as **Stephen Steinberg, *Turning Back: The Retreat from Racial Justice in American Thought and Policy*** (1995); **David Hollinger, *Post-Ethnic America: Beyond Multiculturalism*** (1995); **David M. Reimers, *Unwelcome Strangers: American Identity and the Turn against Immigration*** (1998); **Debra L. DeLaet, *U.S. Immigration Policy in an Age of Rights*** (2000); **Joseph Nevins, *Operation Gatekeeper: The Rise of the "Illegal Alien" and the Remaking of the U.S.-Mexico Boundary*** (2001); **Alice O'Connor, *Poverty Knowledge: Social Science, Social Policy, and the Poor in Twentieth-Century U.S. History*** (2001); and **Hugh Davis Graham, *Collision Course: The Strange Convergence of Affirmative Action and Immigration Policy in America*** (2002).

The much-contested cultural scene comes into view in **Lawrence Grossberg, *We Gotta Get Out of This Place: Popular Conservatism and Postmodern Culture*** (1992); **Alan Nadel, *Flatling on the Field of Dreams: Cultural Narratives in the Films of President Reagan's America*** (1995); **Fred Goodman, *Mansion on the Hill: Dylan, Young, Geffen, Springsteen, and the Head-On Collision of Rock and Commerce*** (1997); **Robert Kolker, *Cinema of Loneliness: Penn, Kubrick, Scorsese, Spielberg, Altman*** (rev. ed., 2000); **Robert Brent Toplin, *Reel History: In Defense of Hollywood*** (2002); and **Virginia Postel, *The Substance of Style: How the Rise of Aesthetic Value is Remaking Commerce, Culture, and Consciousness*** (2003).

The many other excellent and suggestive studies relevant to themes in this chapter include **Juan P. Garcia, ed., *Mexican Americans in the 1990s*** (1997); **John D'Emilio, William B. Turner, and Urvashi Vaid, eds., *Creating Change: Sexuality, Public Policy, and Civil Rights*** (2000); **Ellen Messer-Davidow, *Disciplining Feminism: From Social Action to Academic Discourse*** (2002); **Frank Wu, *Yellow: Race in America Beyond Black and White*** (2002); **Rickie Sollinger, *Beggars and Choosers: How the Politics of Choice Shapes Adoption, Abortion, and Welfare in the United States*** (2002); and **Sara Evans, *Tidal Wave: How Women Changed America at Century's End*** (2003).

AMERICAN JOURNEY ONLINE
AND
 INFOTRAC COLLEGE EDITION

Visit the source collections at www.ajaccess.wadsworth.com and
infotrac.thomsonlearning.com and use the Search function with
the following key terms to explore documents, images, audio
and video clips, articles, and commentary related to the material
in this chapter.

Immigration Act of 1965
Refugee Act of 1980
Information Revolution
Bill Gates
Human Genome Project
Cesar Chavez
United Farm Workers
AIDS
Racial profiling
Congressional Black Caucus
(CBC)

Indian Bill of Rights
Native American Rights Fund
Chicano/Chicana
La Raza Unida
Asian Pacific Planning Council
(APPCON)
National Asian Pacific American
Network Council
Affirmative Action
Neoconservatives
Religious Right

GRADE AIDS

Visit the Liberty Equality Power Companion Web Site for resources specific to
this textbook: http://history.wadsworth.com/murrin_LEP4e

 The CD in the back of this book and the U.S. History Resource Center at
http://history.wadsworth.com/u.s./ offer a variety of tools to help you succeed in
this course, including access to quizzes; images; documents; interactive simulations,
maps, and timelines; movie explorations; and a wealth of other sources.

Chapter 31

Power and Politics since 1974

© James L. Amos/Corbis.

FREEWAY ARTISTRY IN ATLANTA
As suburbs spread, so did highways. Often graceful in design, as the lines
of this interchange suggest, severely congested highways would nonetheless
challenge America's love affair with the automobile.

CHAPTER OUTLINE

During the three decades after the Second World War, the national government continually expanded its power. Most people supported augmenting military and intelligence capabilities to maintain the United States' dominant place in world affairs. They also endorsed the use of governmental power to cushion against economic downturns and to assist needy families.

The Vietnam War and the Watergate scandals (see chapter 29), however, shook people's faith in government. Disillusionment with secrecy, corruption, budget deficits, and failed crusades (especially the intervention in Vietnam and the War on Poverty) bred distrust of power located in Washington. In this environment, divisive debates punctuated political life. During the 1970s and 1980s, questions focused on how to respond to an aging industrial economy, a ballooning federal deficit, and a beleaguered welfare system. Did the country need more governmental activism to address persistent social problems, or would conditions improve if the national government reduced its role? Other highly emotional issues such as abortion, environmental regulation, and taxation policy also created controversy.

When the U.S. economy began to expand during the mid-1980s and entered a lengthy period of growth during the 1990s, cynicism about government seemed to wane a bit. The overhaul of the nation's social welfare programs, plus unexpected budget surpluses and declining crime rates, restored some sense of confidence in government. Still, political debate remained polarized and culminated in the only impeachment trial of a president, Democrat Bill Clinton, in the 20th century. A new Republican president, George W. Bush, promised an administration that would restore political tranquility. The close election of 2000, a sharp economic downturn, and increasingly bitter partisan debates, however, further polarized American life.

Disagreements also focused on foreign policy. Should the United States set aside anticommunism to pursue other goals, as Democratic President Jimmy Carter (1977–81) initially urged, or should it wage the Cold War even more vigorously, as his successor, Republican Ronald Reagan (1981–89), advocated? After 1989, when the Cold War ended unexpectedly, the United States needed to reshape its foreign policy for a new post–Cold War world, one that after the attacks of September 11, 2001, in New York City and Washington, D.C., seemed as dangerous as ever before.

C H A P T E R F O C U S

♦ How were the presidencies of Gerald Ford (1974–77) and Jimmy Carter shaped by the legacies of Watergate and the Vietnam War?

♦ What conservative agenda, in both domestic and foreign policy, did Ronald Reagan's Republican administration construct?

♦ What forces and events contributed to the end of the Cold War?

♦ Around what policies and appeals did President Bill Clinton reorient the Democratic Party's domestic appeal? What was Clinton's post–Cold War agenda in foreign policy?

♦ How did the presidency of George W. Bush seek to change both domestic and foreign policy, especially in the wake of the attacks of September 11, 2001?

The Caretaker Presidency of Gerald Ford (1974–1977)

When Richard Nixon resigned from the presidency in August 1974, Gerald Ford became the first person to serve as vice president and then as president without having been elected to either office. Ford promised to salve the wounds of the 1960s and early 1970s. Drawing on political ties from his long career in the House of Representatives, Ford hoped to reestablish the presidency as a focus of national unity. But Ford's ability to "heal the land," as he put it, proved limited. A genial, unpretentious former football star who preferred his public entries to be accompanied by the fight song of his alma mater, the University of Michigan, rather than by "Hail to the Chief," Ford appeared a weak, indecisive president.

C H R O N O L O G Y

1974	Nixon resigns and Ford becomes president; Ford soon pardons Nixon
1975	South Vietnam falls to North Vietnam • Ford asserts U.S. power in *Mayaguez* incident
1976	Jimmy Carter elected president • OPEC sharply raises oil prices
1978	Carter helps negotiate Camp David peace accords on Middle East
1979	Soviet Union invades Afghanistan • Sandinista party comes to power in Nicaragua • U.S. hostages seized in Iran
1980	Reagan elected president • U.S. hostages in Iran released
1981	Reagan tax cut passed
1983	U.S. troops removed from Lebanon • U.S. troops invade Grenada • Reagan announces SDI ("Star Wars") program
1984	Reagan defeats Walter Mondale
1986	Reagan administration rocked by revelation of Iran-*Contra* affair
1988	George H. W. Bush defeats Michael Dukakis in presidential election
1989	Communist regimes in Eastern Europe collapse; Berlin Wall falls • Cold War, in effect, ends
1990	Bush angers conservative Republicans by agreeing to a tax increase
1991	Bush orchestrates Persian Gulf War against Iraq
1992	Bill Clinton defeats Bush and third-party candidate Ross Perot in presidential race
1993	Congress approves North American Free Trade Agreement (NAFTA)
1994	Republicans gain control of both houses of Congress and pledge to enact their Contract with America • Special prosecutor Kenneth Starr takes over the investigation of Whitewater allegations
1995	World Trade Organization (WTO) created
1996	The Personal Responsibility and Work Opportunity Reconciliation Act becomes the first major overhaul of the national welfare system since the 1930s • Clinton defeats Robert Dole in the presidential race
1997	Congress and the White House agree on legislation aimed at reducing taxes and rolling back the federal deficit
1998	Republicans lose House seats in off-year election • Republican-controlled House impeaches Clinton
1999	Senate fails to convict Clinton on impeachment charges • Clinton orders bombing campaign against Serbia
2000	Longest economic expansion in U.S. history continues • George W. Bush defeats Gore in close, hotly disputed election
2001	Large tax cuts passed • Al Qaeda suicide squads crash passenger airplanes into World Trade Center and Pentagon on September 11 • Patriot Act passed • U.S. military campaign ousts Taliban from power in Afghanistan
2002	Midterm elections strengthen Republican majorities in House and Senate
2003	U.S. invades Iraq and overthrows Saddam Hussein • Huge federal budget deficits return

Trying to Whip Stagflation

Ford's plan to rebuild his own party around an updated version of the moderate Republicanism of the 1950s quickly foundered. His appointment of Nelson Rockefeller as vice president infuriated the New Right, and his granting of a presidential pardon to former President Nixon, in September 1974, proved widely unpopular. Ford's approval rating plummeted.

Economic problems dominated the domestic side of the 865-day Ford presidency. Focusing on rising prices, rather than on increasing unemployment, the Ford administration touted a program called "Whip Inflation Now" (WIN). It offered a one-year income tax surcharge and cuts in federal spending as solutions to inflation. Prices, however, defied the predictions of prevailing economic wisdom and crept higher. As both prices and unemployment rose—continuing the condition known during Nixon's presidency as "stagflation"—Ford abandoned WIN. Unemployment reached 8.5 percent, and the inflation rate topped 9 percent during 1975.

Meanwhile, Ford clashed with the Democratic-controlled Congress over how to deal with stagflation. Ford, who vetoed nearly 40 spending bills during his brief presidency, eventually acquiesced to a congressional economic program that included a tax cut, an increase in unemployment benefits, an unbalanced federal budget, and a limited set of controls over oil prices. Democrats charged that Ford could not implement coherent programs of his own, and many Republicans complained that he could not stand up to Democrats in Congress.

Foreign Policy

As he struggled with economic problems at home, Ford steered the nation through its final involvement in the war in Southeast Asia. After assuming office, Ford pledged a renewal of U.S. military support to the government in South Vietnam if it ever became directly menaced by North Vietnam. The antiwar mood in Congress and throughout the country, however, made fulfilling this commitment impossible. North Vietnam's armies, sensing final victory, moved rapidly through the South in March 1975, and Congress, relieved that U.S. troops had finally been withdrawn after the 1973 Paris peace accords, refused to reintroduce U.S. military personnel.

Spring 1975 brought new communist victories. In early April, Khmer Rouge forces in Cambodia drove a U.S.-backed government from the capital of Phnom Penh, and on April 30, 1975, North Vietnamese troops overran the South Vietnamese capital of Saigon, renaming it Ho Chi Minh City. Debate over U.S. policy in Indochina again became contentious. Former "doves" lamented the lives lost and money wasted, while former "hawks" derided their country's "failure of will."

Within this charged atmosphere, Ford tried to demonstrate that the United States could still assert its power. In May 1975, a contingent of Khmer Rouge boarded a U.S. ship, the *Mayaguez*, and seized its crew. Secretary of State Henry Kissinger, declaring that it was time to "look ferocious," convinced Ford to order a rescue mission and bombing strikes against Cambodia. This military response, along with pressure on the Khmer Rouge from China, secured the release of the *Mayaguez* and its crew. The president's approval ratings briefly shot up, but the incident did little to allay doubts about Ford's leadership. The White House seemed primarily interested in looking tough, and the United States lost more men than it saved during the *Mayaguez* rescue. Meanwhile, the president's other foreign policy initiatives, which included extending Nixon's policy of détente with the Soviet Union and pursuing a peace treaty for the Middle East, achieved little. Gerald Ford increasingly appeared a caretaker president.

The Election of 1976

Conservative Republicans rallied behind Ronald Reagan and nearly denied Ford the GOP presidential nomination in 1976. Reagan, once a movie actor and the governor of California from 1966 to 1974, ignited his campaign by abandoning specific policy proposals and by highlighting his image as a "true conservative" who, unlike Ford, stood apart from political insiders in Washington. Ford had already won just enough delegates in the early primaries, however, to eke out a narrow, first-ballot victory at the Republican Party's national convention.

The Democrats did turn to an outsider, James Earl (Jimmy) Carter, the former governor of Georgia. A retired naval officer, with a degree in engineering, Carter had worked on the nuclear submarine program before abandoning a military career to return to Plains, Georgia, and run his family's peanut farming business. Later, Carter entered state politics, gaining the reputation of being a social moderate and a fiscal conservative. When he announced his presidential candidacy in 1976, few people took notice; no governor, after all, had captured the White House since Franklin Roosevelt in 1932.

With Watergate still a vivid memory, Carter's campaign emphasized personal character. Highlighting his small-town roots, Carter pledged to "give the government of this country back to the people of this country." A devout Baptist, Carter campaigned as a born-again Christian. Touting his record as a successful governor, he asked people to "help me evolve an efficient, economical, purposeful, and manageable government for our nation." In order to balance the Democratic ticket, he picked a member of the

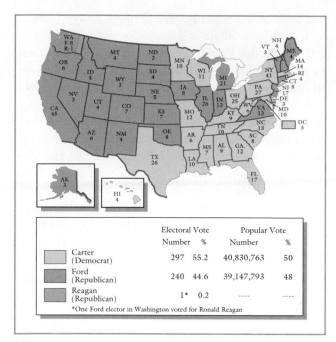

MAP 31.1 PRESIDENTIAL ELECTION, 1976

This map shows the low voter turnout and the very close election that made Jimmy Carter president. Notice how Carter, from Georgia, drew votes from Southern states.

U.S. Senate, Walter Mondale of Minnesota, as his running mate. In November, Carter won a narrow victory over Ford.

Carter's triumph rested on a diverse, transitory coalition. Tapping his regional appeal, Carter carried every southern state except Virginia. Although he ran well among southern whites who belonged to fundamentalist and evangelical churches, his victory in the South depended on a strong turnout among African Americans, the beneficiaries of federal voter protection measures enacted during the 1960s. Carter courted younger voters by promising to pardon most Vietnam-era draft resisters. With the floundering economy a major concern, Walter Mondale's appeal to party loyalists helped Carter narrowly capture three key states that had long been Democratic strongholds—New York, Pennsylvania, and Ohio. Even so, Carter defeated Ford by less than 2 million popular ballots and by only 56 electoral votes. Voter turnout in 1976 hit its lowest mark since the end of the Second World War; only about 54 percent of eligible voters went to the polls.

Jimmy Carter's One-term Presidency (1977–1981)

Jimmy Carter's lack of a popular mandate and his outsider image posed serious handicaps. Powerful constituencies, including both business and labor, feared that Carter might prove an unpredictable leader. Moreover, many Democratic members of Congress, especially those first elected in the aftermath of Watergate, stressed their independence from the White House. In 1976, most of them, after all, rolled up higher vote totals in their states than the Carter-Mondale ticket. Carter also seemed a regional, rather than a national, figure. Although some veteran Washington people joined his cabinet, he relied on the Georgians on his White House staff, a small cadre of advisers that the Washington press corps dubbed the Georgia Mafia. After leaving government, Carter reflected on his difficulties: "I had a different way of governing. . . . I was a southerner, a born-again Christian, a Baptist, a newcomer."

Welfare and Energy Initiatives

Carter found himself caught between advisers who claimed that the national government was already exercising too much power and ones who argued that Washington was doing too little to address social and economic problems at home.

In contrast to Richard Nixon, who had unveiled a bold Family Assistance Plan (FAP) before retreating, Carter immediately temporized on welfare policy. His staff split over offering a revised version of FAP, which would have emphasized monetary assistance to low-income families, and creating several million new public service jobs, which would be underwritten by Washington. Opposed to increasing federal spending, Carter nonetheless asked Congress for a compromise program that included both additional spending on existing social programs and job creation but nothing that resembled Nixon's FAP initiative. Carter's proposal failed in Congress, and the drive to overhaul the social welfare system stalled for nearly a decade.

Carter pushed harder on energy issues. The United States obtained 90 percent of its energy from fossil fuels, and this dependence, especially on petroleum imported from abroad, worried policy makers. In 1973 and again in 1976, the Organization of Petroleum Exporting Countries (OPEC), a cartel dominated by oil-rich nations in the Middle East, dramatically raised the price of crude oil and precipitated acute shortages across the globe, particularly in the United States. As gasoline became both expensive and scarce, drivers quickly wearied of high prices and long lines at service stations. Carter promised to make the United States less dependent on imported fossil fuel.

The President charged James Schlesinger, a veteran of the Nixon and Ford administrations and head of a new Department of Energy, with developing a sweeping energy plan. Schlesinger outlined ambitious goals: (1) decrease U.S. reliance on foreign oil and natural gas; (2) expand domestic energy production through new tax incentives and deregulation of natural gas production; (3) levy new taxes to discourage gasoline use; (4) foster conservation by encouraging energy-saving measures; and (5) promote nonpetroleum energy sources, especially coal and nuclear power. Neither Carter nor Schlesinger consulted Congress or even some members of the president's own administration. Instead, in April 1977, the president suddenly announced an energy proposal that included more than 100 interrelated provisions.

Congress quickly rejected the plan. Legislators from oil-producing states opposed higher taxes on gasoline, and critics of corporate power blocked deregulation of domestic oil and natural gas production. Meanwhile, environmentalists charged that greater use of coal would consequently increase air pollution. Most Americans, meanwhile, ignored Carter's plea that the struggle with energy problems amounted to "the moral equivalent of war." Carter continued to press for energy conservation; for development of renewable sources, such as solar and wind-generated energy; and for greater use of nuclear power.

The nuclear option generated sharp controversy. Boosters of atomic research programs during the early days of the Cold War had promised that giant nuclear reactors would provide a cheap, almost limitless supply of energy. The cost of building and maintaining them, however, far exceeded the original estimates, and critics saw the reactors as grave safety risks. A 1979 incident seemingly offered a graphic illustration of the danger when the malfunction of a reactor at Three Mile Island, Pennsylvania, nearly produced a nuclear meltdown. Responding to growing public concern, power companies canceled orders for new reactors, and nuclear power industry expansion halted. Meanwhile, OPEC oil prices continued to skyrocket, from $1.80 a barrel in 1971 to nearly $30 a decade later, at the end of Carter's presidency.

A Faltering Economy

Carter inherited economic problems—especially stagflation—from the Nixon and Ford years, but rising oil prices heightened inflationary pressures during his own presidency. Carter pledged to lower both unemployment and inflation, to stimulate greater economic growth, and to balance the federal budget (which showed a deficit of about $70 billion in 1976). Instead, by 1980 the economy had virtually stopped expanding, unemployment (after temporarily dipping) was again rising, and inflation was topping 13 percent. Most voters told opinion pollsters that their own economic conditions had dramatically deteriorated while Carter occupied the White House.

Economic difficulties spread beyond individuals. New York City, beset by long-term economic and social problems and short-term fiscal mismanagement, faced bankruptcy. The nation's largest city could neither meet its financial obligations nor borrow new money through the normal channels. Private bankers and public officials had to secure congressional "bailout" legislation that granted federal loan guarantees to New York City.

The Big Apple's troubles, although different in scale from those of other cities, were hardly unique. According to one estimate, Chicago lost 200,000 manufacturing jobs during the 1970s. Bricks from demolished, industrial-era buildings in St. Louis became one of that city's leading exports. Increasing numbers of people living in central cities across the country could find only low-paying, short-term jobs with no fringe benefits. Many found no employment at all. Rising crime rates, deteriorating downtowns, and shrinking tax revenues afflicted most urban areas, even as inflation further eroded the buying power of city budgets.

What explains the economic dislocation of the late 1970s? Tax cuts, increased governmental spending on

© 1980 Time Inc., Reprinted by permission.

"IS CAPITALISM WORKING?"

In 1980, even *Time* magazine wondered about the economic future of the United States. Persistent economic problems—especially high rates of inflation and unemployment—dominated the Ford and Carter presidencies.

public works projects, and actions by the Federal Reserve Board were aimed at stimulating recovery. These measures, however, also drove price inflation. Meanwhile, ever-rising international oil prices triggered a series of increases for gasoline and home heating fuel that rippled through the economy. These severe inflationary pressures brought high interest rates and a loss of confidence and investment, choking off productivity and economic growth.

Conservative economists and business groups charged that domestic programs favored by most congressional Democrats contributed to economic distress. Increasing the minimum wage and vigorously enforcing safety and antipollution regulations, they argued, drove up the cost of doing business and forced companies to raise prices to consumers. During his last two years in office, Carter seemed to agree, in part, with this analysis. Defying most Democrats in Congress, he cut spending for many social programs; sought to reduce capital gains taxes to encourage investment; and inaugurated a process of "deregulating" various industries, beginning with the transportation sector.

Negotiating Foreign Disputes

In foreign, as in domestic policy, Carter promised new directions. On his first day in office, he granted amnesty to most Vietnam-era draft resisters. He soon declared that he would not be afflicted by an "inordinate fear of communism" and would place concern for human rights at the center of U.S. foreign policy. After four years, however, his foreign policy initiatives were in disarray. Republican Ronald Reagan's "get-tough-again" presidential campaign of 1980 would link Carter with ineptitude in foreign affairs.

Although skillful in small-group negotiations, Carter had little experience working with long-term foreign policy issues. Furthermore, his top advisers—Cyrus Vance as secretary of state and Zbigniew Brzezinski as national security adviser—pursued contradictory agendas. Brzezinski favored a hard-line, anti-Soviet policy with an emphasis on military muscle; Vance preferred to avoid confrontations and to engage in quiet diplomacy. Pulled in divergent directions, Carter's foreign policy seemed to waffle. Still, Carter set some important new directions, emphasizing negotiation in particular trouble spots of the world and making human rights a priority.

Carter's faith in negotiations and in his personal skill as a facilitator yielded some success in Latin America and the Middle East. On the issue of the Panama Canal, which had been the object of diplomatic negotiations for 13 years, Carter adroitly secured treaties that granted Panama increasing authority over the waterway to culminate in full

Panamanian control in 2000. U.S. ownership of the canal, a legacy of turn-of-the-20th century expansionism, he argued, continued to fuel anti-Yankee sentiment not just in Panama but throughout Latin America. In addition, Carter convinced skeptical U.S. senators, whose votes he needed to secure any treaty, that the canal was no longer the economic and strategic necessity it had once been.

Carter's personal touch also emerged during the Camp David peace talks of 1978. Relations between Egypt and Israel had been strained since the Yom Kippur War of 1973, when Israel had repelled an Egyptian attack and had seized the Sinai Peninsula and territory along the West Bank (of the Jordan River). Reviving earlier Republican efforts to mediate the Arab-Israeli conflict, Carter brought Menachem Begin and Anwar Sadat, leaders of Israel and Egypt, respectively, to the presidential retreat at Camp David. After 13 days of bargaining, the three leaders announced the framework for a negotiating process and a peace treaty. Middle East tensions hardly vanished, but these Camp David Accords kept alive high-level discussions, lowered the level of acrimony between Egypt and Israel, and bound both nations to the United States through Carter's promises of economic aid.

In Asia and Africa, the Carter administration also emphasized accommodation. Building on Nixon's initiative, Carter expanded economic and cultural relations with China and finally established formal diplomatic ties with the People's Republic on New Year's Day 1979. In Africa, Carter abandoned Kissinger's reliance on white colonial regimes and supported the transition of Zimbabwe (formerly Rhodesia) to a government run by its black majority.

Campaigning for Human Rights Abroad

Carter's foreign policy became best known for an emphasis on human rights. Cold War alliances with anticommunist dictatorships, Carter believed, were undermining U.S. influence in the world. In the long run, Carter's policy helped encourage worldwide support for human rights issues. The trend toward democratization, which occurred in many nations during the 1980s and 1990s, could be partly traced back to Carter's stress on human rights.

The immediate impact of Carter's human rights policy, however, proved ambiguous. Because his administration sometimes ignored this matter in specific circumstances, many of America's most repressive allies, such as Ferdinand Marcos in the Philippines, continued their dictatorial ways. Moreover, Carter's own rhetoric about human rights helped justify uprising against other long-standing dictator-allies in Nicaragua and Iran. Revolutions in these countries, fueled by resentment against the United States, brought anti-American regimes to power and presented Carter with difficult choices.

In Nicaragua, the Sandinista movement toppled the repressive regime of Anastasio Somoza, whom the United States had long supported. The Sandinistas, initially a coalition of moderate democrats and communists, soon tilted toward a militant Marxism and began to expropriate private property. Carter opposed this turn in Nicaragua but concluded he could not immediately change it. Republican critics charged that Carter's policies had given a green light to communism throughout Central America and pledged to oust Nicaragua's Sandinista-controlled government.

Confronting Problems in Iran and Afghanistan

If events in Nicaragua eroded Carter's standing, those in Iran and Afghanistan all but shattered it. The United States had steadfastly supported Shah Reza Pahlavi, who had reigned in Iran since an American-supported coup in 1953, with military and economic aid. The Shah's overthrow, in January 1979, by revolutionary movement spearheaded by Islamic fundamentalists thus signaled a massive rejection of U.S. influence in oil-rich Iran. When the Carter administration allowed the deposed Shah to enter the United States for medical treatment in November 1979, a group of Iranians (with the tacit support of their government) seized the U.S. embassy compound in Tehran and 66 American hostages. Iranians demanded the return of the Shah in exchange for the release of the Americans.

Carter's critics saw this "hostage crisis" as proof of his incompetence. In response, Carter talked tough; levied economic reprisals against Iran; and, over the objections of Cyrus Vance (who subsequently resigned), sent a military mission to rescue the hostages. The effort proved an embarrassing failure, and Carter never could resolve the situation. After his defeat in the 1980 election, diplomatic efforts finally freed the hostages, but the United States and Iran remained at odds.

Criticism of Carter also focused on the Soviet Union's invasion of Afghanistan in December 1979, a move primarily sparked by Soviet fear of the growing influence of Islamic fundamentalists along its borders. Carter's opponents, however, saw this episode as a sign that Soviet leaders viewed the United States, under Carter's leadership, as too weak to contain their expansionism. Charged with suffering from the "post-Vietnam syndrome," a failure to act decisively in foreign affairs, Carter tried to respond in

nonmilitary ways. He halted grain exports to the Soviet Union (angering his farm constituency), organized a boycott of the 1980 Olympic Games in Moscow, withdrew a new Strategic Arms Limitation Treaty (SALT) from the Senate, and revived registration for the military draft. Still, Republicans (along with some Democrats) charged Carter with allowing American power and prestige to decline.

The Election of 1980

For a time, when Senator Edward Kennedy of Massachusetts entered the party's 1980 presidential primaries, it seemed that Democrats themselves might deny Carter a second term. Although Kennedy's challenge eventually fizzled, it did underscore Carter's vulnerability. Kennedy popularized anti-Carter themes that Republicans gleefully embraced. "It's time to say no more hostages, no more high interest rates, no more high inflation, and no more Jimmy Carter," went one of Kennedy's stump speeches. More than one-third of the Democrats who supported Kennedy in the final Democratic primaries (most of which Kennedy won) told pollsters they probably would vote Republican in the general election. As Carter entered the fall campaign, he seemed a sure loser.

Republican candidate Ronald Reagan exuded confidence. He stressed his opposition to many domestic social programs and his support for a stronger national defense. His successful primary campaign glossed over specific details, promised massive tax cuts, and highlighted an optimistic vision of a rejuvenated America and a supply of movie-inspired quips. To remind voters of the economic problems associated with Carter's presidency, Reagan asked repeatedly, "Are you better off now than you were four years ago?" He would quickly answer his own question by invoking what he called a "misery index," which added the rate of inflation to the rate of unemployment.

Reagan seized an issue that the Democratic Party had long regarded its own: economic growth. In 1979, one of Jimmy Carter's advisers had gloomily portrayed the nation's economic problems as so severe that there was "no way we can avoid a decline in our standard of living. All we can do is adapt to it." In contrast, Reagan promised that sharp tax cuts would bring back the kind of economic expansion the nation had enjoyed during the 1950s and 1960s. During a crucial television debate, when Carter charged that Reagan's upbeat proposals lacked specificity, a smiling Reagan spotlighted Carter's apparent pessimism by repeatedly quipping, "There you go again!"

Reagan (and his running mate, George H. W. Bush) won the November presidential election with slightly more than 50 percent of the popular vote. (John Anderson, a middle-of-the-road Republican who ran an independent campaign for the White House, won about 7 percent.) Reagan's vote total in the Electoral College, however, overwhelmed Carter's: 489 to 49. Moreover, Republicans took 12 Senate seats away from Democrats, gaining control of the Senate for the first time since 1954.

Noting Reagan's slim majority in the popular vote, old-line Democrats underestimated his political clout. They portrayed 1980 as more of a defeat for Carter than a victory for the Republicans and the New Right. By reducing expenditures for domestic programs and lowering taxes on capital gains, according to their analysis, Carter had alienated traditional Democrats. Moreover, these Democrats told themselves that Reagan's sophisticated media campaign temporarily misled voters; in due course,

they claimed, Reagan would be unmasked as a media-manufactured president.

These same Democrats, however, refused to recognize that their party's domestic agenda had been steadily losing support for more than a decade and failed to acknowledge the appeal of the New Right. In 1980, voters ousted seven prominent Democratic senators, including former presidential candidate George McGovern. The real income of the average American family, which had advanced at an annual rate of nearly 3 percent per year between 1950 and 1965, rose only 1.7 percent per year between 1965 and 1980, with the worst times coming after 1973. In this economic climate, middle-income taxpayers who were struggling to make ends meet found Democratic social

---

M U S I C A L   L I N K   T O   T H E   P A S T

Hip-hop Leaps In

Songwriters: E. Fletcher, M. Glover, C. Chase, S. Robinson

Title: "The Message" (1982)

Performers: Grandmaster Flash and the Furious Five

Black radio formats in the early 1980s were staid and conservative, favoring easy listening, corporate-associated artists such as Lionel Richie. According to Nelson George, New York–based black music professionals "were so office-bound, taking meetings with managers and listening to tapes from song publishers [in midtown Manhattan], that they failed to venture up the road to Harlem and the South Bronx, where, in the middle of the nation's most depressing urban rot, something wonderful was happening." That "wonderful" innovation was hip-hop music, which began in the mid-1970s with DJs utilizing other artists' records (Chic's "Good Times" was a perennial favorite) as instrumental backing tracks for live rappers. Hip-hop assembled elaborate rhyming stories, messages, and braggings—often improvised on the spot.

Although early hits such as the Sugar Hill Gang's 1979 "Rapper's Delight" promoted a lightweight party mood, "The Message" presented a sobering litany of inner-city ghetto life: police brutality, junkies, pimps, homeless people "pissing on the stairs," and random violence, punctuated with the mantra of "sometimes it makes me wonder, how I keep from going under." It presaged the even harder-edged, more politically minded and economically successful rap artists, such as Public Enemy, NWA, and KRS-One. Despite commercial

success ("The Message" was a top-five R&B hit), major label executives veered away from the angry black, mostly male performers of rap music until the mid-1980s. Like other controversial American music innovations such as bebop and rock 'n' roll, rap was initially confined to independent label distribution.

Hip-hop also introduced revolutionary musical approaches. DJ Grandmaster Flash, who was unable to afford studio recording time in the mid-1970s, created his own backing tracks by manipulating turntables and vinyl records in new ways. He, along with DJ Kool Herc, pioneered the effects of "scratching" (turning records manually to make the needle repeat brief lengths of groove) and "phasing" (altering turntable speeds to change the sound of recordings). These and other new technologies helped construct the soundscapes that brought a harsh urban atmosphere to life in "The Message."

---

1. Can a turntable be viewed as a musical instrument?
2. If so, what does this use of a century-old technology say about the historical atmosphere that gave birth to hip-hop?
3. What might it say about the role of technology in musical change?

For additional sources related to this feature, visit the CD accompanying this text or the *Liberty, Equality, Power* Web site at:

http://history.wadsworth.com/murrin_LEP4e

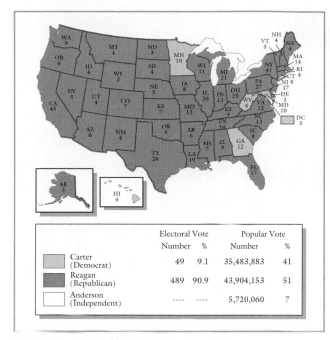

MAP 31.2   PRESIDENTIAL ELECTION, 1980

Compare this map with the one showing the election of Jimmy Carter four years earlier. What factors might explain such a sudden downturn in Democratic fortunes?

welfare measures far less palatable than during more prosperous times.

The 1970s had dampened support for ambitious domestic programming. Still, most traditional Democrats continued to talk about how to improve, and even expand, the social welfare system they had constructed since the New Deal of the 1930s. The New Right, on the other hand, advocated a significant reduction in government spending programs. It decried public housing, for example, as a waste of tax dollars and denounced Aid to Families with Dependent Children (AFDC) and food stamps as socially debilitating for their recipients and a drag on the nation's economy. The New Right's antigovernment rhetoric increasingly resonated with voters, including some longtime Democrats.

🌎 Ronald Reagan's "New Morning in America" (1981–1989)

Ronald Reagan's advisers quickly crafted a bold conservative agenda. A taxpayer revolt that had swept through California politics during the late 1970s provided a model for his administration's attack on "tax-and-spend" policy making at the federal level. (The situation was ironic, however, because California's tax revolt had emerged in

response to increases while Reagan had served as the state's governor.) Across the country, people increasingly responded to the tax-reduction message.

In addition, Reagan courted the New Right. He opposed abortion, advocated prayer in school, extolled "family values," urged radical tax reductions, and offered new approaches to affirmative action and energy policy. Conservative religious figures, including Jerry Falwell and Pat Robertson, former Democrats, joined Reagan's new Republican coalition. Even Jimmy Carter's own Southern Baptists, who had rallied behind him in 1976, along with born-again Christians across the country, began flocking to Reagan. By touting "color-blind" social policies and by bringing conservative African Americans and Hispanics into his administration, the president could effectively court white (especially male) voters who were upset over affirmative action, while avoiding the charge that he was making racially charged appeals. "Guaranteeing equality of treatment is the government's proper function," Reagan proclaimed at one of his first presidential press conferences.

Pursuing Supply-Side Economics

To justify cutting taxes, Reagan touted "supply-side economics." This economic theory held that sizable tax reductions would stimulate growth by putting more money in the hands of both producers and consumers, thereby curing the economic stagnation of the 1970s. Reagan pushed a tax-reduction plan through Congress during summer 1981. It significantly reduced taxes for people who earned high incomes and already possessed significant wealth. Taxes on businesses also were slashed to encourage investment in new facilities and equipment. Most Democrats, who had supported more limited tax reductions during Carter's presidency, endorsed Reagan's plan. At the same time, the Federal Reserve Board under Paul Volcker, a Carter appointee, kept interest rates high in hopes of driving down inflation.

After a severe economic downturn in 1981 and 1982, the worst since the Great Depression of the 1930s, the economy rebounded and entered a vibrant period of noninflationary growth. Between 1983 and 1986, the economy added more than 11 million new jobs. By 1986, the GNP was steadily climbing, and the inflation rate rested at less than 2 percent. Although unemployment figures stubbornly refused to drop, Reagan's supporters called the turnaround an "economic miracle" and hailed a "Reagan revolution."

This revival sparked debate over several issues, particularly the cumulative impact of Reagan's budget deficits and the consequences of the economic expansion. On the first issue—budget deficits—Reagan's critics complained that he had not matched tax cuts with budget reductions. Although Reagan constantly inveighed against budget deficits and big spenders, his administration rolled up an extraordinary record of deficits and spending. Despite some upward revision in tax rates after his first round of tax-cutting, annual deficits tripled to nearly $300 billion during Reagan's eight-year presidency. To finance such spending, the United States borrowed abroad and piled up the largest foreign debt in the world. Reagan's "revolution," critics charged, brought short-term recovery for some people by courting a long-term budget crisis that harmed low-income people who relied more heavily on government programs. Future generations, these observers argued, would pay dearly for the soaring government debt of the 1980s.

© Jeff Lowenthal/Woodfin Camp.

FARM FORECLOSURES

During the early 1980s, many Midwest farmers endured hard times. Farm foreclosures—followed by auctions of land, equipment, and personal property—swept across the Farm Belt during Ronald Reagan's first term as president.

On the second issue—the grassroots impact of the expansion—Reagan's supporters and opponents argued over the distribution of the new economic growth. Reagan partisans insisted that a booming economy would ultimately benefit all Americans. In contrast, critics saw a "Swiss-cheese" economy, one full of holes. Farmers in the Midwest, especially battered during the 1981–82 recession, watched falling crop prices hamper their ability to pay back the high-interest loans they had contracted during the inflation-ridden 1970s. The value of land, a small farmer's primary asset, plummeted. A series of mortgage foreclosures, reminiscent of the 1930s, hit the farm states, and the ripple effect decimated the economies of small towns. At the same time, those urban families who found only low-paying jobs and declining welfare benefits also puzzled over talk of a booming economy. Many jobs created during the 1980s came in the service sector and offered relatively low wages and few, if any, fringe benefits. In 1981, the average weekly paycheck was $270; measured in constant dollars, the same check was worth only $254 in 1991. The minimum wage, when adjusted for inflation, fell in value throughout Reagan's presidency.

The economic changes of the Reagan era fell especially hard on disadvantaged groups. People with educational credentials and marketable skills could make significant economic gains. The number of African American families earning a solid middle-class income more than doubled between 1970 and 1990. College graduates of African descent could expect incomes comparable to those of their white classmates, partly as a result of affirmative action hiring plans put in place by the Nixon and Carter administrations. Many people, therefore, could afford to leave problem-plagued inner-city neighborhoods. The story of mobility looked very different, however, for those who remained persistently unemployed, an underclass who seemed trapped in declining urban centers. At the end of the 1980s, one-third of all African American families lived in poverty, and the number earning less than $15,000 per year had doubled since 1970. In inner cities, less than half of African American children were completing high school, and more than 60 percent were unemployed. Throughout America, the gap between the well-off and the disadvantaged widened significantly during the 1980s.

Broadening the New Right Agenda

Reagan moved aggressively on several domestic issues. In 1981, he summarily fired the nation's air traffic controllers when their union refused to halt a nationwide strike. Overall, union membership continued to decline, as both the Reagan administration and most large businesses pursued aggressive antiunion strategies during the 1980s. The percentage of unionized workers fell to just 16 percent by the end of Reagan's presidency. Workers recognized that the balance of power was tilting against them and increasingly turned away from strikes as an economic weapon.

The president also placed a conservative stamp on the federal legal system. Almost immediately, he nominated a Supreme Court justice, Sandra Day O'Connor (the first woman to sit on the Court), who initially seemed a staunch conservative, particularly on social questions and criminal justice matters. During Reagan's first term, when the Republican Party controlled the Senate, Reagan also named prominent conservative jurists, such as Robert Bork and Antonin Scalia, to lower federal courts. The New Right, which had decried the "rights revolution" of the Supreme Court, welcomed the influx of judges from the political right. Civil libertarians complained that the federal courts were becoming less hospitable to legal claims made by criminal defendants, labor unions, and political dissenters. By 1990, because of retirements, about half of all federal judges had reached the bench during Ronald Reagan's presidency. Reagan also looked for staunch conservatives to fill nonjudicial appointments. He staffed his department of justice with lawyers who were eager to end the rights revolution and—in line with the "color-blind" approach to racial issues—to sidetrack affirmative action programs.

Reagan, who had campaigned in 1980 on a promise not only to halt the growth of government power but to roll back its reach, could claim only limited success in fulfilling this pledge. He appointed James Watt, an outspoken critic of environmental legislation, as secretary of the interior, the department that guides the nation's conservation policy. Watt angered environmentalists by supporting the "sagebrush rebellion," in which western states demanded fewer restrictions on the use of public land within their borders. Emotional battles broke out over private use of resources in federal wilderness areas. Particularly in the timber states of the Pacific Northwest, people hotly debated whether endangered species, such as rare bird populations, should be protected to the detriment of economic activities such as timber cutting. Reagan's first two appointees to the Department of Energy actually proposed eliminating the cabinet office they headed—an idea that Congress blocked. Reagan mused about abolishing the Department of Education and often criticized programs espoused by his own secretary of education. Able to fill most of the administrative agencies with conservatives, the president sought to ease regulations on businesses by relaxing enforcement of the safety and environmental laws that conservative economists continued to blame for driving up costs.

After taking office in 1981, Reagan promised to break OPEC's oil monopoly by encouraging the development of new sources of supply. Ignoring environmentalists' calls to break U.S. dependence on fossil fuels by promotion of renewable sources, Reagan and his successor George H. W. Bush followed a "cheap oil" policy. The tapping of new supplies of oil at home, together with rivalries among OPEC members, weakened OPEC's hold on the world market and reduced energy costs, which remained moderate throughout the economic boom of the 1990s.

Reagan tinkered with social welfare policy. He eliminated funding for some programs, most notably the Comprehensive Employment and Training Act (CETA), established during Richard Nixon's first term, and reduced funding for others, such as food stamps. Reagan proved to be much more conservative on domestic issues than Nixon, who had allowed social expenditures to increase, had courted some labor union leaders, and had advanced his guaranteed income program, FAP. Nevertheless, Reagan pledged that Washington would maintain a "safety net" for those in true need of governmental assistance.

Controversy surrounded the reach of this safety net. Critics complained about the increasing number of people whose total package of income and public benefits fell below what the federal government defined as the "poverty level." The burden of Reagan-era cutbacks seemed to fall disproportionately on female-headed households and on children. By the end of the 1980s, one of every five children was being raised in a household whose total income fell below the official poverty line. Meanwhile, many older people continued to benefit from a revision, during the 1970s, in the nation's most popular welfare program, Social Security. As a consequence of the arrangement called "indexing," Social Security payments automatically increased along with the rate of inflation. Larger Social Security checks, along with Medicare benefits, enabled millions of older Americans to do relatively well during the Reagan years.

Despite sometimes sharp debate, especially over the economic downturn of 1981–82 and the soaring federal deficit, Reagan remained a popular leader. His genial optimism seemed unshakable. He even appeared to rebound quickly—although close observers noted a clear decline in his energies—after being shot by a would-be assassin in March 1981. No matter what problems beset his administration, criticism never stuck to Reagan, whom one frustrated Democrat dubbed the "Teflon president."

Routing the Democrats, 1984

Democrats continually underestimated the appeal of Reagan and his policies—a miscalculation that doomed their own 1984 presidential effort. Walter Mondale, Jimmy Carter's vice president, ran on a platform calling for "the eradication of discrimination in all aspects of American life" and for an expansion of national social welfare programs. Mondale also proposed higher taxes to fund his agenda.

Republicans ran a textbook-perfect campaign. They labeled Mondale's support from labor unions and civil-rights groups as a vestige of the old politics of "special interests" and his tax proposal as a return to the "wasteful" policies popularly associated with the stagflation of the 1970s. Mondale's running mate, Representative Geraldine Ferraro of New York, the first woman to stand for president or vice president on a major party ticket, became another symbol of kowtowing to special interests—in this case, feminist and pro-choice groups. Reagan's speeches predicted a bright, tranquil future for America. Republican campaign ads—accompanied by the slogan "It's Morning Again in America" and by the sound of "I'm Proud to Be an American"—portrayed a glowing landscape of bustling small towns and lush farmlands. The 1984 presidential election ended with Mondale carrying only his home state of Minnesota and the District of Columbia. In 1964, the Republican Party had hit bottom with Barry Goldwater's defeat; 20 years later, Ronald Reagan's reelection capped a remarkable revival for the GOP. By regaining control of Congress, however, Democrats could continue to claim that Reagan's personal popularity counted for more than the appeal of his New Right policies.

Reagan's Second Term

Although the economy continued to expand, charges of corruption and mismanagement also marked Reagan's second term. The process of deregulating the banking system became linked to individual malfeasance and, more

HISTORY THROUGH FILM

The First Movie-Star President

Ronald Reagan began his presidency in Hollywood, where he lived and worked before entering politics during the 1960s. The political career of the "great communicator" built on, rather than broke with, his days in Hollywood. His media advisers could count on directing a seasoned professional. Reagan always knew where to stand; how to deliver lines flawlessly; how to convey emotions through both body language and dialogue; and when to melt into the background so that supporting players on his presidential team might carry a crucial scene.

Reagan's movies provided a rehearsal for the role he would play in the White House. Initially, Reagan's opponents expected that his old film parts, particularly *Bedtime for Bonzo* (1947), in which he co-starred with a chimpanzee, would become political liabilities. Instead of disavowing his Hollywood days, Reagan accentuated his fluency with film-related references. His efforts to cheer on the nation during the 1980s consciously invoked his favorite film role, that of the 1920s Notre Dame football star, George Gipp, whom Reagan played in *Knute Rockne, All American* (1940). Similarly, when tilting with a Democratic-controlled Congress over tax policy, Reagan invoked Clint Eastwood's famous screen character "Dirty Harry" when promising to veto any tax increase. "Go ahead, make my day," he taunted. On another occasion, he cited *Rambo* (1982) as a possible blueprint for dealing with countries that had seized American hostages. As he freely drew on lines from Hollywood motion pictures, Reagan occasionally seemed unable to separate "reel" from "real" life. During one session with reporters, he referred to his own dog as "Lassie," the canine performer who had been Reagan's Hollywood contemporary during the 1940s and 1950s.

Life in Hollywood also provided a prologue to President Reagan's conservative policies. Early in his film career, Reagan appeared in four films as the same character, a government agent named Brass Bancroft. In these B-grade thrillers, Reagan defined a popular image that he later deployed in politics: that of a confident leader who maintained a clear distinction, especially in foreign policy, between (good) friends and (evil) foes. One of the Brass Bancroft series, entitled *Murder in the Air* (1940), even featured a science-fiction-style "death ray" that resembled the Strategic Defense Initiative armaments that President Reagan would champion more than 40 years later.

broadly, to risky speculation that critics called "casino capitalism." These issues loomed particularly large in the savings and loan industry. Encouraged by lax oversight from federal regulators, many savings and loan institutions (S&Ls) overextended loans to risky ventures, particularly in real estate, and incurred financial obligations far beyond their means. Hundreds of S&Ls fell insolvent. The people and the businesses to which these institutions had loaned money faced financial disaster. The federal agency that regulated S&Ls predicted an impending crisis as early as spring 1985, but both the Reagan administration and Congress, hoping to delay any decisive response until after the 1988 election, ignored the warning.

Finally, in 1989, Congress had to act. Its bailout plan, designed to save some S&Ls and to transfer assets from failed institutions to still-solvent ones, proved inordinately expensive. Even as taxpayers began paying the costs of executing the plan, corruption plagued its execution. Large, well-connected commercial banks purchased the remaining assets of bankrupt S&Ls at bargain-basement prices. By the time the Treasury Department stepped in, some five years later, most of the larger S&Ls had already been sold. As a consequence, the banking industry went through a sudden, unplanned consolidation.

During Reagan's second term, the White House and Congress danced around two long-term domestic issues: reduction of the federal deficit and overhaul of the social welfare system. First, the Gramm-Rudman-Hollings Act of 1985 mandated a balanced federal budget by 1991. Neither Congress nor the Reagan administration, however,

Subsequent film roles refined this early Hollywood image. Poor eyesight kept him out of combat during the Second World War, but Reagan served long hours as an Army Air Corps officer, making movies in support of the war effort. He appeared as a military hero in films such as *For God and Country* (1943) and often provided upbeat voiceovers, once even sharing a soundtrack with President Franklin Roosevelt. He also starred, on loan from the Air Corps, in *This Is the Army* (1943), one of the most successful of Hollywood's military-oriented musicals.

After the war, Reagan increasingly directed his energies toward Hollywood's own Cold War politics. His tenure as the communist-fighting president of the Screen Actors Guild likely speeded his conversion from New Deal Democrat to right-leaning Republican. In his final onscreen roles, Reagan usually portrayed the kind of independent, rugged individualist—often in westerns such as *Law and Order* (1953)—whom he would later lionize in his political speeches.

Nancy Reagan, who co-starred with her husband in *Hellcats of the Navy* (1957) and later as the nation's First Lady, perceptively summed up the relationship between

© Bettmann/Corbis.

Ronald Reagan as the "Gipper" in *Knute Rockne, All American*.

Reagan the actor and Reagan the political leader. "There are not two Ronald Reagans," she observed. During the 1980s, movie and political culture became intertwined and embodied in the same charismatic leader, Ronald Wilson Reagan.

Courtesy, Ronald Reagan Library.

REAGAN RIDES

A latecomer to politics, the former motion picture star often used cowboy imagery to counter charges that he was too old for national leadership.

seemed eager to implement this goal or the larger one of reducing the still-soaring government deficit. Second, the Family Support Act of 1988 required states to inaugurate work training programs and to move people, including mothers receiving AFDC payments, off the welfare rolls. This law, its critics worried, failed to guarantee that its work training provision would actually result in people finding—and keeping—jobs. Yet, despite their limitations, Gramm-Rudman-Hollings and the Family Support Act set policy makers on a course that culminated in comprehensive budget-reduction and welfare-overhaul packages nearly a decade later.

Conservatives would eventually hail Ronald Reagan as the Moses of the New Right, but during his second term, some early supporters on the New Right looked balefully at his domestic record. The 1986 resignation of Warren Burger allowed Reagan to elevate William Rehnquist to the Chief Justice position and to tap Antonin Scalia, an even more conservative jurist, to replace Rehnquist as an

associate justice on the Supreme Court. In 1987, however, the Senate rebuffed Reagan's attempt to nominate Robert Bork, a particular favorite of the New Right, to the High Court. Bork's rejection enraged conservatives, some of whom blamed Reagan for not working hard enough on Bork's behalf. Meanwhile, the religious wing of the New Right chafed at what it considered Reagan's tepid support of its antiabortion crusade. Reagan also appeared to show little interest in altering the structure of Social Security or social welfare arrangements.

Although never lacking for critics, the "Reagan revolution" succeeded in advancing much of the New Right's agenda and in significantly changing the nation's political vocabulary. "Liberalism" no longer connoted a set of government programs that would stimulate the economy and build prosperity for all. Instead, Republicans made "liberal" a code word for wasteful social programs devised by a bloated federal government that gouged hardworking people and squandered their dollars. The term "conservative," as used by New Right Republicans, came to mean economic growth, curtailment of governmental power, and support for traditional sociocultural values. The once-dominant Democratic Party seemed to face an uncertain future.

Renewing the Cold War

Reagan quickly established foreign policy themes that emphasized building American power in the world. Carter's policies, he claimed, represented a "Vietnam syndrome" of passivity and a "loss of will." In contrast to Carter's grant of amnesty for Vietnam War resisters, Reagan declared that the war had been a "noble cause" that the government had refused to win. Although Reagan did not repudiate Carter's human rights policy, he employed it in a renewed Cold War, highlighting the Soviet Union's mistreatment of its Jewish population and ethnic minorities.

The Defense Buildup

The United States, Reagan claimed, had "unilaterally disarmed" during the 1970s, while the Soviets had staged a massive military buildup. He denounced the "evil empire" of the Soviet Union and dismissed critics of his foreign policy as the "Blame-America-First Crowd." They were "the strangest collection of misfits, loony tunes, and squalid criminals since the advent of the Third Reich."

Closing what Reagan called America's "window of vulnerability" against Soviet military power proved expensive. Even though Reagan's tax cuts reduced government revenues, the White House sought dramatic increases in military spending. The Pentagon launched programs to enlarge the Navy and to modernize strategic nuclear forces. It also deployed new missiles throughout Western Europe. At the height of Reagan's military buildup, the Pentagon was purchasing about 20 percent of the nation's manufacturing output.

In 1984, Reagan proposed the most expensive defense system in history—a space-based shield against any missile hurled toward the United States. Beginning as a nebulous hope, the Strategic Defense Initiative (SDI) soon had its own Pentagon agency that sought $26 billion, over five years, just for start-up research. Controversy swirled around SDI. Critics dubbed it "Star Wars" and shuddered at its astronomical costs. Although most scientists dismissed the initiative as impossible to implement, Congress voted appropriations for SDI, and Reagan steadfastly clung to the idea of a defensive shield. SDI dominated both strategic debates at home and arms talks with the Soviet Union.

Greater defense spending had another strategic dimension. Secretary of Defense Caspar Weinberger predicted that, as the Soviets increased the burden on their own faltering economy in order to compete in the accelerating arms race, the Soviet Union might collapse under the economic strain. This scenario, an implicit goal of the containment policy since the NSC-68 blueprint of 1950, increasingly tantalized the Reagan administration.

Reagan's foreign policy agenda included many nonmilitary initiatives. In a new "informational" offensive, the administration funded a variety of conservative groups around the world and established Radio Martí, a Florida station beamed at Cuba and designed to discredit Fidel Castro's communist government. When the United Nations agency UNESCO adopted an anti-American tone and called for a New World Information Order that would reduce the influence of U.S.-originated news and information, Reagan cut off U.S. contributions to UNESCO and demanded changes in UN operations. The Reagan administration also championed free markets, urging other nations to minimize tariffs and restrictions on foreign investment. The Caribbean Basin Initiative, for example, rewarded with U.S. aid those small nations in the Caribbean region that adhered to free-market principles.

The CIA, now headed by William Casey, stepped up its "covert" activities. Some of these became so obvious that they hardly qualified as covert. It was no secret, for example, that the United States sent aid to anticommunist forces in Afghanistan, many of them radical Muslim fundamentalist groups, and to the opponents of the Sandinista government in Nicaragua, the *contras*. At the time, however, Washington acknowledged neither the extent nor the nature of its assistance.

Deploying Military Power

In renewing a global Cold War, Reagan promised vigorous military support to "democratic" revolutions anywhere, a move designed to constrain the Soviet Union's sphere of influence. Reagan's UN representative, Jeane Kirkpatrick, wrote that "democratic" forces included almost any movement, no matter how autocratic, that was noncommunist. The United States thus funded opposition military movements in countries aligned with the Soviet Union: Ethiopia, Angola, South Yemen, Cambodia, Grenada, Cuba, Nicaragua, and Afghanistan. Reagan called the participants in such anticommunist insurgencies "freedom fighters," although few had any visible commitment to democratic values or institutions.

The Reagan administration also deployed U.S. military power, first in southern Lebanon in 1982. Here, Israeli troops were facing off against Lebanese Muslims supported by Syria and the Soviet Union. Alarmed by Muslim gains, the Reagan administration convinced Israel to withdraw and sent 1,600 American marines as part of a "peacekeeping force" to restore stability. Muslim fighters, however, turned against the Americans. After a suicide commando mission into a U.S. military compound killed 241 marines, Reagan decided that this ill-defined undertaking could never win public support. He subsequently pulled out U.S. troops and disengaged from Lebanon. Another military intervention seemed more successful. In October 1983, Reagan sent 2,000 U.S. troops to the tiny Caribbean island of Grenada, whose socialist leader was forging ties with Castro's Cuba. U.S. troops overthrew the government and installed one that was friendly to American interests.

Buoyed by Grenada, the Reagan administration fixed its sights on Nicaragua. Here, the Sandinista government was trying to strengthen ties with Cuba and to break Nicaragua's historic dependence on the United States. The Reagan administration responded by augmenting U.S. military forces in neighboring Honduras, conducting training exercises throughout Central America, stepping up a campaign of economic pressure and anti-Sandinista propaganda. Most important, it gave increased support to the *contras*. Meanwhile, the Reagan administration supported the harsh dictatorships in nearby El Salvador and Guatemala in order to prevent other leftist insurgencies from gaining ground in Central America.

These initiatives in Central America became the most controversial aspect of Reagan's foreign policy. Regimes supported by the Reagan administration were clearly implicated in human-rights abuses, not only against their own people but also against American nuns, journalists, and humanitarian-aid workers. Mounting evidence of brutality and corruption among the Nicaraguan *contras* fueled growing criticism. In 1984, the Democratic-controlled Congress broke with the president's policy and barred further military aid to the *contras*.

The Reagan administration quickly sought to avoid the congressional ban. It encouraged wealthy American conservatives and foreign governments to donate money to the *contras*. In June 1984, at a top-secret meeting of the National Security Planning Group, Reagan and his top advisers discussed the legality of pressing "third parties" to contribute to the *contra* cause. Reagan ended the meeting with a bid for secrecy: "If such a story gets out, we'll all be hanging by our thumbs in front of the White House."

Meanwhile, violence continued to escalate throughout the Middle East. Militant Islamic groups increased attacks against Israel and Western powers; bombings and the kidnapping of Western hostages became more frequent. Apparently, Libya's Muammar al-Qaddafi and Iranian leaders encouraged such activities. In spring 1986, the United States launched an air strike into Libya against Qaddafi's personal compound. The bombs killed Qaddafi's young daughter, but Qaddafi and his government survived. Despite what looked like a long-range assassination attempt against a foreign leader (an action outlawed by Congress), Americans generally approved of using strong measures against sponsors of terrorism and hostage-taking.

The Iran-*Contra* Controversy

In November 1986, a magazine in Lebanon claimed that the Reagan administration was selling arms to Iran in order to secure the release of Americans being held hostage by Islamic militants. The alleged deal stood in clear conflict with the Reagan administration's pledge that it would not sell arms to Iran and would never reward hostage-taking by negotiating for the release of captives. During the 1980 campaign, Reagan had made hostages in Iran a symbol of U.S. weakness under Carter. When Iranian-backed groups continued to kidnap Americans during his presidency, it seemed that Reagan had begun seeking a clandestine way to recover hostages.

As Congress began to investigate the arms-for-hostages charge, matters turned even more bizarre. It appeared that the Reagan administration had not only sold arms to Iran but had channeled profits from these deals to the *contra* forces in Nicaragua as a means of circumventing the congressional ban on U.S. military aid. Oliver North, who worked in the office of the national security adviser, had directed the effort, working with shadowy international arms dealers and private go-betweens. North's covert machinations seemingly violated both the stated

policy of the White House and an act of Congress. Pundits soon dubbed the episode, reminiscent of the constitutional crisis of the Nixon era, as Irangate.

In the end, however, the Iran-*Contra* controversy never reached the proportions of Watergate. In contrast to Richard Nixon, who had temporized, Ronald Reagan stepped forward and testified (through a deposition) that he could remember no details about either the release of hostages or the funding of the *contras*. His management skills might deserve criticism, Reagan admitted, but he had intended to break no law or to violate any presidential promise. Meanwhile, Vice President George H. W. Bush, whom investigators initially linked to some of North's machinations, steadfastly claimed ignorance about any arms deals. Oliver North even became a New Right celebrity as a result of his artful dodging during televised hearings into the Iran-*Contra* affair. North had destroyed so many documents and had left so many false paper trails that congressional investigators struggled even to compile a simple narrative of events. North and several others connected to the Reagan administration were convicted of felonies, including falsification of documents and lying to Congress, but appellate courts later overturned these verdicts. Finally, in 1992, just a few days before the end of his presidency, George H. W. Bush pardoned six former Reagan-era officials connected to the Iran-*Contra* controversy.

The Beginning of the End of the Cold War

Although Reagan's first six years in office had revived the Cold War confrontation, his last two years saw a sudden thaw in U.S.–Soviet relations. The economic cost of superpower rivalry was burdening both nations. Moreover, changes within the Soviet Union were eliminating the reasons for confrontation. Mikhail Gorbachev, who became general secretary of the Communist Party in 1985, was a new style of Soviet leader. Gorbachev understood the challenge of technological change in Western democracies, as their economies and communications became globally integrated. He also realized that his isolated country faced economic stagnation and an environmental crisis brought on by decades of poorly planned industrial development. To redirect the Soviet Union's course, he withdrew Soviet troops from Afghanistan, reduced commitments to Cuba and Nicaragua, proclaimed a policy of *glasnost* ("openness"), and began to implement *perestroika* ("economic liberalization") at home.

Gorbachev's policies brought him acclaim throughout the West and stirred winds of change. He began summit meetings with the United States to discuss arms control. At Reykjavik, Iceland, in October 1986, Reagan shocked both Gorbachev and his own advisers by proposing a wholesale ban on nuclear weapons. Although negotiations at Reykjavik stumbled over Gorbachev's insistence that the United States abandon its Star Wars program, the next year Gorbachev dropped that condition. In December 1987, Reagan and Gorbachev signed a major arms treaty that reduced each nation's supply of intermediate-range missiles and allowed for on-site verification, which the Soviets had never before permitted. The next year, Gorbachev scrapped the policy that forbade any nation under Soviet influence from renouncing communism. In effect, Gorbachev declared an end to the Cold War. Within the next few years, the Soviet sphere of influence—and the Soviet Union itself—would cease to exist.

The First Bush Presidency (1989–1993)

During his first term, Ronald Reagan became America's most popular president since Franklin Roosevelt, but even before the Iran *Contra* affair, his presidential image and influence were beginning to fade. Even as some members of the New Right were criticizing the president for failing to vigorously support their agenda, economic problems—especially the growing federal deficit and disarray in the financial sector—sparked calls for more assured leadership from the White House. Despite criticism of Reagan's leadership at home, Cold War détente boosted the 1988 presidential prospects of his heir-apparent, Vice President George H. W. Bush.

The Election of 1988

Bush easily gained the Republican nomination. Born into a prominent Republican family and educated at Yale, Bush had moved from Connecticut to Texas and entered the oil business as a young man. His lengthy political résumé included time in the House of Representatives and a stint as director of the CIA. To court the New Right, which was decidedly lukewarm to his candidacy, Bush chose Senator J. Danforth Quayle, a staunch conservative better known for his golfing prowess than his legislative skills, as a running mate. Suddenly elevated into the national spotlight, the youthful senator from Indiana delighted political comedians, who found his verbal blunders a rich source for new material.

Governor Michael Dukakis of Massachusetts emerged as the Democratic presidential candidate. Hoping to distance himself from the disastrous Democratic effort in 1984, Dukakis avoided talk of new domestic programs and higher taxes. Instead, he spoke about bringing com-

petence and honesty to the White House and boasted of knowing, as a result of his gubernatorial experience, how to mobilize private expertise and to handle economic matters. Dukakis gambled that a cautious campaign, devoid of bold promises, could defeat Bush, who lacked Reagan's charisma.

The election of 1988, the last of the Cold War era, became best known for its negative campaigning, especially by Republican strategists. Pro-Bush television commercials usually presented Dukakis bathed in shadows and always showed him with a frown on his face. The campaign's most infamous ad linked Dukakis to Willie Horton, an African American inmate who had been charged with rape while on furlough from a Massachusetts prison. While seeming to play "the race card," the ad charged that Dukakis, whom Bush identified as a "card-carrying member of the American Civil Liberties Union," was soft on crime. As one media analyst quipped, the Bush campaign almost made it appear that Willie Horton was Dukakis's running mate.

Bush did emerge the winner in 1988 but by a relatively narrow margin. A quick glance at the 1988 returns might suggest that he had comfortably carried both the popular vote and the electoral college. Yet, the Republican ticket carried so many states by such a small margin that several relatively minor shifts in voter turnouts, especially among black and Latino voters who failed to support Dukakis as enthusiastically as they had backed Mondale four years earlier, could have given the victory to the Democrats. Dukakis bested Mondale's 1984 performance with 111 electoral votes. Outside the South, which Bush swept, Dukakis carried more than 500 counties that had supported Reagan in 1984. Overall, voter turnout was the lowest of any national election since 1924, and polls suggested that many voters considered neither George H. W. Bush nor Michael Dukakis worthy of being president. At the same time, their ballots allowed the Democrats to retain control of both houses of Congress.

Although the New Right hoped Bush would build on the Reagan presidency, his campaign prompted distrust about his commitment to its agenda. Might not his campaign slogan about a "kinder, gentler America" imply a veiled criticism of Reagan's domestic policies? Could conservatives believe Bush when he promised "no new taxes"? Once in the White House, Bush angered the New Right by agreeing to an increase in the minimum wage and by failing to veto the Civil Rights Act of 1991, a law that critics charged with establishing "quotas" for the "preferential hiring" of women and people of color in business and government. Most important, in 1990, Bush apparently broke his antitax pledge, the issue on which New Right leaders came to judge his worthiness as Reagan's successor, when he agreed to an upward revision in tax rates in order to deal with the rising federal deficit. Although Bush's move began a process that would eventually temporarily eliminate the deficit, the New Right bitterly denounced his decision.

Meanwhile, the national government, divided between a Democratic-controlled Congress and a Republican-occupied White House, increasingly appeared to suffer from gridlock. Any hope of addressing key domestic issues, especially reorganization of the health care and social welfare systems, vanished. Worse, the economic growth of the Reagan years began slowing, and the budget deficit continued expanding. George H. W. Bush's chances for a second term seemed to depend on his record in foreign, rather than domestic, policy.

The End of the Cold War

During the first Bush presidency, the Soviet Union collapsed. As other communist states toppled like dominoes, the international order underwent its greatest transformation since the end of the Second World War.

Beginning in 1989, political change swept through Eastern and Central Europe. In Poland, the anticommunist labor party, Solidarity, ousted the pro-Soviet regime. The pro-Moscow government in East Germany fell in November 1989, and both West and East Germans hacked down the Berlin Wall. Divided since the Second World War, Germany began the difficult process of reunification. Popular movements similarly forced out communist governments throughout Eastern Europe. Yugoslavia quickly

disintegrated, and warfare ensued as rival ethnic groups re-created separate states in Slovenia, Serbia, Bosnia, and Croatia. The Baltic countries of Latvia, Lithuania, and Estonia, which had been under Soviet control since the Second World War, declared their independence. Most dramatic, the major provinces that had constituted the Soviet Union assumed self-government. The president of the new state of Russia, Boris Yeltsin, put down a coup by hard-line communists in August 1991, and he soon solidified his political position. In December 1991, the Russian Parliament ratified Yeltsin's plan to abolish the Soviet Union and replace it with 11 republics, loosely joined in a commonwealth arrangement.

As the map of Europe changed, the United States needed to create diplomatic relations with the new countries. In December 1991, Congress authorized $400 million for helping the Soviet Union's successor states, especially Ukraine, dismantle their nuclear weaponry, and it later allotted an equivalent amount for promoting democracy in the new European states.

More broadly, the administration of George H. W. Bush pressed a program of international economic integration. During the mid-1980s, huge debts that Third World nations owed to U.S. banks had threatened the international banking system, but most of these obligations had been renegotiated by 1990. Market economies, which replaced centrally controlled ones, began to emerge in the former communist states; Western Europe moved toward economic integration; and the nations of the Pacific Rim were seeing steady economic growth. At the same time, President Bush pressed for the North American Free Trade

BERLIN WALL, 1989

Berliners celebrated the end of the Cold War by chiseling away at the Berlin Wall, which the communist East German state had erected in 1962 to prevent the flow of refugees to West Berlin. Pieces of the Berlin Wall became coveted symbols of the fall of communism.

© Owen Franken/Corbis.

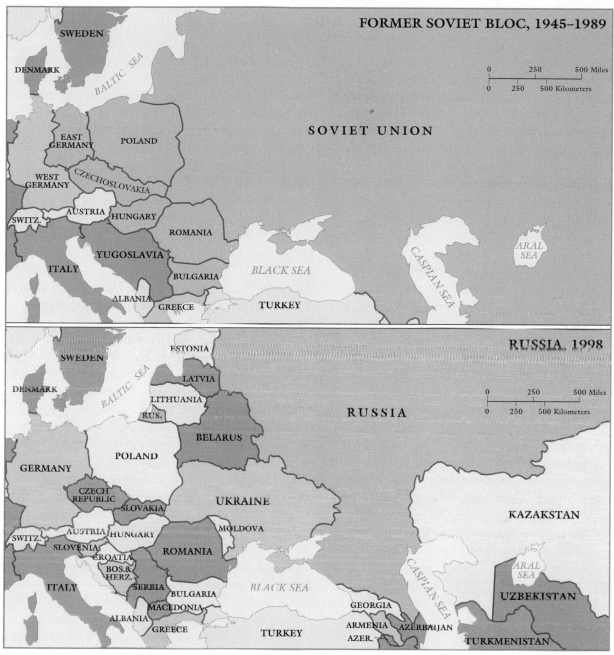

MAP 31.3   COLLAPSE OF THE SOVIET BLOC

These contrasting maps show the Soviet Union and the countries it dominated before and after the fall of communist governments. What countries in Eastern Europe escaped Russian control after 1989? What new countries emerged out of the old Soviet Union?

Agreement (NAFTA), which would eliminate tariff barriers and join Canada, the United States, and Mexico in the largest free-market zone in the world.

As the likelihood of armed conflict with the Soviet Union faded, the Bush administration also set about redefining national security. The end of the Cold War weakened support for the leftist insurgencies in Central America that had preoccupied the Reagan administration.

Nicaraguans voted the Sandinistas, who became just another political party in a multiparty system, out of office. Supported by the United States, the United Nations assisted both El Salvador and Guatemala in turning their armed conflicts into electoral ones. The Pentagon pondered new missions for its military forces. Future action, its planners predicted, would take the form of rapid, sharply targeted strikes rather than lengthy military campaigns.

The armed forces might even serve in the "war against drugs," an effort that Bush had promised during his 1988 presidential campaign.

General Manuel Noriega, the president of Panama, was deeply involved in the drug trade. The Reagan administration had secured an indictment for drug trafficking against Noriega and had mounted a program of economic pressure, which only deepened his reliance on drug revenue. Confronting Noriega posed a potentially embarrassing problem for the Bush administration because the anticommunist general had been recruited as a CIA "asset" during the mid-1970s, when Bush was the agency's director. Nevertheless, the United States needed a friendly, stable government in Panama in order to complete the transfer of the Panama Canal to Panamanian sovereignty by 2000, and Bush finally decided to topple the mercurial Noriega. In a military incursion called Operation Just Cause and broadcast live on television, U.S. Marines landed in Panama in December 1989, pinpointed Noriega's whereabouts, and laid siege to his headquarters. Noriega soon surrendered, faced extradition to Florida, and was imprisoned in 1992 after a conviction for trafficking in cocaine.

Although a relatively minor episode, the Panamanian operation carried major implications. On the one hand, using military force in a region that was long sensitive to U.S. intervention sparked controversy in Latin America, and deposing the leader of a foreign government by unilateral military action raised questions of international law. Yet, this episode, which involved 25,000 U.S. troops but brought few casualties, provided a new model for post–Cold War military strategy. The Pentagon firmed up existing plans for phasing out some older military bases, particularly in Germany and the Philippines, and for creating highly mobile, rapid deployment forces. A test of this new strategy came in the Persian Gulf War.

The Persian Gulf War

On August 2, 1990, President Saddam Hussein of Iraq ordered his troops to occupy the neighboring, oil-rich emirate of Kuwait. Within a day, Iraq's forces had taken control of Kuwait, a move that caught the United States off guard. Although Iraq had been moving troops to its border with Kuwait and denouncing Kuwaiti producers for cooperating with U.S. oil interests, American intelligence forecasters had not expected an immediate invasion. Now, however, they warned that Iraq's next target might be Saudi Arabia, the largest oil exporter in the Middle East and a longtime ally of the United States.

Moving swiftly, Bush orchestrated a multilateral, international response. He convinced the Saudi government, initially concerned about allowing Western troops

on sacred Islamic soil, to accept a U.S. military presence in Saudi Arabia. Four days after Iraq's invasion of Kuwait, Bush launched Operation Desert Shield by sending 230,000 troops to protect Saudi Arabia. After consulting with European leaders, he approached the United Nations, which denounced Iraqi aggression, ordered economic sanctions against Iraq, and authorized the United States to lead an international force to restore the government of Kuwait if Saddam Hussein's troops had not withdrawn by January 15, 1991. Bush assembled a massive coalition force, ultimately nearly 500,000 troops from the United States and some 200,000 from other countries. He also persuaded Congress to approve a resolution backing the use of force. Although Bush claimed a moral obligation to rescue Kuwait, his policy makers spoke frankly about the economic threat that Hussein's aggression posed for the oil-dependent economies of the United States and its coalition allies. Secretary of State James Baker summed up the danger in one word: "Jobs."

Just after the January 15 deadline passed, the United States launched an air war on Iraq. "Pools" of journalists, whose movements were carefully controlled by the Pentagon, highlighted the new role of women in America's modernized military and hailed its apparently innovative technology, especially the antimissile missile called the "Patriot." Television networks showed Patriots, in video game fashion, intercepting and downing Iraqi "Scud" missiles. (Later, careful studies significantly revised claims about the stellar performance of the Patriot missiles.) After six weeks of devastating aerial bombardment, General Colin Powell ordered a ground offensive against Iraq on February 24. Coalition forces, enjoying air supremacy, decimated Saddam Hussein's armies over the next four days. U.S. casualties were relatively light (148 deaths in battle). Estimates of Iraqi casualties ranged from 25,000 to 100,000 deaths. Although the conflict had lasted scarcely six weeks, it took an enormous toll on highways, bridges, communications, and other infrastructure facilities in both Iraq and Kuwait.

In a controversial decision, Bush stopped short of ousting Saddam Hussein, a goal that the UN had never approved and that military advisers had considered costly to achieve. Instead, the United States, backed by the UN, maintained its economic pressure, ordered the dismantling of Iraq's nuclear and bacteriological capabilities, and enforced "no-fly" zones over northern and southern Iraq to help protect the Kurds and Shi'a Muslims from Hussein's continued persecution. The Persian Gulf War temporarily boosted George H. W. Bush's popularity and seemed to assure his reelection in 1992.

Yet, with a second term resting on his international record, Bush seemed increasingly unable to articulate

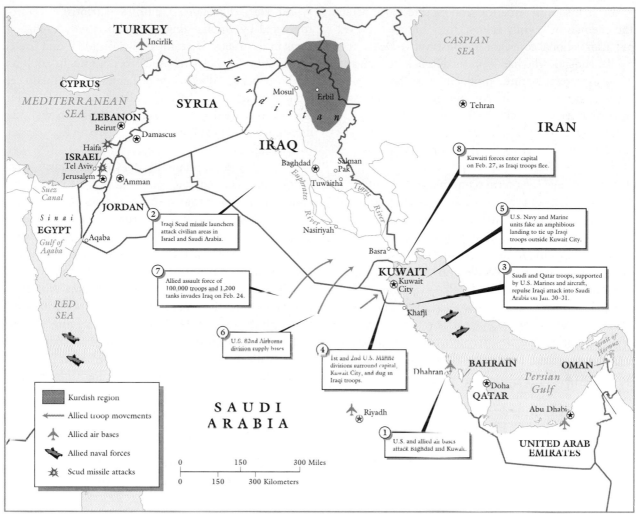

MAP 31.4 PERSIAN GULF WAR, 1991
After Iraq invaded Kuwait, the United States marshaled forces in neighboring areas to attack. Notice the positioning of U.S. air, naval, and land forces. What countries hosted American bases?

long-term strategic goals for a post–Cold War world. Turmoil broke out in some of the former Soviet provinces, and Russia struggled to develop an economy based on private property and market mechanisms. Full-scale warfare erupted among the states of the former Yugoslavia, with Serbs launching a brutal campaign of territorial aggrandizement and "ethnic cleansing" against Bosnian Muslims. In the Far East, Japan's still-growing economy prompted Americans to grumble about "unfair" competition. In Africa, when severe famine struck the country of Somalia, Bush ordered U.S. troops to establish humanitarian supply lines, but the American public remained wary of this military mission.

Ultimately, voters judged Bush's record on foreign affairs as something of a muddle. He assembled and held together an international coalition against Iraq, construc-

tively assisted the transition in Russia and Eastern Europe at the end of the Cold War, and advanced a global process of economic integration. As the old reference points of containing the Soviet Union disappeared between 1989 and 1992, however, George H. W. Bush failed to effectively articulate a new vision that could inspire people and firmly establish his reputation as a world leader.

The Election of 1992

The inability to portray a coherent vision of either domestic or foreign policy threatened Bush's reelection and forced concessions to the New Right. Dan Quayle, although clearly a liability with voters outside his conservative constituency, returned as Bush's running mate. The president allowed New Right activists, who talked about "a religious war" for "the soul of America" and pictured Democrats as the enemies of "family values," to dominate the 1992 Republican national convention. Conservative Democrats and independents, who had supported Ronald Reagan and Bush in the previous three presidential elections, found this rhetoric no substitute for policies that addressed domestic concerns, particularly the sluggish economy.

Bush's Democratic challenger, Governor William Jefferson Clinton of Arkansas, zeroed in on economic issues. Bill Clinton promised to increase governmental spending for job creation and long-term economic growth. Addressing a concern that cut across partisan lines, he promised a comprehensive revision of the nation's health care system. On other domestic issues, Clinton almost sounded like a Republican. "It's time to end this [welfare] system as we know it," Clinton insisted. "People who can work ought to go to work, and no one should be able to stay on welfare forever." He campaigned as a "new Democrat" who would reduce taxes for middle-class Americans, cut the federal deficit, and shrink the size of government. Clinton, in short, made it difficult for Bush to label him as a "big government liberal."

A focus on economic questions also helped deflect attention from the sociocultural issues on which Bill Clinton was vulnerable. As a college student, he had not only avoided service in Vietnam but had also demonstrated against the Vietnam War while in England as a Rhodes Scholar. When Bush, a decorated veteran of the Second World War, challenged Clinton's patriotism, Clinton countered by emphasizing, rather than repudiating, his roots in the 1960s. He campaigned on MTV and touted his affection for (relatively soft) rock music. In addition, he chose Senator Albert Gore of Tennessee, a Vietnam veteran, as his running mate. Bill and Hillary Rodham Clinton acknowledged past problems in their personal relationship but defended their marriage as a loving, ongoing partnership.

The 1992 election brought Bill Clinton a surprisingly easy victory. The quixotic campaign of Ross Perot, a billionaire from Texas who spent more than $60 million of his own money on a third-party run for the White House, attracted 19 million popular, but no electoral, votes. Perot's candidacy, which denounced the "mess" in Washington and urged people to "take back our country," likely hurt insider Bush more than outsider Clinton. With Perot in the race, Clinton garnered only 43 percent of the popular vote but won 370 electoral votes by carrying 32 states and the District of Columbia. Bush won a majority only among white Protestants in the South. In contrast, Clinton carried the Jewish, African American, and Latino vote by large margins and even gained a plurality among people who had served in the Vietnam War. He also ran well among independents who had supported Reagan and Bush during the 1980s. Perhaps most surprising, about 55 percent of eligible voters went to the polls, a turnout that reversed 32 years of steady decline in voter participation.

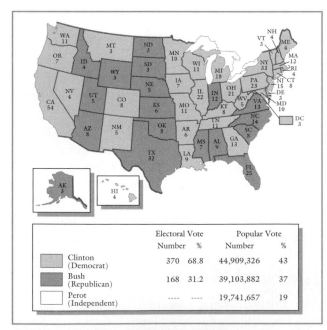

		Electoral Vote		Popular Vote	
		Number	%	Number	%
	Clinton (Democrat)	370	68.8	44,909,326	43
	Bush (Republican)	168	31.2	39,103,882	37
	Perot (Independent)	----	----	19,741,657	19

MAP 31.5 PRESIDENTIAL ELECTION, 1992
Notice the substantial number of votes cast for an independent candidate, Ross Perot. How did Perot's vote totals affect the mandate that Bill Clinton had as president?

The Presidency of Bill Clinton (1993–2001)

Bill Clinton, the first Democratic president in 12 years and the first chief executive from the baby boom generation, brought an image of youth, vitality, and cultural diversity to Washington. The inaugural celebration included different balls for different musical tastes; one (broadcast live on MTV) featured rock 'n' roll from the Vietnam War era. Clinton's initial cabinet included three African Americans and two Latinos; three cabinet posts went to women. His first nominee to the Supreme Court was Ruth Bader Ginsburg, only the second woman to sit on the Court. As representative to the United Nations, Clinton named Madeleine Albright, who would become the country's first female secretary of state during his second term.

Clinton's First Two Years

Clinton gave his supporters several victories on domestic issues. He ended the Reagan era's ban on abortion counseling in family planning clinics; pushed through Con-

CLINTON WAILS SAX DURING HIS PRESIDENTIAL CAMPAIGN

Bill Clinton eagerly identified himself as a New Democrat and as a member of the rock 'n' roll generation.

gress a family leave program for working parents; established the Americorps program, which allowed students to repay their college loans through community service; and secured passage of the Brady Bill, which instituted a five-day waiting period on handgun purchases. Limited college-loan and youth training programs also received funding. An anticrime bill, passed in 1994, provided federal funds to put more police officers on the streets; it also contained more money for prison construction and a controversial "three strikes and you're out" provision, which mandated a lifetime prison sentence for a third felony conviction.

Clinton obtained new economic legislation. His 1993 deficit-reduction plan, which required a tie-breaking vote of Vice President Al Gore to pass the Senate, featured a tax-increase and spending-cut package aimed at reducing the federal deficit and eventually lowering interest rates as a means of stimulating economic growth. The plan also included a provision that expanded an existing governmental program, called the earned tax credit, which provided annual cash bonuses to low-income workers with children.

In contrast, Clinton's hope of reshaping the nation's health care system quickly collapsed. Hillary Rodham Clinton led a task force that produced a complex plan that few people understood; even worse, virtually no one liked what they could decipher. Republicans effectively used the health care proposal, which quickly died in Congress, to paint Clinton as just another advocate of big government. Meanwhile, talk-radio shows, especially that of arch-conservative Rush Limbaugh, featured nonstop criticism of the Clinton White House for bungling the health care issue and for raising taxes. As the welfare rolls soared to an all-time high of 14.4 million people in 1994, Clinton delayed any effort at an overhaul.

Clinton also faced personal problems. Hillary Rodham Clinton's prominent role in the failed heath care effort fueled criticism of her public activities. The Clintons' joint involvement in financial dealings in Arkansas—particularly those connected to a bankrupt savings and loan institution and to a failed land development called Whitewater—drew criticism. In August 1994, a three-judge panel appointed Kenneth Starr, a conservative Republican, to replace the independent prosecutor appointed in January. Charged with investigating the Whitewater affair, Starr moved aggressively to expand his inquiry into new allegations and seemed intent on securing an indictment against at least one of the Clintons.

A Republican Congress, A Democratic White House

The November 1994 elections brought a dramatic, unexpected GOP victory that was spearheaded by New Right strategists, particularly Newt Gingrich, a member of Congress from Georgia. Republicans secured control of both houses of Congress for the first time in 40 years; they won several new governorships, gained ground in most state legislatures, and made significant headway in many city and county elections, particularly across the South. Newt Gingrich hailed these gains as a mandate for an ambitious agenda that the New Right called a Contract with America. It aimed at rolling back federal spending and a variety of governmental programs and regulations.

Congressional Republicans, however, soon overplayed their hand. Opinion polls suggested that people distrusted Gingrich, who became Speaker of the House of Representatives, more than they did Clinton. Moreover, surveys also showed little support for the immediate "revolution" against federal programs that Gingrich and the New Right

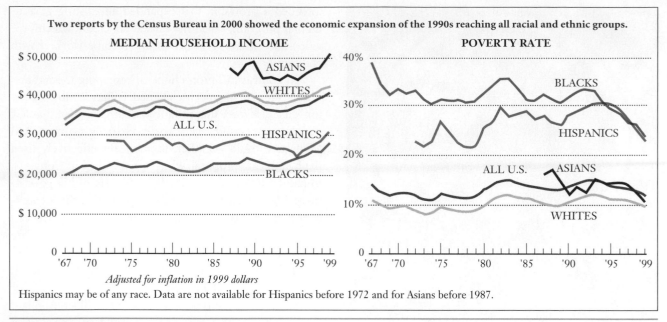

Two reports by the Census Bureau in 2000 showed the economic expansion of the 1990s reaching all racial and ethnic groups.

MEDIAN HOUSEHOLD INCOME

POVERTY RATE

Adjusted for inflation in 1999 dollars

Hispanics may be of any race. Data are not available for Hispanics before 1972 and for Asians before 1987.

INCOME AND POVERTY IN THE LATE 20TH CENTURY

were seeking. When conflict between the Democratic president and the GOP Congress over budget issues led to two brief shutdowns of many government agencies, most people blamed congressional Republicans, rather than the Clinton White House, for the situation.

Most important, a revived U.S. economy buoyed Clinton's presidency. Alan Greenspan, chairman of the Federal Reserve Board, gained a reputation for economic wizardry, particularly for his ability to keep inflation in check through adroit management of interest rates. Low rates of inflation, accompanied by steady economic growth, spurred millions of new jobs. The stock market, before forming a speculative "bubble" at the end of the 1990s, soared. Old-line Democrats often complained that benefits of this Clinton-era expansion were distributed unequally. The agricultural economy continued to push smaller farmers off the land; the gap between earnings of corporate executives and ordinary workers grew steadily larger; and the wealthiest 10 percent of households still owned 90 percent of the nation's stockholdings. Yet, most people did see their economic fortunes improve. Unemployment figures fell steadily, and real income began to grow for the first time in nearly 15 years.

An overhaul of the social welfare system boosted Clinton's political capital. The president, whose 1996 State of the Union address declared that "the era of big government is over," and congressional Republicans cooperated on the long-delayed welfare issue. The Personal Responsibility and Work Opportunity Reconciliation Act of 1996 represented a series of compromises that pleased Republicans more than Democrats. Relatively uncontroversial

sections of the law tightened collection of child support payments and reorganized nutrition and child-care programs. Clinton, while voicing concern about provisions that cut the food stamp program and benefits for recent immigrants, embraced the law's central feature. It replaced the AFDC program, which provided funds and basic social services to poor families headed by single unemployed women, with a flexible system of block grants to individual states. Under the new program, entitled Temporary Assistance to Needy Families (TANF), the 50 states were to design, under broad federal guidelines, their own welfare-to-work programs.

TANF, which effectively replaced the national welfare system created during the New Deal and Great Society, provoked bitter controversy. Its proponents claimed that TANF would encourage states to experiment with new programs that would reduce their welfare costs and create job opportunities. Critics worried that its provisions, including those that limited a person to five years of government assistance during his or her lifetime and authorized states to cut off support if recipients failed to find employment within two years, underestimated the difficulty that people without job skills faced. They also feared the impact that TANF might have on the daily lives of children, especially if states provided inadequate child care, nutritional, and medical care programs. By deferring any protracted debate over these difficult issues, however, the new welfare law effectively removed several potential domestic issues from the political campaign of 1996, a turn that especially helped Bill Clinton.

The huge growth in the productivity of workers, partly due to the computer revolution, buttressed the economic boom of the late 1990s.

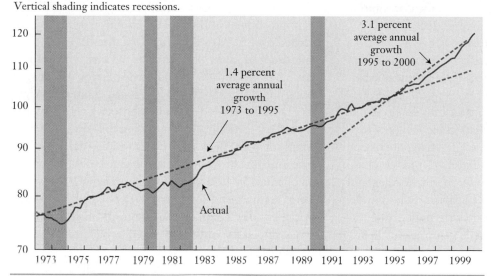

Output per hour in the nonfarm business sector
Index, 1992 = 100
Vertical shading indicates recessions.

PRODUCTIVITY GROWTH, 1973–2000

Sources: Department of Commerce (Bureau of Economic Analysis) and Department of Labor (Bureau of Labor Statistics).

Victory and Impeachment

The election of 1996 capped Clinton's political comeback. Clinton and Gore, riding the economic expansion, defeated Republicans Robert Dole and Jack Kemp by about the same margin they had beaten George H. W. Bush and Dan Quayle in 1992. Clinton, the first Democratic president since Franklin Roosevelt to win back-to-back terms, continued to run especially well among African Americans, women, and Hispanic voters. Republicans did retain control of Congress and gained several new governorships, but Democrats still held a majority of the seats in the 50 state legislatures, a sign that many voters believed that ticket-splitting (voting for both Democrats and Republicans) need not produce gridlock.

After the election, Clinton and congressional Republicans cooperated by passing legislation that established a timetable for reducing the federal deficit. Clinton's 1998 State of the Union address proclaimed that the budget deficit would inevitably disappear, and the president began to negotiate with congressional Republicans about what to do with potential surpluses. He also launched a "national conversation" about racial issues, pressed for programs to improve education, and secured a measure extending health care coverage to several million children from low-income families. The White House even seemed poised, in early 1998, to work with congressional Republicans on reshaping Social Security and Medicare programs.

The nation's political life during 1998 and early 1999, however, revolved not around legislative initiatives but around charges about the president's personal behavior. Kenneth Starr's inquiry finally narrowed to the question of whether the president had been concealing sexual encounters with female employees. Although Clinton unequivocally denied wrongdoing, Republicans pressed forward, claiming that Clinton's efforts to fend off Starr amounted to "obstruction of justice." In response, the president's defenders charged Starr with pursuing a partisan vendetta and with coordinating his efforts with that of New Right activists, especially those bankrolling a civil lawsuit that charged Clinton with sexual harassment while serving as governor of Arkansas. Internet sites and 24/7 cable news channels—relatively new additions to the informational matrix—competed to provide the latest tidbits on the Clinton-Starr battle. Meanwhile, with economic statistics continuing to show solid growth, Clinton's approval ratings rose, while Starr's plummeted.

The president's denials of any personal indiscretion crumbled after Starr obtained irrefutable evidence of his relationship with a young intern named Monica Lewinsky. Facing both a widening criminal investigation and a lingering civil lawsuit, the president's problems went beyond personal embarrassment. Republican opponents insisted that his public actions, particularly a deposition in the lawsuit for sexual harassment (which a federal judge had actually dismissed in April 1998), justified his ouster from the White House. Democrats denounced Clinton's behavior but insisted that his private failings hardly merited removal from public office. Partisan passions, both inside Congress and in the media, intensified as political invective mingled with legal debate over what constituted the kind of "high crimes and misdemeanors" that the Constitution required for the impeachment of a president.

Throughout all of the controversy, Clinton's approval rating, which remained consistently higher than those of any of his Republican critics, provided a formidable barrier against his ouster from the presidency. After making Clinton their primary target during the off-year election of 1998, the GOP actually lost five seats in the House of Representatives. (For the first time since 1934, the opposition party failed to gain House seats in an off-year election.) Even worse for the New Right, Clinton's main antagonist in Congress, House Speaker Newt Gingrich, resigned when a long-term extramarital affair became public. Still, the Republican majority in the lame-duck House of Representatives sent two articles of impeachment (one for perjury and another for obstruction of justice) against Clinton to the Senate on December 19, 1998. Although no one expected that Republicans could attract enough Democratic senators to secure the two-thirds vote required by the Constitution to remove Clinton, only the second president in U.S. history to face an impeachment trial, bipartisan attempts to find an alternative sanction failed. After a month-long trial, which concluded on February 12, 1999, Republican senators failed to muster even a bare majority on either article of impeachment.

Clinton's popularity actually grew during and after the impeachment imbroglio. Economic growth, carefully watched over by Alan Greenspan, continued. Unemployment dropped under 4 percent for the first time in more than 30 years, and the economic expansion that began during the Bush presidency and lasted more than eight years ranked as the longest in U.S. history. Crime statistics dropped dramatically, and the welfare rolls shrank to one-seventh of their 1994 high, or 2.2 million families. The earned income tax credit, whose expansion the president had obtained in 1993, provided more than $30 billion in federal assistance to low-income workers with families. On the eve of Clinton's departure from office, nearly 70 percent of poll respondents believed he had been an effective political leader.

On the surface, the national political climate seemed to change between 1992 and 2000. Clinton and other New Democrats succeeded in reviving their party's fortunes. Once reviled by Ronald Reagan as the party of the "misery index," the Democrats became associated with economic growth, full employment, low inflation, and fiscal responsibility. The White House and congressional Republicans even found common ground on issues such as overhauling the welfare system and reducing the federal deficit. A person who generated bitter enemies, Clinton also engendered equally fervent support, particularly from African Americans. Author Toni Morrison joked that Clinton, who had grown up in a multiracial community, might be considered the nation's first "black president." The success of the earned income tax credit allowed Clinton to retain a strong base among low-income families. Polls indicated that, overall, Americans lost some of their previous cynicism about government.

Environmental Policy

Clinton's years in office expanded environmental protection. His administration negotiated plans to manage and protect old-growth forests in the Pacific Northwest, to implement a conservation framework in nine national forests in the Sierra Nevada,

The percentage of the public who approved of the way the presidents handled the economy clearly correlates with the unemployment rate. Note the rise in unemployment around 1982, 1992, and 2002, and the presidential approval ratings for those same years.

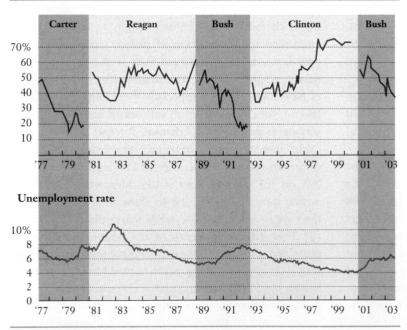

ELECTIONS AND EMPLOYMENT

and to handle the crowds of tourists in Yosemite National Park. In more controversial moves, Clinton's secretary of the interior, Bruce Babbitt, set aside 16 new national monuments and blocked road construction and logging in 58 million acres of wild areas in national forests. Building on records of his Republican predecessors, his administration placed 5.6 million new surface and underwater acres under federal protection. New approaches to environmental management often sought to promote change through incentives rather than penalties. In 1997, for example, the Conservation Reserve Program, a farm subsidy program that previously paid farmers to remove land from tillage, now extended payment to farmers who would restore wetlands on their properties in order to decrease polluted runoff into streams and preserve wildlife habitat.

The U.S. government, however, often seemed to be one of the country's most flagrant polluters. Toward the end of the Reagan administration, the secretary of energy had admitted that the government's nuclear facilities had been lax in enforcing safety measures and estimated that cleanup would cost more than $1 billion. The revelation of hazardous conditions at sites where atomic weapons had been produced shocked nearby residents, who feared they might have suffered radiation poisoning. Workers at the sites had been inadequately warned about radiation, even though government officials knew of its dangers. Moreover, medical records, long suppressed by the government, revealed that people living downwind of nuclear test sites in the 1940s and 1950s had experienced an abnormally high incidence of cancer, leukemia, and thyroid disorders. In 1993, Clinton's new energy secretary released records relating to radiation testing and experimentation and promised programs to inform and compensate victims. The legacy of other kinds of military-related toxic pollutants also became evident as many of the nation's bases were closed down during the 1990s.

The environmental movement increasingly focused on international, as well as national, ecological dangers. Those hazards included global warming (the "greenhouse effect"); holes in the ozone layer caused by chlorofluorocarbons (CFCs); massive deforestation and desertification with accompanying climatic changes; pollution of the oceans; and the rapid decline of biological diversity among both plant and animal species. A so-called Earth Summit was held in Brazil in 1992, and a conference in Cairo in 1994 took up global population issues. Fear that environmental restrictions could harm economic growth and disagreements over mechanisms to measure and enforce agreed-on targets, however, slowed the progress of the international environmental movement. Solutions to global problems required worldwide cooperation toward "sustainable development," and international meetings on environmental issues became more frequent. Conventions in Vienna in 1985, Montreal in 1987, London in 1990, Kyoto in 1997, and The Hague in 2000 worked toward establishing international standards on emissions of CFCs and greenhouse gases.

© Tom Prettyman/PhotoEdit.

AIR QUALITY IN LOS ANGELES: GOOD DAYS AND BAD

During the 1960s, before the introduction of federal air-quality laws, a layer of thick smog that endangered public health hung over the Los Angeles basin 80 percent of the time. By the late 1990s, *left,* the bad old days seemed to be over. Yet, enough bad days still occurred, *right,* that during two of every five days the air quality level failed to meet minimum safety levels, despite the introduction of pollution controls.

Post–Cold War Foreign Policy

For nearly a half century, anticommunism and rivalry with the Soviet Union had shaped U.S. foreign policy. The United States now began to redefine national security. Throughout his presidency, Bill Clinton articulated an expansive, internationalist vision: promoting free-market policies, improving relations with the UN, expanding NATO, advancing human rights and democracy abroad, reducing nuclear threats, and working on global environmental and health concerns. Critics charged that his administration lacked any overall vision or framework; defenders claimed that Clinton's apparent flexibility was a virtue in the fragmented post–Cold War world.

One of the most perplexing issues involved when, and under what conditions, to use U.S. military power in localized conflicts. Several trouble spots sparked debate. In Somalia, U.S. troops, under the umbrella of a UN mission, had been assisting a humanitarian effort to provide food and relief supplies for that African nation since May 1992. The effort, however, cost the lives of 18 American servicemen, who were killed in factional fighting. Under heavy domestic criticism for undertaking an ill-defined mission, Clinton ordered a pullout during spring 1994. The next year, recalling criticism over Somalia, Clinton withheld support from a UN peacekeeping effort in Rwanda, where 500,000 Tutsis died during a genocidal civil war.

In Haiti, closer to home, U.S. interests seemed clearer, and Clinton vowed to help reinstall the ousted president, Jean-Bertrand Aristide. In September 1994, U.S. troops, in cooperation with the UN, landed in Haiti. Last-minute negotiations by former president Jimmy Carter persuaded the Haitian military to step aside. After six months, with Aristide back in office, the United States handed over responsibility for keeping civil order to UN forces.

The United States, through NATO, also sent troops into former Yugoslavia to stop Bosnian Serbs from massacring Bosnian Muslims. The U.S. military remained in Bosnia to oversee a cease-fire and peace-building process in the U.S.-brokered Dayton (Ohio) accords of 1995.

In March 1999, Clinton supported a NATO bombing campaign in Kosovo, a province of Serbia. NATO leaders and Clinton insisted that this controversial use of military force was necessary to protect ethnic Albanian Muslims, who constituted nearly 90 percent of Kosovo's population, from an "ethnic cleansing" program directed by Serbia's president Slobodan Milosevic. As NATO's bombs systematically decimated Serbia's economic infrastructure, Milosevic stepped up his campaign and forced hundreds of thousands of ethnic Albanians to flee from Kosovo into neighboring countries. Finally, in June 1999, after 78 days

of bombardment, Serbia withdrew its forces and, watched over by NATO troops, ethnic Albanians returned to Kosovo. In fall 2000, Serbs repudiated Milosevic, turned him out of office, and elected a president who was more friendly to multiethnic democracy and to the West. As in Bosnia, however, American and other allied troops remained as peacekeepers.

These military initiatives provoked controversy in the United States. Republican critics accused Clinton of an erratic policy with no clear guiding principles about when and how to employ force. They were especially suspicious of cooperation with UN forces and sought clearer exit strategies. Defenders of Clinton's policy continued to argue that flexibility and working with allied forces were strengths, not weaknesses, in the post–Cold War world. In 2000, disputes over a military assistance operation called Plan Colombia, undertaken to combat drug cartels and guerrilla fighters in that country, suggested that the issue of when and how to organize military intervention would remain a contentious one.

Clinton's post–Cold War agenda also included working to promote accords among antagonists in the trouble spots of Northern Ireland and the Middle East. In summer 2000, Clinton brought Israeli and Palestinian heads of state to Camp David in an unsuccessful effort to broker peace, an issue to which he devoted his energy in the closing hours of his administration.

Clinton sought to shape new policies on weapons of mass destruction and terrorism. He dismantled some of the U.S. nuclear arsenal and tried to curtail the potential danger from other nuclear powers. When the former Soviet Union's nuclear stockpile became dispersed among several independent states, the Clinton administration feared dangerous weapons might find their way onto the black market and into the hands of terrorists. In early 1994, it increased economic aid to Ukraine, then the third greatest nuclear power in the world, in return for promises to disarm its 1,600 warheads. In the same year, highly secret Project Sapphire transferred enriched uranium stocks from Kazakhstan to storage facilities in the United States. Jimmy Carter helped negotiate a complicated agreement with North Korea over nuclear weapons, signed in 1994. In return for American help in constructing safe, light-water nuclear reactors for its energy needs, North Korea agreed to begin dismantling its nuclear program and permit international inspections, promises it later violated. The United States also successfully pressed many nations to sign a new Nuclear Nonproliferation Treaty in spring 1995. In early 1998, Clinton went to the brink of war with Iraq to maintain international inspections of Saddam Hussein's weapons programs, but after enduring punishing air

Madeleine Albright:
A Woman on the World Stage

The second woman to represent the United States as its ambassador to the United Nations and the first to serve as Secretary of State, Madeleine Albright (1937–) took a circuitous route to diplomatic fame. Born Marie Jana Korbel in Czechoslovakia, she left for Great Britain during the 1930s when her father, a prominent Czech diplomat, took his family out of the reach of the Nazis. After the communist coup of 1948 ended a brief return to Czechoslovakia, the family of Joseph Korbel settled in Denver, Colorado, where he became a college professor. Madeleine, now a teenager, attended a private school for girls.

After graduating from Wellesley College, Madeleine married journalist Joseph Albright in 1959 and devoted much of the 1960s to raising three children. At the same time, though, she began graduate study at Columbia University under the tutelage of Zbigniew Brzezinski. Initially a firm supporter of U.S. involvement in the Vietnam War, Madeleine gradually came to see American intervention as a disastrous mistake. Finally receiving her Ph.D. in international studies in 1976, she went to work for Brzezinksi, then Jimmy Carter's National Security Adviser. Shortly after Carter's 1980 defeat left Madeleine Albright without a political position, her husband's decision to seek a divorce left her, at age 45, with the need to pursue new options. On returning to Wellesley in 1984, for the 25th anniversary of her graduation, she listed "Divorce and Ronald Reagan" as the "lows" in an otherwise successful life.

Madeleine Albright soon plunged into the interlocking worlds of Democratic Party politics and foreign affairs. Bill Clinton's eight-year presidency gave her the chance to serve as UN ambassador and, then, as Secretary of State during the 1990s. Shortly after becoming Secretary of State, Madeleine Albright, raised a Catholic, learned that three of her grandparents had been Jewish and had died in Nazi concentration camps. This news,

she later observed, inclined her to see international issues, especially those related to genocide, in a more intensely personal light.

Albright gained the reputation of being a shrewd, tough-minded negotiator—and an often witty observer of the diplomatic scene. One of her most poignant moments, she recalled, was her first flight into Prague, Czechoslovakia, with President Clinton. Visiting there and listening to a band play the Czech national anthem, "Where Is My Home," she recalled the strange international journey she had taken to become America's top policy maker.

© Reuters NewMedia Inc./Corbis.

MADELEINE ALBRIGHT RETURNING TO HER NATIVE CZECHOSLOVAKIA, 2000

The secretary of state speaks under a statue of Tomas Masaryk, president of Czechoslovakia before the Second World War, in a celebration to mark the 150th anniversary of his birth.

strikes, Iraq still expelled the investigators. International terrorists bombed the World Trade Center in New York City in 1993, the U.S. embassies in Kenya and Tanzania in 1998, and a U.S. battleship docked in Yemen in 2000. These escalating attacks by Islamic militants raised alarm about future plots.

Globalization

The Clinton administration placed high priority on lowering trade barriers and expanding the global marketplace—a process called "globalization." Building on the Reagan-Bush legacy, Clinton argued that globalization would boost prosperity and foster democracy around the world.

Clinton enthusiastically backed the North American Free Trade Agreement (NAFTA), which projected cutting tariffs and eliminating other trade barriers between the United States, Canada, and Mexico over a 15-year period. After adding weak new provisions on labor and environmental issues, in December 1993 he muscled NAFTA through Congress in a close vote that depended on Republican support and faced fierce opposition from labor unions. Then, in early 1995, Mexico's severe debt crisis and a dramatic devaluation of its peso prompted Clinton to extend a $20 billion loan from America's Exchange Stabilization Fund. Although unprecedented and controversial, this loan stabilized the Mexican economy and, within a few years, had been repaid with $1 billion in interest.

Clinton's administration frequently used economic enticements to persuade other nations to embrace globalization and the more than 300 trade agreements signed between 1993 and 2001. His trade negotiators completed the so-called Uruguay Round of the General Agreement on Tariffs and Trade (GATT) in late 1993, and in early 1995, GATT was replaced by a more powerful World Trade Organization (WTO), created to enlarge world trade by implementing new agreements and mediating disputes. Anxious to move China toward capitalism, Clinton reversed his election-year position and granted China, despite its dismal record on human rights, equal trading status with other nations. In October 1999, the Clinton administration agreed to back China's entry into the WTO in exchange for a promise to liberalize its policies toward the United States and other potential trading partners. Clinton argued that increased trade with China would contribute to long-term pressures for democratization there. Similarly, in February 1994, the United States ended its 19-year-old trade embargo against Vietnam.

Clinton claimed that the effort to expand trade, along with the emerging free-market economies in Eastern Europe and Latin America, provided the framework for global prosperity. When Asian economies faltered during 1998, he supported acting with the International Monetary Fund (IMF) to provide huge emergency credits to reform and restore financial systems from Korea to Indonesia. Everywhere he went, Clinton extolled the "new century" in which "liberty will spread by cell phone and cable modem."

The Presidency of George W. Bush (2001–)

Bill Clinton's popularity in the polls remained high as he neared the end of his term. After one of the closest elections in U.S. history, however, his Republican successor began to take the country in very different directions. George W. Bush, son of the nation's 41st president, assumed the mantle of Ronald Reagan and determined to vigorously pursue the New Right agenda that Clinton's presidency had interrupted.

The Long Election

A retro aura surrounded the presidential campaign of 2000. Al Gore reappeared, this time as the Democratic presidential nominee. The Republican ballot, for the fifth time in the last six elections, bore the name of Bush—that of George W. Bush. The younger Bush selected Richard (Dick) Cheney, who had served in his father's administration, as the GOP's vice-presidential running candidate. The presidential ballot also included a third-party challenger: Ralph Nader, the veteran activist. Nader ran as the candidate of the Green Party and ultimately attracted less than 3 percent of the popular vote, a far less impressive showing than Ross Perot's in 1996.

The tepid campaign stirred few passions. George W. Bush cited his record as governor of Texas as a sign that he could work with Democrats, attract a following among African Americans and Hispanics, and pursue "compassionate conservatism." While the Bush camp stayed "on message," Gore's disorganized campaign struggled to articulate coherent themes. By distancing himself from Clinton, the vice president likely squandered his primary asset, eight years of economic prosperity. The turnout was relatively light; barely 50 percent of the eligible voters went to the polls. Following a pattern that had been in place since the Reagan era, the popular vote highlighted the gender, racial, and ethnic differences between the two parties. According to exit polls, Bush attracted 54 percent of the votes cast by men but only 43 percent of those from women. He received 38 percent of his votes from Latinos,

MAP 31.6 PRESIDENTIAL ELECTION, 2000

Although Gore won the popular vote, Bush won the electoral vote after a bitter dispute involving ballots in Florida. Note the possible impact of third-party candidates.

RECOUNTING VOTES IN PALM BEACH COUNTY, FLORIDA

The slow process of interpreting voters' intentions from improperly punched ballots with "hanging chads" helped complicate the effort to recount votes in Florida.

37 percent from Asian Americans, and 9 percent from African Americans.

The election of 2000 produced a near dead heat. Republicans narrowly maintained control of the House of Representatives, and the Senate ended up evenly split between the two parties. Gore carried the popular vote by about 500,000 ballots. The only tally that mattered, the one in the electoral college, remained so close that the identity of the next president turned on who had gained the 25 electoral votes from Florida, where about 1,000 votes separated the candidates and where Bush's brother Jeb served as governor and Republicans controlled the legislature.

Partisan fervor, which was muted during the campaign, suddenly flared as, for a month, no clear winner emerged in Florida. After counting all absentee ballots, Republican officials in Florida declared Bush, by a margin of 930 votes, to be the winner. Democrats complained that many circumstances, particularly antiquated voting machines, had distorted the count, and they sued to force hand recounts in several counties where the Gore total seemed abnormally low. More than 50 lawsuits, by both Democrats and Republicans, soon dotted court dockets; both parties, particularly the GOP, flooded Florida with cadres of lawyers and demonstrators; and an even greater number of media personnel saturated the Sunshine State. When the early recounts seemed to be reducing Bush's already slim margin, Republicans charged that Democrats were "stealing" his victory. Statisticians advised that no procedure for hand counting so many disputed ballots, in such a close election, could ever yield a universally agreed-upon result.

Finally, the U.S. Supreme Court, in two 5–4 opinions, chose the new president. After first issuing a temporary injunction, halting all manual recounts in Florida, the Court's conservative Republicans (over the dissents of two moderate Republicans and two Democrats) declared, on December 12, 2000, that conducting these recounts only in the contested counties violated the Constitution. In addition, the same justices insisted that, because of Florida's timetable for reporting to the electoral college, there could not be any statewide recount of the November ballots. At this point, Gore conceded defeat, and George W. Bush became the 43rd president of the United States.

A Conservative Domestic Agenda

Several divisive domestic issues soon dominated Bush's presidency. First, signs of a downturn in the overall economy, accompanied by a plunge in a badly overvalued and fraud-plagued stock market, seemed to herald the end of the Clinton-era boom. The revenue surpluses of the late 1990s, at both the national and state levels, began dwindling and promised to become, once again, growing

AP/Wide World Photos.

GEORGE W. SHOWS TEXAS STYLE
George W. Bush emerged victorious despite losing the popular vote to Democrat Al Gore.

deficits. Consumer confidence declined as corporate accounting scandals rocked Wall Street and sent several major companies into bankruptcy. The Bush administration quickly urged a controversial tax cut, which Democrats charged favored the wealthiest 1 percent of the population, to provide an economic stimulus. The president's critics also complained that a White House energy plan, based on easing restrictions on drilling and regulations on pricing, primarily benefited large gas and oil companies, many of which were headquartered in Texas. Finally, the Bush administration pressed an educational policy that sought mandatory, nationwide testing of children, as a means of determining which schools were teaching effectively. In addition, it called for government-financed vouchers, which promised federal money for parents who wished to transfer their children from failing public to private schools.

Bush's initiatives, which were far bolder than either his campaign rhetoric or his loss of the popular vote might have suggested, faced a divided Congress. A revised tax plan, which passed in June 2001, mandated substantial cuts that were to be phased in gradually, and an educational measure required the nationwide testing of students but not vouchers. Opposition to Bush's plans mounted after James Jeffords, a Republican senator from Vermont who invariably voted against the GOP anyway, became an independent and thus gave the Democrats brief control of the Senate.

Foreign Policy Changes Course

Foreign policy, an area in which Bush initially admitted to having little background, soon pushed most domestic issues to the side. On September 11, 2001, 19 suicide commandos of Middle Eastern descent seized four jetliners, already airborne and fully loaded with flammable fuel, and attempted to use them as high-octane, human-guided missiles. Two planes toppled the twin towers of New York's World Trade Center; another ripped into the Pentagon building in Washington; and only the courageous action of several passengers on a fourth plane (which crashed in Pennsylvania) prevented a second attack in the nation's capital. More than 3,000 people, including several hundred passengers and an even larger number of police and fire officers in New York City, perished.

Bush, donning the mantle of a war-time president, declared a "war on terror," and his popularity soared. Tracing the attack to Afghanistan and to Osama bin Laden, an Islamic fundamentalist from a wealthy Saudi Arabian family who headed the Al Qaeda terrorist network, the Bush administration sponsored a multinational force that, in December 2001, toppled the Taliban regime that had been dominating Afghanistan with bin Laden's help. American-led forces installed a pro-U.S. government in Afghanistan's capital city of Kabul but failed to secure the countryside or to capture bin Laden and his top lieutenants.

Meanwhile, President Bush announced a dramatic new foreign policy initiative. Denouncing all terrorist networks and any nation sponsoring terrorism or accumulating weapons of mass destruction, he proclaimed the Bush Doctrine. It declared that the United States now assumed the authority to wage preventive war against any force, including any foreign nation, that endangered American security. The United States, in other words, would not simply respond to direct and immediate threats, as it had done throughout the 20th century, and even during the Cold War era, but would mount preemptive military strikes, whenever and wherever it seemed necessary, to safeguard U.S. interests. Implementation of the Bush Doctrine, the White House predicted, would cost about as much (in constant dollars) as the United States had spent during all of the Second World War and during the early years of the

GROUND ZERO, SEPTEMBER 11, 2001

The South Tower of the World Trade Center collapses as the North Tower burns, after terrorists commandeered two airliners and used them as deadly missiles. The attack, widely compared to Pearl Harbor, provoked the Bush administration to declare a "war on terrorism."

The Bush administration's tough and unilateralist foreign policy remained popular enough to help the Republicans, despite worsening economic conditions, expand their political base. In the election of 2002, the GOP gained control of the U.S. Senate and picked up several additional seats in the House. As a result, the White House secured yet another tax cut, again touted as an economic stimulus, which Democrats once more condemned for tilting toward the rich. Rejecting this claim and downplaying the impact of a record federal budget deficit, the White House insisted that its tax plan would restore prosperity to an economy that had already shed nearly 3 million jobs during the initial years of the Bush presidency. The partisan pitch of political rhetoric steadily increased—in the halls of Congress, on talk-radio shows, and on the 24/7 news channels. New Right pundits, such as Ann Coulter and Rush Limbaugh, charged Democrats with slandering conservatives and with endangering national security; spokespeople on the left, such as Al Franken and Michael Moore, condemned the New Right for lying about its domestic and foreign agenda, including the war in Iraq, and asking future generations to pay for a war on terrorism while the wealthiest members of the current generation enjoyed tax decreases.

As Osama bin Laden dropped from sight and Al Qaeda reorganized, the Bush administration shifted its attention to Iraq and Saddam Hussein, the old nemesis of the president's father, who tightly controlled one of the richest oil basins in the world. The so-called neocons in the National Security Council and the Pentagon, who favored a unilateral war against Hussein, tilted with Secretary of State Colin Powell, who tried to gain international support for U.S. action. At Powell's insistence, the White House did press the UN and other nations to support a military strike to topple Hussein on the claim that his regime, which had been avoiding the weapons inspections mandated by the Gulf War settlement of 1991, was both aiding terrorists and stockpiling weapons of mass destruction. Although Great Britain and several smaller nations signed on, the UN and major powers such as France and Germany rebuffed the United States.

After failing to gain UN support, the Bush administration and a "coalition of the willing" launched an air and ground assault against Iraq on March 20, 2003. Although

Cold War. The president's approval ratings, which had earlier hovered around 50 percent, soared nearly 40 points. Coupled with the president's tax-cutting, however, these expenditures brought back a huge national deficit.

The White House kept the nation, and particularly the media, focused on its war against terrorism. Revelations about massive corporate scandals, which included Enron and other businesses that had supported Bush's political campaign, failed to divert attention from foreign issues. Reluctant to challenge the White House, congressional Democrats joined Republicans in passing the White-House–supported Patriot Act, which gave the executive branch broad latitude over the surveillance and detention of people it considered threats to national security.

the self-proclaimed liberators encountered more resistance than the Bush administration initially predicted, Saddam's regime fell in less than two months. On May 1, President Bush landed on the deck of the aircraft carrier *Abraham Lincoln* and proclaimed an end to the combat phase of his Iraqi mission. This carefully crafted media event quickly rebounded against the president as resistance to the American-dominated occupation, which aimed at creating a pro-U.S. government and an economic order closely tied to U.S. companies in post-Saddam Iraq, grew steadily wider and increasingly more lethal. By fall 2003, more Americans had died from hostile fire *after* Bush's landing on the *Abraham Lincoln* than *before* his declaration.

Meanwhile, attacks on Americans in Iraq expanded to include deadly assaults against aid workers from the United Nations, the Red Cross, and various other international relief agencies. Anti-Western groups from outside Iraq, it appeared, were joining the battle there as well as in Afghanistan, where the U.S.-backed government in Kabul retained a tenuous hold on power. Although early supporters of action against Saddam Hussein had suggested that Iraqi oil revenues could pay for the costs of any U.S. military action there, by fall 2003, the president had to ask Congress for $87 billion to fund just the immediate costs of the fighting and rebuilding activity in Iraq and Afghanistan. The lack of international support for U.S. action meant that, unlike in the 1991 Persian Gulf War, most of the costs would be borne by American taxpayers.

The White House insisted that the political and economic reconstruction of Iraq remained on track, but public opinion polls revealed growing doubts in the United States about the Bush policy. Had the administration misinterpreted or exaggerated intelligence information about Saddam's supposed cache of weapons of mass destruction, which could not be found after his fall? Did its claim that American-led forces would be hailed as liberators badly misread the situation in Iraq? Had there been an appropriate planning process for postwar stabilization in Iraq? As spokespeople for the Bush administration portrayed their goal of building a democratic Iraq as being similar to the successful operations in Japan and Germany during the 1940s, critics saw the Iraqi situation looking more like the failed crusade in Vietnam during the 1960s. As the cost of the occupation in both money and human life escalated, discussion in both the United States and overseas

U.S. SOLDIERS IN BAGHDAD, NOVEMBER 2003
After a relatively short military campaign to overthrow Saddam Hussein, U.S. forces struggled to bring stability to Iraq. Here, troops respond to a rocket attack on the Iraqi Oil Ministry and two hotels in central Baghdad.

© Damir Sagolj/Reuters NewMedia Inc./Corbis.

slowly turned to whether the Bush administration could devise alternative policies to achieve its overly optimistic goals for a post-invasion Iraq.

Conclusion

Two outsized personalities dominated American political life in the late 20th century: Ronald Reagan and Bill Clinton. The "Reagan revolution" of the 1980s saw the emergence of a new conservative movement that had been born in the shadow of Lyndon Johnson's Great Society. New Right Republicans distrusted extending federal government power, advocated sharp tax cuts, and stressed a sociocultural agenda emphasizing traditional values. The dozen years of Republican dominance in the White House from 1980 to 1992 significantly shifted the terms of political debate to the right. The once-proud label of "liberal" became a term that politicians of both parties sought to avoid.

During the 1990s, the Republican agenda met its match in Bill Clinton, a New Democrat. Clinton blunted the Republican surge by adopting a fairly conservative economic agenda (e.g., slashing the federal deficit, reshaping the welfare system, and downsizing the federal bureaucracy). At the same time, he supported other issues that were heatedly opposed by many Republicans: abortion rights, gun control, affirmative action, and environmental protection. During his presidency, Clinton moved the Democratic Party away from its big-government agenda of the 1960s and 1970s.

In foreign policy, Reagan's military buildup coincided with the last years of the Cold War. By contrast, Clinton's emphasis on economic globalization addressed the post–Cold War environment.

The first president to take office in the 21st century, George W. Bush, recalled and built on the policies of the Reagan years. Polling data in early 2004, however, suggested that the electorate remained evenly split in their party loyalties.

Reagan and Clinton, both charismatic, media-savvy, two-term presidents, inspired intense adoration and passionate dislike. Together, their administrations tried to redraw the political landscape. In their shadows, Americans continued to negotiate the difficult balances among liberty, equality, and power.

SUGGESTED READINGS

For differing views of the political trends that came together during the 1980s, see **Garry Wills,** *Reagan's America: Innocents at Home* (1987); **Thomas Byrne and Mary D. Edsall,** *Chain Reaction: The Impact of Race, Rights, and Taxes on American Politics* (1992); **Burton J. Kaufman,** *The Presidency of James Earl Carter* (1993); **John W. Sloan,** *The Reagan Effect: Economics and Presidential Leadership* (1999); **Frances Fitzgerald,** *Way Out There in the Blue: Reagan and Star Wars and the End of the Cold War* (2000); **Lisa McGirr,** *Suburban Warriors: The Origins of the New American Right* (2001); **John Schoenwald,** *A Time for Choosing: The Rise of Modern American Conservatism* (2001); and **W. Carl Biven,** *Jimmy Carter's Economy: Policy in an Age of Limits* (2002).

Very different perspectives on the post-Reagan political scene appear in **Bob Woodward,** *The Agenda: Inside the Clinton White House* (1994) and *The Choice* (1996); **Theodore Lowi and Benjamin Ginsburg,** *Embattled Democracy: Politics and Policy in the Clinton Era* (1995); **David Mervin,** *George Bush and the Guardian Presidency* (1996); **Kenneth Baer,** *Reinventing Democrats: The Politics of Liberalism from Reagan to Clinton* (2000); **Steven F. Schier, ed.,** *The Postmodern Presidency: Bill Clinton's Legacy in U.S. Politics* (2000); **John Robert Greene,** *The Presidency of George Bush* (2000); **Haynes Johnson,** *The Best of Times: America in the Clinton Years* (2001); **David Halberstam,** *War in a Time of Peace* (2001); **Joe Conanson and Gene Lyons,** *The Hunting of the President: The Ten-Year Campaign to Destroy Bill and Hillary Clinton* (2001); and **Sidney Blumenthal,** *The Clinton Wars* (2003).

The electoral contest that elevated George W. Bush to the presidency is analyzed in **Gerald M. Pomper, et al.,** *The Election of 2000: Reports and Interpretations* (2000); **Richard Posner,** *Breaking the Deadlock: The 2000 Election and the Courts* (2001); and **Jeffrey Toobin,** *Too Close to Call* (2001).

The controversy surrounding George W. Bush's early tenure in the White House, and especially its relationship to the attacks of 9/11, is reflected in titles such as **Fred H. Halliday,** *Two Hours That Shook the World: September 11, 2001: Causes and Consequences* (2002); **Bob Woodward,** *Bush At War* (2002); **Craig Calhoun, Paul Price, and Ashley Timmer, eds.,** *Understanding September 11* (2002); **David Frum,** *The Right Man: The Surprise Presidency of George W. Bush* (2003); **Stephen Hess and Marvin Kalb, eds.,** *The Media and the War on Terrorism* (2003); **Gerald Posner,** *Why America Slept: The Failure to Prevent 9/11* (2003); **Williamson Murray and Major General Robert H. Scales, Jr.,** *The Iraq War: A Military History* (2003); and **Joanne Meyerowitz, ed.,** *History and September 11th* (2003).

 AMERICAN JOURNEY ONLINE
AND
INFOTRAC COLLEGE EDITION

Visit the source collections at www.ajaccess.wadsworth.com and infotrac.thomsonlearning.com and use the Search function with the following key terms to explore documents, images, audio and video clips, articles, and commentary related to the material in this chapter.

Gerald R. Ford	North American Free Trade
Jimmy Carter	Agreement (NAFTA)
Ronald Reagan	Kenneth Starr
Iran-*Contra*	Clinton impeachment
Star Wars (SDI)	George W. Bush
Persian Gulf War	September 11, 2001
Bill Clinton	War on Terrorism
Ross Perot	

GRADE AIDS

Visit the Liberty Equality Power Companion Web Site for resources specific to this textbook: http://history.wadsworth.com/murrin_LEP4e

The CD in the back of this book and the U.S. History Resource Center at http://history.wadsworth.com/u.s./ offer a variety of tools to help you succeed in this course, including access to quizzes; images; documents; interactive simulations, maps, and timelines; movie explorations; and a wealth of other sources.

Appendix

The Declaration of Independence

The Constitution of the United States of America

Admission of States

Population of the United States

Presidential Elections

Presidential Administrations

Justices of the U.S. Supreme Court

The Declaration of Independence

THE UNANIMOUS DECLARATION OF THE THIRTEEN UNITED STATES OF AMERICA

When in the Course of human events it becomes necessary for one people to dissolve the political bands which have connected them with another, and to assume among the Powers of the earth, the separate and equal station to which the Laws of Nature and of Nature's God entitle them, a decent respect to the opinions of mankind requires that they should declare the causes which impel them to the separation.

We hold these truths to be self-evident, that all men are created equal, that they are endowed by their Creator with certain unalienable Rights, that among these are Life, Liberty and the pursuit of Happiness. That to secure these rights, Governments are instituted among Men, deriving their just Powers from the consent of the governed. That whenever any Form of Government becomes destructive of these ends, it is the Right of the People to alter or to abolish it, and to institute new Government, laying its foundation on such principles and organizing its Powers in such form, as to them shall seem most likely to effect their Safety and Happiness. Prudence, indeed, will dictate that Governments long established should not be changed for light and transient causes; and accordingly all experience hath shewn, that mankind are more disposed to suffer, while evils are sufferable, than to right themselves by abolishing the forms to which they are accustomed. But when a long train of abuses and usurpations, pursuing invariably the same Object evinces a design to reduce them under absolute Despotism, it is their right, it is their duty, to throw off such Government, and to provide new Guards for their future security. Such has been the patient sufferance of these Colonies; and such is now the necessity which constrains them to alter their former Systems of Government. The history of the present King of Great Britain is a history of repeated injuries and usurpations, all having in direct object the establishment of an absolute Tyranny over these States. To prove this, let Facts be submitted to a candid world.

Text is reprinted from the facsimile of the engrossed copy in the National Archives. The original spelling, capitalization, and punctuation have been retained. Paragraphing has been added.

He has refused his Assent to Laws, the most wholesome and necessary for the public good.

He has forbidden his Governors to pass Laws of immediate and pressing importance, unless suspended in their operation till his Assent should be obtained; and when so suspended, he has utterly neglected to attend to them.

He has refused to pass other Laws for the accommodation of large districts of people, unless those people would relinquish the right of Representation in the Legislature, a right inestimable to them and formidable to tyrants only.

He has called together legislative bodies at places unusual, uncomfortable, and distant from the depository of their Public Records, for the sole Purpose of fatiguing them into compliance with his measures.

He has dissolved Representative Houses repeatedly, for opposing with manly firmness his invasions on the rights of the People.

He has refused for a long time, after such dissolutions, to cause others to be elected; whereby the Legislative Powers, incapable of Annihilation, have returned to the People at large for their exercise; the State remaining in the mean time exposed to all the dangers of invasion from without, and convulsions within.

He has endeavoured to prevent the Population of these States; for that purpose obstructing the Laws for Naturalization of Foreigners; refusing to pass others to encourage their migrations hither, and raising the conditions of new Appropriations of Lands.

He has obstructed the Administration of Justice, by refusing his Assent to Laws for establishing Judiciary Powers.

He has made Judges dependent on his Will alone, for the tenure of their offices, and the amount and payment of their salaries.

He has erected a multitude of New Offices, and sent hither swarms of Officers to harass our People, and eat out their substance.

He has kept among us, in times of peace, Standing Armies without the Consent of our legislatures.

He has affected to render the Military independent of and superior to the Civil Power.

He has combined with others to subject us to a jurisdiction foreign to our constitution, and unacknowledged by our laws; giving his Assent to their Acts of pretended Legislation:

For Quartering large bodies of armed troops among us:

For protecting them, by a mock Trial, from Punishment for any Murders which they should commit on the Inhabitants of these States:

For cutting off our Trade with all parts of the world:

For imposing Taxes on us without our Consent:

For depriving us in many cases, of the benefits of Trial by Jury:

For transporting us beyond Seas to be tried for pretended offences:

For abolishing the free System of English Laws in a neighbouring Province, establishing therein an Arbitrary government, and enlarging its Boundaries so as to render it at once an example and fit instrument for introducing the same absolute rule into these Colonies:

For taking away our Charters, abolishing our most valuable Laws, and altering fundamentally the Forms of our Governments:

For suspending our own Legislatures, and declaring themselves invested with Power to legislate for us in all cases whatsoever.

He has abdicated Government here, by declaring us out of his Protection, and waging War against us.

He has plundered our seas, ravaged our Coasts, burnt our towns, and destroyed the lives of our people.

He is at this time transporting large Armies of foreign Mercenaries to compleat the works of death, desolation and tyranny, already begun with circumstances of Cruelty and perfidy scarcely parallelled in the most barbarous ages, and totally unworthy the Head of a civilized nation.

He has constrained our fellow Citizens taken Captive on the high Seas to bear Arms against their Country, to become the executioners of their friends and Brethren, or to fall themselves by their Hands.

He has excited domestic insurrections amongst us, and has endeavoured to bring on the inhabitants of our frontiers, the merciless Indian Savages, whose known rule of warfare, is an undistinguished destruction of all ages, sexes and conditions.

In every stage of these Oppressions We have Petitioned for Redress in the most humble terms: Our repeated Petitions have been answered only by repeated injury. A Prince, whose character is thus marked by every act which may define a Tyrant, is unfit to be the ruler of a free People.

Nor have We been wanting in attentions to our British brethren. We have warned them from time to time of attempts by their legislature to extend an unwarrantable jurisdiction over us. We have reminded them of the circumstances of our emigration and settlement here. We have appealed to their native justice and magnanimity, and we have conjured them by the ties of our common kindred to disavow these usurpations, which, would inevitably interrupt our connections and correspondence. They too have been deaf to the voice of justice and of consanguinity. We must, therefore, acquiesce in the necessity, which denounces our Separation, and hold them, as we hold the rest of mankind, Enemies in War, in Peace Friends.

WE, THEREFORE, the Representatives of the UNITED STATES OF AMERICA, in General Congress, Assembled, appealing to the Supreme Judge of the world for the rectitude of our intentions, do, in the Name, and by Authority of the good People of these Colonies, solemnly publish and declare, That these United Colonies are, and of Right ought to be FREE AND INDEPENDENT STATES; that they are Absolved from all Allegiance to the British Crown, and that all political connection between them and the State of Great Britain, is and ought to be totally dissolved; and that, as Free and Independent States, they have full Power to levy War, conclude Peace, contract Alliances, establish Commerce, and to do all other Acts and Things which Independent States may of right do. And for the support of this Declaration, with a firm reliance on the protection of divine Providence, we mutually pledge to each other our Lives, our Fortunes and our sacred Honor.

The Constitution of the United States of America

We the People of the United States, in Order to form a more perfect Union, establish Justice, insure domestic Tranquility, provide for the common defence, promote the general Welfare, and secure the Blessings of Liberty to ourselves and our Posterity, do ordain and establish this Constitution for the United States of America.

ARTICLE I.

SECTION 1. All legislative Powers herein granted shall be vested in a Congress of the United States, which shall consist of a Senate and House of Representatives.

SECTION 2. The House of Representatives shall be composed of Members chosen every second Year by the People of the several States, and the Electors in each State shall have the Qualifications requisite for Electors of the most numerous Branch of the State Legislature.

No Person shall be a Representative who shall not have attained to the Age of twenty five Years, and been seven Years a Citizen of the United States, and who shall not, when elected, be an Inhabitant of that State in which he shall be chosen.

Representatives and direct Taxes[1] shall be apportioned among the several States which may be included within this Union, according to their respective Numbers, which shall be determined by adding to the whole Number of free Persons, including those bound to Service for a Term of Years, and excluding Indians not taxed, three fifths of all other Persons.[2] The actual Enumeration shall be made within three Years after the first Meeting of the Congress of the United States, and within every subsequent Term of ten Years, in such Manner as they shall by Law direct. The Number of Representatives shall not exceed one for every thirty Thousand, but each State shall have at Least one Representative; and until such enumeration shall be made, the State of New Hampshire shall be entitled to chuse three; Massachusetts eight; Rhode Island and Providence Plantations one; Connecticut five; New York six; New Jersey four; Pennsylvania eight; Delaware one; Maryland six; Virginia ten; North Carolina five; South Carolina five; and Georgia three.

When vacancies happen in the Representation from any State, the Executive Authority thereof shall issue Writs of Election to fill such Vacancies.

The House of Representatives shall chuse their Speaker and other Officers; and shall have the sole Power of Impeachment.

SECTION 3. The Senate of the United States shall be composed of two Senators from each State, chosen by the Legislature thereof, for six Years; and each Senator shall have one Vote.[3]

Immediately after they shall be assembled in Consequence of the first Election, they shall be divided as equally as may be into three Classes. The Seats of the Senators of the first Class shall be vacated at the Expiration of the second Year, of the second Class at the Expiration of the fourth Year, and of the third Class at the Expiration of the sixth Year, so that one third may be chosen every second Year; and if Vacancies happen by Resignation, or otherwise, during the Recess of the Legislature of any State, the Executive thereof may make temporary Appointments until the next Meeting of the Legislature, which shall then fill such Vacancies.[4]

No Person shall be a Senator who shall not have attained to the Age of thirty Years, and been nine Years a Citizen of the United States, and who shall not, when elected, be an Inhabitant of that State for which he shall be chosen.

The Vice President of the United States shall be President of the Senate, but shall have no Vote, unless they be equally divided.

The Senate shall chuse their other Officers, and also a President pro tempore, in the Absence of the Vice President, or when he shall exercise the Office of President of the United States.

Text is from the engrossed copy in the National Archives. Original spelling, capitalization, and punctuation have been retained.

[1]Modified by the Sixteenth Amendment.
[2]Replaced by the Fourteenth Amendment.
[3]Superseded by the Seventeenth Amendment.
[4]Modified by the Seventeenth Amendment.

The Senate shall have the sole Power to try all Impeachments. When sitting for that Purpose, they shall be on Oath or Affirmation. When the President of the United States is tried, the Chief Justice shall preside: And no Person shall be convicted without the Concurrence of two thirds of the Members present.

Judgment in Cases of Impeachment shall not extend further than to removal from Office, and disqualification to hold and enjoy any Office of honor, Trust or Profit under the United States: but the Party convicted shall nevertheless be liable and subject to Indictment, Trial, Judgment and Punishment, according to Law.

SECTION 4. The Times, Places and Manner of holding Elections for Senators and Representatives, shall be prescribed in each State by the Legislature thereof, but the Congress may at any time by Law make or alter such Regulation, except as to the Places of chusing Senators.

The Congress shall assemble at least once in every Year, and such Meeting shall be on the first Monday in December, unless they shall by Law appoint a different Day.[5]

SECTION 5. Each House shall be the Judge of the Elections, Returns and Qualifications of its own Members, and a Majority of each shall constitute a Quorum to do Business; but a smaller Number may adjourn from day to day, and may be authorized to compel the Attendance of absent Members, in such Manner, and under such Penalties as each House may provide.

Each House may determine the Rules of its Proceedings, punish its Members for disorderly Behaviour, and, with the Concurrence of two thirds, expel a Member.

Each House shall keep a Journal of its Proceedings, and from time to time publish the same, excepting such Parts as may in their Judgment require Secrecy; and the Yeas and Nays of the Members of either House on any question shall, at the Desire of one fifth of those Present, be entered on the Journal.

Neither House, during the Session of Congress, shall, without the Consent of the other, adjourn for more than three days, nor to any other Place than that in which the two Houses shall be sitting.

SECTION 6. The Senators and Representatives shall receive a Compensation for their Services, to be ascertained by Law, and paid out of the Treasury of the United States. They shall in all Cases, except Treason, Felony and Breach of the Peace, be privileged from Arrest during their Attendance at the Session of their respective Houses, and in going to and returning from the same; and for any Speech or Debate in either House, they shall not be questioned in any other Place.

No Senator or Representative shall, during the Time for which he was elected, be appointed to any civil Office under the Authority of the United States, which shall have been created, or the Emoluments whereof shall have been encreased during such time; and no Person holding any Office under the United States, shall be a Member of either House during his Continuance in Office.

SECTION 7. All Bills for raising Revenue shall originate in the House of Representatives; but the Senate may propose or concur with Amendments as on other Bills.

Every Bill which shall have passed the House of Representatives and the Senate shall, before it become a Law, be presented to the President of the United States; If he approve he shall sign it, but if not he shall return it, with his Objections to that House in which it shall have originated, who shall enter the Objections at large on their Journal, and proceed to reconsider it. If after such Reconsideration two thirds of that House shall agree to pass the Bill, it shall be sent, together with the Objections, to the other House, by which it shall likewise be reconsidered, and if approved by two thirds of that House, it shall become a Law. But in all such Cases the Votes of both Houses shall be determined by yeas and Nays, and the Names of the Persons voting for and against the Bill shall be entered on the Journal of each House respectively. If any Bill shall not be returned by the President within ten Days (Sundays excepted) after it shall have been presented to him, the Same shall be a Law, in like Manner as if he had signed it, unless the Congress by their Adjournment prevent its Return, in which Case it shall not be a Law.

Every Order, Resolution, or Vote to which the Concurrence of the Senate and House of Representatives may be necessary (except on a question of Adjournment) shall be presented to the President of the United States; and before the Same shall take Effect, shall be approved by him, or being disapproved by him shall be repassed by two thirds of the Senate and House of Representatives, according to the Rules and Limitations prescribed in the Case of a Bill.

SECTION 8. The Congress shall have power To lay and collect Taxes, Duties, Imposts and Excises, to pay the Debts and provide for the common Defence and general Welfare of the United States; but all Duties, Imposts and Excises shall be uniform throughout the United States;

To borrow Money on the credit of the United States;

To regulate Commerce with foreign Nations, and among the several States, and with the Indian Tribes;

To establish an uniform Rule of Naturalization, and uniform Laws on the subject of Bankruptcies throughout the United States;

To coin Money, regulate the Value thereof, and of foreign Coin, and fix the Standard of Weights and Measures;

---

[5]Superseded by the Twentieth Amendment.

To provide for the Punishment of counterfeiting the Securities and current Coin of the United States;

To establish Post Offices and post Roads;

To promote the Progress of Science and useful Arts, by securing for limited Times to Authors and Inventors the exclusive Right to their respective Writings and Discoveries;

To constitute Tribunals inferior to the supreme Court;

To define and punish Piracies and Felonies committed on the high Seas, and Offences against the Law of Nations;

To declare War, grant Letters of Marque and Reprisal, and make Rules concerning Captures on Land and Water;

To raise and support Armies, but no Appropriation of Money to that Use shall be for a longer Term than two Years;

To provide and maintain a Navy;

To make Rules for the Government and Regulation of the land and naval Forces;

To provide for calling forth the Militia to execute the Laws of the Union, suppress Insurrections and repel Invasions;

To provide for organizing, arming, and disciplining, the Militia, and for governing such Part of them as may be employed in the Service of the United States, reserving to the States respectively, the Appointment of the Officers, and the Authority of training the Militia according to the discipline prescribed by Congress;

To exercise exclusive Legislation in all Cases whatsoever, over such District (not exceeding ten Miles square) as may, by Cession of particular States, and the Acceptance of Congress, become the Seat of the Government of the United States, and to exercise like Authority over all Places purchased by the Consent of the Legislature of the State in which the Same shall be, for the Erection of Forts, Magazines, Arsenals, dock-Yards, and other needful Buildings;—And

To make all Laws which shall be necessary and proper for carrying into Execution the foregoing Powers, and all other Powers vested by this Constitution in the Government of the United States, or in any Department or Officer thereof.

SECTION 9. The Migration or Importation of such Persons as any of the States now existing shall think proper to admit, shall not be prohibited by the Congress prior to the Year one thousand eight hundred and eight, but a Tax or duty may be imposed on such Importation, not exceeding ten dollars for each Person.

The Privilege of the Writ of Habeas Corpus shall not be suspended, unless when in Cases of Rebellion or Invasion the public Safety may require it.

No Bill of Attainder or ex post facto Law shall be passed.

No Capitation, or other direct, Tax shall be laid, unless in Proportion to the Census or Enumeration herein before directed to be taken.

No Tax or Duty shall be laid on Articles exported from any State.

No Preference shall be given by any Regulation of Commerce or Revenue to the Ports of one State over those of another: nor shall Vessels bound to, or from, one State, be obliged to enter, clear, or pay Duties in another.

No Money shall be drawn from the Treasury, but in Consequence of Appropriations made by Law, and a regular Statement and Account of the Receipts and Expenditures of all public Money shall be published from time to time.

No Title of Nobility shall be granted by the United States: And no Person holding any Office of Profit or Trust under them, shall, without the Consent of the Congress, accept of any present, Emolument, Office, or Title, of any kind whatever, from any King, Prince, or foreign State.

SECTION 10. No State shall enter into any Treaty, Alliance, or Confederation; grant Letters of Marque and Reprisal; coin Money; emit Bills of Credit; make any Thing but gold and silver Coin a Tender in Payment of Debts; pass any Bill of Attainder, ex post facto Law, or Law impairing the Obligation of Contracts, or grant any Title of Nobility.

No State shall, without the Consent of the Congress, lay any Imposts or Duties on Imports or Exports, except what may be absolutely necessary for executing its inspection Laws: and the net Produce of all Duties and Imposts, laid by any State on Imports or Exports, shall be for the Use of the Treasury of the United States; and all such Laws shall be subject to the Revision and Controul of the Congress.

No State shall, without the Consent of Congress, lay any Duty of Tonnage, keep Troops, or Ships of War in time of Peace, enter into any Agreement or Compact with another State, or with a foreign Power, or engage in War, unless actually invaded, or in such imminent Danger as will not admit of delay.

ARTICLE II.

SECTION 1. The executive Power shall be vested in a President of the United States of America. He shall hold his Office during the Term of four Years, and, together with the Vice President, chosen for the same Term, be elected, as follows:

Each State shall appoint, in such Manner as the Legislature thereof may direct, a Number of Electors, equal to the whole Number of Senators and Representatives to which the State may be entitled in the Congress: but no Senator or Representative, or Person holding an Office of Trust or Profit under the United States, shall be appointed an Elector.

The Electors shall meet in their respective States, and vote by Ballot for two Persons, of whom one at least shall not be an Inhabitant of the same State with themselves. And they shall make a List of all the Persons voted for, and of the Number of Votes for each; which List they shall sign and certify, and transmit sealed to the Seat of the Government of the United States, directed to the President of the Senate. The President of the Senate shall, in the Presence of the Senate and House of Representatives, open all the Certificates, and the Votes shall then be counted. The Person having the greatest Number of Votes shall be the President, if such Number be a Majority of the whole Number of Electors appointed; and if there be more than one who have such Majority, and have an equal Number of Votes, then the House of Representatives shall immediately chuse by Ballot one of them for President; and if no Person have a Majority, then from the five highest on the List the said House shall in like Manner chuse the President. But in chusing the President, the Votes shall be taken by States, the Representation from each State having one Vote; A quorum for this Purpose shall consist of a Member or Members from two thirds of the States, and a Majority of all the States shall be necessary to a Choice. In every Case, after the Choice of the President, the Person having the greatest Number of Votes of the Electors shall be the Vice President. But if there should remain two or more who have equal Votes, the Senate shall chuse from them by Ballot the Vice President.[6]

The Congress may determine the Time of chusing the Electors, and the Day on which they shall give their Votes; which Day shall be the same throughout the United States.

No Person except a natural born Citizen, or a Citizen of the United States, at the time of the Adoption of this Constitution, shall be eligible to the Office of President, neither shall any Person be eligible to that Office who shall not have attained to the Age of thirty five Years, and been fourteen Years a Resident within the United States.

In Case of the Removal of the President from Office, or of his Death, Resignation, or Inability to discharge the Powers and Duties of the said Office, the Same shall devolve on the Vice President, and the Congress may by Law provide for the Case of Removal, Death, Resignation or Inability, both of the President and Vice President, declaring what Officer shall then act as President, and such Officer shall act accordingly, until the Disability be removed, or a President shall be elected.[7]

The President shall, at stated Times, receive for his Services, a Compensation, which shall neither be encreased nor diminished during the Period for which he shall have been elected, and he shall not receive within that Period any other Emolument from the United States, or any of them.

Before he enter on the Execution of his Office, he shall take the following Oath or Affirmation:—"I do solemnly swear (or affirm) that I will faithfully execute the Office of President of the United States, and will to the best of my Ability, preserve, protect and defend the Constitution of the United States."

SECTION 2. The President shall be Commander in Chief of the Army and Navy of the United States, and of the Militia of the several States, when called into the actual Service of the United States; he may require the Opinion, in writing, of the principal Officer in each of the executive Departments, upon any Subject relating to the Duties of their respective Offices, and he shall have Power to grant Reprieves and Pardons for Offences against the United States, except in Cases of Impeachment.

He shall have Power, by and with the Advice and Consent of the Senate, to make Treaties, provided two thirds of the Senators present concur; and he shall nominate, and by and with the Advice and Consent of the Senate, shall appoint Ambassadors, other public Ministers and Consuls, Judges of the supreme Court, and all other Officers of the United States, whose Appointments are not herein otherwise provided for, and which shall be established by Law; but the Congress may by Law vest the Appointment of such inferior Officers, as they think proper, in the President alone, in the Courts of Law, or in the Heads of Departments.

The President shall have Power to fill up all Vacancies that may happen during the Recess of the Senate, by granting Commissions which shall expire at the End of their next Session.

SECTION 3. He shall from time to time give the Congress Information of the State of the Union, and recommend to their Consideration such Measures as he shall judge necessary and expedient; he may, on extraordinary Occasions, convene both Houses, or either of them, and in Case of Disagreement between them, with Respect to the Time of Adjournment, he may adjourn them to such Time as he shall think proper; he shall receive Ambassadors and other public Ministers; he shall take Care that the Laws be

---

[6]Superseded by the Twelfth Amendment.

[7]Modified by the Twenty-fifth Amendment.

faithfully executed, and shall Commission all the Officers of the United States.

SECTION 4. The President, Vice President and all civil Officers of the United States, shall be removed from Office on Impeachment for, and Conviction of, Treason, Bribery, or other high Crimes and Misdemeanors.

ARTICLE III.

SECTION 1. The judicial Power of the United States, shall be vested in one supreme Court, and in such inferior Courts as the Congress may from time to time ordain and establish. The Judges, both of the supreme and inferior Courts, shall hold their Offices during good Behaviour, and shall, at stated Times, receive for their Services, a Compensation, which shall not be diminished during their Continuance in Office.

SECTION 2. The judicial Power shall extend to all Cases, in Law and Equity, arising under this Constitution, the Laws of the United States, and Treaties made, or which shall be made, under their Authority;—to all Cases affecting Ambassadors, other public Ministers and Consuls;—to all Cases of admiralty and maritime Jurisdiction;—to Controversies to which the United States shall be a Party;—to Controversies between two or more States;—between a State and Citizens of another State;[8]—between Citizens of different States,—between Citizens of the same State claiming Lands under Grants of different States, and between a State, or the Citizens thereof, and foreign States, Citizens or Subjects.

In all Cases affecting Ambassadors, other public Ministers and Consuls, and those in which a State shall be Party, the supreme Court shall have original Jurisdiction. In all the other Cases before mentioned, the supreme Court shall have appellate Jurisdiction, both as to Law and Fact, with such Exceptions, and under such Regulations as the Congress shall make.

The Trial of all Crimes, except in Cases of Impeachment, shall be by Jury; and such Trial shall be held in the State where the said Crimes shall have been committed; but when not committed within any State, the Trial shall be at such Place or Places as the Congress may by Law have directed.

SECTION 3. Treason against the United States, shall consist only in levying War against them, or in adhering to their Enemies, giving them Aid and Comfort. No Person shall be convicted of Treason unless on the Testimony of two Witnesses to the same overt Act, or on Confession in open Court.

[8]Modified by the Eleventh Amendment.

The Congress shall have Power to declare the Punishment of Treason, but no Attainder of Treason shall work Corruption of Blood, or Forfeiture except during the Life of the Person attainted.

ARTICLE IV.

SECTION 1. Full Faith and Credit shall be given in each State to the public Acts, Records, and judicial Proceedings of every other State. And the Congress may by general Laws prescribe the Manner in which such Acts, Records and Proceedings shall be proved, and the Effect thereof.

SECTION 2. The Citizens of each State shall be entitled to all Privileges and Immunities of Citizens in the several States.

A Person charged in any State with Treason, Felony, or other Crime, who shall flee from Justice, and be found in another State, shall on Demand of the executive Authority of the State from which he fled, be delivered up, to be removed to the State having Jurisdiction of the Crime.

No Person held to Service or Labour in one State, under the Laws thereof, escaping into another, shall, in Consequence of any Law or Regulation therein, be discharged from such Service or Labour, but shall be delivered up on Claim of the Party to whom such Service or Labour may be due.

SECTION 3. New States may be admitted by the Congress into this Union; but no new State shall be formed or erected within the Jurisdiction of any other State, nor any State be formed by the Junction of two or more States, or Parts of States, without the Consent of the Legislatures of the States concerned as well as of the Congress.

The Congress shall have Power to dispose of and make all needful Rules and Regulations respecting the Territory or other Property belonging to the United States; and nothing in this Constitution shall be so construed as to Prejudice any Claims of the United States, or of any particular State.

SECTION 4. The United States shall guarantee to every State in this Union a Republican Form of Government, and shall protect each of them against Invasion; and on Application of the Legislature, or of the Executive (when the Legislature cannot be convened) against domestic Violence.

ARTICLE V.

The Congress, whenever two thirds of both Houses shall deem it necessary, shall propose Amendments to this Constitution, or, on the Application of the Legislatures of two thirds of the several States, shall call a Convention for proposing Amendments, which, in either Case, shall be valid to all Intents and Purposes, as Part of this Constitution, when ratified by the Legislatures of three fourths of the several States, or by Conventions in three fourths thereof, as the one or the other Mode of Ratification may be proposed by the Congress; Provided that no Amendment which may be made prior to the Year One thousand eight hundred and eight shall in any Manner affect the first and fourth Clauses in the Ninth Section of the first Article; and that no State, without its Consent, shall be deprived of its equal Suffrage in the Senate.

ARTICLE VI.

All Debts contracted and Engagements entered into, before the Adoption of this Constitution, shall be as valid against the United States under this Constitution, as under the Confederation.

This Constitution, and the Laws of the United States which shall be made in Pursuance thereof; and all Treaties made, or which shall be made, under the Authority of the United States, shall be the supreme Law of the Land; and the Judges in every State shall be bound thereby, any Thing in the Constitution or Laws of any State to the Contrary notwithstanding.

The Senators and Representatives before mentioned, and the Members of the several State Legislatures, and all executive and judicial Officers, both of the United States and of the several States, shall be bound by Oath or Affirmation, to support this Constitution; but no religious Test shall ever be required as a Qualification to any Office or public Trust under the United States.

ARTICLE VII.

The Ratification of the Conventions of nine States, shall be sufficient for the Establishment of this Constitution between the States so ratifying the Same.

Done in Convention by the Unanimous Consent of the States present the Seventeenth Day of September in the Year of our Lord one thousand seven hundred and Eighty seven and of the Independence of the United States of America the Twelfth. In witness whereof We have hereunto subscribed our Names,

Articles in Addition to, and Amendment of, the Constitution of the United States of America, Proposed by Congress, and Ratified by the Legislatures of the Several States, Pursuant to the Fifth Article of the Original Constitution.

AMENDMENT I [9]

Congress shall make no law respecting an establishment of religion, or prohibiting the free exercise thereof; or abridging the freedom of speech, or of the press; or the right of the people peaceably to assemble, and to petition the Government for a redress of grievances.

AMENDMENT II

A well regulated Militia, being necessary to the security of a free State, the right of the people to keep and bear Arms shall not be infringed.

AMENDMENT III

No Soldier shall, in time of peace, be quartered in any house, without the consent of the Owner, nor in time of war, but in a manner to be prescribed by law.

AMENDMENT IV

The right of the people to be secure in their persons, houses, papers, and effects, against unreasonable searches and seizures, shall not be violated, and no Warrants shall issue, but upon probable cause, supported by Oath or affirmation, and particularly describing the place to be searched, and the persons or things to be seized.

AMENDMENT V

No person shall be held to answer for a capital or otherwise infamous crime, unless on a presentment or indictment of a Grand Jury, except in cases arising in the land or naval forces, or in the Militia, when in actual service in time of War or public danger; nor shall any person be subject for the same offence to be twice put in jeopardy of life or limb; nor shall be compelled in any criminal case to be a witness against himself, nor be deprived of life, liberty, or property, without due process of law; nor shall private property be taken for public use, without just compensation.

AMENDMENT VI

In all criminal prosecutions, the accused shall enjoy the right to a speedy and public trial, by an impartial jury of the State and district wherein the crime shall have been

---

[9] The first ten amendments were passed by Congress September 25, 1789. They were ratified by three-fourths of the states December 15, 1791.

committed, which district shall have been previously ascertained by law, and to be informed of the nature and cause of the accusation; to be confronted with the witnesses against him; to have compulsory process for obtaining witnesses in his favor, and to have the Assistance of Counsel for his defence.

AMENDMENT VII

In suits at common law, where the value in controversy shall exceed twenty dollars, the right of trial by jury shall be preserved, and no fact tried by a jury, shall be otherwise reexamined in any Court of the United States, than according to the rules of the common law.

AMENDMENT VIII

Excessive bail shall not be required, nor excessive fines imposed, nor cruel and unusual punishments inflicted.

AMENDMENT IX

The enumeration in the Constitution, of certain rights, shall not be construed to deny or disparage others retained by the people.

AMENDMENT X

The powers not delegated to the United States by the Constitution; nor prohibited by it to the States, are reserved to the States respectively, or to the people.

AMENDMENT XI[10]

The Judicial power of the United States shall not be construed to extend to any suit in law or equity, commenced or prosecuted against one of the United States by Citizens of another State, or by Citizens or Subjects of any Foreign State.

AMENDMENT XII[11]

The Electors shall meet in their respective States and vote by ballot for President and Vice-President, one of whom, at least, shall not be an inhabitant of the same State with themselves; they shall name in their ballots the person voted for as President, and in distinct ballots the person voted for as Vice-President, and they shall make distinct lists of all persons voted for as President, and of all persons voted for as Vice-President, and of the number of votes for each, which lists they shall sign and certify, and transmit sealed to the seat of the government of the United States, directed to the President of the Senate;—The President of the Senate shall, in the presence of the Senate and House of Representatives, open all the certificates and the votes shall then be counted;—The person having the greatest number of votes for President, shall be the President, if such number be a majority of the whole number of Electors appointed; and if no person have such majority, then from the persons having the highest numbers not exceeding three on the list of those voted for as President, the House of Representatives shall choose immediately, by ballot, the President. But in choosing the President, the votes shall be taken by states, the representation from each state having one vote; a quorum for this purpose shall consist of a member or members from two-thirds of the states, and a majority of all the states shall be necessary to a choice. And if the House of Representatives shall not choose a President whenever the right of choice shall devolve upon them, before the fourth day of March next following, then the Vice-President shall act as President, as in the case of the death or other constitutional disability of the President.—The person having the greatest number of votes as Vice-President, shall be the Vice-President, if such number be a majority of the whole number of Electors appointed, and if no person have a majority, then from the two highest numbers on the list, the Senate shall choose the Vice-President; a quorum for the purpose shall consist of two-thirds of the whole number of Senators, and a majority of the whole number shall be necessary to a choice. But no person constitutionally ineligible to the office of President shall be eligible to that of Vice-President of the United States.

AMENDMENT XIII[12]

SECTION 1. Neither slavery nor involuntary servitude, except as a punishment for crime whereof the party shall have been duly convicted, shall exist within the United States, or any place subject to their jurisdiction.

SECTION 2. Congress shall have power to enforce this article by appropriate legislation.

AMENDMENT XIV[13]

SECTION 1. All persons born or naturalized in the United States, and subject to the jurisdiction thereof, are citizens of the United States and of the State wherein they

---

[10]Passed March 4, 1794. Ratified January 23, 1795.
[11]Passed December 9, 1803. Ratified June 15, 1804.

[12]Passed January 31, 1865. Ratified December 6, 1865.
[13]Passed June 13, 1866. Ratified July 9, 1868.

reside. No State shall make or enforce any law which shall abridge the privileges or immunities of citizens of the United States; nor shall any State deprive any person of life, liberty, or property, without due process of law; nor deny to any person within its jurisdiction the equal protection of the laws.

SECTION 2. Representatives shall be apportioned among the several States according to their respective numbers, counting the whole number of persons in each State, excluding Indians not taxed. But when the right to vote at any election for the choice of electors for President and Vice-President of the United States, Representatives in Congress, the Executive and Judicial officers of a State, or the members of the Legislature thereof, is denied to any of the male inhabitants of such State, being twenty-one years of age, and citizens of the United States, or in any way abridged, except for participation in rebellion, or other crime, the basis of representation therein shall be reduced in the proportion which the number of such male citizens shall bear to the whole number of male citizens twenty-one years of age in such State.

SECTION 3. No person shall be a Senator or Representative in Congress, or elector of President and Vice-President, or hold any office, civil or military, under the United States, or under any State, who, having previously taken an oath, as a member of Congress, or as an officer of the United States, or as a member of any State legislature, or as an executive or judicial officer of any State, to support the Constitution of the United States, shall have engaged in insurrection or rebellion against the same, or given aid or comfort to the enemies thereof. But Congress may by a vote of two-thirds of each House, remove such disability.

SECTION 4. The validity of the public debt of the United States, authorized by law, including debts incurred for payment of pensions and bounties for services in suppressing insurrection or rebellion, shall not be questioned. But neither the United States nor any State shall assume or pay any debt or obligation incurred in aid of insurrection or rebellion against the United States, or any claim for the loss or emancipation of any slave; but all such debts, obligations, and claims shall be held illegal and void.

SECTION 5. The Congress shall have the power to enforce, by appropriate legislation, the provisions of this article.

AMENDMENT XV[14]

SECTION 1. The right of citizens of the United States to vote shall not be denied or abridged by the United States or by any State on account of race, color, or previous conditions of servitude—

SECTION 2. The Congress shall have power to enforce this article by appropriate legislation.

AMENDMENT XVI

The Congress shall have power to lay and collect taxes on incomes, from whatever source derived, without apportionment among the several States, and without regard to any census or enumeration.

AMENDMENT XVII[15]

The Senate of the United States shall be composed of two Senators from each State, elected by the people thereof, for six years; and each Senator shall have one vote. The electors in each State shall have the qualifications requisite for electors of the most numerous branch of the State legislatures.

When vacancies happen in the representation of any State in the Senate, the executive authority of such State shall issue writs of election to fill such vacancies: *Provided,* That the legislature of any State may empower the executive thereof to make temporary appointments until the people fill the vacancies by election as the legislature may direct.

This amendment shall not be so construed as to affect the election or term of any Senator chosen before it becomes valid as part of the Constitution.

AMENDMENT XVIII[16]

SECTION 1. After one year from the ratification of this article the manufacture, sale, or transportation of intoxicating liquors within, the importation thereof into, or the exportation thereof from the United States and all territory subject to the jurisdiction thereof for beverage purposes is hereby prohibited.

SECTION 2. The Congress and the several States shall have concurrent power to enforce this article by appropriate legislation.

SECTION 3. This article shall be inoperative unless it shall have been ratified as an amendment to the Constitution by the legislatures of the several States, as provided in the Constitution, within seven years from the date of the submission hereof to the States by the Congress.

---

[14]Passed February 26, 1869. Ratified February 2, 1870.

[15]Passed May 13, 1912. Ratified April 8, 1913.
[16]Passed December 18, 1917. Ratified January 16, 1919.

AMENDMENT XIX[17]

The right of citizens of the United States to vote shall not be denied or abridged by the United States or by any State on account of sex.

Congress shall have power to enforce this article by appropriate legislation.

AMENDMENT XX[18]

SECTION 1. The terms of the President and Vice-President shall end at noon on the 20th day of January, and the terms of Senators and Representatives at noon on the 3d day of January, of the years in which such terms would have ended if this article had not been ratified; and the terms of their successors shall then begin.

SECTION 2. The Congress shall assemble at least once in every year, and such meeting shall begin at noon on the 3d day of January, unless they shall by law appoint a different day.

SECTION 3. If, at the time fixed for the beginning of the term of the President, the President elect shall have died, the Vice-President elect shall become President. If a President shall not have been chosen before the time fixed for the beginning of his term, or if the President elect shall have failed to qualify, then the Vice-President elect shall act as President until a President shall have qualified; and the Congress may by law provide for the case wherein neither a President elect nor a Vice-President elect shall have qualified, declaring who shall then act as President, or the manner in which one who is to act shall be selected, and such person shall act accordingly until a President or Vice-President shall have qualified.

SECTION 4. The Congress may by law provide for the case of the death of any of the persons from whom the House of Representatives may choose a President whenever the right of choice shall have devolved upon them, and for the case of the death of any of the persons from whom the Senate may choose a Vice-President whenever the right of choice shall have devolved upon them.

SECTION 5. Sections 1 and 2 shall take effect on the 15th day of October following the ratification of this article.

SECTION 6. This article shall be inoperative unless it shall have been ratified as an amendment to the Constitution by the legislatures of three-fourths of the several States within seven years from the date of its submission.

AMENDMENT XXI[19]

SECTION 1. The eighteenth article of amendment to the Constitution of the United States is hereby repealed.

SECTION 2. The transportation or importation into any State, Territory, or possession of the United States for delivery or use therein of intoxicating liquors, in violation of the laws thereof, is hereby prohibited.

SECTION 3. This article shall be inoperative unless it shall have been ratified as an amendment to the Constitution by conventions in the several States, as provided in the Constitution, within seven years from the date of the submission hereof to the States by the Congress.

AMENDMENT XXII[20]

No person shall be elected to the office of the President more than twice, and no person who has held the office of President, or acted as President, for more than two years of a term to which some other person was elected President shall be elected to the office of the President more than once.

But this Article shall not apply to any person holding the office of President when this Article was proposed by the Congress, and shall not prevent any person who may be holding the office of President, or acting as President, during the term within which this Article becomes operative from holding the office of President or acting as President during the remainder of such term.

AMENDMENT XXIII[21]

SECTION 1. The District constituting the seat of Government of the United States shall appoint in such manner as the Congress may direct:

A number of electors of President and Vice President equal to the whole number of Senators and Representatives in Congress to which the District would be entitled if it were a State, but in no event more than the least populous State; they shall be in addition to those appointed by the States, but they shall be considered, for the purposes of the election of President and Vice President, to be electors appointed by the State; and they shall meet in the District and perform such duties as provided by the twelfth article of amendment.

SECTION 2. The Congress shall have power to enforce this article by appropriate legislation.

---

[17]Passed June 4, 1919. Ratified August 18, 1920.
[18]Passed March 2, 1932. Ratified January 23, 1933.

[19]Passed February 20, 1933. Ratified December 5, 1933.
[20]Passed March 12, 1947. Ratified March 1, 1951.
[21]Passed June 16, 1960. Ratified April 3, 1961.

AMENDMENT XXIV[22]

SECTION 1. The right of citizens of the United States to vote in any primary or other election for President or Vice President, or for Senator or Representative in Congress, shall not be denied or abridged by the United States or any State by reason of failure to pay any poll tax or other tax.

SECTION 2. The Congress shall have power to enforce this article by appropriate legislation.

AMENDMENT XXV[23]

SECTION 1. In case of the removal of the President from office or of his death or resignation, the Vice President shall become President.

SECTION 2. Whenever there is a vacancy in the office of the Vice President, the President shall nominate a Vice President who shall take office upon confirmation by a majority vote of both Houses of Congress.

SECTION 3. Whenever the President transmits to the President pro tempore of the Senate and the Speaker of the House of Representatives his written declaration that he is unable to discharge the powers and duties of his office, and until he transmits them a written declaration to the contrary, such powers and duties shall be discharged by the Vice President as Acting President.

SECTION 4. Whenever the Vice President and a majority of either the principal officers of the executive department or of such other body as Congress may by law provide, transmit to the President pro tempore of the Senate and the Speaker of the House of Representatives their written declaration that the President is unable to discharge the powers and duties of his office, the Vice President shall immediately assume the powers and duties of the office of Acting President.

Thereafter, when the President transmits to the President pro tempore of the Senate and the Speaker of the House of Representatives his written declaration that no inability exists, he shall resume the powers and duties of his office unless the Vice President and a majority of either the principal officers of the executive department or of such other body as Congress may by law provide, transmit within four days to the President pro tempore of the Senate and the Speaker of the House of Representatives their written declaration that the President is unable to discharge the powers and duties of his office. Thereupon Congress shall decide the issue, assembling within forty-eight hours for that purpose if not in session. If the Congress, within twenty-one days after receipt of the latter written declaration, or, if Congress is not in session, within twenty-one days after Congress is required to assemble, determines by two-thirds vote of both Houses that the President is unable to discharge the powers and duties of his office, the Vice President shall continue to discharge the same as Acting President; otherwise, the President shall resume the powers and duties of his office.

AMENDMENT XXVI[24]

SECTION 1. The right of citizens of the United States, who are eighteen years of age or older, to vote shall not be denied or abridged by the United States or by any State on account of age.

SECTION 2. The Congress shall have power to enforce this article by appropriate legislation.

AMENDMENT XXVII[25]

No law, varying the compensation for the service of the Senators and Representatives, shall take effect, until an election of Representatives shall have intervened.

---

[22]Passed August 27, 1962. Ratified January 23, 1964.
[23]Passed July 6, 1965. Ratified February 11, 1967.

[24]Passed March 23, 1971. Ratified July 5, 1971.
[25]Passed September 25, 1789. Ratified May 7, 1992.

ADMISSION OF STATES

Order of admission	State	Date of admission	Order of admission	State	Date of admission
1	Delaware	December 7, 1787	26	Michigan	January 26, 1837
2	Pennsylvania	December 12, 1787	27	Florida	March 3, 1845
3	New Jersey	December 18, 1787	28	Texas	December 29, 1845
4	Georgia	January 2, 1788	29	Iowa	December 28, 1846
5	Connecticut	January 9, 1788	30	Wisconsin	May 29, 1848
6	Massachusetts	February 6, 1788	31	California	September 9, 1850
7	Maryland	April 28, 1788	32	Minnesota	May 11, 1858
8	South Carolina	May 23, 1788	33	Oregon	February 14, 1859
9	New Hampshire	June 21, 1788	34	Kansas	January 29, 1861
10	Virginia	June 25, 1788	35	West Virginia	June 20, 1863
11	New York	July 26, 1788	36	Nevada	October 31, 1864
12	North Carolina	November 21, 1789	37	Nebraska	March 1, 1867
13	Rhode Island	May 29, 1790	38	Colorado	August 1, 1876
14	Vermont	March 4, 1791	39	North Dakota	November 2, 1889
15	Kentucky	June 1, 1792	40	South Dakota	November 2, 1889
16	Tennessee	June 1, 1796	41	Montana	November 8, 1889
17	Ohio	March 1, 1803	42	Washington	November 11, 1889
18	Louisiana	April 30, 1812	43	Idaho	July 3, 1890
19	Indiana	December 11, 1816	44	Wyoming	July 10, 1890
20	Mississippi	December 10, 1817	45	Utah	January 4, 1896
21	Illinois	December 3, 1818	46	Oklahoma	November 16, 1907
22	Alabama	December 14, 1819	47	New Mexico	January 6, 1912
23	Maine	March 15, 1820	48	Arizona	February 14, 1912
24	Missouri	August 10, 1821	49	Alaska	January 3, 1959
25	Arkansas	June 15, 1836	50	Hawaii	August 21, 1959

POPULATION OF THE UNITED STATES

Year	Total population	Number per square mile	Year	Total population	Number per square mile	Year	Total population	Number per square mile
1790	3,929	4.5	1808	6,838		1826	11,580	
1791	4,056		1809	7,031		1827	11,909	
1792	4,194		1810	7,224	4.3	1828	12,237	
1793	4,332		1811	7,460		1829	12,565	
1794	4,469		1812	7,700		1830	12,901	7.4
1795	4,607		1813	7,939		1831	13,321	
1796	4,745		1814	8,179		1832	13,742	
1797	4,883		1815	8,419		1833	14,162	
1798	5,021		1816	8,659		1834	14,582	
1799	5,159		1817	8,899		1835	15,003	
1800	5,297	6.1	1818	9,139		1836	15,423	
1801	5,486		1819	9,379		1837	15,843	
1802	5,679		1820	9,618	5.6	1838	16,264	
1803	5,872		1821	9,939		1839	16,684	
1804	5,065		1822	10,268		1840	17,120	9.8
1805	6,258		1823	10,596		1841	17,733	
1806	6,451		1824	10,924		1842	18,345	
1807	6,644		1825	11,252		1843	18,957	

Figures are from *Historical Statistics of the United States, Colonial Times to 1957* (1961), pp. 7, 8; *Statistical Abstract of the United States: 1974*, p. 5, Census Bureau for 1974 and 1975; and *Statistical Abstract of the United States: 1988*, p. 7.

Note: Population figures are in thousands. Density figures are for land area of continental United States.

(continued)

POPULATION OF THE UNITED STATES, CONTINUED

Year	Total population	Number per square mile	Year	Total population[1]	Number per square mile	Year	Total population[1]	Number per square mile
1844	19,569		1897	72,189		1950	150,697	50.7
1845	20,182		1898	73,494		1951	154,878	
1846	20,794		1899	74,799		1952	157,553	
1847	21,406		1900	76,094	25.6	1953	160,184	
1848	22,018		1901	77,585		1954	163,026	
1849	22,631		1902	79,160		1955	165,931	
1850	23,261	7.9	1903	80,632		1956	168,903	
1851	24,086		1904	82,165		1957	171,984	
1852	24,911		1905	83,820		1958	174,882	
1853	25,736		1906	85,437		1959	177,830	
1854	26,561		1907	87,000		1960	178,464	60.1
1855	27,386		1908	88,709		1961	183,642	
1856	28,212		1909	90,492		1962	186,504	
1857	29,037		1910	92,407	31.0	1963	189,197	
1858	29,862		1911	93,868		1964	191,833	
1859	30,687		1912	95,331		1965	194,237	
1860	31,513	10.6	1913	97,227		1966	196,485	
1861	32,351		1914	99,118		1967	198,629	
1862	33,188		1915	100,549		1968	200,619	
1863	34,026		1916	101,966		1969	202,599	
1864	34,863		1917	103,414		1970	203,875	57.5[2]
1865	35,701		1918	104,550		1971	207,045	
1866	36,538		1919	105,063		1972	208,842	
1867	37,376		1920	106,466	35.6	1973	210,396	
1868	38,213		1921	108,541		1974	211,894	
1869	39,051		1922	110,055		1975	213,631	
1870	39,905	13.4	1923	111,950		1976	215,152	
1871	40,938		1924	114,113		1977	216,880	
1872	41,972		1925	115,832		1978	218,717	
1873	43,006		1926	117,399		1979	220,584	
1874	44,040		1927	119,038		1980	226,546	64.0
1875	45,073		1928	120,501		1981	230,138	
1876	46,107		1929	121,700		1982	232,520	
1877	47,141		1930	122,775	41.2	1983	234,799	
1878	48,174		1931	124,040		1984	237,001	
1879	49,208		1932	124,840		1985	239,283	
1880	50,262	16.9	1933	125,579		1986	241,596	
1881	51,542		1934	126,374		1987	234,773	
1882	52,821		1935	127,250		1988	245,051	
1883	54,100		1936	128,053		1989	247,350	
1884	55,379		1937	128,825		1990	250,122	70.3
1885	56,658		1938	129,825		1991	254,521	
1886	57,938		1939	130,880		1992	245,908	
1887	59,217		1940	131,669	44.2	1993	257,908	
1888	60,496		1941	133,894		1994	261,875	
1889	61,775		1942	135,361		1995	263,434	
1890	63,056	21.2	1943	137,250		1996	266,096	
1891	64,361		1944	138,916		1997	267,901	
1892	65,666		1945	140,468		1998	269,501	
1893	66,970		1946	141,936		1999	272,700	
1894	68,275		1947	144,698		2000	281,400	
1895	69,580		1948	147,208		2001	286,909	
1896	70,885		1949	149,767		2002	289,947	

[1]Figures after 1940 represent total population including armed forces abroad, except in official census years.

[2]Figure includes Alaska and Hawaii.

PRESIDENTIAL ELECTIONS

Year	Number of states	Candidates[1]	Parties	Popular vote	Electoral vote	Percentage of popular vote[2]
1789	11	**George Washington**	No party designations		69	
		John Adams			34	
		Minor Candidates			35	
1792	15	**George Washington**	No party designations		132	
		John Adams			77	
		George Clinton			50	
		Minor Candidates			5	
1796	16	**John Adams**	Federalist		71	
		Thomas Jefferson	Democratic-Republican		68	
		Thomas Pinckney	Federalist		59	
		Aaron Burr	Democratic-Republican		30	
		Minor Candidates			48	
1800	16	**Thomas Jefferson**	Democratic-Republican		73	
		Aaron Burr	Democratic-Republican		73	
		John Adams	Federalist		65	
		Charles C. Pinckney	Federalist		64	
		John Jay	Federalist		1	
1804	17	**Thomas Jefferson**	Democratic-Republican		162	
		Charles C. Pinckney	Federalist		14	
1808	17	**James Madison**	Democratic-Republican		122	
		Charles C. Pinckney	Federalist		47	
		George Clinton	Democratic-Republican		6	
1812	18	**James Madison**	Democratic-Republican		128	
		DeWitt Clinton	Federalist		89	
1816	19	**James Monroe**	Democratic-Republican		183	
		Rufus King	Federalist		34	
1820	24	**James Monroe**	Democratic-Republican		231	
		John Quincy Adams	Independent Republican		1	
1824	24	**John Quincy Adams**	Democratic-Republican	108,740	84	30.5
		Andrew Jackson	Democratic-Republican	153,544	99	43.1
		William H. Crawford	Democratic-Republican	46,618	41	13.1
		Henry Clay	Democratic-Republican	47,136	37	13.2
1828	24	**Andrew Jackson**	Democratic	647,286	178	56.0
		John Quincy Adams	National Republican	508,064	83	44.0
1832	24	**Andrew Jackson**	Democratic	687,502	219	55.0
		Henry Clay	National Republican	530,189	49	42.4
		William Wirt	Anti-Masonic	33,108	7	2.6
		John Floyd	National Republican		11	

[1]Before the passage of the Twelfth Amendment in 1804, the Electoral College voted for two presidential candidates; the runner-up became vice president. Figures are from *Historical Statistics of the United States, Colonial Times to 1957* (1961), pp. 682–83; and the U.S. Department of Justice.

[2]Candidates receiving less than 1 percent of the popular vote have been omitted. For that reason the percentage of popular vote given for any election year may not total 100 percent.

(continued)

PRESIDENTIAL ELECTIONS, CONTINUED

Year	Number of states	Candidates	Parties	Popular vote	Electoral vote	Percentage of popular vote[1]
1836	26	**Martin Van Buren**	Democratic	765,483	170	50.9
		William H. Harrison	Whig		73	
		Hugh L. White	Whig	739,795	26	
		Daniel Webster	Whig		14	
		W. P. Mangum	Whig		11	
1840	26	**William H. Harrison**	Whig	1,274,624	234	53.1
		Martin Van Buren	Democratic	1,127,781	60	46.9
1844	26	**James K. Polk**	Democratic	1,338,464	170	49.6
		Henry Clay	Whig	1,300,097	105	48.1
		James G. Birney	Liberty	62,300		2.3
1848	30	**Zachary Taylor**	Whig	1,360,967	163	47.4
		Lewis Cass	Democratic	1,222,342	127	42.5
		Martin Van Buren	Free Soil	291,263		10.1
1852	31	**Franklin Pierce**	Democratic	1,601,117	254	50.9
		Winfield Scott	Whig	1,385,453	42	44.1
		John P. Hale	Free Soil	155,825		5.0
1856	31	**James Buchanan**	Democratic	1,832,955	174	45.3
		John C. Frémont	Republican	1,339,932	114	33.1
		Millard Fillmore	American	871,731	8	21.6
1860	33	**Abraham Lincoln**	Republican	1,865,593	180	39.8
		Stephen A. Douglas	Democratic	1,382,713	12	29.5
		John C. Breckinridge	Democratic	848,356	72	18.1
		John Bell	Constitutional Union	592,906	39	12.6
1864	36	**Abraham Lincoln**	Republican	2,206,938	212	55.0
		George B. McClellan	Democratic	1,803,787	21	45.0
1868	37	**Ulysses S. Grant**	Republican	3,013,421	214	52.7
		Horatio Seymour	Democratic	2,706,829	80	47.3
1872	37	**Ulysses S. Grant**	Republican	3,596,745	286	55.6
		Horace Greeley	Democratic	2,843,446	[2]	43.9
1876	38	**Rutherford B. Hayes**	Republican	4,036,572	185	48.0
		Samuel J. Tilden	Democratic	4,284,020	184	51.0
1880	38	**James A. Garfield**	Republican	4,453,295	214	48.5
		Winfield S. Hancock	Democratic	4,414,082	155	48.1
		James B. Weaver	Greenback-Labor	308,578		3.4
1884	38	**Grover Cleveland**	Democratic	4,879,507	219	48.5
		James G. Blaine	Republican	4,850,293	182	48.2
		Benjamin F. Butler	Greenback-Labor	175,370		1.8
		John P. St. John	Prohibition	150,369		1.5
1888	38	**Benjamin Harrison**	Republican	5,477,129	233	47.9
		Grover Cleveland	Democratic	5,537,857	168	48.6
		Clinton B. Fisk	Prohibition	249,506		2.2
		Anson J. Streeter	Union Labor	146,935		1.3

[1]Candidates receiving less than 1 percent of the popular vote have been omitted. For that reason the percentage of popular vote given for any election year may not total 100 percent.

[2]Greeley died shortly after the election; the electors supporting him then divided their votes among minor candidates.

Year	Number of states	Candidates	Parties	Popular vote	Electoral vote	Percentage of popular vote[1]
1892	44	**Grover Cleveland**	Democratic	5,555,426	277	46.1
		Benjamin Harrison	Republican	5,182,690	145	43.0
		James B. Weaver	People's	1,029,846	22	8.5
		John Bidwell	Prohibition	264,133		2.2
1896	45	**William McKinley**	Republican	7,102,246	271	51.1
		William J. Bryan	Democratic	6,492,559	176	47.7
1900	45	**William McKinley**	Republican	7,218,491	292	51.7
		William J. Bryan	Democratic; Populist	6,356,734	155	45.5
		John C. Wooley	Prohibition	208,914		1.5
1904	45	**Theodore Roosevelt**	Republican	7,628,461	336	57.4
		Alton B. Parker	Democratic	5,084,223	140	37.6
		Eugene V. Debs	Socialist	402,283		3.0
		Silas C. Swallow	Prohibition	258,536		1.9
1908	46	**William H. Taft**	Republican	7,675,320	321	51.6
		William J. Bryan	Democratic	6,412,294	162	43.1
		Eugene V. Debs	Socialist	420,793		2.8
		Eugene W. Chafin	Prohibition	253,840		1.7
1912	48	**Woodrow Wilson**	Democratic	6,296,547	435	41.9
		Theodore Roosevelt	Progressive	4,118,571	88	27.4
		William H. Taft	Republican	3,486,720	8	23.2
		Eugene V. Debs	Socialist	900,672		6.0
		Eugene W. Chafin	Prohibition	206,275		1.4
1916	48	**Woodrow Wilson**	Democratic	9,127,695	277	49.4
		Charles E. Hughes	Republican	8,533,507	254	46.2
		A. L. Benson	Socialist	585,113		3.2
		J. Frank Hanly	Prohibition	220,506		1.2
1920	48	**Warren G. Harding**	Republican	16,143,407	404	60.4
		James N. Cox	Democratic	9,130,328	127	34.2
		Eugene V. Debs	Socialist	919,799		3.4
		P. P. Christensen	Farmer-Labor	265,411		1.0
1924	48	**Calvin Coolidge**	Republican	15,718,211	382	54.0
		John W. Davis	Democratic	8,385,283	136	28.8
		Robert M. La Follette	Progressive	4,831,289	13	16.6
1928	48	**Herbert C. Hoover**	Republican	21,391,993	444	58.2
		Alfred E. Smith	Democratic	15,016,169	87	40.9
1932	48	**Franklin D. Roosevelt**	Democratic	22,809,638	472	57.4
		Herbert C. Hoover	Republican	15,758,901	59	39.7
		Norman Thomas	Socialist	881,951		2.2

[1]Candidates receiving less than 1 percent of the popular vote have been omitted. For that reason the percentage of popular vote given for any election year may not total 100 percent.

(continued)

PRESIDENTIAL ELECTIONS, CONTINUED

Year	Number of states	Candidates	Parties	Popular vote	Electoral vote	Percentage of popular vote[1]
1936	48	**Franklin D. Roosevelt**	Democratic	27,752,869	523	60.8
		Alfred M. Landon	Republican	16,674,665	8	36.5
		William Lemke	Union	882,479		1.9
1940	48	**Franklin D. Roosevelt**	Democratic	27,307,819	449	54.8
		Wendell L. Willkie	Republican	22,321,018	82	44.8
1944	48	**Franklin D. Roosevelt**	Democratic	25,606,585	432	53.5
		Thomas E. Dewey	Republican	22,014,745	99	46.0
1948	48	**Harry S Truman**	Democratic	24,105,812	303	49.5
		Thomas E. Dewey	Republican	21,970,065	189	45.1
		J. Strom Thurmond	States' Rights	1,169,063	39	2.4
		Henry A. Wallace	Progressive	1,157,172		2.4
1952	48	**Dwight D. Eisenhower**	Republican	33,936,234	442	55.1
		Adlai E. Stevenson	Democratic	27,314,992	89	44.4
1956	48	**Dwight D. Eisenhower**	Republican	35,590,472	457	57.6
		Adlai E. Stevenson	Democratic	26,022,752	73	42.1
1960	50	**John F. Kennedy**	Democratic	34,227,096	303	49.9
		Richard M. Nixon	Republican	34,108,546	219	49.6
1964	50	**Lyndon B. Johnson**	Democratic	43,126,506	486	61.1
		Barry M. Goldwater	Republican	27,176,799	52	38.5
1968	50	**Richard M. Nixon**	Republican	31,785,480	301	43.4
		Hubert H. Humphrey	Democratic	31,275,165	191	42.7
		George C. Wallace	American Independent	9,906,473	46	13.5
1972	50	**Richard M. Nixon**	Republican	47,169,911	520	60.7
		George S. McGovern	Democratic	29,170,383	17	37.5
1976	50	**Jimmy Carter**	Democratic	40,827,394	297	50.0
		Gerald R. Ford	Republican	39,145,977	240	47.9
1980	50	**Ronald W. Reagan**	Republican	43,899,248	489	50.8
		Jimmy Carter	Democratic	35,481,435	49	41.0
		John B. Anderson	Independent	5,719,437		6.6
		Ed Clark	Libertarian	920,859		1.0
1984	50	**Ronald W. Reagan**	Republican	54,281,858	525	59.2
		Walter F. Mondale	Democratic	37,457,215	13	40.8
1988	50	**George H. Bush**	Republican	47,917,341	426	54
		Michael Dukakis	Democratic	41,013,030	112	46
1992	50	**William Clinton**	Democratic	44,908,254	370	43.0
		George H. Bush	Republican	39,102,343	168	37.4
		Ross Perot	Independent	19,741,065		18.9
1996	50	**William Clinton**	Democratic	45,628,667	379	49.2
		Robert Dole	Republican	37,869,435	159	40.8
		Ross Perot	Reform	7,874,283		8.5
2000	50	**George W. Bush**	Republican	50,456,062	271	47.9
		Albert Gore	Democratic	50,996,582	266	48.4
		Ralph Nader	Green	2,858,843		2.7

[1]Candidates receiving less than 1 percent of the popular vote have been omitted. For that reason the percentage of popular vote given for any election year may not total 100 percent.

PRESIDENTIAL ADMINISTRATIONS

President	Vice President	Secretary of State	Secretary of Treasury	Secretary of War	Secretary of Navy	Postmaster General	Attorney General
George Washington 1789–1797	John Adams 1789–1797	Thomas Jefferson 1789–1794 Edmund Randolph 1794–1795 Timothy Pickering 1795–1797	Alexander Hamilton 1789–1795 Oliver Wolcott 1795–1797	Henry Knox 1789–1795 Timothy Pickering 1795–1796 James McHenry 1796–1797		Samuel Osgood 1789–1791 Timothy Pickering 1791–1795 Joseph Habersham 1795–1797	Edmund Randolph 1789–1794 William Bradford 1794–1795 Charles Lee 1795–1797
John Adams 1797–1801	Thomas Jefferson 1797–1801	Timothy Pickering 1797–1800 John Marshall 1800–1801	Oliver Wolcott 1797–1801 Samuel Dexter 1801	James McHenry 1797–1800 Samuel Dexter 1800–1801	Benjamin Stoddert 1798–1801	Joseph Habersham 1797–1801	Charles Lee 1797–1801
Thomas Jefferson 1801–1809	Aaron Burr 1801–1805 George Clinton 1805–1809	James Madison 1801–1809	Samuel Dexter 1801 Albert Gallatin 1801–1809	Henry Dearborn 1801–1809	Benjamin Stoddert 1801 Robert Smith 1801–1809	Joseph Habersham 1801 Gideon Granger 1801–1809	Levi Lincoln 1801–1805 John Breckinridge 1805–1807 Caesar Rodney 1807–1809
James Madison 1809–1817	George Clinton 1809–1813 Elbridge Gerry 1813–1817	Robert Smith 1809–1811 James Monroe 1811–1817	Albert Gallatin 1809–1814 George Campbell 1814 Alexander Dallas 1814–1816 William Crawford 1816–1817	William Eustis 1809–1813 John Armstrong 1813–1814 James Monroe 1814–1815 William Crawford 1815–1817	Paul Hamilton 1809–1813 William Jones 1813–1814 Benjamin Crowninshield 1814–1817	Gideon Granger 1809–1814 Return Meigs 1814–1817	Caesar Rodney 1809–1811 William Pinkney 1811–1814 Richard Rush 1814–1817
James Monroe 1817–1825	Daniel D. Tompkins 1817–1825	John Quincy Adams 1817–1825	William Crawford 1817–1825	George Graham 1817 John C. Calhoun 1817–1825	Benjamin Crowninshield 1817–1818 Smith Thompson 1818–1823 Samuel Southard 1823–1825	Return Meigs 1817–1823 John McLean 1823–1825	Richard Rush 1817 William Wirt 1817–1825
John Quincy Adams 1825–1829	John C. Calhoun 1825–1829	Henry Clay 1825–1829	Richard Rush 1825–1829	James Barbour 1825–1828 Peter B. Porter 1828–1829	Samuel Southard 1825–1829	John McLean 1825–1829	William Wirt 1825–1829
Andrew Jackson 1829–1837	John C. Calhoun 1829–1833 Martin Van Buren 1833–1837	Martin Van Buren 1829–1831 Edward Livingston 1831–1833 Louis McLane 1833–1834 John Forsyth 1834–1837	Samuel Ingham 1829–1831 Louis McLane 1831–1833 William Duane 1833 Roger B. Taney 1833–1834 Levi Woodbury 1834–1837	John H. Eaton 1829–1831 Lewis Cass 1831–1837 Benjamin Butler 1837	John Branch 1829–1831 Levi Woodbury 1831–1834 Mahlon Dickerson 1834–1837	William Barry 1829–1835 Amos Kendall 1835–1837	John M. Berrien 1829–1831 Roger B. Taney 1831–1833 Benjamin Butler 1833–1837
Martin Van Buren 1837–1841	Richard M. Johnson 1837–1841	John Forsyth 1837–1841	Levi Woodbury 1837–1841	Joel R. Poinsett 1837–1841	Mahlon Dickerson 1837–1838 James K. Paulding 1838–1841	Amos Kendall 1837–1840 John M. Niles 1840–1841	Benjamin Butler 1837–1838 Felix Grundy 1838–1840 Henry D. Gilpin 1840–1841

(continued)

PRESIDENTIAL ADMINISTRATIONS, CONTINUED

President	Vice President	Secretary of State	Secretary of Treasury	Secretary of War
William H. Harrison 1841	John Tyler 1841	Daniel Webster 1841	Thomas Ewing 1841	John Bell 1841
John Tyler 1841–1845		Daniel Webster 1841–1843 Hugh S. Legaré 1843 Abel P. Upshur 1843–1844 John C. Calhoun 1844–1845	Thomas Ewing 1841 Walter Forward 1841–1843 John C. Spencer 1843–1844 George M. Bibb 1844–1845	John Bell 1841 John C. Spencer 1841–1843 James M. Porter 1843–1844 William Wilkins 1844–1845
James K. Polk 1845–1849	George M. Dallas 1845–1849	James Buchanan 1845–1849	Robert J. Walker 1845–1849	William L. Marcy 1845–1849
Zachary Taylor 1849–1850	Millard Fillmore 1849–1850	John M. Clayton 1849–1850	William M. Meredith 1849–1850	George W. Crawford 1849–1850
Millard Fillmore 1850–1853		Daniel Webster 1850–1852 Edward Everett 1852–1853	Thomas Corwin 1850–1853	Charles M. Conrad 1850–1853
Franklin Pierce 1853–1857	William R. King 1853–1857	William L. Marcy 1853–1857	James Guthrie 1853–1857	Jefferson Davis 1853–1857
James Buchanan 1857–1861	John C. Breckinridge 1857–1861	Lewis Cass 1857–1860 Jeremiah S. Black 1860–1861	Howell Cobb 1857–1860 Philip F. Thomas 1860–1861 John A. Dix 1861	John B. Floyd 1857–1861 Joseph Holt 1861
Abraham Lincoln 1861–1865	Hannibal Hamlin 1861–1865 Andrew Johnson 1865	William H. Seward 1861–1865	Salmon P. Chase 1861–1864 William P. Fessenden 1864–1865 Hugh McCulloch 1865	Simon Cameron 1861–1862 Edwin M. Stanton 1862–1865
Andrew Johnson 1865–1869		William H. Seward 1865–1869	Hugh McCulloch 1865–1869	Edwin M. Stanton 1865–1867 Ulysses S. Grant 1867–1868 John M. Schofield 1868–1869
Ulysses S. Grant 1869–1877	Schuyler Colfax 1869–1873 Henry Wilson 1873–1877	Elihu B. Washburne 1869 Hamilton Fish 1869–1877	George S. Boutwell 1869–1873 William A. Richardson 1873–1874 Benjamin H. Bristow 1874–1876 Lot M. Morrill 1876–1877	John A. Rawlins 1869 William T. Sherman 1869 William W. Belknap 1869–1876 Alphonso Taft 1876 James D. Cameron 1876–1877

Secretary of Navy	Postmaster General	Attorney General	Secretary of Interior
George E. Badger 1841	Francis Granger 1841	John J. Crittenden 1841	
George E. Badger 1841 Abel P. Upshur 1841–1843 David Henshaw 1843–1844 Thomas Gilmer 1844 John Y. Mason 1844–1845	Francis Granger 1841 Charles A. Wickliffe 1841–1845	John J. Crittenden 1841 Hugh S. Legaré 1841–1843 John Nelson 1843–1845	
George Bancroft 1845–1846 John Y. Mason 1846–1849	Cave Johnson 1845–1849	John Y. Mason 1845–1846 Nathan Clifford 1846–1848 Isaac Toucey 1848–1849	
William B. Preston 1849–1850	Jacob Collamer 1849–1850	Reverdy Johnson 1849–1850	Thomas Ewing 1849–1850
William A. Graham 1850–1852 John P. Kennedy 1852–1853	Nathan K. Hall 1850–1852 Sam D. Hubbard 1852–1853	John J. Crittenden 1850–1853	Thomas McKennan 1850 A. H. H. Stuart 1850–1853
James C. Dobbin 1853–1857	James Campbell 1853–1857	Caleb Cushing 1853–1857	Robert McClelland 1853–1857
Isaac Toucey 1857–1861	Aaron V. Brown 1857–1859 Joseph Holt 1859–1861 Horatio King 1861	Jeremiah S. Black 1857–1860 Edwin M. Stanton 1860–1861	Jacob Thompson 1857–1861
Gideon Welles 1861–1865	Horatio King 1861 Montgomery Blair 1861–1864 William Dennison 1864–1865	Edward Bates 1861–1864 James Speed 1864–1865	Caleb B. Smith 1861–1863 John P. Usher 1863–1865
Gideon Welles 1865–1869	William Dennison 1865–1866 Alexander Randall 1866–1869 William M. Evarts 1868–1869	James Speed 1865–1866 Henry Stanbery 1866–1868 O. H. Browning 1866–1869	John P. Usher 1865 James Harlan 1865–1866
Adolph E. Borie 1869 George M. Robeson 1869–1877	John A. J. Creswell 1869–1874 James W. Marshall 1874 Marshall Jewell 1874–1876 James N. Tyner 1876–1877	Ebenezer R. Hoar 1869–1870 Amos T. Akerman 1870–1871 G. H. Williams 1871–1875 Edwards Pierrepont 1875–1876 Alphonso Taft 1876–1877	Jacob D. Cox 1869–1870 Columbus Delano 1870–1875 Zachariah Chandler 1875–1877

(continued)

PRESIDENTIAL ADMINISTRATIONS, CONTINUED

President	Vice President	Secretary of State	Secretary of Treasury	Secretary of War	Secretary of Navy
Rutherford B. Hayes 1877–1881	William A. Wheeler 1877–1881	William M. Evarts 1877–1881	John Sherman 1877–1881	George W. McCrary 1877–1879 Alexander Ramsey 1879–1881	R. W. Thompson 1877–1881 Nathan Goff, Jr. 1881
James A. Garfield 1881	Chester A. Arthur 1881	James G. Blaine 1881	William Windom 1881	Robert T. Lincoln 1881	William H. Hunt 1881
Chester A. Arthur 1881–1885		F. T. Frelinghuysen 1881–1885	Charles J. Folger 1881–1884 Walter Q. Gresham 1884 Hugh McCulloch 1884–1885	Robert T. Lincoln 1881–1885	William E. Chandler 1881–1885
Grover Cleveland 1885–1889	T. A. Hendricks 1885	Thomas F. Bayard 1885–1889	Daniel Manning 1885–1887 Charles S. Fairchild 1887–1889	William C. Endicott 1885–1889	William C. Whitney 1885–1889
Benjamin Harrison 1889–1893	Levi P. Morton 1889–1893	James G. Blaine 1889–1892 John W. Foster 1892–1893	William Windom 1889–1891 Charles Foster 1892–1893	Redfield Procter 1889–1891 Stephen B. Elkins 1891–1893	Benjamin F. Tracy 1889–1893
Grover Cleveland 1893–1897	Adlai E. Stevenson 1893–1897	Walter Q. Gresham 1893–1895 Richard Olney 1895–1897	John G. Carlisle 1893–1897	Daniel S. Lamont 1893–1897	Hilary A. Herbert 1893–1897
William McKinley 1897–1901	Garret A. Hobart 1897–1899 Theodore Roosevelt 1901	John Sherman 1897–1898 William R. Day 1898 John Hay 1898–1901	Lyman J. Gage 1897–1901	Russell A. Alger 1897–1899 Elihu Root 1899–1901	John D. Long 1897–1901
Theodore Roosevelt 1901–1909	Charles Fairbanks 1905–1909	John Hay 1901–1905 Elihu Root 1905–1909 Robert Bacon 1909	Lyman J. Gage 1901–1902 Leslie M. Shaw 1902–1907 George B. Cortelyou 1907–1909	Elihu Root 1901–1904 William H. Taft 1904–1908 Luke E. Wright 1908–1909	John D. Long 1901–1902 William H. Moody 1902–1904 Paul Morton 1904–1905 Charles J. Bonaparte 1905–1906 Victor H. Metcalf 1906–1908 T. H. Newberry 1908–1909
William H. Taft 1909–1913	James S. Sherman 1909–1913	Philander C. Knox 1909–1913	Franklin MacVeagh 1909–1913	Jacob M. Dickinson 1909–1911 Henry L. Stimson 1911–1913	George von L. Meyer 1909–1913
Woodrow Wilson 1913–1921	Thomas R. Marshall 1913–1921	William J. Bryan 1913–1915 Robert Lansing 1915–1920 Bainbridge Colby 1920–1921	William G. McAdoo 1913–1918 Carter Glass 1918–1920 David F. Houston 1920–1921	Lindley M. Garrison 1913–1916 Newton D. Baker 1916–1921	Josephus Daniels 1913–1921

Postmaster General	Attorney General	Secretary of Interior	Secretary of Agriculture	Secretary of Commerce and Labor	
David M. Key 1877–1880 Horace Maynard 1880–1881	Charles Devens 1877–1881	Carl Schurz 1877–1881			
Thomas L. James 1881	Wayne MacVeagh 1881	S. J. Kirkwood 1881			
Thomas L. James 1881 Timothy O. Howe 1881–1883 Walter Q. Gresham 1883–1884 Frank Hatton 1884–1885	B. H. Brewster 1881–1885	Henry M. Teller 1881–1885			
William F. Vilas 1885–1888 Don M. Dickinson 1888–1889	A. H. Garland 1885–1889	L. Q. C. Lamar 1885–1888 William F. Vilas 1888–1889	Norman J. Colman 1889		
John Wanamaker 1889–1893	W. H. H. Miller 1889–1893	John W. Noble 1889–1893	Jeremiah M. Rusk 1889–1893		
Wilson S. Bissel 1893–1895 William L. Wilson 1895–1897	Richard Olney 1893–1895 Judson Harmon 1895–1897	Hoke Smith 1893–1896 David R. Francis 1896–1897	J. Sterling Morton 1893–1897		
James A. Gary 1897–1898 Charles E. Smith 1898–1901	Joseph McKenna 1897–1898 John W. Griggs 1898–1901 Philander C. Knox 1901	Cornelius N. Bliss 1897–1898 E. A. Hitchcock 1898–1901	James Wilson 1897–1901		
Charles E. Smith 1901–1902 Henry C. Payne 1902–1904 Robert J. Wynne 1904–1905 George B. Cortelyou 1905–1907 George von L. Meyer 1907–1909	Philander C. Knox 1901–1904 William H. Moody 1904–1906 Charles J. Bonaparte 1906–1909	E. A. Hitchcock 1901–1907 James R. Garfield 1907–1909	James Wilson 1901–1909	George B. Cortelyou 1903–1904 Victor H. Metcalf 1904–1906 Oscar S. Straus 1906–1909	

Postmaster General	Attorney General	Secretary of Interior	Secretary of Agriculture	Secretary of Commerce	Secretary of Labor
Frank H. Hitchcock 1909–1913	G. W. Wickersham 1909–1913	R. A. Ballinger 1909–1911 Walter L. Fisher 1911–1913	James Wilson 1909–1913	Charles Nagel 1909–1913	
Albert S. Burleson 1913–1921	J. C. McReynolds 1913–1914 T. W. Gregory 1914–1919 A. Mitchell Palmer 1919–1921	Franklin K. Lane 1913–1920 John B. Payne 1920–1921	David F. Houston 1913–1920 E. T. Meredith 1920–1921	W. C. Redfield 1913–1919 J. W. Alexander 1919–1921	William B. Wilson 1913–1921

(continued)

PRESIDENTIAL ADMINISTRATIONS, CONTINUED

President	Vice President	Secretary of State	Secretary of Treasury	Secretary of War	Secretary of Navy	Postmaster General	Attorney General
Warren G. Harding 1921–1923	Calvin Coolidge 1921–1923	Charles E. Hughes 1921–1923	Andrew W. Mellon 1921–1923	John W. Weeks 1921–1923	Edwin Denby 1921–1923	Will H. Hays 1921–1922 Hubert Work 1922–1923 Harry S. New 1923	H. M. Daugherty 1921–1923
Calvin Coolidge 1923–1929	Charles G. Dawes 1925–1929	Charles E. Hughes 1923–1925 Frank B. Kellogg 1925–1929	Andrew W. Mellon 1923–1929	John W. Weeks 1923–1925 Dwight F. Davis 1925–1929	Edwin Denby 1923–1924 Curtis D. Wilbur 1924–1929	Harry S. New 1923–1929	H. M. Daugherty 1923–1924 Harlan F. Stone 1924–1925 John G. Sargent 1925–1929
Herbert C. Hoover 1929–1933	Charles Curtis 1929–1933	Henry L. Stimson 1929–1933	Andrew W. Mellon 1929–1932 Ogden L. Mills 1932–1933	James W. Good 1929 Patrick J. Hurley 1929–1933	Charles F. Adams 1929–1933	Walter F. Brown 1929–1933	J. D. Mitchell 1929–1933
Franklin Delano Roosevelt 1933–1945	John Nance Garner 1933–1941 Henry A. Wallace 1941–1945 Harry S Truman 1945	Cordell Hull 1933–1944 E. R. Stettinius, Jr. 1944–1945	William H. Woodin 1933–1934 Henry Morgenthau, Jr. 1934–1945	George H. Dern 1933–1936 Harry H. Woodring 1936–1940 Henry L. Stimson 1940–1945	Claude A. Swanson 1933–1940 Charles Edison 1940 Frank Knox 1940–1944 James V. Forrestal 1944–1945	James A. Farley 1933–1940 Frank C. Walker 1940–1945	H. S. Cummings 1933–1939 Frank Murphy 1939–1940 Robert Jackson 1940–1941 Francis Biddel 1941–1945
Harry S Truman 1945–1953	Alben W. Barkley 1949–1953	James F. Byrnes 1945–1947 George C. Marshall 1947–1949 Dean G. Acheson 1949–1953	Fred M. Vinson 1945–1946 John W. Snyder 1946–1953	Robert P. Patterson 1945–1947 Kenneth C. Royall 1947 — Secretary of Defense — James V. Forrestal 1947–1949 Louis A. Johnson 1949–1950 George C. Marshall 1950–1951 Robert A. Lovett 1951–1953	James V. Forrestal 1945–1947	R. E. Hannegan 1945–1947 Jesse M. Donaldson 1947–1953	Tom C. Clark 1945–1949 J. H. McGrath 1949–1952 James P. McGranery 1952–1953
Dwight D. Eisenhower 1953–1961	Richard M. Nixon 1953–1961	John Foster Dulles 1953–1959 Christian A. Herter 1957–1961	George M. Humphrey 1953–1957 Robert B. Anderson 1957–1961	Charles E. Wilson 1953–1957 Neil H. McElroy 1957–1961 Thomas S. Gates 1959–1961		A. E. Summerfield 1953–1961	H. Brownell, Jr. 1953–1957 William P. Rogers 1957–1961
John F. Kennedy 1961–1963	Lyndon B. Johnson 1961–1963	Dean Rusk 1961–1963	C. Douglas Dillon 1961–1963	Robert S. McNamara 1961–1963		J. Edward Day 1961–1963 John A. Gronouski 1961–1963	Robert F. Kennedy 1961–1963
Lyndon B. Johnson 1963–1969	Hubert H. Humphrey 1965–1969	Dean Rusk 1963–1969	C. Douglas Dillon 1963–1965 Henry H. Fowler 1965–1968 Joseph W. Barr 1968–1969	Robert S. McNamara 1963–1968 Clark M. Clifford 1968–1969		John A. Gronouski 1963–1965 Lawrence F. O'Brien 1965–1968 W. Marvin Watson 1968–1969	Robert F. Kennedy 1963–1965 N. deB. Katzenbach 1965–1967 Ramsey Clark 1967–1969

Secretary of Interior	Secretary of Agriculture	Secretary of Commerce	Secretary of Labor	Secretary of Health, Education and Welfare	Secretary of Housing and Urban Development	Secretary of Transportation
Albert B. Fall 1921–1923 Hubert Work 1923	Henry C. Wallace 1921–1923	Herbert C. Hoover 1921–1923	James J. Davis 1921–1923			
Hubert Work 1923–1928 Roy O. West 1928–1929	Henry C. Wallace 1923–1924 Howard M. Gore 1924–1925 W. J. Jardine 1925–1929	Herbert C. Hoover 1923–1928 William F. Whiting 1928–1929	James J. Davis 1923–1929			
Ray L. Wilbur 1929–1933	Arthur M. Hyde 1929–1933 Roy D. Chapin 1932–1933	Robert P. Lamont 1929–1932 William N. Doak 1930–1933	James J. Davis 1929–1930			
Harold L. Ickes 1933–1945	Henry A. Wallace 1933–1940 Claude R. Wickard 1940–1945	Daniel C. Roper 1933–1939 Harry L. Hopkins 1939–1940 Jesse Jones 1940–1945 Henry A. Wallace 1945	Frances Perkins 1933–1945			
Harold L. Ickes 1945–1946 Julius A. Krug 1946–1949 Oscar L. Chapman 1949–1953	C. P. Anderson 1945–1948 C. F. Brannan 1948–1953	W. A. Harriman 1946–1948 Charles Sawyer 1948–1953	L. B. Schwellenbach 1945–1948 Maurice J. Tobin 1948–1953			
Douglas McKay 1953–1956 Fred Seaton 1956–1961	Ezra T. Benson 1953–1961	Sinclair Weeks 1953–1958 Lewis L. Strauss 1958–1961	Martin P. Durkin 1953 James P. Mitchell 1953–1961	Oveta Culp Hobby 1953–1955 Marion B. Folsom 1955–1958 Arthur S. Flemming 1958–1961		
Stewart L. Udall 1961–1963	Orville L. Freeman 1961–1963	Luther H. Hodges 1961–1963	Arthur J. Goldberg 1961–1963 W. Willard Wirtz 1962–1963	A. H. Ribicoff 1961–1963 Anthony J. Celebrezze 1962–1963		
Stewart L. Udall 1963–1969	Orville L. Freeman 1963–1969	Luther H. Hodges 1963–1965 John T. Connor 1965–1967 Alexander B. Trowbridge 1967–1968 C. R. Smith 1968–1969	W. Willard Wirtz 1963–1969	Anthony J. Celebrezze 1963–1965 John W. Gardner 1965–1968 Wilbur J. Cohen 1968–1969	Robert C. Weaver 1966–1968 Robert C. Wood 1968–1969	Alan S. Boyd 1966–1969

(continued)

PRESIDENTIAL ADMINISTRATIONS, CONTINUED

President	Vice President	Secretary of State	Secretary of Treasury	Secretary of Defense	Postmaster General[1]	Attorney General	Secretary of Interior	Secretary of Agriculture
Richard M. Nixon 1969–1974	Spiro T. Agnew 1969–1973 Gerald R. Ford 1973–1974	William P. Rogers 1969–1973 Henry A. Kissinger 1973–1974	David M. Kennedy 1969–1970 John B. Connally 1970–1972 George P. Schultz 1972–1974 William E. Simon 1974	Melvin R. Laird 1969–1973 Elliot L. Richardson 1973 James R. Schlesinger 1973–1974	Winton M. Blount 1969–1971	John M. Mitchell 1969–1972 Richard G. Kleindienst 1972–1973 Elliot L. Richardson 1973 William B. Saxbe 1974	Walter J. Hickel 1969–1971 Rogers C. B. Morton 1971–1974	Clifford M. Hardin 1969–1971 Earl L. Butz 1971–1974
Gerald R. Ford 1974–1977	Nelson A. Rockefeller 1974–1977	Henry A. Kissinger 1974–1977	William E. Simon 1974–1977	James R. Schlesinger 1974–1975 Donald H. Rumsfeld 1975–1977		William B. Saxbe 1974–1975 Edward H. Levi 1975–1977	Rogers C. B. Morton 1974–1975 Stanley K. Hathaway 1975 Thomas D. Kleppe 1975–1977	Earl L. Butz 1974–1976
Jimmy Carter 1977–1981	Walter F. Mondale 1977–1981	Cyrus R. Vance 1977–1980 Edmund S. Muskie 1980–1981	W. Michael Blumenthal 1977–1979 G. William Miller 1979–1981	Harold Brown 1977–1981		Griffin Bell 1977–1979 Benjamin R. Civiletti 1979–1981	Cecil D. Andrus 1977–1981	Robert Bergland 1977–1981
Ronald W. Reagan 1981–1989	George H. Bush 1981–1989	Alexander M. Haig, Jr. 1981–1982 George P. Shultz 1982–1989	Donald T. Regan 1981–1985 James A. Baker 1985–1988 Nicholas F. Brady 1988–1989	Caspar W. Weinberger 1981–1987 Frank C. Carlucci 1987–1989		William French Smith 1981–1985 Edwin Meese 1985–1988 Richard Thornburgh 1988–1989	James G. Watt 1981–1983 William P. Clark 1983–1985 Donald P. Hodel 1985–1989	John R. Block 1981–1986 Richard E. Lyng 1986–1989
George H. Bush 1989–1993	J. Danforth Quayle 1989–1993	James A. Baker 1989–1992 Lawrence S. Eagleburger 1992–1993	Nicholas F. Brady 1989–1993	Richard Cheney 1989–1993		Richard Thornburgh 1989–1990 William Barr 1990–1993	Manuel Lujan 1989–1993	Clayton Yeutter 1989–1990 Edward Madigan 1990–1993
William Clinton 1993–2001	Albert Gore 1993–2001	Warren M. Christopher 1993–1996 Madeleine K. Albright 1997–2001	Lloyd Bentsen 1993–1994 Robert E. Rubin 1994–1999 Lawrence H. Summers 1999–2001	Les Aspin 1993–1994 William J. Perry 1994–1996 William S. Cohen 1997–2001		Janet Reno 1993–2001	Bruce Babbitt 1993–2001	Mike Espy 1993–1994 Dan Glickman 1995–2001
George W. Bush 2001–	Richard B. Cheney 2001–	Gen. Colin L. Powell 2001–	Paul H. O'Neill 2001–2002 John W. Snow 2003–	Donald H. Rumsfeld 2001–		John Ashcroft 2001–	Gale A. Norton 2001–	Ann M. Veneman 2001–

[1]On July 1, 1971, the Post Office became an independent agency. After that date, the postmaster general was no longer a member of the Cabinet.

[2]Acting secretary.

Secretary of Commerce	Secretary of Labor	Secretary of Health, Education and Welfare		Secretary of Housing and Urban Development	Secretary of Transportation	Secretary of Energy	Secretary of Veterans Affairs	Secretary of Homeland Security
Maurice H. Stans 1969–1972 Peter G. Peterson 1972 Frederick B. Dent 1972–1974	George P. Shultz 1969–1970 James D. Hodgson 1970–1973 Peter J. Brennan 1973–1974	Robert H. Finch 1969–1970 Elliot L. Richardson 1970–1973 Caspar W. Weinberger 1973–1974		George W. Romney 1969–1973 James T. Lynn 1973–1974	John A. Volpe 1969–1973 Claude S. Brinegar 1973–1974			
Frederick B. Dent 1974–1975 Rogers C. B. Morton 1975 Elliot L. Richardson 1975–1977	Peter J. Brennan 1974–1975 John T. Dunlop 1975–1976 W. J. Usery 1976–1977	Caspar W. Weinberger 1974–1975 Forrest D. Matthews 1975–1977		James T. Lynn 1974–1975 Carla A. Hills 1975–1977	Claude S. Brinegar 1974–1975 William T. Coleman 1975–1977			
Juanita Kreps 1977–1981	F. Ray Marshall 1977–1981	Joseph Califano 1977–1979 Patricia Roberts Harris 1979–1980		Patricia Roberts Harris 1977–1979 Moon Landrieu 1979–1981	Brock Adams 1977–1979 Neil E. Goldschmidt 1979–1981	James R. Schlesinger 1977–1979 Charles W. Duncan, Jr. 1979–1981		

		Secretary of Health and Human Services	Secretary of Education					
		Patricia Roberts Harris 1980–1981	Shirley M. Hufstedler 1980–1981					
Malcolm Baldridge 1981–1987 C. William Verity, Jr. 1987–1989	Raymond J. Donovan 1981–1985 William E. Brock 1985–1987 Ann Dore McLaughlin 1987–1989	Richard S. Schweiker 1981–1983 Margaret M. Heckler 1983–1985 Otis R. Bowen 1985–1989	Terrell H. Bell 1981–1985 William J. Bennett 1985–1988 Lauro Fred Cavazos 1988–1989	Samuel R. Pierce, Jr. 1981–1989	Drew Lewis 1981–1983 Elizabeth H. Dole 1983–1987 James H. Burnley 1987–1989	James B. Edwards 1981–1982 Donald P. Hodel 1982–1985 John S. Harrington 1985–1989		
Robert Mosbacher 1989–1991 Barbara Franklin 1991–1993	Elizabeth Dole 1989–1990 Lynn Martin 1992–1993	Louis Sullivan 1989–1993	Lamar Alexander 1990–1993	Jack Kemp 1989–1993	Samuel Skinner 1989–1990 Andrew Card 1990–1993	James Watkins 1989–1993	Edward J. Derwinski 1989–1993	
Ronald H. Brown 1993–1996 William M. Daley 1997–2000 Norman Y. Mineta 2000–2001	Robert B. Reich 1993–1996 Alexis M. Herman 1997–2001	Donna E. Shalala 1993–2001	Richard W. Riley 1993–2001	Henry G. Cisneros 1993–1996 Andrew M. Cuomo 1997–2001	Federico F. Peña 1993–1996 Rodney E. Slater 1997–2001	Hazel O'Leary 1993–1996 Federico F. Peña 1997–1998 Bill Richardson 1998–2001	Jesse Brown 1993–1997 Togo D. West, Jr.[2] 1998–2001	
Donald L. Evans 2001–	Elaine L. Chao 2001–	Tommy G. Thompson 2001–	Roderick R. Paige 2001–	Melquiades R. Martinez 2001–	Norman Y. Mineta 2001–	Spencer Abraham 2001–	Anthony Principi 2001–	Tom Ridge 2001–

JUSTICES OF THE U.S. SUPREME COURT

Name	Term of Service	Years of Service	Appointed By	Name	Term of Service	Years of Service	Appointed By
John Jay	1789–1795	5	Washington	Rufus W. Peckham	1895–1909	14	Cleveland
John Rutledge	1789–1791	1	Washington	Joseph McKenna	1898–1925	26	McKinley
William Cushing	1789–1810	20	Washington	Oliver W. Holmes, Jr.	1902–1932	30	T. Roosevelt
James Wilson	1789–1798	8	Washington	William R. Day	1903–1922	19	T. Roosevelt
John Blair	1789–1796	6	Washington	William H. Moody	1906–1910	3	T. Roosevelt
Robert H. Harrison	1789–1790	—	Washington	Horace H. Lurton	1910–1914	4	Taft
James Iredell	1790–1799	9	Washington	Charles E. Hughes	1910–1916	5	Taft
Thomas Johnson	1791–1793	1	Washington	Willis Van Devanter	1911–1937	26	Taft
William Paterson	1793–1806	13	Washington	Joseph R. Lamar	1911–1916	5	Taft
John Rutledge[1]	1795	—	Washington	**Edward D. White**	1910–1921	11	Taft
Samuel Chase	1796–1811	15	Washington	Mahlon Pitney	1912–1922	10	Taft
Oliver Ellsworth	1796–1800	4	Washington	James C. McReynolds	1914–1941	26	Wilson
Bushrod Washington	1798–1829	31	J. Adams	Louis D. Brandeis	1916–1939	22	Wilson
Alfred Moore	1799–1804	4	J. Adams	John H. Clarke	1916–1922	6	Wilson
John Marshall	1801–1835	34	J. Adams	**William H. Taft**	1921–1930	8	Harding
William Johnson	1804–1834	30	Jefferson	George Sutherland	1922–1938	15	Harding
H. Brockholst Livingston	1806–1823	16	Jefferson	Pierce Butler	1922–1939	16	Harding
Thomas Todd	1807–1826	18	Jefferson	Edward T. Sanford	1923–1930	7	Harding
Joseph Story	1811–1845	33	Madison	Harlan F. Stone	1925–1941	16	Coolidge
Gabriel Duval	1811–1835	24	Madison	**Charles E. Hughes**	1930–1941	11	Hoover
Smith Thompson	1823–1843	20	Monroe	Owen J. Roberts	1930–1945	15	Hoover
Robert Trimble	1826–1828	2	J. Q. Adams	Benjamin N. Cardozo	1932–1938	6	Hoover
John McLean	1829–1861	32	Jackson	Hugo L. Black	1937–1971	34	F. Roosevelt
Henry Baldwin	1830–1844	14	Jackson	Stanley F. Reed	1938–1957	19	F. Roosevelt
James M. Wayne	1835–1867	32	Jackson	Felix Frankfurter	1939–1962	23	F. Roosevelt
Roger B. Taney	1836–1864	28	Jackson	William O. Douglas	1939–1975	36	F. Roosevelt
Philip P. Barbour	1836–1841	4	Jackson	Frank Murphy	1940–1949	9	F. Roosevelt
John Catron	1837–1865	28	Van Buren	**Harlan F. Stone**	1941–1946	5	F. Roosevelt
John McKinley	1837–1852	15	Van Buren	James F. Byrnes	1941–1942	1	F. Roosevelt
Peter V. Daniel	1841–1860	19	Van Buren	Robert H. Jackson	1941–1954	13	F. Roosevelt
Samuel Nelson	1845–1872	27	Tyler	Wiley B. Rutledge	1943–1949	6	F. Roosevelt
Levi Woodbury	1845–1851	5	Polk	Harold H. Burton	1945–1958	13	Truman
Robert C. Grier	1846–1870	23	Polk	**Fred M. Vinson**	1946–1953	7	Truman
Benjamin R. Curtis	1851–1857	6	Fillmore	Tom C. Clark	1949–1967	18	Truman
John A. Campbell	1853–1861	8	Pierce	Sherman Minton	1949–1956	7	Truman
Nathan Clifford	1858–1881	23	Buchanan	**Earl Warren**	1953–1969	16	Eisenhower
Noah H. Swayne	1862–1881	18	Lincoln	John Marshall Harlan	1955–1971	16	Eisenhower
Samuel F. Miller	1862–1890	28	Lincoln	William J. Brennan, Jr.	1956–1990	34	Eisenhower
David Davis	1862–1877	14	Lincoln	Charles E. Whittaker	1957–1962	5	Eisenhower
Stephen J. Field	1863–1897	34	Lincoln	Potter Stewart	1958–1981	23	Eisenhower
Salmon P. Chase	1864–1873	8	Lincoln	Byron R. White	1962–1993	31	Kennedy
William Strong	1870–1880	10	Grant	Arthur J. Goldberg	1962–1965	3	Kennedy
Joseph P. Bradley	1870–1892	22	Grant	Abe Fortas	1965–1969	4	Johnson
Ward Hunt	1873–1882	9	Grant	Thurgood Marshall	1967–1994	24	Johnson
Morrison R. Waite	1874–1888	14	Grant	**Warren E. Burger**	1969–1986	18	Nixon
John M. Harlan	1877–1911	34	Hayes	Harry A. Blackmun	1970–1994	24	Nixon
William B. Woods	1880–1887	7	Hayes	Lewis F. Powell, Jr.	1971–1987	15	Nixon
Stanley Matthews	1881–1889	7	Garfield	**William H. Rehnquist[2]**	1971–	—	Nixon
Horace Gray	1882–1902	20	Arthur	John P. Stevens III	1975–	—	Ford
Samuel Blatchford	1882–1893	11	Arthur	Sandra Day O'Connor	1981–	—	Reagan
Lucius Q. C. Lamar	1888–1893	5	Cleveland	Antonin Scalia	1986–	—	Reagan
Melville W. Fuller	1888–1910	21	Cleveland	Anthony M. Kennedy	1988–	—	Reagan
David J. Brewer	1890–1910	20	B. Harrison	David Souter	1990–	—	Bush
Henry B. Brown	1890–1906	16	B. Harrison	Clarence Thomas	1991–	—	Bush
George Shiras, Jr.	1892–1903	10	B. Harrison	Ruth Bader Ginsburg	1993–	—	Clinton
Howell E. Jackson	1893–1895	2	B. Harrison	Stephen G. Breyer	1994–	—	Clinton
Edward D. White	1894–1910	16	Cleveland				

Note: Chief justices appear in bold type.

[1]Acting chief justice; Senate refused to confirm appointment.

[2]Chief justice from 1986 on (Reagan administration).

Photo Credits

Images not referenced below are in the public domain.

Chapter 17

p. 534: Winslow Homer, Sunday Morning in Virginia, 1877. Cincinnati Art Museum John J. Emery Fund. Acc.#1924.247; **p. 537:** Courtesy Chicago Historical Society; **p. 539 (left):** Reproduced from the Collections of the Library of Congress; **p. 539 (right):** Reproduced from the Collections of the Library of Congress; **p. 541 (top):** Reproduced from the Collections of the Library of Congress; **p. 541 (bottom):** © Bettmann/Corbis; **p. 542:** Reproduced from the Collections of the Library of Congress; **p. 543 (left):** © Stock Montage, Inc.; **p. 543 (right):** From the Collections of the Library of Congress; **p. 545:** From the Collections of the Library of Congress; **p. 548:** © Corbis; **p. 553:** © Bettmann/Corbis; **p. 554:** From the Collections of the Library of Congress; **p. 556:** © Bettmann/Corbis; **p. 558:** The Granger Collection, New York

Chapter 18

p. 562: Frederic Remington, "A Dash for Timber" oil on canvas, 1889. 1961.381. © Amon Carter Museum, Fort Worth, Texas; **p. 564:** Nebraska State Historical Society; **p. 568:** Erwin E. Smith Collection of the Library of Congress on deposit at the Amon Carter Museum, Fort Worth; **p. 569:** By courtesy of the National Portrait Gallery, London; **p. 570:** Smithsonian Institution, Bureau of American Ethnology; **p. 571:** © John Springer Collection/Corbis; **p. 577:** © The Granger Collection

Chapter 19

p. 582: The Kansas State Historical Society Topeka, Kansas; **p. 586:** The Museum of the City of New York; **p. 587:** © Bob Krist/Corbis; **p. 591:** From the Collections of the Library of Congress; **p. 593:** © Bettmann/Corbis; **p. 595:** © Bettmann/Corbis; **p. 598:** North Wind Picture Archives; **p. 599:** © Bettmann/Corbis; **p. 600:** Kansas State Historical Society; **p. 603:** From the Collections of the Library of Congress

Chapter 20

p. 608: John Sloan, The City from Greenwich Village, 1922. National Gallery of Art. Gift of Helen Farr Sloan, 1970.I. I.; **p. 611:** © Lake County Museum/Corbis; **p. 614:** © Bettmann/Corbis; **p. 615:** © Bettmann/Corbis; **p. 617:** State Historical Society of Wisconsin; **p. 618:** Brown University Archives; **p. 622:** © Bettmann/Corbis; **p. 624:** Victor Joseph Gatto Triangle Fire, March 25, 1911. Oil on canvas, 19 x 28 inches. Museum of the City of New York, 54.75, Gift of Mrs. Henry L. Moses; **p. 626:** © Bettmann/ Corbis;

p. 628: From the Collections of the Library of Congress; **p. 631:** Underwood Photo Archives; **p. 632:** The Granger Collection, New York; **p. 633:** © Bettmann/ Corbis; **p. 635:** © Picture Desk/Kobal Collection/20th Century Fox; **p. 636:** © Bettmann/Corbis

Chapter 21

p. 638: Culver Pictures; **p. 641:** Culver Pictures; **p. 642:** George Bellows, "Cliff Dwellers" 1913. oil on canvas. Los Angeles County Museum of Art, Los Angeles County Fund; **p. 643:** Brown Brothers; **p. 645:** Columbia University Library; **p. 648:** © Hulton Artchive/Getty Images; **p. 652:** Reproduced from the Collections of the Library of Congress; **p. 654:** © Bettmann/Corbis; **p. 656:** © Bettmann/ Corbis; **p. 657:** © Bettmann/Corbis; **p. 659:** From the Collections of the Library of Congress; **p. 662:** Brown Brothers; **p. 664:** Reproduced from the Collections of the Library of Congress; **p. 667:** © Picture Desk/Kobal Collection/20th Century Fox

Chapter 22

p. 670: Culver Pictures; **p. 673:** Smithsonian Institution Photo No. 85-14366; **p. 674:** © Hulton-Deutsch Collection/Corbis; **p. 676:** The Granger Collection, New York; **p. 677:** Chicago Historical Society; **p. 679:** From the Collections of the Library of Congress; **p. 680 (top):** © Bettmann/Corbis; **p. 680 (bottom):** The Granger Collection; **p. 682:** © Corbis; **p. 684:** The Granger Collection, New York; **p. 685:** The Granger Collection, New York; **p. 689:** © Bettmann/Corbis; **p. 690:** © Underwood & Underwood/ Corbis; **p. 691:** North Wind Picture Archives; **p. 694:** Brown Brothers

Chapter 23

p. 698: Mary Evans Picture Library; **p. 702:** Imperial War Museum, London; **p. 704:** Records of the Women's International League for Peace and Freedom, U.S. Section, Swarthmore College Peace Collection; **p. 706:** The Granger Collections, New York; **p. 709:** © Corbis; **p. 710:** © Digital Images © The Museum of Modern Art/ Licensed by Scala/Art Resource, NY; **p. 713:** National Archives photo; **p. 714:** Reproduced from the Collections of the Library of Congress; **p. 715:** National Archives; **p. 717:** Imperial War Museum; **p. 718:** New York Times, 1919; **p. 719:** © UPI-Bettmann/Corbis; **p. 721:** © Corbis; **p. 723:** Library & Archives Division, Historical Society of Western Pennsylvania, Pittsburgh, Pa; **p. 725:** © Picture Desk/Kobal Collection/Paramount; **p. 726:** © 1995 Estate of Ben Shahn/ VAGA, New York. Collection of Whitney Museum of

American Art; **p. 727:** From the Collections of the Library of Congress

Chapter 24

p. 730: The Dance Club, or The Jazz Party, 1923 (oil on canvas) by Roberts, William Patrick (1895–1980) Leeds Museums and Galleries (City Art Gallery)/The Bridgeman Art Library. Reproduced by permission of the Treasury Solicitor (administrator of the estate of John David Roberts); **p. 735:** The Granger Collection, New York; **p. 737 (top):** From the Collections of the Library of Congress; **p. 737 (bottom):** © Bettmann/Corbis; **p. 739:** © Corbis; **p. 741:** Brown Brothers; **p. 742:** Brown Brothers; **p. 743:** © Bettmann/Corbis; **p. 746:** Brown Brothers; **p. 748:** From the Collections of the Library of Congress; **p. 751:** Brown Brothers; **p. 753:** The Granger Collection; **p. 755:** National Portrait Gallery, Smithsonian Institution/Art Resource, NY; **p. 756:** © Bettmann/Corbis; **p. 759:** Security Pacific Colleciton/Los Angeles Public Library; **p. 760:** © Leonard de Selva/Corbis; **p. 761:** The Granger Collection, New York

Chapter 25

p. 764: The Granger Collection, New York; **p. 766:** From the Collections of the Library of Congress; **p. 769:** © Bettmann/Corbis; **p. 771:** © Bettmann/Corbis; **p. 774:** From the Collections of the Library of Congress; **p. 775:** From the Collections of the Library of Congress; **p. 776:** FDR Library; **p. 777:** © Bettmann/Corbis; **p. 779:** © Lester Lefkowitz/Corbis; **p. 781:** © UPI-Bettmann/Corbis; **p. 782:** Detroit Industry, North Wall, 1932-1933, Diego Rivera. Gift of Edsel B. Ford. Photograph © 1991 The Detroit Institute of Arts; **p. 785:** The Granger Collection; **p. 786:** The Granger Collection, New York; **p. 789:** AP/Wide World Photos; **p. 790:** Michael Barson Collection/Past Perfect; **p. 791:** From the Collections of the Library of Congress; **p. 794:** From the Collections of the Library of Congress

Chapter 26

p. 800: Hoover Institute Archives, Stanford University. U560; **p. 806:** © Bettmann/Corbis; **p. 807:** © UPI-Bettmann/Corbis; **p. 809:** San Diego Historical Society; **p. 813:** © AFP/Corbis; **p. 817:** National Archives #127-N-69559-A; **p. 820 (both):** © UPI-Bettmann/Corbis; **p. 822:** National Archives; **p. 823:** © Bettmann/Corbis; **p. 824:** Reproduced from the Collections of the Library of Congress; **p. 825:** From the Collections of the Library of Congress; **p. 826:** © Corbis; **p. 827:** © Bettmann/Corbis; **p. 830:** FDR Library

Chapter 27

p. 836: Michael Barson Collection/Past Perfect; **p. 839:** The Granger Collection, New York; **p. 841:** Courtesy of the George C. Marshall Research Library, Lexington, Virginia; **p. 842:** Courtesy of the Truman Library; **p. 846:** Courtesy of the Truman Library; **p. 850:** © Archive Photos; **p. 853:** © Sunset Boulevard/Corbis Sygma; **p. 854:** From the Collections of the Library of Congress; **p. 859:** Courtesy of the Minnesota Historical Society; **p. 860:** © Bettmann/Corbis; **p. 861:** Michael Barson Collection/Past Perfect; **p. 865:** Michael Barson Collection/Past Perfect

Chapter 28

p. 868: The Granger Collection, New York; **p. 872:** © AP/Wide World Photo; **p. 877 (top):** © UPI-Bettmann/Corbis; **p. 877 (bottom):** © Elliott Erwitt/Magnum Photos Inc.; **p. 879:** © Joe Munroe/Photo Researchers; **p. 882:** From the Collections of the Library of Congress; **p. 883:** © Corbis; **p. 886:** © UPI-Bettmann/Corbis; **p. 888:** AP/Wide World; **p. 893:** © UPI-Bettmann/Corbis; **p. 896:** © UPI-Bettmann/Corbis; **p. 897:** © Danny Lyon/Magnum Photos, Inc.; **p. 898:** AP/Wide World Photos; **p. 901:** © John Springer Collection/Corbis

Chapter 29

p. 904: © Joseph Sohm; ChromoSohm Inc./Corbis; **p. 907 (both):** George Tames/NYT Pictures; **p. 913:** AP/Wide World Photos; **p. 914:** The Granger Collection, New York; **p. 918:** © Bettmann/Corbis; **p. 919:** © UPI-Bettmann/Corbis; **p. 921:** © Corbis; **p. 923 (top):** © UPI-Bettmann/Corbis; **p. 923 (bottom):** © UPI-Bettmann/Corbis; **p. 928:** © Bettmann/Corbis; **p. 929:** © UPI-Bettmann/Corbis

Chapter 30

p. 936: © Richard Nowitz/Corbis; **p. 941:** © Paul Conklin/PhotoEdit; **p. 944 (all):** California Department of Transportation; **p. 946:** © Ted Streshinsky/Corbis; **p. 947:** © Karen Su/Corbis; **p. 950:** © Archive Photos/Fotos International; **p. 953:** © Picture Desk/Kobal Collection/ Lucasfilm/20th Century Fox; **p. 958:** © Bettmann/Corbis; **p. 961:** AP/Wide World Photos; **p. 962 (top):** Bill Pugliano/Gamma-Liaison Network; **p. 962 (bottom):** © Gary A. Conner/PhotoEdit; **p. 963:** © Ralf-Finn Hestoft/Corbis; **p. 965:** © Nik Wheeler/Corbis; **p. 966:** AP/Wide World Photos; **p. 967:** © Bettmann/Corbis

Chapter 31

p. 972: © James L. Amos/Corbis; **p. 977:** © 1980 Time Inc, Reprinted by permission; **p. 982:** © Jeff Lowenthal/Woodfin Camp; **p. 985:** © Bettmann/Corbis; **p. 986:** Courtesy, Ronald Reagan Library; **p. 990:** © Owen Franken/Corbis; **p. 995:** © Reuters NewMedia Inc/Corbis; **p. 999 (both):** © Tom Prettyman/PhotoEdit; **p. 1001:** © Reuters Newmedia Inc/Corbis; **p. 1003:** © Corbis; **p. 1004:** AP/Wide World Photos; **p. 1005:** © Lee Snider/ Corbis; **p. 1006:** © Damir Sagolj/Reuters Newmedia Inc/Corbis

Index

in federal hiring, 860
toward Filipinos, 681
after First World War, 726–728
Harlem Renaissance, white prejudice, and, 757
toward Hispanics, 619
Holocaust and, 813
immigrant restriction and, 749–750
imperialism and, 673
Johnson, Jack, and, 634–635
Kennedy, John F., and, 894
King, Martin Luther, Jr., and, 888
legal and criminal justice systems and, 960
Mexican Americans and, 758, 759
Montgomery bus boycott and, 888
in Nazi Germany, 802
toward new immigrants, 620
in New South, 577–578
in North, 543
quotas and, 749–750
racial fitness and, 619
of Roosevelt, Theodore, 658, 686, 692
school desegregation and, 886–887
in Second World War, 800, 815, 827–831
Social Darwinism and, 619
in South Africa, 848
in Spanish-American War, 677–679
stereotypes and, 619
in *Tarzan, the Ape Man*, 688–689
Truman's fight against, 860–861
urban-suburban issues in, 891
Voting Rights Act (1965) and, 909
of wealthy, 619
Race riots, 699
in Atlanta, 577
after First World War, 727
in Omaha, 656
during Reconstruction, 544, 545
in Springfield, Illinois, 655
in Wilmington, North Carolina, 577
Racial discrimination. *See* Discrimination; Race and racism
Racial equality. *See* Equality; Race and racism
Racial profiling, 960
Racial superiority, 619
Radar, 809, 821
Radcliffe, 590
Radford, Arthur, 871
Radiation
after atomic bombings, 819
environmental damage from, 926
nuclear testing and, 872
poisoning by, 999
Radical Republicans, 536–538, 544–545
Radicals and radicalism
capitalism and, 632
critics of New Deal, 783

farmers as, 745
First World War and, 718, 723
IWW and, 646–647
labor and feminist, 636
and Red Scare, 725–726
in 74th Congress, 783
Radio, 733
black, 980
fireside chats of Franklin D. Roosevelt, 773
New Right on, 969
in 1920s, 736
in rural areas, 746
Radioactivity. *See* Radiation
Radio Asia, 871
Radio Free Europe, 871
Radio Liberty, 871
Radio Martí, 987
"Radio priest," 781
RAF. *See* Royal Air Force (RAF)
Railroads, 611
Asian labor for, 622
black workers on, 628
cattle frontier and, 566, 567
economic growth and, 584–585
expansion of (1870–1890), 565 (map)
First World War mobilization of, 708
gauges of, 576
granger laws and, 584–585
labor for, 623
land grants to, 563
mail-order houses and, 588
in New South, 576
overcapacity and, 584
pools in, 613
rate-cutting wars of, 584
refrigerated rail cars and, 567
regulation of, 585
standard time zones and, 585
technological advances for, 585
westward expansion and, 564
in Wisconsin, 654, 655
Ramona (Jackson), 573
Ranching
cattle drives and, 566–567
growth of frontier, 565–567, 566 (map)
longhorn cattle and, 566–567
open-range grazing and, 567
reforms in, 567
R&D. *See* Research and development (R&D)
RAND corporation, 848
Randolph, A. Philip, 757, 827, 860
Range wars, 567
Rape, crisis centers for, 957
Rate-cutting wars, of railroads, 584
Ratification, of Versailles Treaty, 722
Rationing, in Second World War, 821
Rauschenbusch, Walter, 640–641

Raw materials, Japanese need for, 808
Ray, James Earl, 921
Reading. *See* Literacy
Reading Railroad, 598, 659
Reagan, Ronald, 909
antiwar movement and, 915
arms treaty and, 989
as California governor, 981
Cold War and, 986–988
domestic policy of, 981–983, 985–986
election of 1980 and, 979–981, 981 (map)
election of 1984 and, 983–984
foreign policy of, 974
HUAC hearings and, 851
impact of, 1006
Iran-*Contra* and, 988
military deployment and, 987–988
as movie actor, 984–985
New Right and, 981, 982–983
S&L crisis and, 985
second term of, 984–986
Reagon, Bernice Johnson, 897, 899
Real estate, African American agents in, 629
Realism, 641
about cowboys-and-Indians conflict, 562
magazine illustrations and, 589
middle class interest in, 642–643
"Reality shows," 954
Real wages, in 1870–1900, 594
Rearmament
of Germany, 848
naval, 804
Rebellions. *See* Revolts and rebellions
Rebel without a Cause (film), 917
Recession(s). *See also* Depressions (financial); Economy
of 1937–1938, 797
Reciprocal Trade Agreement (1934), 796
Reconnaissance flights, disarmament and, 871
Reconstruction, 534–560, 550, 551 (map), 552–553
Black Codes during, 540
black officeholders in, 551
carpetbaggers and, 551–552
completion of formal, 546–547
Compromise of 1877 and, 559
congressional, 542–545
constitutional conventions during, 546–547, 546 (map)
election of 1868 and, 548–549
end of, 560
Fifteenth Amendment and, 547
Fourteenth Amendment and, 544, 547
Freedmen's Bureau and, 540–541
freedpeople during, 541–542